A GATEWAY TO SINDARIN

A Gateway to Sindarin

A GRAMMAR OF AN ELVISH LANGUAGE FROM J. R. R. TOLKIEN'S *Lord of the Rings*

David Salo

THE UNIVERSITY OF UTAH PRESS

Salt Lake City

© 2004 by The University of Utah Press. All rights reserved.
First paperback printing 2007

The Defiance House Man colophon is a registered trademark
of the University of Utah Press. It is based upon a four-foot-tall,
Ancient Puebloan pictograph (late PIII) near Glen Canyon, Utah.

11 10 2 3 4 5

LIBRARY OF CONGRESS CATALOGING-IN PUBLICATION DATA

Salo, David, 1969–
A gateway to Sindarin: a grammar of an Elvish language
from J.R.R Tolkien's Lord of the rings /
David Salo.
p. cm.
Includes bibliographical references.
ISBN 978-0-87480-912-1 (paperback : alk. paper)
1. Sindarin (Artificial language)—Grammar.
I. Title.
PM8780.S35 2004
499'.99—dc22
2004008124

www.UofUpress.com

Printed by Sheridan Books, Inc., Ann Arbor, Michigan
Interior printed on recycled paper with 50% post-consumer content.

CONTENTS

List of Tables xi
Preface xiii
List of Abbreviations xvi

1. The History of Sindarin 3
  The First Age 3
    The Lindāi (§ 1.1) 3
    The Sindar in Beleriand (§ 1.2) 4
    The Noldor (§ 1.3) 5
    The Edain (§ 1.4) 7
    The end of the First Age (§ 1.5) 7
  The Second Age 8
    The Eldar in Beleriand (§ 1.6) 8
    The migrations of the Sindar of Doriath (§ 1.7) 9
    The migrations of the Noldor (§ 1.8) 9
    Númenor (§ 1.9) 10
  The Third Age 12
    The kingdoms of the Elves (§ 1.10) 12
    The kingdoms of Men (§ 1.11) 13
    The end of the Third Age (§ 1.12) 15
    Timeline (§ 1.13) 15

2. The Sounds of Sindarin 19
  Sounds found in Classical Sindarin (§ 2.1) 19
  Syllable divisions (§ 2.2) 22
  Light and heavy syllables (§ 2.3) 23
  Open and closed syllables (§ 2.4) 23
  Stress accent (§ 2.5) 23
  Long consonants (§ 2.6) 24
  Sounds found in Middle Sindarin or Sindarin dialects (§ 2.7) 24
  Sounds found in Old Sindarin (§ 2.8) 25
  Sounds found in Common Eldarin (§ 2.9) 25

3. Sindarin Writing Systems 26
The *Certhas Daeron* (§ 3.1) 26
The mode of Beleriand (§ 3.2) 27
The alphabetic mode of Gondor (§ 3.3) 28
The consonantal mode of Gondor (§ 3.4) 29

4. Historical Phonology of Sindarin 31
Changes Preceding Common Eldarin (§§ 4.1–6) 34
Early Changes in Common Eldarin (§§ 4.7–21) 34
Lindarin Changes (§§ 4.22–32) 37
Changes in Sindarin Only (§§ 4.33–77) 38
Old Sindarin to Middle Sindarin (§§ 4.78–115) 44
Sandhi Changes (§§ 4.116–68) 51
Middle Sindarin to Classical Sindarin (§§ 4.168–215) 60
Postclassical Sindarin (§§ 4.216–20) 66
Sound Changes in Sindarin Dialects (§§ 4.221–48) 67

5. Mutations 73
Consonant Mutations 73
The soft mutation (§ 5.1) 73
The nasal mutation (§ 5.2) 75
The stop mutation (§ 5.3) 77
The liquid mutation (§ 5.4) 78
The mixed mutation (§ 5.5) 79
Medial mutations (§ 5.6) 80
Vowel Mutations 82
The *a*-affection (§§ 5.7–8) 82
The *i*-affection (§ 5.9) 83
Primary final affection 83
Primary internal affection 84
Secondary affection 87
Double affection (§ 5.10) 89
Ablaut (§ 5.11) 90

6. Nouns 93
The genitive (§ 6.1) 93
Plurals (§§ 6.2–11) 94
Vowel mutation plurals (§ 6.2) 94
Unusual *i*-final plurals 95
-h plurals (§ 6.3) 95
-u plurals (§ 6.4) 96

Double affection plurals (§ 6.5) 96
Defective singulars (§ 6.6) 96
Suffix plurals (§ 6.7) 98
-in plurals (§ 6.8) 98
-ath plurals (§ 6.9) 98
-rim, -hoth, and *-waith* (§ 6.10) 98
The dative (§ 6.11) 100
The accusative (§ 6.12) 100
The vocative (§ 6.13) 100

7. Adjectives 101
Mutation of postpositioned adjectives (§ 7.1) 101
Mutation and prepositioned adjectives (§ 7.2) 101
Lenition (§ 7.3) 102
Quasi-genitive adjectives (§ 7.4) 102
Mutation and monosyllables (§ 7.5) 103
Plurality (§ 7.6) 103

8. Pronouns 105
Personal Pronouns (§§ 8.1–6) 105
Demonstratives (§§ 8.7–9) 108
Other Pronouns (§§ 8.10–13) 109
Interrogative pronouns (§ 8.10) 109
Relative pronouns (§ 8.11) 109
Indefinite pronouns (§ 8.12) 110
Reconstructed pronouns (§ 8.13) 110

9. Verbs 111
Overview (§ 9.1) 111
Personal endings (§ 9.2) 111
The infinitive (§ 9.3) 112
The present tense (§ 9.4) 112
The impersonal (§ 9.5) 113
The present participle (§ 9.6) 113
The gerund (§ 9.7) 114
The future tense (§ 9.8) 115
The past tense (§§ 9.9–13) 115
The past passive participle (§ 9.14) 120
The perfect active participle (§ 9.15) 120
The imperative (§ 9.16) 121
The verb *to be* (§ 9.17) 121
Verb Paradigms 122

10. Adverbs, Prefixes, and Prepositions 139

11. Conjunctions 148

12. The Article 149
- Overview (§ 12.1) 149
- Forms of the article (§ 12.2) 149
- Singular nominative/accusative article (§ 12.3) 149
- Singular genitive article (§ 12.4) 149
- Singular prepositional article (§ 12.5) 150
- Plural article (§ 12.6) 150
- Examples (§ 12.7) 151
- The article with collective plurals (§ 12.8) 151
- Plural prepositional article (§ 12.9) 152

13. Interjections 153

14. Word Formation 154
- Roots (§ 14.1) 154
- Nouns 156
  - Simple nouns (§ 14.2) 156
  - Nasalized nouns (§ 14.3) 157
  - Nouns with strengthened nasals (§ 14.4) 158
  - Nouns with doubled finals (§ 14.5) 158
  - Nouns with vocalized initial nasals (§ 14.6) 159
  - Nouns with Suffixes 159
    - Immediate suffixes (§ 14.7) 159
    - Mediate suffixes (§ 14.8) 161
    - Unchangeable mediate suffixes (§ 14.9) 162
- Adjectives 166
  - Simple adjectives (§ 14.10) 166
  - Nasalized adjectives (§ 14.11) 167
  - Adjectives with strengthened nasals (§ 14.12) 167
  - Adjectives with doubled finals (§ 14.13) 168
  - Adjectives with Suffixes 168
    - Immediate suffixes (§ 14.14) 168
    - Mediate suffixes (§ 14.15) 169
    - Unchangeable mediate suffixes (§ 14.16) 169
- Verbs 171
  - Simple verbs (§ 14.17) 171
  - Nasalized verbs (§ 14.18) 171

Verbs with Suffixes 172
Immediate suffixes (§ 14.19) 172
Mediate suffixes (§ 14.20) 172

15. Compound Words and Names 173
Overview (§ 15.1) 173
Tatpurusha compounds (§ 15.2) 173
Karmadharaya compounds (§ 15.3) 174
Bahuvrihi compounds (§ 15.4) 176
Prepositional compounds (§ 15.5) 176
Dvigu compounds (§ 15.6) 176
Double comparatives (§ 15.7) 176
Dvandva compounds (§ 15.8) 177
Improper compounds (§ 15.9) 177
Formation of Compound Words 178
Overview (§ 15.10) 178
Changes in Element-Initial Consonants (§§ 15.11–18) 178
Changes in Element-Final Consonants (§§ 15.19–29) 183
Liquid mutation (§ 15.30) 187
Vowel and diphthong shortenings (§ 15.31) 188
Consonant simplification (§ 15.32) 189

16. Loanwords in Sindarin 191

17. Syntax 194
Noun phrases (§ 17.1) 194
Composite noun phrases (§ 17.2) 194
Appositive noun phrases (§ 17.3) 195
Genitive noun phrases (§ 17.4) 195
Conjunct noun phrases (§ 17.5) 197
Noun and adjective phrase (§ 17.6) 197
Noun and prepositional phrase (§ 17.7) 198
Noun and complementizer phrase (§ 17.8) 199
Determiner phrases (§ 17.9) 199
Adjective phrases (§ 17.10) 201
Prepositional phrases (§ 17.11) 201
Preposition and pronoun (§ 17.12) 201
Preposition and noun phrase (§ 17.13) 201
Preposition and determiner phrase (§ 17.14) 202
Conjunct prepositional phrases (§ 17.15) 202
Complementizer phrases (§ 17.16) 202

Sentence structure: verbless sentences (§ 17.17) 203
- Noun-phrase sentences (§ 17.18) 203
- Noun-and-prepositional-phrase sentences (§ 17.19) 203
- Adjectival sentences (§ 17.20) 204

Sentence structure: verbal sentences(§ 17.21) 204
- Normal VS(O)-type sentences (§ 17.22) 204
- Sentences with omitted subject pronouns (§ 17.23) 205
- Sentences with subject topicalization (§ 17.24) 206
- Sentences with object topicalization (§ 17.25) 206
- Sentences with verb topicalization (§ 17.26) 206

Conjunct sentences (§ 17.27) 207

Extrasentential elements (§ 17.28) 207
- Vocatives (§ 17.29) 207
- Adverbials (§ 17.30) 208

Appendix 1. Extant Texts in Sindarin 211

Appendix 2. A Sindarin-English Glossary 234

Appendix 3. Eldarin Roots 294

Appendix 4. An English-Sindarin Glossary 317

Appendix 5. Sindarin Names 337
- Names of Persons and Creatures 339
- Names of Things 359
- Names of Places 366

Appendix 6. Miscellanea 395
- Sindarin Names of the Valar, Valier, and Maiar 395
- Sindarin Numbers 399
- Sindarin Month and Day Names 400

Glossary of Linguistic Terms 404

Annotated Bibliography 416

Addendum 436

TABLES

4.1. Consonantal Phonology of Common Eldarin 35
4.2. Vocalic Phonology of Common Eldarin 35
4.3. Consonantal Phonology of Old Sindarin 43
4.4. Vocalic Phonology of Old Sindarin 43
4.5. Consonantal Phonology of Middle Sindarin 60
4.6. Vocalic Phonology of Middle Sindarin 60
4.7. Consonantal Phonology of Classical Sindarin 66
4.8. Vocalic Phonology of Classical Sindarin 66
5.1. Synopsis of Initial Consonant Mutations 81
6.1. Sindarin *i*-Affection Plurals 95

PREFACE

This book is a description of Sindarin, one of the many invented languages of author and linguist J. R. R. Tolkien. Sindarin, like Tolkien's other languages, was a new invention, not based on any existing natural or artificial language. Unlike Esperanto and similar inventions, Tolkien's languages were not intended to be "ideal" languages but plausibly realistic ones. By the end of his life Tolkien had established fairly complete descriptions of at least two of these languages, the "Elvish" tongues called *Quenya* and *Sindarin*, and knew them well enough to compose poetic and prose texts in them.

Tolkien constructed for Quenya and Sindarin a lengthy sequence of changes from an ancestral "protolanguage." This history is, as Tolkien intended, comparable to the historical development of natural languages and, like them, can be usefully analyzed with the tools and techniques of historical linguistics. Within the invented historical framework Quenya and Sindarin are "related"; both are descendants of the protolanguage *Common Eldarin*, and they share a framework of "roots" from which their vocabulary is derived by a series of rule-based modifications.

Tolkien began to work on the Elvish languages in the 1910s and continued to make changes in them until his death in 1973. Although only a portion of Tolkien's work on his languages has been published, more than enough is available to allow and justify a description of Sindarin; there is, especially, a superfluity of evidence regarding such things as the formation of the vocabulary, the composition of compound words and names, and the phonetic history of the languages, of which this book will give an account. Where gaps occur, they have been filled in by educated guesswork marked as such.

Sindarin was one of the latest of Tolkien's languages to be developed. Although it can be traced back to a language that Tolkien called "Gnomish" or *Goldogrin*, invented in the 1910s, that language was quite unlike Sindarin in its internal history and morphology, despite a small overlap in vocabulary. This language would pass through many more stages of development, not all well known since the relevant documents have not yet been published. One published specimen dating from the early 1930s contains only three words known from Sindarin, whereas Quenya specimens from the same period are, despite some differences in vocabulary and morphology, much closer to the Quenya of *The Lord of the Rings*. Tolkien's non-Quenya Elvish language did not become recognizably Sindarin until the end of the 1930s, when Tolkien had finished *The Hobbit* and was beginning work on *The Lord of the Rings*. Even in the earliest drafts of *The Lord of the Rings*, some of the names are inconsistent with Sindarin and contain some novel words, such as *narod* 'red' and *palath* 'iris', that would not be seen again. These superseded forms and other early words, names, and structures are not found in this book, which undertakes to represent Sindarin in the stage it had reached from c. 1939 onward.

At its inception this language was not called Sindarin but Noldorin, referring to a later superseded version of Tolkien's mythology in which Sindarin was the language of the Noldor Elves and not of the Elves called Sindar. That mythology had been altered by the time of the publication of *The Lord of the Rings*. The change in name from Noldorin to Sindarin did not coincide with a change in structure or vocabulary. We will therefore call this language Sindarin, even though some of the words and specimens referred to were called "Noldorin" at the time of their invention.

The Sindarin presented in this book—which I have called "Classical Sindarin"—has been slightly regularized in spelling, since the material available, created at different stages in Tolkien's life, adopts a variety of "dialectal" forms and orthographic styles. The basis of the regularization is Tolkien's orthography in *The Lord of the Rings*, and the focus of this work is the Sindarin spoken by Elves and humans in Tolkien's Third Age, during which the events of *The Lord of the Rings* take place. Other variants receive attention when appropriate.

The "roots" of the attested vocabulary have been corrected, and in some cases constructed, to allow for Tolkien's repeated changes of mind about the contents and origin of his Elvish vocabulary. The new roots are intended to be entirely consistent with the phonological development of the language as this development can be demonstrated from other words with known roots. In the Sindarin glossary a number of words have been introduced to help elucidate the relationship between words that have been recorded; for example, given the recorded gerund *nestad* 'healing', it has been thought appropriate to list the unrecorded verb *nesta-* 'heal'.

Throughout the data in the appendices (and where appropriate in the body of the book) all of these new words, constructions, and corrections have been indicated by various signs, especially ! for a word or form constructed by deduction from other words and # for an altered or regularized spelling; these are carefully distinguished from the sign *, used to indicate reconstructed forms of words within the imagined history of the language. Superscript numbers distinguish words of the same form but of distinct origin and meaning.

In the course of writing this book I have had input from a number of people who read some of the chapters in draft form and made comments or suggestions. These people include Lisa Star, Helge Fauskanger, Benct Philip Jonsson, Edward Kloczko, and not least, my enormously patient wife, Dorothea Salo, without whom this book would probably never have been finished. I am also grateful for the very helpful comments and suggestions from the reviewers of this book.

I bear sole responsibility for the choice of treatment of the material, decisions on what to include and exclude, interpretations of all doubtful points, and the actual writing. Any defects—and there are doubtless many—in this book are therefore entirely my own.

This volume is not and cannot be the last or most accurate word on Sindarin. Although it is as consistent as possible with the published material, it has not been possible to take the large amount of unpublished material into account. This book must therefore contain errors large and small. Nonetheless, within the limits of the available source material, I believe this work to be accurate in general and in most points of detail. I hope it will furnish the necessary groundwork for future investigation into Sindarin. For those who wish to learn Sindarin, such errors as there may be should not affect their ability to read Sindarin texts or to construct their own.

ABBREVIATIONS

Be	[the language of the] Bëorian Edain
CE	Common Eldarin
CS	Classical Sindarin
DorS	Sindarin dialect of Doriath
Dr	[the language of the] Drúedain
Hal	Haladic
Kh	Khuzdul
MNS	Middle North Sindarin
MS	Middle Sindarin
N	Noldorin dialect of Sindarin
NS	North Sindarin dialect
OS	Old Sindarin
Oss	Ossiriandic Nandorin
Q	Quenya
S	Sindarin
SE	Silvan Elvish (Nandorin)

A GATEWAY TO SINDARIN

1

The History of Sindarin

Tolkien imagined the language of Sindarin as the end product of a history set within his created or "secondary" world. The peculiar characteristics of this Elvish language were imagined as deriving from periods of separation, isolation, and renewed contact with other Elvish languages. Description of the language is therefore assisted by a description of its invented history.

THE FIRST AGE

§ 1.1. The Lindāi

The Sindarin language was originally an Elvish speech whose roots are traceable to the first awakening of the *Quendi* (the Elves' original name for themselves, meaning 'the people') at a place in eastern Middle-earth called Cuiviénen (Sindarin *Nen Echui* 'Water of Awakening') in the 1050th year after the beginning of the Two Trees (YT [Year of the Trees]; each of these years was about nine and a half solar years long).

In the beginning the Quendi all spoke one language, which was of their own creation. They were, however, divided into three clans, each of which would eventually develop its own distinctive dialect. These clans were the Minyar (also called the Vanyar or Ingwer), the Tatyar (or Noldor) and the Nelyar, who called themselves *Lindāi* (in Quenya, *Lindar*) 'singers' because "they sang before they could speak with words."[1]

In YT 1105 the Quendi divided into two groups, the *Eldar* (*Edelōi) 'people of the journey' and the *Avari* (*Abarī) 'the refusers'. The Eldar began to travel from Cuiviénen into the West. In their journey to the West each clan traveled separately, and because the Lindāi made up more than half the Eldar and were the least eager to depart (*WJ*, p. 382), they were always the furthest behind on the road; so they were called the *Teleri* 'the hindmost'. The language of the Teleri may have begun to change in small

1. *The War of the Jewels*, p. 382. Subsequent references to this source will be cited parenthetically in the text as *WJ*.

ways from the language of the other Quendi even before the separation of the Eldar and Avari (see *WJ*, p. 410); however, these differences became even greater during the course of the journey, by the end of which the Teleri were speaking a dialect quite distinct from the speech of the Vanyar and the Noldor.

Before the Teleri had crossed the Misty Mountains, a large faction of the clan departed down the River Anduin, forsaking the journey; these became known as the *Nandor* 'those who turn back'. In YT 1128 the Teleri crossed the Ered Luin and entered the northwestern land of Beleriand.

In YT 1150 the Teleri divided again: one group crossed the Great Sea into the West, while the other group, for various reasons, remained in Beleriand and were separated from their relatives. These Teleri who remained became the people who were eventually called the Sindar 'Grey-Elves'.

§ 1.2. The Sindar in Beleriand

Among the Sindar one group remained by the Falas, the shores of the Great Sea. They became a separate folk from the other Sindar, calling themselves *Telir* (Teleri) or *Eglain* 'the forsaken', although they were known by others as *Falathrim* 'the folk of the Falas'. Over the course of the years their speech became different from that of the other Sindar, retaining some archaic features (*WJ*, p. 380).[2]

The majority of the Sindar, however, lived east of the Falathrim, as far as the mountains of Ered Luin, especially in the woods of Doriath in the midmost parts of Beleriand.

Some of the Sindar removed to the northwest, into the cool and misty country that lay around the lake of *Mithrim*, or of the Grey-folk, for so they called themselves and the land in which they dwelt. They also came to speak a dialect unlike that of the southern Sindar. The language of the Sindar was therefore divided into three distinct dialects, of Mithrim, of the Falas, and of central Beleriand, although in no case were the differences so great that one Elf could not converse with another (*WJ*, p. 411n12). Together all the dialects were known to the Noldor as Sindarin, the Grey-Elven tongue.

The Sindar did not call their own language *Sindarin*. When they were the only Elves in Beleriand, they would not have had any word to distinguish themselves from other Elves; their own name for themselves was

2. See also *The Peoples of Middle-earth*, p. 385 (subsequent references to this source will be cited parenthetically in the text as *PME*).

in-Edhil 'the Elves' (*WJ*, p. 378), and their language was *Edhellen* 'Elvish'. Only the Noldor ever called them the *Sendrim* 'Sindar'.

Before the Sindar had arrived in Beleriand, a small Dwarvish folk lived in the West of the land (*WJ*, p. 408), and the larger Dwarves crossed the Ered Luin into Beleriand about YT 1250. Around YT 1350, a part of the Nandor who had resumed the westward journey entered Beleriand and resided in the East, under the Ered Luin in the country called Ossiriand. They were known as the Green-Elves. Later a few of the Avari entered Beleriand from the South (*WJ*, p. 377). Dwarves, Green-Elves, and Avari had their own languages but used Sindarin in their dealings with the Elves of Beleriand.

During the long peace before the return of the evil power called *Morgoth* 'the Dark Enemy' to Beleriand in YT 1495, the Sindarin language was first written down in the cirth 'runes' invented and later revised by the loremaster Daeron. The cirth were mostly used for writing names and brief inscriptions, since Sindarin song and history was primarily oral (*WJ*, pp. 14, 20). Sindarin did not change very fast in that time, and over a period of about thirty-three hundred solar years it only changed as much as a later unwritten language might change in five hundred years (*WJ*, p. 24). This form of the language is called Old Sindarin in this book.

After Morgoth returned and began to attack the Sindar, many of them retreated to Doriath and became concentrated there, surrounded by a magical "Girdle" of enchantment that outsiders could not penetrate. After this time the Elves of Doriath became a separate people called the *iathrim* 'people of the fence'; their language lagged behind the changes that took place in the Sindarin spoken elsewhere in Beleriand, and in later days it was considered archaic, rich, and courteous.[3]

§ 1.3. The Noldor

In YT 1497 the first company of the Noldor (the Fëanorians) returned from across the Western Sea and entered the land of the Mithrim, and they were followed by another company of Noldor in YT 1500 (after YT 1500 the dates are given in ordinary solar years, abbreviated YS [Years of the Sun]). The speech of the Noldor was Quenya, an Eldarin language that by this time had diverged so much from Sindarin that speakers of the two languages could not understand each other.

---

3. *Unfinished Tales*, p. 76 (subsequent references to this source will be cited parenthetically in the text as *UT*); see also *WJ*, p. 312.

The Noldor, fewer in number than the Sindar, tended to adopt Sindarin after their arrival.[4] They first learned the northern Sindarin dialect and took Sindarin names in it, since they first entered the northern lands of Hithlum and Mithrim. The Noldor probably gave the name *Sindar* 'grey ones' to the whole people because the first Sindar that the Noldor met were the Mithrim or Grey-folk (*WJ*, pp. 410–11n11). In the years that followed, the Noldor spread out through Beleriand—some remaining in Mithrim, others moving into the empty lands north and east of Doriath.

In YS 67 Thingol, king of the Sindar, issued a decree that the Quenya speech should not be openly spoken in Beleriand and that the Sindar should not speak or answer to it (*WJ*, pp. 26, 43–44). After that time Quenya died out as a spoken language even among the Noldor, although it continued to be used in writing (*RK*, p. 406; *WJ*, p. 26; *PME*, p. 400n). Quenya only survived as a spoken language in the hidden city of Gondolin (founded in the YS 116); nonetheless, most of the Gondolindrim spoke Sindarin, but because they were cut off from later changes in the language, their speech remained archaic (*PME*, pp. 370, 374n16; *WJ*, p. 201; *UT*, p. 44).

In later years, in the lands they controlled, the Noldor merged with the Sindar into one people speaking the Sindarin tongue (*WJ*, p. 378). The Quenya words and devices used by the Noldor gradually found their way into the common Sindarin language, except in Doriath, where a purer speech was preserved (*WJ*, p. 26). The Noldor also lent to Sindarin their script, the *tengwar* of Fëanor. This writing became so commonly used, even among the Sindar, that the Runes of Daeron fell largely into disuse and when used were spelled according to the usual usages of the tengwar script (*PME*, p. 298).

At the height of their power the Noldor held all Beleriand and Hithlum except for the Falas, Doriath, and Ossiriand. Their kingdoms were Hithlum and Mithrim; Tol Sirion, in the pass of Sirion; the northern hills of Dorthonion; the east marches, between Dorthonion and the Ered Luin; and the height of Amon Ereb, in the south of East Beleriand. The people of Nevrast, Noldor and Sindar alike, removed to the hidden city of Gondolin in the western mountains of Dorthonion. The largest kingdom had its seat in the caves of Nargothrond but extended all along the river Narog from the Ered Wethrin to the sea and included all of West Beleriand except the Falas and the forest of Brethil, the last of which was controlled by Doriath.

In most of these realms, which were either in lands formerly inhabited by the Mithrim or by few or no Sindar at all, the Northern Sindarin first

---

4. *Return of the King*, p. 406 (subsequent references to this source will be cited parenthetically in the text as *RK*); *WJ*, p. 26.

learned by the Noldor was spoken; but in Nargothrond, the largest kingdom, the people originally spoke the same tongue as that of Doriath. It can be deduced that the Sindarin of Nargothrond was the standard of comparison, since the Sindarin of all the other kingdoms of Beleriand is characterized either as dialectal (the Falas, Hithlum, Mithrim, Dorthonion, East Beleriand) or archaic (Doriath, Gondolin).

§ 1.4. The Edain

Beginning in the year of the Sun 310, the three tribes or "houses" of the Edain 'humans' crossed the Ered Luin into Beleriand. They dwelt first in Estolad, in East Beleriand; but later many of them received lands in Beleriand from the Eldar. Although each house kept its own tongue for daily use, Sindarin was widely learned among them both for speech with the Eldar and as a common tongue for use in speech with Edain of another house (*WJ*, pp. 219, 223; *PME*, pp. 308, 368).

The House of Bëor settled in the land of Ladros, in the eastern parts of Dorthonion, where some learned the North Sindarin of the lords of the Noldor (*PME*, 368). The House of Marach, who under their lord, Hador, settled in Dor-lómin, the southernmost part of Hithlum, also used North Sindarin, which alone was spoken in the dwelling of Hador (*WJ*, p. 224). The House of Haleth, after many wanderings, settled in Brethil by the leave of King Thingol. Despite an early preference for their own language, by the time their realm came to an end, they had abandoned their native speech for daily use and had adopted Sindarin (*WJ*, p. 283; *PME*, p. 372n4).

§ 1.5. The end of the First Age

The Elvish kingdoms ultimately fell either to Morgoth or to their own civil wars: Dorthonion and Tol Sirion fell in YS 455; Ladros in 456; Hithlum, Dor-lómin, and the northern realms of the Fëanorians in 472; the Falas in 473; Nargothrond in 495; Brethil in 501; Doriath in 507; and Gondolin in 510. The Eldar and the Edain were driven back to refuges on the Island of Balar, in Arvernien, and about the mouths of Sirion in the South. All varieties of Sindarin were spoken in the Havens, as well as the Mannish speeches of the houses of Hador and Bëor. At the Havens the first great literary monument of Sindarin that was later preserved was written, the *Narn i Chîn Húrin* by Dírhaval (or Dírhavel) of the House of Hador (*PME*, p. 370; *WJ*, p. 313).

The Havens of Sirion were destroyed by the Fëanorians of Amon Ereb in 538; Ereb was captured by Morgoth in 544, and the Fëanorians also went to the Island of Balar. That war, however, ended with the defeat of Morgoth by an army led from the West. In the war Beleriand was destroyed and sank beneath the sea. Only the easternmost parts of Beleriand and Ossiriand were saved; this land afterward became part of the Elvish kingdom of Lindon.

This period, the last 590 years of the First Age, was a period of very rapid change in the Sindarin language due to the breakup of the language into even more isolated dialects and the influence of the Noldor and the Edain. The transitional language of this period is called Middle Sindarin in this book.

THE SECOND AGE

§ 1.6. The Eldar in Beleriand

After the fall of Beleriand many of the Noldor returned to the island of Tol Eressëa in the West. Many of the Sindar went with them, so Sindarin came to be one of the languages spoken in Tol Eressëa.

Others of the Sindar remained in Lindon, along with some of the Noldor, including High King Gil-galad, ruler of Lindon and the lands beyond the northern Ered Luin as far as the Great and Little Lune (*PME*, p. 313); Galadriel, his kinswoman; Celeborn of Doriath, who ruled over the Sindar of Lindon south of the river Lune as a vassal of Gil-galad (PME, p. 328n65); Círdan the Shipwright, lord of the Havens founded at the mouth of the Lune in the first year of the Second Age (SA 1); Celebrimbor of the Fëanorians; and Elrond, son of Eärendil.

In this time Sindarin took the form that it would have for the next two ages whenever it was written or spoken with correctness and courtesy—a language that might be called "Classical" Sindarin. The main element in the formation of this speech seems to have been the dialect of Nargothrond and perhaps the dialects of Doriath and Gondolin. Despite its former prevalence in Beleriand, the North Sindarin dialect seems to have had little effect on this standardized speech.

The Sindarin words and names recorded in the histories of the First Age (such as the *Grey Annals* of Beleriand)[5] are not necessarily those used by the people living at the time of which the histories tell. The words are, in-

---

5. See *WJ*, pp. 1–172.

stead, those that were current at the beginning of the Second Age, and the names of people and places were, like other words, altered to fit the style of the language at that time (*WJ*, p. 26). It may have been at this time that the second great work of Sindarin literature, the *Lay of Leithian* (mentioned in the *Grey Annals*), was written.

§ 1.7. The migrations of the Sindar of Doriath

Late in the First Age or early in the Second, some of the Sindar departed Beleriand, either crossing the Ered Luin into the wide lands of Eriador in the East or sailing from the Havens to the southern coasts. These were for the most part Sindar of Doriath, who did not wish to be ruled by the Noldor (*UT*, pp. 247, 259).

Those who went east passed over the Misty Mountains and came into the woods on either side of the Vale of Anduin, where many of the Silvan Elves (a branch of the Nandor) dwelt. One of these Sindar, Oropher, founded a realm over the Silvan Elves in the south of Greenwood the Great east of Anduin. Amdír, who ruled Lórien west of Anduin, was probably another of these Sindar (*UT*, pp. 236, 243, 256, 259). At first the outnumbered Sindar tended to merge with the Silvan Elves, often adopting the Silvan language for speech rather than teaching Sindarin to the Nandor (*UT*, p. 259; *WJ*, p. 381); if the Nandor learned to write, however, they doubtless wrote in Sindarin (*UT*, p. 257).

The Sindar who went south founded a new haven at the mouths of the rivers Morthond and Ringló that lasted well into the Third Age. This was called Edhellond, the Elf-haven. In later years they were joined by some of the Silvan Elves who wished to live near the sea (*PME*, p. 329n67).

§ 1.8. The migrations of the Noldor

After some centuries of the Second Age had passed, some of the mixed Noldor and Sindar of Lindon began to travel eastward. Their foremost leaders were Galadriel, Celeborn, and Celebrimbor. To the west of the Misty Mountains, bordering the great Dwarf-mansion of Khazad-dûm (where the metal *mithril* had recently been discovered), they founded the great realm of Eregion and its city of Ost-in-Edhil in the eighth century SA. Galadriel passed over the Misty Mountains and entered the realms of Lórien and the Greenwood. In the latter realm her intrusion, combined with the growing power of Khazad-dûm—and perhaps the Men of the Vales of Anduin, with whom the Dwarves were allied (*PME*, pp. 303–5)—

caused Oropher to remove his folk to a part of the Greenwood north of the Gladden Fields (*UT*, p. 258). In later years he continued to move northward, until at the end of the age his folk were dwelling in the Emyn Duir, the Dark Mountains in the north of the Greenwood (*UT*, p. 280n14).

In SA 1693 Sauron, a former servant of Morgoth, made war against the Eldar of Eregion. Despite the assistance of the Elves of Lindon and Lórien, Eregion was destroyed and its people scattered. In SA 1697 some of the fugitives joined with the army from Lindon and retreated to Imladris, a hidden valley on a branch of the Bruinen River, where they established a refuge. Other fugitives made their way across the mountains to Lórien (*UT*, pp. 243, 257). At the end of the war (SA 1701) the Eldar decided to maintain Imladris as a stronghold in eastern Eriador, under Elrond, but the realm of Eregion was never reestablished (*UT*, p. 239). In these wars the people of Lindon abandoned their lands east of the Ered Luin (*PME*, p. 330n75). At this time Elves also began to sail west over sea from Edhellond.[6]

§ 1.9. Númenor

The Edain who had fought against Morgoth in Beleriand migrated (SA 32–c. 80) to the island of Elenna in the middle of the Great Sea, where they established the realm of Númenor (*PME*, pp. 144–45).

These Edain were mostly of the houses of Hador and Bëor; few if any of the people of Haleth had survived the destruction of Brethil, and their language was no longer spoken (*PME*, pp. 372n4, 374n17). The Bëorians settled mostly in the western districts of the island, and except for some rural areas in which their ancient tongue continued to be spoken, this people spoke Sindarin as a daily speech, used by all classes (*PME*, p. 329; *UT*, pp. 194, 215n9).

The rest of the island was inhabited by Edain of the House of Hador, whose daily tongue was their own Adûnaic. But most of them knew at least a little Sindarin, and the noble and learned families of Númenor also learned Sindarin in childhood and spoke it familiarly among themselves or even as a native language (*PME*, p. 329). The purity of this Sindarin was maintained by the long-established contacts that Númenor had with the Eldar of Eressëa and of Lindon (*UT*, p. 215n9).

---

6. *Adventures of Tom Bombadil*, p. 8 (subsequent references to this source will be cited parenthetically in the text as *ATB*).

It may have been in Númenor that the third great monument of Sindarin literature was written, *The Tale of the Fall of Gondolin and of the Rising of the Star*, which treated of Eärendil and his father, Tuor. In Númenor also the *Lay of Leithian* was put into prose as the *Tale of Beren, Son of Barahir* (or *Tale of the Nightingale*),[7] and in Númenor was made, from the traditions remembered by the Edain and by the Eldar of Lindon and Eressëa, the great compilation of the lore of the Elder Days known as *The Silmarillion* (*PME*, p. 357).

After the reign of Tar-Atanamir the Great (SA 2035–2221) the use of Sindarin declined in Númenor, for the kings became hostile to the Eldar and all that was associated with them. In the reign of Tar-Ancalimon, son of Atanamir (SA 2221–2386), the partisans of the king began to abandon the use of Sindarin and only taught their children Adûnaic (*UT*, p. 221). By the time of the reign of Ar-Adûnakhôr (SA 2899–2962) Sindarin had fallen out of common use, and it was no longer permitted to teach it or speak it openly or in the hearing of the king; but those Númenóreans known as the Faithful, who remained friendly to the Eldar, continued to speak it privately among themselves.[8]

Ar-Gimilzôr (SA 3102–77) at last banned any use of Sindarin, public or private, and ordered many books that had been written in the Elvish tongues burned. He also forbade the landing of any of the Eldar from Eressëa and removed the Faithful from the Westlands (where they had mostly dwelt) to the eastern harbor of Rómenna (*Silm*, p. 268; *UT*, p. 223).

During this time many of the Faithful fled Númenor and established refuges in Middle-earth. The greatest of these refuges was Pelargir, near the mouths of the Anduin, established in SA 2350 in the reign of Tar-Ancalimon; but a family of the Faithful also established a colony in Belfalas, not far from Edhellond (*UT*, p. 316n39).

In SA 3319 Elenna was destroyed in a great earthquake and drowned beneath the waves. Only a handful of the Elf-friends, led by Elendil the Tall, escaped to the western shores of Middle-earth. But even in the colonies of the Faithful, which were friendly to the Númenórean exiles, Sindarin was little known (*RK*, p. 407); and the common speech of the realms that Elendil and his sons established in Middle-earth was a form of Adûnaic, mixed with languages of other peoples, which came to be known as Adûni or Westron (*PME*, p. 316).

---

7. *Morgoth's Ring*, p. 373.

8. *RK*, p. 316; *The Silmarillion*, p. 267 (subsequent references to this source will be cited parenthetically in the text as *Silm*); *UT*, p. 222.

THE THIRD AGE

§ 1.10. The kingdoms of the Elves

The Second Age closed with the great assault of Sauron against the Númenórean and Elvish kingdoms, which destroyed an entire generation of Elvish rulers (Gil-galad, Amdîr, Oropher). Lindon was then ruled by Cîrdan the Shipwright and remained little changed for the rest of the Third Age.

In the Third Age, exiles from Eregion combined with the earlier Sindarin settlers and made the woodland realm of Lórien less Silvan and more Sindarin in character (*UT*, pp. 243, 257). By the year 1981 of the Third Age the Silvan tongue was dying out (*UT*, p. 241). After Amroth departed for Edhellond and was replaced by Galadriel and Celeborn, Silvan was lost altogether, leaving only a few words and names in the Sindarin tongue of Lórien. The Sindarin of Lórien was, however, a dialect distinctive enough in "accent" that strangers might not recognize it as Sindarin (*RK*, p. 405n; *UT*, p. 257).

Around TA 1000 Sauron reappeared in the south of the Greenwood, which now came to be called Mirkwood. Thranduil retreated from Sauron farther northward, and in the hills in the northeast of the wood not far from the Lonely Mountain and the Long Lake he established underground halls like those of Menegroth in the First Age (*UT*, p. 259).

In northern Mirkwood both Sindarin and Silvan were spoken, although there seems to be some confusion between the dialectal Sindarin of Mirkwood and the native Silvan tongue. According to one account Silvan had been replaced entirely by Sindarin, as in Lórien (*UT*, p. 257); according to another Sindarin was used only in the house and family of Thranduil (*UT*, p. 256); and according to a third "the Silvan Elves of Thranduil's realm did not speak S[indarin] but a related language or dialect."[9] The name of Legolas, son of Thranduil, was said to have been in a woodland dialect of Sindarin.[10] Since the Sindar of Mirkwood came originally from Doriath, their dialect may always have been distinct from the common Sindarin of other Elves, which had undergone strong Noldorin influences.

The Elvish haven of Edhellond at the mouth of the Morthond continued for many years of the Third Age. Many of its folk were Silvan Elves, and it was somehow associated with Amroth of Lórien even at this early date: the land about was called the country of Amroth (*UT*, p. 175), and the nearby Númenórean citadel of Belfalas was called *Dol Amroth* 'Amroth's Hill'.

---

9. *The Letters of J. R. R. Tolkien*, p. 425n.
10. Ibid., p. 282.

The number of Elves dwelling there steadily dwindled, and after the last ship set sail from its haven in 1981 it became part of the kingdom of Gondor (*UT*, pp. 241–42).

At the end of the Third Age the four remaining Elvish realms were small, widely scattered, and often hidden, but they retained a tenuous contact with each other. Pilgrims from Rivendell (Imladris) often journeyed at least as far as the Tower Hills, the easternmost outpost of Lindon.[11] There were also secret but frequent communications between Rivendell and Lórien.[12] Contact between the Elves of Lórien and their kin in Mirkwood had long ago been lost (*FR*, p. 352), but after the Battle of Five Armies (TA 2941) and the rise of the Beornings, the passes of the Misty Mountains became safe enough for messengers to go from Mirkwood to Rivendell.[13]

§ 1.11. The kingdoms of Men

The Númenórean exiles, or Dúnedain, established two kingdoms in Middle-earth: Arnor, in Eriador, and Gondor, about the southern Anduin and the Bay of Belfalas. In these kingdoms Westron was the language of daily speech, but as in the early years of Númenor, the noble and literate people of the kingdoms also learned Sindarin and made their names for persons and places in this tongue (*RK*, p. 406n1; *PME*, pp. 315, 330n73). Many used it as a daily speech, and in some families it became a native language. Despite some changes in the language, it remained fairly pure, being taught in the schools "according to forms and grammatical structure of ancient days" (*PME*, p. 330n74; see also *RK*, p. 406). The Dúnedain did not, however, teach Sindarin to people of other nations, and knowledge of it became a mark of Númenórean descent (*PME*, p. 315).

The Kingdom of Arnor broke into petty states early in the Third Age (861), the last of which was entirely destroyed in 1975. The Dúnedain that remained became wanderers, ranging over a wide area between the Baranduin and the Bruinen, going as far north as the ruins of Fornost Erain and south to Sarn Ford (*FR*, pp. 161, 202; *RK*, p. 273; *UT*, p. 341; *ATB*, p. 21). They also remained in touch with Imladris, where their chieftains were raised (*FR*, p. 323). They appear to have retained a good knowledge of Sindarin and were able to compose verse in it (*RK*, p. 342).

---

11. *The Road Goes Ever On*, pp. 65–66; *PME*, p. 313.

12. *The Fellowship of the Ring* (subsequent references to this source will be cited parenthetically in the text as *FR*), p. 287.

13. *The Hobbit*, p. 245; *FR*, pp. 241, 253, 309.

Development of the Elvish Languages

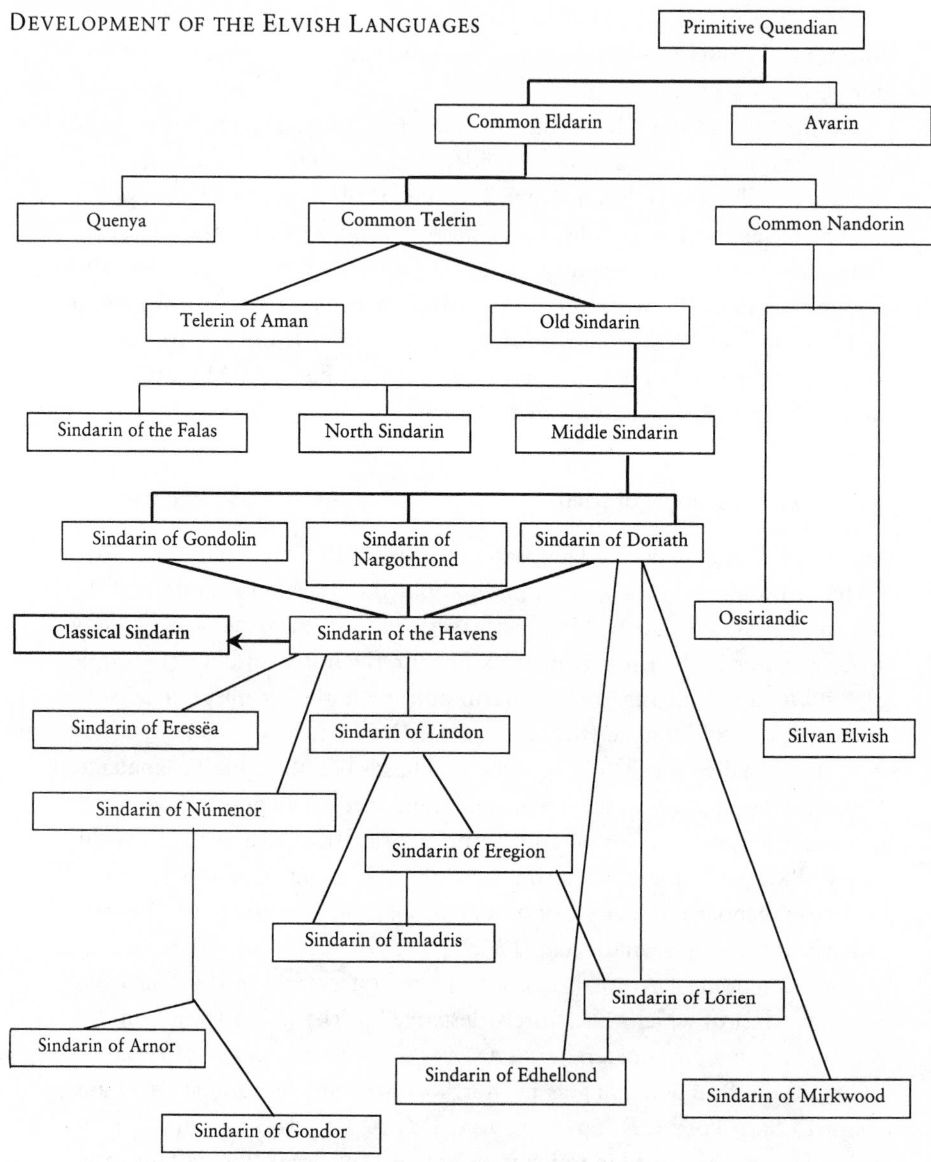

The realm of Gondor lasted to the end of the Third Age. The noble families of Gondor usually knew some Sindarin (*UT*, p. 399; *PME*, pp. 316n2, 332), but only a few used it as a daily speech. "These," it is said, "dwelt mostly in Minas Tirith and the townlands adjacent, and in the land of the tributary princes of Dol Amroth" (*RK*, p. 407). It is likely that the persistence of Sindarin in Dol Amroth owed something to the city's proximity to the ancient haven of Edhellond and to the Elvish ancestry that its princes claimed (*UT*, p. 248; *PME*, p. 221). It was used in speech if the speaker "wanted to be polite,"[14] that is, to address another person in a respectful manner. Despite a decline in the Sindarin-speaking population of Gondor, at the end of the Third Age there were probably more Dúnedain of Gondor who spoke Sindarin than there were Sindarin-speaking Elves in Lindon, Rivendell, and Lórien all together.[15] In the last years of the Third Age, as a result of the marriage (2943) of Thengel of Rohan to Morwen of Lossarnach (whose family was from Belfalas), Sindarin came to be spoken also by the kings of Rohan (*PME*, p. 316n2; *RK*, p. 350; *UT*, p. 286).

§ 1.12. The end of the Third Age

The Third Age ended with the fall of Sauron and the departure of Elrond and Galadriel over the sea. Imladris and Lórien thereafter declined, but Gondor and Rohan became powerful, and the realm of Arnor was reestablished. Elves from Lórien returned to the southern woods of Mirkwood, which was now called Eryn Lasgalen, the Wood of Greenleaves. A new colony of Sindarin-speaking Elves was also made in Gondor, for Legolas son of Thranduil brought Elves from the Wood into the fief of Ithilien, where they would remain until they decided to depart into the West (*RK*, pp. 234, 360, 362, 378).

§ 1.13. Timeline

VALIAN YEARS (FROM THE BEGINNING OF THE TWO TREES)

1050	The Quendi awake at Cuiviénen. Beginning of *Primitive Quendian*.
1085	Oromë (Araw) comes to Cuiviénen.
1105	Separation of the Eldar from the Avari. Beginning of the Great Journey. *Common Eldarin*.
1115	The Eldar halt east of the Misty Mountains. The Nandor leave the march of the Eldar and pass south down the Anduin. End of *Common Telerin*.
1128	The Teleri cross the Blue Mountains (Ered Luin) and enter Beleriand.

14. *Letters*, p. 425.
15. Ibid.

1132	The Vanyar and Noldor depart across the sea.
1150	The Teleri under Olwë depart across the sea. Beginning of *Old Sindarin.*
1152	Elwë (Elu Thingol) becomes king of the remaining Teleri (Sindar).
1250	The Dwarves enter Beleriand.
1300	Building of Menegroth. Daeron, loremaster of Thingol, devises the runes (cirth).
1330	Orcs and other evil creatures enter Beleriand.
1350	Denethor of the Nandor leads the Green-Elves into Beleriand.
1495	Ungoliant enters Beleriand.
1497	Morgoth assaults Beleriand. Thingol withdraws within the Girdle of Melian. The Noldor of Fëanor enter Hithlum.
1500	The Noldor of Fingolfin enter Hithlum. The rising of the Sun and Moon. End of *Old Sindarin.* Beginning of *Middle Sindarin.*

YEARS OF THE SUN: FIRST AGE

6	Thingol grants the Noldor lands north and east of Doriath.
20	Mereth Aderthad. The Noldor adopt Sindarin for general use.
52–102	Finrod establishes the realm of Nargothrond west of Doriath.
60–445	The Siege of Angband.
64–116	Turgon builds the hidden city of Gondolin.
67	Thingol forbids the open use of Quenya within his realms.
310–14	The Three Houses of the Edain enter Beleriand.
390	The House of Haleth settles in Brethil.
410	The House of Bëor settles in Ladros.
c. 420	The House of Hador settles in Dor-lómin.
455–56	Dagor Bragollach. Destruction of Dorthonion and Ladros. Taking of Tol Sirion. Turgon establishes refuges on the Isle of Balar.
472	Nírnaeth Arnediad. Destruction of Hithlum, Dor-lómin, and the northern lordships of the sons of Fëanor.
473	Destruction of the Falas. The Falathrim establish refuges in Balar and the mouths of Sirion.
495	Fall of Nargothrond.
501	Civil war and end of the domain of Brethil.
503	Invasion of Doriath and death of Elu Thingol.
507	The realm of Doriath destroyed by the Fëanorians.

510	Fall of Gondolin.
511	Survivors of Gondolin escape to the mouths of Sirion.
538	The havens of Sirion destroyed by the Fëanorians.
544	Destruction of the refuges of the Fëeanorians. They flee to Balar.
545–87	The War of Wrath.
590	End of the First Age. End of *Middle Sindarin*.

Years of the Sun: Second Age

1	The Grey Havens and the kingdom of Lindon are established by Círdan and Gil-galad. Beginning of *Classical Sindarin*.
32–c. 82	The Edain under Elros sail to Númenor.
Early Second Age	Sindar depart from Lindon; realms are established in Lórien (by Amdír) and Greenwood the Great (by Oropher), as well as the havens of Edhellond at the mouth of Morthond.
c. 700	The realm of Eregion established.
c. 750	Building of Ost-in-Edhil, chief city of Eregion.
Mid-Second Age	Oropher removes north of the Gladden.
1693–1701	War of the Elves and Sauron. Eregion destroyed. Establishment of Imladris under Elrond (1697). Many of Eregion's inhabitants flee to Imladris or Lórien. Ships begin to sail over sea from Edhellond. Lindon abandons its provinces in Eriador.
Later Second Age	Oropher moves north to the Emyn Duir.
2221–2386	Reign of Tar-Ancalimon. The "King's Men" in Númenor abandon the use of Sindarin. The 'Faithful' Númenóreans begin to make settlements of their own on the coasts of Middle-earth, including Pelargir and Belfalas.
2899–2962	Reign of Ar-Adûnakhôr. Suppression of Sindarin in Númenor begins.
3102–77	Reign of Ar-Gimilzôr. Use of Sindarin outlawed in Númenor.
3319	Fall of Númenor.
3320	Elendil and his sons establish the realms of Arnor and Gondor in Middle-earth.
3429–41	War of the Last Alliance. Defeat of Sauron. Deaths of Amdír, Oropher, Gil-galad, Elendil. Amroth and Thranduil become kings of their people in Lórien and the Greenwood.

Years of the Sun: Third Age

2	Isildur killed at the Gladden Fields. Separation of Arnor and Gondor.
861	Division of Arnor into petty kingdoms.
933	Gondor takes Umbar.
c. 1000	Sauron enters southern Mirkwood. Thranduil removes to northeastern Mirkwood.
c.1350	Rhudaur ruled by Hillmen.
1409	Angmar invades the northern kingdoms. The Dúnedain abandon Rhudaur.
1448	Gondor loses Umbar.
1601	The Halflings settle the largely abandoned royal demesne of Arthedain and name it "The Shire."
1636	The Great Plague desolates much of Eriador. The Dúnedain die out in Cardolan.
Mid-Third Age	The Silvan Elvish tongue is gradually abandoned in Lórien.
1810–1944	Gondor briefly holds Umbar.
1974–75	Angmar destroys Arthedain. The Dúnedain of Arthedain become a wandering people.
1980–81	A Balrog appears in Moria. Many Elves of Lórien, including their king Amroth, flee south. Amroth is lost. Galadriel and Celeborn take up the rule of Lórien. End of the haven of Edhellond.
2050	Death of the last king of Gondor, which is now ruled by Stewards.
2510	Gondor gives the province of Calenardhon to the Éothéod of the North; it is later known as Rohan.
2901	Gondor abandons Ithilien.
2941	Battle of the Five Armies.
2953	Thengel becomes king of Rohan. Sindarin begins to be spoken in Edoras.
3018–19	The War of the Ring. Sauron finally defeated. Reestablishment of the Kingdom of Arnor.
3021	End of the Third Age. Many of the Eldar depart from Middle-earth.

2

The Sounds of Sindarin

Below are listed the sounds found in Sindarin and its ancestors, represented by (1) Tolkien's conventional transcription of Sindarin, (2) a phonemic transcription used in this book for Elvish languages other than Quenya and Classical Sindarin,[1] and (3) the International Phonetic Alphabet.

§ 2.1. Sounds found in Classical Sindarin

1.	2.	3.	
a	a	ɑ	like *a* in English *father*.
á	ā	[ɑː]	the same sound as *a* but prolonged for about twice as long.
ae	ae	[ae̯]	like the *i* in English *high* (but ending with the sound of Sindarin *e* rather than Sindarin *i*). Occasionally written *ai* in nonfinal syllables (e.g., *Aiglos*, *Gwaihir*).
ai	ai	[aj]	like the *i* in English *high* (but clearly beginning with the sound of Sindarin *a*). Occasionally used for *ae* in nonfinal syllables.
au	au	[aw]	like the *ou* in English *proud* (but clearly beginning with the sound of Sindarin *a*).
aw	au	[aw]	the same as *au*.
b	b	[b]	like English *b*.
c	k	[k]	always like English *k* in *skill*, even before *e* and *i*; *celeb* 'silver' = keleb. Not aspirated initially.
ch	x	[x]	like the *ch* in Scottish *loch* (not that in English *chill*). In the pronunciation of Sindarin in Gondor this sound became *h* (except finally, where it was pronounced *k*), and that change has been shown in the writing of a few names, such as *Rohan* and *Elrohir*.

1. These symbols were suggested by Mr. Benct Philip Jonsson.

chw	xƕ	[xʍ]	like *ch* + *hw*.
d	d	[d]	like English *d*.
dh	ð	[ð]	like the voiced *th* of English *those*, *blithe*.
e	e	[ɛ]	like *e* of English *bed*.
é	ē	[eː]	the same sound as Sindarin *e* but prolonged for about twice as long.
ei	ei	[ej]	like the *ay* of English *May*.
f	f, v	[f], [v]	like the *f* of English *fair*, except at the end of words and before *n*, where it is used to represent the sound of *v* (as in English *of*): *Nindalf*, *Fladrif*, *Lefnui* = Nindalv, Fladriv, Levnui.
g	g	[g]	like the *g* of English *gift*, *get*, never as in *gem*; *gîl* 'star' begins as in English *gilt*.
gw	gw	[gw]	like the *gw* in *bigwig*.
h	h	[h]	like the *h* of English *hill*, *ahead* when by itself (without any other accompanying consonant).
hw	ƕ	[ʍ]	a voiceless *w*, like the *wh* of English *wheel*, *whale* (when pronounced differently from *weal*, *wail*).
i^1	i	[i]	like the *i* in English *marine*.
i^2	j	[j]	*i* initially before a vowel has the consonantal sound of *y* in *yes*, *your*; as in *Ioreth*, *Iarwain* = Yoreth, Yarwain. It is spelled thus to distinguish it from the vowel *y* (see below).
í	ī	[iː]	the same sound as i^1 but prolonged for about twice as long.
l	l	[l][ʎ]	like the *l* of English *less*, *lift* (not the "dark" *l* of *ball*), palatalized (given a sound somewhat like that of the *lli* in *million*) between *e* or *i* and a consonant, or finally after *e* or *i*. *l* is voiceless (see *lh*) after voiceless fricatives, e.g., *f*, *th*.
lh	ḽ	[l̥]	a voiceless *l* (usually derived from initial *sl-*). It occurred initially and also after voiceless fricatives (e.g., *f*, *th*), where it is spelled *l*, as in the name *Delduthling*.
m	m	[m]	like English *m*.
n	n	[n], [ŋ]	like English *n*; before *c* or *g* like *ng* in English *ring*.
ng	ŋ, ŋg	[ŋ], [ŋg]	initially, finally, and before consonants other than *r*, *l*, or *w* like *ng* in English *ring*, *kingdom*; between vowels or before *r*, *l*, and *w* like the *ng* in English *linger*, *hungry*.

nth	nþ, nth	[nθ], [nth]	when the syllable break falls between *n* and *th* (*n·th*), pronounced like the *nth* in English *anthem*; when it falls between *nt* and *h* (*nt·h*) pronounced like the *nth* in English *anthill.*
o	o	[ɔ]	like the *o* in (British) English *hot* but more rounded.
ó	ō	[ɔ:]	the same sound as *o* but prolonged for about twice as long.
oe	oe	[ɔɛ̯]	similar to *oy* in English *toy* (but ending with the sound of Sindarin *e* rather than Sindarin *i*).
p	p	[p]	like English *p* in *spy*, not aspirated initially
ph	f	[f]	the same sound as *f*, used where the *f* sound occurs at the end of a word, as in *alph* 'swan' (to distinguish it from final -*f* = v); where the *f* sound is related to or derived from a *p*, as in *i·Pheredhil* 'the Half-Elves' (*peredhel*) or *arphen* 'nobleman'; in the middle of some words where it represents a formerly long -*ff*- (from *-*pp*-), *p* + *h*, *n* + *p*, etc., as in *aphadon* 'follower' or the names *Celepharn*, *Araphant.*
r	r	[r]	always a trilled *r*, never lost before consonants. *r* is voiceless (see *rh*) after voiceless fricatives, e.g., *f, h.*
rh	r̭	[r̥]	a voiceless *r* (usually derived from older initial **sr*-); it occurred initially and also after voiceless fricatives (e.g., *f, th*), where it is spelled *r* (as in *lathron*).
s	s	[s]	always voiceless, like the *s* of English *say*, *loose*; there was no sound like the *s* in English *as*, *user*, in Classical Sindarin or its descendant dialects.
t	t	[t]	like English *t* in *stair*, not aspirated initially.
th	þ	[θ]	the English voiceless *th* of *thick*, *path.*
u	u	[u]	the sound of *u* in English *brute.*
ú	ū	[u:]	the same sound as *u* but prolonged for about twice as long.
ui	ui	[uj]	similar to the sound of *oui* in French *Louis* but pronounced as a single syllable.
v	v	[v]	the *v* of English, not used finally. See *f.*
w	w	[w]	like English *w.*
y	y	[y]	like the sound of *u* in French *vu.*

For a classification of these sounds by type and position see Table 4.7.

Of these sounds, the consonants *b*, *c*, *d*, *f*, *g*, *h*, *hw*, i^2, *l*, *lh*, *m*, *n*, *p*, *r*, *rh*, *s*, *t*, *th*, and the clusters *bl*, *br*, *cl*, *cr*, *dr*, *fl*, *gl*, *gr*, *gw*, *pr*, and *tr* appear in absolute initial position; the consonants *b*, *ch*, *chw*, *d*, *dh*, *f*, *g*, *h*, i^2, *l*, *m*, *n*, *ng*, *r*, *th*, *v*, *w*, and the clusters *br*, *chl*, *chr*, *dr*, *dhr*, *fl*, *fr*, *ml*, *mr*, *thl*, *thr*, *vl*, and *vr* can appear in lenited initial position; and the consonants *b*, *ch*, *d*, *dh*, *f* (spelled *ph*), *g*, *l*, *m*, *n*, *ng*, *r*, *s*, *th*, *v* (spelled *f*), *w*, and the clusters *fn*, *lch*, *lph*, *ll*, *lt*, *lv* (spelled *lf*), *mp*, *nc*, *nd*, *nt*, *rch*, *rdh*, *rn*, *rth*, *rv* (spelled *rf*), *sg*, *sp*, and *st* appear in final position.

§ 2.2. Syllable divisions

A syllable of a Sindarin word consists of a vocalic core (every syllable *must* have at least one vowel) and attached consonants. If a word has only one vowel, short or long, it has only one syllable, no matter how many consonants it has; both *i* and *brand* are alike a single syllable.

The simplest syllable is just a vowel (short or long), as in *a*, *i*, *o*, or the initial syllables of *a·nor* or *ú·an*. A vowel can be preceded by one or two consonants: *dû*, *dú·ath*, *gwî*, *bre·thil*. A vowel can be followed by up to two consonants: *ad*, *ag·lar*, *ast*, *lant·hir*. A syllable can also consist of a diphthong with associated consonants, e.g., *ae·wen*, *mae·thor*, *dui·nath*, *goe·ol*, *gwai·hir*, *duin·hir*. The elements of a diphthong are never split between two syllables; *duin* not *!du·in*, *laeg* not *!la·eg*.

If more than one consonant begins a syllable, the second consonant must be *l*, *r*, or *w* (the last only in the cluster *gw*): *cram*, *pres·'tan·neth*, *gwaew*; *gon·dren*, *an·gren*, *an·'glen·na*, *an·gwedh*.

When no consonant follows a vowel, and the two vowels do not form a diphthong (*ae*, *ai*, *au*, *ei*, *oe*, or *ui*) together, the break between syllables falls between the vowels: *ae·ar*, *rí·an*, *goe·ol*, *'fi·ri·on*.

When a single consonant follows a vowel, the syllable break almost always comes before the following consonant, except where that is final: *ta·lan*, *o·rod*, *'se·re·gon*. The notable exception involves *m*, for which see below (§ 2.6).

When only two consonants follow each other in the middle of a word, the syllable division *always* falls between them, whether they can begin a syllable or not: *idh·ren*, *oth·lonn*, *nes·'tad·ren*, *baug·ron*.

When three consonants (four or more cannot occur) follow each other in the middle of a word, the syllable break can fall either between the first and second consonant or between the second and the third. The first instance, which is by far the more common, occurs when the second and third consonants are a permissible beginning to a word or a syllable; that is, when the third consonant is *l*, *r*, or *w*: *nin·glor*, *an·drath*, *lhin·gril*, *dan·gweth*, *Or·christ*. In the few remaining cases the syllable break occurs before the third consonant: *lant·hir*, *Pant·hael*.

§ 2.3. Light and heavy syllables

Syllables can be separated into the classes of light (or short) and heavy (or long). A light syllable usually takes less time to say than a heavy one. A light syllable consists of a single short vowel, either by itself or preceded by one or more consonants. All other syllables are heavy: those containing a long vowel, a diphthong, or a short vowel followed by one or more consonants.

Monosyllables such as *a* or *na* are light; *dû* is heavy because it contains a long vowel; *nae*, *goe*, and *glaw* because they contain diphthongs; *ed*, *dan*, *ost*, and *nand* because they end in one or more consonants; and *glân*, *dîr*, and *laer* for combinations of these reasons.

§ 2.4. Open and closed syllables

A different distinction, of some importance in the history of Sindarin, is that between open and closed syllables. Open syllables are those followed only by a single consonant or none (including those with long vowels and diphthongs); closed syllables are those followed by more than one consonant. All closed syllables are heavy, but open syllables may be either light or heavy. The overall tendency in both Quenya and Sindarin was to shorten long vowels in closed syllables or to prevent short ones from lengthening.

§ 2.5. Stress accent

In Sindarin a strong stress fell on one syllable in most words. Nouns, adjectives, and most verbs of one syllable tended to receive a strong stress; other monosyllabic particles (articles, prepositions, conjunctions, interjections) received a lighter stress.

In words of two syllables primary stress fell in all cases on the first syllable. In these cases the stress has not been marked. In words of three or more syllables the principal stress fell on either the second syllable from the end (penultimate) or the third from the end (antepenultimate). Stress fell on the penultimate vowel when that was heavy, e.g., *a·'dui·al*, *an·'nú·naid*, *ce·'ned·ril*, *e·'dhel·harn*. Stress fell on the antepenultimate when the penultimate vowel was light (regardless of the quality of the penultimate), e.g., *a·'da·na·dar*, *'ae·a·ron*, *'ag·la·reb*, *'ci·ri·on*, *'dú·na·dan*, *E·'ri·a·dor*.

§ 2.6. Long consonants

When consonants are written double, they are pronounced long, e.g., *nn* = [n:]. Exception may be made for *mm* and *ss*. In Classical Sindarin these no longer contrasted with *m* and *s* in any position; *mm* and *ss* had not occurred initially, and medially and finally original *m* and *s* had changed. Consequently, the same word might be written with either single or double *m* and *s*. The word here spelled *bessain* is actually found spelled as *besain* (both pronounced [besajn]); the spelling has been altered to conform to the Sindarin orthographic norm, in which [s] was almost always spelled *ss* between vowels. No such norm existed for the representation of [m], which was indiscriminately represented by *mm* or *m*; e.g., the same word was spelled both *lamad* and *lammad* (both pronounced [lamad]).

But even when not followed by another consonant, *m* closed the previous syllable, so that primary stress in a word of more than two syllables should in CS always fall on a penultimate vowel preceding *m*, as in the words and names *min·'lam·ad*, *Tu·'ram·arth*, *Nae·'ram·arth*. Exceptions occur when the vowel before *m* arose from svarabhakti (as in *'Eg·la·mar*, earlier **'Egl·mar*) and in names of Quenya origin, such as *An·'ge·li·mir* < **An·'ca·li·mir*, *'Bo·ro·mir* < **'Vo·ro·mir*; in such cases the names kept their original accentuation and were necessarily written with a single *m*.

§ 2.7. Sounds found in Middle Sindarin or Sindarin dialects but not in Classical Sindarin

bh	ƀ	[β]	a fricative b (like the *b* in Spanish *saber*).
gh	ʒ	[ɣ]	a fricative g (like the g in Spanish *agua*).
mh	ṽ	[ṽ]or[β̃]	similar to *v* but nasalized like *m*.
oe	ö	[œ]	like the *eu* in French *bleu*.
oei	öi	[œj]	like the *euille* in French *feuille*.
	ǭi	[ɒ:j]	like the *awy* in English *lawyer*.
	ɸ	[ɸ]	similar to f, but with the lips together rather than with teeth touching lips.

§ 2.8. Sounds found in Old Sindarin but not in Middle or Classical Sindarin

e	ė	?[ɪ]	an allophone of short *i* (when final), usually transcribed *e*; possibly with the sound of *i* in English *kiss*.
hy	ç	[ç]	something between the sound of *h* in *hue* and the sound of *sh* in *leash*; or like the sound of *ch* in German *ich*.
hl	ḽ	[l̥]	the same as *lh*.
hm	m̭	[m̥]	a voiceless *m*.
hn	ṋ	[n̥]	a voiceless *n*.
hr	r̭	[r̥]	the same as *rh*.
iu	iu	[iw]	like *u* in English *cute*.
kh	k^h	[k^h]	*k* followed by a strong aspiration or breath.
	ṃ	[ṃ]	a syllabic *m*, like the *m* in English *prism*.
	ṇ	[ṇ]	a syllabic *n*, like the *en* in English *frozen*.
	ŋ̣	[ŋ̣]	a syllabic ŋ.
mb	m͡b	[m͡b]	a prenasalized *b* (only initial).
nd	n͡d	[n͡d]	a prenasalized *d* (only initial).
ŋg	ŋ͡g	[ŋ͡g]	a prenasalized *g* (only initial).
o	ȯ	?[ʊ]	an allophone of short *u* (when final), usually transcribed *o*; possibly with the sound of *oo* in English *look*.
ǭ, ō	ō	[ɒː]	like the sound of *aw* in English *law* but prolonged.
ph	p^h	[p^h]	*p* followed by a strong aspiration or breath.
th	t^h	[t^h]	*t* followed by a strong aspiration or breath.

§ 2.9. Sounds found in Common Eldarin but not in Sindarin

æ	æ	[æː]	like the *a* in *hat* but prolonged.
dy	d^j	[ɟ]	between the *d* in *duke* and the *j* in *joy*.
eu	eu	[ew]	*e* followed by *u* but pronounced as one syllable.
gw	g^w	[g^w]	similar to the *Gw* in *Gwendolyn*.
gy	g^j	[g^j]	a palatalized *g*, similar to the the *g* in *gules*.
khy	k^{hj}	[k^{hj}]	a palatalized k^h, similar to the *c* in *cue*.
kw	k^w	[k^w]	similar to the *qu* in *queen*.
ky	k^j	[k^j]	a palatalized *k*, like the *c* in *cue*, but not aspirated.
ny	n^j	[ɲ]	similar to the *n* in English *menu*.
ty	t^j	[c]	between the *t* in *tune* and the *ch* in *church*.

3

Sindarin Writing Systems

Sindarin might be written in several ways, depending both on the set of letters used and the assignment of values to those letters. In all of the systems, however, the spelling was nearly phonemic: in most cases, a single symbol stood for a single distinctive sound (in a few cases, one symbol stood for a combination of sounds). In this the writing systems differed both from the English alphabet and from the romanized transcription of Sindarin. Sindarin words therefore should not be transcribed by following the romanized conventions but according to the way they are actually pronounced; e.g. *alph* should be transcribed as if it were spelled *alf*, and *nef* should be transcribed as if it were spelled *nev*. Since they represent single sounds, *ch, dh, hw, lh, mh, rh, th,* are always represented by single symbols, never by (for instance) *c+h*.

§ 3.1. The *Certhas Daeron*

The first complete system for writing Sindarin was the *Certhas Daeron*, a modification of a more ancient and arbitrary runic alphabet made by Daeron, the minstrel and loremaster of King Thingol of Doriath.

The Certhas in its later forms—the Angerthas of Eregion, Moria, and Erebor, which were applied to Quenya, Khuzdul, and Mannish languages— became long, complex, and inconsistent. The original Angerthas Daeron, used only for the writing of Sindarin, was a relatively short (38–41 cirth) and consistent system.

The cirth of the original Certhas Daeron were:
p [cirth], *b* [cirth], *f* [cirth], *v* [cirth], *m* or *mh* [cirth]; *t* [cirth], *d* [cirth], *th* [cirth], *dh* [cirth], *n* [cirth]; *c* [cirth], *g* [cirth], *ch* [cirth], *gh* [cirth], *ŋ* [cirth]; *r* [cirth], *rh* [cirth], *l* [cirth], *lh* [cirth]; *s* [cirth] or [cirth], *ss* [cirth]; *i* (vowel or consonant) [cirth], *u* or *w* [cirth], *ui* or *y* (vowel) [cirth], *e* [cirth], *a* [cirth], *o* [cirth], *oi* or ö [cirth], *h* [cirth]. Long vowels were written either by doubling the vowel letter or by putting a dot on each side of the vowel, e.g. *ú* [cirth]. The sound of hw was written [cirth].

In a slightly revised form the Certhas provided distinctive cirth for *hw, m* and *mh, w, y,* ö, and some of the long vowels: *p*, *b*, *f*, *v*, *hw* *, *m* *, *mh* *; *t*, *d*, *th*, *dh*, *n*; *c*, *g*, *ch*, *gh*, *ŋ*; r, rh, l, lh; s, ss; i (vowel or consonant), u, w *, y (vowel) *, e, é *, a, á *, o, ó *, ö *, *h* derived from *s* *, *h* derived from *ch*. (Asterisks indicate characters varying from the older Certhas.) This was the ideal form of the Certhas; in actual usage , , and might all be used for either *s* or *h*.

The Certhas above represented the sounds of archaic Sindarin. By the Third Age, had become identical in sound with , had become entirely silent, and had become identical in sound with . Third Age Sindarin could therefore be written with as few as thirty-four cirth.

It will be noted that the long vowel sounds frequently appear to consist of two fused or overlapping versions of the short vowel cirth. This is most obvious in ; but it can also be distinguished in and . There is no certh for long *í*, which could be written with two i's in sequence.

It should also be noted that the front vowels and consist of the corresponding back vowels and with a small drawn under or through them; that is, *y* and *ö* were effectively written as *ui* and *oi* respectively, with the *i* being the equivalent of a diacritical mark.

Later alterations of the Certhas Daeron were made by the Noldor in Eregion. Most of these alterations involved the introduction of symbols to represent the sounds of Quenya and other languages, and so did not affect the representation of Sindarin. The most important changes were the introduction of for *h* (because had been reassigned to represent the non-Sindarin sound of *ch* in *chair*) and the introduction of a sign for *ú* . In addition, the Angerthas of Eregion employed several single signs to represent groups of consonants, some of which could be used in Sindarin: *mb* (since was no longer needed to represent *mh*), *gw*, *chw*, *ŋgw*, *nw*, *ŋg*, *nd* or .

§ 3.2. The mode of Beleriand

Other modes of writing Sindarin were drawn from the *tengwar* (*tîw* in Sindarin), a system invented by the Noldo Fëanor in Valinor for writing Quenya, and brought by him and his people to Middle-earth, where it was extensively used by both elves and men.

The oldest known application of tengwar to Sindarin is found on the West gate of Moria, which must have been in common use in Eregion; it is called the "mode of Beleriand." In it, as in the cirth, each vowel is represented by a separate letter. These were *i*, *u*, *y*, *e*, *a*, *o*. When long, they were distinguished with an acute accent, called *andaith* 'long mark': .

Diphthongs ending in *i* were indicated by two dots above the first letter of the diphthong: ui ei ai ; diphthongs ending in *e* either had a small above the first letter or were followed by : *ae* or , *oe* or ; the diphthong *au* was written with a "w-curl" above the first letter .

The consonants were *p* , *b* , *f* , *v* , *hw* , *m* , *mm* ; *t* , *d* , *th* , *dh* , *n* , *nn* ; *c* , *g* , *ch* , *ŋ* ?; *w* ; *r* , *rh* , *l* , *lh* ; *s* , *ss* ; *h* . Stops preceded by a nasal were indicated by a bar over the corresponding nonnasalized stop, e.g. *nt* *nd* *mp* *mb* *ŋc* *ŋg* . A consonantal *i* could have been indicated by the dotted long carrier , as in the alphabetic mode of Gondor.

§ 3.3. The alphabetic mode of Gondor

Other applications of the tengwar were used in Gondor. The Beleriandic mode had used the third series of the tengwar for velars, in accordance with Quenya custom; in Gondor, where the third series was a palatal series, the fourth series was used as a velar series in writing both Westron and Sindarin. The men of Gondor used both an alphabetic and a consonantal mode, in which the vowels were written by diacriticals or tehtar.

In the former mode, the tengwar used were *p* , *b* , *f* , *v* , *hw* , *m* *; *t* , *d* , *th* , *dh* , *n* *; *c* *, *g* *, *ch* *, *ŋ* *?; *w* ; *r* * (rarely), *rh* , *l* , *lh* , *s* , *ss* , **i* (consonantal) or , *h* . Stops preceded by a nasal were, as in the mode of Beleriand, indicated by a bar over the corresponding non-nasalized stop, e.g. *nt* *nd* *mp* *mb* *ŋc* * *ŋg* *; *nn* and *mm* were similarly written and ; a following *w* was indicated by the w-curl above the preceding consonant, e.g. *gw* .

For **mh* was used. (Asterisks indicate characters varying from the mode of Beleriand).

The vowels were identical in every respect to those used in the mode of Beleriand, except that at the end of a word *c* was written with a small downstroke.

§ 3.4. The consonantal mode of Gondor

The consonantal mode was identical in terms of consonants to the alphabetic mode except that tended to be more common than for *r*, although was preferred at the ends of words. was used for consonantal *i*. What was used for *w* is unknown; but it was presumably either or .

Short vowels were indicated by vowel marks (tehtar) supported by the following consonant, or by a short carrier when no consonant followed; long vowels were always indicated by the long carrier.

i was indicated by a single dot, e.g. *i* ; *í* and *î* ; *il*

u was indicated by a curl open to the left, e.g. *u* ; *ú* and *û* ; *ul*

y was indicated by two dots next to each other horizontally, e.g. *y* ; *ý* ; *yl*

e was indicated by the acute accent, e.g. *e* ; *é* and *ê* ; *el*

a was indicated by three dots in an upright triangular pattern, e.g. *a* ; *á* and *â* ; *al*

o was indicated by a curl open to the right, e.g. *o* ; *ó* and ; *ol*

Diphthongs were shown by a tehta representing the first element above a tengwa representing the second element. Thus *ui* was , *ei* was , and *ai* was ; *ae* was and *oe* was ; *au* is not attested, but was presumably either or .

In two inscriptions shown in *J.R.R. Tolkien, Artist and Illustrator* (nos. 194 and 195, p. 197), the name *Lúthien Tinúviel* is spelled according to a mode identical to that above except that the tehtar are above the consonants that precede them rather than those that follow them; i.e. the name is written and not .

English Transcription: *Túrin Turambar Dagnir Glaurunga*

Early *Certhas Daeron*:

Late *Certhas Daeron*:

Angerthas of Eregion:

Mode of Beleriand:

Mode of Gondor, alphabetic:

Mode of Gondor, consonantal:

4

Historical Phonology of Sindarin

This chapter lists all the sound changes that can be shown to have occurred between the period of Common Eldarin (in some instances earlier) and the development of Classical Sindarin; it concludes with some notes on the known characteristic features of the Sindarin dialects.

This list should be used with some caution. It is by intention chronological; that is, the sound changes listed later assume the existence of earlier sound changes and cannot be adequately understood without reference to them. However, the mere act of creating such a list is misleading in two ways: it suggests that sound change is both punctual (occurring at a single moment in time) and linear (occurring one at a time).

As to punctuality, it may be true that some sound changes occur over a fairly short period; others, however, may take centuries to become established. In some cases sound change may involve the very gradual alteration of one sound into another; the change of Eldarin *ā* to Old Sindarin *ǭ* may be one such example, the sound gradually coming to be pronounced further back and with more rounding over centuries.

In other cases sound change may involve the coexistence of two distinct sounds, one of which supplants the other (the replacement of Quenya þ by *s* is a notable instance). Even in these cases change may be gradual, as it may take a long time for the population using the older sounds to die out or convert to the new sounds.

The idea of chronological linearity is even less tenable. In any evolving language many different sound changes occur at the same time. Where one is not an obvious condition for another, it may be difficult or impossible to know which one occurred first. In this list the order of the sound changes is in many cases arbitrary and has often been governed by the desire to keep related changes together. That does not mean that they necessarily precede later developments—except in cases where they have an obvious impact on those developments.

The reconstructed forms that are postulated need not, therefore, be taken as forms that actually have existed at some given time. The necessity of separating particular sound changes and ordering them linearly leads to some absurdities, such as the reconstruction of **lemmmbas* (*lembas*) (§ 4.121) as a form between **lennembass* and **lembass*; in all probability the assimilation of *nn* to following *m* (§ 4.121) and the shortening of the sequence *-nnm-* (§§ 4.129, 4.140) occurred concurrently and over a brief span of time. If this caution is kept in mind, however, the list is a useful guide both to the actual changes and the general sequence in which they took place.

A note on stress

The Common Eldarin language, like its descendant languages and probably its ancestor language, placed a strong stress on at least one syllable of polysyllabic words and possibly in many cases a weaker but still significant stress on another. The stress patterns were, however, entirely altered in the descendant languages of Quenya and Sindarin; they can only be deduced from phonetic developments in the history of these languages, which do not necessarily occur for all words. It is therefore impossible to reconstruct with complete accuracy the original stress patterns of the words in Common Eldarin. However, it is often necessary to refer to these stresses to explain developments in Sindarin. Typically, a vowel in a stressed syllable might be lengthened or even (in the earliest period) changed to a diphthong, whereas a vowel in an unstressed syllable might be shortened or even omitted altogether. Examples include the vowel shortening in § 4.14 and the syncope in §§ 4.3 and 4.35; the ablaut lengthenings of the vowels (see § 5.11) are perhaps evidence of a primitive stress.

It seems that roots originally consisting of two syllables (see appendix 2) were usually accented on one or the other vowel (the particular vowel varying with the root); however, it cannot be assumed that a root vowel was always stressed. For instance, in the case of *glaw*, derived from a root √ŋAL, the root vowel was entirely lost; this type of loss occurred more often in derivative roots, where at least one derivative vowel was usually maintained, as in *claur* and *aglar*, from √KAL-ÁR and √Á-KAL-AR.

It would also seem that many Sindarin suffixes maintained at least a secondary accent (which was lost at an early date in Quenya—the most archaic of the related languages—shortening the destressed vowel); this explains such suffixes as *-ol* < *-'ālā, Q *-ala* < *-alā. Some of these were also destressed at an early stage of Sindarin, for example *-en* < *-'ēnā next to *-in* < *-ēnē.

The stress accent only shifted to the positions found in Classical Sindarin at the end of the Middle Sindarin phase; following this stress shift, old long vowels were often shortened.

In the list of rules that follows, the rules describing the sound changes taking place in Sindarin from the earliest forms of Elvish to the division of Sindarin into many dialects (also described, insofar as they are known) are set forth in a modified version of featural notation, followed by a prose description. Since the featural notation may be somewhat opaque, even to many acquainted with the more traditional vocabulary of phonetics, the following definitions are given:

Voiced = [+voice]
Unvoiced = [–voice]
Stop = [–sonorant –continuant]
Fricative = [–sonorant +continuant]
Nasal = [+sonorant –continuant +nasal]
Aspirate = [+spread glottis]
Liquid = [+sonorant +continuant +consonantal]
Semivowel or Glide = [+sonorant +continuant –consonantal]
Sibilant = [–sonorant +continuant +strident]
Labial = [+labial]
Labialized velar = [+labial +dorsal]
Dental or Alveolar = [+coronal]
Palatalized alveolar [+coronal –anterior]
Velar = [+dorsal]
Palatalized velar [+dorsal –back]
C = consonant
V = vowel
S = segment
S_0 = any number of segments
ø = no sound
= word boundary
+ = morpheme boundary
$ = syllable boundary
α place = a variable, defined by place of articulation

CHANGES PRECEDING COMMON ELDARIN

§4.1	[+dorsal][w] > [+dorsal +labial][ø] Velars immediately followed by *w* became labialized velars.	*atakwē > *atak^{w}ē (adab) *laikwāā > *laik^{w}ā (laeb) *jagwē > *jag^{w}ē (iaw) *neŋwi > *neŋ^{w}i (nem)
§4.2	ø > g^{w} / / $ŋ^{w}$___V $ŋ^{w}$ became $ŋ^{w}g^{w}$ before vowels.	*neŋ^{w}i > *neŋ^{w}g^{w}i (nem) *liŋ^{w}i > *liŋ^{w}g^{w}i (lim)
§4.3	V [–stress] > ø / #(C)V[+stress]C___C In a number of instances the second vowel in some words constructed to (V)CVCVC roots disappeared when unstressed, producing the structure (V)CVCC.	*'okot-ō > *oktō (auth) *'esed-ē > *esdē (îdh) *'misid-ē > *misdē (mîdh) *'misik-ā > *miskā (mesg) *'masag-ā > *masgā (mae) *'usuk^{w}-ē > *usk^{w}ē (osp) *'akalar-ē > *aklarē (aglar) *'atalant-ā > *atlantā (adlant)
§4.4	*s* > [+voiced] / ___ [–sonorant –continuant +voiced] *s* became *z* before voiced stops.	*esdē > *ezdē (îdh) *misdē > *mizdē (mîdh) *masgā > *mazgā (mae)
§4.5	[–continuant +voice α place]$_1$ [+sonorant +nasal α place]$_2$ > 2 1 Voiced stops followed by nasals with the same place of articulation undergo metathesis: *dn*, *bm* > *nd*, *mb*.	*labmē > *lambē (lam) *adnō > *andō (and)
§4.6	[+long] > [–long] / ___CC Long vowels became short in closed syllables.	*nōssē > *nossē (nos)

See Tables 4.1 and 4.2 for phonology at this stage.

EARLY CHANGES IN COMMON ELDARIN

§4.7	[–sonorant –continuant] > [–voice –spread] / ___ [+coronal –voice] *d* and t^{h} became *t* before *s*; k^{h} became *k* before *s*; *d* and t^{h} became *t* before *t*; k^{h} and *g* became *k* before *t*.	*sjadslā > *sjatslā (hathol) *k^{h}ot^{h}sē, *lot^{h}sē > *k^{h}otsē, *lotsē (hoth, loth) *lok^{h}sē > *loksē (laus) *sjadtā > *sjattā (hast) *wedtā > *wettā (gwest) *kot^{h}tā > *kottā (cost) *nedt- > *nett- (nest) *rik^{h}ta- > *rikta- (ritha-) *wegte > *wekte (gwaith)

TABLE 4.1
CONSONANTAL PHONOLOGY OF COMMON ELDARIN (consonant combinations in italics)

	Bilabials		Alveolars		Palatalized Alveolars		Palatalized Velars		Velars		Labialized Velars		Glottal
Unaspirated stops	p	b	t	d	t^j	d^j	k^j	g^j	k	g	k^w	g^w	
	sp		*st*				sk^j		*sk*				
Aspirated stops	p^h	t^h					kh^j		k^h				
Nasalized stops		m͡b		n͡d				ŋ͡g^j		ŋ͡g		ŋ^w͡g^w	
Nasals	*sm*	m	*sn*	n		n^j							
Trills			*sr*	r									
Fricatives			s	z		*sj*						*sw*	h
Approximants			*sl*	l				j				w	

TABLE 4.2
VOCALIC PHONOLOGY OF COMMON ELDARIN (rounded vowels in italics)

	Simple Vowels		Diphthongs Ending in *-i*		Diphthongs Ending in *-u*	
	Front	Back	Front	Back	Front	Back
High	i, ī	*u, ū*		ui	iu	
	ē	*ō*				
Mid	e	*o*	ei	oi	eu	ou
Low		a, ā		ai		au

§4.8 ø > s / *t*__*t*
t became *ts* before *t*.

*sjattā > *sjatstā (hast)
*wettā > *wetstā (gwest)
*kottā > *kotstā (cost)
*nett- > *netst- (nest)

§4.9 *t* > ø / __*st*
t disappeared before *st*.

*netstaki- > *nestaki- (nestegi-)
*sjatstā > *sjastā (hast)
*wetstā > *westā (gwest)
*kotstā > *kostā (cost)
*netst- > *nest- (nest)

§4.10 [–sonorant –continuant +coronal] > [α place] / ___
[–sonorant –continuant α place]
t or *d* assimilated to a following stop: *tp* > *pp*, *tk* > *kk*, *dg* > *gg*,
even across a word boundary, in the case of a preceding preposition.

*etpeles > *eppeles (ephel)
*etkoirē > *ekkoirē (echuir)
*aud·galadā > *aug·galadā (o galadh)
*et·kirjā > *ek·kirjā (e chair, v. cair)
*et·parmā > *ep·parmā (e pharf, v. parf)

§4.11	t_1k_2 > 2 1 In one exceptional case, *tk* metathesized into *kt* (the usual change being *tk* > *kk*, as in § 4.10 above).	*etkelē > *ektelē (eithel)
§4.12	[+nasal] > [–labial –dorsal] / ___[+coronal –nasal] *m* and *ŋ* became *n* when preceding *t*, *d*.	*glimta- > *glinta- (glinna-) *glimd- > *glind- (glind) *kemtano > *kentano (cennan) *wiŋta- > *winta- (Q. winta-)
§4.13	V[–long +high +tense] > [–tense] / ___# Final *-i* and *-u* became *-ė* and *-ȯ* (probably phonetically [ɪ] and [ʊ]).	*niŋʷkʷi > *niŋʷkʷė (nimp) *smalu > *smalȯ (mâl) *raŋku > *raŋkȯ (ranc)
§4.14	V[+long –stress] > [–long] / [+stress] ___ Condition: not ___#. Unstressed long vowels become short, unless they are final.	*'tʰaurēnā > *'tʰaurenā (thoren) *'luktjēnē > *'luktjenē (luithien)
§4.15	*ō* > *ā* / *w*___# Final *-wō* became *-wā*.	*nidwō > *nidwā (nedhu)
§4.16	*ā* > *ē* / [*t*][+labial]___# Final *-wā* or *-mā* became *-wē* or *-mē* when attached to a root ending in *-t*.	*katwā > *katwē (cadu) *jatmā > *jatmē (ianu)
§4.17	*u* > ø / *ā* ___ *āu* became *ā*.	*rāu > *rā (raw)
§4.18	[–sonorant –continuant +nasal] > [+nasal +syllabic][–sonorant –continuant] In certain instances, *ŋ͡g* > *ŋ͡g* *m͡b* > *ṃb*, *n͡d* > *ṇd*, creating an extra syllable at the beginning of the word.	m͡bartā > ṃbartā (amarth) n͡dūnēē > ṇdūnē (annûn) ŋ͡golē > ŋ̣golē (angol) ŋ͡gʲō > ŋ̣gʲō (OS ango)
§4.19	V > ø / ___+V The final vowel of a preceding element of a compound word disappeared before a following element beginning with a vowel.	*smalda + ornē > *smaldornē (mallorn)
§4.20	V + *j* > ø + *i* The final vowel of a preceding element in a compound also disappeared before a following element beginning with *j*, which became *i*.	*anda + jēn > *andiēn (ennin)
§4.21	C_1V > ø / ___C_1 Haplology: a consonant and the vowel immediately following disappeared when preceding a consonant identical to the first.	*ostotiriondō > *ostiriondō (ostirion) *kʰelkakaraksē > *kʰelkaraksē (Helcharaes) *tuilelindō > *tuilindō (tuilinn)

	Haplology might also occur when the consonants were merely similar, occurring at the same place of articulation.	*enda n͡dorē > *endorē (ennor)

LINDARIN CHANGES BEFORE THE SEPARATION OF THE SINDAR

§4.22	*g^w > gw* / {#___} {V___} *g^w* became *gw* when initial or following a vowel.	*g^wet^h- > *gwet^h- (gweth) *jag^{w}ē > *jagwē (iaw)
§4.23	[+labial +dorsal] > [–dorsal] All remaining labiovelars became labials: *k^w* became *p*; *$ŋ^wk^w$* became *mp*; *$ŋ^wg^w$* became *mb*.	*k^wantā > *pantā (pant) *atak^{w}ē > *atapē (adab) *usk^{w}ē > *uspē (osp) *niŋ^{w}k^{w}ė > *nimpė (nimp) *neŋ^{w}g^{w}ė > *nembė (nem)
§4.24	*b > w / ___d* *b* became *w* before *d*.	*glibdā > *gliwdā (glûdh)
§4.25	*g > w* / V[+back]___*d* *g* became *w* between a back vowel and *d*.	*k^{h}agdā > *k^{h}awdā (haudh)
§4.26	*g > j* / V[–back]___*d* *g* became *j* between a front vowel and *d*.	*negdē > *nejdē (nîdh)
§4.27	*z > j* / ___ C[–sonorant –continuant +voice] *z* became *j* before a voiced stop.	*mizdē > *mijdē (mîdh) *mazgā > *majgā (mae)
§4.28	*iw > jū* / [+coronal]___ Following a dental consonant, *iw* became *jū*; the *u* became long in compensation to maintain the prosodic length of the diphthong.	*tiwkā > *tjūkā (tûg) *gliwdā > *gljūdā (glûdh) *siwlē > *sjūlē (hûl)
§4.29	C [+coronal –strident][*j*] > [+coronal –anterior][ø] / #___ Initial alveolar consonants followed by *j* were palatalized.	*tjūkā > * t^jūkā (tûg) *gljūdā > * gl^jūdā (glûdh)
§4.30	[+coronal –anterior –strident] > [+anterior] / #(C)___ Initial palatalized alveolar consonants were depalatalized: *t^j, d^j, n^j, l^j > t, d, n, l.*	*t^jalja- > *talja- (teilia-) *d^jelipa > *delipa (deleb) *n^jarna > *narna (narn) *t^jūkā > *tūkā (tûg) *gl^jūdā > *glūdā (glûdh)
§4.31	*m > n* / ___[+sonorant +continuant –consonantal] *m* became *n* before the glides *j* and *w*.	*ramja- > *ranja- (renia-) *k^{h}amwā > *k^{h}anwā (hanu)
§4.32	*j > i* / ___V Prevocalic *-j-* (not part of a palatalized consonant) > *-i-*.	*gājā > *gāiā (goe) *kirjā > *kiriā (cair) *sirjondō > *siriondō (sirion)

CHANGES IN SINDARIN ONLY

(Following the Split between the Sindar and the Amanyar Teleri)

§4.33	V[-high] *i* > *ī* / ___# Diphthongs occurring at the ends of words (*āi*, *ēi*, *ōi*) became *ī*.	*lassēi > *lassī (lais, pl. of las) *galadāi > *galadī (gelaidh, pl. of galadh)
§4.34	#C V[+stress] [*r*] V [–stress] CC > #C V[–stress] [*r*] V [+stress] CC The stress accent shifts from an initial stressed syllable to a following closed syllable when the stressed syllable precedes r.	*'tarasta- > *ta'rasta- (trasta-) *'peresta- > *pe'resta (presta-) *'kirikta- > *ki'rikta (critha-)
§4.35	V[–stress] > ø / ___[*r*] V[+stress] An unstressed vowel (usually in a CVCVC root) immediately preceding a stressed vowel in the next syllable was frequently syncopated before a liquid (*l* or *r*).	*ba'randa- > *branda- (brand) *mo'roko- > *mroko- (brôg) *ŋa'lā > *ŋlā (glaw) *ta'rasta- > *trasta- (trasta-) *ki'rikta- > *krikta- (critha-) *k^ha'rasse- > *k^hrasse- (rhas)
§4.36	[+nasal] > [–sonorant –nasal] / #___C [+sonorant +continuant] Initial *mr*- became *br*-, *ŋl*- became *gl*-.	*mrokō > *brokō (brôg) *ŋlā > *glā (glaw)
§4.37	V[+long] > V[–long] / VS_0___# The final long vowels of polysyllabic words were reduced in length. *-ā*, *-ē*, *-ī*, *-ō*, *-ū* > *-a*, *-e*, *-i*, *-o*, *-u*.	*kirjā > *kirja (cair) *lassē > *lasse (las) *ŋ͡golodō > *ŋ͡golodo (golodh) *kundū > *kundu (cund) *ŋg^jō > *ŋg^jo (OS ango)
§4.38	*ŋ* > [–sonorant] / #___ Initial *ŋ*- was regularly fortified to *ŋg*-. But in one instance *ŋ* was irregularly deleted.	*ŋalata > *ŋgalata (galad) *ŋōle > ōle (ûl)
§4.39	[+dorsal –back] > [+back] Palatalized velars were depalatalized: *k^j*, *k^{hj}*, *g^j*, *ŋg^j* > *k*, *k^h*, *g*, *ŋg*.	*ŋg^jo > *ŋgo (OS ango) *sk^japat > *skapat (habad) *k^jelepe > *kelepe (celeb) *k^{hj}aratė > *k^haratė (harad) *g^jerna > *gerna (gern)
§4.40	[+nasal +syllabic] > *a* [–syllabic] ṃ, ṇ, ŋ̣ > am, an, aŋ	*ṃbarta > *ambarta (amarth) *ŋ̣gole > *aŋgole (angol) *ṇdūne > *andūne (annûn) *ŋ̣go > *aŋgo (OS ango)
§4.41	*h* > ø / ___V *h* disappeared before vowels.	*hanwa > *anwa (anu) *hekla > *ekla (egol) *helwe > *elwe (elu) *mahi > *mai (mae, pl. of maw) *tehi > *tei (tî, pl. of tê) *mahitė > *maitė (maed)

§4.42	*h* > *g* / ___[+nasal] *h* became *g* before nasal consonants.	*dohme > *dogme (daw) *kuhna > *kugna (cûn) *wahna > *wagna (gwaen) *tahna > *tagna (taen)
§4.43	*h* > [–sonorant +coronal –voice α continuant] / ___[–sonorant +coronal –voice α continuant] *h* assimilated to following voiceless dentals, becoming *t* before *t* and *s* before *s*.	*wahte > *watte (gwath) *wahta- > *watta- (gwatha-) *mahta- > *matta- (matha-) *wahse > *wasse (gwas)
§4.44	V[–long] [*h*] > V [+long] ø / ___*r* *h* disappeared before *r*, and the preceding vowel became long.	*dohra > *dōra (dûr) *wahra > *wāra (gwaur) *tehra > *tēra (tîr)
§4.45	V[–long] [*h*] > [+long]ø / ___#	*kuh > *kū (cû) *mah > *mā (maw)
§4.46	[–sonorant –continuant –voice] > [+voice] / ___ [+nasal] Voiceless stops became voiced before nasals (*pn*, *tn*, *tm*, *kn*, *km* > *bn*, *dn*, *dm*, *gn*, *gm*).	*kelepna > *kelebna (celefn) *lepnāia > *lebnāia (lefnui) *jatma > *jadma (ianu) *nakma > *nagma (naew) *rakme > *ragme (raew) *et·n͡dore > *ed·n͡dore (e ndor) *et·m͡bar > *ed·m͡bar (e mbar)
§4.47	[–sonorant –continuant –dorsal] > [+sonorant +nasal] / ___ [+nasal] Labial and dental stops became nasal before nasals: *bn* > *mn*, *dn* > *nn*, *dm* > *nm*. In the case of a preposition preceding a noun, this change could take place across a word boundary.	*kelebna > *kelemna (celefn) *lebna > *lemna (lefn) *lebnāia > *lemnāia (lefnui) *jadma > *janma (ianu) *aud·menel > *aun·menel (o menel) *ed·n͡dore > *en·n͡dore (e ndor) *ed·m͡bar > *en·m͡bar (e mbar)
§4.48	*n* > *l* / *l*___ *ln* > *ll*	*k^{h}alna > *k^{h}alla (hall) *skelna > *skella (hell)
§4.49	*n* > t^h / t^h___ *n* assimilated to a preceding t^h.	*pat^{h}na > *pat^{h}t^{h}a (path)
§4.50	t^h > *t* / ___t^h t^ht^h > tt^h	*pat^{h}t^{h}a > *patt^{h}a (path)
§4.51	*m* > *w* / [+coronal]___ *m* > *w* / [+nasal +dorsal]___ *nm* (< *nm*, *tm*, *dm*) > *nw*, *thm* > *thw*, *ŋm* > *ŋw*	*janme > *janwe (ianu) *k^{h}it^{h}me > *k^{h}it^{h}we (hithu) *pat^{h}ma > *pat^{h}wa (pathu) *teŋme > *teŋwe (têw)
§4.52	*t* > *d* / *n*___ Occasionally (irregularly) *nt* developed into *nd*.	*lanta > *landa (land) *atlanta > *atlanda (adland)

§4.53	[–sonorant –continuant –voice –spread] > ø / ___# Voiceless unaspirated stops disappeared finally.	*nelek > *nele (nêl) *orot > *oro (ôr) *skapat > *skapa (OS sk^{h}apa > *hâb, altered to habad)
§4.54	*m* > ø / ___# *m* disappeared finally.	*kaim > *kai (cae)
§4.55	t^h > [–spread] / ___# -t^h became -*t* when final.	*k^{h}ōt^{h} > *k^{h}ōt (hûd)
§4.56	V[–high –low +long] > V[+high] Long *ē* and *ō* became *ī* and *ū*.	*jēn > *jīn (în) *k^{h}ērȯ > *k^{h}īrȯ (hîr) *dōme > *dūme (dû) *dōra > *dūra (dûr)
§4.57	*i* > ø / ___*ī* *i* disappears before long *ī*.	*andiīn > *andīn (ennin)
§4.58	V [+low +back –round] > V [–low +round] *ā* > *ǭ*	*rā > *rǭ (raw) *wāra > *wǭra (gwaur)
§4.59	[–high –low] > [+high] / ___*i* *ei* > *ii*; *oi* > *ui*	*wei > *wii (gwî) *eide > *iide (îdh) *neire > *niire (nîr) *neitė > *niitė (nîd) *neine > *niine (nîn) *ekkoire > *ekkuire (echuir) *moina > *muina (muin) *oire > *uire (uir) *poika > *puika (puig) *roime > *ruime (ruiw)
§4.60	*e* > [+high] / ___*u* *eu* > *iu*	*leuka > *liuka (lŷg) *sneuma > *sniuma (nŷw) *beuia > *biuia (buia-) *beuro > *biuro (bŷr) *n͡deuro > *n͡diuro (dŷr) *p^{h}euia > *p^{h}iuia (fuia-)
§4.61	*ū* > [–long] / ___*i* *ūi* > *ui*	*jūia > *juia (ui) *andūia > *anduia (annui) *t^{h}ūia- > *t^{h}uia- (thuia-)
§4.62	*i* > ø / ___*ui* *j* > ø / ___*ui* *jui* and *iui* became *ui*.	*biuia- > buia- *p^{h}iuia- > *p^{h}uia- (fuia-) *piuia- > puia- *tiuia- > tuia- *juia- > *uia (ui)

§4.63	*n* > [α place] / ___ [–continuant] *n* assimilated to the place of articulation of a following stop.	*in·peredeli > *im·peredeli (i-pheredil, v. peredhel) *in·kalari > *iŋ·kalari (i-chelair, v. calar) *in·beleki > *im·beleki (i-melig, v. beleg) *in·m͡bari > *im·m͡bari (i-mbair, v. bâr) *in·ŋ͡golodi > *iŋ·ŋ͡golodi (in-gelydh, v. golodh)
§4.64	[–sonorant –continuant] > [+spread] / C [–strident]___ *t, p, k* became t^h, p^h, k^h after another consonant, except *s*. *pp, tt, kk* > pp^h, tt^h, kk^h	*rapp- > *rapp^h- (raph) *petta > *pett^{h}a (peth) *lokko > *lokk^{h}o (loch) *ep·parma > *ep·p^{h}arma (e pharf, v. parf) *et·taware > *et·t^{h}aware (e thawar, v. tawar) *ek·kirja > *ek·k^{h}irja (e chair, v. cair)
	mp, nt, ŋk > mp^h, nt^h, $ŋk^h$	*nimpė > *nimp^{h}ė (nimp) *pentasse > *pent^{h}asse (pennas) *aŋka > *aŋk^{h}a (anc)
	This includes stops following prepositions and articles that had become attached to the following word.	*im+peredeli > *im+p^{h}eredeli (i-pheredil) *aŋ + kalari > *aŋ + k^{h}alari (a chelair)
	rp, rt, rk > rp^h, rt^h, rk^h	*arpen- > *arp^{h}en- (arphen) *garta > *gart^{h}a (garth) *karka > *kark^{h}a (carch) *kirka > *kirk^{h}a (cerch) *urko > *urk^{h}o (orch)
	lp, lt, lk > lp^h, lt^h, lk^h	*alpa > *alp^{h}a (alph) *kalpa > *kalp^{h}a (calph) *salpa > *salp^{h}a (salph) *talta > *talt^{h}a (talt) *telko > *telk^{h}o (telch) *sulka > *sulk^{h}a (solch)
	kt > kt^h	*okto > *okt^{h}o (auth) *wekte > *wekt^{h}e (gwaith)
§4.65	[–sonorant –continuant] > [+spread] / #s___ Initial *sp, st, sk* > sp^h, st^h, sk^h .	*spaŋga > *sp^{h}aŋga (fang) *staŋga > *st^{h}aŋga (thang) *skapa > *sk^{h}apa (habad)
§4.66	[+sonorant] > [–voice] / [–sonorant +continuant –voice]___ *n, m, r, l, w,* and *j* became voiceless after	*snarda > *sṋarda (nardh) *smalȯ > *sm̭alȯ (mâl) *sruska > *sr̭uska (rhosg)

voiceless fricatives. This was a continuing change that operated throughout the history of Sindarin, wherever these sounds came in contact.

*slūkė > *sḽūkė (lhûg)
*lansra- > *lansr̭a- (lathra-)
*swesta > *sƕesta (hwest)
*sjasta > *sçasta (hast)

§4.67 *s* > [–continuant +spread] / *t*___
ts became *tt*^{h}.

*natse > *natt^{h}e (nath)
*litse > *litt^{h}e (lith)
*lotse > *lott^{h}e (loth)
*natsr̭o > *natt^{h}r̭o (nathron)

§4.68 *t* > [ø] / ___*t*^{h}C
tt^h*r* simplified to *t*^{h}*r*.

*natt^{h}r̭o > *nat^{h}r̭o (nathron)

§4.69 *s* > ø / #___[+sonorant –voice]
s disappeared before voiceless *n*, *m*, *r*, *l*, *ƕ*, and *ç* at the beginning of a word.

*sm̭alȯ > *m̭alȯ (mâl)
*sṋarda > *ṋarda (nardh)
*sr̭uska > *r̭uska (rhosg)
*sḽūkė > *ḽūkė (lhûg)
*sƕesta > *ƕesta (hwest)
*sçasta > *çasta (hast)
*sçūle > *çūlē (hûl)

§4.70 *s* [+sonorant –voice] > ø [+sonorant –voice +long] / V___
s assimilates to a following voiceless sonorant after a vowel.
This may also have taken place after the article or prepositions.

*besṋo > *beṋṋo (benn)
*asm̭alinde > *am̭m̭alinde (emlinn)
*ambasḽūkė > *ambaḽḽūkė (amlug)

*i·sr̭īwe > *i·r̭r̭īwe (!i-rîw, v. rhîw)
*na·sr̭īwe > *na·r̭r̭īwe (!na-rîw, v. rhîw)

§4.71 *s* > *h* / V___ V
s became *h* between vowels,

*glisė > *glihė (glî)
*gǭsa > gǭha (gaw)
*olosi > *olohi (ely, pl. of ôl)
*pisina > *pihina (pihen)
*pisia > *pihia (paich)
*i·sarna > *i·harna (i-harn, v. sarn)
*os·atani > *oh·atani (o hEdain, v. o2, adan)

but remained where it was protected by a preceding consonant.

*apsa (aes)
*tarsa (tas)
*in·satrondi (i-sedryn)

§4.72 *s* > ø / ___#
Final *s* was deleted.

*olos > *olo (ôl)
*peles > *pele (pêl)
*t^{h}eles > t^{h}ele (thêl)
*kǭs > *kǭ (caw)

§4.73 *s* > ø / ___+C
s was also deleted before a morpheme boundary followed by a consonant.

*peles+n͡dore > *pele+n͡dore (pelennor)

§4.74 *a* [–stress] > *i* / *j*__CV[+stress]
Unstressed *a* became *i* between *j* and a stressed syllable.
*ja'ƀǭn > *jiƀǭn (Ivon)
*ja'ƀanneββe > *jiƀanneββe (Ivanneth)

§4.75 *j* > ø / __*i*
j disappeared before *a* following *i*.
*jiƀǭn > *iƀǭn (Ivon)
*jiƀanneββe > *iƀanneββe (Ivanneth)
*jīn > *īn (în)

§4.76 *ii* > *ī*
*iide > *īde (îdh)
*miide > *mīde (mîdh)

§4.77 *o* [+stress] > *a* / *w*__
Stressed *wo-* > *wa-*.
*'wolott^{h}e > *'walott^{h}e (gwaloth)

See Tables 4.3 and 4.4 for phonology at this stage.

TABLE 4.3
CONSONANTAL PHONOLOGY OF OLD SINDARIN (consonant combinations in italics)

	Bilabials		Alveolars		Palatals		Velars		Labialized Velars		Glottal
Unaspirated stops	p	b	t	d			k	g	*gw*		
Aspirated stops	p^h *sp^h*		t^h *st^h*				k^h *sk^h*				
Nasalized stops		m͡b		n͡d				ŋ͡g			
Nasals	m̭	m	ṋ	n				ŋ			
Trills			r̭	r							
Fricatives			s		ç				ƕ-		h
Approximants			ḽ	l		j				w	

Table 4.4
VOCALIC PHONOLOGY OF OLD SINDARIN (rounded vowels in italics)

	Simple Vowels		Diphthongs Ending in *-i*		Diphthongs Ending in *-u*	
	Front	Back	Front	Back	Front	Back
High	i, ī	*u*, *ū*		ui	iu	
Mid	e	*o*				ou
Low		a, *ǭ*		ai		au

OLD SINDARIN TO MIDDLE SINDARIN

§4.78	[–sonorant –continuant +nasal] > [–nasal] / #___ Absolutely initial nasalized stops denasalized: *n͡d-*, *m͡b-*, *ŋ͡g-* > *d-*, *b-*, *g-*.	*ŋ͡galata > *galata (galad) * n͡dore > *dore (dôr) * m͡bando > *bando (band)
§4.79	[–sonorant –continuant +nasal] > [+sonorant +continuant][–nasal] Remaining nasalized stops, n͡d, m͡b, ŋ͡g (as in compounds) became *nd*, *mb*, *ŋg* also after an article or preposition.	*balan͡dore > *balandore (balannor) *dakan͡dīr > *dakandīr (dagnir) *um͡barta > *umbarta (úmarth) *moriŋ͡gūle > *moriŋgūle (morgul) *i·m͡bar > *i·mbar (i-mâr) *ina·n͡dore > *ina·ndore (e ndor)
§4.80	[–sonorant –continuant +spread] > [+continuant] Aspirates became fricatives: *p^h*, *t^h*, *k^h* > *ϕ*, *β*, x. *pp^h*, *tt^h*, *kk^h* > *pϕ*, *tβ*, *kx*	*p^{h}alasse > *ϕalasse (falas) *t^{h}unda > *βunda (thond) *k^{h}auda > *xauda (haudh) *k^{h}īt^{h}ė > *xīβė (hîth) *epp^{h}ele > *epϕele (ephel) *ett^{h}uile > *etβuile (ethuil) *rokk^{h}o > *rokxo (roch) *ep·p^{h}arma > *ep·ϕarma (e pharf) *et·t^{h}aware> *et·βaware (e thawar) *ek·k^{h}irja > *ek·xiria (e chair)
§4.81	[–sonorant –continuant] > [+continuant] / ___[–sonorant +continuant] Stops became fricatives before a following fricative: *pϕ tβ*, *kx* > *ϕϕ*, *ββ*, *xx* *kβ*> *xβ*, *tβ* > *ββ* *ks* > *xs* *ps* > *ϕs*	*datβa > *daββa (dath) *epϕele > *eϕϕele (ephel) *rokxo > *roxxo (roch) *ep·ϕarma > *eϕ·ϕarma (e pharf) *et·βaware > *eβ·βaware (e thawar) *ek·xirja > *ex·xiria (e chair) *okβo > *oxβo (auth) *lukβe > *luxβe (luith) *wekβe > *wexβe (gwaith) *nekβe > *nexβe (naith) *tekβa > *texβa (taith) *litβe > *liββe (lith) *lokse > *loxse (laus) *takse > *taxse (taes) *lapse > *laϕse (laes) *tupse > *tuϕse (taus) *apsa > *aϕsa (aes)
§4.82	*ϕ* > [–labial +dorsal] / ___*s* *ϕs* > *xs*	*laϕse > *laxse (laes) *tuϕse > *tuxse (taus) *aϕsa > *axsa (aes)
§4.83	*s* > [–strident] / *l*___ *ls* > *lβ*	*falsa > falβa- (faltha-) *olsa > olβa- (oltha-)

§4.84	[+sonorant +nasal –voice] > [+voice] Voiceless nasals became voiced: *m̭- > m-*, *ṋ- > n-*; *m̭m̭ > -mm-*, *-ṋṋ- > -nn-*.	*m̭alina > *malina (malen) *ṋarda > *narda (nardh) *am̭m̭alinde > *ammalinde (emlinn) *beṋṋo > *benno (benn)
§4.85	*s* > ø / ___C [–sonorant +continuant –strident] *sβ*, *sϕ*, *sx* > *β*, *ϕ*, *x*	*sβaŋga > *βaŋga (thang) *sxarwe > *xarwe (haru) *sϕaŋga > *ϕaŋga (fang)
§4.86	[–sonorant –continuant +voice] > [+continuant] / [+sonorant –nasal] ___ [+sonorant] First lenition: voiced stops (*d*, *b*, *g*) became fricatives (*ð*, *ƀ*, *ʒ*) when preceded by a vowel or liquid and followed by a vowel, liquid, nasal, or glide.	*golodo > *goloðo (golodh) *narda > *narða (nardh) *kulda > *kulða (coll) *xauda > *xauða (haudh) *nidwa > *niðwa (nedhu) *i·dolo > *i·ðolo (i-dhôl, v. dôl) *abaro > *aƀaro (avar) *i·baraβil > *i·ƀaraβil (i-vereth, v. bereth) *maiga > *maiʒa (mae) *nagma > *naʒma (naew) *ragme > *raʒme (raew) *dagno > *daʒno (daen) *wagna > *waʒna (gwaen) *regna > *reʒna (rain) *logna > *loʒna (loen) *kugna > *kuʒna (cûn) *i·galada > *i·ʒalaða (i-'aladh, v. galadh) *ina·danβa > *ina·ðanβa (e-dant) *ina·glata > *ina·ʒlata (en-glad)
§4.87	*ʒ > u* / ___C[+sonorant] *uʒ > uu*	*kuʒna > *kuuna (cûn) *suʒlȯ > *suulȯ (sûl) *tuluʒme > *tuluume (tulu)
§4.88	*u > u* / ___[+high] *u > u* / [+high] ___ *u > u* / ___[C] [+nasal] *u > u* / ___[C] [+high +round] *u > o* elsewhere *u* became *o*, except when part of the sequences *ju*, *iu*, *ui*, and *uu* or when followed by a nasal, by *u* or *w* in the next syllable, or by a final *ȯ* (< short *u*).	*kulða > *kolða (coll) *tuliie > *toliie (teli) *usϕe > *osϕe (osp) But these remained: *urukȯ (urug) *kurwe (curu) *lumbe (lûm) *liuka (lŷg) *kuuna (kûn) *uile (uil)
§4.89	*u > u* or *o* / ___*x*C In some words *uxβ* and *uxs* became *oxβ* and *oxs*,	*suxβa- > *soxβa (sautha-) *tuxse > *toxse (taus) These remained:

	but in others they remained unchanged.	*gruxβa- (gruitha-) *nuxβa- (nuitha-) *juxβa- (iuitha-)
§4.90	*x* > *u* / *o*___[–sonorant +continuant] Between *o* and a fricative, *x* became *u*, and *ox* became *ou*.	*loxse > *louse (laus) *toxse > *touse (taus) *oxβa > *ouβa (auth) *soxβa- > *souβa- (sautha-)
§4.91	[–sonorant +continuant +dorsal] > *i* / V___C *x* and *ʒ* became *i* between a vowel and a consonant.	*rixβa- > *riiβa- (ritha-) *krixβa- > *kriiβa- (critha-)
	ix, *iʒ* > *ii*	*rixβa- > *riiβa- (ritha-) *krixβa- > *kriiβa- (critha-) *riʒna > *riina (rîn)
	ex, *eʒ* > *ei*	*exβa- > eiβa- (eitha-) *wexβe > *weiβe (gwaith) *texβa > *teiβa (taith) *reʒna > *reina (rain) *keʒle > *keile (cail)
	ax, *aʒ* > *ai*	*maxβa- > *maiβa- (maetha-) *taxβa- > *taiβa- (taetha-) *jaxβa > *jaiβa (iaetha-) *axsa > *aisa (aes) *taxse > *taise (taes) *maʒla > *maila (mael) *saʒra > *saira (saer) *waʒna > *waina (gwaen) *daʒno > *daino (daen) *raʒme > *raime (raew) *naʒma > *naima (naew)
	oʒ > *oi* (Exceptionally, *oʒ* might become *ou*; cf. § 4.90.)	*loʒna > *loina (loen) *doʒme > *doume (daw)
	ux > *ui*	*gruxβa- > gruiβa- (gruitha-) *nuxβa- > nuiβa- (nuitha-) *juxβa- > juiβa- (iuitha-)
§4.92	*u* > [+front] / *i*___ *u* > [+front] / *j*___ Condition: not ___*i* *u* became *y* after *i* or *j*; it remained, however, in the sequence *jui-*.	*liuka > *liyka (lŷg) *julma > *jylma (ylf) *juiβa- (iuitha-) remained
§4.93	*i* > *y* / ___*y* *j* > *y* / ___*y* *i* and *j* assimilated to following *y*.	*liyka > *lyyka (lŷg) *jylma > *yylma (ylf)

§4.94 [–high –low –long] > [+high] / ___$ S_0 [i] (V)#
[+low –long] > [–low] / ___$ S_0 [i] (V)#
First (raising) *i*-affection. Short *e*, *a*, *o* raised to *i*, *e*, *u* in the syllable before a following *i* (no matter how many consonants intervened); the sequence *ie* became *ii* (later *i*).

*lassi > *lessi (lais)
*atani > *ateni (edain)
*eleni > *elini (elin)
*pelehi > *pelihi (peli)
*olohi > *oluhi (ely)
*tolli > *tulli (tyll)
*bania > *benia (bain)
*kalaria > *kaleria (celair)
*minielði > *miniilði (mínil)

§4.95 [+high –long] > [–high –low] / ___C(S_0)*a*
a-affection. Short *i* and *u* lowered to *e* and *o* before a final *-a* (< *-ā*).

*ina > *ena (en)
*ina·ðanβa > *ena·ðanβa (en-dant)
*pihia > *pehia (paich)
*miska > *meska (mesg)
*tunda > *tonda (tond)
*tuluka > *toloka (tolog)

§4.96 *i* > [–high] / ___*ia*

*miniia > *mineia (minai)

§4.97 [+back +round] > [–back] / ___(C)*i*(V)#
Second (fronting) *i*-affection changes *o* to *ö* and *u* to *y* [*a* no longer existed before an affecting *i*].

*ronia > *rönia (rain)
*oluhi > *olyhi (ely)
*goluði > *golyði (gelydh)
*miriuni > *miriyni (miryn)
*raŋxui > *raŋxyi (rengy)
*malui > *malyi (mely)

§4.98 *au* > ǭ
au became ǭ

*nauko > *nǭko (naug)
*bauia > *bǭia (boe)

§4.99 C(C)$_1$ *i*$_2$ > 2 1 / ___(V)#
C(C)$_1$ *i*$_2$ > 2 1 / ___(V)+
i following one or more consonants at or near the end of a word or before a morpheme boundary came to precede the consonant(s), changing preceding *i* to *ii*, *e* to *ei*, *ö* to *öi*, *y* to *yi*, *ǭ* to *ǭi*, *ū* to *ūi*.

*elini > *eliin (elin)
*pelihi > *peliih (peli)
*βinie > *βiine (thîn)
*lessi > *leiss (lais)
*ateni > *atein (edain)
*xapeti > *xapeit (hebaid)
*elϕi > *eilϕ (eilph)
*nerni > *neirn (nern)
*ϕeŋgi > *ϕeiŋg (feng)
*pehia > *peiha (paich)
*keʒia > *keiʒa (cai)
*keria > *keira (cair)
*kaleria > *kaleira (celair)
*rönia > *röina (ruin)
*föria > *föira (fuir)
*golyði > *golyið (gelydh)
*miriyni > *miriyin (miryn)
*nǭki > nǭik (noeg)
*dūri > *dūir (duir)
*rūnia > *rūina (ruin)
*kiria+tano > *kiira+tano (círdan)

§4.100 *h* > ø / ___#
Final *h* (< *s*) disappeared.

*peliih > *pelii (peli)
*olyih > *olyi (ely)

§4.101 *h* > *x* / *i*___
h became *x* following *i*.

*peiha > *peixa (paich)

§4.102 ø > *g* / #___*w*
Initial *w* became *gw*.
But *w* remained after a previous article.
Possibly later, initial *gw* appeared after articles and prepositions ending in *-n*, possibly on the analogy of words beginning with *gr-* and *gl-*.

*weiβe > *gweiβe (gwaith)
*waina > *gwaina (gwaen)
*i·weiβe > *i·weiβe (i·waith)
*in·waili > *iŋ·gwaili (in-gwael)
cf.*iŋ·glati (in-glaid, v. glâd) (see § 4.138)

§4.103 *a*[–stress] > *o* / *gw*___
gwa- (unstressed) > *gwo* (gwo-, go-)

§4.104 V[+back] > V[–low –back] / ___S_0 (V[–low –back]) V[+high –back]
Internal *i*-affection: *a*, *o*, and *u* were fronted to *e*, *ö*, and *y* in syllables preceding a syllable containing *i*, *ī*, *ei*, *ii*, *öi*, *yi*; in most compounds this did not occur or was reversed;

*arein > *erein (erain)
*ambyin > *embyin (emyn)
*andīn > *endīn (ennin)
*xalatirno > *xeletirno (heledir)
*ammalinde > *emmelinde (emlinn)
*olyi > *ölyi (ely)
*tulyiss > *tylyiss (tylys)
*atanateir > *eteneteir (edenedair)
*kaleira > *keleira (celair)
*baraβil > *bereβil (bereth)
*aranion > *erenion (Ereinion)
*gwonotiata > *gwönötiata (genediad)
*balariande > *beleriande (Beleriand)
*raŋxyi > *reŋxyi (rengy)
*malyi > *melyi (mely)

it did occur, however, in a few compounds.

*alϕaxīrȯ > *elϕexīrȯ (Elphir)

§4.105 ø > *i* / *e*___C [+voice +coronal] *i*
i was sometimes inserted between *e* and *l*, *n*, *r*, or *ð* preceding another *i*.

*elianwe > *eilianwe (eilian)
*teliene > *teiliene (teilien)
*ereniono > *ereiniono (Ereinion)
*gölöðiende > *gölöiðiende (Geleidhien)

§4.106 V[–long] (C) > ø / V(C)___#
Apocope. Words of more than one syllable lost their final vowel or (if ending in a consonant and the vowel preceding the consonant was short) the final vowel + consonant.

*gwönötiata > *gwönötiat (genediad)
*bereβil > *bereβ (bereth)
*doume > *doum (daw)
*elen > *el (êl)
*baraha > *barah (bara)
*mineia > *minei (minai)

	But final syllables containing long vowels or diphthongs remained.	*iβīl > *iβīl (ithil) *anǭr > *anǭr (anor) *endīn > *endīn (ennin)
	So did most plurals.	*erein > *erein (erain), etc.
§4.107	*h* > ø / ___# Final *h* resulting from apocope disappeared.	*barah > bara *atar > adar
§4.108	[–sonorant –continuant –voice] > [+voice] / V___ Second lenition: voiceless stops following vowels became voiced (*p*, *t*, *k* > *b*, *d*, *g*).	*grot > grod *nǭk > *nǭg (naug) *gwönötiat > *gwönödiad (genediad) *xepeit > *xebeid (hebaid) *kapr > *kabr (cabor) *makl > *magl (magol) *i·taur > i-daur, v. taur *i·palaβ > *i·balaβ (i-balath, v. palath) *i·kū > *i·gū (i-gû, v. cû) *ena·taur > *ena·daur (e-daur)
§4.109	ø > *u* / ǭ___C ǭ before a consonant became *ǭu*;	*gwǭn > *gwǭun (gwaun) *anǭr > *anǭur (anor) *xaðǭd > *xaðǭud (hadhod)
	but ǭ before a vowel remained unchanged.	*nǭig > *nǭig (noeg) *gǭi > *gǭi (goe)
§4.110	[+back –high +round] > [+low –round –long] / ___*u* *ou* and *ǭu* became *au*.	*doum > *daum (daw) *lous > laus (laus) *nouβa- > nauβa- (nautha-) *souβa- > sauβa- (sautha-) *gwǭun > gwaun *anǭur > *anaur (anor) *xaðǭud > *xaðaud (hadhod)
§4.111	*i* > ø / [+high –back]___ *yi* > *y*, *ii* > *i*	*pelii > peli *embyin > *embyn (emyn, v. amon) *ölyi > *öly (ely, v. ôl) *gölyið > gölyð (gelydh, v. golodh) *tylyiss > *tylyss (tylys, v. tulus) *miniil > *minil (mínil, v. miniel) *reŋxyi > *reŋxy (rengy, v. ranc) *melyi > *mely (mely, v. mâl) *riina > *rin (rîn)
§4.112	C [+nasal] > [–sonorant +continuant –voice –nasal] / ___ + [–sonorant +continuant –voice] A nasal consonant assimilates to an immediately following voiceless fricative	*aran+βorn > *araββorn (Arathorn) *in+βiw > *iββiw (i-thîw, v. têw) *im+ɸanβ > *iɸɸant (iphant) *iŋ+xeleir > *ixxeleir (i-chelair, v. calar)

belonging to another morpheme; *nβ*, *mφ*, *ŋx* > *ββ*, *φφ*, *xx*.

§4.113 [+nasal] > ø / ___ C [–sonorant +continuant +coronal]

A nasal consonant disappears before the consonants *β*, *φ*, *x*, *s* when followed by a liquid (e.g., *nβr̭* > *βr̭*, *mφr̭* > *φr̭*, *ŋxḽ* > *xḽ*, *nsr̭* > *sr̭*).

*taŋxḽ > *taxḽ (tachol)
*panβr̭ed > *paβr̭ed (pathred)
*nimφr̭ed > *niφr̭ed (niphred)
*lansr̭a- > *lasr̭a- (lathra-)
*aŋ·xr̭aban > *a·xr̭aban (a chraban, v. craban)

§4.114 [–sonorant –continuant +voice] > [+sonorant +continuant +nasal] / [V] [+nasal] ___ [+sonorant –nasal]

mb, *nd*, *ŋg* became *mm*, *nn*, *ŋŋ* after a vowel and before a vowel or a liquid.

*lambass > *lammass (lammas)
*handass > *hannass (hannas)
*endīn > *ennīn (ennin)
*umbarβ > *ummarβ (úmarth)
*pelendor > Pelennor
*elendor > Elennor
*glambren > glamren
*i·mbar > *i·mmar (i-mâr, v. bâr)
*i·ndor > *i·nnor (i-nôr, v. dôr)
*i·ŋgūl > *i·ŋŋūl (i-ngûl, v. gûl)
*in·döryn > *in·nöryn (i-neryn, v. doron)
*im·belig > *im·melig (i-melig, v. beleg)
*iŋ·geleið > *iŋ·ŋeleið (in-gelaidh, v. galadh)
*in·drūʒedein > *in·nrūʒedein (in·Drúedain)
*im·breβil > *im·mreβil (i-mrethil, v. brethil)
*iŋ·gleid > *iŋ·ŋleid (in-glaid, v. glâd)
*ambadir > *ammadir (amdir)
*drambabaur > *drammabaur (drambor)
*glambeðring > *glammeðring (Glamdring)
*glambexoβ > glammexoβ (glamhoth)
*rembemīr > *remmemīr (remmir)
*lambaβaŋk > lammaβaŋk (lamthanc)
*andadeiβ > *annadeiβ (andaith)
*andaðuin > *annaðuin (Anduin)
*andanest > *annanest (annest)
*andaφalass > *annaφalass (Anfalas)
*lindexir > *linnexir (Linhir)

*aŋgahabar > *aŋŋahabar (Anghabar)

nd, *mb*, *ŋg* remained when final. *nd*, *mb*, *ŋg* also did not change when they were the initial sounds of the second element in a compound word (and so followed an entirely unstressed syllable).

*lamb (lam), brand, *aŋg (ang)
*gondo+ndor > *gonno+ndor (Gondor)
*aŋga+mband > *aŋŋa+mband (Angband)

And so also after *ena·(en-): *aŋga+mbar > *aŋŋa+mmar (Angmar) is anomalous.

*ena·mbar (e-mbar) remained

§4.115 V > ø / ___+
Loss of composition vowels. Vowels connecting the different parts of a compound word were lost.

*maiga+xeneb > *maig+xeneb (maecheneb)
*roxxo+xīr > *roxx+xīr (rochir)
*elɸe+xīr > *elɸ+xīr (Elphir)
*ena·ðanβ > *en·ðanβ (e-dant)
*ena·daur > *en·daur (e-daur, v. taur)
*ena·ʒlad > *en·ʒlad (en-glad, v. glâd)
*ena·mbar > *en·mbar (e-mbar, v. bâr)
and many more.

Sometimes the vowel eliminated was not historically a composition vowel but was synchronically misunderstood as one.

*neleð+orn > *nelðorn (understood as nele+ðorn) (neldor)
*elem+bereβ > *elmbereβ (understood as ele+mbereβ) (Elbereth)

SANDHI CHANGES

§4.116 *h* > ø / ___C
h was deleted before a following consonant.

*barahnaur > *baranaur (Baranor)

§4.117 [–sonorant +continuant –voice] > [–continuant] / [+nasal] ___#
[–sonorant +continuant –voice] > [–continuant] / [+nasal] ___+
Remaining *nβ*, *mɸ*, *ŋx* became *nt*, *mp*, *ŋk* finally and before a morpheme boundary.

*kanβ > kant (cant)
*limɸ > limp
*xamɸ > *xamp (hamp)
*raŋx > raŋk (ranc)
*panβ+hail > *panthail (Panthael)
*aŋx+alagaun > *aŋkalagaun (Ancalagon)
*nimɸ+rass > *nimprass (Nimras)

§4.118 [–sonorant +continuant –voice] > [+sonorant –continuant +voice +nasal] / [+nasal] ___
Remaining medial *nβ*, *mɸ*, *ŋx* became *nn*, *mm*, *ŋŋ*.

*penβass > *pennass (pennas)
*daŋxen > *daŋŋen (dangen)
*reŋxy > *reŋŋy (rengy)
*limɸida- > *limmida- (limmida-)

§4.119	*ð* > ø / ___ [+nasal] *ð* was deleted before a nasal.	*eleðndor > *elendor (Elennor) *heleðmorn > *helemorn (Helevorn) *goloðmīr > *golomīr (Golovir)
§4.120	[+sonorant +continuant +coronal –voice +long] > [+voice –long] / S___ Long voiceless liquids became shortened and voiced after any consonant or vowel.	*limmḽḽūg > *limmlūg (limlug) *ammr̭r̭ūn > *ammrūn (amrûn) *an·r̭r̭īw > *an·rīw (a 'rîw) *en·r̭r̭ūn > *en·rūn (e·'rûn) *i·r̭r̭ūn > *i·rūn (i·rûn)
§4.121	*n* > [α place] / [–sonorant] *n*, short or long, assimilates to a following stop, fricative, or nasal.	*kelebrinbaur > *kelebrimbaur (Celebrimbor) *briβaunmbar > *briβaummbar (Brithombar) *annūnminass > *annūmminass (Annúminas) *nīnʒlaur > *nīŋʒlaur (ninglor) *βoronŋil > *βoroŋŋīl (Thorongil) *arngīr > *arŋgīr (argir) *arnʒonaβ > *arŋʒonaβ (Argonath) *mornben > *mormben (morben) *mornmegil > *mormmegil (Mormegil) *βinngoll > βiŋŋgoll (Thingol) *lennmbass > *lemmmbas (lembas) *en·mbar > *em·mbar (e-mbar) *en·ʒlad > *eŋ·ʒlad (en-glad) *aun·menel > *aum·menel (o menel)
§4.122	*ʒ* > ø / C___C *ʒ* disappeared between consonants.	*kelebʒrond > *kelebrond (Celebrond) *maigʒlīn > *maiglīn (Maeglin) *menegʒroβ > *menegroβ (Menegroth) *raβʒlauriel > *raβlauriel (Rathlóriel) *galaðʒlauriel > *galaðlauriel (Galadlóriel) *nauƀʒrod > *nauƀrod (Novrod) *dūmʒwaβ > *dūmwaβ (dúath) *tarʒlaŋk > tarlaŋk (tarlanc)
§4.123	*ð* > [–continuant] / ___ [–sonorant –continuant +voice] *ð* became *d* before voiced stops.	*arðgalen > Ardgalen
§4.124	*ð* > [–continuant] / ___ l *ð* became *d* before *l*.	*galaðlauriel > *galadlauriel (Galadlóriel)

§4.125	ð > [–continuant] / C+___ ð became *d* at the beginning of a morpheme following a consonant.	*karag+ðūr > karagdūr (Caragdûr) *ann+ðuin > annduin (Anduin) *baran+ðuin > Baranduin *glamm+ðriŋg > glammdriŋg (Glamdring) *gas+ðil > gasdil *gūl+ðūr > gūldūr (guldur) *mall+ðuin > mallduin (Malduin) *nel+ðorn (so analyzed) > neldorn (neldor) *en+ðant > en·dant (e-dant)
	But ð- was retained after a vowel.	*fanui-ðol > fanuiðol (Fanuidhol)
§4.126	*w* > ø / V___+C *w* disappeared after a vowel at the end of a morpheme before a consonant.	*gwaiw+hīr > *gwaihīr (Gwaehir) *gwaiw+raun > *gwairaun (Gwaeron)
§4.127	*m* [–long] > [–sonorant +continuant] / [+sonorant –nasal]___ *m* became *ṽ* after a vowel, semivowel or liquid.	*daum > *dauṽ (daw) *kaim > *kaiṽ (caew) *tuim > *tuiṽ (tuiw) *rīm > *rīṽ (rîw) *dūm > *dūṽ (dû) *ϕalm > *ϕalṽ (falf) *ylm > *ylṽ (ylf) *parm > *parṽ (parf) *helemorn > *heleṽorn (helevorn) *ϕormen > *ϕorṽen (forven) *galmorn > *galṽorn (forven) *mallmegil > *mallṽegil (malvegil) *dūmwaβ > dūṽwaβ (dúath) *lemn > *leṽn (lefn) *udumn > *uduṽn (udûn) *gwelwmen > *gwelwṽen (gwelwen) *i·medui > *i·ṽedui (i-vedui, v. medui) dagmor
	m remained in other instances.	raβmallen (rathmallen) rasmund *annūmminass (Annúminas) *mormmegil (Mormegil) *remmmīr (remmir)
	m occasionally remained after *l*.	gilmiβ (Gilmith)
§4.128	*n* > [–sonorant +continuant –nasal] / ___*r* *n* became ð before *r*.	*onrond > *oðrond (odhron) *onrill > *oðrill (odhril) *inr > *iðr (idhor) *īn+rind > * īðrind (idhrinn) *karan+rass > *karaðrass (Caradhras) *in·reiss > *ið·reiss (idh-rais, v. ras)

In one, possibly archaic, case *n* remained before r.

*aran-rūβ > aranrūβ (Aranrúth)

§4.129 C [+long] > [–long] / ___C
A long or double consonant became short when preceding another consonant.

*ellroxxxīr > elroxxīr (Elrohir)
*hallbarad > Halbarad
*mallbeβ > malbeβ (Malbeth)
*mallduin > Malduin
*mellndīr > *melndīr (meldir)
*orxalldaur > *orxaldaur (Orchaldor)
*ammdir > *amdir (Amdir)
*drammbaur > *drambaur (drambor)
*glammdring > *glamdring (glamdring)
*glammxoβ > *glamxoβ (glamhoth)
*remmmīr > *remmīr (remmir)
*lammβaŋk > lamβaŋk (lamthanc)
*anndeiβ > *andeiβ (andaith)
*annduin > Anduin
*annnest > annest
*annɸalass > *anɸalas (Anfalas)
*gonnndor > *gonndor (Gondor)
*lemmmbas > *lemmbas (lembas)
*linnxir > *linxir (Linhir)
*aŋŋhabar > aŋhabar (Anghabar)
*aŋŋmband > *aŋmband (Angband)
*βiŋŋgoll > *βiŋgol (Thingol)
*lassbelin > lasbelin
*lassgalen > lasgalen
*gossβīr > *gosβīr (Gostir)
*ɸalassr̭imb > *ɸalasr̭imb (Falathrim)
*nossḽīr > *nosḽīr (nothlir)
*roxxxīr > *roxxīr (rochir)
*em·mbar > e-mbar, v. bâr
*im·mbeir > *i·mbeir (i-mbair, v. bâr)
*in·nrūʒedein >*i·nrūʒedein (in-Drúedain, v. Drúadan)
*im·mreβil > *i·mreβil (i-mrethil, v. brethil)
*iŋ·ŋleid > *i·ŋleid (in-glaid, v. glâd)
*iŋ·ŋgölyð > *i·ŋgölyð (in-gelydh, v. golodh)

§	Rule	Examples
		*en·ndor > e ndor, v. dôr *en·mbar > e mbar, v. bâr
§4.130	*x* > *h* / #___ *x* became *h* at the beginning of a word, but remained after the article *i*.	*xarad > harad *xaðaud > *haðaud (hadhod) *xr̭ass > *hr̭ass (rhas) *i·xarad (i-Ĉharad)
§4.131	*h* > ø / #___*r̭* *h* disappeared before *r* (which was voiceless following *h*).	*hr̭ass > r̭ass (rhas)
§4.132	*x* > *h* / C+___ Condition: C not +sonorant +continuant *x* also became *h* at the beginning of a morpheme following a consonant, but not after *w*, liquids, or vowels.	*araud+xīr > *araudhīr (Arothir) *maig+xeneb > *maigheneb (maecheneb) *elϕ+xīr > *elϕhīr (Elphir) *rox+xīr > *roxhīr (rochir) *glam+xoβ > glamhoβ (glamhoth) *duin+xīr > *duinhīr (Duinhir) *loss+xoβ > *losshoβ (Lossoth) *galað+xīr > *galaðhīr (Galathir) *elwxīl (Eluchíl), *eruxīn (Eruchín), *orxall (orchal) remained unchanged
§4.133	[–sonorant –continuant +voice] > [–voice] / ___[–sonorant +continuant –voice] Voiced stops (*b*, *d*, *g*) became voiceless (*p*, *t*, *k*) before *h* and *β*.	*kelebharn > *kelepharn (Celepharn) *aigβeliond > *aikβeliond (Aecthelion) *belegβor > *belekβor (Belecthor) *maigheneb > *maikheneb (maecheneb) *araudhīr > *arauthīr (Arothir)
§4.134	[–sonorant –continuant –voice] > [+continuant] ___ *h* Voiceless stops *p*, *t*, *k* became voiceless fricatives *f*, *β*, *x* preceding *h*.	*kelepharn > *keleϕharn (Celepharn) *maekheneb > *maexheneb (maecheneb) *arauthir > *arauβhir (Arothir)
§4.135	*ð* > [–voice] / ___[–voice] *ð* became *β* before a voiceless sound.	*galaðhīr > *galaβhīr (Galathir) *galaðβiliaun > *galaββiliaun (Galathilion)
§4.136	*h* > ø / [–sonorant –continuant –voice] ___ *h* disappeared after voiceless fricatives.	*keleϕharn > *kelefarn (Celepharn) *maixheneb > *maixeneb (maecheneb) *arauβhīr > *arauβīr (Arothir) *galaβhīr > *galaβīr (Galathir) *elϕhīr > *elϕīr (Elphir) *roxhīr > *roxīr (rochir)

*losshoβ > lossoβ (Lossoth)
*gwaβhīr > *gwaβīr (Gwathir)

§4.137 *p* > ø / *m*___C
p disappeared between *m* and another consonant.

*nimpdill > *nimdill (Nimdil)
*nimpƀreβil > nimbreβil (Nimbrethil)
*nimploββ > nimloββ (Nimloth)
*nimprass > nimras (Nimras)

§4.138 *ʒ* > [–continuant] / [+nasal] ___
ʒ became *g* after nasals.

*nīŋʒlaur > *nīŋglaur (ninglor)
*arŋʒonaβ > *arŋgonaβ (Argonath)
*daŋʒweβ > daŋgweβ (dangweth)
*βūriŋʒweβil > *βūriŋgweβil (Thuringwethil)
*eŋ·ʒlad > *eŋ·glad (en-glad)

§4.139 *ƀ* > [–continuant] / C+___
Condition: not *r*___
ƀ- became *b*- in most instances when following a consonant;
but *ƀ* remained after *r*.

*halƀarad > Halbarad
*nimƀreβil > nimbreβil (Nimbrethil)

*herƀenn (hervenn), *arƀeleg (Arveleg) remained

§4.140 $[+nasal]_0$ > ø / C [+sonorant] ___ C [+voice]
Nasals disappeared between a nasal or liquid and a voiced consonant.

*arŋgīr > *argīr (argir)
*arŋgonaβ > argonaβ (Argonath)
*mormben > morben
*mormmegil > Mormegil
*karnnen > karnen (Carnen)
*elmbereβ > elbereβ (Elbereth)
*mornndor > Mordor
*briβaummbar > *briβaumbar (Brithombar)
*βoronndīr > *βorondīr (Thorondir)
*linndīr > *lindīr (Lindir)
*herndīr > *herdīr (herdir)
*gilndīss > *gildīss (Gildis)
*lemmbass > *lembass (lembas)
*aŋmband > *aŋband (Angband)
*mōrŋgoβ > *mōrgoβ (Morgoth)

Nasals were retained before semivowels.

dornhoβ (Dornhoth)
*ϕornwobel (Fornobel) remained unchanged

§4.141 [+nasal] > ø / C_a___ C_b
Condition: a = b
Nasals were lost between two stops of the same place of articulation.

*ϕeredndīr > *ϕereddīr (feredir)
*belegŋgurβ > *beleggurβ (Belegurth)

§4.142 [–sonorant –continuant +voice] > ø / [C] [+nasal] ___
Remaining *nd* and *mb* became the nasals *n* and *m* after nonnasal stops and fricatives, after semivowels and vowels, or after nasals following nonliquids.

*dagndīr > *dagnīr (dagnir)
*goβmbaug > *goβmaug (Gothmog)
*lemnndīr > *lemnnīr (lefnir)
*kurwndīr > *kurwnīr (Curunír)
*eglmbar > *eglmar (Eglamar)

§4.143 *t* > ø / *s*___C
st simplifies to *s* before a consonant.

*bastgorn > basgorn
*ostgiliaβ > osgiliaβ (Osgiliath)
*ostϕorod > *osϕorod (Osforod)

§4.144 *s* > *β* / ___ C [+sonorant +continuant +coronal]
s became *β* before liquids *l* and *r*.

*ϕalasr̭imb > *ϕalaβr̭imb (Falathrim)
*nosḽīr > *noβḽīr (nothlir)
*osr̭ond > oβr̭ond (othrond)
*losḽand > loβḽand (lothlann)
*ϕalasr̭en > *ϕalaβr̭en (falathren)
*lasr̭a- > *laβr̭a- (lathra-)

§4.145 *β* > [–continuant] / *s*___
β became *t* after *s*.

*gosβīr > *gostīr (Gostir)

§4.146 ø > *d* / *n*___ C [+sonorant +continuant]
n became *nd* before a following liquid consonant,

*anross > *andross (Andros)
*i·nrūʒedein > *in·drūʒedein (in-Drúedain)
*ϕinlass > *ϕindlass (Finglas)

unless the following consonant was a *d*.

*ϕinraud (Finrod)

§4.147 ø > *g* / *ŋ* ___ [+sonorant +continuant]
ŋ became *ŋg* before *l*, *r*, *w*-.

*aŋweð > aŋgweð (Angwedh)
*aŋrist > aŋgrist (Angrist)
*riŋloʒ > *riŋgloʒ (Ringló)
*i·ŋleid > *iŋgleid (in-glaid)
*iŋ·wanūr > *iŋ·gwanūr (in-gwanur)

§4.148 *nd* > [–coronal +dorsal] / ___l
nd became *ŋg* before *l*.

*ϕindlas > *ϕiŋglas (Finglas)

§4.149 *ṽ* > ø / *w*___
ṽ disappeared after *w*.

*gwelwṽen > gwelwen

§4.150 *ṽ* > *w* / *l*___
lṽ sometimes became *lw*,

*lalṽen > lalwen
*lalṽorn > *lalworn (lalorn)
*gilṽen > gilwen

but elsewhere remained.

*galṽorn (galvorn) remained

§4.151 *w* > ø / ___[+round]
w disappeared before *o*, *ö*, and *ǭ*.

*gwǭin > *gǭin (goen)
*gwolass > *golass (golas)
*gwönödiad > *gönödiad (genediad)
*lalworn > lalorn

*ɸornwobel > *ɸornobel (Fornobel)
*ɸorwoxell > *ɸoroxell (Forochel)
*arwonoded > aronoded (aronoded)

§4.152 ʒ > *i* / C[+sonorant +continuant +coronal] ___V
rʒ, *lʒ* usually became *ri*, *li* before a vowel.

*tarʒass > *tariass (tarias)
*þalʒond > *þaliond (thalion)
*þelʒynd > *þeliynd (thelyn, v. thalion)
*dīrʒell > *dīriell (Díriel)
but *delʒoss > *deloss (delos)

§4.153 *i* > ø / ___*y*
The sequence *iy* became *y*.

*miriyni > *miryni (miryn)
*þeliynd > *þelynd (thelyn)

§4.154 ʒ > ø / $\$S_0$C___#
ʒ disappeared at the end of a polysyllable.

*ekþelʒ > ekþel (ecthel)

§4.155 ʒ > *a* / [–high] C___#
ʒ became *a* at the end of monosyllables following *a* and *e*.

*þelʒ > þela (thela)
*tarʒ > tara

§4.156 ʒ > *i* / [+high] C___#
ʒ became *i* at the end of monosyllables following *i*.

*þeilʒ > þeili (theili)
*ɸilʒ > *ɸili (fili)

§4.157 *ð* > *l* / *l*___
The sequence *lð* became *ll*.

*kolð > koll (coll)
*golðr > *gollr (gollor)

§4.158 *n* > *l* / ___*l*
The sequence *nl* sometimes became *ll* but sometimes remained.

*miþrenlass > *miþrellass (Mithrellas)
*minlammad (minlamad)

§4.159 *n* > ø / V[+long] ___*n*
n might disappear after a long vowel before another *n*.

*nīnnimp > *nīnimp (nínim)

§4.160 *r* > *l* / *l*___
The sequence *lr* sometimes became *ll*, especially when the second element was a suffix, but usually remained in compound words and names.

*eðelrimb > *eðellimb (edhellim)
*eðelren > eðellen (edhellen)
*kalrond > *kallond (callon)
Elrond
*elross (Elros)

§4.161 *r* > *l* / ___*l*
The sequence *rl* sometimes became *ll*,

*glewerlind > *glewellind (Glewellin)
*erloþ > elloþ (elloth)

but often remained.

Forlond remained

§4.162 *r* > ø / ___*r*
The sequence *rr* sometimes simplified to *r* but often remained.

*airrandīr > *airandīr (Aerandir)
*aglarrond > Aglarond
*telerrimb (Telerrim) remained
*çast > hast

§4.163 *ç > h*
ç became *h*.

*çūl > hūl (hûl)

§4.164 V[+high] V[+high] > [+high +long]
uu, *yy*, and *ii* became *ū*, *ȳ*, and *ī*.

*βiin > *βīn (thîn)
*lyyg > *lȳg (lŷg)
*tuluuṽ > *tulūṽ (tulu)

§4.165 Accent shift: the stress accent shifted from its original free placement to a regular system based on syllable length, falling on the first syllable of almost all dissyllables, on the penultimate syllable of polysyllables if that syllable was closed (followed by more than one consonant, or containing a diphthong), and on the antepenultimate if the penultimate syllable was open (followed by only one or no consonant) and short.

§4.166 [+long] > [–long]
Condition not ___ C [+sonorant +coronal]
Change in quantity. In polysyllables ī and ū became short; however, they remained long in a number of instances when they preceded *n*, *l*, or *r*;

kīrdan (círdan), mīrdan (mírdan), *dīrneiβ (dírnaith), *nīrnaiβ (nírnaeth), *hīrill (híril), mīriel (míriel), nīniel (níniel), *nīnimp (nínim), *nīnui (nínui), anīra (aníra), tīra (tíra), sīla (síla), dīnen (dínen), eruxīn (eruchín), *kurwnīr (curunír), *annūneid (annúnaid), *kūraun (cúron), *rūnen (rhúnen)

ǭi was also reduced to *ǫi*, and *ūi* to *ui*

*ĝǭi > *gǫi (goe)
*rūin > ruin

§4.167 V > [+long] / #(C)(C)V(C)#
All vowels, short or long, became long in monosyllables when followed by only a single final consonant or none. All vowels remained short in monosyllables when followed by two final consonants, e.g., *nand*, *ost*, *anc*.
In polysyllables *a* and *e* were almost always short.

*tal > tāl (tâl)
*hen > hēn (hên)
*dor > dōr (dôr)

See Tables 4.5 and 4.6 for phonology at this stage.

Table 4.5
Consonantal Phonology of Middle Sindarin

	Labials	Interdentals	Alveolars	Palatals	Velars	Labialized Velars	Glottal
Unaspirated stops	p b		t d		k g	*gw*	
Nasals	m		n		ŋ		
Trills			r̭- r				
Fricatives	ɸ ƀ	þ ð	s-		x ʒ		h
Nasal fricative	ṽ						
Approximants			ḽ- l	j		ƕ- -w	

Table 4.6
Vocalic Phonology of Middle Sindarin (rounded vowels in italics)

	Simple Vowels		Diphthongs Ending in -i		Diphthongs Ending in -u	
	Front	Back	Front	Back	Front	Back
High	i, y	*u*		ui		
Mid	e, ö	*o*	ei, öi	oi		
Low		a		ai, ǫi		au

MIDDLE SINDARIN TO CLASSICAL SINDARIN

§4.168 *au* > *o*

au was reduced to *o* when it became unstressed, and usually in polysyllables,

*anaur > anor
*raudon > rodon
*daulen > dolen
*jaureþ > joreþ (Ioreth)
*balraug > balrog
*bauldaug > Boldog
*goþmaug > goþmog (Gothmog)
*nauƀrod > *noƀrod (Novrod)
*gilþauniell > gilþoniel (Gilthoniel)
*r̭auƀaniond > *r̭oƀaniond (Rhovanion)
*aug·galað > *og·galað (o galadh)
*aum·menel > *om·menel (o menel)

especially in words containing *kaun* (con, -gon), *naur* (-nor), *paur* (-bor), *raun* 'moon' (-ron), *taur* 'king' (-dor), *glaur* (glor-), *jaur* (ior-), *aur* (or-).

*arþauriend > *arþōriend (Arthórien)
*anauriend > *anōriend (Anórien)
*glaureðel > glōreðel (Glóredhel)

au often appears as *ō* in a stressed open syllable, especially when followed by an open syllable.

*glauriel > glōriel (glóriel)
*naurui > nōrui (nórui)
*auðel > ōðel (ódhel)

au was retained in all monosyllables, and in words containing the elements *gaur*, *taur* 'forest', *thaur*, *faug*, *draug*, *baug*, and other polysyllabic words closely related to them; it was also usually retained in the element *naug*, but *naug* was sometimes shortened to *nog*.

au was also retained before *ṽ* and *w*.

*arauṽ (Araw), *rauwross (Rauros)

§4.169 C [+long] > [–long] / ___V [+long +stress]
A long consonant was shortened immediately preceding a long stressed syllable.

*tinnūṽiell > *tinūṽiell (tinúviel)

§4.170 V[–long] C [+voice +dorsal] > V [+long] ø / ___C
ʒ and *ŋ* disappeared between a vowel and a consonant, usually with compensatory lengthening of the previous vowel (except where that was part of a diphthong).

*druʒweiβ > drūweiβ (Drúwaith)
*tuʒʒor > *tūʒor (Tuor)
*uiʒloss > *uiloss (Uilos)
*jaʒw > jāw (iaw)

§4.171 [+voice +dorsal] > ø / ___ [–consonantal]
ʒ and *ŋ* disappeared before vowels and *w*.

*teŋw > *tēw (têw)
*uiŋal > uial
*i·ŋīl > i·īl (i-'îl v. gîl)
*maʒid > *maid (maed)
*loʒeg > loeg
*guruβʒoss > *guruβoss (guruthos)
*delʒoss > *deloss (delos)
*i·ʒalað > i·alað (i-'aladh)

§4.172 V[+voice +dorsal] > V [+long] ø / ___#
At the end of a word, *ʒ* disappeared, and the preceding vowel became long.

*loʒ > lō (lô)

This sometimes happened with *ʒ* and *ŋ* in the middle of words as well.

*teŋw > *tēw (têw)
*riʒiss > *riiss > *rīss (rîs)
*riʒann >*rīann (rían)
*druʒin > *drūin (drúin, v. drû)

But *tuʒor > Tuor, not *Túor.

§4.173 *ṽ* > *w* / V[+high]___#
ṽ > *w* / V[+high]___C
Final -*ṽ* became *w* between a high vowel and a consonant or at the end of a word.

*dūṽ > *dūw (dû)
*dūṽlind > *dūwlind (dúlinn)
*dūṽhirion > *dūwhirion (Dúhirion)
*dūṽwaβ > *dūwwaβ (dúath)
*uduṽn > *uduwn (udûn)
*eruṽ > *eruw (eru)
*tulūṽ > *tulūw (tulu)

*dauṽ > *dauw (daw)
*hīṽ > *hīw (hîw)
*naiṽ > *naiw (naew)
*tuiṽ > tuiw
*nȳṽ > nȳw (nŷw)

§4.174 *ƀ > w / ai___*
ƀ became *w* following *ai*.

*glaiƀ > *glaiw (glaew)

§4.175 *w* > ø / ___CC
w disappeared before more than one consonant.

*delduwβḽiŋg > delduβḽiŋg (Delduth̭ling)
(for thling cf. § 4.225)

§4.176 *uw > ū*
w following *u* disappeared, and the *u* became long by compensatory lengthening.

*duw > dū (dû)
*uwan > ūan (úan)
*nuwath > nūath (núath)
*duwlind > *dūlind (dúlinn)
*uduwn > *udūn (udûn)
*eruw > erū (eru)
*tulūw > *tulū (tulu)

§4.177 *w* > ø / *au*___
w disappeared after *au*.

*dauw > *dau (daw)
*nauw > *nau (naw)
*rauwross > *rauross (rauros)

§4.178 V [+long] > [–long] / $C___#
A long final vowel became short when in a polysyllabic word.

*erū > eru
*tulū > tulu

§4.179 ø > *x* / V___*ƕ*V
ƕ became *xƕ* between vowels.

*i·ƕest > *i·xƕest (i-chwest, v. hwest)

§4.180 [–sonorant +continuant +labial] > [+labial +coronal]
Bilabial *ɸ* and *ƀ* became labiodental *f* and *v*.

*rīƀ > rīv (rîf)
*noƀrod > Novrod

§4.181 *ṽ* > [+labial +coronal –nasal]
ṽ merges into *v*.

*ylṽ > ylv (ylf)
*gorṽ > gorv (gorf)
*sileṽrill > silevrill (silevril)
*tinūṽiell > tinūviell (tinúviel)

§4.182 V > ø / [+stress] ___ [+stress]
Short unstressed *o* disappears between stressed syllables.

*ˌnaro'goβr̭ond > *nar 'goβr̭ond (Nargoth̭rond)

§4.183 *r* > *s* / ___*s*
rs became *ss*.

*tars > tass (tas)

§4.184 [–sonorant +continuant –voice +long] > [–long]
Long *ββ*, *ff*, *xx*, *ss* became *β*, *f*, *x*, *s*.

*effel > efel (ephel)
*roxxir > roxir (rochir)
*laββ > laβ (lath)
*lass > las

		*bessein > *besein (besain) *lossen > losen (lossen; the older *ss* spelling was generally retained between vowels) *ef·farv > *e·farv (e pharf) *eþ·þawar > *e·þawar (e thawar) *ex·xeir > *e·xeir (e chair)
§4.185	[–sonorant –continuant +voice +long] > [–long] Long or double voiced stops became short.	*fereddir > feredir *beleggurþ > belegurþ (Belegurth) *og·galað > *o galað (o galadh)
§4.186	*m* > ø / *m*___ *mm* became *m*. *mm* was often, however, retained in spelling: lammen, am meril.	*ammarþ > amarþ (amarth) *annūmminass > *annūminass (Annúminas) *ummarþ > *umarþ (úmarth) *om·menel > o menel *ammon > amon
§4.187	*n* > ø / V[–long]___#CV Final *-n* in preposed articles and prepositions consisting of a short vowel + n (*in*, *an*, *en*) was dropped before words beginning with a single consonant. There are some exceptions, such as Taur en-Faroth. *n* was retained if more than one consonant followed. *n* was also retained after long vowels or in polysyllables.	*en·dinw > *e·dinw (e-dinu) *en·dant > e-dant *in·sedryn > i sedryn *in·nögyþ > *i·nögyþ (i-negyth, v. nogoth) *in·leis > *i·leis (i-lais, v. las) *eŋ·glad (en-glad) *in·drūedein (in-drúedain) *īn·fein (în phain) erin·doloþen (erin dolothen)
§4.188	ö > [–front +high] / ___*i* The diphthong *öi* became *ui*	*röin > ruin *föir > fuir
§4.189	ö > [–round] ö became *e*	*gönödiad > genediad *önyd > enyd gölyð > gelyð (gelydh, v. golodh)
§4.190	*i* > [–high] / [–high +back] ___ The diphthong *ai* became *ae*, and *oi* and *ǫi* became *oe*.	*dain > daen *gwain > gwaen *nǫig > noeg *loin > loen
§4.191	*w* > ø / S_0\$(C)VC___# Final *-w* was lost following a consonant in words of more than one syllable.	*kurwfinw > *kurwfin (Curufin) *finarfinw > Finarfin *iþildinw > iþildin (ithildin) *eilianw > eilian
§4.192	ø > *o* / C ___ C [+sonorant +continuant] # Final *r* and *l* after a consonant became *-or*, *-ol* (see note in § 4.196 below)	*taxl > taxol (tachol) *magr > magor

§4.193 ø > o / C___ *r* C
r between consonants became *or*.
*dagrlind > Dagorlind

§4.194 ø > *a* / C *l* ___ C
l between consonants became *la* (see note in § 4.196 below)
*eglmar > Eglamar
*maglðūr > maglaðūr (Magladhûr)

§4.195 *w* > *u* / C___#
Final *w* after a consonant became u.
*tinw > tinu
*kurw > kuru (curu)
*janw > janu (ianu)

§4.196 *w* > *u* / C___C
w also became *u* between consonants.
Note: The introduction of new light syllables did not generally cause the accent to shift; thus '*eglamar*, '*kurunīr* remained accented on the first syllable even though the new vowels preceded an originally double consonant. However, if addition of a new vowel at the end pushed the stress forward beyond the antepenultimate, the stress probably moved toward the end. The introduction of the vowel in *Dagorlind*, *Dagorlad*, may, however, have altered the accentuation as the new syllable was heavy.
*kurwfin > kurufin (Curufin)
*kurwnīr > kurunīr (Curunír)
*'menelvagr > me'nelvagor (Menelvagor)

§4.197 *i* > ø / *e*___*r*C#
ei reduced to *e* before *r* followed by a consonant.
*neirn > nern
*keirð > kerð (cerdh, certh)

§4.198 *i* > ø / *e*___*ŋg*#
ei also reduced to *e* before ŋg.
*feiŋg > feŋg (feng)

§4.199 *e* > [+low +back] / ___*i*C(C)#
ei > *ai* in mono- and final syllables.
*leis > lais
*edein > edain
*erein > erain

Condition: not ___*il*C#
But *ei* remained before *l* followed by a consonant.
eilf (eilph, v. alph)

§4.200 *ŋ* > ø / # ___ *ŋ*
Initial *ŋŋ* became *ŋ*.
*i·ŋŋuruþ > *i·ŋuruþ (i-nguruth, v. guruth)
*iŋ·ŋelaið > i·ŋelaið (i-ngelaidh, v. galadh)

§4.201 *ŋ* > [–nasal –sonorant] / *ŋ*___
Medial -*ŋŋ*- > -*ŋg*-.
*þoroŋŋil > þoroŋgil (Thorongil)
*daŋŋen > daŋgen (dangen)

§4.202 *g* > ø / *ŋ*___#
Final -*ŋg* became -*ŋ*.
*aŋg > aŋ (ang)

§4.203 *b* > ø / *m*___#
Final -*mb* became -*m*.
*lamb > lam

§4.204 *p* > ø / $C(C)V*m*___
Final *-mp* became *-m* in polysyllables.
*nīnimp > *nīnim (nínim)

§4.205 *l* > ø / $S_0$$(C)Vl___#
Final *-ll* simplifies to *-l* in polysyllables.
*oðrill > oðril (odhril)
*orxall > orxal (orchal)
*tinūviell > tinūviel (tinúviel)

§4.206 *u* > *ū* / #(C)C ___*m*#
u became long in monosyllables preceding *m*.
*tum > tūm (tûm)
*kum > kūm (cûm)

§4.207 *u* > *ū* / ___*m*V
And sometimes even in polysyllables when *m* preceded a vowel.
*umarþ > ūmarþ (úmarth)

§4.208 *t* > ø / $*s*___#
Final *-st* in polysyllables commonly became *-s;*
*imladrist > Imladris
also in monosyllables in adjectival or genitive phrases.
*rast morþil > ras morþil (Ras Morthil)

§4.209 *n* > ø / $*r*___#
Final *-rn* in polysyllables could become *-r;* but final *-rn* was usually retained.
*heledirn > heledir
*eþirn > *eþir (ethir)
basgorn, edhelharn

§4.210 *w* > ø / *ui*___
Final *w* might be lost following *ui;* but such words could also be written with final *w*.
exuiw > exui (echui)
ruiw > rui

§4.211 *ð* > ø / *r*___#
Final *ð* was (rarely) lost following *r*.
karð > kar (car)

§4.212 *d* > *nd* / $S_0$$*n*___#
Final *-nd* became *-nn* in polysyllables.
*roxand > *roxann (Rohan)
*aerlind > aerlinn
*loþḽand > loþḽann (Lothlann)

§4.213 *n* > ø / S_0 $ S $ *n*___#
Final *-nn* became *-n* in words of more than two syllables.
*seregonn > seregon
*iþilienn > iþilien (Ithilien)
*gondolinn > Gondolin
*beleriann > Belerian

‡Final *-nd* was often kept in compounds where the final element was a monosyllable, especially *-rond*, *-þond* (*-thond*), *-lond*, *-gund* (< *cund*), and *-ind*. Sometimes even final *-nn* was reduced to *-n* in dissyllables, e.g., *taeglinn > *taeglin*, *roxann > *roxan (Rohan). Moreover, the final element **-nand* always appears as *-nan*: *mornand > *Mornan*; and the final ending **-ond* usually appears as *-on*: *oðrond > oðron (*odhron*).

§4.214 *d* > ø / *n*___#
Final *-nd* became *-n* in monosyllables used in adjectival or genetive phrases.
*fend hollen > Fen Hollen
*amon hend > Amon Hen
*nand elmoþ > nan elmoþ (Nan Elmoth)

§4.215 *þ* > *s* / *þ*V_0___ — *ūþaeþ > ūþaes (úthaes)

þ dissimilated to *s* when the preceding consonant was *þ*. This did not occur in compounds; e.g., Mitheithel did not become !Mitheisel.

See Tables 4.7 and 4.8 for phonology at this stage.

TABLE 4.7
CONSONANTAL PHONOLOGY OF CLASSICAL SINDARIN
(consonant combinations in italics)

	Labials	Interdentals	Alveolars	Palatals	Velars	Labialized Velars	Glottal
Unaspirated stops	p b		t d		k g	*gw*	
Nasals	m		n		ŋ		
Trills			r̥- r				
Fricatives	f v	þ ð	s		-x-	*-xƕ-*	h
Approximants			l̥- l	j		ƕ-	-w

TABLE 4.8
VOCALIC PHONOLOGY OF CLASSICAL SINDARIN (rounded vowels in italics)

	Simple Vowels		Diphthongs Ending in -e		Diphthongs Ending in -i		Diphthongs Ending in -u	
	Front	Back	Front	Back	Front	Back	Front	Back
High	i, *y*	*u*				ui		
Mid	e	*o*		oe	ei			
Low		a		ae		ai		au

POSTCLASSICAL SINDARIN

§4.216 *x* > *h* / V___V

In Sindarin as pronounced in Gondor, perhaps due to the Westron substrate, *x* was often softened to *h* between vowels.

roxir (rochir) > rohir
roxan > Rohan
*gwaexir > Gwaehir
baraxir > Barahir
*gwaxaedir (gwachaedir) > gwahaedir

§4.217 *x* > *k* / ___#

Also in the pronunciation of Gondor, *x* became *k* finally (in pronunciation, probably not in spelling).[1]

balx (balch) > balk
lax (lach) > lak

1. See Unfinished Tales, pp. 318–19n49.

§4.218 *aeg* > *ēg*
ae > *ē*
In some Sindarin dialects (including Gondor and Mirkwood) ae was pronounced ē.

laeg > lēg

§4.219 $l_1m_2 > 2\ 1$
In dialectal Sindarin some consonant clusters underwent metathesis, e.g., *-ml-* > *-lm-*.

egamloβ > egalmoβ (Egalmoth)

§4.220 *y* > [–round]
In Gondor *-y-* was usually pronounced *-i-*.

emyn > *emin
enyd > *enid

SOUND CHANGES IN SINDARIN DIALECTS

Noldorin

Noldorin (S !*Golodhren*) is the name used for a distinct Sindarin dialect, possibly that spoken in Gondolin. Although doubtless perfectly intelligible to other speakers of Sindarin, it had a number of very distinctive features, both phonological and morphological.

§4.221 Initial *m̭* and *ṋ* may have remained in some varieties of Noldorin (cf. §§ 4.66, 4.69, and 4.84).

N hmâl = S mâl
N hniof = S nŷw

§4.222 The change of *iu* and *ju* to *y* (§§ 4.92, 4.93) did not occur in Noldorin, and the resulting *u* was lowered to *o* by following *a* in accordance with § 4.88 or § 4.95.
This *io* could become *eo* in some variants.
S *lŷg* would therefore correspond to N **liog*.

*diuro > *dioro > N dior (S dŷr)
*julma > *jolma > N iolf (S ylf)
*ṋiuma > *ṋioma > ṋiov or niov (N hniof, ṋiof) (S ṋŷw) (N bior, bëor = S bŷr)

§4.223 *d* > [–coronal +dorsal] / ___*l*
The sequence *-dl-* usually became *-gl-* in Noldorin (cf. § 4.148).

galadlōriel (S Galadlóriel) > N galaglōriel (Galaglóriel)
medlin (so in S) > N meglin
edleðron (S edledhron) > N egleðron (egledhron)

§4.224 *ð* > *t* / *l*___#
Final *-lð* became *-lt* in Noldorin (cf. § 4.157)

*dolð > dolt (S doll)
*malð > malt (S mall)

§4.225 ø > *β* / #___C [+sonorant +continuant –voice]
Initial *r̭*, *ḽ* became *βr̭*, *βḽ*.

r̭ibi- > βr̭ibi- (S rhibi-, N thribi-)
ḽiŋg > βḽiŋg > βḽiŋ (S lhing, N thling)

	Exceptions were the words *rhosg* and *rhûn* (and its relatives), which were as in Sindarin; but these may have arisen from related roots beginning with *R-* instead of *S-R-*.	
§4.226	*β* > [+labial] / #___C [+sonorant +continuant –voice] Initial *β̭r̭*, *β̭ḽ* often became *fr̭*, *fḽ*.	β̭r̭oss > fr̭oss (S rhoss) β̭ḽaew > β̭ḽaew > fḽaew (S lhaew)
§4.227	ø > *x* / #___ *ƕ* Initial *ƕ* became *xƕ* (cf. § 4.179).	ƕest (S hwest) > xƕest (N chwest)
§4.228	C [+sonorant +continuant +voice] > [–voice] / #___ Initial *r*, *l* became *β̭*, *ḽ* (transcribed *rh-*, *lh-*).	randir (so in S) > r̭andir (N rhandir) lend (so in S) > ḽend (N lhend)
§4.229	*ǫ* > [+high] / ___i **ǫi* became *ui* rather than *oe* in all instances (cf. § 4.190). This change may have occurred very early, before the change of *w* to *gw* (§ 4.102), since *w* was lost in **wǭia* > **wuia* > **uia* > N *ui* (corresponding to S *goe*); on the other hand, the loss of *w* may have been a change particular to this one word (it is not seen elsewhere), in which case the Sindarin equivalent should perhaps be *oe*.	N bui = S boe N guin = S goen (v. gwaun)
§4.230	*a* > [–low +round] / ___*e* *ae* (< *ai) often became *oe* (cf. § 4.190). This change took place after the change of *az* to *ai* (§ 4.27) and after the loss of medial *h* (§ 4.41) but before the change of *ax* and *aʒ* to *ai* (§ 4.91); in any case, only *ae* is found in Noldorin.	mael (S) > N moel laeb (S) > N lhoeb
§4.231	*öi* did not dissimilate to *ui* (cf. § 4.188), in which case it became *ei* by § 4.189.	röin > N rein föir > N feir
§4.232	*ei* failed to become *ai* in mono- and final syllables (cf. § 4.199).	bein (S bain) remained as N bein
§4.233	*i* > ø / *e*___ *ei* was often shortened to *e*, especially in plural formations.	N edeb = S edaib (v. adab) N oeges = S aegais (v. aegas) N eder = S edair (v. adar) N belen = S belain (v. balan) N feles = S felais (v. falas) N rhovel = S rovail (v. roval) N seleb = S selaib (v. salab) N elf = S eilph (v. alph)

But cf. also _teleif_ (S telaif, v. talaf) and _hebeid_ (S hebaid, v. habad); and beside _eder_ and _belen_ are also _edeir_ and _belein._

§4.234 *_o_ either sometimes failed to raise before _i_ in the next syllable, or it was later lowered (cf. § 4.94), when following an _o_ in the previous syllable; for whatever reason, many plurals (e.g., *goloði, *olohi) show no raising but only fronting of _o_ to _ö_ (§ 4.97), metathesis of final _i_ (§ 4.99), internal _i_-affection (§ 4.104), and, in some words, the late change of _ö_ to _e_ (§ 4.189). Some of these also showed a progress from _ei_ to _e_ identical to that in § 4.233 above.

*goloði > *golöði > *golöið > N gölöið > N geleið
= S gölydh, gelydh (v. golodh)
*orodi > *orödi > *oröid > *öröid > N ereid, ered
= S eryd, ered (v. orod)
*doroni > *doröni > *doröin > *döröin > N derein
= S deryn (v. doron)
*boroni > *boröni > *boröin > *böröin > N berein
= S beryn (v. bôr and cf. § 6.6)
And so also elei (v. ôl), therein (v. thôr), terein (v. tôr); rather exceptionally included is gwedeir pl. of gwador.

§4.235 _y_ > [+back] / ___ _i_
*_o_ not preceded by _o_ in the previous syllable did raise to _u_ (§ 4.94) and probably was fronted (§ 4.97) to _y_, but the combination *_yi_ resulting from metathesis (§ 4.99) normally became _ui_ in Noldorin (cf. the Sindarin development *_yi_ > _y_, § 4.111).

N emuin = S emyn (v. amon)
N egledhruin = S edledhryn (v. edledhron)
N miruin = S miryn (v. mirion)

Noldorin also showed _y_ (as in S) in many instances, however.

yrch (v. orch), yrn (v. orn), thelyn (v. thalion)

§4.236 Noldorin also had a distinct system of consonant mutations. There does not, however, seem to be enough information to reconstruct the entire system of Noldorin mutations.

The soft mutation (see § 5.1) seems to have been on the same general lines as that of Noldorin; however, it was used in genitives, unmutated in Sindarin.

N Ennyn Dhurin = S Ennyn Durin 'doors of Durin'
N Aran Voria = S Aran Moria 'king of Moria'
N Bered Ondrath = S Beraid Gondrath 'towers of (the) causeway'
N Pennas Hilevril = S Pennas Silevril 'account of the Silmarils'
N ínias Veleriand = S ínias Beleriand 'annals of Beleriand'

Noldorin used a different nasal mutation with words beginning in voiceless stops. And also in voiced stops.

N i-ndiw (or i-nniw?) = S i-thiw 'the letters'
N Cerch i-mBelain = S Cerch i-Melain 'sickle of the Valar'
(cf. S Taur i-Melegyrn)

The mutation appears to have been the same as in Sindarin before nasalized stops.

N Mîr in-Geleidh = S Mîr in-Gelydh 'jewel of the Noldor'
N Haudh i-Ndengin = S Haudh i-nDengin 'barrow of the slain'

Dialect of Doriath

The peculiar features of the Sindarin dialect of Doriath can only be hypothesized from a few names associated with the area.

§4.237 *x* > *u* / *u*___*β*
**ux* became **uu* (and so to long *ū*) before β (cf. §§ 4.87, 4.91).

*luxβiene > *luuβiene (DorS Lúthien; cf. S luithien)
*aranruxβ- > *aranruuβ- (DorS Aranrúth)

§4.238 *o* > *u* / ___[+nasal]
o was raised to *u* before a nasal.

*long > *lung (DorS Mablung; cf. S lung)

§4.239 *n* remained before *r* (cf. § 4.128).

*aranrūβ (DorS Aranrúth) remained unchanged rather than becoming Aradhrúth.

North Sindarin

North Sindarin was spoken over a wide area, including Hithlum, Dorthonion, and the lands of the sons of Fëanor. Only a few words of this dialect are known, but they show that it had established a distinctive character very early.

§4.240 ǭ did not change to *au* (cf. § 4.98).

*nǭƀa > NS nǭv = S †naw

§4.241 In some (uncertain) conditions, ǭ became *u*.

*arǭme > NS Arum = S Araw
*-lǭme (from Q lómë) > NS *-lum* in Hithlum

§4.242 *m* did not become *ṽ* or *v* (cf. §§ 4.127, 4.149–50, 4.173, 4.176–77).

NS Arum = S Araw
NS Celegorm = S Celegorf

§4.243 Final *-nw* became *-m* (cf. §§ 4.191, 4.195)

*kurwfinw > NS Curufim, S Curufin

§4.244 *a*-affection (§ 4.95) may not have taken place in some instances.

lǭmina > NS *lǭmin (borrowed as S lómin)

§4.245 nt^h, mp^h, and $ŋk^h$ changed to *nt*, *mp*, *ŋk* and not to *nβ*, *mɸ*, *ŋx*; cf. §§ 4.80, 118.

*pent^hasse > *pentasse > NS !pentas, S pennas

Unknown Dialects

§4.246 In an unspecified "southern Sindarin" dialect, medial *nβ*, *mɸ*, and *ŋx* did not change to *nn*, *mm*, *ŋŋ* but remained unchanged. Cf. § 4.117 and Appendix 6.

*kanβui > Dial. canthui, S !cannui
eŋxui > Dial. enchui, S !engui

§4.247 In the same dialect, *nβ*, *mɸ*, *ŋx*, and *lβ* later changed to long voiceless consonants: *ṋṋ*, *m̭m̭*, *ŋ̭ŋ̭*, and *ḽḽ*.

*rimɸa- > Dial. !rim̭m̭a-, S. rimma-
*tolβa- > Dial. !toḽḽa-, S. toltha-

§4.248 *s* > [–continuant +spread glottis α place] / [–sonorant –continuant α place]
In a Sindarin dialect of unknown affiliation the sequences *ks* and *ps* became *kk^h^* and *pp^h^* respectively and eventually *x*, *f*. Cf. §§ 4.67, 4.81–82, and 4.91. It is possible that this is the normal Sindarin development and that the forms in which *ks* and *ps* changed to **is* > *es* are actually Noldorin.

*karakse > *karakk^h^e > karax (*carach*), S (N?) *caraes*

5

Mutations

CONSONANT MUTATIONS

The initial consonants of most Sindarin words characteristically undergo regular changes under various circumstances, including following a certain word, such as an article or preposition; taking a certain grammatical role, such as direct object; or occupying the second position in a compound.

These changes, or *mutations*, fall into five classes: the soft mutation; the nasal mutation; the stop mutation; the liquid mutation; and the mixed mutation. There is not enough evidence to reconstruct every detail of the mutation system; the attempt has been made, within the scope of what is known about the phonological history of Sindarin, but because the system does not necessarily follow strictly from historical processes of sound change (much may, for instance, have been changed by analogy with other forms), it is possible that much is mistaken. The least well attested of the reconstructions are marked with a preceding *!*.

There is no evidence at all for the mutation of Sindarin *hw*, except that Sindarin is known to have had the sounds of both *hw* and *chw*. In what follows it has been assumed that *hw* has a distribution similar to that of *h*; but that is no more than a guess. For a synopsis of the consonant mutations described below see Table 5.1.

§ 5.1. The soft mutation

The soft mutation is the most common mutation. It occurs after the singular definite article and relative pronoun *i*; after many prepositions ending in a vowel such as *na*, *nu*, *trî*; after the negative prefix *u-* or *ú-*; in nouns that serve as the direct objects of verbs; in some adjectives, and always pronominal adjectives, modifying nouns; in the second element of most compounds; in nouns modified by preceding adjectives; in words immediately following an imperative verb, other than the subjects of those verbs (e.g., *caro* > *garo* in *avo garo* 'don't do', *si* > *hi* in *edro hi* 'open now', *gaer* > *aer* in *no aer* 'be holy').

The soft mutation is as follows:

Voiceless stops	become	voiced stops:
t	becomes	*d*
p	becomes	*b*
c	becomes	*g*
Nonnasal voiced stops and *m*	become	voiced fricatives:
d	becomes	*dh*
b	becomes	*v*
g	becomes	'(zero)
m	becomes	*v*

The change of *g* to zero (formerly the voiced fricative ʒ) can be especially confusing, particularly when it occurs in the combinations *gl*, *gr*, and *gw*:

gl	becomes	*'l*
gr	becomes	*'r*
gw	becomes	*'w*
Original nasal voiced stops	become	nasals:
(n)d	becomes	*n*
(m)b	becomes	*m*
(n)g	becomes	*ng*
Voiceless liquids	become	liquids:
lh	becomes	*l*
rh	becomes	*r*
Other changes:		
s	becomes	*h*
h	becomes	*ch*
hw	becomes	*!chw*

The consonants *f*, *l*, *n*, *r*, and *th* remain unchanged.

The soft mutation results from a series of sound changes that affected consonants following vowels and preceding another vowel, a semivowel, or a liquid. Mutation usually happened because the prefixed element (article or preposition) came to be regarded, effectively, as part of the word. For example, the combination **i taure* 'the forest' became joined as **i-taure* (the dash represents the close connection between the two words); later the normal change of intervocalic *t* to *d* (§ 4.108) occurred, transforming **i-taur* into **i-daur*.

In chronological sequence the sound changes were as follows:

s to *h* between vowels (§ 4.71);
voiced stops to fricatives (§ 4.86). The fricative corresponding to *g* later disappeared (see § 4.171) and was replaced, at least in writing, by a *gasdil*, or stopgap ('), indicating a hiatus between vowels. The gasdil is, however, rarely found in transcribed Sindarin when not initial (it is never transcribed, and perhaps was not written, in compounds), and it was not reflected in the pronunciation of the Third Age;
w to *gw* (§ 4.102);
voiceless stops to voiced stops (§ 4.108);
voiced stops following a nasal (already altered from nasalized stops, § 4.79) became nasals themselves (§ 4.114); (the spelling *i-ngûl* represents *i-ŋūl*).
voiceless *lh* and *rh* to *l* and *r* in medial position (§ 4.120);
m to *v*; in a few texts *v* derived from *m* was written with a modified form of *m*, usually transcribed *mh* (§§ 4.127 and 4.181);
initial *ch* to *h* (§ 4.130);
loss of medial *ŋ* (§ 4.171);
hw to *chw* in medial position (§ 4.179).

§ 5.2. The nasal mutation

The nasal mutation occurred after the plural article *in*; the prepositions *an*, *dan*, and *min*; and after some pronominal forms, such as *în* 'his own'.

Voiceless stops		become	voiceless fricatives:
	t	becomes	*th*
	p	becomes	*ph*
	c	becomes	*ch*
Nonnasal voiced stops		become	nasals:
	d	becomes	*n*
	b	becomes	*m*
	g	becomes	*ng*

When these stops occur before another consonant, however, they often remain stops:

dr	becomes	*n-dr*
gr	becomes	*n-gr*
gl	becomes	*n-gl*
gw	becomes	*n-gw*

but

	br	becomes	*!mr*
	bl	becomes	*!ml*
Nasal voiced stops		become	nasals + stops:
	(n)d	becomes	*nd*
	(m)b	becomes	*mb*
	(n)g	becomes	*ng*
Voiceless liquids		become	liquids:
	lh	becomes	*!l*
	rh	becomes	*!r*
Other changes:			
	h	becomes	*ch*
	hw	becomes	*!chw*

The consonants *f*, *l*, *m*, *n*, *r*, *s*, and *th* remained unchanged; but *n* became *dh* when it preceded *r*.

The nasal mutation resulted from the early contact of a noun with a preceding article or preposition ending in *-n*. For example, **in·tali* 'the feet' became aspirated in Old Sindarin as **in·tʰali* (§ 4.64); then **in·ƀali* (§ 4.80), **iƀ·ƀeil* (§ 4.112), and in Classical Sindarin *i-thail* (§ 4.184).

The relevant changes in chronological order were as follows:

- *n* to *m* before following labial, *ŋ* before following velar consonants (§ 4.63);
- stops become aspirates *pʰ*, *tʰ*, *kʰ* after *n* (§ 4.64);
- aspirates become fricatives *ɸ*, *ƀ*, *x* (§ 4.80);
- assimilation of nasals to following aspirate (§ 4.112);
- loss of nasals before *ɸr*, *ƀr*, *xr* (§ 4.113);
- *nd*, *mb*, *ŋg* to *nn*, *mm*, *ŋŋ* (§ 4.114);
- voiceless *lh* and *rh* to *l* and *r* in medial position (§ 4.120);
- *n* to *dh* before *r* (§ 4.128);
- shortening of long *nn*, *mm*, *ŋŋ* before a consonant (§ 4.129);
- *nr* to *ndr* (§ 4.146);
- *ŋr* to *ŋgr*, *ŋl* to *ŋgl* (§ 4.147);
- **n·w* (with *w* from *gw*) apparently became *ŋgw* by analogy with these (§ 4.102);
- shortening of *ɸɸ*, *ƀƀ*, and *xx* (§ 4.184);
- loss of *n* before a single following consonant (§ 4.187);
- initial *ŋŋ* to *ŋ* (§ 4.200).

ng represents the sound *ŋg*, as distinct from *ŋ*; thus the spelling *an golodh* [a ŋgoloð], beside *i ngolodh* [i ŋoloð]. When Sindarin is written in *tengwar* or cirth, such devices are, of course, unnecessary.

§ 5.3. The stop mutation

The stop mutation occurred after the prepositions o, *ed*, *ned*, and the related prefixes.

Voiceless stops		become	voiceless fricatives:
	t	becomes	*!th*
	p	becomes	*!ph*
	c	becomes	*!ch*
Nasal voiced stops			become nasals + stops:
	(n)d	becomes	*!nd*
	(m)b	becomes	*!mb*
	(n)g	becomes	*!n-g*
Voiceless liquids		become	liquids:
	lh	becomes	*!l*
	rh	becomes	*!r*
Other changes:			
	h	becomes	*!ch*
	hw	becomes	*!chw*

The consonants *b*, *d*, *f*, *g*, *l*, *m*, *n*, *r*, *s*, and *th* remain. The final *d* of *ed* before *s*, *f*, or *th* becomes identical to those consonants.

Although the existence of a separate stop mutation, resulting from the contact of the initial consonant of a word with a previous stop (usually *t* or *d*), cannot be doubted, there is little direct evidence for it except for *ed* before *s*, *f*, and *th*, and o before *m* and *g* (and presumably other voiced stops); in all these cases the initial consonant remains unchanged. The mutations shown here are deduced from the history of similar clusters in Sindarin, especially those including the prefix *ed-*. But since these are sometimes at odds with the known form of the mutation (cf. *es sîr* 'out of a river' with *ethir* 'out-flow', 'river mouth'), the results are dubious. Probably the most reliable are the mutations of the voiceless stops; the mutations of the voiceless liquids and semivowels are very nearly sheer guesses.

The following sound changes are suggested as evidence for or examples of the stop mutation:

assimilation of *t* or *d* to a following stop (§ 4.10);
voicing of *t* before a nasal (§ 4.46);
nasalization of *t* or *d* before a nasal (§ 4.47);
aspiration of stops following a previous stop (§ 4.64);
alteration of *tsr* to $t^{h}r$ (§§ 4.67 and 4.68);
aspirates to fricatives (§ 4.80);
assimilation of a stop to a following fricative (§ 4.81);
shortening of long fricatives (§ 4.185).

§ 5.4. The liquid mutation

The liquid mutation is found only with prepositions and prefixed elements ending in *-l* or *-r*, including *ar-* 'noble', *ar-* 'without', *er-* 'one, alone', *nel-* 'three, tri-', *or* 'above', and sometimes *mor-* 'dark, black'.

Voiceless stops		become	voiced stops:
	t	becomes	*!th*
	p	becomes	*!ph*
	c	becomes	*!ch*
Nonnasal voiced stops		become	voiced fricatives:
	d	becomes	*!dh*
	b	becomes	*!v*
	g	becomes	*!zero*
	gl	becomes	*!l*
	gr	becomes	*!r*
	gw	becomes	*!w*
Nasal *m* becomes fricative			
	m	becomes	*!v*
Nasal voiced stops		become	stops:
	(n)d	becomes	*!d*
	(m)b	becomes	*!b*
	(n)g	becomes	*!g*
Voiceless liquids		become	liquids:
	lh	becomes	*!l*
	rh	becomes	*!r*
Other changes:			
	h	becomes	*!ch*
	hw	becomes	*!chw*

The consonants *f*, *l*, *n*, *r*, *s*, and *th* remain.

The liquid mutation resulted from the early contact of a liquid with another consonant. It is unattested outside of words with prefixes ending in *-r*. Its unique elements occur in the following sound changes:

- aspiration of stops following a previous consonant, e.g., *rt* > *rt*^{h} (§ 4.64);
- the preservation of *s* after *r* (§ 4.71);
- aspirates to fricatives, e.g., *rt*^{h} > *rβ* (§ 4.80);
- voiceless *lh* and *rh* to *l* and *r* in medial position (§ 4.120);
- the retention of *ch* after *r* (§ 4.132);
- elimination of nasals between a liquid and a voiced consonant, changing, e.g., *rnd* > *rd* (§ 4.140).

Other changes resemble those of the soft mutation (see § 5.1).

§ 5.5. The mixed mutation

The mixed mutation is seen in the genitive article *en* and in a number of prepositions combined with the oblique form of the article *in*: *erin*, *ben*, and *min*.

Voiceless stops		become	voiced stops:
	t	becomes	*d*
	p	becomes	*b*
	c	becomes	*g*
Nasal voiced stops		become	nasal + stop:
	nd	becomes	*nd*
	mb	becomes	*mb*
	ng	becomes	*ng*
Voiceless liquids		become	liquids:
	lh	becomes	*l*
	rh	becomes	*r*
Other changes:			
	s	becomes	*h*
	h	becomes	*!ch*
	hw	becomes	*!chw*

The consonants *b*, *d*, *f*, *g*, *l*, *n*, *r*, and *th* remain. The final *n* of the prefix may have become *dh* before *r*.

The mixed mutation is a combination of original soft mutation, followed by operation of the nasal mutation. (In many cases the condition for the nasal mutation is obscured by a later denasalization of the prefix; see § 4.187.) The mixed mutation operated when a prefix, such as **ena*, ending in a vowel (and so inducing soft mutation), lost that vowel at the time other composition vowels were lost (§ 4.115) and so brought a nasal consonant preceding the vowel into immediate contact with the following consonant. Thus **ena·tinw* was lenited to **ena·dinw*; the loss of the medial vowel resulted in **en·dinw*, and eventually *e-dinu*.

The relevant sound changes were, first of all, the changes relating to the soft mutation up to the loss of composition vowels, namely, §§ 4.71, 4.86, and 4.108 (§ 4.102 was obscured by the analogous development of *gw-* after *n*—as in the case of the nasal mutation—and § 4.114 was inoperative for these prefixes). The remainder of the relevant changes were as follows:

voiceless *lh* and *rh* to *l* and *r* in medial position (§ 4.120);
assimilation of *n* before a following stop, fricative, or nasal (these contacts arising from the loss of the composition vowel) (§ 4.121);
n to *dh* before *r* (§ 4.128);
shortening of long *nn*, *mm*, and *ŋŋ* before a consonant (§ 4.129);
voiced fricatives to stops after a preceding nasal (§§ 4.125, 4.138–9);
**n·w* (with *w* from *gw*) to *n-gw* by analogy with the groups *n-gr*, *n-gl*; cf. *erin gwirith edwen* 'on April 2' (§§ 4.102, 4.147);
loss of *n* before a single following consonant (§ 4.187).

§ 5.6. Medial mutations

Medial mutations are those affecting final consonants that preceded suffixes beginning with a vowel; these reflect either changes to consonants that were preserved finally or changes to finals that were preserved internally.

Medial *-nt-*, *-mp-*, and *-nc-* had become *-nn-*, *-mm-*, and *-ng-* (see §§ 4.64, 4.80, 4.118, 4.201); finally, however, they had been restored (§ 4.117). The following examples show the results of their separate development:

pent (OS **pent^{h}a*) 'story'	*pennas* (OS **pent^{h}asse*) 'history'
nimp (OS **nimp^{h}ė*) 'white'	*nimmida-* (OS **nimp^{h}ita-*) 'whiten'
danc (OS **n̄daŋk^{h}e*) 'slew'	*dangen* (OS **n̄daŋk^{h}ena*) 'slain'

Medial *-mb-* and *-nd-* became *-mm-* and *-nn-* (§ 4.114); final *-mb* was usually reduced to *-m* (§ 4.203).

TABLE 5.1.
SYNOPSIS OF INITIAL CONSONANT MUTATIONS

Mutations	Soft	Nasal	Stop	Liquid	Mixed
	i- 'the'	*an* 'for a'	*ed* 'from a'	*or* 'above'	*en* 'of the'
edhel 'elf'	i-edhel	an edhel	ed edhel	or edhel	en-edhel
taur 'forest'	i-daur	a thaur	e thaur	or thaur	e-daur
trann 'shire'	i-drann	a thrann	e thrann	or thrann	en-drann
parth 'field'	i-barth	a pharth	e pharth	or pharth	e-barth
prestad 'disturbance'	i-brestad	a phrestad	e phrestad	or phrestad	e·mrestad
cant 'shape'	i-gant	a chant	e chant	or chant	e-gant
claur 'splendor'	i-glaur	a chlaur	e chlaur	or chlaur	en-glaur
craban 'crow'	i-graban	a chraban	e chraban	or chraban	en-graban
duin 'river'	i-dhuin	a nuin	e duin	or dhuin	e-duin
draug 'wolf'	i-dhraug	an draug	e draug	or dhraug	en-draug
barad 'tower'	i-varad	a marad	e barad	or varad	e-barad
blabed 'flapping'	i-vlabed	a mlabed	e blabed	or vlabed	e·mlabed
brethil 'birch'	i-vrethil	a mrethil	e brethil	or vrethil	e·mrethil
galadh 'tree'	i-'aladh	a ngaladh	e galadh	or 'aladh	e-galadh
glân 'border'	i-'lan	an glan	e glan	or 'lan	en-glan
graug 'demon'	i-'raug	an graug	e graug	or 'raug	en-graug
gwâth 'shadow'	i-'wath	an gwath	e gwath	or 'wath	en-gwath
megil 'sword'	i-vegil	a(m) megil	e megil	or vegil	e-megil
(*n*)*dôr* 'land'	i-nor	a ndor	e ndor	or dor	e-ndor
(*m*)*bâr* 'house'	i-mar	a mbar	e mbar	or bar	e-mbar
(*n*)*gûl* 'magic'	i-ngul	an gul	en gul	or gul	en-gul
lhûg 'dragon'	i-lug	a lug	ed lug	or lug	e-lug
rhavan 'wild man'	i-ravan	adh ravan	ed ravan	or ravan	e-ravan
sereg 'blood'	i-hereg	a sereg (cf. i sedryn)	es sereg	or sereg	e-hereg
hîth 'mist'	i-chith	a chith	e chith	or chith	e-chith
hwest 'breeze'	i-chwest	a chwest	e chwest	or chwest	e-chwest
naug 'Dwarf'	i-naug	a naug	e naug	or naug	en-naug
fang 'beard'	i-fang	a fang	ef fang	or fang	e-fang
thand 'shield'	i-thand	a thand	eth thand	or thand	e-thand
los 'snow'	i-los	a los	e los	or los	e-los
ras 'horn'	i-ras	adh ras	e ras	or ras	edh-ras

lam (OS **lambe*) 'tongue' *lammas* (OS **lambasse*) 'account of tongues'

hand (OS **k^handa*) 'intelligent' *hannas* (OS **k^handasse*) 'understanding'

Medial *-ss-* was reduced to *-s* at the ends of words but remained internally (§ 4.184).

los (OS **losse*) 'snow' *lossen* (OS **lossena*) 'snowy'

VOWEL MUTATIONS

Because of the disturbing influence of certain nearby vowels or semivowels, Sindarin vowels were commonly transformed in quality in a process that can be called *umlaut* or simply vowel mutation (or affection).

There were two primary kinds of affection: the *a*-affection, so called because it was due to the presence of a final *-a*, and the *i*-affection, which was due to the presence of the vowel *i*. A few words show the effects of both kinds of affection interacting (double affection).

§ 5.7. The *a*-affection

The *a*-affection is seen in the change of the vowels *i* and *u* to *e* and *o* when they preceded a final *a* (later lost) in Old Sindarin (see § 4.94).

The *a*-affection of *i* > *e* can be seen in a number of endings, especially those of adjectives, where there is a fairly regular relationship between adjectives (formerly ending in *-a*) containing *e* and nouns, verbs, or even other adjectives containing *i*:

dem 'sad, gloomy' (OS *dimba) — *dim* 'gloom, sadness' (OS *dimbe)
fern 'dead, mortal' (OS *p^{h}irna) — *firith* 'fading, dying' (OS *p^{h}iritt^{h}e)
hethu 'foggy' (OS *k^{h}it^{h}wa) — *hith* 'mist' (OS *k^{h}īt^{h}e)
rem 'numerous' (OS *rimba) — *rim* 'host' (OS *rimbe)

A number of nouns also ended in *-a*:

dess 'young woman' (OS *ñdissa) next to *dîs* 'woman' (OS *ñdisse)
peg 'small spot' (OS *pika) next to *pigen* 'tiny' (OS *pikina)
rest 'cut' (OS *rist^{h}a) next to *ris* 'ravine' (OS *risse)

As did several endings:

-eb, adjective ending (OS *-ipa)
-ed, gerund ending (OS *-ita)
-en, adjective ending (OS *-ina)
-eth, feminine ending (OS *-itt^{h}a)

Some words lost their *a*-affection when suffixes were attached, and the *a* ceased to be final (in Old Sindarin, such intermediate vowels tended to become less clearly pronounced, approaching the sound of *a* in *about*):

silef 'crystal' (OS *silima) vs. *siliv-ren* 'crystalline' (OS *silima-rina)

celebren 'of silver' (OS **keleprina*)	vs.	*celebrin-dal* 'silver-foot' (OS **keleprinatal*)
thent 'short' (OS **st^{h}int^{h}a*)	vs.	*thinnas* 'short mark' (OS **st^{h}int^{h}asse*)

However, in words of later composition and in words composed by simply joining two elements together (without consideration for their history), the *a*-affection might be retained:

thennath 'short sounds'
silevril 'Silmaril' (OS **silimarille*)

§ 5.8. *a*-affection of *u*

The *a*-affection of *u* is somewhat less transparent, since *u* had already generally changed to *o* before *a*-affection; it was retained only when it either preceded a nasal or preceded a *u*, *w*, or final high *o* (derived from *u*) in the next syllable. There are therefore many cases in which *a*-affection appears to be taking place but that really reflect this older change of *u* to *o*.

Authentic examples of *a*-affection of *u* include the following:

coru 'cunning, wily' (OS **kurwa*)	vs.	*curu* 'craft' (OS **kurwe*)
crom 'left' (OS **krumba*)	vs.	*crum* 'left hand' (OS **krumbe*)
tolog 'stalwart' (OS **tuluka*)	vs.	*tulu* 'support' (OS **tulugme*)
tond 'tall' (OS **tunda*)	vs.	*tund* 'hill' (OS **tundo*)
tong 'tight' (OS **tuŋga*)	vs.	*tû* 'strength' (OS **tugȯ*)

§ 5.9. The *i*-affection

There are three types of *i*-affection: primary final affection, primary internal affection, and secondary affection.

PRIMARY FINAL AFFECTION

Primary final *i*-affection occurred in syllables that were penultimate in Old Sindarin and that preceded either the final vowel *-i* (common as a plural suffix) or a suffix beginning with *-i-*; e.g., *-ie* or *-ia*. In both cases the vowel in the syllable immediately preceding the *i* was raised and fronted; following this, the *i* came to be pronounced *before* the originally preceding consonant and joined with the preceding vowel in a diphthong (sometimes simplified) (see §§ 4.94, 4.97, 4.99, 4.111, 4.153, 4.188–89, 4.197–99).

Under primary final *i*-affection the following vowels are altered:

a	>	ai[1]	*ras* 'horn'	*rais* 'horns'
â	>	ai	*tâl* 'foot'	*tail* 'feet'
e	>	i	*certh* 'rune'	*cirth* 'runes'
ê	>	î	*têw* 'letter'	*tîw* 'letters'
o	>	y	*orn* 'tree'	*yrn* 'trees'
ô	>	ŷ	*dôl* 'hill'	*dŷl* 'hills'
u	>	y	*lunt* 'boat'	*lynt* 'boats'
û	>	ui	*dûr* 'dark' (*sg.*)	*duir* 'dark' (*pl.*)
au	>	oe	*naug* 'Dwarf'	*noeg* 'Dwarves'

The vowels *i*, *î*, *y* and the diphthongs *ae*, *ai*, *ui* are not changed by primary final *i*-affection.

Words containing the final sequences *ie* or *io* change them to *i* or *y* respectively (dropping the first *i*), and if the preceding vowel is an *i*, it may become long (*miniel* 'first Elf', *mínil* 'first Elves') or remain short (*mirion* 'great jewel', *miryn* 'great jewels').

Primary *i*-affection is seen in a few other Sindarin plural words and names formerly ending in *-i*:

*gairossi	>	*Gaerys* 'Ossë'
*kheruni	>	*heryn* 'lady'
*oroni-	>	*eryn* 'woods'

And a few words with the suffixes *-ie* and *-ia*:

*mbassanie	>	*bessain* 'loaf-giver, lady'
*kalaria	>	*celair*
*ambarenia	>	*Emerain*
*ulia	>	*uil* (impersonal form of *elia-*)

In words of one syllable that ended in only one consonant in Middle Sindarin, the vowel was lengthened; it also became long in the plural (e.g., *têw* 'letter'; *tîw* 'letters').

Primary internal affection

Primary internal *i*-affection occurred in syllables immediately preceding a vowel *i* anywhere in a word, except as final vowel. This was even true of *i*

1. In words ending in two consonants, of which the first was *l*, *ei* remained unchanged (e.g., *alph* 'swan', *eilph* 'swans'); and in words ending in *ng* or in two consonants of which the first was *r*, it became *e* (e.g., *narn* 'tale', *nern* 'tales', *úgarth* 'misdeed', *úgerth* 'misdeeds', *fang* 'beard', *feng* 'beards'.

in the final syllable of a word, when followed by a consonant (see §§ 4.104–5, 4.189).

The following changes result from primary internal affection:

_a_	becomes	_e_
_o_	becomes	_e_ (archaic ö, spelled oe)

Reliable examples of _u_ are not found.

The vowels _i_ and _e_ remain unchanged, as do diphthongs, long vowels, and any _o_ resulting from the shortening of _au_.

Primary internal _i_-affection occurred in the following circumstances:

1. Before the suffix _-iie_, as in the river name _*Sarniie_ (pebbly) > Serni. This suffix was most commonly found as an infinitive ending for _i_-stem verbs; internal affection also occurred in a number of forms of these verbs containing _-i-_:

cebi (OS _*kapiie_) 'to leap'	_cabed_ (OS _*kapita_) 'a leap'
hedi (OS _*k^{h}atiie_) 'to hurl'	_hador_ (OS _*k^{h}atro_) 'warrior'
degi (OS _*ñdakiie_) 'to slay'	_dangen_ (OS _*ñdank^{h}ena_) 'slain'
tegin (OS _*tukiie_) 'I lead'	_tôg_ (OS _*tukė_)[2] 'leads'

2. Before the suffix _-ia-_ (infinitive _-io_), common to a large group of verbs and their derivatives:

renio (OS _*raniǭbe_) 'to wander'	_randir_ (OS _*randīr[o]_) 'wanderer'
pelio (OS _*paliǭbe_) 'to spread'	_palath_ (OS _*palatt^{h}e_) 'surface'
erio (OS _*oriǭbe_) 'to rise'	_ortho_ (OS _*ort^{h}ǭbe_) 'to raise'
eglerio (OS _*aklariǭbe_) 'to glorify'	_aglar_ (OS _*aklare_) 'glory'
genediad (OS _*wonotiata_) 'reckoning'	_gonoded_ (OS _*wonotita_) 'count, number'

3. Before the suffix _-il-_ (usually feminine):

brennil (OS _*brandille_) 'lady'	_brannon_ (OS _*brandondo_) 'lord'
gwethil (OS _*gwat^{h}ille_) 'shadow-woman'	_gwath_ (OS _*gwat^{h}a_) 'shadow'
ernil (OS _*arnilo_) 'prince'	_arn_ (OS _*arna_) 'royal'

The short version of the suffix was lost in Sindarin (_bereth_ [OS _*barat^{h}il_] 'spouse, queen').

2. OS _u_ had become _o_ in most cases (see § 4.88).

4. Before a number of other suffixes containing _-i-_:

> _-ig_: _lhewig_ 'ear'; cf. _lhaw_ 'ears'
> _-id_, _-in_: _thenid_, _thenin_ 'firm, true, abiding' (OS _*st^{h}anite_, _*st^{h}anine_)
> _-ien_: _telien_ (or _teilien_) (OS _*taliene_) 'play' (But note: _Anórien_ [archaic _*Anauriend_] not _!Anerien_, since the _o_ is long and arises from a diphthong.)
> _-iand_: _Beleriand_; cf. _Balar_
> _-in_ (articular ending): _erin_ 'on'; cf. _or_ 'above'
> _-ndir_: _ceredir_ (OS _*karita-ndīro_) 'maker'; cf. _feredir_ (OS _*sp^{h}arata-ndīro_) 'hunter' (Most compound words ending in _-ndir_ do not show internal _i_-affection [e.g., _randir_ 'wanderer', _dagnir_ 'slayer'].)

5. In a few compound words and names, where the second element contains _i_, especially where the independent meaning of at least one part of the compound was not known or remembered:

> _heledirn_ (OS _*sk^{h}alatirno_) 'kingfisher'
> _emlinn_ (OS _*am̭m̭alinde_) 'yellowhammer'
> _medli_ (OS _*mada-glihe_) 'honey-eater, bear' (cf. _mad-_ 'eat')
> _edegil_ 'seven stars, the Big Dipper' (cf. _odog_ 'seven')
> _Glewellin_ 'song of gold' (cf. _glawar_ 'golden light')
> _Elphir_ 'swan-lord' (cf. _alph_ 'swan')
> _Belthil_ 'divine radiance' (cf. _Balan_ 'Vala')
> _Ethring_ (probably) 'cold crossing' (cf. _athrad_ 'ford')

And the following words containing _în_ 'year':

> _edinor_ 'anniversary day' (cf. _ad_ 'again')
> _penninor_ 'last day of the year' (cf. _pant_ 'full, complete')
> _ennin_ 'long year, year of the Valar' (cf. _and_ 'long')

In most compound words, however, the first element remains unaffected.

6. Sometimes when an adjective ending in _-en_ takes its stem form (ending with _-in-_; see section on _a_-affection above) in composition:

> _Melthinorn_ 'golden tree' (cf. _malthen_ 'golden')
> _Celebrindal_ 'silver foot' (cf. _celebren_ 'silver')

7. In many borrowings of words and names from Quenya, the names were hyper-Sindarized, with affection introduced before any _i_ in the word:

Q _*Ancalimírë_ 'brilliant jewel'	>	S _Angelimir_
Q _Atandil_ 'friend of the Edain'	>	S _Edennil_

Q *Anardil* 'friend of the Sun'	>	S *Enerdhil*
Q *Arien* 'Sun-maiden'	>	S *Eirien*
Q *macil* 'sword'	>	S *megil*

In a few cases, when the vowel *a* precedes an *i* that itself precedes another vowel (which is still syllabic in Sindarin), especially before *l*, *r*, *n*, the change is to *ei*:

teilia- (< *telia-* < OS **talia-*) 'play'
einior (< **eniaur* < OS **aniǭra*) 'elder'
Ereinion (< **Erenion* < OS **Araniono*) 'son of kings'
Feiniel (< **Feniel* < OS **Spʰanielle*) 'white lady'
Eirien (< **Erien* < Q *Arien*) 'Sun-maiden'

This change is by no means universal: e.g., *Beleriand* (not *!Beleiriand*), *eglerio* (not *!egleirio*).

Secondary affection

Secondary affection occurred as a result of the presence in a word of a vowel that had been altered from primary *i*-affection (whether final or internal): affecting vowels thus include *i*, *y*, *ei* (which became *ai* in later Sindarin), and *e*. Secondary affection can affect not just a single vowel but a whole series of vowels through a word (see § 4.104).

The following changes result from secondary affection:

a	becomes	*e*
o	becomes	*e* (archaic ö, transcribed *oe*)
u	becomes	*y*

The vowels *i* and *e* remain unchanged, as do diphthongs, long vowels, and any *o* resulting from the shortening of *au*.

Secondary affection is most commonly found in plurals:

Before *ai*:

aran 'king'	*erain* 'kings'
calardan 'lampwright'	*celerdain* 'lampwrights'
adanadar 'father of the Edain'	*edenedair* 'fathers of the Edain'

Before *i*:

angren 'of iron' (*sg.*)	*engrin* 'of iron' (*pl.*)
morben 'dark Elf'	*merbin* 'dark Elves'
abonnen 'one after-born'	*ebennin* 'those after-born'

But cf. *gódhel* 'Noldo' > *gódhil* 'Noldor'.

Before y:

amon 'hill'	*emyn* 'hills'
golodh 'Noldo'	*gelydh* 'Noldor'
aphadon 'follower'	*ephedyn* 'followers'
tulus 'poplar'	*tylys* 'poplars'

In compound words the first element can be found unaffected, but plurals usually show affection throughout (e.g., *morchant* 'shadow' > *morchaint* 'shadows').

Secondary affection is also found in words with *-i-* suffixes (e.g., *-ia*, *-ie*) in Old Sindarin:

bessain 'bread-giver' (OS **m̃bassanie*)
celair 'brilliant' (OS **kalaria*)

Secondary affection is also sometimes found in prefixes to affected forms of verbs:

esgeri 'to cut around'	and	*osgar* 'cuts around'
genedio 'count'	and	*gonod-* 'count up'

But not in other cases, such as *ortheri* 'to conquer'.

And in most words in which internal *i*-affection has already taken place, e.g.: *Ereinion*, *Beleriand*, *ceredir*, *feredir*, *bereth*, *edegil*, *heledirn*, *Glewellin*, *Edennil*, *Enerdhil*.

Sometimes a prefix remained unaffected:

Angelimir (*an* + *celimir*)
Arnediad (*ar* + *nediad*)

The common form *ered* for mountains, instead of the expected *eryd*, may be attributable to its usual position as a prefix to a longer word, thus undergoing secondary instead of primary affection (e.g., *Ered Wethrin* for *Eredwethrin*); it may also, however, be due to the influence of Noldorin or similar Sindarin dialects on Classical Sindarin (see § 4.234).

Secondary *i*-affection can be classed as a form of vowel harmony in which certain sequences of vowels must have common characteristics (e.g., front pronunciation); here, every short *a*, *o*, or *u* preceding a front vowel (*ei*, *y*, *i*, *e*) was fronted to *e*, *ö*, *y*.

In some words *i*-affection was not found where it might be expected:
1. It does not occur in most compounds where the independent meaning of each part of the compound was retained or remembered:

ostirion (*ost-tirion*) 'fortress, watchtower', not *!estirion*
alfirin (*al-firin*) 'immortal', not *!elfirin*
amdir (*am-tir*) 'hope', not *!emdir*
galadhrim (*galadh-rim*) 'tree people', not *!geledhrim*

This includes most proper names:

Galion, not *!Gelion*
Doriath, not *!Deriath*

2. Where the *i* did not appear until after the historical stage of affection:

tarias (OS **targasse*) 'stiffness', not *!terias*
thalion (OS **stʰalgǭna*) 'steadfast', not *!thelion*

3. Possibly by analogy with other related words:

odhril 'mother' by analogy with *odhron* 'parent, father', not *!edhril*

4. Inexplicably, in some cases:

erchamion 'one-handed', not *!erchemion*
thonion 'having pines', not *!thenion*

§ 5.10. Double affection

When a word ended with the sequence *-ia*, both *i*-affection and *a*-affection occurred. Although the historical interaction of these affections is complex (see §§ 4.94–95, 4.97, 4.99, 4.166, 4.188, 4.199), the results are simple:
The vowels *a*, *e*, and *i* before *-ia* became first *ei*, then *ai*; *o* and *u* before *-ia* became first *öi*, then *ui*; and *ū* before *-ia* became *ui* directly:

fain 'white' (OS **spʰania*); cf. *fân* 'cloud' (OS **spʰana*)
cai 'fence' (MS **keiʒ*, OS **kegia*)
paich 'syrup' (OS **pihia*), cf. *pihen* 'juice' (OS **pihina*)
cair 'ship' (OS **kiria*); cf. *cîr* 'ships' (OS **kirii*)
fuir 'right hand' (OS **pʰoria*); cf. *forn* 'northern'
ruin 'track' (OS **runia*)
ruin 'fiery red' (OS **rūnia*)

§ 5.11. Ablaut

Ablaut refers to a regular alteration between different grades of vowels. This alteration goes back to the common Eldarin tongue and may originally reflect different degrees of stress on the root vowel. Three grades can be distinguished: normal, long, and strong.

The normal grade originally consisted of the short vowels. The long grade consisted of the same vowels, lengthened. In the strong grade they became diphthongs. Ablaut only occurred in vowels in open syllables (that is, vowels followed by no more than one consonant).

Common Eldarin Ablaut (Reconstructed)

Normal	Long	Strong
a	ā	ā
e	ē	*ae
i	ī	ai
o	ō	*ao
u	ū	au

The diphthongs **ae* and **ao* are uncertain; they may have been realized at some point as the monophthongs ǣ and ǭ. The strong and middle grades of *a*, both being ā, cannot be distinguished.

In Old Sindarin the long vowels and diphthongs underwent some changes:

Old Sindarin Ablaut

Normal	Long	Strong
a	ǭ	ǭ
e	ī	ai
i	ī	ai
o	ū	au
u	ū	au

Further changes occurred in Classical Sindarin:

Classical Sindarin Ablaut

Normal	Long	Strong
a	au/o	au/o
e	i	ae
i	i	ae

o	u	au/o
o, u	u	au/o

Some examples of long ablaut follow:

a:
√BAD *baudh* 'judgment' cf. *badhron* 'judge'
√DAR *daur* 'pause, league' cf. *daro* 'stop'

e:
√KHER *hîr* 'master, lord' cf. *herdir* 'master'
√MEL *mîl* 'love, affection' cf. *mellon* 'friend'

i:
√MIR *mîr* 'jewel'

o:
√ÑGOT *gûd* 'enemy' cf. *goth* 'enemy'
√KHOTH *hûd* 'assembly' cf. *hoth* 'horde'
√BORON *brûn* 'long endured' cf. *boron* 'steadfast'

u:
√TUG *tû* 'muscle, sinew' cf. *tong* 'taut'

Some examples of strong ablaut follow here:

e:
√WED *gwaedh* 'bond, troth' cf. *gwedhi* 'to bind'
√NDER *daer* 'bridegroom' cf. *dîr* (long ablaut) 'man'

i:
√G-LIR *glaer* 'lay' cf. *gliri* 'to sing'
√KHIM *haew* 'custom' cf. *hîw* 'sticky'
√ŋGIL *gael* 'pale, glimmering' cf. *gîl* 'star'
√SLIW *lhaew* 'sickly, sick' cf. *lhîw* 'sickness'
√MIW *maew* 'gull'
√LIB *glaew* 'salve'
√MIL *mael* 'lust'
√MIK *maeg* 'sharp'

o:
√MOR *maur* 'gloom' cf. *morn* 'black'
√ROD *raudh* 'cavernous' cf. *rosta-* 'excavate'

u:
√UR *aur* 'day' cf. *ûr* (long ablaut) 'fire, heat'
√RUK *graug*, *raug* 'demon' cf. *gruitha-* 'to terrify'

√NUK *naug* 'Dwarf, stunted' cf. *nuitha-* 'to cut short, stunt'
√TUR *taur* 'vast, mighty' cf. *tûr* (long ablaut) 'mastery'
√THU *thaw* 'rotten' cf. *thû* (long ablaut) 'stench'
√NUT *naud* 'bound'

Ablaut variation occurs in a number of words used as prefixes, e.g., *hîr*, *iaur*, *taur*[1], *naur*; these are often found as *her-*, *iar-*, *tar-*, *nar-* (beside expected *hir-*, *ior-*, *tor-*, *nor-*). This development probably originates from an ancient pattern in which the root occurred in a closed syllable (in which long vowels were always shortened; see § 4.6), as in *Narwain* < **narwinya* 'new sun', later generalized to other instances. Thus we have *Nardhol* 'hill of fire', *Targon* 'high commander', *Iarwain* 'eldest', and *hervenn* 'husband' next to *Torhir* 'high lord', *Iorhael* 'old and wise', and *Hirgon* 'lord commander'.

6

Nouns

Sindarin nouns are not marked for case by any overt morpheme. The case of a Sindarin noun in a sentence can be determined from its position, its lenition, and any preceding prepositions. When a Sindarin noun is accompanied by the definite article, the form of the article also can indicate the case of the noun (see chapter 12).

§ 6.1. The genitive

Sindarin nouns indicating possession, material, or salient characteristic exemplify the genitive case. When a noun without the definite article is in the genitive, it appears as an unlenited noun placed immediately after what it modifies (e.g., *ennyn Durin* 'gates of Durin'). When the noun does have the definite article, it takes the appropriate lenition (see §§ 12.4, 12.6), but the phrase with article and noun is still in the position immediately after the modified noun (e.g., *Ernil i-Pheriannath* 'Prince of the Halflings'). In some instances the genitive is expressed with the preposition *na* (see *na*, chapter 10): *mîr n(a) Ardhon* 'jewel of the world'. Very rarely the genitive noun appears lenited: *Nan Laur* 'valley of golden light'.

Monosyllables used in genitive phrases are usually shortened when the vowel is *â*, *ê*, or *ô* (cf. § 15.31):

bâr + erib	>	*Bar Erib* 'Dwelling of the Lonely Ones'
nên + echui	>	*Nen Echui* 'Water of Awakening'
dôl + Amroth	>	*Dol Amroth* 'Hill of Amroth'

But the vowel *î* remains long:

sîr + ninglor	>	*Sîr Ninglor* 'river of (the) gladden-flower'
mîr + in-gelydh	>	*Mîr in-Gelydh* 'Jewel of the Noldor'

In genitive phrases monosyllables ending in consonant clusters also tend to simplify those clusters (cf. § 15.32):

amon + hend	>	*Amon Hen* 'hill of (the) eye'
nand + curunír	>	*Nan Curunír* 'wizard's Vale'
rast + maewrim	>	*Ras Maewrim* 'cape of gulls'
toll + Morwen	>	*Tol Morwen* 'island of Morwen'

There are a very few instances in which there appears to be a suffix *-a* indicating the genitive:

Dagnir Glaurunga (instead of *!Dagnir Glaurung*) 'Slayer of Glaurung'
Bar Bëora 'House of Bëor'
Nothlir Haletha 'Familiy Line of Haleth'
Nothlir Maracha 'Family Line of Marach'

However, all three of these occur with names, at least two of which were intended to be non-Sindarin. It is possible that the ending is not Sindarin either; a similar ending occurred in the language of the Haladin. It is certain that it is not connected with the Quenya genitive affix *-o*, since all final vowels disappeared in Sindarin. Possibly *-a* is an originally independent postposition that was later attached to the noun.

Since Quenya genitive plurals often end in *-ion*, it might be supposed that the endings *-on* and *-ion* seen in some Sindarin noun phrases or compounds, such as *Caras Galadhon* or *Dorthonion*, might be a genitive plural case ending. However, the Old Sindarin cognate ending **-io* would only appear in Sindarin as a vowel mutation indistinguishable from the plural: *Ered Nimrais* = OS **oroti nimp*^{h}*irassio* 'Mountains of White Peaks'. It is more likely that the *-on* and *-ion* endings are forms of the adjectival endings seen in such words as *brithon* 'pebbly, of pebbles'; *erchamion* 'having one hand' (see § 14.16).

PLURALS (§§ 6.2–10)

§ 6.2. Vowel mutation plurals

The most common plural of Sindarin nouns and adjectives is the vowel mutation plural. Several different plurals in Common Eldarin (*-āi*, *-ēi*, *-ī*, *-ōi*) had merged in an Old Sindarin plural ending in *-i* (see §§ 4.33, 4.37), which was later lost after changing the previous vowel. There was also an Old Sindarin plural in *-ui*, which had developed in a slightly different way, although in Classical Sindarin the *-ui* plurals tended to be reformed to resemble the other plurals.

The Old Sindarin *-i* plural gave rise to primary final *i*-affection (see § 5.9) of the vowel in the last syllable of the word (or of the vowel of the only syllable, if there is but one). Any syllables preceding the last show

TABLE 6.1
SINDARIN *i*-AFFECTION PLURALS

Original Vowel	Becomes in Nonfinal Syllables	Becomes in Final Syllables	Singular	Plural
a, â	e	ai	las	lais
			tâl	tail
			adan	edain
e, ê	e	i, î	sen	sin
			têw	tîw
			edhel	edhil
i, î	i	i, î	gîl	gîl
			gilith	gilith
o, ô	e (< *ö)	y, ŷ	pôd	pŷd
			onod	enyd
u	y	y	tulus	tylys
û	ú, u	ui	dûr	duir
ŷ		ŷ	mŷl	mŷl
ai		ai	taith	taith
ae	ae	ae	gwael	gwael
			aegas	aegais
au	au, ó	oe	naug	noeg
			roval	rovail
			ódhel	ódhil
ie		i	miniel	mínil
io		y	mirion	miryn
ui	ui	ui	luin	luin
			annui	annui

secondary *i*-affection (§ 5.9). Pluralization by *i*-affection is the normal type of plural in Classical Sindarin.

Table 6.1 shows the developmental scheme of general Sindarin plurals. Single vowels in monosyllables that had originally been open syllables became overlong in both singulars and plurals: thus the plural of *têw* is *tîw*.

Before syllables containing *ui* (and probably also *oe* and *ae*, although examples do not occur) vowels did not undergo *i*-affection: the plural of *annui* 'western' is *annui*, not *!ennui*.

Unusual *i*-final plurals (§§ 6.3–6.6)

§ 6.3. -*h* plurals

In Old Sindarin, Common Eldarin *h* was lost in all positions. Thus a word that ended primitively in -*h* lost that *h*, and the preceding vowel became long. The final *i* of the plural, following the *h*, became part of a diphthong. Thus CE **mah* 'hand' became **mā*; CE **mahi* 'hands' became **mai*. These became OS **mǭ*, **mai*, and Sindarin *maw*, pl. *mae* (which were archaic by the Classical period). Other *-h* plurals would be

**-eh*, **-ih* > *-î*; **-ehi*, **-ihi* > *-î* (cf. **tehi* > **tei* > *tî* 'lines', plural of *tê* 'line')
**-oh*, *-uh* > *-û*; **-ohi*, **-uhi* > *-ui* (e.g. *cû* 'bow', **cui* 'bows').

§ 6.4. *-u* plurals

Original final *-ui* became *y*, through *i*-affection of the *u*, producing a plural with final *-y* and internal affection (cf. §§ 4.104, 4.111):

ranc 'arm' [OS **raŋk*^{h}*ȯ*], *rengy* 'arms' [OS **raŋk*^{h}*ui*]
mâl 'pollen' [OS **malȯ*], *mely* 'pollens' [OS **malui*]

But these also have the "regular" plurals *rainc* and *mail*, formed by analogy with the normal *i*-final plurals.

§ 6.5. Double-affection plurals

Words containing *-ai-* arising from double affection (see § 5.10) show the following types of plurals:

Words containing *-ai-* arising from *-a-* would also have plurals containing *-ai-*:

fain 'white' (*sg.*) [OS **sp*^{h}*ania*] *fain* 'white' (*pl.*) [OS **sp*^{h}*anii*]

Words containing *-ai-* arising from *e* and *i* have plurals containing *-i-*:

cair 'ship' [OS **kiria*] *cîr* 'ships' [OS **kirii*]
cai 'fence' [OS **kegia*] *cî* 'fences' [OS **kegii*]

Words containing *-ui-* arising from *o* or *u* have plurals containing *-y-*:

fuir 'right hand' [OS **p*^{h}*oria*] *fŷr* 'right hands' [OS **p*^{h}*orii*]
ruin 'track' [OS **runia*] *rŷn* 'tracks' [OS **runii*]

That is, the plural is the final *i*-affection of the original vowel in Old Sindarin.

§ 6.6. Defective singulars

In a number of words the singular form of a noun lacks an original final syllable, part of the stem, that appears in the plural or in the first element of some compounds. Such words give the appearance of having had irregular plural suffixes added to them:

singular	stem	plural
ael 'pool'	_aelin-_	_aelin_
_êl_ 'star'	_elen-_	_elin_
fêr 'beech'	_feren-_	_ferin_
thôr 'eagle'	_thoron-_	_theryn_
bôr 'faithful man'	_boron-_	_beryn_
_ôr_ 'mountain'	_orod-_	_eryd_
nêl 'tooth'	_neleg-_	_nelig_
_ôl_ 'dream'	_olo-_	_ely_
pêl 'fenced field'	_pele-_	_peli_
thêl 'sister'	_thele-_	_theli_

These plurals were formed on a word ending in a consonant in Common Eldarin, which had plurals with one more syllable than the singular: OS _*ailin_ 'pool' pl. _*ailini_ 'pools'. These lost their final syllables (beginning with the final vowel), becoming _*ail_ and _*ailin_, which normally altered to _ael_ and _aelin_ in Sindarin.

The plurals are subject to the same _i_-affections as normal _i_-plurals:

*oro, pl. _*oroti_	>	_ôr_, _eryd_ 'mountains'
*nele, pl. _*neleki_	>	_nêl_, _nelig_ 'teeth'
*elen, pl. _*eleni_	>	_êl_, _elin_ 'stars'
*aran, pl. _*arani_	>	_âr_, _erain_ 'kings'
*feren, pl. _*fereni_	>	_fêr_, _ferin_ 'beeches'
*boron, pl. _*boroni_	>	_bôr_, _beryn_ 'faithful vassals'
*thoron, pl. _*thoroni_	>	_thôr_, _theryn_ 'eagles'

Other differences result from a loss of final _s_ (which had become _h_ medially but been lost finally in Old Sindarin):

*olo, pl. _*olohi_	>	_ôl_, _ely_ 'dreams'
*pele, pl. _*pelehi_	>	_pêl_, _peli_ 'fenced fields'
*thele, pl. _*thelehi_	>	_thêl_, _theli_ 'sisters'

When final vowels were lost, leaving a final _ʒ_ after _l_ or _r_, the _ʒ_ became vocalized to _a_ if unpalatalized, _i_ if palatalized, and the main vowel was affected as if it were a monosyllable:

OS _*_p^{h}_elga_, pl. _*_p^{h}_elgi_ > MS _*ϕelʒ_, pl. _*ϕilʒ_ > CS _fela_, pl. _fili_ 'caves'

OS *st^helga, pl. *st^helgi > MS *flelȝ, pl. *flilȝ > CS *thela*, pl. *thili* 'spear points'
OS *st^halga, pl. *st^halgi > MS *flalȝ, pl. *fleilȝ > CS *thala*, pl. *theili* 'stalwart'
OS **targa*, pl. **targi* > MS **tarȝ*, pl. **teirȝ* > CS *tara*, pl. *teiri* 'tough'

One common irregular plural is *ered*, plural of *orod* (next to the also attested *eryd*). This might be a result of assimilation of the second vowel to the first, but that would not explain why other comparable words (e.g., *onod* 'ent', pl. *enyd*) do not show this change. The form is perhaps to be explained by the element usually appearing in quasi-compounds with a plural modifier and so only receiving a secondary affection (e.g., *Ered-wethrin*, *Ered-luin*).

§ 6.7. Suffix plurals

In a number of words the basic form is the plural, and singulars are formed by suffixes attached to the plural, such as *-od*, *-og*, *-ig*:

filig 'small birds' — *filigod* 'small bird'
glam 'orcs' — *glamog* 'orc'
gwanûn 'pair of twins' — *gwanunig* 'twin'
lhaw 'pair of ears' — *lhewig* 'ear'

and perhaps

lind 'song' — *linnod* 'verse'

§ 6.8. *-in* plurals

A few words (all monosyllables) show a plural (of unknown origin) ending in *-in*:

caun 'prince' (< Q *cáno*), pl. *conin* 'princes'
drû 'wild man' (< Druic **druȝu*), pl. *drúin* 'wild men'

It is possible that this plural is used, like the genitive ending *-a*, primarily with words of non-Sindarin origin.

§ 6.9. *-ath* plurals

All words can take a plural ending *-ath* (see § 14.9); this differs from the normal plurals, as it indicates not merely multiplicity of number but that the plural is considered as a single group. It is therefore called a *collective plural*. Thus the normal plural of *êl* 'star', *elin*, means 'a number of stars, some stars, so-and-so many stars', whereas the collective plural *elenath* means 'the stars as a group, all the stars of heaven'.

Monosyllabic words whose stems contain the vowel *i* and end in the dental resonants *r*, *l*, or *n* have the plural suffix in the form *-iath*:

lîn 'pool'	*liniath* 'pools'
sîr 'river'	*siriath* 'rivers'
gîl 'star'	*giliath* 'stars'
fair 'mortal'	*firiath* 'mortals'
sain 'new'	*siniath* 'news' (derived from the adjective)

If a word had ended in a consonant cluster in Middle Sindarin, which had been simplified in Classical Sindarin, the cluster reappears before the *-ath* plural:

las 'leaf'	*lassath* 'leaves'
lam 'tongue'	*lammath* 'tongues'
perian 'halfling' [MS **periand*]	*periannath* 'halflings'

Internal *mm* may also be written *m* in some cases, however, resulting in spellings like *lamath*.

Clusters that were retained may be subject to medial consonant mutations (§ 5.6):

tump 'hump'	*tummath* 'humps'
tinc 'metal'	*tingath* 'metals'
cant 'shape'	*cannath* 'shapes'

Words ending in *-or* deriving from original postconsonantal *-r* take plurals in *-orath*: *dagor*, pl. *dagorath* 'battles'. But words ending in *-ol* from postconsonantal *-l* have their plurals in *-lath*: *nagol*, pl. *naglath* 'teeth'. There is insufficient evidence to show whether this is a general rule or simply represents an irregular development in the case of *dagor*, whereby the plural was reformed on the analogy of the single.

§ 6.10. *-rim*, *-hoth*, and *-waith*

The suffix *-rim* (originating from a noun meaning 'multitude'; see § 14.9) is used to mark plurals, especially of peoples but also of things: *onodrim* 'ents', *orodrim* 'mountains'. It may appear as *-lim* after nouns ending in *-l*: *edhellim* 'Elves'.

Other endings with similar significance are *-hoth* 'horde' and *-waith* 'people', but these are usually given to peoples (occasionally animals);

-hoth particularly refers to less friendly peoples, and *-waith* is limited to peoples of human or Elvish shape. Words containing these elements may also be considered compounds.

orchoth 'Orcs'	*forodwaith* 'north-folk'
dornhoth 'Dwarves'	*Eluwaith* 'people of Elu'
lossoth 'snow-people'	*tawarwaith* 'silvan folk'
gaurhoth 'werewolves'	*gaurwaith* 'wolvish folk'

§ 6.11. The dative

Words functioning as datives (expressing recipients and beneficiaries) are usually preceded by the preposition *an* (functioning like *to* in English) (see chapter 10), but this role can also be indicated by word position, following a direct object, which comes after the verb: *Onen i-Estel Edain* 'I gave hope to the Edain'.

§ 6.12. The accusative

Nouns functioning as accusatives, that is, direct objects of verbs (including commands), are usually given the soft mutation (§ 5.1), if not preceded by an article. The lenited object usually follows the verb but does not need to come immediately after the verb:

e aníra suilad mhellyn în 'he wants to meet his friends'
eglerio Daur a Berhael! 'praise Frodo and Samwise!'
lasto beth! 'listen to (the) word!'

There is no mutation when the noun is the subject of the command: *lacho calad!* 'flame light!' (i.e., the light is commanded to "flame").

The gerund, when used as the complement of a verb (see § 9.7), is not lenited: *e aníra tírad* 'he wants to see'.

Nouns in apposition to an accusative, but not immediately following the verb, are not lenited: *tírad i Cherdir Perhael Condir* 'to see the Master Samwise, Mayor' (not **i Cherdir Berhael, Gondir . . .*).

§ 6.13. The vocative

Words and names used in direct address are never mutated:

A Elbereth Gilthoniel!
A Hîr Annûn!

Other case relations are indicated by prepositions (see chapter 10).

7

Adjectives

The Sindarin adjective almost always follows the noun it modifies; exceptions are typically poetic. The adjective normally agrees with the noun it modifies in number. Some nouns, such as *eryn* 'woods', which may have been plural in origin (OS ? **oroni*), were always construed as singular, e.g., *eryn galen* 'green woods'.

§ 7.1. Mutation of postpositioned adjectives

When an adjective beginning with a consonant susceptible to mutation follows the noun that it modifies, it may undergo soft mutation (see § 5.1):

calen 'green'	*parth galen* 'green lawn'
dínen 'silent'	*dor dhínen* 'silent land'
daer 'great'	*athrad dhaer* 'great ford'
gwathren 'shadowy'	*ered wethrin* 'shadowy mountains'
morn 'black'	*eryn vorn* 'black wood'
tirnen 'watched, guarded'	*talath dirnen* 'guarded plain'

This mutation can even occur when the adjective follows the noun at some distance:

tiriel 'gazing'	*ithil síla diriel* 'a gazing moon shines'.

§ 7.2. Mutation and prepositioned adjectives

In the rare instances where the adjective precedes the vowel, it remains without mutation:

silivren 'crystalline'	*silivren míriel aglar* 'crystalline jeweled glory'
galadhremmen 'tree-woven'	*galadhremmin ennorath* 'tree-woven lands of middle-earth'
sarn 'stony'	*sarn athrad* 'stony ford'

However, the noun *following* the adjective may be mutated:

caber 'spike' (pl. *cebir*)	*sarn gebir* 'stone spikes'
tûm 'valley'	*carn dûm* 'red valley'

§ 7.3. Lenition

Adjectives or descriptive phrases after proper names are regularly lenited:

glân 'white'	*Curunír Lân* 'Saruman the White'
glos 'snow-white'	*Rodwen Los* 'Rodwen the White'
glórindol 'golden-headed'	*Hador Lórindol* (Glórindol) 'Hador the Goldenheaded'
pen-adar 'fatherless'	*Iarwain Ben-adar* (Pen-adar) 'Iarwain the Fatherless'

But nouns in apposition to names are unlenited, e.g., Elbereth Gilthoniel.

In many adjective phrases the adjective fails to lenite. In some cases this may be due to the adjective's being in quasi composition with the noun: *Barad-dûr* 'Dark Tower' (not *barad dhûr*). But in most cases the adjective simply remains unlenited where it might be expected to lenite. There is no obvious pattern:

beleg 'great'	*cû beleg* 'great bow'
baran 'brown'	*dol baran* 'brown hill'
dûr 'dark'	*emyn duir* 'dark mountains'
daer 'great'	*lond daer* 'great haven'
dínen 'silent'	*rath dínen* 'silent street'
galadhon 'of trees'	*caras galadhon* 'city of trees'
gwaeren 'windy'	*côf gwaeren* 'windy bay'
haeron 'distant'	*dor haeron* 'distant land'
hithoel 'cool with mist'	*nen hithoel* 'water cool with mist'
hollen 'closed'	*fen hollen* 'closed door'
mithren 'grey'	*ered mithrin* 'grey mountains'
rhúnen 'eastern'	*talath rhúnen* 'east valley'
tathren 'of willows'	*nan tathren* 'vale of willows'

§ 7.4. Quasi-genitive adjectives

Sindarin adjectives derived from nouns (especially ending in *-en*, *-ion*, *-on*, *-ren*) are often used with a quasi-genitive significance in compounds or adjectival phrases:

aewen 'of birds'	*lin-aewen* 'lake of birds'
thonion 'of pines'	*dor-thonion* 'land of pines'
galadhon 'of trees'	*caras galadhon* 'fortress of trees'
ningloron 'of golden water-flowers'	*loeg ningloron* 'pools of golden water-flowers'
gilion 'of stars'	*or-gilion* 'day of stars, starry day'
dúhirion 'of streams of darkness'	*nan-duhirion* 'valley of streams of darkness'
edhellen 'of Elves, Elvish'	*annon edhellen* 'gate of Elves, Elvish gate'
nestadren 'of healing'	*bair nestedrin* 'houses of healing'

§ 7.5. Mutation and monosyllables

Monosyllables in adjective phrases show vowel shortenings and consonant reductions comparable to those in genitive phrases and compounds (cf. §§ 6.1, 15.31–32):

dôl 'hill' + *baran*	>	*Dol Baran* 'brown hill'
dôr 'land' + *glamren*	>	*Dor Lamren* 'echoing land'
toll 'island' + *calen*	>	*Tol Galen* 'green island'
fend 'door' + *hollen*	>	*Fen Hollen* 'closed door'
nand 'vale' + tathren	>	*Nan-tathren* 'willowy vale'

§ 7.6. Plurality

Adjectives form plurals by *i*-affection (see § 5.9), in agreement with any nouns they modify:

SINGULAR ALONE	PLURAL
calen 'green'	*celin*
gwathren 'shadowy'	*gwethrin*
dangen 'slain'	*dengin*
abonnen 'born after'	*ebennin*
morn 'black'	*myrn*

In a noun phrase

aegas angren 'iron peak'	*aegais engrin* 'iron peaks'
amon dûr 'dark hill'	*emyn duir* 'dark hills'
athrad angren 'iron crossing'	*ethraid engrin* 'iron crossings'
bar nestadren 'healing house'	*bair nestedrin* 'healing houses'

nel or *neleg morn* 'black tooth'	*nelig myrn* 'black teeth'
orod angren 'iron mountain'	*eryd engrin* 'iron mountains'
orod 'wathren 'grey mountain'	*eryd 'wethrin* 'grey mountains'
pin galen 'green ridge'	*pinnath gelin* 'green ridges'

In a compound

niben-nog 'petty-Dwarf'	*nibin-noeg* 'petty-Dwarves'

8

Pronouns

The pronouns of Sindarin are scantily attested in the available material. To some extent these can be supplemented by comparison with Quenya, but the list of pronouns remains very partial.

PERSONAL PRONOUNS

Unlike Sindarin nouns and adjectives, the personal pronouns appear to be declined for the nominative, genitive, dative, and accusative cases. Sindarin personal pronouns fall into categories based on person (first, second, third); number (singular and plural); and, in the second person, into respectful and familiar categories.

§ 8.1. The first-person singular pronoun

Nominative: *im* 'I'
Genitive: *!nîn*, *nín* 'my, mine'
Dative: *anim*, *enni* 'for me, to me, me' (as indirect object)
Accusative: *nin* 'me' (as direct object)

This pronoun derives from two stems, one of which appears as *im* and has a possible Common Eldarin reconstruction **iŋwi*, **iŋgwi*, Old Sindarin **imbė*; this could in turn derive either from the root √IŋG 'first' or from a root √ŋWI. The other stem is √NI, which appears in other Eldarin languages, especially in verbal affixes. It is possible that √NI and √ŋWI are ancient alternate forms.

Im must descend directly from OS **imbė*; the dative *anim* shows the preposition *an* 'for' prefixed to the same pronoun. This formation must be of relatively recent date, as the prefix *an* did not undergo mutation to *en-*. This mutation is, however, seen in a form of similar derivation, *enni*, in which the preposition *an* precedes the bare root *ni*.

Nín 'my' and *nin* are probably variants of a single pronoun consisting of the root √NI and the suffix *-n(a)*, which could mean either 'to' or 'of'. The OS form was either **nin* or **nīna*; possibly both occurred.

For the first-person singular only, a suffix *-en* (from OS **-ena*, ultimately from the root √NI) meaning 'my' is attested in the word *lammen* (translated as 'my tongue' in *The Return of the Shadow*, p. 463) as well as the word *guren* 'my heart' (from *gûr* 'heart'). It is possible that other suffixes exist, but none have been attested yet, whereas genitive pronouns are fairly well attested (e.g., *adar nín* 'my father', *bar nín* 'my home'). The difference between the *-en* suffix and the *nín* pronoun is uncertain; perhaps the former was used with inalienable possessions, such as parts of one's mind or body.

§ 8.2. The first-person plural pronoun

Nominative: *!men* 'we'
Genitive: *!mîn* (as a modifier, *vîn*) 'our, ours'
Dative: *ammen* 'for us, to us'
Accusative: *mín* 'us'

All of these forms derive from the root √ME, which also appears in verbal affixes and some pronominal forms. The form **me* might be supposed to be the most basic, but the attested form *ammen* shows the prefixation of the preposition *an-* to a suffixed form *-men*. This suffixed *men* is also most likely a nominative form; cf. *im* and *anim* in §8.1. The genitive and accusative forms *mîn* and *mín* can be derived from CE **mēn* or *mēna* and would yield OS **mīn(a)*, S *mîn*.

§ 8.3. The second-person pronoun

The second-person respectful pronoun occurs in the following forms:

Nominative: *!le* 'thou'
Genitive: *lîn* 'thy, thine'
Dative: *le !alle* 'for thee, to thee'
Accusative: *!len* 'thee'

The second-person root was √D-, but this appeared as *l-* in Quenya. The Sindarin respectful pronoun *le* (probably referring to both singular and plural persons) appears to have been borrowed and modified from the Quenya respectful pronoun *elye*, or the pronominal ending *-lye*. As such, it may have acquired a quite distinct declension; nonetheless, it is here represented as if it were consistent with the original Sindarin pronouns.

The second-person familiar pronoun is not attested.

§ 8.4. The third-person pronoun

As far as can be told, gender is assigned "naturally" in the third-person pronoun; male and female persons take appropriate pronouns, and ungendered objects are neuter.

	Singular	Plural
Masculine:	*ho/hon/hono* 'he'	*hyn* 'them'
Feminine:	*he/hen/hene* 'she'	*hin* 'them'
Neuter:	*ha/han/hana* 'it'	*hain* 'them'

The three forms given are variants. The middle one is probably normal. The functions of the short and long forms are unknown.

§ 8.5. The general pronoun

Nominative: *e* 'he, she[?]'
Genitive: *în* 'his, her[?], hers[?]'
Dative: *!ane* 'for him, to him, for her[?] to her[?]'
Accusative: *!en* 'him, her[?]'

This pronoun does not appear to be gender marked (where attested it is used for masculine) and so may operate for either gender. It possibly derives from a root √H-, although this root is not otherwise attested. The genitive *în* probably comes from a form like CE **hēna* (or *ēna*), OS *īn(a)*. It is also possible that this pronoun is related to the article *i*.

This pronoun is used to refer to the subject of a sentence or clause.

§ 8.6. Nonreflexive pronoun

When a person other than the subject is referred to, the pronoun **te* is used to distinguish that person from the subject; *te*, therefore, is not expected to have a nominative form:

Genitive: *!tîn* (as a modifier, *dîn*)
Dative: *!athe*
Accusative: *!ten* (usually *!den*)

This pronoun is perhaps derived from a root √T- 'that', used to refer to something secondary within the knowledge of the person spoken to. *Athe* is a reconstructed form from *a·the*, equivalent to *an* + *te*.

Plural forms of the general pronoun are not attested.

DEMONSTRATIVES

Demonstrative pronouns are not known to be declined for case. They can, however, be marked for number (singular, plural).

§ 8.7. The near demonstrative

The near demonstrative, *si/sin* 'this', is not attested as such but is suggested by the presence of the root √SI, related forms in Quenya, and derivative forms in Sindarin. It refers to items close (physically or mentally) to one.

The word *si* is also used adverbially, to mean 'now'; when not initial it is usually lenited to *hi*. It is doubtless related to the Quenya *sí* and *sín*, meaning 'now'.

The term *sí* means 'here' and is usually unlenited. It possibly comes from CE **sīse*, OS **sī* or *sīhe*, a locative case form meaning 'in this (place)'.

Also possible, but completely unattested, are the following case formations:

!sidh [OS **sid*] 'hither', 'to this (place)'
!senn [OS **sinna*] 'hither', 'to this (place)'
!sil [OS **sillo*] 'hence', 'from this (place)'

Also deriving from √SI is the demonstrative adjective *sen* (plural *sin*), usually placed after the noun it modifies and lenited as *hen* or *hin*; the noun modified also takes the article. This adjective comes from OS **sina*, pl. **sini*: *i-dêw hen* 'this letter', *i-thîw hin* 'these letters'.

§ 8.8. The distant demonstrative

This pronoun is used for things at some distance (physically or mentally) from one, usually things associated with the person one is speaking to.

The pronoun *!ta* 'that, it' is suggested by Quenya *ta*. Possibly it could also be used to mean 'then, at that time'. The plural of this pronoun is attested with the lenited form *di* (unlenited *ti*) 'those, them'.

The pronoun *!taw* 'there' is suggested by OS *tǭ*. It could come from CE **tāse*, a locative form meaning 'in that (place)'.

Also possible, but completely unattested, are the following case formations:

!tadh (OS **tad*) 'thither', 'to that (place)'
!tann (OS **tanna*) 'thither', 'to that (place)'
!tal (OS **tallo*) 'thence', 'from that (place)'

Also parallel to the Sindarin *sen*, *sin* should be a demonstrative adjective *!tan*, pl. *!tain*, usually lenited as *dan*, *dain*. This would come from OS **tana*, pl. **tani*: *i-dêw dan* 'that letter', *i-thîw dain* 'those letters'.

§ 8.9. The far-distant demonstrative

This pronoun is used for things distant from both the speaker and the person spoken to.

The pronoun *!ent* 'that yonder' is suggested by Q *enta*. Applied to time, it could mean 'at an indefinitely distant time'.

The form *ennas* 'there, in that place yonder' derives from OS **entasse*, a locative case form of **enta*. This form is attested.

Also possible, but completely unattested, are the following case formations:

> *!ennadh* (OS **entad*) 'to that place yonder'
> *!ennan* (OS **entanna*) 'to that place yonder'
> *!ennal* (OS **entallo*) 'from that place yonder'

A demonstrative adjective form *!ennan*, pl. *!ennain*, is possible, but, perhaps more likely, the forms *!ent* (OS **enta*), pl. *!int* (OS **enti*) would be used.

OTHER PRONOUNS

§ 8.10. Interrogative pronouns

The only known interrogative pronoun is *man* 'who?', related to Quenya *man* 'who?', or *mana* 'what?'. But by comparison with the demonstrative pronouns, one can also reconstruct the words *!ma* 'when?' and *!maw* or *!mas* 'where?'

§ 8.11. Relative pronouns

The most common relative pronoun (used to introduce relative clauses or phrases that explain the characteristics of some other word) to be used is *i*; but this properly means 'the, that, the one that' and was in origin identical to the article (see §12.3). Its plural form was *in*, or *i* with nasal mutation (see §5.2), exactly as the article (see §12.6); this is seen in the name *Gyrth i Chuinar* '(the) dead (ones) who live', which probably originally meant '(the) dead, those (ones) living'. However, a form without plural agreement (*i* with soft mutation) is seen in the equivalent form *Firn i Guinar* 'dead who live'; both *chuinar* and *guinar* have the basic form *cuinar* 'they live'.

An independent relative pronoun may have existed, equivalent to Quenya *ya-*; if so it may have had the forms *ia* 'which, at which time', *iaw*, or *ias* 'where'. Possibly related to Quenya *ya-* is the relative pronoun *ai*, found after the plural demonstrative *ti* (lenited *di*) in *di ai gerir úgerth* 'those who do misdeeds'. The exact distribution of *ai* (as opposed to *i*) is unclear; *ai* induces the soft mutation in the verb *cerir*, so it becomes *gerir*.

§ 8.12. Indefinite pronouns

Indefinite pronouns stood in the place of a subject in a sentence for which there was, properly, no subject; they can be represented by such words as *one*, *they*, or simply as passives.

Three such pronouns are known:

pen, an enclitic pronoun meaning 'one, somebody'; usually lenited as *ben*. It came from Common Eldarin **kʷen* 'a person'.

aen, a pronoun perhaps meaning 'they' (in the abstract) and taking a plural verb, is attested in the phrase *i sennui Panthael estathar aen* 'he whom they [aen] rather [sennui] shall [i.e., should] name Panthael [Full-wise]'.

ten (lenited *den*) following a verb, attested in the phrase *caro den i innas lín* 'may your will be done', literally 'may one [ten] do [caro] the will of you [i innas lín]'.

§ 8.13. Reconstructed pronouns

The following pronouns can be reconstructed by comparison with Quenya and Telerin but are not attested:

!aeben, pl. *!aebin* 'whoever', also translated as 'if anyone': e.g., *aeben Hiritha hilevril a hebitha, e firitha* 'whoever shall find a Silmaril and keep it, he shall die' or 'if anyone shall find and keep a Silmaril, he shall die'.

!ilphen, pl. *!ilphin* 'everyone'

Possibly in some of these words the element *nad* 'thing' can be substituted to act as a form used for things instead of persons: *!aenad*, pl. *!aenaid* 'whatever thing', *!illad*, pl. *!illaid* 'everything'.

9

Verbs

§ 9.1. Overview

Sindarin verbs fall into two categories (also seen in Quenya): *i*-stems and *a*-stems. An *i* is the final vowel of the present stem of the *i*-stems, and an *a* is the final vowel of the present stem of the *a*-stems. Verbs of the *i*-stem variety are almost always formed directly from the verbal root; *a*-stem verbs may be formed directly from the root but are also formed from the root plus some suffix—most frequently suffixes derived from older **-ta*, **-ja*, or **-ra*.

The *i*-stem verbs show internal affection (see § 5.9) in a number of instances, e.g., *cebi* 'to leap', *câb* 'leaps'.

The **-ja-* verbs show internal affection throughout and the suffix *-ia-*, e.g., *beria-* 'protect', from a root √BAR.

The ending of **-ta*-stem verbs appears variously as *-da* (after vowels), *-tha* (after *l*, *r*, or original *k* and *g*), *-ta* (after *s*), and *-na* (after *n*).

§ 9.2. Personal endings

These endings are found in the published examples of Sindarin:

	Singular		Plural	
1st person	*-n*	'I'	*-m*	'we'
3rd person	–	'he, she, it'	*-r*	'they'

The first-person endings derive from CE pronominal suffixes: *-n* from CE **-ni* 'I' and *-m* from CE **-mmē* 'we' (perhaps from older **-me*). No second-person endings are found in published material, but they would presumably also have been derived from pronominal endings: CE **-de* or **-le* for polite forms, becoming *-dh* or *-l* in CS; CE **-ke* for familiar ones, becoming *-g* in CS (or perhaps **-kke* > *-ch*).

The third-person plural ending *-r* most likely comes from a common plural ending **-re*, also seen in the plurals of Quenya nouns and verbs. The zero ending of the third-person singular may derive from the pronominal endings **-so* 'he' and **-se* 'she', which would have become OS **-ho*, *-he*, then **-h*, and finally zero.

When a verb is used following a personal pronoun (see §§ 8.1–5), the personal endings can be omitted; *im echant* 'I made' vs. *echannen* 'I made'.

§ 9.3. The infinitive

The infinitive is an abstract word denoting verbal action, with several different usages. It can be used with verbs indicating ability, e.g., *neledhi gar* 'he/she can enter'. There is no evidence of it being used as a noun or to indicate purpose.

The infinitive is characterized by the ending *-i* with internal *i*-affection for *i*-stems and by the ending *-o* for *a*-stems:

i-stems	*cebi* 'to leap'
a-stems (root)	*naro* 'to tell'
a-stems (*-ja* suffix)	*renio* 'to wander'
a-stems (*-ta* suffix)	*isto* 'to know'

The *-i* ending of *i*-stem infinitives derives from a CE ending **-ijē*, in OS **-iie* (e.g., **kapiie > cebi*); the *-o* ending of the *a*-stem infinitives comes from a CE ending **-ābi* or **-ābē* (which may include an element related to the preposition *be* 'like, as'). The **-ābē* ending became OS **-ǭbe* (e.g., OS **narǭbe* 'to tell'), later **-auv*, **-au*, and at last CS *-o*.

§ 9.4. The present tense

The present tense of a verb may indicate either of the two following: an action currently taking place: *le nallon sí di nguruthos* 'I am crying to you under the horror of death'; or a state that is generally the case but not necessarily going on at the present more than any other time (i.e., there is no *now* implied): *hebin estel* 'I keep hope, I have kept hope'; *i aran aníra suilannad vellyn în* 'the king wants to greet his friends'. It thus performs the tasks of a present, an aorist, and to some extent a perfect tense.

The present tense of the verb is formed by adding the personal endings to the present stem:

cebi 'to leap' (OS **kapiie*)

1s. *cebin* 'I leap' (OS **kapinė*)	1p. *cebim* 'we leap' (OS **kapimme*)

3s. *câb* 'he/she/it leaps' (OS **kapė*, CE **kapi*)
3p. *cebir* 'they leap' (OS **kapire*)

naro 'to tell' (OS **narǭbe*)

1s. *naron* 'I tell' (OS **narǭnė*)
1p. *naram* 'we tell' (OS **naramme*)
3s. *nara* 'he/she/it tells' (OS **narah-*)
3p. *narar* 'they tell' (OS **narare*)

Both *renio* and *isto* are formed like *naro*.

The first-person singular of the *a*-stem verbs shows the original long *ā* of the stem. CE **narāni* 'I tell' became OS **narǭnė*, MS **naraun*, and CS *naron*. In the first-person plural the *ā* is shortened because it occurs in a closed syllable; in the third-person forms it is short, possibly because the original accent fell on the root instead of on the suffix.

The third-person singular of *i*-stem verbs has no ending at all and does not show internal *i*-affection. It derives originally from the bare present stem **kapi*, which became OS **kapė*; the change of final *-i* to *-ė* prevented *i*-affection from taking place. The vowel of a monosyllable followed by only one consonant tended to be lengthened.

§ 9.5. The impersonal

The *a*-stem verbs may have distinctive impersonal forms. These forms denote actions that have no agents. These could be events, such as the weather, for which no agent is usually attributed: *uil* 'it rains'; or purely abstract grammatical functions: *boe*, 'it is necessary, one must'.

Impersonal forms arose from the plain stem of an *a*-stem verb without additional ending:

CE **mbauja-* > OS **mbauia-* > *boe*
CE **ulja-* > OS **ulia-* > *uil*

Contrast the possible personal verb form CE **mbaujas-* 'he or she compels' > OS **mbauiah-* > **boea*, and CE **uljas-* > OS **uliah-* > **elia*.

§ 9.6. The present participle

The present participle is an adjective formed from the verb. It indicates that the word it modifies is either currently engaging in or habitually engaged in an action: *Elbereth . . . o menel palandiriel* 'Elbereth . . . gazing afar from heaven'.

The present participle is formed by adding the suffix *-l* to the present stem. This suffix was originally **-la* and therefore induced *a*-affection in the *i*-stem, raising the *-i-* of the stem to *-e-*. The *-a-* of *a*-stems was lengthened, becoming *-ǭ-*, *-au-*, and finally *-o-*. Thus the endings were *-el* for the *i*-stems and *-ol* for the *a*-stems.

cabel 'leaping' (OS **kapila*)
narol 'telling' (OS **narǭla*)
reniol 'wandering' (OS **raniǭla*)
istol 'knowing' (OS **istǭla*)

Those *i*-stem roots whose root vowel is *i*, and that end in either L, R, or N, often introduce an *i* after the L, R, or N before suffixes beginning with a vowel; so from *tiri* 'to gaze' comes *tiriel* 'watching, gazing'.

No plural forms of present participles are recorded, and, as in Quenya, they probably did not exist.

§ 9.7. The gerund

The gerund is a verbal noun, indicating an action considered as an abstract entity, without any reference to the time at which the action took place. It can be used simply as a noun, and some gerunds have ceased to have a direct connection with a verb; e.g. *suilad* 'greeting' next to *suilanno* 'to greet' (i.e., 'give greeting'; the verb *suilo*, if it existed, is not known to be used in the sense 'to greet'). But most gerunds come directly from verbs still in use, e.g., *cabed* 'a leaping', 'a leap' from *cebi* 'to leap'. The gerund can also be used as the complement of a verb, in which case it is best translated as an infinitve: *e aníra tírad* 'he wants to see'.

The gerund is formed by the addition of the suffix *-d* (OS **-ta*). This follows the stem vowel, which underwent *a*-affection (see § 5.7) in the case of *i*-stem verbs; the endings are therefore *-ed* for the *i*-stems, *-ad* for the *a*-stems.

cabed 'a leaping, a leap' (OS **kapita*)
narad 'a telling' (OS **narata*)
reniad 'a wandering' (OS **raniata*)
istad 'a knowing, knowledge' (OS **ist*^{h}*ata*)

Gerunds ending in *-ed* form plurals ending in *-id*, and gerunds ending in *-ad* form plurals ending in *-aid*, both with internal *i*-affection (see § 5.9): *cebid* 'leaps, leapings'; *neraid* 'tellings'.

§ 9.8. The future tense

The future tense indicates events that will take place in the future; it can also indicate a present intention:

le linnathon 'I will sing to you, I mean to sing to you'
i aran anglennatha i Varanduiniant 'the king will approach the Brandywine Bridge, the king intends to approach the Brandywine Bridge'.

The future tense is formed by adding the element *-tha-*, conjugated like an *a*-stem verb, to the present stem. The origin of this *-tha-* is unknown; possibly it was originally an independent auxiliary verb.

1s. *cebithon* 'I shall leap'	*narathon* 'I shall tell'
1p. *cebitham* 'we shall leap'	*naratham* 'we shall tell'
3s. *cebitha* 'he/she/it will leap'	*naratha* 'he/she/it will tell'
3p. *cebithar* 'they will leap'	*narathar* 'they will tell'
1s. *reniathon* 'I shall wander'	*istathon* 'I shall know'
1p. *reniatham* 'we shall wander'	*istatham* 'we shall know'
3s. *reniatha* 'he/she/it will wander'	*istatha* 'he/she/it will know'
3p. *reniathar* 'they will wander'	*istathar* 'they will know'

§ 9.9. The past tense

The past, or preterite, tense indicates an event that took place sometime in the past: *Celebrimbor teithant i thiw* 'Celebrimbor drew the letters'. It may also indicate a completed action, although it probably cannot indicate an event that is still going on: *im hain echant* 'I made them, I have made them'.

The past tense was formed in at least four different ways in Sindarin: (A) nasal affixation, (B) reduplication, (C) ablaut, and (D) addition of the suffixes *-nt* and *-s*.

§ 9.10. (A) Nasal affixation

Nasalization is a common method of forming past tenses for short stems, that is, *i*-stems or *a*-stems based on roots with the structure Consonant-Vowel-Consonant (CVC). A new past stem was formed from the root by infixing a nasal *before* the final consonant of a root when that was a stop or nasal (*n* before T, D, N; *m* before P, B, M; *ŋ* before K, G). When the final consonant of a root was R or L, *n* was suffixed rather than infixed. The *n* suffix remained in *-rn-*, but **-ln-* regularly became *-ll-*. Perhaps the nasal infixation results from metathesis of a stop and a following *n* suffix; if so, it must take place very early, because nasal infixation is found in both Quenya and Sindarin.

The personal endings are found after both the connecting vowels *-i-* and *-e-*. Perhaps the connecting vowel *-i-* is to be used with *i*-stem verbs, after the analogy of the present tense.

cebi 'to leap'
1s. *cemmin* 'I leaped' (OS **kampʰinė*)
1p. *cemmim* 'we leaped' (OS **kampʰimme*)
3s. *camp* 'he/she/it leaped' (OS **kampʰė*, CE **kampi*)
3p. *cemmir* 'they leaped' (OS **kampʰire*)

gwedhi 'to bind'
1s. *gwennin* 'I bound' (OS **wendinė*)
1p. *gwennim* 'we bound' (OS **wendimme*)
3s. *gwend* 'he/she/it bound' (OS **wendė*, CE **wendi*)
3p. *gwennir* 'they bound' (OS **wendire*)

naro 'to tell'
1s. *narnen* 'I told' (OS **narnenė*)
1p. *narnem* 'we told' (OS **narnemme*)
3s. *narn* 'he/she/it told' (OS **narne*)
3p. *narner* 'they told' (OS **narnere*)

teli 'to come'
1s. *tellin* 'I came' (OS **tullinė*, CE **tulneni?*)
1p. *tellim* 'we came' (OS **tullimme*)
3s. *toll* 'he/she/it came' (OS **tulle*)
3p. *teller* 'they came' (OS **tullere*)

galo 'to grow'
1s. *gallen* 'I grew' (OS **gallenė*, CE **galneni*)
1p. *gallem* 'we grew' (OS **gallemme*)
3s. *gall* 'he/she/it grew' (OS **galle*)
3p. *galler* 'they grew' (OS **gallere*)

When the vowel *u* originally occured in a root, it is preserved before a nasal, as in the past tense of *sogo*, although elsewhere it became *o*:

sogo 'to drink'
1s. *sungen* 'I drank' (OS **suŋkʰenė*)

1p. *sungem* 'we drank' (OS *$*su\eta k^{h}emme$*)
3s. *sunc* 'he/she/it drank' (OS *$*su\eta k^{h}e$*)
3p. *sunger* 'they drank' (OS *$*su\eta k^{h}ere$*)

Historically unjustified past-tense formations might be formed analogically; e.g., 3s. *dramp* (as if from **drap-*) rather than **dramm* (from **dram-*), thus agreeing with other verbs containing *-mme*, like *cemmin* and *camp* above.

dravo 'to hew'
1s. *drammen* 'I hewed' (OS **drammenė*)
1p. *drammem* 'we hewed' (OS **drammemme*)
3s. *dramp* 'he/she/it hewed' (OS **dramme*, but as if from *$*dramp^{h}e$*)
3p. *drammer* 'they hewed' (OS **drammere*)

Adjectival verbs containing the suffix *-da* have a nasal inserted before the suffix, creating the past suffixes *-nt*, *-nn-*.

nimmido 'to make white'
1s. *nimminnen* 'I made white' (OS *$*nimp^{h}int^{h}en\dot{e}$*)
1p. *nimminnem* 'we made white' (OS *$*nimp^{h}int^{h}emme$*)
3s. *nimmint* 'he/she/it made white' (OS *$*nimp^{h}int^{h}e$*)
3p. *nimminner* 'they made white' (OS *$*nimp^{h}int^{h}ere$*)

tangado 'to make firm'
1s. *tangannen* 'I made firm' (OS *$*ta\eta k^{h}ant^{h}en\dot{e}$*)
1p. *tangannem* 'we made firm' (OS *$*ta\eta k^{h}ant^{h}emme$*)
3s. *tangant* 'he/she/it made firm' (OS *$*ta\eta k^{h}ant^{h}e$*)
3p. *tanganner* 'they made firm' (OS *$*ta\eta k^{h}ant^{h}ere$*)

§ 9.11. (B) Reduplication

Reduplication takes place only in verbs based on a CVC root. Originally a short vowel identical in quality to the root vowel was placed before the root, and the root vowel underwent long ablaut (see § 5.11).

The initial consonant of the root underwent soft mutation (see § 5.1). Where there was no initial consonant, the reduplicated prefix (augment) was either lost or fused with the root vowel, e.g., *a* + *ā* > *ā*. Personal suffixes are connected to the stem by the vowel *-e-*.

ceri 'to make'
1s. *agoren* 'I made' (OS **akǭrenė*)
1p. *agorem* 'we made' (OS **akǭremme*)

3s. *agor* 'he/she/it made' (OS **akǭre*)
3p. *agorer* 'they made' (OS **akǭrere*)

anno 'to give' (probably for an older **ano* or **eni*)
1s. *onen* 'I gave' (OS **ǭnenė* < CE **a-āneni*)
1p. *onem* 'we gave' (OS **ǭnemme*)
3s. *aun* 'he/she/it gave' (OS **ǭne*)
3p. *oner* 'they gave' (OS **ǭnere*)

This formation was said to be "usual in Sindarin 'strong' or primary verbs" (*WJ*, p. 415n30), but in fact examples are much rarer than those of the nasal past. One might expect such formations as **udul* 'he/she/it came', **idir* 'he/she/it watched', **egin* 'he/she/it saw', etc., but these are not in fact found. Possibly reduplication is more usual with roots containing *-a-*. This formation also does not seem to be used as a basis for past passive participles (see below).

§ 9.12. (C) Ablaut

The strong ablauted past occurs only in verbs with CVC roots. The stem consists merely of the root itself with the vowel in strong grade (see § 5.11); its suffixes are perhaps the same as those of the reduplicated past.

delio or *doltho* 'to hide' (probably replacing an older **dolo*)
1s. *dolen* 'I hid' (OS **daulenė*)
1p. *dolem* 'we hid' (OS **daulemme*)
3s. *daul* 'he/she/it hid' (OS **daule*)
3p. *doler* 'they hid' (OS **daulere*)

thoro 'to fence'
1s. *thoren* 'I fenced' (OS *t^{h}*aurenė*)
1p. *thorem* 'we fenced' (OS *t^{h}*auremme*)
3s. *thaur* 'he/she/it fenced' (OS *t^{h}*aure*)
3p. *thorer* 'they fenced' (OS *t^{h}*aurere*)

Pasts of this form are rare and were probably replaced by analogical formations by the period of Classical Sindarin.

§ 9.13. (D) Addition of suffix

The suffixed past is normal for all verbs that add an affix to the root to form the stem: e.g., *-ta* stems, *-ja* stems, *-ra* stems, etc. These verbs add the ending *-nt*, *-nn-* to the stem.

This is the most common type of past ending and is often substituted for the other types: *gwedhant* 'he/she/it bound' superseded *gwend*; *sogant* 'he/she/it drank' existed alongside *sunc*. Other such pairs include *danc* and *dagant* from *dag-* 'slay'; *dramp* and *dravant* from *drav-* 'hammer'; *hamp* and *havant* from *hav-* 'sit'.

renio 'to wander'
1s. *reniannen* 'I wandered' (OS **raniant*^{h}*enė*)
1p. *reniannem* 'we wandered' (OS **raniant*^{h}*emme*)
3s. *reniant* 'he/she/it wandered' (OS **raniant*^{h}*e*)
3p. *renianner* 'they wandered' (OS **raniant*^{h}*ere*)

teitho 'write, draw'
1s. *teithannen* 'I drew' (OS **tekt*^{h}*ant*^{h}*enė*)
1p. *teithannem* 'we drew' (OS **tekt*^{h}*ant*^{h}*emme*)
3s. teithant 'he/she/it drew' (OS **tekt*^{h}*ant*^{h}*e*)
3p. *teithanner* 'they drew' (OS **tekt*^{h}*ant*^{h}*ere*)

The suffix in verbs whose stem ended in *-nn* could be reduced by haplology (loss of a syllable when two similar syllables followed each other):

danno 'fall'
1s. *dannen* 'I fell' (OS **dant*^{h}*ene*, **dant*^{h}*ant*^{h}*enė*)
1p. *dannem* 'we fell' (OS **dant*^{h}*emme*, **dant*^{h}*ant*^{h}*emme*)
3s. *dant*, *dannant* 'he/she/it fell' (OS **dant*^{h}*e*, **dant*^{h}*ant*^{h}*e*)
3p. *danner* 'they fell' (OS **dant*^{h}*ere*, **dant*^{h}*ant*^{h}*ere*)

There was also a past tense suffix that added *-s*, *-ss-* to the stem. This suffix is found attached to the *-ta* verbs. It is also found in the composite form *-a-s*, *-a-ss-* with CVC root verbs that originally ended in the alveolar stops *t* and *d* (appearing in Sindarin as *t*, *d*, *th*, or *dh*). Examples are *mudas* (past of *muda-*), *istas* (past of *ista-* [beside *sint*]), and *edledhas* (past of *edledhi* [beside *edlent*]). However, this past tense may have been preserved only in the Noldorin dialect of Sindarin, as we have *teithant* from the *-ta* verb *teitha-* but not *teithas*.

The **-sse* suffix may originate from CE **-nsē*, with *n*-infixation comparable to the CE **-ntē* suffix.

1s. *mudassen* 'I toiled' (OS **mūtassenė*)
1p. *mudassem* 'we toiled' (OS **mūtassemme*)
3s. *mudas* 'he/she/it toiled' (OS **mūtasse*)
3p. *mudasser* 'they toiled' (OS **mūtassere*)

§ 9.14. The past passive participle

The past passive participle was an adjective showing a present state that had resulted from a past action, whether occurring only once or still continuing and so not necessarily existing only in the past; e.g., *talath dirnen* 'guarded plain' implied a plain that was still guarded.

The past passive participle was formed by suffixing the ending *-en* (OS *-ena*) to the past stem. Consonants preceding the ending took medial mutation. The past participle had a plural ending *-in* (OS *-eni*), with secondary *i*-affection (see § 5.9) through the rest of the word.

The past participles can therefore be classified in the same way as the past tenses:

	Singular	Plural
(A)	*tirnen*	*tirnin* 'having been watched'
	dangen	*dengin* 'having been slain'
(C)	*dolen*	*dolin* 'having been hidden'
	thoren	*thorin* 'having been fenced'
(D)	*teithannen*	*teithennin* 'having been written'
	prestannen	*prestennin* 'having been altered'

Past participles made from past tense B (reduplication) are not attested.

A number of adjectives and nouns derived from older past participial formations that were independent of the formation of the past tense; such adjectives lacked the *-en* suffix:

daen 'one who is slain, corpse' OS **<ñdagno*, corresponding to the later formation OS **<ñdaŋk^{h}ena > dangen*.

narn 'tale' OS **narna*, probably corresponds to a past participle *narnen*.

eglenn 'exiled' OS **etlenna* < CE **etlednā*, probably corresponds to a past participle *eglennen* (OS **etlendena*)

naud 'bound' OS **nauta*, probably corresponds to a past participle *noden* (OS **nautena*) or *nunnen* (OS **nunt^{h}ena*).

neithan 'wronged' OS **nekt^{h}ana*, probably corresponds to a past participle *neithannen* (OS **nekt^{h}ant^{h}ena*).

§ 9.15. The perfect active participle

The perfect active participle was an adjective that indicated that one had completed an action before beginning another one; it was thus normally used in conjunction with another verb: *na-chaered tíriel . . . linnathon* 'having gazed to a distance . . . I will sing' or 'after gazing to a distance . . . I will sing; *ithil ammen síla díriel* 'the moon shines white after watching (for) us'. With the past tense it could even be translated as 'when . . . (then) . . .'; e.g., *cíniel veldis nín, hen suilonen* 'having seen my friend, I greeted her' or 'when I saw my friend, I greeted her'.

This participle was probably derived from adding the participial ending *-la* to the stem of a perfect verb formed by long ablaut of the root (where possible) and the suffix *-ie*. This verb form still existed in Quenya, but no examples of it are found in Sindarin. As with the present participle, there do not appear to be any plural forms.

cebi (*cab-*) — *cóbiel* 'after leaping' (OS **kǭpiela*, CE **kāpijēlā*)
naro — *nóriel* 'after telling' (OS **nǭriela*, CE **nārijēlā*)
ceni (*cen-*) — *cíniel* 'after seeing' (OS **kīniela*, CE **kēnijēlā*)
tiri — *tíriel* 'after watching' (OS **tīriela*)
teli (*tol-*) — *túliel* 'after coming' (OS **tūliela*)
eglerio (*aglar-*) — *aglóriel* 'after glorifying' (OS **aklǭriela*)
renio (*ran-*) — *róniel* 'after wandering' (OS **rǭni(i)ela*)
lasto — *lestiel* 'after listening' (OS **last^{h}iela*)

§ 9.16. The imperative

The imperative was used to express commands or wishes. It consisted of the unaffected present stem followed by the suffix *-o* (in both singular and plural), originally a separate interjection *A!*, *O!*, in OS **ǭ*: *cabo* 'jump!', *edro* 'open!', *daro* 'stop!', *tiro* 'look!', *eglerio* 'praise!', *lasto* 'listen!'.

§ 9.17. The verb *to be*

The only forms of a verb *to be* extant in Sindarin are the gerund *nad* (OS **nata*) 'being, thing' and the imperative *no* (OS **nǭ ǭ*) 'Be!'. From these forms, however, and from comparison with the Quenya verb *ná*, it is possible to extrapolate the following (possible) forms for this verb:

Infinitive: *naw* (OS **nǭbe*)

Present tense:
1s. *naun*, *non* (OS **nǭnė*) 'I am'
1p. *nam* (OS **namme*) 'we are'
3s. *naw*, *no* (OS **nǭ*) 'he/she/it is'
3p. *nar* (OS **nare*) 'they are'

Present participle: *naul* (OS **nǭla*) 'being'

Gerund: *nad* (OS **nata*) 'a being, a thing'

Future tense:
1s. *nathon* 'I will be'
1p. *natham* 'we will be'
3s. *natha* 'he/she/it will be'
3p. *nathar* 'they will be'

Past tense
1s. *nónen* (OS **nǭnenė*) 'I was'
1p. *nónem* (OS **nǭnemme*) 'we were'
3s. *naun*, *non* (OS **nǭne*) 'he/she/it was'
3p. *nóner* (OS **nǭnere*) 'they were'

Past passive participle: *naun* (OS **nǭna*) 'been'

Perfect active participle: *nóniel* (OS **nǭniela*) 'having been'

Imperative: *naw*, *no* (OS **nǭ ǭ*) 'Be!'

Where alternative forms containing *au* (or *aw*) and *o* are found, the forms with *au* (*aw*) may be used where the word takes a strong stress in the sentence, the forms with *o* when (as often) it is weakly stressed (e.g., when next to a noun or adjective): *Si gwanwen no Bar i Melain* 'Now Valimar is lost'; *Aerennil non cirion* 'Eärendil was a mariner'.

VERB PARADIGMS

Sindarin verbs fall into three main categories: *i*-stems, simple *a*-stems, and complex *a*-stems. Following a paradigm of a verb in each of these classes are given the verbs that are conjugated according to that paradigm. All forms of the verb are listed except the first- and third-person plurals of past and present, which may be deduced from the first-person singular of their respective tenses by substituting the endings *-im*, *-ir* for *-in* in the *i*-stems, and *-am*, *-ar* for *-on* in the *a*-stems; and the first-person singular and the first- and third-person plural of the future, which may be deduced from the third-person singular by substituting the endings *-on*, *-am*, and *-ar* for *-a*. Second-person forms are not known with certainty for any tense of the verb. Past tense forms in first-person singular *-essin* or *-assen* and in third-person singular *-as* may optionally be substituted for first-person singular *-ennin* or *-annen* or third-person singular *-ant* when the last consonant of the stem is *t*, *d*, *th*, or *dh*.

Example of an *i*-stem verb

Had 'hurl'
Infinitive: *hedi* 'to hurl'
Gerund: *haded* 'hurling'

VERB TENSE OR FORM	SINGULAR	PLURAL
Present tense		
1st person	*hedin* 'I hurl'	*hedim* 'we hurl'
3rd person	*hâd* 'he/she/it hurls'	*hedir* 'they hurl'
Act. part.	*hadel* 'hurling'	*hadel* 'hurling'
Imperative	*hado* 'hurl!'	*hado* 'hurl!'
Past tense		
1st person	*hennin* 'I hurled'	*hennim* 'we hurled'
3rd person	*hant* 'he/she/it hurled'	*hennir* 'they hurled'
Act. part.	*hódiel* 'having hurled'	*hódiel* 'having hurled'
Pass. part.	*hannen* '(having been) hurled'	*hennin* '(having been) hurled'
Future tense		
1st person	*hedithon* 'I will hurl'	*heditham* 'we will hurl'
3rd person	*heditha* 'he/she/it will hurl'	*hedithar* 'they will hurl'

ABBREVIATIONS

1 first person	pl. plural
3 third person	pp. passive participle
ap. active participle	pr. present
fut. future	pt. past
ger. gerund	sg. singular
inf. infinitive	‡ archaic

i-stems with root ending in a stop or fricative

Bad- 'walk'
inf. *bedi*, ger. *baded*, pr.1sg. *bedin*, pr.3sg. *bâd*, pr.ap. *badel*, imp. *bado*, pt.1sg. *bennin*, pt.3sg. *bant*, pt.ap. *bódiel*, pt.pp.sg. *bannen*, pt.pp.pl. *bennin*, fut.3sg. *beditha*.
Conjugated like *bad-* are *gad-* 'catch', *had-* 'hurl', *mad-* 'eat'.

Cab- 'leap'

inf. *cebi*, ger. *cabed*, pr.1sg. *cebin*, pr.3sg. *câb*, pr.ap. *cabel*, imp. *cabo*, pt.1sg. *cemmin*, pt.3sg. *camp*, pt.ap. *cóbiel*, pt.pp.sg. *cammen*, pt. pp.pl. *cemmin*, fut.3sg. *cebitha*.

Conjugated like *cab-* are *blab-* 'flap', *hab-* 'clothe', *mab-* 'grasp'.

Dag- 'slay'

inf. *degi*, ger. *daged*, pr.1sg. *degin*, pr.3sg. *dâg*, pr.ap. *dagel*, imp. *dago*, pt.1sg. *dengin* or *dagannen*, pt.3sg. *danc* or *dagant*, pt.ap. *dógiel*, pt.pp.sg. *dangen*, pt.pp.pl. *dengin*, fut.3sg. *degitha*.

Conjugated like *dag-* is *nag-* 'bite'.

Gwedh- 'bind'

inf. *gwedhi*, ger. *gwedhed*, pr.1sg. *gwedhin*, pr.3sg. *gwêdh*, pr.ap. *gwedhel*, imp. *gwedho*, pt.1sg. *gwennin* (archaic) or *gwedhannen*, pt.3sg. ‡*gwend* or *gwedhant*, pt.ap. *gwídhiel*, pt.pp.sg. ‡*gwennen* or *gwedhannen*, pt.pp.pl. ‡*gwennin* or *gwedhennin*, fut.3sg. *gwedhitha*.

Hav- 'sit'

inf. *hevi*, ger. *haved*, pr.1sg. *hevin*, pr.3sg. *hâf*, pr.ap. *havel*, imp. *havo*, pt.1sg. *hemmin* or *hevennin*, pt.3sg. *hamp* or *havant*, pt.ap. *hóviel*, pt.pp.sg. *hammen*, pt.pp.pl. *hemmin*, fut.3sg. *hevitha*.

Lav- 'lick'

inf. *levi*, ger. *laved*, pr.1sg. *levin*, pr.3sg. *lâf*, pr.ap. *lavel*, imp. *lavo*, pt.1sg. *lemmin*, pt.3sg. *lam*, pt.ap. *lóviel*, pt.pp.sg. *lammen*, pt.pp.pl. *lemmin*, fut.3sg. *levitha*.

Nod- 'tie'

inf. *nedi*, ger. *noded*, pr.1sg. *nedin*, pr.3sg. *nôd*, pr.ap. *nodel*, imp. *nodo*, pt.1sg. *nynnin*, pt.3sg. *nunt*, pt.ap. *núdiel*, pt.pp.sg. *nunnen*, pt.pp.pl. *nynnin*, fut.3sg. *neditha*.

Ped- 'speak'

inf. *pedi*, ger. *peded*, pr.1sg. *pedin*, pr.3sg. *pêd*, pr.ap. *pedel*, imp. *pedo*, pt.1sg. *pennin*, pt.3sg. *pent*, pt.ap. *pídiel*, pt.pp.sg. *pennen*, pt.pp.pl. *pennin*, fut.3sg. *peditha*.

Redh- 'sow'

inf. *redhi*, ger. *redhed*, pr.1sg. *redhin*, pr.3sg. *rêdh*, pr.ap. *redhel*, imp. *redho*, pt.1sg. *rennin*, pt.3sg. *rend*, pt.ap. *rídhiel*, pt.pp.sg. *rennen*, pt.pp.pl. *rennin*, fut.3sg. *redhitha*.

Rib- 'rush, flow'
inf. *ribi*, ger. *ribed*, pr.1sg. *ribin*, pr.3sg. *rîb*, pr.ap. *ribiel*, imp. *ribo*, pt.1sg. *rimmin*, pt.3sg. *rimp*, pt.ap. *ríbiel*, pt.pp.sg. *rimmen*, pt.pp.pl. *rimmin*, fut.3sg. *ribitha*.
Conjugated like *rib-* is *rhib-* 'scratch'.

Tog- 'lead'
inf. *tegi*, ger. *toged*, pr.1sg. *tegin*, pr.3sg. *tôg*, pr.ap. *togel*, imp. *togo*, pt.1sg. *tyngin*, pt.3sg. *tunc*, pt.ap. *túgiel*, pt.pp.sg. *tungen*, pt.pp.pl. *tyngin*, fut.3sg. *tegitha*.

Stop/fricative-final i-stem verbs with prefixes

Adleg- 'set free'
inf. *adlegi*, ger. *adleged*, pr.1sg. *adlegin*, pr.3sg. *adleg*, pr.ap. *adlegel*, imp. *adlego*, pt.1sg. *adlengin*, pt.3sg. *adlenc*, pt.ap. *adlígiel*, pt.pp.sg. *adlengen*, pt.pp.pl. *adlengin*, fut.3sg. *adlegitha*.

Edledh- 'go into exile'
inf. *edledhi*, ger. *edledhed*, pr.1sg. *edledhin*, pr.3sg. *edledh*, pr.ap. *edledhel*, imp. *edledho*, pt.1sg. *edlennin* or *edledhassen*, pt.3sg. *edlent* or *edledhas*, pt.ap. *edlídhiel*, pt.pp.sg. *edlennen*, pt.pp.pl. *edlennin*, fut.3sg. *edledhitha*.
Conjugated like *edledh-* is *neledh-* 'go into'.

Gonod- 'count'
inf. *genedi*, ger. *gonoded*, pr.1sg. *genedin*, pr.3sg. *gonod*, pr.ap. *gonodel*, imp. *gonodo*, pt.1sg. *genennin*, pt.3sg. *gonont*, pt.ap. *gonúdiel*, pt.pp.sg. *gononnen*, pt.pp.pl. *genennin*, fut.3sg. *geneditha*.

Govad- 'meet'
inf. *gevedi*, ger. *govaded*, pr.1sg. *gevedin*, pr.3sg. *govad*, pr.ap. *govadel*, imp. *govado*, pt.1sg. *gevennin*, pt.3sg. *govant*, pt.ap. *govódiel*, pt.pp.sg. *govannen*, pt.pp.pl. *gevennin*, fut.3sg. *geveditha*.
Conjugated like *govad-* are *echad-* 'make', *trevad-* 'traverse'.

Nestag- 'insert'
inf. *nestegi*, ger. *nestaged*, pr.1sg. *nestegin*, pr.3sg. *nestag*, pr.ap. *nestagel*, imp. *nestago*, pt.1sg. *nestengin*, pt.3sg. *nestanc*, pt.ap. *nestógiel*, pt.pp.sg. *nestangen*, pt.pp.pl. *nestengin*, fut.3sg. *nestegitha*.

i-stems with root ending in sonorant (r, l , n)

Can- 'cry out'
inf. *ceni*, ger. *caned*, pr.1sg. *cenin*, pr.3sg. *cân*, pr.ap. *canel*, imp. *cano*, pt.1sg. *cennin*, pt.3sg. *cann*, pt.ap. *cóniel*, pt.pp.sg. *cannen*, pt.pp.pl. *cennin*, fut.3sg. *cenitha*.

Car- 'make'
inf. *ceri*, ger. *cared*, pr.1sg. *cerin*, pr.3sg. *câr*, pr.ap. *carel*, imp. *caro*, pt.1sg. *agoren*, pt.3sg. *agor*, pt.ap. *córiel*, pt.pp.sg. *coren* (or *carnen*), pt.pp.pl. *corin* (or *cernin*), fut.3sg. *ceritha*.

Cen- 'see'
inf. *ceni*, ger. *cened*, pr.1sg. *cenin*, pr.3sg. *cên*, pr.ap. *cenel*, imp. *ceno*, pt.1sg. *cennin*, pt.3sg. *cenn*, pt.ap. *cíniel*, pt.pp.sg. *cennen*, pt.pp.pl. *cennin*, fut.3sg. *cenitha*.

Gar- 'hold'
inf. *geri*, ger. *gared*, pr.1sg. *gerin*, pr.3sg. *gâr*, pr.ap. *garel*, imp. *garo*, pt.1sg. *gernin* or *gerennin*, pt.3sg. *garn* or *garant*, pt.ap. *góriel*, pt.pp.sg. *garnen*, pt.pp.pl. *gernin*, fut.3sg. *geritha*.
Conjugated like *gar-* is *dar-* 'stop'.

Gor- 'warn, counsel'
inf. *geri*, ger. *gored*, pr.1sg. *gerin*, pr.3sg. *gôr*, pr.ap. *gorel*, imp. *goro*, pt.1sg. *gernin*, pt.3sg. *gorn*, pt.ap. *gúriel*, pt.pp.sg. *gornen*, pt.pp.pl. *gernin*, fut.3sg. *geritha*.
Conjugated like *gor-* is *nor-* 'run' (?).

Hal- 'lift'
inf. *heli*, ger. *haled*, pr.1sg. *helin*, pr.3sg. *hâl*, pr.ap. *halel*, imp. *halo*, pt.1sg. *hellin*, pt.3sg. *hall*, pt.ap. *hóliel*, pt.pp.sg. *hallen*, pt.pp.pl. *hellin*, fut.3sg. *helitha*.

Pel- 'fade'
inf. *peli*, ger. *peled*, pr.1sg. *pelin*, pr.3sg. *pêl*, pr.ap. *pelel*, imp. *pelo*, pt.1sg. *pellin*, pt.3sg. *pell*, pt.ap. *píliel*, pt.pp.sg. *pellen*, pt.pp.pl. *pellin*, fut.3sg. *pelitha*.
Conjugated like *pel-* is *thel-* 'intend'.

Tir- (also *tiria-*) 'watch'
inf. *tiri*, ger. *tired*, pr.1sg. *tirin*, pr.3sg. *tîr*, pr.ap. *tiriel*, imp. *tiro*, pt.1sg. *tirnin*, pt.3sg. *tirn*, pt.ap. *tíriel*, pt.pp.sg. *tirnen*, pt.pp.pl. *tirnin*, fut.3sg. *tiritha*.
Conjugated like *tir-* are *fir-* 'die', *gir-* 'shudder', and *glir-* 'sing'.

Tol- 'come'
inf. *teli*, ger. *toled*, pr.1sg. *telin*, pr.3sg. *tôl*, pr.ap. *tolel*, imp. *tolo*, pt.1sg. *tellin*, pt.3sg. *toll*, pt.ap. *túliel*, pt.pp.sg. *tollen*, pt.pp.pl. *tellin*, fut.3sg. *telitha.*
Conjugated like *tol-* is *hol-* 'close'.

Yr- 'run'
inf. *yri*, ger. *yred*, pr.1sg. *yrin*, pr.3sg. *ŷr*, pr.ap. *yrel*, imp. *yro*, pt.1sg. *yrnin*, pt.3sg. *yrn*, pt.ap. *iúriel*, pt.pp.sg. *yrnen*, pt.pp.pl. *yrnin*, fut.3sg. *yritha.*

Sonorant-final i-stem verbs with prefixes

Orthel- 'roof'
inf. *ortheli*, ger. *ortheled*, pr.1sg. *orthelin*, pr.3sg. *orthel*, pr.ap. *orthelel*, imp. *orthelo*, pt.1sg. *orthellin*, pt.3sg. *orthell*, pt.ap. *orthíliel*, pt.pp.sg. *orthellen*, pt.pp.pl. *orthellin*, fut.3sg. *orthelitha.*

Orthor- 'conquer'
inf. *ortheri*, ger. *orthored*, pr.1sg. *ortherin*, pr.3sg. *orthor*, pr.ap. *orthorel*, imp. *orthoro*, pt.1sg. *orthernin*, pt.3sg. *orthorn*, pt.ap. *orthúriel*, pt.pp.sg. *orthornen*, pt.pp.pl. *orthernin*, fut.3sg. *ortheritha.*

Oscar- 'amputate'
inf. *esceri*, ger. *oscared*, pr.1sg. *escerin*, pr.3sg. *oscar*, pr.ap. *oscarel*, imp. *oscaro*, pt.1sg. *escernin*, pt.3sg. *oscarn*, pt.ap. *oscóriel*, pt.pp.sg. *oscarnen*, pt.pp.pl. *escernin*, fut.3sg. *esceritha.*

Palandir- 'watch from afar'
inf. *palandiri*, ger. *palandired*, pr.1sg. *palandirin*, pr.3sg. *palandir*, pr.ap. *palandiriel*, imp. *palandiro*, pt.1sg. *palandirnin*, pt.3sg. *palandirn*, pt.ap. *palandíriel*, pt.pp.sg. *palandirnen*, pt.pp.pl. *palandirnin*, fut.3sg. *palandiritha.*

Trenar- 'recount'
inf. *treneri*, ger. *trenared*, pr.1sg. *trenerin*, pr.3sg. *trenar*, pr.ap. *trenarel*, imp. *trenaro*, pt.1sg. *trenoren*, pt.3sg. *trenor*, pt.ap. *trenóriel*, pt.pp.sg. *trenoren*, pt.pp.pl. *trenorin*, fut.3sg. *treneritha*

EXMPLE OF A SIMPLE *a*-STEM VERB

Fara-	'hunt'
Infinitive:	*faro* 'to hunt'
Gerund:	*farad* 'hunting'

VERB FORM OR TENSE	SINGULAR	PLURAL
Present tense		
1st person	*faron* 'I hunt'	*faram* 'we hunt'
3rd person	*fara* 'hunts'	*farar* 'they hunt'
Act. part.	*farol* 'hunting'	*farol* 'hunting'
Imperative	*faro* 'hunt!'	*faro* 'hunt!'
Past tense		
1st person	*farnen* 'I hunted'	*farnem* 'we hunted'
3rd person	*farn* 'he/she/it hunted'	*farner* 'they hunted'
Act. part.	*fóriel* 'having hunted'	*fóriel* 'having hunted'
Pass. part.	*farnen* '(having been) hunted'	*fernin* '(having been) hunted'
Future tense		
1st person	*farathon* 'I will hunt'	*faratham* 'we will hunt'
3rd person	*faratha* 'he/she/it will hunt'	*farathar* 'they will hunt'

Conjugated like *fara-* is *nara-* 'tell.'

Aphada- 'follow'
inf. *aphado*, ger. *aphadad*, pr.1sg. *aphadon*, pr.3sg. *aphada*, pr.ap. *aphadol*, imp. *aphado*, pt.1sg. *aphannen*, pt.3sg. *aphant*, pt.ap. *aphódiel*, pt.pp.sg. *aphannen*, pt.pp.pl. *ephennin*, fut.3sg. *aphadatha*.
Conjugated like *aphada-* is *athrada-* 'cross'.

Ava- 'refuse'
inf. *avo*, ger. *avad*, pr.1sg. *avon*, pr.3sg. *ava*, pr.ap. *avol*, imp. *avo*, pt.1sg. *ammen*, pt.3sg. *am*, pt.ap. *óviel*, pt.pp.sg. *ammen*, pt.pp.pl. *emmin*, fut.3sg. *avatha*.

Banga- 'trade'
inf. *bango*, ger. *bangad*, pr.1sg. *bangon*, pr.3sg. *banga*, pr.ap. *bangol*, imp. *bango*, pt.1sg. *bangen*, pt.3sg. *banc*, pt.ap. *bengiel*, pt.pp.sg. *bangen*, pt.pp.pl. *bengin*, fut.3sg. *bangatha*.

Drava- 'beat'
inf. *dravo*, ger. *dravad*, pr.1sg. *dravon*, pr.3sg. *drava*, pr.ap. *dravol*, imp. *dravo*, pt.1sg. *drammen* or *dravannen*, pt.3sg. *dram* (‡*dramp*)

or *dravant*, pt.ap. *dróviel*, pt.pp.sg. *drammen*, pt.pp.pl. *dremmin*, fut.3sg. *dravatha*.

Gala- 'grow'
inf. *galo*, ger. *galad*, pr.1sg. *galon*, pr.3sg. *gala*, pr.ap. *galol*, imp. *galo*, pt.1sg. *gallen*, pt.3sg. *gall*, pt.ap. *góliel*, pt.pp.sg. *gallen*, pt.pp.pl. *gellin*, fut.3sg. *galatha*.

Gawa- 'howl'
inf. *gawo*, ger. *gawad*, pr.1sg. *gawon*, pr.3sg. *gawa*, pr.ap. *gawol*, imp. *gawo*, pt.1sg. *gonen*, pt.3sg. *gaun*, pt.ap. *gówiel*, pt.pp.sg. *gonen*, pt.pp.pl. *gonin*, fut.3sg. *gawatha*.

Groga- 'feel terror'
inf. *grogo*, ger. *grogad*, pr.1sg. *grogon*, pr.3sg. *groga*, pr.ap. *grogol*, imp. *grogo*, pt.1sg. *grungen*, pt.3sg. *grunc*, pt.ap. *grúgiel*, pt.pp.sg. *grungen*, pt.pp.pl. *gryngin*, fut.3sg. *grogatha*.

Laba- 'hop'
inf. *labo*, ger. *labad*, pr.1sg. *labon*, pr.3sg. *laba*, pr.ap. *labol*, imp. *labo*, pt.1sg. *lammen*, pt.3sg. *lamp*, pt.ap. *lóbiel*, pt.pp.sg. *lammen*, pt.pp.pl. *lemmin*, fut.3sg. *labatha*.

Loda- 'float'
inf. *lodo*, ger. *lodad*, pr.1sg. *lodon*, pr.3sg. *lôd*, pr.ap. *lodol*, imp. *lodo*, pt.1sg. *lunnen*, pt.3sg. *lunt*, pt.ap. *lúdiel*, pt.pp.sg. *lunnen*, pt.pp.pl. *lynnin*, fut.3sg. *lodatha*.

Mela- 'love'
inf. *melo*, ger. *melad*, pr.1sg. *melon*, pr.3sg. *mela*, pr.ap. *melol*, imp. *melo*, pt.1sg. *mellen* or *melannen*, pt.3sg. *mell* or *melant*, pt.ap. *míliel*, pt.pp.sg. *mellen*, pt.pp.pl. *mellin*, fut.3sg. *melatha*.

Pada- 'walk on a path'
inf. *pado*, ger. *padad*, pr.1sg. *padon*, pr.3sg. *pada*, pr.ap. *padol*, imp. *pado*, pt.1sg. *pannen*, pt.3sg. *pant*, pt.ap. *pódiel*, pt.pp.sg. *pannen*, pt.pp.pl. *pennin*, fut.3sg. *padatha*.

Conjugated like *pada-* is *rada-* 'make a way'.

Síla- 'shine with silver light'
inf. *sílo*, ger. *sílad*, pr.1sg. *sílon*, pr.3sg. *síla*, pr.ap. *sílol*, imp. *sílo*, pt.1sg. *sillen*, pt.3sg. *sill*, pt.ap. *síliel*, pt.pp.sg. *sillen*, pt.pp.pl. *sillin*, fut.3sg. *sílatha*.

Tíra- 'see'
inf. *tíro*, ger. *tírad*, pr.1sg. *tíron*, pr.3sg. *tíra*, pr.ap. *tírol*, imp. *tíro*, pt.1sg. *tirnen*, pt.3sg. *tirn*, pt.ap. *tíriel*, pt.pp.sg. *tirnen*, pt.pp.pl. *tirnin*, fut.3sg. *tíratha*.
Conjugated like *tíra-* is *aníra-* 'desire'.

Thora- 'fence'
inf. *thoro*, ger. *thorad*, pr.1sg. *thoron*, pr.3sg. *thora*, pr.ap. *thorol*, imp. *thoro*, pt.1sg. *thoren*, pt.3sg. *thaur*, pt.ap. *thóriel*, pt.pp.sg. *thoren*, pt.pp.pl. *thorin*, fut.3sg. *thoratha*.

Toba- 'roof'
inf. *tobo*, ger. *tobad*, pr.1sg. *tobon*, pr.3sg. *toba*, pr.ap. *tobol*, imp. *tobo*, pt.1sg. *tummen*, pt.3sg. *tump*, pt.ap. *túbiel*, pt.pp.sg. *tummen*, pt.pp.pl. *tymmin*, fut.3sg. *tobatha*.

Verbs with -ida and -ada suffixes

Gannada- 'harp'
inf. *gannado*, ger. *gannadad*, pr.1sg. *gannadon*, pr.3sg. *gannada*, pr.ap. *gannadol*, imp. *gannado*, pt.1sg. *gannen*, pt.3sg. *gannant*, pt.ap.*gennediel*, pt.pp.sg. *gannen*, pt.pp.pl. *gennin*, fut.3sg. *gannadatha*.

Nimmida- 'whiten'
inf. *nimmido*, ger. *nimmidad*, pr.1sg. *nimmidon*, pr.3sg. *nimmida*, pr.ap. *nimmidol*, imp. *nimmido*, pt.1sg. *nimminnen*, pt.3sg. *nimmint*, pt.ap. *nimmidiel*, pt.pp.sg. *nimminnen*, pt.pp.pl. *nimminnin*, fut. 3sg. *nimmidatha*.
Conjugated like *nimmida-* is *limmida-* 'moisten.'

Tangada- 'establish'
inf. *tangado*, ger. *tangadad*, pr.1sg. *tangadon*, pr.3sg. *tangada*, pr.ap. *tangadol*, imp. *tangado*, pt.1sg. *tangannen*, pt.3sg. *tangant*, pt.ap. *tengediel*, pt.pp.sg. *tangannen*, pt.pp.pl. *tengennin*, fut.3sg. *tangadatha*.
Conjugated like *tangada-* are *dagrada-* 'make war' and *lathrada-* 'eavesdrop'.

Example of a complex *a*-stem verb

Oltha- 'dream'
Infinitive: *oltho* 'to dream'
Gerund: *olthad* 'dreaming'

VERB FORM OR TENSE	SINGULAR	PLURAL
Present tense		
1st person	*olthon* 'I dream'	*oltham* 'we dream'
3rd person	*oltha* 'dreams'	*olthar* 'they dream'
Act. part.	*olthol* 'dreaming'	*olthol* 'dreaming'
Imperative	*oltho* 'dream!'	*oltho* 'dream!'
Past tense		
1st person	*olthannen* 'I dreamed'	*olthannem* 'we dreamed'
3rd person	*olthant* 'he/she/it dreamed'	*olthanner* 'they dreamed'
Act. part.	*elthiel* 'having dreamed'	*elthiel* 'having dreamed'
Pass. part.	*olthannen* '(having been) dreamed'	*elthennin* '(having been) dreamed'
Future tense		
1st person	*olthathon* 'I will dream'	*olthatham* 'we will dream'
3rd person	*olthatha* 'he/she/it will dream'	*olthathar* 'they will dream'

Conjugated like *oltha-* is *ovra-* 'abound'.

Athra- 'cross'
inf. *athro*, ger. *athrad*, pr.1sg. *athron*, pr.3sg. *athra*, pr.ap. *athrol*, imp. *athro*, pt.1sg. *athrannen*, pt.3sg. *athrant*, pt.ap. *ethriel*, pt.pp.sg. *athrannen*, pt.pp.pl. *ethrennin*, fut.3sg. *athratha*.
Conjugated like *athra-* are *bartha-* 'doom', *faltha-* 'foam', *hamma-* 'clothe', *lacha-* 'flame', *narcha-* 'rend', *tamma-* 'knock', *dagra-* 'do battle', *glavra-* 'babble', *gwathra-* 'overshadow', *lathra-* 'eavesdrop', *pathra-* 'fill', *harna-* 'wound', *batha-* 'trample', *nalla-* 'cry out'.

Gonathra- 'entangle'
inf. *gonathro*, ger. *gonathrad*, pr.1sg. *gonathron*, pr.3sg. *gonathra*, pr.ap. *gonathrol*, imp. *gonathro*, pt.1sg. *gonathrannen*,

pt.3sg. *gonathrant*, pt.ap. *genethriel*, pt.pp.sg. *gonathrannen*, pt.pp.pl. *genethrennin*, fut.3sg. *gonathratha*.

Drega- 'flee'
inf. *drego*, ger. *dregad*, pr.1sg. *dregon*, pr.3sg. *drega*, pr.ap. *dregol*, imp. *drego*, pt.1sg. *dregannen*, pt.3sg. *dregant*, pt.ap. *drígiel*, pt.pp.sg. *dregannen*, pt.pp.pl. *dregennin*, fut.3sg. *dregatha*.

Brona- 'last'
inf. *brono*, ger. *bronad*, pr.1sg. *bronon*, pr.3sg. *brona*, pr.ap. *bronol*, imp. *brono*, pt.1sg. *bronannen*, pt.3sg. *bronant*, pt.ap. *brúniel*, pt.pp.sg. *bronannen*, pt.pp.pl. *brenennin*, fut.3sg. *bronatha*.

Complex a-stems with unchanging root vowel

Edra- 'open'
inf. *edro*, ger. *edrad*, pr.1sg. *edron*, pr.3sg. *edra*, pr.ap. *edrol*, imp. *edro*, pt.1sg. *edrannen*, pt.3sg. *edrant*, pt.ap. *edriel*, pt.pp.sg. *edrannen*, pt.pp.pl. *edrennin*, fut.3sg. *edratha*.
Conjugated like *edra-* are *ercha-* 'prick' and *nella-* 'sound bells'.

Dringa- 'beat'
inf. *dringo*, ger. *dringad*, pr.1sg. *dringon*, pr.3sg. *dringa*, pr.ap. *dringol*, imp. *dringo*, pt.1sg. *dringannen*, pt.3sg. *dringant*, pt.ap. *dringiel*, pt.pp.sg. *dringannen*, pt.pp.pl. *dringennin*, fut.3sg. *dringatha*.
Conjugated like *dringa-* are *glinga-* 'dangle' and *rimma-* 'flow like a torrent'.

Baugla- 'oppress'
inf. *bauglo*, ger. *bauglad*, pr.1sg. *bauglon*, pr.3sg. *baugla*, pr.ap. *bauglol*, imp. *bauglo*, pt.1sg. *bauglannen*, pt.3sg. *bauglant*, pt.ap. *baugliel*, pt.pp.sg. *bauglannen*, pt.pp.pl. *bauglennin*, fut.3sg. *bauglatha*.

Cuina- 'be alive'
inf. *cuino*, ger. *cuinad*, pr.1sg. *cuinon*, pr.3sg. *cuina*, pr.ap. *cuinol*, imp. *cuino*, pt.1sg. *cuinannen*, pt.3sg. *cuinant*, pt.ap. *cuiniel*, pt.pp.sg. *cuinannen*, pt.pp.pl. *cuinennin*, fut.3sg. *cuinatha*.

Naegra- 'cause pain'
inf. *naegro*, ger. *naegrad*, pr.1sg. *naegron*, pr.3sg. *naegra*, pr.ap. *naegrol*, imp. *naegro*, pt.1sg. *naegrannen*, pt.3sg. *naegrant*, pt.ap. *naegriel*, pt.pp.sg. *naegrannen*, pt.pp.pl. *naegrennin*, fut.3sg. *naegratha*.

Damma- 'hammer'
inf. *dammo*, ger. *dammad*, pr.1sg. *dammon*, pr.3sg. *damma*, pr.ap. *dammol*, imp. *dammo*, pt.1sg. *dammannen*, pt.3sg. *dammant*,

pt.ap. *demmiel*, pt.pp.sg. *dammannen*, pt.pp.pl. *demmennin*, fut.3sg. *dammatha*.

Irregular complex a-stems

Anna- 'give'
inf. *anno*, ger. *annad*, pr.1sg. *annon*, pr.3sg. *anna*, pr.ap. *annol*, imp. *anno*, pt.1sg. *onen*, pt.3sg. *aun*, pt.ap. *óniel*, pt.pp.sg. *onen*, pt.pp.pl. *onin*, fut.3sg. *annatha*.

Soga- 'drink'
inf. *sogo*, ger. *sogad*, pr.1sg. *sogon*, pr.3sg. *sôg*, pr.ap. *sogol*, imp. *sogo*, pt.1sg. *sungen* or *sogannen*, pt.3sg. *sunc* or *sogant*, pt.ap. *súgiel*, pt.pp.sg. *sungen* or *sogannen*, pt.pp.pl. *syngin* or *segennin*, fut.3sg. *sogatha*.

Verbs ending in -da

Boda- 'prohibit'
inf. *bodo*, ger. *bodad*, pr.1sg. *bodon*, pr.3sg. *boda*, pr.ap. *bodol*, imp. *bodo*, pt.1sg. *bodannen*, pt.3sg. *bodant*, pt.ap. *bódiel*, pt.pp.sg. *bodannen*, pt.pp.pl. *bodennin*, fut.3sg. *bodatha*.

Muda- 'labor'
inf. *mudo*, ger. *mudad*, pr.1sg. *mudon*, pr.3sg. *muda*, pr.ap. *mudol*, imp. *mudo*, pt.1sg. *mudassen*, pt.3sg. *mudas*, pt.ap. *múdiel*, pt.pp.sg. *mudassen*, pt.pp.pl. *mudessin*, fut.3sg. *mudatha*.

Verbs ending in -ia

Beria- 'protect'
inf. *berio*, ger. *beriad*, pr.1sg. *berion*, pr.3sg. *beria*, pr.ap. *beriol*, imp. *berio*, pt.1sg. *beriannen*, pt.3sg. *beriant*, pt.ap. *bóriel*, pt.pp.sg. *beriannen*, pt.pp.pl. *beriennin*, fut.3sg. *beriatha*.
Conjugated like *beria-* are *gleinia-* 'enclose', *henia-* 'understand', *pelia-* 'spread', *penia-* 'set', *renia-* 'stray', *seidia-* 'set aside', *telia-* or *teilia-* 'play'.

Brenia- 'endure'
inf. *brenio*, ger. *breniad*, pr.1sg. *brenion*, pr.3sg. *brenia*, pr.ap. *breniol*, imp. *brenio*, pt.1sg. *breniannen*, pt.3sg. *breniant*, pt.ap. *brúniel*, pt.pp.sg. *breniannen*, pt.pp.pl. *breniennin*, fut.3sg. *breniatha*.

Cuia- 'live'
inf. *cuio*, ger. *cuiad*, pr.1sg. *cuion*, pr.3sg. *cuia*, pr.ap. *cuiol*, imp. *cuio*, pt.1sg. *cuinen*, pt.3sg. *cuin*, pt.ap. *cuiel*, pt.pp.sg. *cuinen*, pt.pp.pl. *cuinin*, fut.3sg. *cuiatha*.
Conjugated like *cuia-* may be *tuia-* 'aprout'.

Delia- 'conceal' (irregular)
inf. *delio*, ger. *deliad*, pr.1sg. *delion*, pr.3sg. *delia*, pr.ap. *deliol*, imp. *delio*, pt.1sg. *dolen* or *deliannen*, pt.3sg. *daul* or *deliant*, pt.ap. *dúliel*, pt.pp.sg. *dolen*, pt.pp.pl. *dolin*, fut.3sg. *deliatha*.

Edledhia- 'go into exile'
inf. *edledhio*, ger. *edledhiad*, pr.1sg. *edledhion*, pr.3sg. *edledhia*, pr.ap. *edledhiol*, imp. *edledhio*, pt.1sg. *edledhiannen*, pt.3sg. *edledhiant*, pt.ap. *edlídhiel*, pt.pp.sg. *edledhiannen*, pt.pp.pl. *edledhiennin*, fut.3sg. *edledhiatha*.

Egleria- 'glorify'
inf. *eglerio*, ger. *egleriad*, pr.1sg. *eglerion*, pr.3sg. *egleria*, pr.ap. *egleriol*, imp. *eglerio*, pt.1sg. *egleriannen*, pt.3sg. *egleriant*, pt.ap. *aglóriel*, pt.pp.sg. *egleriannen*, pt.pp.pl. *egleriennin*, fut.3sg. *egleriatha*.

Elia- 'rain' (impersonal verb)
inf. *elio*, ger. *eliad*, pr.3sg. *ail*, pr.ap. *eliol*, imp. *elio*, pt.3sg. *eliant* or *aul*, pt.ap. *úliel*, pt.pp.sg. *eliannen* or *olen*, pt.pp.pl. *eliennin* or *olin*, fut.3sg. *eliatha*.

Eria- 'rise'
inf. *erio*, ger. *eriad*, pr.1sg. *erion*, pr.3sg. *eria*, pr.ap. *eriol*, imp. *erio*, pt.1sg. *eriannen*, pt.3sg. *eriant*, pt.ap. *úriel*, pt.pp.sg. *eriannen*, pt.pp.pl. *eriennin*, fut.3sg. *eriatha*.
Conjugated like *eria-* are *heria-* 'begin suddenly', and *nedia-* 'count'.

Genedia- 'reckon'
inf. *genedio*, ger. *genediad*, pr.1sg. *genedion*, pr.3sg. *genedia*, pr.ap. *genediol*, imp. *genedio*, pt.1sg. *genediannen*, pt.3sg. *genediant*, pt.ap. *gonúdiel*, pt.pp.sg. *genediannen*, pt.pp.pl. *genediennin*, fut.3sg. *genediatha*.

Gweria- 'betray'
inf. *gwerio*, ger. *gweriad*, pr.1sg. *gwerion*, pr.3sg. *gweria*, pr.ap. *gweriol*, imp. *gwerio*, pt.1sg. *gweriannen*, pt.3sg. *gweriant*, pt.ap. *góriel*, pt.pp.sg. *gweriannen*, pt.pp.pl. *gweriennin*, fut.3sg. *gweriatha*.

Luithia- 'quench'
inf. *luithio*, ger. *luithiad*, pr.1sg. *luithion*, pr.3sg. *luithia*, pr.ap. *luithiol*, imp. *luithio*, pt.1sg. *luithiannen*, pt.3sg. *luithiant*, pt.ap. *luithiel*, pt.pp.sg. *luithiannen*, pt.pp.pl. *luithiennin*, fut.3sg. *luithiatha*.

Siria- 'flow'
inf. *sirio*, ger. *siriad*, pr.1sg. *sirion*, pr.3sg. *siria*, pr.ap. *siriol*, imp. *sirio*, pt.1sg. *siriannen*, pt.3sg. *siriant*, pt.ap. *síriel*, pt.pp.sg. *siriannen*, pt.pp.pl. *siriennin*, fut.3sg. *siriatha*.
Conjugated like *siria-* are *dilia-* 'stop up', *hwinia-* 'twirl', *tiria-* 'watch', *thilia-* 'glister'.

Thia- 'seem'
inf. *thio*, ger. *thiad*, pr.1sg. *thion*, pr.3sg. *thia*, pr.ap. *thiol*, imp. *thio*, pt.1sg. *thiannen*, pt.3sg. *thiant*, pt.ap. *thiel*, pt.pp.sg. *thiannen*, pt.pp.pl. *thiennin*, fut.3sg. *thiatha*.

Thuia- 'breathe'
inf. *thuio*, ger. *thuiad*, pr.1sg. *thuion*, pr.3sg. *thuia*, pr.ap. *thuiol*, imp. *thuio*, pt.1sg. *thuiannen*, pt.3sg. *thuiant*, pt.ap. *thuiel*, pt.pp.sg. *thuiannen*, pt.pp.pl. *thuiennin*, fut.3sg. *thuiatha*.
Conjugated like *thuia-* are *buia-* 'serve', *fuia-* 'abhor', *puia* 'spit', and possibly *tuia-* 'sprout', though *tuia-* may also have been conjugated like *cuia-*.

Verbs ending in -nna

Danna- 'fall'
inf. *danno*, ger. *dannad*, pr.1sg. *dannon*, pr.3sg. *danna*, pr.ap. *dannol*, imp. *danno*, pt.1sg. *dannen*, pt.3sg. *dannant*, pt.ap. *denniel*, pt.pp.sg. *dannen*, pt.pp.pl. *dennin*, fut.3sg. *dannatha*.
Conjugated like *danna-* are *ganna-* 'play a harp', *glanna-*, 'make clear', *gwanna-* 'depart', *panna-* 'open' or 'fill', *suilanna-* 'greet'.

Linna- 'sing'
inf. *linno*, ger. *linnad*, pr.1sg. *linnon*, pr.3sg. *linna*, pr.ap. *linnol*, imp. *linno*, pt.1sg. *linnen*, pt.3sg. *linnant*, pt.ap. *linniel*, pt.pp.sg. *linnen*, pt.pp.pl. *linnin*, fut.3sg. *linnatha*.
Conjugated like *linna-* are *glinna-* 'glance at', *tinna-* 'glint', *thinna-* 'fade', and *minna-* 'enter'.

Onna- 'beget'
inf. *onno*, ger. *onnad*, pr.1sg. *onnon*, pr.3sg. *onna*, pr.ap. *onnol*,

imp. *onno*, pt.1sg. *onnen*, pt.3sg. *onnant*, pt.ap. *enniel*, pt.pp.sg. *onnen*, pt.pp.pl. *ennin*, fut.3sg. *onnatha*.
Conjugated like *onna-* is *edonna-* 'beget'.

Penna- 'slant down'
inf. *penno*, ger. *pennad*, pr.1sg. *pennon*, pr.3sg. *penna*, pr.ap. *pennol*, imp. *penno*, pt.1sg. *pennen*, pt.3sg. *pennant*, pt.ap.*penniel*, pt.pp.sg. *pennen*, pt.pp.pl. *pennin*, fut.3sg. *pennatha*.
Conjugated like *penna-* is *anglenna-* 'approach'.

Verbs ending in -sta

Esta- 'name'
inf. *esto*, ger. *estad*, pr.1sg. *eston*, pr.3sg. *esta*, pr.ap. *estol*, imp. *esto*, pt.1sg. *estannen*, pt.3sg. *estant*, pt.ap. *estiel*, pt.pp.sg. *estannen*, pt.pp.pl. *estennin*, fut.3sg. *estatha*.
Conjugated like *esta-* are *gwesta-* 'swear', *presta-* 'affect', *nesta-* 'heal'.

Gosta- fear exceedingly
inf. *gosto*, ger. *gostad*, pr.1sg. *goston*, pr.3sg. *gosta*, pr.ap. *gostol*, imp. *gosto*, pt.1sg. *gostannen*, pt.3sg. *gostant*, pt.ap. *gestiel*, pt.pp.sg. *gostannen*, pt.pp.pl. *gestennin*, fut.3sg. *gostatha*.
Conjugated like *gosta-* are *rosta-* 'hollow out' and *dosta-* 'burn'.

Ista- 'have knowledge'
inf. *isto*, ger. *istad*, pr.1sg. *iston*, pr.3sg. *ista*, pr.ap. *istol*, imp. *isto*, pt.1sg. *sinnen* or *istassen*, pt.3sg. *sint* or *istas*, pt.ap. *istiel*, pt.pp.sg. *sinnen*, pt.pp.pl. *sinnin*, fut.3sg. *istatha*.

Lasta- 'listen'
inf. *lasto*, ger. *lastad*, pr.1sg. *laston*, pr.3sg. *lasta*, pr.ap. *lastol*, imp. *lasto*, pt.1sg. *lastannen*, pt.3sg. *lastant*, pt.ap. *lestiel*, pt.pp.sg. *lastannen*, pt.pp.pl. *lestennin*, fut.3sg. *lastatha*.
Conjugated like *lasta-* are *hasta-* 'hack through', *nasta-* 'prick', *trasta-* 'harass'.

Mista- 'stray'
inf. *misto*, ger. *mistad*, pr.1sg. *miston*, pr.3sg. *mista*, pr.ap. *mistol*, imp. *misto*, pt.1sg. *mistannen*, pt.3sg. *mistant*, pt.ap. *mistiel*, pt.pp.sg. *mistannen*, pt.pp.pl. *mistennin*, fut.3sg. *mistatha*.
Conjugated like *mista-* is *rista-* 'rend'.

Verbs ending in -tha

Bertha- 'dare'
inf. *bertho*, ger. *berthad*, pr.1sg. *berthon*, pr.3sg. *bertha*, pr.ap. *berthol*, imp. *bertho*, pt.1sg. *berthannen*, pt.3sg. *berthant*, pt.ap. *berthiel*, pt.pp.sg. *berthannen*, pt.pp.pl. *berthennin*, fut.3sg. *berthatha*.
Conjugated like *bertha-* are *adertha-* 'reunite', *ertha-* 'unite', *heltha-* 'strip'.

Breitha- 'break out suddenly'
inf. *breitho*, ger. *breithad*, pr.1sg. *breithon*, pr.3sg. *breitha*, pr.ap. *breithol*, imp. *breitho*, pt.1sg. *breithannen*, pt.3sg. *breithant*, pt.ap. *breithiel*, pt.pp.sg. *breithannen*, pt.pp.pl. *breithennin*, fut.3sg. *breithatha*.
Conjugated like *breitha-* are *adleitha-* 'set free', *eitha-* 'stab', *leitha-* 'set free', *neitha-* 'deprive', *teitha-* 'draw'.

Critha- 'reap'
inf. *critho*, ger. *crithad*, pr.1sg. *crithon*, pr.3sg. *critha*, pr.ap. *crithol*, imp. *critho*, pt.1sg. *crithannen*, pt.3sg. *crithant*, pt.ap. *crithiel*, pt.pp.sg. *crithannen*, pt.pp.pl. *crithennin*, fut.3sg. *crithatha*.
Conjugated like *critha-* is *ritha-* 'jerk'.

Dartha- 'wait'
inf. *dartho*, ger. *darthad*, pr.1sg. *darthon*, pr.3sg. *dartha*, pr.ap. *darthol*, imp. *dartho*, pt.1sg. *darthannen*, pt.3sg. *darthant*, pt.ap. *derthiel*, pt.pp.sg. *darthannen*, pt.pp.pl. *derthennin*, fut.3sg. *darthatha*.
Conjugated like *dartha-* are *awartha-* 'forsake', *gartha-* 'defend', *gwatha-* 'stain', *haltha-* 'screen', *hartha-* 'hope', *nartha-* 'kindle', *partha-* 'arrange'.

Doltha- 'conceal' (irregular)
inf. *doltho*, ger. *dolthad*, pr.1sg. *dolthon*, pr.3sg. *doltha*, pr.ap. *dolthol*, imp. *doltho*, pt.1sg. *dolthannen* or *dolen*, pt.3sg. *dolthant* or *daul*, pt.ap. *delthiel*, pt.pp.sg. *dolthannen*, pt.pp.pl. *delthennin*, fut.3sg. *dolthatha*.

Dortha- 'dwell'
inf. *dortho*, ger. *dorthad*, pr.1sg. *dorthon*, pr.3sg. *dortha*, pr.ap. *dorthol*, imp. *dortho*, pt.1sg. *dorthannen*, pt.3sg. *dorthant*, pt.ap. *derthiel*, pt.pp.sg. *dorthannen*, pt.pp.pl. *derthennin*, fut.3sg. *dorthatha*.
Conjugated like *dortha-* are *hortha-* 'urge on', *ortha-* 'raise', *toltha-* 'fetch', *tortha-* 'wield'.

Gruitha- 'terrify'

inf. *gruitho*, ger. *gruithad*, pr.1sg. *gruithon*, pr.3sg. *gruitha*, pr.ap. *gruithol*, imp. *gruitho*, pt.1sg. *gruithannen*, pt.3sg. *gruithant*, pt.ap. *gruithiel*, pt.pp.sg. *gruithannen*, pt.pp.pl. *gruithennin*, fut.3sg. *gruithatha*.

Conjugated like *gruitha-* are *iuitha-* 'use', *luitha-* 'enchant', *nuitha-* 'stunt'.

Maetha- 'fight'

inf. *maetho*, ger. *maethad*, pr.1sg. *maethon*, pr.3sg. *maetha*, pr.ap. *maethol*, imp. *maetho*, pt.1sg. *maethannen*, pt.3sg. *maethant*, pt.ap. *maethiel*, pt.pp.sg. *maethannen*, pt.pp.pl. *maethennin*, fut.3sg. *maethatha*.

Conjugated like *maetha-* is *taetha-* 'fasten'.

Nautha- 'conceive'

inf. *nautho*, ger. *nauthad*, pr.1sg. *nauthon*, pr.3sg. *nautha*, pr.ap. *nauthol*, imp. *nautho*, pt.1sg. *nauthannen*, pt.3sg. *nauthant*, pt.ap. *nauthiel*, pt.pp.sg. *nauthannen*, pt.pp.pl. *nauthennin*, fut.3sg. *nauthatha*.

Conjugated like *nautha-* is *sautha-* 'drain'.

10

Adverbs, Prefixes, and Prepositions

Adverbs show the relationship of a verb to the rest of the sentence, and prepositions show the relationship of one object or event to another object (e.g., where they stand in spatial or temporal relationship). In Sindarin the two parts of speech can be difficult to distinguish because the same words are often used for both. Early in the history of the Elvish languages many adverbs became commonly used as prefixes to verbs. Many of these elements are attested, but it is likely that even more remain unknown. This chapter provides a list of all known adverbs, prefixes, and prepositions.

ab 'after, behind, following, later' (pref.) [OS **ap*, **apa*] +soft or stop mutation. Used as a prefix with verb forms: *aphada-* (*ab* + *pada-*) 'follow after', *abonnen* (*ab* + *onnen*) 'born after'.

ad 'against' (prep.) 'back, again, re-' (adv.) [OS **at*] + consonant mutation. This preposition comes from the Eldarin root √AT 'two' and originally referred to an action done a second time, particularly an action (beneficial or harmful) done in return for another action. As such, it became closely related in meaning to *dan*.

> *naur ad i ngaurhoth* 'fire against the wargs'
> *aderthad* (*ad* + *erthad*) 'reuniting' (uniting for a second time)
> *aduial* (*ad* + *uial*) 'second twilight'

adel 'behind, in the rear (of)' (prep., adv.) [OS **atele*] + soft mutation; *adel* is derived from the Eldarin √TEL 'be at the end'.

al 'not' (pref.) [OS **al*] + liquid mutation. The prefix *al* is used to negate the meaning of a following noun or adjective. From √LA, reduced simply to **l̥* as a prefix, later expanded again to *al*. Similar in meaning to *ar*, *pen*, and *ú*.

> *alfirin* (*al* + *firin*) 'not mortal, immortal'
> *alchoron* (*al* + *coron*) 'not from Kôr' (an older name for Túna, the hill on which the Noldorin town of Tirion was built)

am 'up, above, over, high' (adv., adj. pref., prep.) [OS **amba*] + soft mutation. As a prefix, *am* indicated that something was in a high place or was moving up toward a high place:

> *ambenn* (*am* + *pend*) 'up-slope, uphill'
> *amdir* (*am* + *tir*) 'looking (tir) up, hope'
> *amloth* (*am* + *loth*) 'high flower, crest'
> *amrûn* (*am* + *rhûn*) 'rising up, sunrise'

As a preposition, *am* meant 'upon, in (a high place)':

> *bair am yrn* 'dwellings upon (the) trees'

Its meaning thus approached that of *or*. It was also a common prefix in names. Opposite of *dad*.

an 'for, to' (prep.); 'for, to, very' (pref.) [OS **an*] + nasal mutation. This was one of the most common words and had a wide range of meanings. It originally came from a √ANA, which indicated, in general, movement in a direction away from the speaker, toward something else. But in Sindarin this meaning had been largely lost, replaced by figurative meanings; *an* could be used of something, good or bad, that one wished to give or bestow on someone else:

> *gurth an glamhoth* 'death to the orcs'
> *aglar (a)ni Pheriannath* 'glory to the Halflings'
> *suilad a Pherhael* (*an* + *Perhael*) 'greeting to Samwise'
> *naur an edraith* 'fire for saving'

Or of an action that might benefit or harm one:

> *edro ammen* (*an* + *men*) 'open for us'
> *hebin estel anim* (*an* + *im*) 'I kept hope for myself'

As a prefix, *an-* could be used with verbs to indicate that they had some particular object or direction:

> *aníra-* (*an* + *íra-*) 'desire, have desire for', as opposed to **íra*, which might simply mean 'have desire'
> *anglenna-* (*an* + *glenna-*) 'go toward, approach', as opposed to **glenna*, which might simply mean 'go, move'

Before adjectives, *an-* might convert the adjective into an adverb: *anann* (*an* + *and*) 'long, for a long time' from the adjective *and* 'long'. Or it could intensify the meaning of the adjective: *apharch* (OS *$app^{h}ark^{h}a$ [*an* +

parch]) 'very dry' from the adjective *parch* 'dry'; *einior* (OS **anjǭra* [*an* + *iaur*]) 'elder, very old' from the adjective *iaur* 'old'.

With attached article the form *nin* (for *anin* or *enin*) is found.

anann 'long, for a long time' (adv.) [OS **an-anda*]. An adverbialized form of the adjective *and* 'long'. See *an*.

ar 'without, not' (pref.) [OS **ar*] + liquid mutation. This prefix was commonly used before nouns; it changed them into adjectives, indicating that what the noun signified was lacking in the thing modified. See, e.g., *arnediad* 'without counting' (*ar* + *nediad*). It originally meant 'outside, beside', but with the change in meaning came close to *al*, *pen*, and *ú*.

ath 'on both sides, across' (pref.) [OS **at^{h}ar or *att^{h}a?*] + soft mutation. Although thought by some to be related to √AT 'two', this prefix may be only a reduced form of *athar* or *athra*. Cf. also *thar*.

> *athrada-* (*ath* + *rada*) 'cross, traverse'
> *athrad* (*ath* + *râd*) 'cross-path', or so it is sometimes interpreted; but it may be a nominal form of a verb *athra-* (from √THAR) 'cross'.

athar 'beyond, across' (prep.) [OS **at^{h}ara*, **at^{h}ra*] + liquid mutation. From a √THAR meaning 'crossing, going over' (e.g., as a bridge). Also used figuratively to refer to something excessive or beyond normal measure in some way: *athar harthad* 'beyond hope'. Cf. *ath*, *athra*, *thar*.

athr-, *athra-* 'across' (pref.). A form of *athar*, used as a prefix. Related to the word *athrad* 'ford', literally 'crossing'; used metaphorically, as in *athrabeth* (*athra* + *peth*) 'speech that goes across', i.e., back and forth in opposition between two people; used of a debate (not necessarily an unfriendly one).

avo 'don't' (adv.) [OS *abǭ*], *av-* 'don't' (pref.) [OS **aba*] + soft mutation. Used before negative imperative verbs. From a √AB 'refuse'.

be 'according to' (prep.) [OS **be*] + soft mutation. Perhaps related to the Quenya preposition and suffix *ve* 'like, as'; the basic meaning may be "in the manner of." The form *ben* shows attached article. It may also be used as an adverbial suffix, in which case it takes the form *-f*: *ben genediad* 'according to the reckoning'.

dad 'down' (adv., pref.) [OS **data*] + soft mutation. Indicates direction of motion. From a √DAT 'fall down'. Similar to *nu*. Opposite of *am*: *dadbenn* 'downhill'.

dan 'against' (prep.), *re-*, *counter-* (pref.) [OS **ñd an*] + nasal mutation. Refers to an action done in return for another action, or reversed, and so similar in meaning to *ad*. The opposite of *an*.

naur dan i ngaurhoth 'fire against the wargs'
danwedh (*dan* + *gwedh*) 'ransom', a pledge or bond (*gwêdh*) given in return for something else
dangweth (*dan* + **gweth*) 'answer', an account given in response to a question

dî[1] 'beneath, under' (prep.) [OS *ñdi*] + soft mutation: *di nguruthos* 'beneath horror of death'. Also has the meaning 'in', perhaps in the sense 'submerged under'. Another preposition with the meaning 'under' is *nu*.

ed, *e*, 'from, out from, out of' (prep.); 'out, away, forth' (pref.) [OS **et*] + stop mutation. Cognate to the Quenya preposition *et*. As a prefix *et-* can indicate action going away from the speaker or his or her thought into another place:

ethir (*ed* + *sîr*) 'outflow, river mouth, where the river flows into the ocean'
ethir (*ed* + *tir*) 'lookout, spy, one who looks into other places'
edledhi (*ed* + **ledhi*) 'to go into exile'
echil (*ed* + *hîl*) 'follower' (going into a new place)

Action that changes something from one state to another:

echui (*ed* + **cui*) 'awakening' (changing from a state of sleep to wakefulness)
echuir (*ed* + **cuir*) 'stirring, coming to life' (changing from death to life)
edonna- (*ed* + *onna-*) 'to beget' (causing a new state)
echedi (*ed* + **cedi*) 'to make, to fashion' (creating a new thing)

Placement on an edge or border, outside some center:

echor (*ed* + **côr*) 'outer circle'
edrain (*ed* + *rain*) 'border'
ephel (*ed* + *pêlouter*) 'fence'

As a preposition, *ed* appears as *e* before most consonants, but as *es*, *ef*, *eth* before *s-*, *f-*, and *th-*.

edregol 'especially, in especial' (adv.) [OS **etrekla*]. Of uncertain origin. Perhaps related to the noun *edraith* 'saving'; in English, *save* as preposition or conjunction means 'except', referring to things or actions that are saved from consideration; but perhaps it could equally well be used for things or actions that are saved *for* special consideration.

en, *e*: see § 12.4. The article.

erin: see *or*.

far 'sufficient, enough, quite' (adv.) [OS **p^{h}ar or *p^{h}ara*]. From a √PHAR 'suffice'.

go, *gwa*- 'together' (pref.) [OS **wo*, *wa*] + soft mutation. Used to indicate motion moving from several places toward a single point or involving more than one person; also to indicate groups or accumulations of things or a special relationship expressed by the word. The word *go* or *gwa* could possibly be used as a comitative preposition meaning 'together with' (as opposed to *ar*), but no example of this use is known.

> *govad*- [*go* + *bad*-] 'meets together'
> *gowest* [*go* + *gwest*] 'contract' (between two people together)
> *gonod* [*go* + *nod*-] 'counts up' (accumulates)
> *golas* [*go* + *las*] 'foliage, collection of leaves'
> *gwaloth* [*gwa* + *loth*] 'collection of flowers'
> *gwanun* [*gwa* + **nûn*] 'pair of twins'

godref 'through together' (adv.) [OS **wotrebe*]. A form of an adverb **tref* 'through', which combines the prepositional prefix *tre*- (see *trî*) and the adverbial suffix *-f* (see *be*). It indicates motion through an opening by a number of people: *neledh neledhi gar godref* 'three can walk in through together'.

him 'continually' (adv.) [OS **k^{h}imbė*]. From a √KHIM 'stick' 'adhere', from which the meanings 'abide', 'continue' are derived: *himring* (*him* + *ring*) 'continually cold'.

io, *ia* 'formerly, ago' (adv.) [OS **jǭ*, *ja*]. From a √JA; related to *iaur* 'old'.

im 'between, in' (prep.) [OS *imbė] + mixed mutation. Cognate to Q *imbe*. This prefix probably comes from a √MI with an early variant √(I)MBI, indicating existence inside something that surrounded one at least on two sides. From this came the meanings 'in' (in the sense 'inside') and 'between'. Cf. *mi*; the preposition is also close in sense to *ned*: *im duinath* 'between the rivers'.

mae 'well' (adv.) [OS **mai*]. May be related to Q *maia* 'beautiful'.

mi 'between' (prep.) [OS **mi*] + soft mutation. Close in meaning to *im* and possibly of the same origin. This preposition is found with attached article as *min*. It is possible that *mi* does not actually exist but that the combination of *im* and the article *-in*, *!imin*, was reduced by aphaeresis to *min*: *minhiriath* 'between the rivers'; cf. *an* + *in* > *!enin* > *'nin in aglar 'ni Pheriannath* 'glory to the Halflings'.

min 'in' (prep.) [OS **min*] + nasal mutation. Usually lenited as *vi(n)*. Related to Q *mi*. Also related to the verb *minna-* 'go in, enter'. Cf. *mi* and *ned*: *vi menel* 'in heaven'.

na 'to, toward, at; of; with, by' (prep.) [OS **na*] + soft mutation. This preposition is of the same origin as *an* and must at one time have had the same meaning; indeed, there is still some overlap between the two in Sindarin, where it has four primary uses:

1. It acts as an allative, indicating the direction toward which an action tends (e.g., *tíriel na chaered* 'looking into the distance');
2. It marks the locative, indicating the place or time of an action (e.g., *na vedui* 'at [the] last [time]');
3. It can be used as a marker of the genitive; this meaning probably derives from the previous one, as the sense of 'belonging to' or 'characterized by' can be deduced from 'at, near, in the close presence of' (e.g., *mîr na Ardhon* 'world's jewel', *orod na thôn* 'mountain of pine (trees)', *taur na chardhîn* 'forest of southern silence');
4. It can also mark the instrumental, indicating the means by which something is done; this is probably also derived from the sense 'close to', and so 'in or by the hands of'.

With attached article its form may have been *nin* (pl.). The name *Sarch nia Chîn Húrin* 'Grave of the Children of Húrin' is perhaps derived from ?*Sarch ni Chîn Húrin*. But this may be identical to the forms mentioned under *an*. In older names a form *nan* with attached article is also found: *Taur nan-Erig* 'Forest of Hollies'. Before words beginning with vowels (especially *a-*) it may be elided to *n*: *mîr na Ardhon* > *mîr n'Ardhon*.

ne 'in' (pref.) [OS **ne*]. Implies motion into the middle of something:

nestegi (*ne* + *stag-*) 'insert, stick in' (i.e., into the midst of something)
neledhi (*ne* + *ledhi*) 'go into, enter'

ned 'in, of (time)' (prep.); [OS **ned*] + stop mutation. This element derives from the √NED, from which also is derived Sindarin *enedh* 'middle'. Its original meaning appears to have been 'in the middle, amidst', and so 'in'. Cf. *im*, *mi*.

ned Echuir 'in (the season of) Echuir'

nef, *nev-* 'here, on this side of' (prep.); 'near' (pref.). Of unknown origin. Opposed to *hae* 'far, distant'.

nef aear 'on this side of the ocean'
nevrast (*nef* + *rast*) 'near shore'

ni, *nia*: see *an*, *na*.

nu 'under' (prep.) + soft mutation [OS **nu*]. From a √NU, an early variant of √NDU 'go down, sink down' (from which come such words as *dûn* 'sunset, west'); that which has gone down is under. With attached article it appears as *nuin*. Similar to *dad*, *di*. Opposite of *or*.

Taur nu-Fuin 'forest under night-shade'
Dagor nuin Giliath (or *Dagor nui Ngiliath*) 'battle under the stars'

o[1], *od* 'from, of' (prep.) [OS **aud*] + stop mutation. From a derivative of a √AWA 'away from', with a suffix *-d(a)* meaning 'to', and so meaning 'to another place away from here'. In Sindarin, however, it had come to mean 'from' in the sense of motion either from or away to another place or even generically indicating origin (in which sense it can be translated 'of'). The form *od* is used when the second word begins with *o-*. With attached article it takes the form *uin*:

Motion from away to here:

aglar penna o menel 'glory falls from heaven'
suilad o Minas Tirith 'greeting from Minas Tirith'
suilad uin aran 'greeting from the king'

Motion from here to away:

tíriel o ennorath 'looking from the middle-lands'

General origin:

edhil o Imladris 'Elves of (or from) Imladris'
Celebrimbor o Eregion 'Celebrimbor of Eregion'

o[2] 'about, concerning' (prep.); *os-* 'around' (pref.) [OS **o*, **oh*]. From a √OS 'around'; that which goes around something is necessarily 'concerned' with it (cf. the two meanings of English *about*). When preceding a word beginning with a vowel, the second word began with *h*:

o hedhil 'about Elves'
oscar (*o* + **scar-*) 'cuts around'

or 'above, over, on' (in space or time) (prep.); 'above, over, high' [OS **or*] + liquid mutation. From a √ORO 'go up, rise'; the opposite of *nu*. That which rises is above other things; what is above something may be on it, and *or* may be used as a locative in time as well as space. Related to the verb *ortha-* 'raise'. Appears as *erin* with suffixed article. Cf. *am*.

erin dolothen Ethuil 'on the eighth of spring'
erin gwirith edwen 'on the second of Gwirith'
orchall (*or* + *hall*) 'eminent, superior, tall' (literally 'overtall')
orfalch 'high ravine'
ortheri (*or* + *tor-*) 'to conquer, to gain mastery over'
ortheli (*or* + *tel-*) 'to roof over'

palan 'far off, over a wide area' (pref.) [Q *palan*]. Used for an action directed to a distance: *palan-diri* 'to look to a great distance'.

pen 'without, lacking, -less' [OS **pen*] + nasal mutation. From a √PEN 'lack'. *al*, *ar*, and *ú* have similar meanings: *pen adar* 'without a father'.

po 'on' [OS **pǭ*] + soft mutation. Usually lenited as *bo*: *bo Geven* 'on earth'.

sennui 'instead, rather' (adv.). Of uncertain origin.

sui 'like, as' (prep.) [OS **siui*]. From CE **sībe* 'like this', combining the pronoun *si* with the preposition *be*, followed by the relative pronoun *i*; OS *siw* + *i* became OS *siui*, Sindarin *sui*: *sui mín* 'like us'.

trî 'through' (prep.) [OS **trī*] *tre-* 'completely, utterly, all the way through' (pref.) [OS **tre-*] + soft mutation. From a √TER 'through'. Cognate to Q *ter*.

trenar (*tre* + *nar*) 'tells the tale through'
trevad (*tre* + *bad*) 'walks through, traverses'

thar 'across, beyond, on the other side' (pref.) [OS **t^{h}ar*] + liquid mutation. Related to *athar*, *ath*, *athra*: *Thar-gelion* 'on the other side of Gelion'.

ú, *u* 'not, without' (adverb, pref.) [OS **ū*] + soft mutation. Reverses or indicates a lack in the meaning of a noun, verb, or adjective, often in a negative sense. Similar in meaning to *al*, *ar*, *pen*.

ú chebin 'I did not keep'
úmarth 'ill-fate'
ubed (*ú* + *pêd*) 'saying no, denial'
úgerth 'misdeed'
udalraph (*ú* + *talraph*) 'without a stirrup'
úthaes 'temptation'

ui 'ever, eternal' (adv., adj.) [OS **ui(o)*]: *uilos* (*ui* + *los*) 'eternal flower'; *uin*: see *o*[1].

11

Conjunctions

Only a few conjunctions are known to exist in Sindarin.

A, *ah*, *ar* 'and, also' [OS **ah*]
The conjunction *a* is used to join two words or phrases. Before another word beginning with *a*-, it takes the form *ah* (e.g., *ah Andreth* 'and Andreth'). This indicates that at one time the conjunction may have had the alternative form **as*, which in Sindarin became *ah*.[1]

Dan 'but, on the other hand' (?)[OS **n̄dan*]
No Sindarin example of the word for *but* is available. However, in Quenya the word used is *nan*, cognate to the Sindarin preposition and prefix *dan*; it is possible that this word may also be used as a conjunction.

Egor 'or, otherwise'
This word is of uncertain origin. It is used to disjoin two words or phrases: *erin dolothen Ethuil . . . egor erin Gwirith edwen* 'on the eighth of Tuilë . . . or on the second of Víressë'.

Sui 'like, as' [OS **sībe i*]
This conjunction joins two phrases expressing things or states that are similar to each other: *bo Geven sui vi Menel* 'as in heaven'

1. The form *ar* 'and' is also found. Although this has not been emended in any of the texts cited in this book, it is clear that Tolkien intended to generally replace *ar* with *a(h)*. The change appears to have taken place in the early 1950s, prior to publication of *The Lord of the Rings*. Neither *a* nor *ar* is followed by any form of consonant mutation, as can be seen in the examples *a galadh*, *a minno*, *ar Meril*, *ar diheno*. In *a Berhael*, *Perhael* is lenited as a direct object, not because of the presence of a preceding conjunction.

12

The Article

§ 12.1. Overview

Sindarin has no indefinite article; common nouns are assumed to be indefinite if there is no article.

The Sindarin definite article *the* is inflected for both number and case; that is, it changes form according to whether it precedes a singular or plural noun and according to whether the noun is the subject or object of the sentence (nominative/accusative), a premodifier of another noun (genitive), or the object of a preposition (prepositional). Before collective nouns the article is usually plural but may be singular.

§ 12.2. Forms of the article

The various forms the article takes may be summarized as follows:

CASE	SINGULAR	PLURAL
Nominative/Accusative	*i* + soft mutation	*in* + nasal mutation
Genitive	*en* + mixed mutation	*in* + nasal mutation
Prepositional	*in* + mixed mutation	*in* + nasal mutation

§ 12.3. Singular nominative/accusative article

The singular article accompanying subject and object nouns in a sentence is *i*. This article always precedes the word it accompanies, and it takes the soft mutation (see § 5.1). It may take the form *ir* when it precedes a word beginning with *i-*: *ir ithil* 'the moon'.

§ 12.4 Singular genitive article

When a definite singular noun modifies another noun as a genitive, the article of the modifying word takes the form *e* or *en* and is followed by the mixed mutation (see § 5.5):

en Andrath 'of the Long Climb'
en·aras 'of the deer'
e·mbar 'of the home'
e·dant 'of the fall'
e·dinúviel 'of the nightingale'
en·êl 'of the star'
en ernil 'of the prince'
en·glad 'of the wood'
e·'rach 'of the curse'
en annûn 'of the west'
en·arwen 'of the noble woman'
e·ndaedhelos 'of the great fear'
en·danwedh 'of the ransom'
en Echoriath 'of the Echoriath'
en·elleth 'of the Elf-woman'
en·faroth 'of the hunters' (collectively)
en·nírnaeth 'of lamentation'

This genitive form *en* of the article probably comes from the sequence *i* + *na* > **ina* > *en*, which combines the article *i* and the genitive preposition *na* (see *na*, chapter 10).

§ 12.5. Singular prepositional article

The prepositional article *in* takes the mixed mutation. It is usually combined with a preceding preposition, retaining the form *-in* after consonants and the vowels *o* (which becomes *u*) and *u*, but reduced to *-n* after the vowels *a*, *e*, and *i*.

PREPOSITION	PREPOSITION WITH ARTICLE	
be	*ben*	'as the'
o	*uin*	'from the' (note change from **oin*)
or	*erin*	'on the'
mi	*min*	'between the'

It is also possible for the article to follow the preposition without change, in which case it appears to take the soft mutation: *dan i ngaurhoth* 'against the wargs'.

§ 12.6. Plural article

The plural article for all cases is *in*; it also precedes the word it accompanies and takes the nasal mutation (see § 5.2); when it precedes a consonant it is reduced to *i* but can usually still be distinguished from the singular article by the nasal mutation.

§ 12.7. Examples

NOMINATIVE/ACCUSATIVE

Singular	Plural
i·êl 'the star'	*in·elin* 'the stars'
i·berian 'the halfling'	*i·pheriain* 'the halflings'
i·gerth 'the rune'	*i·chirth* 'the runes'
i·valan 'the Vala'	*i·melain* 'the Valar'
i·ngaur 'the werewolf'	*in·goer*, *in·gaurhoth* 'the werewolves'

GENITIVE

Singular	Plural
en·adan 'of the human'	*in·edain*, *in·adanath* 'of the humans'
en·adanadar 'of the father of the Edain'	*in·edenedair* 'of the fathers of the Edain'
en·alph 'of the swan'	*in·eilph* 'of the swans'
en·arwen 'of the noblewoman'	*in erwin*, *in arwenath* 'of the noblewomen'
e·mbar 'of the dwelling'	*i·mbair* 'of the dwellings'
e·belegorn 'of the great tree'	*i·melegyrn* 'of the great trees'
e·ndangen 'of the slain one'	*i·ndengin* 'of the slain ones'
en·drúadan 'of the Drû'	*in·drúedain* 'of the Drû-folk'
en·edhel 'of the Elf'	*in·edhil* 'of the Elves'
en·elleth 'of the Elf-woman'	*in·ellith* 'of the Elf-women'
en·golodh 'of the Noldo'	*in·gelydh* 'of the Noldor'
e·gwael 'of the gull'	*in·gwael* 'of the gulls'
e·chên 'of the child'	*i·chîn* 'of the children'
e·las 'of the leaf'	*i·lais* 'of the leaves'
e·mírdan 'of the jewel maker'	*i·mírdain* 'of the jewel makers'
e·mŷl 'of the gull'	*i·mŷl* 'of the gulls'
en·naug 'of the Dwarf'	*i·noeg*, *i·naugrim* 'of the Dwarves'
en·nogoth 'of the Dwarf'	*i·negyth* 'of the Dwarves'
e·beredhel 'of the half-Elf'	*i·pheredhil* 'of the half-Elves'
e·berian 'of the halfling'	*i·pheriain*, *i·pheriannath* 'of the halflings'
e·sadron 'of the faithful one'	*i·sedryn* 'of the faithful ones'
e·dêw 'of the letter'	*i·thiw* 'of the letters'

§ 12.8. The article with collective plurals

Either the singular or the plural article can be used with collective plural nouns.

Singular article: *i·elenath* 'the stars'; *i·gerthas* 'the Runes' (as a group); *i·Wenyn* 'the twins'; *i·ngaurhoth* 'the wolves'; *i·Hendrim* 'the Sindar'.

Plural article: *in·elenath* 'the stars'; *i·pheriannath* 'the Halflings' (as a group); *in·Gwanur* 'the twins'; *in·gaurhoth* 'the wolves'; *in·adanath* 'the Edain' (as a group).

§ 12.9. Plural prepositional article

Like the singular prepositional article, the plural article usually merges with the preceding preposition. Like other plural articles it takes the nasal mutation, but in some cases, perhaps because of association with the singular forms, it is seen taking the mixed mutation:

an	*(a)nin*	*'ni Pheriannath* 'for the halflings'
na	*nan*	*nan erig* 'of the hollies/to the hollies'
nu	*nuin*	*nuin giliath* 'under the stars'

13

Interjections

Sindarin uses four interjections:

A! 'O!' [OS **a*]
This word is used in direct address, immediately preceding the name or title of a person addressed (without lenition).

Alae! 'Ah!' [OS **alaia*]
This word is used when experiencing some deep emotion.

Elo! 'Oh!' or 'Wow!' [OS **el' ǭ*]
An exclamation of wonder, admiration, or delight

Nae! 'Alas!' [OS **nai*]
An exclamation of sadness.

14

Word Formation

§ 14.1. Roots

Relationships between words in Sindarin and the other Eldarin languages can be described in terms of modifications to a short sequence of sounds known as a root. It is possible (although not demonstrable) that some or all of these roots existed at one time as independent words and that the later Eldarin vocabularies developed from the addition of prefixes, suffixes, infixed sounds, or changes in the stress or pitch of these root vowels. It is also possible that many of the roots are purely abstract and have rarely existed independently.

In the earliest (Primitive Quendian) stage of the Elvish languages there was a great deal of variation in the forms of the roots according to rules that cannot now be inferred with any certainty. There exist, for example, a number of roots with the form Velar Consonant-Vowel-L, all referring to light of various kinds: √KAL 'light', √KUL 'golden-red light', √ŋAL 'reflected light', √ŋIL 'glinting silver light'. No guess, however, can be made regarding what original sound sequence these roots derive from or by what sequence of sound changes they assumed their later form. There are also sequences of the same type (e.g., √ŋGOL 'wise') that are evidently unrelated. Hints as to possible relationships of this type are suggested in the list of roots. All roots are cited in a form based on the sounds of Common Eldarin, a later stage of the language.

The most primitive roots appear to have the structures C(onsonant) V(owel), VC, and CVC (the last two can be represented together as [C]VC). In several cases there are roots of a CV structure that are clearly related to roots of a VC structure, sharing the same consonant and vowel, and having related meanings. For instance, √AW and √WA, and √OR and √RO. In such instances it is convenient to describe the root as VCV—e.g., √AWA and √ORO—and to regard the CV form of the root as resulting from the omission of an initial vowel (something that occurs in a number of other cases of V-initial roots).

Another archaic relationship, also somewhat obscure, is that between roots beginning with nasals and those with nasalized stops; e.g., the root √NER (only found in Quenya) 'manly, courageous' and √NDER 'man, male person'; √NU 'under' and √NDU 'go down'; √MI 'in' and √IMBI 'between'.

Later, but still prehistoric, variations in root structure are somewhat more transparent. A very common form of derivation from a CV or (C)VC root is by addition of another consonant. This consonant follows the V of a CV root directly (producing the structure CV-C); e.g., √KWE produces the derived root √KWE-N. After a (C)VC root the consonant follows a vowel with the same value as the primary root vowel, producing the structure (C)VC-VC; e.g., from √BEL 'strong' is derived the root √BEL-EK 'mighty', or from √OR 'go up' is derived √OR-OT 'mountain'. The only root consonants known to be used in this way are D, G, H, K, N, R, S, and T; and in (C)VC-VC roots they follow the consonants J, L, N, P, R, S, T, W.

There are also a number of (C)VCVC roots that cannot be attributed to a (C)VC root. Some of these may be primitive; others may derive from (C)VC roots that no longer exist independently. There are also a few roots that must be described as (C)VCC (e.g., √AJW, √LAJK, √RAWT, √STINT, √TIŋK, √WAJW) although some of these may also be derived from (C)VC or (C)VCVC roots.

Roots were also derived by prefixation, of which vocalic and consonantal prefixes can be distinguished; both occurred only with CVC roots.

Vocalic prefixation was invariably a repetition of the root vowel before the initial consonant or consonant cluster, producing the structure V-CVC(VC): e.g., √A-SKAR, √E-LED, √I-THIL, √O-KOTH, √U-RUK, √A-TALAT.

Consonantal prefixation normally occurred before L and R, and the consonants prefixed were S and G: √S-LOK, √G-LAM, √S-ROT, √G-RUK.

A root could be derived by both prefixation and suffixation: e.g., √A-KAL-AR, √S-RUS-UK.

Another type of prefixation is better described as an alteration between initial nasalized stops and nonnasal voiced stops, a change that is quite independent of similar changes in the Eldarin languages of much later date; e.g., the roots √DAJ and √N-DAJ (both 'great'); √DOL and (Quenya) √N-DOL 'head'; √BEL-EK and Quenya √M-BEL-EK 'mighty'.

NOUNS

§ 14.2. Simple nouns

The largest class of nouns in Common Eldarin was formed by suffixing a vowel (short or long *-a*, *-e*, *-i*, *-o*, or *-u*) to a root. These vowels must often have imparted distinctions of meaning to the root, but it is no longer possible to say with certainty what those were. Only a few very broad generalizations can be made.

The finals *-e* and *-i* were commonly used for the names of female persons and also for abstract nouns referring to verbal actions or events; the finals *-o* and *-u* were often used for the names of males and for persons or agents irrespective of sex; the final *-a* was often used for nouns derived from adjectives or for nouns referring to concrete inanimate objects.

In Sindarin these final vowels were lost, reducing the words to the root itself, with such phonetic changes as it had undergone in Sindarin. It is not always possible to reconstruct the final vowel of such words or to distinguish them from the smaller class of nouns that had no vocalic suffix in Common Eldarin. These two classes, which may be called "simple nouns," are here discussed together.

CVC roots, with or without suffixed vowels, might take normal, long, or strong ablaut (see § 5.11). In Classical Sindarin, vowels in monosyllables with normal ablaut were lengthened when preceding a voiced final consonant; vowels with long or strong ablaut were already long or had become diphthongs. (Examples given below are not necessarily exhaustive, but have been chosen in order to exhibit some of the range of variation in formation of Sindarin words.)

CVC nouns take normal, long, or strong ablaut:

Normal ablaut

gwath √GWATH 'shade', *tâl* √TAL 'foot', *hên* √KHIN 'child', *fîn* √PHIN 'hair', *iôn* √JON 'son', *gûr* √ŋGUR 'death', *fae* √PHAJ 'spirit', *rhaw* √SRAW 'flesh', *naw* √NOW 'idea', *iâ* √JAG 'chasm', *tê* √TEH 'line', *glî* √G-LIS 'honey', *lô* √LOG 'shallow lake', *cû* √KUH 'bow'.

The diphthongs *ae* and *aw* arise from the combination of a vowel with a following J or W in the root; nouns without final consonants arose from the loss of a final G, H, or S.

Long ablaut

These nouns always contain the vowels or diphthongs *au* (*aw*), *î*, *oe*, or *û*: *daur* √DAR 'league', *hîr* √KHER 'master', *rhîw* √SRIW 'winter', *lhûg* √SLOK 'dragon', *tûr* √TUR 'victory', *goe* √GAJ 'terror'.

Strong ablaut

These nouns always contain the diphthongs *ae* or *au*: *cae* √KEM 'earth', *glaer* √LIR 'lay', *maur* √MOR 'gloom', *raug* √RUK 'demon'.

In one instance there was an early syncope of the root vowel, and the stress fell on the final vowel, which was long and remained so throughout Sindarin: *glaw* [OS **ŋglǭ*] √ŋAL 'radiance'.

(C)VCC roots

These roots, few in number, almost always occurred in simple nouns: *aew* √AJW 'bird', *ang* √AŋG 'iron', *cund* √KUND 'prince', *raud* √RAWT 'metal'.

(C)VCVC roots

These roots could occur without syncope or with syncope (omission) of the ultimate or penultimate vowel of the root. The syncopated vowel normally corresponded to the vowel not stressed in the root, but it is not possible to predict from the form of the root whether a noun will show syncope or not.

The following roots occurred without syncope: *adan* √AT2-AN 'man', *celeb* √KJELEP 'silver', *ithil* √I-THÍL 'moon', *golodh* √ŋGOL-OD 'Noldo', *urug* √Ú-RUK 'bogey'.

In many of these roots it is possible to tell if the original word ended in a consonant, since the final syllable was lost in the singular but preserved in the plural: *nêl*, pl. *nelig* √NÉL2-EK 'tooth', *ôr*, pl. *eryd* √ÓR-OT 'mountain'.

Some of these roots showed long ablaut in a stressed syllable (when final): *anor* √A-NÁR 'sun', earlier *anaur*.

Some roots underwent syncope of the penultimate vowel: *brôg* √MORÓK 'bear', *glas* √GAL-ÁS 'joy'. Some of these roots showed long ablaut in the surviving vowel: *draug* √DARÁK 'wolf'.

Some roots underwent syncope of the ultimate vowel: *anc* √Á-NAK 'jaw', *auth* √Ó-KOTH 'war, battle', *cerch* √KÍR-IK 'sickle', *salph* √SALAP 'soup'.

VCVCVC roots

These roots always showed either syncope of the ultimate vowel (e.g., *amarth* √A-MBÁRAT 'fate, doom') or penultimate vowel (e.g., *aglar* √A-KAL-ÁR 'brilliance, glory').

§ 14.3. Nasalized nouns

Many nouns derived from roots ending in the stops B, D, G, K, KH, P, and T, and rarely J and W, inserted a nasal sound (or nasalized the root vowel) before the final stop; this nasal sound became *m* before B and P, *n* before D, T, and J, and *ŋ* before K, KH, G, and W. Final *mb* (from *-mb-* and *-ŋw-*) became *m* in Sindarin, and final *ŋg* became *ŋ* (spelled *ng* in the conventional transcription).

CVC roots: *cam* √KAB 'hand', *gamp* √GAP 'hook', *band* √M-BAD 'custody', *cant* √KAT 'shape', *rŷn* √ROJ 'hound', *ranc* √RAK 'arm', *rinc* √RIKH 'twitch', *peng* √KWIG 'bow', *lim* √LIW 'fish'.

Nasalized nouns derived from roots ending in T occasionally have doublets ending in *-nd*: *land* √LAT 'open space' next to *lant* √LAT 'forest-clearing'.

CVCVC roots, showing penultimate syncope: *cram* √*KARÁB 'cake', *dring* √*DIRÍG 'hammer'.

§ 14.4. Nouns with strengthened nasals

These nouns had roots ending in -M, -N, which they altered to *-mb-*, *-nd-*, yielding the Sindarin finals *-m*, *-nd*, or *-n*.

CVC roots

dam √NDAM 'hammer', *glam* √G-LAM 'din', *gond* √GON 'stone', *hen(d)* √KHEN 'eye'.

CVCVC roots, with penultimate syncope

crûm √KURÚM 'left hand', *dram* √DARÁM 'heavy blow'.

§ 14.5. Nouns with doubled finals

These nouns doubled the final consonant of roots ending in the voiceless stops K and KH, P, T, or the consonants L and S, yielding the Sindarin finals *-ch*, *-ph*, *-th*, *-ll*, *-s*.

CVC roots

ech √EK 'spine', *loch* √LOKH 'ringlet', *raph* √*RAP 'strap', *dath* √DAT 'pit', *peth* √KWE-T 'word', *nell* √NJEL 'bell', *las* √LAS 'leaf'.

CVCVC roots

Without syncope

carach √KÁRAK 'jaws', *canath* √KÁNAT 'farthing'.

With penultimate syncope

bras √BARÁS 'white heat', *brith* √BIRÍT 'gravel', *cris* √KIR-ÍS 'cleft', *rhas* √KHARÁS 'precipice'.

§ 14.6. Nouns with vocalized initial nasals

These nouns had roots beginning with MB, ND, ŋ, or ŋG, of which the nasal portion became vocalized (acquiring sounds similar to the *-en* in *brazen* or the *m* in *prism*). The vocalized *m̥*, *n̥*, *ŋ* sounds became *am*, *an*, *aŋ* in Sindarin: *ambar* √MBAR 'earth', *angol* √ŋGOL 'magic', *angol* √ŋOL 'stench'.

Nouns with Suffixes

A large number of roots—of both (C)VC and (C)VCVC types—took suffixes of the type CV. By the time of Classical Sindarin these suffixes had become an intrinsic part of the words they were attached to and were no longer distinguishable as elements in themselves, making it impossible to construct new words using them.

Since the final vowels were lost, several different suffixes (e.g., **-da*, **-de*, **-do*) often merged into a single suffix (e.g., *-dh*). In most cases it is not possible to pin down the exact meaning of any of these suffixes, but in the few cases where it is possible, the suffix will be quoted in its archaic form (e.g., **-na*). Otherwise only the initial consonant of the root is mentioned.

§ 14.7. Immediate suffixes

Immediate suffixes had no vowel suffixes separating them from the root.

- **-d-*: suffixes beginning with **-d-* (**-da*, **-de*, **-do*) become *-dh* after most consonants, but *-ld-* became *-ll*: *glûdh* √G-LIB 'soap', *haudh* √KHAG 'barrow', *nardh* √SNAR 'knot', *mall* √SMAL 'gold', *sell* √SEL 'daughter'.
- **-j-*: suffixes beginning with **-j-* (**-ja*, **-je*) disappear but induce primary final *i*-affection (§ 5.9): *inc* √IŋK 'guess', *lîn* √LIN 'pool', *thîn* √THIN 'evening'.

The suffix *-ja* induces double affection (§ 5.10): *cair* √KIR 'ship', *fuir* √PHOR 'right hand', *lain* √LAN 'thread', *ruin* √RUN[1] 'track'.

- **-k-*: suffixes beginning with **-k-* (e.g., **-ka*) become *-g*: *rasc* √RAS 'horn', *lŷg* √LEW 'snake'.
- **-l-*: suffixes beginning with **-l-* (**-la*, **-le*, **-lo*, **-lu*) become *-l* after roots ending in a vowel or G, J, W; after other consonants they become *-ol*: *thûl* √THU 'breath'; *cail* √KEG 'fence', *mael* √SMAG 'stain', *sûl* √SUG 'goblet', *cael* √KAJ 'sickness', *cuil* √KOJ 'life', *uil* √UJ 'seaweed', *gaul* √ŋGAW 'wolf howl', *hûl* √SIW 'battle cry', *mŷl* √MIW 'gull'; *magol* √MAK 'sword'; *tegol* √TEK 'pen'.

These suffixes can follow roots that had been nasalized, ablauted, or otherwise altered: *tachol* √TAK [OS **taŋk*^{h}*la* < CE **taŋklā*] 'brooch', *naugol* √NUK [OS **nauklo*] 'Dwarf', *hathol* √SJAD [OS **çat*^{h}*la* < CE **sjatslā*] 'axe'.

The suffix **-la* often referred to instruments: *tegol* 'instrument for writing' (i.e., pen); *magol* 'instrument for striking or cleaving' (i.e., sword); *tachol* 'instrument for fastening' (i.e., brooch), *nagol* 'instrument for biting' (i.e., tooth).

The suffix **-lo* in *naugol* was a diminutive, signifying small size.

-m-*: suffixes beginning with **-m-* (-ma*, **-me*) become *-w* after roots ending in I, J, or a velar (G, H, K, ŋ) following A, E, I; *-f* after roots ending in L or R; *-u* after other consonants; they disappeared following a root ending in the vowels O, U, or a velar following these vowels. After B it underwent metathesis, becoming *-mb-*, and in Classical Sindarin *-m*: *caew* √KAJ 'lair', *tui(w)* √TUJ 'sprout', *saew* √SAG 'poison', *daw* √DO-H 'nighttime', *naew* √NAK jaw, *têw* √TEŋ 'letter'; *half* √SJAL 'seashell', *gorf* √GOR 'impetus'; *hithu* √KHITH 'fog', *ianu* √JAT 'bridge', *tinu* √TIN 'star'; *dû* √DO 'night', *lû* √LU 'time', *tulu* √TULUK 'prop'; *lam* √LAB 'tongue'.

The suffix **-ma* sometimes referred to instruments: *lam* 'that with which one licks' (i.e., tongue); *naew* 'that with which one bites' (i.e., jaw); *nŷw* 'that with which one entangles' (i.e., noose); *ylf* 'that with which one drinks' (i.e., vessel).

The suffix **-me* was used for verbal actions: *gorf* 'a hastening' (i.e., impetus); *raew* 'a reaching' (i.e., fathom); *ruiw* 'a hunting' (i.e., hunt).

-n-*: suffixes beginning with **-n-* (-na*, **-ne*, **-no*, **-nu*) become *-l* after L, *-th* after TH, and *-n* in other cases: *coll* √KOL 'cloak', *ann* √AN 'gift', *daen* √NDAK 'corpse', *drafn* √DARÁM 'hewn log', *duin* √DUJ 'river', *dûn* √NDU 'west', *garn* √GAR 'property', *lefn* √LEB 'one left behind', *nîn* √NEJ 'tear', *taen* √TAH 'summit', *thafn* √STAB 'post', *udûn* √U-TUP 'hell'.

The suffix **-ne* was also used for verbal actions: *duin* 'a flowing' (i.e., river); *annûn* 'the going down' (i.e., west).

The suffix **-na* was primarily used for nouns derived from past participles: *coll* 'thing borne or worn' (i.e., cloak); *ann* 'thing given' (i.e., gift); *garn* 'thing possessed' (i.e., property); *narn* 'thing told' (i.e., tale); *rafn* 'thing extended' (i.e., horn or wing).

The suffix **-no* was used for agents or for personalized forms of past participles: *benn* 'person wedded' (i.e., husband); *daen* 'person slain' (i.e., corpse); *tirn* 'one who watches' (i.e., watcher).

*-*r*-: suffixes beginning with *-*r*- (*-*re*, *-*ro*) become -*r* after J, W, and vowels, -*or* after other consonants: *faer* √PHAJ 'spirit', *baur* √MBAW 'need', *nûr* √(O)NO 'race', *badhor* √BAD 'judge', *cabor* √KAP 'frog', *dagor* √NDAK 'battle'.

These suffixes could follow roots that had been nasalized or otherwise modified: *bachor* √MBAKH [OS **mbaŋk^{h}ro*] 'pedlar', *glamor* √G-LAM [OS **glambr*-] 'echo', *gollor* √ŋGOL [OS **ŋ͡goldro*] 'magician'.

The suffix *-*ro* was very commonly used for agents, although the meaning was sometimes obscured: *cabor* 'one who leaps' (i.e., frog); *gaur* 'one who howls' (i.e., wolf); *bador* 'one who hurls (a spear or arrow)' (i.e., warrior); *tavor* 'one who knocks' (i.e., woodpecker).

*-*s*-: suffixes beginning with *-*s*- (*-*sa*, *-*se*) became -*s* after K, KH, H, and P but -*th* after T or TH: *caraes* √KÁRAK 'hedge of spikes', *laus* √LOKH 'ringlet', *gwas* √WAH 'stain', *aes* √AP^{1} 'meat'; *lith* √LIT 'ash', *loth* √LOTH 'flower'.

*-*sta*: the suffix *-*sta* becomes -*st* in its only occurrence in Sindarin, where it indicates the location of action (derived ultimately from a verbal action noun): *haust* √KHAW 'bed' (place of resting).

*-*t*-: suffixes beginning with *-*t*- (*-*ta*, *-*te*, *-*ti*, *-*to*, *-*tu*) become -*t* after D, L, N, S, TH; -*th* after H, K, R, T: *gwest* √WED 'oath', *dolt* √DOL 'knob', *tint* √TIN 'spark', *ist* √IS 'lore', *cost* √KOTH 'quarrel'; *gwath* √WAH 'stain', *aith* √EK 'spear point', *gurth* √ŋGUR 'death', *meth* √MET 'end'.

*-*the*: the suffix *-*the* becomes -*th* in its only occurrence in Sindarin, where it indicates a verbal action: *nauth* √NOW 'thought'.

*-*w*-: suffixes beginning with *-*w*- (*-*wa*, *-*we*, *-*wi*) become -*b* after roots ending in K following a vowel, -*p* after roots ending in K following S and nasals, -*ph* after roots ending in K following a liquid, *m* after roots ending in ŋ or ŋG, *u* after other consonants, and *w* after vowels and J: *salab* √SALAK 'herb', *osp* √ÚSUK [CE *usk^{w}ē] 'smoke', *alph* √Á-LAK [CE **alk^{w}ā*] 'swan', *nem* √NEŋ 'nose', *curu* √KUR 'skill', *nedhu* √NID 'cushion', *iaew* √JAJ 'scorn'.

These suffixes might also occur after (C)VCC roots: *rim* √RIŋG 'cold pool'.

§ 14.8. Mediate suffixes

Mediate suffixes followed a vowel after the root.

One group of mediate suffixes follows a repetition of the root vowel after the final consonant of the root, in Quenya called *ómataina* (vocalic extension). A few roots (√ER, √KEL, √TEL) had the irregular vocalic extension *-u-* (*eru-*, *kelu-*, *telu-*). These suffixes bear a close resemblance to the immediate suffixes listed above.

**-le* became *-l*: *roval* √RAM 'wing' (also shows long ablaut).

**-me* became *-f* after *-i-* but disappeared after *-u-*: *silif* √SIL 'silver light'; *eru* √ER 'desert', *telu* √TEL 'dome'.

**-ne*, **-na* became *-n*: *calan* √KAL 'daytime', *talan* √TAL[2], 'platform', *celon* [OS **keluna*] √KEL 'river'.

**-no* became *-n*, mostly used for personal or agent nouns: *balan* √BAL 'Vala', *craban* √*KARÁKW 'crow', *lavan* √LAM 'animal', *rhavan* √SRAB 'man not of the Edain'.

**-ndo* became *-nd* (probably a strengthened form of **-no*): *ulunn* √ÚL[2]-UG 'monster'.

**-ro* became *-r*, used for names of persons; related to the immediate suffix *-r*, *-or*: *adar* √AT[1] 'father', *avar* √ABA 'refuser' (i.e., one of the Avari), *teler* √TEL 'person at the end' (i.e., one of the Teleri).

**-sse* became *-s*: *rîs* √RIG 'queen', *tulus* √TJUL 'poplar', *celos* [OS **kelusse*] √KEL 'freshet'.

**-t-* became *-d*: *habad* √SKJAP 'shore', *thorod* √THOR 'torrent'.

**-ti* became *-d*, used in names of directions: *forod* √PHOR 'north', *harad* √KHJAR 'south'.

**-tte* became *-th*, used in abstract and verbal action nouns, following roots ending in the consonants N, L, and R: *gwanath* √(A)WA-N 'death, dying', *meleth* √MEL 'love', *firith* √PHIR 'fading'.

§ 14.9. Unchangeable mediate suffixes

The remainder of the suffixes simply followed the root, or a stem derived from a root, without change, and many could be freely affixed to various word stems to produce words with predictable meanings; they are listed here in their Sindarin form.

-ad[1] [OS **-ata*] is the suffix for gerunds formed from *a*-stem verbs and a few other abstract or collective nouns: *athrad* √A-THAR 'crossing', *avad* √ABA 'refusal', *gawad* √ŋGAW 'howling', *genediad* from *genedia-* √NOT 'reckoning', *hammad* 'clothing' from *hamma-* √KHAP- 'clothe', *lammad* √LAM 'echo'.

-ad[2] [√AT[2]] is a dual suffix, indicating pairs: *galadhad* 'two trees' from *galadh* √GÁL-AD 'tree'.

-aith (of uncertain origin) forms verbal action nouns: *edraith* 'saving', *lalaith* √G-LAD 'laughter'.

-as [OS **-asse*] is the suffix for collective nouns, derivative nouns formed from adjectives, and verbal action nouns; it sometimes takes the form *-ias* after roots containing the vowels E (with long ablaut) or I and ending in N, L, or R. It probably arises from the suffix *-s* [OS **-sse*] following *-a-* as a verbal or adjectival ending, from which it was generalized to other instances: *aegas* √ÁJAK 'peak' (perhaps formerly 'sharpness'), *bellas* 'strength' from *bell* √BEL 'strong', *cannas* 'shaping' from *cant* √KAT 'shape', *certhas* 'alphabet' from *certh* √KIR 'rune', *faras* √SPAR 'hunt', *galas* √GAL 'growth', *hannas* 'understanding' from *hand* √KHAN 'intelligent', *hobas* √KHOP 'harborage', *ínias* √JEN 'annals', *maeas* 'dough' from *mae* √MÁSAG 'soft', *minas* √MIN 'tower', *pennas* 'history' from *pent* √KWE-T 'tale', *tarias* √TÁRAG 'stiffness', *tilias* √TIL 'line of peaks', *tobas* √TUP 'roofing', *thinnas* √STINT 'shortness'.

-ath [OS **-attʰe*] is a general plural suffix, derived from a collective-noun suffix probably related to *-as*. It became *-iath* after roots containing the vowel I and ending in L, N, or R: *conath* (from *caun*[1]) 'cries', *dagorath* 'battles', *duinath* 'rivers', *elenath* 'stars', *gonath* 'stones', *ionnath* 'sons', *lamath* 'voices', *periannath* 'halflings', *sammath* 'chambers', *thoronath* 'eagles', *giliath* √ŋGIL 'stars', *firiath* √PHIR 'mortals', *liniath* √LIN 'pools', *siniath* √SI-N 'news', *siriath* √SIR 'rivers'.

-dir, *-nir* [OS **-ndīr(o)*] is a suffix for agent and personal nouns; its original meaning was 'man, male person': *ceredir* 'maker', *curunír* 'wizard', *dagnir* 'slayer', *feredir* 'hunter', *herdir* 'master', *meldir* 'friend', *randir* 'wanderer'.

-ed[1] [OS **-ita*] is the suffix for gerunds formed from *i*-stem verbs and a few other abstract or collective nouns *-eg* (diminutive, derivative). It is closely related to *-ad*[1]: *cabed* √KAP 'leap', *cared* √KAR 'making', *cened* √KEN 'sight'.

-ed[2] [OS **-ete*] is a suffix for abstract or collective nouns (probably related to *-eth*[1]): *breged* √BERÉK 'violence', *methed* 'end' from *meth* √MET 'last'.

-eg is a diminutive suffix: *loeg* 'pool' from *lô* 'wetland', *nogotheg* 'petty-Dwarf' from *nogoth* 'Dwarf', *pesseg* 'pillow'.

-el[1] [OS **-ella*, **-ello*] meant 'Elf': *miniel* 'Vanya', *gwanwel* 'Elf of Aman', *laegel* 'Green-Elf'.

-el[2] [OS **-elle*] is a general derivative suffix: *finnel* 'tress' from *find*

'hair', *gannel* 'harp', *bathel* 'sharp weapon-blade', *nelladel* 'ringing of bells' from *nellad* of the same meaning.

-el[3] and *-iel*[1] [OS **-elle*, **-ielle*] are suffixes for feminine personal nouns: *riel* √RIG 'crowned maiden', *thoniel* √THAN 'kindler'.

-en[1], meaning uncertain: *lalven* √LÁLAM 'elm-tree'.

-en[2] and *-ien*[1] [OS **-ende*, **-iende*] is a suffix for feminine personal nouns: *rien* √RIG 'queen', *luithien* √LUK 'enchantress'.

-eth[1] [OS **-ett*^{h}*e*] is a suffix for abstract nouns; it is probably derived from the ending *-th* after the vocalic extension *-e-*, generalized to other words: *prestanneth* 'vowel affection' from *prestannen* 'disturbed, affected', *Ivanneth* 'giving of fruits' (month name).

-eth[2] [OS **-itt*^{h}*a*] is a suffix for feminine personal nouns; it takes the form *-ieth* after roots containing I and ending in N, L, or R: *adaneth* 'mortal woman' (from *adan*), *elleth* 'Elf-woman', *firieth* √PHIR 'mortal woman', *naneth* √NAN 'mother', *oneth* √AN 'giver', possibly also *gwilwileth* 'butterfly'.

-hoth [OS **-khott*^{h}*e*] was originally a suffix indicating a large group but now often functions as a collective plural, especially for strange or hostile peoples: *lossoth* 'snow-men', *dornhoth* 'twisted folk, Dwarves', *glamhoth* 'orcs', *orchoth* 'orcs'.

-i [OS **-iie*] is possibly a collective-noun suffix: *serni* 'shingle, pebble-bank' from *sarn* √SAR 'stone'.

-ian[1] formed verbal action nouns: *leithian* 'release' from *leitha-* '(to) release', *orthelian* 'covering, canopy' from *ortheli-* '(to) screen above'.

-ian[2] [OS **-iand-*] is a diminutive suffix: *perian* 'halfling', *mirian* 'penny, small coin'.

-iel[2] means 'daughter' or 'maiden': *tinúviel* 'daughter of twilight'.

-ien[2] formed verbal action nouns: *teilien* 'sport' from *teilia-* 'play'.

-ig created singular nouns from a noun originally having dual meaning: *gwanunig* 'twin' from *gwanun* 'twins', *lhewig* 'ear' from *lhaw* 'pair of ears'.

-il[1] [OS **-il*, **-ille*] is a suffix for feminine personal nouns: *bereth* [OS **barathil*] 'spouse', *brennil* 'lady', *híril* 'lady'.

-il[2] is a diminutive or general derivational suffix: *brethil* 'birch tree', *ernil* 'prince' from *aran* 'king', *niphredil* 'snowdrop'.

-in[1] [OS **-ine*] is possibly derived from an adjective ending: *cerin* √KOR 'mound, circular enclosure'.

-in[2] [OS **-īne* < CE **-ēne*] is used for verbal action nouns: *pelin* √KWEL 'withering'.

-ion[1] is a common patronymic suffix, meaning 'son': *Arathornion* 'son of Arathorn', *Inglorion* 'son of Inglor'.

-ir is used for agent nouns; cf. the immediate suffix *-r*, *-or*: *bauglir* 'oppressor', from *baugla-* 'oppress', from *baug* √MBAW 'oppressive'.

-lim a collective or plural suffix most often found after words ending in *-l*: *edhellim* 'Elves'.

-nd, *-n(n)* [OS **-nde*] appears after various vowels (unconnected with the root vowel) to indicate the name of a country or land:

- *-an*: *Rohan* (‡*Rochand*) 'country of horses', *Cardolan* 'country of red hills'
- *-ian* (‡*-iand*): *Beleriand* 'country of Balar', *Ossiriand* 'country of seven rivers'
- *-ien*: *Anórien* 'country of the sun', *Ithilien* 'country of the moon', *Arthórien* 'country of the enclosed region'
- *-ion*: *Eregion* 'country of hollies', *Rhovanion* 'wild country'
- *-on* (‡*-ond*): *Angolonn* 'country of the Noldor'

-od created singular nouns from an original plural or mass noun: *filigod* 'small bird' from *filig* 'birds', possibly *linnod* 'verse' from *lind* 'song'.

-og created singular nouns from an original plural or mass noun: *glamog* 'orc' from *glam* 'horde, orc-host'.

-on[1] [OS **-on*, **-ondo*] is used for masculine, personal, or agent nouns; it takes the form *-ion* after roots containing the vowel I and ending in L, N, or R, and perhaps in other cases: *bôr* [OS **boron* √BOR] 'trusty man', *aphadon* 'follower', *brannon* 'lord', *cirion* √KIR 'shipman', *ellon* 'male Elf', *faron* √SPAR 'hunter', *firion* √PHIR 'mortal man', *mellon* 'friend', *rochon* 'rider', *rodon* 'Vala', *seron* √SER 'friend', *tauron* 'forester', *thelion* 'one having purpose'.

-on[2] [OS **-ond-*] is an augmentative ending, used for large things; it takes the form *-ion* after roots containing I and ending in L, N, or R: *aearon* 'great ocean', *amon* 'hill', *annon* 'great gate', *ardhon* 'great province', *mirion* √MIR 'great jewel', *sirion* √SIR 'great river', *tirion* √TIR 'great watchtower'.

-os [OS **-osse*] is a derivative suffix similar to *-as*: *alagos* 'windstorm' from *alag* 'rushing'.

-oth [OS **-otthₒ*, **-otthe*] appears variously as a collective, diminutive, or augmentative: *faroth* √SPAR 'hunters', *nogoth* √NUK 'Dwarf', *Lammoth* 'great echo' (place-name) from *lam* 'sound of the voice'.

-red is a suffix for adjectival derivatives, perhaps based on adjectives

ending in *-ren*: *haered* 'remote distance' from *hae* 'far', *niphred* 'pallor, fear' from *nimp* 'white', *pathred* 'fullness' from *pant* 'full'.

-ril is a suffix for feminine personal nouns, derived from the agent suffix *-r* and the feminine ending *-il*[1]: *melethril* 'lover', *odhril* √ON 'female parent', possibly also *lhingril* 'spider'.

-rim [OS **-rimbe*] was originally a suffix indicating a numerous group of persons or things but now often acts as a simple plural: *onodrim* 'ents', *orodrim* 'mountains', *haradrim* 'southrons', *rohirrim* 'horse lords'.

-ron is a suffix for masculine, personal, or agent nouns, derived from the agent suffix *-r* and the ending *-on*[1]: *badhron* 'judge', *callon* 'hero', *hadron* 'warrior', *ithron* 'wizard', *lathron* 'hearer', *nathron* 'weaver', *odhron* 'male parent', *pethron* 'narrator', *thavron* 'carpenter'.

-we [OS **-wega*] is a suffix for masculine personal or agent nouns.

-wen[1] [OS **-wene*] is a suffix for feminine personal or agent nouns.

ADJECTIVES

§ 14.10. Simple adjectives

The construction of adjectives is very similar to that of nouns, and much of what has been said here concerning the phonetic development in Sindarin of endings, ablauted vowels, and so forth is also relevant. The range of variation is somewhat more limited, however. The only known vocalic endings used for simple adjectives were *-ā* and *-i* (OS *-a* and *-è*), and it is usually possible to tell which one was used. Adjectives ending in *-ā* induce *a*-affection (see § 5.7) in roots containing the vowels I or U under normal ablaut. There is little distinction in meaning between the two endings, although the adjectives ending in *-i* seem to have been more commonly used for names of colors.

CVC roots take normal or long ablaut.

-i adjectives, all with normal ablaut: *mîn* √MIN 'first', *mith* √MITH 'grey', *môr* √MOR 'black'.

-ā adjectives from CVC roots display normal, long, or strong ablaut:

Normal ablaut

bâl √BAL 'divine', *dae* √NDAJ 'great', *fôr* √PHOR 'right', *hae* √KHAJ 'remote', *pân* √KWA-N 'all', *târ* √TAR 'high', *ui* √OJ 'eternal'.

Long ablaut

hîw √KHIM 'sticky', *‡naw* √NAB 'hollow', *nîn* √NEN 'wet', *raun* √RAN 'straying', *taur* √TAR 'lofty', *ûr* √UR[2] 'wide'.

Strong ablaut

gael √ŋIL 'pale', *lhaew* √SLIW 'sick', *maeg* √MIK 'sharp', *naud* √NUT 'penetrating', *naug* √NUK 'stunted', *raudh* √ROD 'hollow', *taur* √TUR 'masterful', *thaur* √THUR 'enclosed', *thaw* √THU-S 'rotten'.

(C)VCC roots all show normal ablaut

-*i* adjectives: *gling* √GLIŋG 'hanging', *gwind* √WIND 'pale blue', *limp* √LIŋKW 'wet', *lint* √LINT 'swift', *ring* √RIŋG 'cold'.

-*ā* adjectives: *lend* √LIND 'tuneful, sweet', *thent* √STINT 'short', *laeg* √LAIK 'keen'.

(C)VCVC roots

Roots occurring without syncope included the -*i* adjectives *baran* √BARAN 'brown' and *caran* √KAR[2]-AN 'red' and the following -*ā* adjectives: *alag* √A-LAK 'rushing', *asgar* √A-SKAR 'violent', *bara* √BARA 'eager', *baradh* √BAR-AD 'steep', *celeg* √KJELEK 'swift', *enedh* √E-NED 'middle', *tolog* √TULUK 'stalwart'; with strong ablaut of the penultimate vowel: *arod* √AR[1]-ÁT 'noble'.

Roots reflecting syncope of the penultimate vowel included the -*i* adjective *glân* √ŋAL-AN 'white' and the -*ā* adjectives *brêg* √BERÉK 'quick' and *brûn* √BOR[1]-ÓN 'long established'.

The following -*ā* adjectives show syncope of the ultimate vowel: *laeg* √LÁJ-AK 'green', *mae* √MÁSAG 'soft', *melch* √MÍL-IK 'greedy', *parch* √PÁRAK 'dry', *rhosg* √S-RÚS-UK 'russet', *thala* √STÁL-AG 'stalwart'.

§ 14.11. Nasalized adjectives

CVC roots:

-*i* adjectives: *nimp* √NIKW 'white', *rimp* √RIP 'rushing'.

-*ā* adjectives: *land* √LAD 'wide', *long* √LUG 'heavy', *pant* √KWA-T 'full', *tanc* √TAK 'firm', *tong* √TUG 'tight', *thanc* √STAK 'forked'.

CVCVC roots with penultimate syncope:

-*ā* adjective: *brand* √BAR-ÁD 'high'.

VCVCVC roots:

-*ā* adjective: *adlant* √Á-TALAT 'oblique'. This adjective has a doublet *adlann* 'sloping' with original ending in -*nd*.

§ 14.12. Adjectives with strengthened nasals

CVC roots:

-*i* adjectives: *lhind* √SLIN 'fine', *nind* √NIN 'fragile', *rind* √RIN 'circular', *thind* √THIN 'grey', *hwind* √SWIN 'whirling'.

-*ā* adjectives: *cand* √KAN2 'bold', *dem* √DIM 'sad', *hand* √KHAN 'intelligent', *nend* √NEN 'water', *rem* √RIM 'numerous', *tond* √TUN 'tall', *ûm* √UM 'evil'.

CVCVC roots with penultimate syncope:

-*ā* adjective: *crom* √KURÚM 'left'.

§ 14.13. Adjectives with doubled finals

CVC roots:

-*ā* adjectives: *glos* √G-LOS 'white', *meth* √MET 'last', *ros* √RUS 'reddish'; with suffix: *tithen* √TIT 'little'.

Adjectives with Suffixes

§ 14.14. Immediate suffixes

*-*dā* always follows roots ending in L and may be an early variant of *-*lā* or *-*nā*: *bell* √BEL 'strong'; *coll* √KUL 'hollow'; *doll* √N-DUL 'dark'; *goll* √ŋGOL 'wise'; *mell* √MEL 'dear'.

*-*jā*: *annui* √NDU 'western', *bain* √BAN 'beautiful', *fain* √SPAN 'white', *gwain* √WIN1 'new', *hair* √KHJAR 'left', *mail* √MEL 'dear', *ruin* √RUN2 'burning red', *celair* √KAL-AR 'brilliant'.

*-*kā*: *balch* √ŋGWAL 'cruel', *baug* √MBAW 'tyrannous', *faeg* √SPAJ 'poor', *puig* √POJ 'clean', *tûg* √TIW 'thick'.

*-*lā*: *fael* √PHAJ 'just', *mael* √SMAG 'stained', *sael* √SAJ 'wise'.

*-*nā* (used for adjectives derived from past participles, adjectives of color and material, and other adjectives of characteristic): *cuin* √KOJ 'alive', *cûn* √KUH 'bowed', *fern* √PHIR 'dead', *gern* √GJER 'worn', *hall* √KHAL 'exalted', *hell* √SKEL 'naked', *maen* √MAG 'skilled'; *cefn* √KEM 'earthen', *celefn* √KJELEP 'of silver', *crann* √KAR-ÁN 'ruddy', *donn* √DUN 'swart', *faen* √PHAJ 'white', *morn* √MOR 'dark', *sarn* √SAR 'of stone'; *muin* √MOJ 'dear', *orn* √ORO 'tall', *path* √PATH 'smooth', *raen* √RAG 'crooked', *taen* √TAH 'long', *tofn* √TUB 'deep'; with prefix: *avorn* √BOR1.

*-*rā*: *agor* √AK 'narrow', *dûr* √DO-H 'dark', *gwaur* √WAH 'soiled', *iaur* √JA 'old' (with long ablaut), *lagor* √LAK 'swift', *naer* √NAJ 'sad', *ovor* √UB 'abundant', *saer* √SAG 'bitter'.

*-*tā*: *gorth* √ŋGUR 'dead', *lost* √LUS 'empty', *rost* √ROS 'rainy'.

*-*wā*: *anu* √HAN 'male', *cadu* √KAT 'shaped', *gem* √GEŋG 'sickly', *hethu* √KHITH 'foggy', *laeb* √LÁJ-AK 'fresh', *malu* √S-MAL 'fallow', *naru* √NAR 'red', *talu* √TAL2 'flat'.

§ 14.15. Mediate suffixes

Following vocalic extension

-jā > *-i*: *minai* √MIN (OS **miniia* < CE **minijā*) 'single'.
-k^{w}*ā* > *-b*, from the root √KWA 'full', *ereb* √ER 'alone, lonely'.
-mā > *-f*: *silef* √SIL 'shining silver'
-nā > *-n*: *rhovan* √SRAB 'wild'.
-wā > *-w*: *trîw* √TER 'fine, slender' (with accent falling on the vocalic extension and syncope of the root vowel).

§ 14.16. Unchangeable mediate suffixes

-ail (of uncertain origin) is a derivative suffix: *Trannail* 'of the Shire' from *Trann* 'Shire'.

-an [OS **-ana*] is a past participial suffix used when a suffix had been added to the root: *neithan* [OS **nekthana*] 'wronged, deprived', *eglan* √HEK [OS **eklana*] 'forsaken', *amarthan* [OS **ambart*^{h}*ana*] 'fated'.

-eb [OS **-ipa* < CE **-ik*^{w}*ā*] is a derivative suffix, related to *-kwā*: *aglareb* 'glorious' from *aglar* 'glory'; *caeleb* 'bedridden' from *cael* 'sickness'.

-el[4] [OS **-ila* < CE *-ilā*] is a present participial ending for *i*-stem verbs (cf. *-ol*); it took the form *-iel* following roots containing the vowel I and ending in N, R, or L: *tiriel* √TIR 'seeing'

-en[3] [OS **-ena* < CE **-ēnā*] is a past participial ending, usually added to a past-tense form of a verb: *abonnen* 'born after' (i.e., human), *dangen* 'slain', *dolen* 'hidden', *govannen* 'having met', *gwanwen* 'departed', *hollen* 'closed', *tirnen* 'guarded', *thoren* 'fenced'.

-en[4] [OS **-ina* or **-ena*] is a descriptive or derivative suffix: *beren* 'bold', *calen* 'green', *laden* 'wide', *meren* 'joyous', *niben* 'small', *pihen* 'juicy'; *aewen* 'of birds' from *aew* 'bird', *dínen* 'silent' from *dîn* 'silence', *glóren* 'golden' from *glaur* 'golden light', *remmen* 'tangled' from *rem* 'mesh', *rhúnen* 'eastern' from *rhûn* 'east', *tathren* 'of willow' from *tathor* 'willow tree', *tolothen* 'eighth' from *toloth* 'eight'.

-id [OS **-itè* < CE **-iti*]; takes the form *-ed* when in conjunction with *a-*: *annúnaid* 'western', *maed* 'skilled', *nîd* 'damp', *thenid* 'firm'.

-iel[3] [OS **-ielā*] is a derivative suffix: *glóriel* 'golden' from *glaur* 'golden light', *míriel* 'like jewels' from *mîr* 'jewel', *níniel* 'tearful' from *nîn* 'tear'.

-in[3] [OS **-inė* < CE **-ini*]: *firin* 'mortal', *luin* 'blue', *legin* 'swift', *perin* 'half', *thenin* 'firm', *thurin* 'secret'.

-iol [OS **-ǭla* < CE **-jālā*] is probably an extension of the suffix *-jā*: *eriol* 'alone'.

-ion[2] [OS **-iǭna* < CE **-jānā*] is a derivative ending expressing a characteristic feature; probably an extension of the suffix **-jā*: *erchamion* 'having one hand' from *cam* 'hand', *thonion* 'having pine trees' from *thôn* 'pine'; *dúhirion* 'having dark streams' from *dúhir* 'stream of darkness'.

-ob [OS **-upa* < CE **-uk*^{w}*ā*] is a derivative, usually a pejorative suffix related to *-eb*: *gorthob* 'horrible' from *gorth* 'horror'.

-ol [OS **-ǭla* < CE **-ālā*] is a derivative or present participial suffix (cf. *-el*[4]): *bregol* 'sudden' from *brêg* 'quick', *goeol* 'fell' from *goe* 'terror', *glavrol* 'babbling' from *glavra-* '(to) babble', *hwiniol* 'whirling' from *hwinia-* '(to) whirl'.

-on[3] [OS **-ǭna* < CE **-ānā*] is an ending of characteristic, often derivative, adjectives, probably originating from the suffix *-nā* added to words ending in *-ā*, later generalized to other words; it takes the form *-ion* after roots containing I and ending in L, N, or R: *alagon* 'rushing' from *alag* of the same meaning, *thalion* (OS **sthalgǭna*) 'strong' from *thala* 'stalwart'; *brithon* 'pebbly' from *brith* 'gravel'; *galadhon* 'having trees' from *galadh* 'tree'; *gilion* 'of stars' from *gîl* 'star'; *thilion* 'glistening silver' from *thîl* 'radiance'.

-ren [OS **-rina*] is a derivative suffix; it takes the form *-len* after words ending in *-l*: *angren* 'of iron' from *ang* 'iron', *edhellen* 'Elvish' from *edhel* 'Elf', *glamren* 'echoing' from *glam* 'noise', *gobennathren* 'historical' from *gobennas* 'history'; *gwaeren* 'windy' from *gwaew* 'wind', *gwathren* 'shadowy' from *gwath* 'shadow'; *nestadren* 'of healing' from *nestad* 'healing'; *silivren* 'glittering white' from *silif* 'silver light'.

-ron [OS **-rǭna* < CE **-rānā*] is an extension of the suffix **-rā*: *haeron* 'far, distant'.

-ui [OS **-ūia*] is a derivative suffix, originating from the suffix *-jā* added to words ending in *-ō*, *-ū*, later generalized to other words: *crumui* 'left-handed' from *crûm* 'left hand', *fanui* 'cloudy' from *fân* 'cloud', *hithui* 'misty' from *hith* 'mist', *lefnui* 'fifth' from *leben* 'five', *urui* 'hot' from *ûr* 'heat'.

-wain (of uncertain origin) is a superlative suffix: *iarwain* 'eldest' (normal ablaut) from *iaur* 'old' (long ablaut).

-wen[2] [OS **-wina*] is an ordinal numerical counter, probably an extension of **-wā*: *edwen* 'second'.

-wor, *-war* [OS **-wāra*, **-wara*] is probably an extension of **-wā*: *cadwor*, *cadwar* 'shapely'.

VERBS

Like adjectives, verbs fall into two large classes: *i*-stems and *a*-stems. In all their forms verbs almost always show only normal ablaut, except in verbs with roots ending in vowels. The modes of stem formation are very similar to those of nouns and adjectives and require no further detail here.

§ 14.17. Simple verbs

CVC verbs

i-stems: *bad-* √BAT 'go', *car-* √KAR1 'make', *firi* √PHIR 'fade', *gwedhi* √WED 'bind', *nor-* √*NOR 'run', *pedi* √KWE-T 'speak', *tog-* √TUK 'lead'.

a-stems: *cuia-* √KOJ 'live', *gala-* √GAL 'grow', *groga-* √G-RUK 'feel terror', *síla-* √SIL 'shine'.

CVCC verbs (*a*-stem only): *glinga-* √G-LIŋG 'hang'.

(C)VCVC verbs

Syncope of the penultimate syllable occurred in the *i*-stem *blebi* √PALÁP 'flap' and in the *a*-stems *brona-* √BOR1-ÓN 'endure', *drava-* √DARÁM 'hew', *drega-* √*DERÉK 'flee'.

The following *a*-stems underwent syncope of the ultimate syllable: *bartha-* √MBÁRAT 'doom', *edra-* √ÉT-ER 'open', *ercha-* √É-REK 'prick', *faltha-* √PHÁL-AS 'foam', *ganna-* √ŋGÁNAD 'play a harp', *narcha-* √NÁRAK 'rend', *oltha-* √ÓL-OS 'dream'.

§ 14.18. Nasalized verbs (all *a*-stems)

CVC roots: *banga-* √MBAKH 'trade', *danna-* √DAT 'fall', *hamma-* √KHAP 'clothe', *panna-* √KWA-T 'fill', *penna-* √PED 'slant down'.

CVCVC root with syncope of the penultimate syllable: *dringa-* √DIRÍG 'beat'.

VCVCVC root: *adlanna-* √Á-TALAT '(to) slope'

Verbs with strengthened nasal (all a-stems): *damma-* √NDAM '(to) hammer', *linna-* √LIN2 'sing', *tamma-* √TAM 'knock', and perhaps *minna* √MI-N 'enter'.

Verbs with doubled final: *batha-* √BAT 'trample' (this verb is said to be a "frequentative," representing repeated action), *nalla-* √*NAL 'cry out', *nella-* √NJEL 'sound bells'.

Verbs with Suffixes

§ 14.19. Immediate suffixes

**-ja-* becomes *-ia-*: *beria-* √BAR 'protect', *buia-* √BEW 'serve', *delia-* √DUL 'conceal', *eria-* √ORO 'rise', *henia-* √KHAN 'understand', *nedia-* √NOT 'count', *revia-* √RAM 'fly', *thia-* √THE 'appear', *thuia-* √THU 'breathe'; *brenia-* √BOR^1-ÓN 'endure', *egleria-* √Á-KAL-AR 'glorify'.

**-la-* becomes *-la-*: *baugla-* √MBAW 'oppress' from *baug* √MBAW 'oppressive'

**-na-* becomes *-na-*: *anglenna-* √G-LED 'approach', *cuina-* √KOJ 'be alive', *harna-* √SKAR 'wound'.

**-ra-* becomes *-ra-*: *dagra-* √NDAK 'make war', *glavra-* √G-LAM 'babble', *gwathra-* √WATH 'overshadow', *lathra-* √LAS^2 'listen in', *ovra-* √UB 'abound', *pathra-* √KWA-T 'fill', *naegra-* √NAJAK 'cause pain'.

**-ta-*, although belonging to a large number of dissimilar verbs, includes a class of causative verbs that may be distinguished from non-causative verbs from the same root; e.g., *teli* 'to come' and the *-ta-* verb *toltha-* 'cause to come, fetch'; *eria-* 'rise' and *ortha-* 'cause to rise, raise'. *-ta-* becomes *-da-* after vowels, *-na-* after roots ending in M or N, *-ta-* after roots ending in D or S, and *-tha-* after roots ending in H, K, KH, R, or L: *boda-* √(A)BA 'ban', *muda-* √MO 'labor' (both with long ablaut), *glinna-* √GLIM 'glance at', *anna-* √AN 'give', *gwesta-* √WED 'swear', *ista-* √IS 'have knowledge', *matha-* √MAH 'stroke', *teitha-* √TEK 'draw', *ritha-* √RIKH 'twitch', *tortha-* √TUR 'wield', *toltha* √TUL 'fetch'.

(C)VCVC roots whose accent normally falls on the penultimate syllable have it thrown forward to the ultimate syllable, so all (C)VCVC roots show syncope of the penultimate: *critha-* √KÍR-IK 'reap', *presta-* √PÉRES 'affect', *trasta-* √TÁRAS 'trouble', as well as *breitha-* √BERÉK 'break out suddenly'.

**-t^{h}a-* becomes *-tha-*: *nautha-* √NOW 'conceive'.

§ 14.20. Mediate suffixes

-da- [OS **-ta-*] followed verbs derived from nouns or adjectives, in the latter case having a causative significance: *gannada-* 'play a harp' from *gann(el)* 'a harp', *lathrada-* 'eavesdrop' from *lathr(on)* 'listener', *limmida-* 'moisten' from *limp* 'wet'; *nimmida-* 'make white' from *nimp* 'white'; *tangada-* 'make firm' from *tanc* 'firm'.

15

Compound Words and Names

§ 15.1. Overview

A compound is a word (usually a noun or an adjective) composed of two or more elements that exist or have existed separately as independent words. It is thus distinct from affixation, which attaches elements that never stood alone. It is not uncommon, however, for elements used in compounds (especially names) to cease to be used as independent words. The basic form of a compound is bipartite, e.g., of the form X + Y; compounds with more than two members can usually be analyzed as elaborations of this type, e.g., a compound of the form X + Y + Z should be understood either as (X + Y) + Z or X + (Y + Z).

Two principal kinds of compound can be distinguished: the determinative, in which one of the elements expresses the main idea of the compound, and the others modify it; and the exocentric, in which the compound refers to something other than any of the elements. Two main varieties of determinative compound can be distinguished, known by the Sanskrit names *tatpurusha* and *karmadharaya*.

§ 15.2. Tatpurusha compounds

In a tatpurusha compound the modifying element bears a relationship to the modified element (normally the final one in the compound) similar to that of a word in a prepositional phrase or (in a case language) to a word in an oblique case. In many (but not all) cases a tatpurusha compound of the form X + Y can be translated as 'Y of X'. It will be noticed that the first element bears no marker for number; that the translation can just as well be 'Y of (several) Xes' as 'Y of X'.

The following twelve kinds of tatpurusha compounds can be distinguished by the function of the first element; however, it is important to remember that these are not absolute categories and that a word may fall into more than one. The first element may indicate:

1. the object of a verbal action expressed or implied by the final element: *bas-oneth* 'giver of bread', *hele-dir* 'watcher of fish', *calar-dan* 'maker of lamps', *el-vellon* 'friend of Elves', *gas-dil* 'stopper of gaps', *gon-hir* 'master of stone', *adan-adar* 'father of men', *las-belin* 'withering of leaves', etc.;
2. the parent, possessor, master, or maker of the final element: *eru-chên* 'child of the One', *golo-vir* 'jewel of the Noldor', *Ivon-win* 'maidens of Yavanna', *Elu-waith* 'people of Elu Thingol', etc.;
3. the material of which something is made: *silev-ril* 'brilliant light of silima'; *ang-wedh* 'bond of iron', etc.;
4. the individual items out of which a collective noun is composed: *aeg-lir* 'line of mountain peaks', *dír-naith* 'spearhead of men', *than-gail* 'barrier of shields', etc.;
5. the topic of a thought, feeling, or account: *aer-linn* 'song about the sea', *guruth-os* 'dread of death', etc.;
6. occupation or action: *ceredir* 'man who makes' (or 'man of making'), *faradrim* 'people who hunt' (or 'people of the hunt'); the first element may be simply a verb stem, as in *dagnir* 'man who slays', *Gladhwen* 'maiden who laughs', *Narchost* 'fortress that rends', etc.;
7. the subject or instrument of a verbal action expressed or implied by the final element: *i-phant* 'full of years' (or 'filled with years'), *agar-waen* 'stained with blood', etc.;
8. a characteristic or possession: *bal-rog* 'demon possessing divine power', *curu-nír* 'man having skill', *tin-nu* 'night with stars', *rí-an* 'gift with a crown', *roch-ben* 'person with a horse', etc.;
9. accompaniment: *nír-naeth* 'gnashing of teeth accompanied with tears', etc.;
10. purpose: *cened-ril* 'light for seeing', *cír-bann* 'yard for ships', *lem-bas* 'bread for journeys', *had-lath* 'thong for hurling', etc.;
11. place or time of occurrence: *aer-uil* 'weed in the sea', *cam-lann* 'palm of the hand', *dú-linn* 'singer at night', *eil-ian* 'bridge in the sky', *falath-rim* 'people of the coast', etc.;
12. cause or origin: *in-gem* 'sickness caused by old age', *rom-ru* 'sound arising from horns', etc.

§ 15.3. Karmadharaya compounds

In a karmadharaya compound the different elements of the compound refer to the same thing and so in a sense are equivalent, although they may refer to different aspects of that thing. Often the second element has a general, the first a more restrictive meaning; but this is only a tendency. Different forms of karmadharayas can be distinguished by the type of elements that compose them, as follows:

1. *Noun + noun.* In this type the equation of the two elements is most obvious, e.g., *ereg-dos* 'holly bush, bush that is a holly', *idh-rinn* 'circle of the year, circle which is a year', *oth-ronn* 'fortress-cave, cave that is a fortress', *hery-n* 'woman who is master' (this would not have been generally recognized as a compound by Sindarin speakers). In this class come a number of words ending in *-rim* and *-hoth*, where the ending could be taken as a mere pluralizer: *edhel-rim* 'Elves, people who are Elves', *orod-rim* 'mountains'; *gaur-hoth* 'host of werewolves'. These formations bear some resemblance to collective tatpurusha compounds.

   In a special kind of noun + noun karmadharaya the first element is used as a metaphor for the second. Examples of metaphorical karmadharayas are *cú-ron* 'bow-moon, moon like a bow', *ec-thel* 'point like a thorn', *hith-lain* 'mist-thread, thread like mist'; *lim-lug* 'fish-dragon, dragon like a fish (sea serpent)', *gaur-waith* 'wolf-folk, people like wolves, outlaws'.

   In some cases the two nouns are essentially synonymous, and nothing is added to the idea expressed by one, at most there being some kind of intensification: e.g., *del-os* 'fear-horror', *gor-goroth* 'dread-horror'; they may even be the same noun, as in *gor-gor* 'dread-dread', i.e., 'extreme terror'.
2. *Adjective + noun.* This type is not markedly different from the usual pairing of adjective and noun (although in Sindarin the adjective normally follows the noun): *ar-phen* 'noble person', *an-daith* 'long mark', *mor-gul* 'black sorcery'.

   In a number of cases, however, the compound has a specific meaning not ascertainable from the elements alone: e.g., *mall-orn*, which means 'golden tree' but refers to a very specific kind of tree, and *mor-chant*, which means 'dark shape' but actually refers to shadows cast by the sunlight.
3. *Adverb or adjective + adjective.* This is a fairly uncommon type of compound but easily understood: *ui-los* 'always snow-white', *maec-heneb* 'sharp-eyed'.
4. *Adverb + noun.* In this type of compound an adverbial (or prepositional) prefix modified a noun, usually a verbal derivative: *am-dir* 'looking up', *am-rûn* 'rising up, east', *athra-beth* 'talking across, debate', *thar-bad* 'walking across, crossing', *ú-bed* 'saying no, denial'.

Sometimes the verbal element is implied rather than fully stated: *dan-wedh* 'pledge (given) in return', *dan-waith* 'people (going) back'.

The noun might also be a substantive adjective, in which case the compound is really a variety of no. 3 above: *ú-an* 'unbeautiful (one), monster'.

§ 15.4. Bahuvrihi compounds

An exocentric compound (called in Sanskrit *bahuvrihi*) qualifies something other than what the words of the compound express. It may be either an adjective (expressly qualifying something outside itself) or a noun (with the qualified thing implied). A bahuvrihi of the type X + Y can usually be translated '(something) whose Y is X' or 'having an X Y' or just 'X Y'ed'.

Bahuvrihis can be based on either karmadharaya or tatpurusha compounds; the former are more common in Sindarin. Examples of karmadharaya bahuvrihis include *an-fang*, 'he whose beard is long, (a Dwarf) having a long beard', based on the karmadharaya *an-fang* 'long beard', *lach-enn* 'one whose eyes are like flames, a Noldo Elf having flamelike eyes', based on the metaphorical karmadharaya *lachenn* 'eye like a flame'. Adjectival bahuvrihis are those like *for-gam* 'right-handed'.

One of the few tatpurusha-based bahuvrihis in Sindarin is *tegil-bor* 'pen-fisted, one whose fist holds a pen', referring to a calligrapher, based on the tatpurusha compound *tegilbor* 'a fist with (holding) a pen'.

§ 15.5. Prepositional compounds

A special kind of bahuvrihi, not very common, is one composed of a prepositional phrase. It may be either an adjective, as *pen-adar* 'having no father', or a noun, as *Thar-gelion* 'land beyond Gelion'.

§ 15.6. Dvigu compounds

A *dvigu* compound is a special kind of bahuvrihi in which the first element is a number or its equivalent. Examples include *tad-dal* '(someone) having two feet, biped, bipedal'; *nelthil* '(figure) having three-corners, triangle'; *edeg-il* '(constellation) having seven stars, the Big Dipper'; *ui-al* '(time) having two "lights" (i.e., daytime and nighttime), twilight'.

§ 15.7. Double comparatives

An unusual kind of compound found in Sindarin compares the unexpressed thing represented by the compound to both of its elements, e.g., *elanor* '(flower) like the stars and the sun'; *ithil-din* '(metal) like the moon and the stars'.

§ 15.8. Dvandva compounds

A *dvandva* compound amounts to the sum of its two parts, being essentially a short phrase of the type X (and) Y. Dvandvas are very rare in Sindarin. A possible example is the name of the Sindarin meter *ann-thennath* 'long-shorts', i.e., a meter consisting of long and short syllables. Another example, not technically a dvandva but used as one, is *cúarthol*, probably to be read *cû-ar-thôl* 'bow and helm'.

Names constructed as dvandvas are more frequent than common nouns, especially when composed of adjectives, e.g., *Maed-ros* 'shapely and russet', *Ior-hael* 'old and wise', *Loth-lann* 'empty and wide', *Dun-gortheb* 'black and horrible'; they are also found as noun bahuvrihis, e.g., *Tu-or* 'having strength and vigor'.

§ 15.9. Improper compounds

An *improper* compound (the name does not denote a value judgment) is one in which the usual order of the elements is altered, with the modifying element following and the modified one preceding. These were more common (although not predominant) in Sindarin than in other Eldarin languages, since in normal Sindarin phrases nouns were followed by the adjectives that modified them or by other nouns modifying them as genitives. Such short phrases could easily be compressed into compounds, as *las galen* 'green leaf' > *lasgalen*.

Examples of improper karmadharayas are *bas-gorn* 'round bread, loaf', *gon-drafn* 'hewn stone', *gul-dur* 'dark sorcery', *ní-nim* (< *nîn nimp*) 'white tear, snowdrop-flower', *rim-dad* 'rushing down'. Examples of improper tatpurushas are *aeg-los* 'thorn of snow, icicle'; *os-tirion* 'fortress with a watchtower', *sereg-on* 'blood of stone' (a flower). Examples of improper bahuvrihis include *gal-vorn* '(metal) whose light is black'. Although most of these are of relatively "recent" origin, some date from an earlier period in the development of the language, e.g., *emer-ain* 'middle-land', *tal-f* 'flat of the hand'. These early formations are not usually recognizable as compounds in Sindarin.

A notable example of the improper tatpurusha (of early date) begins with a verbal element and ends with a noun that represents the object of the verb. These include *mad-li* 'eat-honey, (animal) which eats honey', i.e., bear; *tala-gan* 'play-harp, person who plays the harp'. Corresponding to these is the improper karmadharaya beginning with a verbal element: *lath-laeg* 'listen-sharp, one who listens acutely'.

FORMATION OF COMPOUND WORDS

§ 15.10. Overview

The sounds of the elements of compound words are often significantly changed. Three kinds of changes can be distinguished: (1) consonant contact changes, which occur both at the beginning of final elements (§§ 15.11–18) and at the end of initial elements (§§ 15.19–29), along with the unusual mutation induced by liquids (§ 15.30); (2) vowel and diphthong shortenings (§ 15.31); and (3) consonant simplification at the end of words (§ 15.32). For *i*-mutation taking place between compound elements, see § 5.9.

Consonant contact changes are the most complex. Their historical development will, in the main, be found in §§ 4.116–67. The following account simply discusses the results of the development, as they appear synchronically.

Changes in Element-Initial Consonants (§§ 15.11–18)

§ 15.11. Initial consonants

Initial consonants of noninitial elements always show the soft mutation (§ 5.1) when following an element beginning with a vowel (e.g., *ú-*, *ui-*); they often show this mutation after various consonants, but in many cases they remained unmutated.

§ 15.12. Voiceless stops

Voiceless stops (*t-*, *p-*, *c-*) beginning final elements always became voiced stops (*b-*, *d-*, *g-*) (cf. § 4.108):

t- became *d-*

celeb-till > *Celebdil* 'silver point'
tâd-tâl > *tad-dal* 'two-foot'
ereg-tos > *eregdos* 'holly bush'
nîn-talf > *Nindalf* 'wet field'
nimp-till > *nimdil* 'white point'
and-taith > *andaith* 'long mark'
am-tîr > *amdir* 'looking up'

mîr-tân > *mírdan* 'jewel wright'
menel-taur > *Meneldor* 'sky lord'
ú-talraph > *udalraph* 'stirrupless'

p- became *b-*
orod-pen > *orodben* 'mountain-person'
roch-pen > *rochben* 'horse-person'
celebrin-paur > *Celebrimbor* 'silver fist'
dram-paur > *drambor* 'blow of fist'
mall-peth > *Malbeth* 'gold word'
thar-pâd > *Tharbad* 'cross way'
lass-pelin > *Lasbelin* 'leaf fall'
morn-pen > *morben* 'dark person'

c- became *g-*
beleg-cund > *Belegund* 'mighty guardian'
ardh-calen > *Ardgalen* 'green realm'
thand-cail > *thangail* 'shield fence'
naer-caun > *naergon* 'cry of lamentation'
las-calen > *lasgalen* 'green of leaf'
arn-cîr > *argir* 'royal ships'

Apparent exceptions such as *ost-tirion* > *ostirion* and *helch-caraes* > *helcharaes* probably arise from an ancient haplologic syncope, by which *ostotiriond-* became *ostiriond-* > *ostirion*, and k^h*elkakarakse* > k^h*elkarakse* > *helcharaes* (see § 4.21).

§ 15.13. Voiced stops

Voiced stops (*b*, *d*, *g*) beginning final elements either altered to *v*, *dh*, and *'* (zero, or intervocalic hiatus), or remained unchanged:

d- became *dh-* after a vowel (see § 4.86):
fanui-dôl > *Fanuidhol* 'cloudy head'
including the secondary vowel derived from final *l* (cf. § 4.194):
magol + *dûr* > *magladhûr* 'dark sword'
but *d* after other consonants remained unchanged:
Barad-dûr, *Baran-duin*, *gas-dil*, *Mal-duin*.

b- became *v-* after *-r* (see §§ 4.86, 4.139):
her (*hîr-*)*-benn* > *hervenn* 'master-husband'
ar-beleg > *Arveleg* 'mighty king'
b remained after consonants other than *r*: *Hal-barad*, *Nim-brethil*.

g- was lost in almost all instances (§§ 4.86, 4.170):
guruth-gos > *guruthos* 'death-horror'
del-gos > *delos* 'horror'
tû-gôr > *Tuor* 'strength-vigor'
laeg-golas > *Laegolas* 'green foliage'
for-gochel > *Forochel* 'northern ice'
forn-gobel > Fornobel[1] 'northern town'
ui-gâl > *uial* 'both-light, twilight'
including in the combinations *gr-*, *gl-*, and *gw-*:
celeb-grond > *Celebrond* 'silver mace'
maeg-glind > *Maeglin* 'sharp glance'
meneg-groth > *Menegroth* '1000 caves'
rath-glóriel > *Rathlóriel* 'golden bed'
galadh-glóriel > *Galadlóriel* 'golden tree'
ui-gloss > *uilos* 'always white'
naw(nauv-)grod > *Novrod* 'Dwarf cavern'
dû-gwath > *dúath* 'dark shadow'

g- remained *g-* after *-n* (which was lost when following a liquid) (§ 4.140):
arn-gonath > *Argonath* 'noble stones'
nîn-glaur > *ninglor* 'watery-gold'
thoron-gîl > *Thorongil* 'eagle of the star' (see § 4.121, 4.201)

gw following a nasal also remained when it arose from original GW-:
thurin-gwethil > *Thuringwethil* 'secret-shadow-woman'
dan-gweth > *dangweth* 'return-account'
but *gw-* from original W always appears as *w-*, even after a nasal:
forod-gwaith > *Forodwaith* 'north people'
dan-gwêdh > *danwedh* 'ransom'
môr-gwên > *Morwen* 'dark maiden'
gîl-gwên > *Gilwen* 'star maiden'
enedh-gwaith > *Enedhwaith* 'middle people'

after the vowel *u*, *w-* from *gw-* was sometimes retained:
Drû-gwaith > *Drúwaith* 'people of the Druedain'
but sometimes lost:
dû-gwath > *duwath* > *dúath* 'dark shadow'

---

1. The combination *go-* always became *-o-* in composition, even after nasals, since it was derived from earlier **gwo-*, **wo-*.

§ 15.14. *m-*

m- either remained or was lenited to *v-* or even sometimes to *w-*.

m- became *v-* after *dh* and usually after liquids (§§ 4.127, 4.181):

heledh-morn > *Helevorn* 'black glass'
fôr-mên > *forven* 'north way'
gâl-morn > *galvorn* 'black light'
mall-megil > *Malvegil* 'sword of gold'

m became *w* after *l* or *lw* (§§ 4.149–50):

gîl-men > *gilwen* 'star way'
gwelw-men > *gwelwen* 'air way'

In most other cases *m* remained: *annú-minas*, *rem-mir*, *mor-megil*, *rath-mallen*, *ras-mund*, *dag-mor*. It also occasionally remained after *l*: *gil-mith*.

§ 15.15. Compounds without lenition

In a number of cases, where *b*, *d*, *g*, or *m* was the initial of a noun in composition that modified (usually as a genitive; cf. § 6.1) a preceding noun, the consonant remained unlenited:

aur-belain > *Orbelain* 'day of the Valar'
aur-menel > *Ormenel* 'day of heaven'
aur-galadhad > *Orgaladhad* 'day of two trees'
gîl-galad > *Gil-galad* 'star of brilliance'
ost-giliath > *Osgiliath* 'fortress of stars'

§ 15.16. Nasal stops

The originally voiced nasal stops *(n)d* and *(m)b* became the nasals *n* and *m* after nonnasal stops and fricatives, semivowels and vowels, or after nasals following nonliquids (§ 4.142):

dag-(n)dîr > *dagnir* 'slayer'
goth-(m)baug > *Gothmog* 'enemy oppressor'
lefn-(n)dîr > *levnir* 'one left behind'
curu-(n)dîr > *Curunír* 'man with skill'
egol-(m)bar > *Eglamar* 'Elf home'

When following a vowel, *nd* became *nn* (§ 4.114):

pel(e)-(n)dor > *Pelennor* 'enclosure-land' (cf. § 4.73)
eledh-(n)dôr > *Elennor* 'Elf land' (cf. § 4.119)

In other instances *(n)d*, *(m)b*, *(ŋ)g*, acted just like *d*, *b*, and *g*:

(n)d and *(ŋ)g* merged with a previous *d* and *g* (§ 4.141):
farad-dîr > *feredir* 'hunter'
beleg-gurth > *belegurth* 'great death'

and after nasals, liquids, and voiced stops following nasals they remained *d*, *b*, and *g*:

thoron-dîr > *Thorondir* 'eagle-man'
lind-dîr > *Lindir* 'singer'
her-dîr > *herdir* 'master-man'
gîl-dîs > *Gildis* 'star-woman'
morn-dôr > *Mordor* 'black land'
lend-bas > *lembas* 'way bread'
ang-band > *Angband* 'iron prison'
môr-goth > *Morgoth* 'black enemy'
brithon-bâr > *Brithombar* 'Brithon dwelling'

One exception occurred in the name *ang-(m)bâr* > *Angmar* 'land of iron'.

§ 15.17. Voiceless fricatives

Voiceless *th-* became *t-* after *s-* (see § 4.145):
gos-thîr > *Gostir* 'dread-countenance'
Otherwise *th-* remained: *ec-thelion*, *gala-thilion*, *caran-thir*, *lam-thanc*, *dur-thang*.

s- became *h-* (see § 4.71):
calen-sâd > *Calenhad* 'green spot'
lind-sîr > *Linhir* 'song-stream'
dîr-sael > *Dírhael* 'wise man'
pant-sael > *Panthael* 'all wise'
dû-sirion > *dúhirion* 'having dark streams'

Both *h-* arising from *s-* and original *h-* disappeared after fricatives (see § 4.136):

gwath-sîr > *Gwathir* 'shadow stream'
celeb-sarn > *Celepharn*[2] 'silver stone'
galadh-hîr > *Galathir* 'master of trees'

---

2. The voiced stop *b* had earlier become the voiceless fricative *f* before *h* (see § 4.134).

arod-hîr > *Arothir*[3] 'noble master'
maeg-heneb > *maecheneb*[4] 'sharp-eyed'
alph-hîr > *Elphir* 'swan master'
roch-hîr > *rochir* 'horse master'
loss-hoth > *Lossoth* 'snow horde'

h appears as *ch* after vowels and *-r* (cf. § 4.132):
elu-hîl > *Eluchíl* 'heir of Elwe'
eru-hîn > *Eruchín* 'children of Eru'
or-hall > *orchall* 'high-tall'
ar-hîr-iôn > *erchirion* 'son of a noble lord'
But *ch* was often softened to *h* (see § 4.216):
gwaew-hîr > **gwaechir* > *Gwaehir* 'wind master'
bara-hîr > *barachir* > *Barahir* 'eager master'
In other instances *h* remained: *duin-hir*, *glam-hoth*.

In all instances *f* remained: *an-falas*, *glor-findel*, *os-forod*, *bel-falas*.

§ 15.18. Liquids

lh- became *l-*; *rh-* became *r-* (§ 4.120):
lim-lhûg > *limlug* 'fish-dragon (sea serpent)'
am-rhûn > *amrûn* 'uprising, east'

r- occasionally assimilated to a preceding *-l* (§ 4.160):
edhel-rim > *edhellim* 'Elf people'

In all other instances *r-* remained: *galad-riel*, *mith-rill*, *galadhrim*, *land-roval*, *dam-raud*, *teler-rim*, *menel-rond*.
In all instances *l* remained: *onod-ló*, *mab-lung*, *taeg-lin*, *mith-lond*, *nim-loth*, *aer-linn*, *ring-ló*.

Changes in Element-Final Consonants (§§ 15.19–29)

§ 15.19. Final voiced stops

Final consonants of initial elements usually remained unchanged, but the following exceptional variations occurred:

Final voiced stops (*b*, *d*, *g*) became voiceless before the voiceless fricatives *th-*, and *f-* (see §§ 4.134, 4.136):

3. The voiced stop *d* had earlier become the voiceless fricative *th* before *h*.
4. The voiced stop *g* had earlier become the voiceless fricative *ch* before *h*.

aeg-thelion > *Aecthelion* 'sharp-willed one'
beleg-thôr > *Belecthor* 'great eagle'

Before *h* or *s* they combined to form the fricatives *f* (*ph*), *th*, *ch*:

celeb-sarn > *Celepharn* 'silver stone'
arod-hîr > *Arothir* 'noble lord'
maeg-heneb > *maecheneb* 'sharp-eyed'

§ 15.20. Final *-ch*

-ch was sometimes softened to *-h-* (§ 4.216):

roch-hîr > *rochir*, *rohir* 'horse-lord'

§ 15.21. Final *-dh*

-dh disappeared before fricatives and before original *m* and *n* (§§ 4.119, 4.135):

galadh-thilion > *Galathilion* 'silver-shining tree'
eledh-(n)dôr > *Elennor* 'land of Elves'
heledh-morn > *Helevorn* 'black glass'

-dh became *th* before *h* (which disappeared) (§§ 4.135–36):

galadh-hîr > *Galathir* 'lord of trees'

-dh became the stop *-d* before nonnasal stops (§ 4.123):

ardh-calen > *Ardgalen* 'green region'

and also before *l-* (or *gl-*) (§ 4.124):

galadh-glóriel > *Galadlóriel* 'golden tree'

-dh was retained elsewhere:

galadh-rim > *Galadhrim* 'tree-people'
enedh-gwaith > *Enedhwaith* 'middle-folk'

§ 15.22. Final *-l* and *-ll*

-ll was reduced to *-l-* before a following consonant (§ 4.129):

orchall-taur > *Orchaldor* 'eminent lord'
mall-peth > *Malbeth* 'word of gold'
mall-duin > *Malduin* 'gold river'
mell-dîr > *meldir* 'lover'
hall-barad > *Halbarad* 'tall tower'
ell-rochir > *Elrohir* 'Elf knight'

Final *-ol* often appears as *-la-* (§ 4.194):

**egol* + *(m)bâr* > *Eglamar* 'Elf home'
**magol* + *dûr* > *Magladhûr* 'dark sword'

§ 15.23. Final voiceless stops preceded by nasals

-mp became *-m* before stops and liquids (§ 4.137):
nimp-till > *nimdil* 'white point'
nimp-brethil > *Nimbrethil* 'white birch'
nimp-loth > *Nimloth* 'white flower'
nimp-ras > *Nimras* 'white horn'
-nc was retained:
anc-alagon > *Ancalagon* 'rushing jaw'

§ 15.24. Final *-n* and *-nd*

-nd became *-n* before a following consonant (§§ 4.114, 4.129):
and-taith > *andaith* 'long mark (in writing)'
gond-dôr > *gondor* 'stone land'
and-nest > *annest* 'central gate'
and-duin > *anduin* 'long river'
and-falas > *anfalas* 'long coast'
lind-sîr > *linhir* 'song river'
Both *-n* and *-nd* became *-m* before the labial sounds *p-*, *b-*, *m-* (§ 4.121):
celebrin-paur > *Celebrimbor* 'silver fist'
lend-bas > *lembas* 'way bread'
brithon-bâr > *Brithombar* 'Brithon dwelling'
annûn-minas > *Annúminas* 'west tower'
Both *-n* and *-nd* became *-ŋ*(transcribed *-n*) before the velar sounds *c-*, *g-* (§ 4.121):
thind-coll > *Thingol* (*thiŋgol*) 'grey cloak'
nîn-glaur > *ninglor* 'watery gold'
thoron-gîl > *Thorongil* 'eagle star'
-n normally became *-dh* before *r-* (§ 4.128):
caran-ras > *Caradhras* 'red horn'
eglan-rim > *Egladhrim* 'Elves of the Falas'
But in one (archaic or dialectal) case it remained:
aran-rûth > *Aranrúth* 'king('s) anger'
-n was sometimes assimilated to following *l-* (§ 4.158):
mithren-las > *Mithrellas* 'grey leaf'
but sometimes remained:
mîn-lammad > *minlamad* 'one sound'
-nd remained before *r-* (§ 4.146):
and-ros > *Andros* 'long foam'

unless a *d* was the next consonsant (§ 4.146):
find-raud > *Finrod* 'hair-champion'
-nd became *-ŋg* before *l-* (§§ 4.146, 4.148):
find-las > *Finglas* 'hair (of) leaf'
-n following *-l-* or *-r-* was usually lost when preceding another consonant (§ 4.140):
arn-cîr > *argir* 'royal ships'
morn-pen > *morben* 'dark person'
arn-gonath > *Argonath* 'royal stones'
morn-ndôr > *Mordor* 'black land'
morn-megil > *Mormegil* 'black sword'
carn-nen > *Carnen* 'red water'
n after *-l-* and *-r-* was preserved before voiceless fricatives and original *g(w)* deriving from *w* (§ 4.140):
dorn-hoth > *dornhoth* 'thrawn people'
forn-g(w)obel > *Fornobel* 'northern town' (cf. § 4.151)

§ 15.25. Final *-ng*

-ng (ŋ) became *-ng* (ŋg) before *l-*, *r-*, and *w-* (§ 4.147):
ang-rist > *Angrist* 'iron cleaver'
ring-lô > *Ringló* 'cold pool'
ang-gwêdh > *angwêdh* 'iron bond'
but *-ng* usually remained *ŋ* (§ 4.129):
ang-band > *Angband* (*aŋband*) 'iron prison'
ang-habar > *Anghabar* (*aŋhabar*) 'iron delving'

§ 15.26. Final *-r*

Final *-r* sometimes coalesced with a following *r-* (§ 4.162):
aer-randir > *Aerandir* 'sea wanderer'
aglar-rond > *Aglarond* 'cavern of glory'

(This coalescence possibly resulted from an early syncope or from analogy with forms showing such syncope: *aklarerondo* > *aklarondo* > *aglarond*); often, however, both *r*'s were retained: *Telerrim*, *Rohirrim*, *Arroch*.

-r occasionally assimilated to a following *l-* (§ 4.161):
glawar-lind > *glewellin* 'song of gold'

§ 15.27. Final *-s* and *-st*

-s appeared as *-ss* (its older form) before vowels (cf. § 4.184):
cris-aeg > *crissaeg* 'cleft peak'
Aros-iach > *Arossiach* 'ford of Aros'
-st became *-s* before stops and fricatives (§ 4.143):
bast-corn > *basgorn* 'round bread'
ost-giliath > *Osgiliath* 'fortress of stars'
ost-forod > *Osforod* 'fortress of the North'
-s and *-st* were changed to *th* before liquids *l* and *r* (§ 4.144):
falas-rim > *Falathrim* 'people of the shore'
nos-lîr > *nothlir* 'family lineage'
ost-rond > *othrond* 'fortress-cave'
lost-land > *Lothlann* 'empty and wide'

§ 15.28. Final *-u(v)* and *-au(v)*

-u and *-au* arising from **-uv* or **-auv* (§§ 4.173, 4.176–77) appeared as *-uv* or *-ov* before a suffix beginning with a vowel or *r* (or *gr*):
naw(nauv)-grod > *Novrod* 'hollow cave'
tinnu(v)-iell > *Tinúviel* 'daughter of twilight'

§ 15.29. Final *-w*

-w was lost before a consonant (§ 4.126):
gwaew-hîr > *gwaihir*, *gwaehir* 'wind master'
gwaew-raun > *gwaeron* 'wind month'

§ 15.30. Liquid mutation

A number of elements, including endings in *-r* or *-l*, came into contact with consonants even before the loss of composition vowels. These included *ar-* 'noble', *er-* 'one, alone', *mor-* 'dark', *nel-* 'three', and *or-* 'high'. Following *r* or *l*, voiceless stops *t*, *p*, and *c* became fricatives *th*, *f* (*ph*), and *ch*:

ar + pen > *arphen* 'noble person'
er + camion > *erchamion* 'one-handed'
mor + cant > *morchant* 'dark shape'
mor + till > *morthil* 'dark spike'
nel + till > *nelthil* 'three-corner, triangle'

§ 15.31. Vowel and dipthong shortenings

The long vowels *â*, *ê*, and *ô* in monosyllables were generally shortened when they became part of a compound.

â became *a*:

celebrin-tâl > *celebrindal* 'silver foot'

calen-sâd > *Calenhad* 'green spot'

mîr-tân > *mírdan* 'jewel smith'

thar-pâd > *tharbad* 'cross way'

tâl-raph > *talraph* 'foot-strap, stirrup'

ê became *e*:

môr-gwên > *Morwen* 'dark maiden'

ô became *o*:

môr-cai > *Morgai* 'black hedge'

dag-môr > *Dagmor* 'slay-dark'

môr-dôr > *Mordor* 'black land'

î and *û* were also sometimes shortened but often remained long (although not as long as in monosyllables; they are then marked with an acute accent, *í* and *ú*, instead of the circumflex).

î became *i*:

gwath-sîr > *Gwathir* 'shadow-river'

odog-gîl > *Edegil* 'seven stars'

dag-dîr > *dagnir* 'slayer'

hîr-rim > *hirrim* 'masters'

gîl-dîs > *Gildis* 'star-woman'

am-tîr > *amdir* 'upward looking'

leben-nîn > *Lebennin* 'five waters'

î became *í*:

rî-ann > *Rían* 'crown gift'

am-dîr > *Amdír* 'uprising man'

mîr-tân > *mírdan* 'jewel wright'

nîr-naeth > *nírnaeth* 'tear-lamentation'

dîr-naith > *dírnaith* 'man-spearhead'

nîn-nimp > *nínim* 'white tear'

curu-dîr > *curunír* 'skill-man'

eru-hîn > *Eruchín* 'children of God'

dîr-sael > *Dírhael* 'wise man'

û became *u*:

tû-gôr > *Tuor* 'strength-vigor'

gûl-dûr > *guldur* 'dark magic'
ûr-gwên > *Urwen* 'heat-maiden'
û became *û* or *ú*:
barad-dûr > *barad-dûr* 'dark tower'
carag-dûr > *caragdûr* 'dark crag'
cû-raun > *cúron* 'bow-moon, crescent'
cû-thalion > *cúthalion* 'strong bow'

The vowels *î* and *û* remained long before *-n* and *-r*, especially in the initial syllable of a disyllable, or the final syllable of a trisyllable, although not always even in these instances.

Long vowels were also retained when they compensated for a lost consonant, especially earlier *ʒ* or *v*:

onod-lô (**-loʒ*) > *Onodló* 'ent-pool'
*dû-(*duv-)lind* > dúlinn 'night-singer'
au likewise normally became *o*, both initially and finally:
aeg-naur > *Aegnor* 'fell fire'
bal-raug > *balrog* 'monster of power'
glaur-findel > *Glorfindel* 'golden tress'
raud-naur > *Rodnor* 'noble fire'
au occasionally remained (see § 4.168):
gaur-hoth > *gaurhoth* 'wolf horde'
naug-rim > *naugrim* 'Dwarf people'

§ 15.32. Consonant simplification

Final consonant clusters were often shortened in compound words:

-a (from original *ʒ*) disappeared (§ 4.122, 4.154–55):
tara-lanc > *tarlanc* 'stiff-neck'
êg-thela > *ecthel* 'thorn-spear point'
-ll became *-l* (§ 4.205):
cened-rill > *cenedril* 'sight-reflection, mirror'
celeb-till > *celebdil* 'silver tine'
-mp became *-m* (§ 4.204):
nîn-nimp > *nínim* 'white tear'
-nd became *-nn* in disyllables (§ 4.212):
aerlind > *aerlinn* 'sea-song'
lost-land > *lothlann* 'empty and wide'

-nd became *-n* in words of more than two syllables (§ 4.213):
sereg-gond > *seregon* 'blood of stone'

For exceptions to the above two rules see § 4.213.

-nw became *-n* (§ 4.191):
ithil-dinw > *ithildin* 'moon-star'
curw-finw > *Curufin* 'skill-Finwe'
el-ianw > *eilian* 'sky-bridge'

-rn became *-r* (§ 4.209):
**hâl* + *tirn* > *heledir* 'fish watcher'
ed-tirn > *ethir* 'out-looker, spy'

-st became *-s* (§ 4.208):
imlad-rist > *Imladris* 'glen of the cleft'

16

Loanwords in Sindarin

Although the vocabulary of Classical Sindarin was derived for the most part from Old Sindarin, in its long history Sindarin borrowed many words from other languages. These loanwords were usually adapted to Sindarin's phonetic style.

The greatest number of borrowings are from Quenya, which is not surprising given the long period of contact between the Noldor and the Sindar in Beleriand and the Noldor's adoption of Sindarin as their spoken tongue. These words often referred to specific knowledge that the Noldor obtained in the West (which had been unavailable to the Sindar), to cultural peculiarities of the Noldor, or to details of their technology.

The religious beliefs of the Noldor contributed the Quenya words *Eru*[2] 'the One' (Q *Eru*), *fân* in the sense 'apparitional form of a Vala' (Q *fana*), and *iaun* 'holy place' (Q *yána*).

Noldorin cosmology contributed the words *menel* 'heaven' (Q *menel*) and *gilwen* or *gilith* 'space, region where the stars are' (Q *ilmen*).

The knowledge of the Noldor concerning human beings (who had not appeared in Beleriand at the time of the return of the Noldor) was reflected in the words *adan* 'man' (Q *atan*) and *fair* 'mortal' (Q *firya*).

Quenya also contributed the words *silef*[2] 'an unbreakable crystal of Noldorin manufacture' (Q *silima*), *tegil* 'pen' (Q *tecil*), and possibly *sigil*[1] 'knife '(Q *sicil*). Also from Quenya was the element *athe-* in *athelas* (Q *aþëa*, *asëa*), and the Quenya name *arien* for the personified Sun appears to have been borrowed as the name of the daisy, *eirien*.

Other words also probably borrowed from Quenya, for less obvious reasons, were *arth* 'noble' (Q *arta*), *caun*[3] 'commander' (Q *cáno*), *lalaith* 'laughter' (Q *lala-* 'laugh'), *lant*[1] 'fall' (Q *lanta*), *le* 'thou' (Q *elye*), *palan* 'far' (Q *palan*), *sam* 'chamber' (Q *sambë*), *Send* 'one of the Sindar' (Q *Sinda*), and *sûl*[2] 'wind' (Q *súlë*).

In form these words were sometimes borrowed entire (e.g., *Eru*, *menel*, *palan*) or with only the loss of a final vowel (which was rare in Sindarin):

fân, *lant*, *sûl*, and *sam* (probably borrowed in the form **samb*). But greater changes were sometimes required to adapt a Quenya word to Sindarin form: in Sindarin the consonants *t*, *p*, *c* did not occur between vowels (they had been changed to *d*, *b*, *g*; see § 4.108), and this process was also followed in adapting Quenya words to Sindarin: *atan* > *adan*, *tecil* > *tegil*, *sicil* > *sigil*. In Sindarin *t*, *p*, and *c* also did not exist following *l* or *r* (they had changed in this position to *th*, *ph*, or *ch*; see § 4.64), and the Noldor also imitated this procedure in adapting Quenya to Sindarin: *arta* > *arth*. Long *á*, common in Quenya but rare in Sindarin, was altered to the diphthong *au*: *yána* > *iaun* (where *i* before a vowel represents the same sound as *y*), *cáno* > *caun* (cf. §§ 4.58, 4.109–10).

Quenya originally had a sound *þ*, which had generally been altered to *s* before the return of the Noldor to Beleriand. This was sometimes preserved as Sindarin *th* (*athelas*, the place-name *Hithlum* = Q *Híþilómë*) but often appears as Sindarin *s* in borrowed words, this fact in itself clearly marking the words as of Quenya origin: *sam*, *Send*, *sûl*.

A few more complex phonological processes were occasionally imitated in the Quenya loans, e.g., *i*-affection (*Send*, *silef*) or double affection (*fair*).

Many names, usually referring to the Noldor themselves or places they had named, were rendered into Sindarin form. Some simply replaced each Quenya element with a cognate Sindarin element, producing an intelligible name in Sindarin. Some such names were *Amrod* (Q *Ambaráto*), *Amros* (Q *Ambarussa*), *Angrod* (Q *Angaráto*), *Caranthir* (Q *Carnistir*), *Celebrimbor* (Q *Telperinquar*), *Finrod* (Q *Findaráto*), *Galadriel* (Q *Altáriel*), *Morgoth* (Q *Moringoþo*), (*Amon*) *Uilos* (Q *Oiolossë*).

In other names new elements were introduced that were not found in Sindarin: *Aegnor* (Q *Aicanáro*), *Argon* (Q *Aracáno*), *Celegorm* (Q *Tyelcormo*), *Fingon* (Q *Findecáno*), *Inglor* (Q *Ingalaurë*), *Maglor* (Q *Macalaurë*), *Turgon* (Q *Turucáno*), where the elements *aica*, *cáno*, *ormo*, *inga*, and *maca* have no Sindarin equivalents.

Sometimes an equivalent Sindarin element was introduced that was not exactly cognate to the Quenya element: *Edhel-los*, for example, represented *Elda-lótë*.

Sometimes the elements were rearranged: *Ras Arphain* for *Ar-fanyarassë*.

Other names were simply made to resemble the Quenya originals, without any attempt to use Sindarin elements: *Aerendil* (Q *Eärendil*), *Angelimir* (Q *Ancalimir*), *Arnor* (Q *Arnanórë*), *Boromir* (Q *Voromírë*), *Edennil* (Q *Atandil*), *Enerdhil* (Q *Anardil*), *Huan* (Q *Huan*), *Idril* (Q *Itarillë*), *Lalwen* (Q *Lalwendë*), *Tûn* (Q *Túna*).

Sometimes only one Sindarin element was introduced, while the rest remained similar to Quenya: Fëanor for *Fëanáro* (with *naur*, *-nor* for *náro*), *Gondolin(d)* for *Ondolindë* (with *gond* for *ondo*), *Hithlum* for *Hísilómë* (with *hîth* for *hísë*).

Sometimes new Sindarin names were constructed from elements of different Quenya names, e.g., *Maedros* from *Maitimo Russandol.*

An acceptable Sindarin-seeming name could occasionally be made just by joining a Sindarin word with a Quenya name of appropriate form: *loth* + *Lórien* became *Lothlórien*. Or an acceptable Sindarin suffix could replace a Quenya one: *Írith*, *Íreth* for *Írissë*.

Sometimes names were given the forms they would have had in Sindarin if they had descended from the same origin as the Quenya, whether or not they made sense in Sindarin: *Finu* (Q *Finwë*), *Angolonn* (Q *Ingolondë*), and *Balannor* (Q *Valandor* [= *Valinor*]). An exceptional variant of this type of conversion was *Fingolfin* for *Nolofinwë*, where the element *Fin* (for *Finwë*) was prefixed to the whole name.

Sindarin also borrowed name elements from some of its more divergent dialects, only slightly modifying them for use; this appears to be the origin of the element *lómin* 'echoing' in *Dor-lómin* and *Eryd Lómin*, a borrowing from North Sindarin; and the names *Dior*, *Mablung*, *Lúthien*, and *Aranrúth* may show peculiarities of the dialect of Doriath.

Khuzdul provided only a few words: here the difficult (to the Sindar) sounds of the Dwarvish language were very substantially altered. Khuzdul *khazâd* 'Dwarves' gave S *hadhod* 'Dwarf' (older **xaðaud*); Khuzdul *kheled* 'glass' gave S *heledh*. The Khuzdul epithet *felakgundu* 'hewer of caves' was rendered in Sindarin as *Felagund* or *Felagon.*

The language of the Green-Elves of Ossiriand lent the element *lind* (S *linn*, *glinn*) 'song' in the words *lindel*, *lindedhel*, and the name *Lindon*, and probably the element *oss* 'seven' in the names *Ossir*, *Ossiriand.*

The language of the Drúedain lent only their name for themselves, *druʒu*, which became Sindarin *drû* (probably borrowed as **druʒ*).

The Mannish language of the Bëorian people contributed the word *rêd* 'heir', at least in the name Eluréd.

17

Syntax

Syntax is the description of the construction of sentences and the phrases that compose them. Although the number of complete Sindarin sentences is very small (see appendix 1), it is still possible to make some generalizations; these are most reliable for the shorter phrases, which are more abundantly attested. The following account will therefore begin by describing these phrases and then turn to a characterization of larger sentence structures.

Sindarin is a rather consistently *head-left* language. That means that in any phrase, which consists of the *head* or main word and any word or phrase that modifies the head, the head will be on the left. Thus nouns are followed by the nouns, adjectives, or prepositional phrases that modify them in noun phrases; prepositions are followed by their complements in prepositional phrases; determiners are followed by the noun phrases that complement them in determiner phrases, and so on. The rare exceptions are noted below.

§ 17.1. Noun phrases

Noun phrases consist at minimum of a single pronoun, noun, or name: *im* 'I', *edhel* 'an Elf', *Eregion* 'Hollin', *Perhael* 'Samwise', etc. Noun phrases may also consist of a noun combined with another noun or noun phrase, with adjectives, with prepositional phrases, or with complementizer phrases.

§ 17.2. Composite noun phrases

Complex noun phrases consist of a noun and other words or phrases, e.g., another noun phrase. There are two principal types of noun phrases consisting of two nouns (or noun phrases) adjoining each other: the *appositive noun phrase* and the *genitive noun phrase*.

§ 17.3. Appositive noun phrases

In appositive noun phrases the two nouns or noun phrases used refer to the same being(s):

Herdir Perhael 'Master Samwise'
Elbereth Gilthoniel 'Elbereth Star-kindler'

A pronoun and a noun can also stand in apposition:

im Narvi 'I, Narvi'
im Tinúviel 'I, Nightingale'
men Eruchín 'we children of God'

One of the two phrases can be a genitive phrase (underlined) (see § 17.4):

Durin aran Moria 'Durin, king of Moria'
Beren iôn Barahir 'Beren, son of Barahir'

One of the two phrases can be a noun phrase containing an adjective (underlined) (see § 17.6): *Meril bess dîn* 'Rose, his wife'.

Two composite noun phrases can stand in apposition to each other: *Taur a Perhael Conin en Annûn* 'Frodo and Samwise, princes of the West'.

§ 17.4. Genitive noun phrases

In genitive phrases the second noun or noun phrase modifies or restricts the first, which is the head, or main word of the phrase. The functions of the genitive are extremely varied; genitive nouns can refer to possessors, agents, objects of action, subject matter, habitual inhabitants or users, creators, spheres of rule or control, associated emotions, associated persons and places, characteristic qualities, constituent elements, intensifiers, and so on. However, in all cases the function is adequately represented by use of the English preposition *of*:

ennyn Durin 'doors of Durin'
aran Moria 'king of Moria'
fennas nogothrim 'gate of the Dwarves'
gil galad 'star of brilliance'
hîn Húrin 'children of Húrin'
certhas Daeron 'runic alphabet of Daeron'
aglar elenath 'glory of stars'
peth lammen 'word of my tongue'

pennas silevril 'account of silmarils'
dagor dagorath 'battle of battles'

The second element of a genitive phrase (underlined) is frequently a determiner phrase (see § 17.9):

dor en·ernil 'the land of the prince'
cabed en·aras 'the leap of the deer'
bar en·danwedh 'the house of the ransom'
ost in·edhil 'the fortress of the Elves'
dant i·lais 'the fall of the leaves'
ernil i·pheriannath 'the prince of the halflings'
tol in·gaurhoth 'the island of the wolves'

Although genitive phrases consisting of two nouns are the most common, either half of the genitive phrase may be a noun phrase of any degree of complexity. For example, a genitive phrase may contain two nouns or noun phrases in conjunction as modifiers of the head (underlined):

athrabeth Finrod ah Andreth 'debate of Finrod and Andreth'
aran Gondor ar Arnor 'King of Gondor and Arnor'
dor cú ar thol 'land of bow and helm'
narn e·dant gondolin ar orthad en·êl 'the tale of the fall of Gondolin and the raising of the star'

Genitive phrases can be nested inside each other, the head of each phrase remaining on the left; that is, the second element of the genitive phrase can itself be a genitive phrase (underlined):

ínias dor Rodyn 'annals of (the) land of (the) Valar'
emyn hen Dúnadan 'hills of (the) eye of (the) Númenórean'

The second element can also be a noun in apposition with another noun or noun phrase: *narn Beren iôn Barahir* 'tale of Beren son of Barahir'.

The second element of the genitive phrase can be a noun phrase including a prepositional phrase: *aerlinn in-edhil o Imladris* 'sea-song of the Elves of Rivendell'.

The second element of the genitive phrase can be a noun phrase including a complementizer phrase: *dor gyrth i-chuinar* 'land of (the) dead that live'.

Either of the elements in a genitive phrase can be modified by an adjective:

<u>côf gwaeren</u> Bêl '<u>windy bay</u> of Bêl'
<u>cirith forn</u> en andrath '<u>northern pass</u> of the long-climbing-road'.
hîr <u>i·Mbair Annui</u> 'lord <u>of the Western Lands</u>'

§ 17.5. Conjunct noun phrases

A noun phrase can consist of two or more noun phrases conjoined by an *and* (*ah* before vowels; earlier *ar*):

loth a galadh 'flower and tree'
Taur a Perhael 'Frodo and Samwise'
Finrod ah Andreth 'Finrod and Andreth'
Gondor ar Arnor 'Gondor and Arnor'
cû ar thôl 'bow and helm'

§ 17.6. Noun and adjective phrase

Adjectival noun phrases consist of a head noun or noun phrase normally followed by an adjective (underlined) or adjective phrase (see § 17.10), which is sometimes lenited. In exceptional cases the adjective precedes the noun, in which case the noun is lenited. The adjective agrees in number with the noun:

annon <u>edhellen</u> '<u>Elvish</u> door'
parth <u>galen</u> '<u>green</u> lawn'
genediad <u>Drannail</u> '<u>Shire</u> Reckoning'
bas <u>ilaurui</u> '<u>daily</u> bread'
ithryn <u>luin</u> '<u>blue</u> wizards'

A noun can also be modified by a longer adjective phrase: *Elbereth Gilthoniel <u>o menel palan-diriel</u>* 'Elbereth Star-kindler <u>gazing afar from heaven</u>'.

In reverse order the adjective precedes the noun:

<u>sarn</u> athrad '<u>stony</u> ford'
<u>carn</u> dûm '<u>red</u> valley'
<u>galadhremmin</u> ennorath '<u>tree-woven</u> middle-lands'

In poetry adjectives can be placed before the noun phrase they modify for reasons of rhyme or meter:

<u>silivren</u> penna *<u>míriel</u>* / o menel aglar elenath
'the <u>crystalline</u> <u>jeweled</u> glory of the stars slants down from heaven'

An adjective can even modify a pronoun that is not overtly expressed:

[im] palan-díriel . . . le linnathon
'[I] having gazed afar . . . will sing to you'

Numbers, unlike most adjectives, come before the nouns they modify:

leben tail 'five feet'
cf. *tad-dail* 'two-footed'

The genitive pronouns *nín* 'my', *mín* 'our', *lín* 'your', *în* 'his own', and *tín* 'his' are treated like adjectives and are always found lenited (e.g., *mín* becomes *vín* and *tîn* becomes *dín*), since they are only attested following the nouns they modify. The demonstrative adjective *hen* 'this' (plural *hin* 'these') behaves the same way (being originally the lenited forms of **sen*, **sin*):

tîw hin 'these letters'
bar nín 'my home'
úgerth vín 'our misdeeds'
mellyn în 'his own friends'
bess dîn 'his wife'
ionnath dîn 'his sons'
sellath dîn 'his daughters'

Adjectives following these words receive the nasal mutation, e.g., *în phain* 'all of his'. Adjectives may also precede the genitive pronoun: *bas ilaurui vín* 'our daily bread'.

§ 17.7. Noun and prepositional phrase

A noun phrase can consist of a noun head followed by a prepositional phrase (underlined) (see § 17.11) that modifies the noun:

Celebrimbor o Eregion 'Celebrimbor of Eregion'
edhil o Imladris 'Elves from Imladris'
bronwe athar harthad 'endurance beyond hope'
rath a chelerdain 'street for lampwrights'
bair am yrn 'houses up in trees'
taur im duinath 'wood between rivers'
taur na neldor 'wood of beech'
edaib na nestad 'houses of healing'
mîr n' ardhon 'jewel of (the) world'
orod na thôn 'mountain of pine'
taur nu fuin 'wood under night'

dor nu fauglith 'land under choking ash'
emyn nu fuin 'mountains under night'
taur nan erig 'wood of the hollies'
dagor nuin giliath 'battle under the stars'

A following prepositional phrase can function as an adjective, in which case the preposition and noun may be treated as one word:

innas lín bo Geven 'your will on Earth'
nírnaeth arnediad (= *ar nediad*) 'lamentation without count'
iarwain ben-adar (= *pen adar*) 'oldest (person) without a father'

§ 17.8. Noun and complementizer phrase

A noun phrase can consist of a noun or noun phrase followed by a modifying complementizer phrase (underlined) (see § 17.16):

gyrth i chuinar 'dead (people) who live'
adar nín i vi menel 'my father who (is) in heaven'
mín i gohenam di 'us who forgive them'
di ai gerir úgerth 'those who do misdeeds'
i-Cherdir Perhael i sennui Panthael estathar aen 'Mayor Samwise, who should rather be called Fullwise'

§ 17.9. Determiner phrases

Determiner phrases consist of various forms of the article *i* 'the' followed by a noun phrase (which may itself consist of bare noun, noun conjunct, noun + adjective, etc.). The article agrees in number with the noun and is inflected in the genitive singular (*en* 'of the').

Singular determiner phrases:

i·annon 'the door'
i·aran Gondor ar Arnor 'the king of Gondor and Arnor'
i·Cherdir Perhael 'the master Samwise'

Determiner phrases with abstract nouns (this Sindarin construction is notably unlike English usage):

i·estel 'Hope'
i·nírnaeth 'Lamentation'

Determiner phrases inflected in the genitive:

en annûn 'of the West'
e·mbar 'of the home'
e·ndaedhelos 'of the great fear'
en·danwedh 'of the ransom'
e·dinúviel 'of the nightingale'
en·êl 'of the star'
en ernil 'of the prince'
en·nírnaeth 'of lamentation'

Plural determiner phrases:

in·edhil 'the Elves'
i·mbair 'the dwellings'
i·thiw 'the letters'
in·gwanur 'the twins'
i·pheriannath 'the halflings'
i·lais 'the leaves'
i·chîn 'the children'
i·naugrim 'the Dwarves'
i·melegyrn 'the great trees'
i·ndengin 'the slain (ones)'
in·drúedain 'the Drû-folk'
in·gaurhoth 'the wolves'

Nouns modified by possessive pronouns and demonstrative adjectives usually also take a determiner:

i thiw hin 'these letters'
i arnad lín 'your kingdom'
i eneth lín 'your name'
i mbas ilaurui vín 'our daily bread'
i úgerth vín 'our misdeeds'
e-mbar nín 'of my home'

A noun that is modified by a determined noun may itself be understood as determined without the further addition of an article:

ered en·Echoriath 'the mountains of the Echoriath'
orthad en·êl 'the raising of the star'

§ 17.10. Adjective phrases

An adjective phrase may consist simply of an adjective, e.g., *calen* 'green', or an adjective combined with other modifiers. Adjective phrases may include adverbs (e.g., *mae govannen* 'well met') or by prepositional phrases used adverbially, which can either precede or follow the adjective:

> *o menel palan-diriel* 'gazing afar from heaven'
> *na-chaered palandíriel o galadhremmin ennorath* 'having gazed afar to the distance from the tree-woven middle-lands'

An adjective phrase can include a phrase indicating extent or degree; in the following example a noun phrase indicates extent: *leben tail brand* 'five feet high'

§ 17.11. Prepositional phrases

Prepositional phrases consist of prepositions followed by a pronoun, a determiner phrase, or noun phrase (or, perhaps, a determiner phrase with null determiner).

§ 17.12. Preposition and pronoun

Prepositions merge with a following pronoun:

> *anim* 'for me'
> *ammen* 'for us'
> *enni* 'for me'

§ 17.13. Preposition and noun phrase

The most typical prepositional phrase consists of a preposition followed by a noun, which takes the appropriate consonant mutation:

> *am yrn* 'up in trees'
> *a chelerdain* 'for lampwrights'
> *athar harthad* 'beyond hope'
> *bo Geven* 'on Earth'
> *di nguruthos* 'under horror of death'
> *im duinath* 'between rivers'
> *vi Menel* 'in heaven'
> *na vedui* 'at last'

na-chaered 'to a distance'
na neldor 'of beech'
ned Echuir 'in Echuir'
nef aear 'on this side of (the) sea'
nu fuin 'under night'
o *menel* 'from heaven'
u dalraph 'without a stirrup'

§ 17.14. Preposition and determiner phrase

These prepositional phrases consist of a preposition followed by a determiner phrase (§ 17.9). The article *in* (see §§ 12.5, 12.9) is usually merged with the preceding preposition:

ben genediad Drannail 'according to the Shire reckoning'
erin dolothen Ethuil 'on the eighth of Ethuil'
erin Gwirith edwen 'on Gwirith second'
uin aran 'from the king'
min hiriath 'between the rivers' (taken as singular)

'ni Pheriannath 'to the halflings'
dan i ngaurhoth 'against the wolf-host'
nan erig 'of/to the hollies'
nuin giliath 'under the stars'

§ 17.15. Conjunct prepositional phrases

Two prepositional phrases can be joined together by conjunctions such as *ar* 'and' and *sui* 'as':

a Pherhael ar am Meril 'to Samwise and to Rose'
bo Geven sui vi Menel 'on Earth as in Heaven'

§ 17.16. Complementizer phrases

A complementizer phrase consists of the complementizer *i* ('that', 'who', 'whom', 'which') followed by a sentence. If followed directly by the verb, the verb takes the same mutations as a noun following a nominative determiner: soft mutation for the singular, nasal mutation for the plural:

ai gerir úgerth '(they) who do misdeeds'
i chuinar '(they) who live'

> *i . . . Panthael estathar aen* '(he) whom . . . they should call Full-wise'
> *i gohenam di* '(we) who forgive them'
> *i vi menel* '(he) who (is) in heaven'

§ 17.17. Sentence structure: verbless sentences

Many sentences in Sindarin can be constructed without having any overt verb; the implied verb is usually some form of *to be*. Verbless sentences include those consisting of just a noun phrase, of a noun and one or more prepositional phrases, or of an adjective phrase with or without a noun.

§ 17.18. Noun-phrase sentences

A sentence can consist of just a single noun phrase, in which case it is usually an assertion of the existence of the person or thing denoted:

> *yrch* '(there are) Orcs'
> *ennyn Durin aran Moria* '(these are) the doors of Durin, king of Moria'
> *ernil i pheriannath* '(that is) the prince of the Halflings'
> *ered en echoriath, ered e·mbar nín* '(these are) the mountains of Echoriath, (these are) the mountains of my home'.

§ 17.19. Noun-and-prepositional-phrase sentences

A sentence can consist of a noun phrase and a prepositional phrase (or multiple prepositional phrases), in which case the sentence has a jussive sense. These are distinct from noun-phrase sentences, as the prepositional phrase does not form part of the noun phrase but rather functions adverbially to the unexpressed verb *to be*. The prepositional phrases are underlined in the examples below:

> *naur an edraith ammen* '(let there be) fire for saving for us'
> *gurth an glamhoth* '(let there be) death to the Orcs'
> *naur dan i ngaurhoth* '(let there be) fire against the wolf-host'
> *aglar 'ni pheriannath* '(let there be) glory to the halflings'
> *a Pherhael . . . suilad uin aran* '(let there be) a greeting to Samwise . . . from the King'

The last example shows the placement of the prepositional phrase *a Pherhael* in presentential position (see § 17.30 below).

§ 17.20. Adjectival sentences

A sentence can consist of a single adjective phrase, when what the adjective (below, *govannen*) applies to is obvious: *mae govannen!* '(you are) well met!'

A sentence can also consist of a predicative adjective phrase preceding a noun phrase: *leben tail brand i annon* 'five feet high (is) the door'.

§ 17.21. Sentence structure: verbal sentences

The basic word order of a verbal sentence is Verb-Subject (-Object) or VS(O). The *subject* is a noun phrase (of any length) performing the action of the verb; the *object* is the recipient of the action. Only *transitive* verbs require an object; *intransitive* verbs need no object, and sentences containing intransitives may have the structure VS.

External to this basic order is a presentential position in which the *topic* or emphasized phrase can be placed. This *topic position* can be filled by either subject or object, although subject topicalization is far more common. When subject or object appears in the topic position, it does not appear in the normal word order; thus, it appears to have moved from its normal place to the topic position. Topicalization of the subject creates the apparent order SVO; topicalization of the object creates the order OVS. The effect of such sentences can be approximated by the use of the "cleft sentence"; e.g., *It is I, Narvi, who made them.* But the cleft sentence creates a rather stronger emphasis than Sindarin topicalization does.

When the object of a verb is a pronoun rather than a noun phrase, it normally precedes the verb, producing the word order OVS. In such cases it is possible for the verb to be moved to the topic position, producing the order VOS, or for the subject to be topicalized, producing the order SOV.

In the sentences below, *verbs* are in italics, subjects are underlined once, and **objects** are in bold.

§ 17.22. Normal VS(O)-type sentences:

Transitive: VSO

aníra i aran . . . *suilannad* **mhellyn în phain** 'the king *desires* . . . **to greet all his friends**'.

caro den **i innas lín** '*may* one *do* **your will**' (= may your will be done).

If the verb governs an infinitive, the sentence has the normal VSO order: verb-subject-infinitive (-object).

Transitive: VSIO

aníra i aran . . . *suilannad* **mhellyn în phain** 'the king *desires* . . . **to greet all his friends**'.

Intransitive: VS

tôl acharn 'vengeance *is coming*'
pedo mellon '*may* a friend *speak*'
lacho calad '*may* light *flame*'
drego morn '*may* darkness *flee*'
tolo i arnad lín '*may* your kingdom *come*'
cuio i pheriain '*may* the halflings *live*'
penna míriel o menel aglar elenath! 'the glory of the stars *slants* down like jewels from heaven!'

The verb *na-* 'to be' together with an adjective creates a single verb phrase, e.g., *no aer* 'be holy'. This verb phrase functions like a single verb, so the following sentence also has VS structure: *no aer* i eneth lín '*may* your name *be holy*'.

VSO sentences with pronominal objects become OVS.

Transitive: OVS

le *linnon* im Tinúviel 'I, Nightingale, *sing* to **you**'.

§ 17.23. Sentences with omitted subject pronouns

Sentences with a first or second person *pronoun* subject may omit the pronoun, creating a V(O) structure.

Transitive: VO

lasto **beth lammen** '*listen* to **the word of my tongue**'
ónen **i-Estel** Edain 'I *gave* **Hope** to the Edain'
ú-chebin **estel** anim 'I *do* not *keep* **hope** for myself'

Intransitive: V

Edro '*Open!*'
Daro '*Stop!*'
Eglerio '*Praise!*'

VO sentences with pronominal objects become OV.

Transitive: OV

le *linnathon* 'I *will sing* to **you**'.
le *nallon* 'I *cry* out to **you**'.

§ 17.24. Sentences with subject topicalization (SV[O]-type sentences)

Transitive: SVO

Celebrimbor o Eregion *teithant* **i thiw hin.** 'Celebrimbor of Eregion *wrote* **these letters**'.

e *aníra tírad* **i-Cherdir Perhael.** 'He *desires* to see **Master Samwise**'.

Aragorn . . . *anglennatha* **i-Varanduiniant.** 'Aragorn . . . *will approach* **the Brandywine-Bridge**'.

Intransitive: SV

Guren *bêd* enni. 'My heart *speaks* for me'.

Neledh *neledhi* gar godref. 'Three *can go* through together'.

SVO sentences with pronominal objects become SOV, the object pronoun preceding the verb.

Transitive: SOV

im Narvi **hain** *echant.* I, Narvi, *made* **them**'.

Sentences containing infinitives have the order subject-verb-infinitive (-object), or SVI(O) if the subject is topicalized. Note that the infinitive, unlike noun objects following a verb, is not subject to soft mutation:
e *aníra tírad* **i-Cherdir Perhael.** 'He *desires* to see **Master Samwise**'.

But the infinitive may also be placed in topic position together with the subject, producing the order SIV(O):

neledh *neledhi gar* godref 'three can go through together'.

§ 17.25. Sentences with object topicalization

OV sentence with object topicalization:

Daur a Berhael . . . *eglerio*! **'Frodo and Samwise,** *praise* (them)!'

Note that the lenition of *Taur a Perhael*, the objects of *eglerio*, remains, despite the appearance of the noun phrase in the topic position.

§ 17.26. Sentences with verb topicalization

There are rare exceptions in which the verb is topicalized and so precedes an object pronoun.

Transitive: VO

Tiro **nin.** '*Watch over* **me**'.

§ 17.27 Conjunct sentences

A sentence can consist of two or more independent clauses conjoined by the conjunction *a* or *ar* 'and'. Each independent clause below is underlined separately:

Pedo mellon a minno. 'Say "friend" and enter' (or 'Let a friend speak and enter').

Leben tail brand i annon, a neledh neledhi gar godref. 'Five feet high is the door and three can enter together'.

Anno ammen sír imbas ilaurui vín ar diheno ammen i úgerth vín. 'Give to us today our daily bread and forgive us our misdeeds'.

Aragorn . . . anglennatha i·Varanduiniant ar ennas aníra i aran . . . suilannad mhellyn în phain. 'Aragorn . . . will approach the Brandywine Bridge and he desires . . . to greet all his friends'.

§ 17.28. Extrasentential elements

Elements not intrinsic to the sentence structure, such as vocatives and verb modifiers (adverbials) do not have fixed positions within the sentence structures outlined above but are found in *extrasentential* positions, either before or after the sentence. Adverbials, in addition, can be found immediately following the verb they modify.

§ 17.29. Vocatives

Vocatives (nouns or noun phrases used to directly address a person or thing) usually occur at the beginning of a sentence. In the following examples the vocatives are underlined, and verbs are italicized:

Ae adar nín . . . *no* aer i eneth lín. 'O my father . . . *may* your name *be* holy'.

A Elbereth Gilthoniel . . . *penna* . . . aglar elenath. 'O Elbereth Starkindler . . . the glory of the stars . . . *slants* down'.

A Hîr Annûn gilthoniel, le *linnon* im Tinúviel! 'O Lady of the West, star-kindler, I *cry* to you, I, Nightingale!'

A Elbereth Gilthoniel o menel palan-diriel le *nallon* sí di' nguruthos. 'O Elbereth Star-kindler watching afar from heaven, I *cry* to you under horror of death!'

Annon edhellen, *edro* hi ammen. 'O Elvish gate, *open* now for us.'

Fennas nogothrim, *lasto* beth lammen. 'O doorway of Dwarves, *listen* to the word of my tongue'.

loth a galadh *lasto* dîn. 'O flower and tree, *listen* silent(?)'.

Less often, vocatives are inserted at the end of a sentence (whether or not that sentence is embedded in another):

Ai, na vedui, Dúnadan! 'Ah, at last, Dúnadan!'
Noro lim, Asfaloth! Run swiftly (?), Asfaloth!
A *tiro* nin, Fanuilos. 'O *watch over* me, Ever-white'.

§ 17.30. Adverbials

Verbs are typically modified either by adverbs or by prepositional phrases (more rarely, by noun phrases) that modify the verb in some way, indicating, for instance, the *place where* the action takes place, the *place from which* the action originates, the *place to which* the action tends, the *time when* the action takes place, the person *for whom* the action is done, the *manner in which* (i.e., how) and the *extent to which* (i.e., how much) the action is done.

These adverbs or adverbial prepositional phrases cannot be inserted inside a noun phrase, determiner phrase, or prepositional phrase. Their normal position is right after the verb; however, they can also appear in the extrasentential positions at the beginning or end of a sentence (including embedded sentences). In the following examples adverbials are underlined, and verbs are italicized.

Adverbials occurring after the verb:

Anno ammen sír i mbas ilaurui vín. '*Give* to us today our daily bread'.
Diheno ammen i úgerth vín. '*Forgive* to us our misdeeds

Ambiguous adverbials (both after verb and at the end of the sentence):

Guren *bêd* enni. 'My heart *speaks* for me'.
Edro hi ammen '*Open* now for us.
Le *nallon* sí di nguruthos. 'I *cry* to you here under horror of death'.
Neledh *neledhi gar* godref. 'Three *can enter* together'.
Le *linnathon* nef aear sí nef aearon. 'I *will sing* to you on this side of the sea, here on this side of the great sea'.
Loth a galadh *lasto* dîn. 'Flower and tree, *listen* silently'.
Noro lim. '*Run* lightly' (?).

Adverbials at the end of the sentence:

Cuio i pheriain anann. '*May* the halflings *live* for a long time'.
Ú-*chebin* estel anim. 'I *keep* no hope for myself'.
Aragorn . . . *anglennatha* i-Varanduiniant erin dolothen Ethuil. 'Aragorn . . . *will approach* the Brandywine Bridge on the eighth of Ethuil'.

ai *gerir* úgerth ammen 'who *do* misdeeds to us'
Ónen i-Estel Edain. 'I *gave* Hope to Men'.

Adverbials at the beginning of the sentence:

Ennas *aníra* i aran . . . suilannad mhellyn în phain. 'There the king *wants* . . . to greet all his friends'.

Edregol e *aníra* tírad i-Cherdir Perhael. 'He especially *wants* to see Mayor Samwise'.

Si loth a galadh *lasto*. 'Now flower and tree, *listen*'.

Adverbials can also be used in verbless sentences (cf. § 17.19):

A Pherhael ar am Meril, Suilad. 'To Samwise and to Rose, [let there be] Greeting'.

Some exceptions are found in poetry. In the sentence below, the adjective *míriel* has been moved before the prepositional phrase *o menel* for the sake of a rhyme:

Penna míriel o menel aglar elenath. 'The jeweled glory of the stars *slants* down from heaven'.

A more normal order might have been "Penna o menel aglar míriel elenath," in which the prepositional phrase follows the verb.

Appendix 1

Extant Texts in Sindarin

For more information on particular words or names, see also appendices 2, 3, 4, and 5.

§ A1.1

Lúthien's song (from *The Lay of Leithian Recommenced*, Cant. III, ll. 99–103)[1]

Ir Ithil ammen Eruchín
menel-vîr síla díriel
si loth a galadh lasto dîn!
A Hîr Annûn gilthoniel,
le linnon im Tinúviel!

[The Moon, having watched for us Children of Eru
shines like a jewel in the sky
now flower and tree, listen silent!
O Lady of the West, star-kindler,
I sing to you, I, Nightingale!]

Ir: possibly the singular article *i* 'the' followed by antihiatic *-r* before a following *i* (to avoid the contraction *i ithil* > *iithil* > *íthil*). Modifies *Ithil.*

Ithil: noun, 'moon'; subject of *síla*. Expanded form of the root √THIL by reduplication of root vowel, meaning 'the Shining One'.

ammen: pronoun, 'for us' = *an* 'for' + *men* 'us', indirect object of *síla* (the moon's shining provides an indirect benefit for the Eruchín by giving its light).

Eruchín: tatpurusha noun compound, 'Children of God', in apposition to *ammen*. Contains Eru 'the One, God' (probably a borrowing from Quenya) and *hîn* 'children', plural of *hên*. Modeled on Q *Eruhíni*. Agrees with *(am)men*.

1. *Lays of Beleriand*, p. 354.

menel-vîr: tatpurusha noun compound, in apposition to *Ithil*, meaning 'jewel [*mîr*] in the sky [*menel*]'. The second element in the compound takes the soft mutation, as it is modified by the first element.

síla: third-person singular *a*-stem verb, 'shines with white or silver light'. From the lengthened stem *síl-* of the root √SIL; apparently a derivative form, suggesting a more immediate verbal form **sili-*.

díriel: lenited form of the past active participle *tíriel* 'having watched', modifying *Ithil*; or (perhaps less likely) modifying *loth* and *galadh* in the next phrase. The lenition may indicate that it does not stand on its own but modifies a preceding noun. The participle indicates the condition under which the main verb *síla* takes place.

si: adverb, 'now', modifying *lasto*; not to be confused with the related *sí* 'here'.

loth: noun, 'flower', vocative.

a: conjunction, 'and', joining *loth* and *galadh*.

galadh: noun, 'tree', vocative, unlenited.

lasto: imperative *ta*-stem verb, 'listen!, may (so-and-so) listen'. Addressed to *loth* and *galadh*.

dîn: perhaps an adverb 'silently', modifying *lasto*, but also perhaps a noun 'silence' (cf. *Amon Dîn* 'Hill of Silence,' 336). The phrase *lasto dîn* could mean 'listen to the silence' (but in this case perhaps it should be lenited as *dhîn*). However, *dîn* may be the lenited form of a pronoun *tîn* 'him, her', which would be the object of *lasto*; the sense would, however, be unclear, as the antecedent of the pronoun is not obvious; it is unlikely to be *ithil*, as the moon is not noticeably noisy.

A: interjection 'O', used before following vocatives.

Hîr: noun, usually 'lord, master'. But the context here indicates that the word should be read as feminine, referring to Varda. Probably the whole phrase *Hîr Annûn* was a calque on Q *Herunúmen* or *Númeheru* 'lord of the West', a phrase that could be used to refer to any of the Valar, regardless of sex.

Annûn: noun in genitival-adjectival position (following the noun modified, *hîr*), 'the West', as a direction, and the region of the Blessed Land of Aman.

gilthoniel: tatpurusha noun compound, 'Kindler of the Stars' (a Sindarin appellation for Varda), composed of *gîl* 'star' and *thoniel* 'kindler'. The last may be a derivative of a Sindarin verbal stem **thaun-* 'kindle, set light to' with a suffix *-iel* indicating a feminine agent. The form **thaun* refers to a creative activity in the distant past and should be properly understood as 'she who had kindled stars' rather than 'she who has and is kindling stars'. *Thoniel* might also be thought of as the perfect active participle of a verb **than-* (see § 9.15). In apposition to *Hîr Annûn*.

le: second-person reverential pronoun, 'thee' (see § 8.3), indirect object of *linnon*.

linnon: present tense verb, first-person singular, 'I sing'.

im: first-person singular personal pronoun 'I', subject of *linnon*. This pronoun is obviously not directly related to the usual pronominal root √NI. The final consonant *-m* indicates that in the past it had a long *-mm* or *-mb* (since *-m-* became *-v-*, *-w-*). Possibly the word derives from a root √ŋWI distantly related to √NI.

Tinúviel: A nickname of Lúthien, meaning 'nightingale'. It combines the noun *tinnú(v)* 'starlit dusk, twilight' and the feminine ending *-iell*, meaning 'woman, maiden, daughter'. The noun *tinnú* combines *tinu* 'star' and *dû* 'darkness, night'. The exact Q equivalent was *Tindómiel*, a name actually borne by a daughter of Elros Tar-Minyatur of Númenor, Lúthien's great-grandson. In apposition to *im*.

§ A1.2

Battle cry of the Edain of Dor-Lómin[2] (from the *Narn i Chîn Húrin*)

Lacho calad! *Drego morn*!
[Flame Light! Flee Night!]

lacho: imperative verb, 'flame!' or 'may it flame!', connected to the noun *lach* 'flame'.

calad: noun, similar to *galad*, also meaning 'light', but from the root √KAL; subject of *lacho* (the thing being exhorted to flame).

drego: imperative verb 'flee!'

morn: noun, 'darkness, night', subject of *drego*.

§ A1.3

Tuor's battle cry (from *Of Tuor and His Coming to Gondolin*)[3]

Gurth an Glamhoth!
[Death to the Yelling-horde!]

Gurth: noun 'death'. Subject of an unexpressed imperative 'be'; e.g., 'may death be for the Glamhoth', i.e., may they die.

---

2. *UT*, p. 65.
3. Ibid., p. 39.

an: preposition 'for, to', governing *glamhoth*, taking the nasal mutation (§ 5.2).
glamhoth: noun, 'yelling-horde', a Sindarin word for Orcs; containing the elements *glam* 'confused noise, clamor' and *hoth* 'horde, unorganized mass of people'; often used as quasi-plural suffix (see § 14.9).

§ A1.4

Voronwë's exclamation (from *Of Tuor and His Coming to Gondolin*)[4]

Alae! Ered en Echoriath, ered e·mbar nín!

[Ah! The Mountains of the Encircling Fence, the mountains of my home!]

Alae!: Interjection, 'Ah!'. Spoken when deeply moved by some sight.
Ered: noun, 'mountains', irregular plural of *orod* 'mountain'. Vocative.
en: articular genitive prefix, 'of the'.
en Echoriath: 'of the Encircling Fence'; the name *Echoriath* is a karmadharaya compound of *echor* 'outer circle' (**etkor-*) and *iath* 'fence': [fence forming a circle round about].
e·mbar: 'of home'; *en* plus a form of the noun *bâr* 'home', showing the mixed mutation (§ 5.5).
nín: pronoun 'my', modifying *bâr*; obviously related to *nin* 'me', and the first-person stem √NI; but not absolutely clear whether a genitive form, a possessive adjective, or a pronoun in adjectival position. Cf. *în*, *dîn*, for which similar questions pertain.

§ A1.5

Húrin's words to Lorgan[5]

Tôl acharn!

[Vengeance comes!]

tôl: third-person singular, present-tense verb 'comes', an endingless form used by *i*-stem verbs (see § 9.4); from OS **tule*, earlier **tuli*. (In one version of this phrase,[6] for reasons that are uncertain, *tôl* was emended to *tûl*.)
acharn: noun 'vengeance'. Possibly from a primitive past participle **atkarna*, from a verb **atkari-* 'do back or in return to someone'.

---

4. Ibid., p. 40.
5. *WJ*, p. 254.
6. Ibid., p. 301n19.

§ A1.6

Celebrimbor's inscription on the West Gate of Moria[7]

Ennyn Durin Aran Moria: pedo mellon a minno. Im Narvi hain echant: Celebrimbor o Eregion teithant i thiw hin.

[Gates of Durin, king of Moria: Say "friend" and enter (or: Let a friend speak and enter). I, Narvi, made them: Celebrimbor of Eregion wrote these letters].

Ennyn: noun, 'gates' (plural of *annon*). Subject of a descriptive sentence; to be understood as 'these are the gates'.

Durin: proper noun. The name of the Dwarf king of Moria. Here modifying *ennyn* as a genitive.

aran: noun, 'king'. In apposition to *Durin*.

Moria: proper noun 'Black Chasm', a karmadharaya compound of *môr* 'black' and *iâ* 'chasm'.

pedo: imperative of the verb *pedi* 'to speak, say' meaning 'speak' or, with a third-person subject, 'may he (or she) speak'.

mellon: noun, 'friend' (or 'beloved' [*mell*] 'person' [-*on*]); quoted object of the verb *pedo*; as a quotation it is not lenited. It can also be understood as the subject of *pedo*; 'let a friend speak', 'may a friend speak'. It is probably not a vocative, since if it were, Gandalf's interpretation of it as 'if you are a friend, speak' would be less intelligible.

a: conjunction, 'and'.

minno: imperative verb, 'enter'; from a verb **minna-*, derived from a root √MI 'in'.

im: personal pronoun, first-person singular 'I', subject of *echant*.

Narvi: proper noun, name of a Dwarvish craftsman; probably from the Old Icelandic name *Narfi*. In apposition to *im*.

hain: pronoun 'them'; object of *echant*. Plural of the neuter demonstrative pronoun *han*.

echant: endingless past tense of verb *echad-*, *echedi* 'to make'; personal endings are not necessary when a personal pronoun is used with the verb. The past tense is created by nasal infixion in the stem (see § 9.10).

Celebrimbor: the Sindarin form of a Quenya name *Telperinquar*; containing the elements *celebrin-* (uncompounded form *celebren*) 'of silver' and *paur* 'fist, hand'.

o: preposition, 'from', governing *Eregion*. Subject of *teithant*.

---

7. *FR*, pp. 318–19.

Eregion: proper noun, name of a place *Hollin* 'holly-land'; contains *ereg* 'holly-tree' and the place-name suffix *-ion(d)* also seen in *Rhovanion* 'Wilderland'.
teithant: past tense of a verb *teitha-* (earlier **tekta-*) 'write'; showing the suffixation of an ending *-nt*.
i thiw: plural noun 'the letters'; singular *têw*, plural *tîw*; showing nasal mutation after the plural article *in* (here reduced to *i*). The noun *thiw* is shortened from *thîw*. Object of *teithant*.
hin: demonstrative adjective 'these'; plural of *hen* 'this', agreeing with plural *tîw*; from OS **sina*, 'this' (pl. **sini*).

An earlier version of this text[8] with identical meaning read: *Ennyn Dhurin Aran Vória. Pedo mellon a minno. Im Narvi hain echant. Celebrimbor (Celebrimmor) o Eregion teithant i·ndíw (i·nníw) thin.* (The tengwar inscription reads Celebrimmor, i·nníw, but the Roman-letter transcription reads Celebrimbor, i·ndíw).

These variants reflect the lenition of genitives (*Durin* > *Dhurin*, *Mória* > *Vória*) and a different result from the contact of the plural article *in* and the noun *tîw*, in which *n* + *t* became *nn* or *nd* instead of *þ*. See § 4.236. A different demonstrative is used, *then* instead of *hen*.

§ A1.7

"The Secret Door" (from a sketch of Thror's Map)[9]

Lheben teil brann i annon ar neledh neledhi gar godrebh.

[Five feet high the door and three can walk in through together.]

This is a Noldorin phrase (see §§ 4.221–36); the Classical Sindarin equivalent would probably be *Leben tail brand i annon, a neledh neledhi gar godref.*

Leben: the numeral 'five', modifying *tail*.
tail: 'feet'; a unit of measure, expressed in the length of a foot (*tâl*). A simple plural following the number (although it could also be interpreted as a genitive: 'five of feet'). The phrase *leben tail* modifies *brand*.
brand: adjective 'high'. Predicate of *annon*; the verb *is* is implied (Five feet high is the door . . .).

8. *Treason of Isengard*, p. 182; and *J. R. R. Tolkien: Artist and Illustrator*, illustration 152, p. 158.

9. *Tolkien: Artist and Illustrator*, illustration 85, p. 92.

i annon: 'the door, the gate'; subject to the predicate *brand*.

a neledh: 'and three'; *neledh* 'three' stands for "three persons," but takes a singular verb, *gar*.

neledhi: infinitive 'to walk in', from *ne-* 'in', and *ledhi* 'to walk'; OS **neledie*.

gar: third-person singular verb 'can, is able'. Governing the infinitive *neledhi*.

godref: adverb 'through together'; contains the elements *go-* 'through', and *tre-* 'through', with an adverbializing suffix *-f* related to *be* 'like, as'. OS **wotrebe*. Modifies *neledhi*.

§ A1.8

Gilraen's linnod[10]

Onen i-Estel Edain;
Ú-chebin estel anim.
[I gave Hope to Men;
I did not keep hope for myself.]

Onen: 'I gave'. Augmented past tense (see § 9.11) of *anta-* 'give'. The pronoun *im* 'I' is here unexpressed, and the person must therefore be shown by the personal ending *-n*.

i-Estel: 'the Hope'. A proper name, given to Aragorn as a youth, but here used punningly in its common sense; referring both to Gilraen's personal hopes and to the hopes of the Dúnedain (for their eventual restoration and the defeat of Sauron) and also to Aragorn himself, as the vehicle of those hopes.

Edain: 'Men' (as opposed to Elves; especially, the Dúnedain of the West). Plural of *adan* 'man'. Here it functions as an indirect object; being in a postsentential adverbial position, it could be understood in a more general sense as *with respect to Men*.

Ú: 'not'; modifying *hebin*, causing soft mutation (§ 5.1).

chebin: 'I keep'; lenited form of *hebin*. An *i*-stem with the first-person ending *-n*.

anim: 'for myself'; *an* 'for' + *im* 'I'. Modifying *hebin*.

---

10. *Return of the King*, p. 342.

§ A1.9

Glorfindel's call to Aragorn[11]

Ai na vedui Dúnadan! Mae govannen!

[Hail, well met at last, Dúnadan!]

Although represented in two sentences as printed, the above is probably to be understood as a single sentence: *Ai, na vedui, Dúnadan, mae govannen.*

Ai: Hail! interjection.

na: preposition taking the soft mutation (§ 5.1) 'to, toward, at', governing *medui*.

vedui: lenited form of *medui* 'last'; *na vedui* means 'at last'. This prepositional phrase functions adverbially, modifying the adjective *govannen.*

Dúnadan: Vocative noun. Dúnadan was a nickname for Aragorn, meaning 'Númenorean', a compound of *Dûn* 'West' and *adan* 'man'.

mae: adverb, 'well', modifying *govannen.*

govannen: 'met' (together); a past participle of the verb *govad-*, infinitive *gevedi* 'to come together', a compound of *go-* (< **gwa*) 'together' and *bedi* 'come', past participle *bannen.* Agreeing with *Dúnadan.*

Glorfindel greets Frodo with a similar greeting: *Hail, and well met at last*! (*FR*, 222).

§ A1.10

Glorfindel's call to his horse[12]

Noro lim, noro lim, Asfaloth!

The exact meaning of this is unknown; from the context it may be guessed that it means something like 'run lightly' or 'run swiftly'. The usual meaning of *lim* is, however, 'light, clear, sparkling'. *Noro* is evidently an imperative. The name of the horse, Asfaloth, probably contains the element *loth* 'flower'; the first element may be *asfal*, which could be derived from the root √SPAL 'foam, froth', with reduplication of root vowel (*A-SPAL*), if the usual development of interior *-sp-* in Sindarin was *-sf-*; this remains unknown.

11. *FR*, p. 222.
12. Ibid., p. 225.

§ A1.11

"Aerlinn in Edhil o Imladris" (The Sea Song of the Elves of Rivendell)[13]

A Elbereth Gilthoniel,
silivren penna míriel
o menel aglar elenath!
Na-chaered palan-díriel
o galadhremmin ennorath,
Fanuilos, le linnathon
nef aear, sí nef aearon!

[O Queen of the Stars, Kindler of the Stars,
the crystalline brilliance of the stars, like jewels
slants down from heaven.
After gazing far into the distance
from the middle lands, enmeshed in trees,
I will sing to you, (lady with) ever-white veil,
on this side of the sea, here on this side of the great ocean.]

A: interjection 'O', introducing a vocative.

Elbereth: vocative noun; Sindarin name of the *Valië Varda* 'Queen of the Stars'. A tatpurusha compound composed of *êl* 'star' (< **elen*) and *bereth* 'spouse, queen' (< **barathil*). The preservation of *-b-* unlenited in the compound is due to early contact (**elembarathil*) and then a syncope (**elmbereth* > *Elbereth*). (See §§ 4.115, 4.140.)

Gilthoniel: see § A1.1 above. In apposition to *Elbereth*; unlenited vocative.

silivren: adjective, 'made of silima'. *Silima* was the magical diamondlike substance used by Fëanor to make the Silmarils (S *silevril*). The Quenya noun, deriving from an adjective **silimā*, meant 'shining with silver light' and corresponded to Sindarin *silef*, in composition *silif* (see § 5.7). The common suffix *-ren* can indicate the substance of which something is made, its nature, or appearance; e.g. *celebren* 'of silver', *mithren* 'grey', *gwathren* 'shadowy'. Modifies *aglar* (line 3).

penna: *a*-stem verb, 'slants down', formed by nasalization of the root √PED. Governed by *aglar*.

míriel: an adjective, meaning 'jewel-like', also modifying *aglar*. The adjective combines the noun *mîr* 'jewel' and an adjectival ending *-iel* (distinct from that in *Gilthoniel*), related to an adjectival ending *-ion*; it can be seen in the name *Rathlóriel*, containing the adjective **glóriel* 'golden

13. Ibid., p. 250; see also *Return of the King*, p. 308; and *The Road Goes Ever On*, pp. 62–67.

colored', derived from *glaur*, 'golden light'. It is not a verbal form.

o: a preposition, meaning 'from', governing the noun *menel*, taking stop mutation; derived from primitive Eldarin **aud*.

menel: noun, 'heaven, the sky'; a compound meaning 'region of the stars', combining Sindarin *men* 'direction, region, way' and *êl* 'star', based on a Quenya compound of the same form. The retention of initial *m* is due to the presence of a stop mutation (see § 5.3) following *o*.

aglar: noun, 'glory, brilliance'. Subject of *penna*.

elenath: noun, 'stars' containing the noun *elen* and a group plural suffix *-ath*; it thus means 'the group of all the stars in the sky'. Modifying *aglar* as genitive.

na: a preposition meaning 'to, toward', taking the soft mutation, governing *haered*.

chaered: lenited form of noun *haered* 'what is far off', from the adjective *hae* 'far away' with the nominalizing suffix *-red* attached; see § 14.9.

palan-: adverbial prefix, 'far off, over a wide area'.

díriel: lenited form (following the prefix) of the perfect active participle *tíriel*, from the verb *tiri-* 'look toward, watch, guard', thus meaning 'having watched'. The verb may, in fact, be *palandir-* and have the meaning 'look far and wide (through a palantír)', referring to one of the crystal seeing-stones of the Númenoreans; one set at the tower of Elostirion on the Emyn Beraid looked out toward the sea, the island of Tol Eressëa, and Taniquetil. See § 9.15 for the formation of the perfect active participle.

galadhremmin: plural adjectival tatpurusha compound, 'woven with trees', composed of *galadh* 'tree' and the adjective *remmen* 'woven, tangled', itself derived from the noun *rem* 'mesh, net' with the adjectival suffix *-en*; modifying the following noun, *ennorath*. (Adjectives usually follow nouns in Sindarin, but the normal word order has been modified to fit the verse structure.) The initial *g*, following the preposition *o*, is further evidence for a distinct stop mutation (§ 5.3).

ennorath: plural noun, 'central lands', with the same group plural as in *elenath*. The noun *ennor* 'middle-land, Middle-earth' comes from an ancient compound showing haplology (loss of a medial syllable), **endorē* < **enda-ndorē* 'middle land'.

Fanuilos: another appellation for *Varda*, a karmadharaya compound meaning 'Always White Appearance'. The elements are *fân* 'cloud, veil, magical body of a Vala', *ui* 'always', *glos* 'dazzling white (the color of snow, *loss*)'.

le: second-person reverential pronoun, 'thee', agreeing with *Fanuilos*, object of *linnathon*.

linnathon: first-person singular future of the *a*-stem verb *linna-* 'sing, chant', from the root √LIN, which refers to musical sound, either of water or of a voice.
nef: preposition, 'near, on this side of' (the opposite of *hae*; *cis-* as opposed to *trans-*). Origin uncertain. Governs *aear*.
aear: noun, 'sea'; either from the root √AJ-AR or a lenited form of *gaear* (root √GAJ), with soft mutation from preceding *nef*.
sí: adverb, 'here', from a root √SI.
aearon: noun, 'ocean'; intensive of *aear*, with the suffix *-on*[2] 'great' (see § 14.9).

Older version:[14]

O Elbereth Gilthoniel
Sir evrin pennar óriel [> íriel]
Dir [> Lír] avos-eithen míriel
Bel daurion sel aurinon
Pennáros evrin ériol.

[This cannot be certainly interpreted. See below § A1.16.]

§ A1.12

Gandalf's spells of fire[15]

Naur an edraith ammen!
Naur dan i ngaurhoth!

[(Let there be) fire for our salvation!
(Let there be) fire against the wargs!]

Naur: noun, 'fire', subject of an implied imperative *be*.
an: preposition, 'to, for', indicating purpose; modifying *edraith*.
edraith: noun, 'saving', object of *an*; etymology obscure.[16]
ammen: pronoun, 'for us', indirect object, but here acting almost like a genitive in relation to *edraith*.
dan: preposition, 'against' (related to the root √NDAN 'back, in reverse, in return'; this replaced *ad* 'again')[17] governing *gaurhoth*.
i ngaurhoth: noun, 'the wargs'; soft mutation of *gaurhoth*, karmadharaya compound of *gaur* 'wolf, werewolf' and the quasi-plural suffix *hoth* 'hoste, horde'.

---

14. *Return of the Shadow*, p. 394, *Sauron Defeated*, p. 112.
15. *FR*, pp. 304, 312.
16. *The Treason of Isengard*, pp.169, 175.
17. Ibid., p. 187.

§ A1.13

Gandalf's spell of opening[18]

Annon edhellen, edro hi ammen!
Fennas nogothrim, lasto beth lammen!

[Elvish gate, open now for us!
Gateway of the Dwarf-folk, listen to the word of my tongue!]

Annon: noun, 'great gate', containing *and* 'gate' (Q *ando*) and the suffix -*on* 'great' (cf. *aearon* above, § A1.11). Vocative or subject of *edro*.

edhellen: adjective, 'Elvish' modifying *annon*. Combines *edhel* 'Elf' and the adjectival suffix -*ren* (§ 14.16).

edro: imperative verb, 'open!'

ammen: see §A1.12

hi: lenited form of adverb *si* 'now', modifying *edro*, lenited because directly following an imperative verb.

fennas: noun, 'gateway'; extended form of *fend* 'door' (cf. *Fen Hollen*, the 'Closed Door' leading to the Tombs of the Stewards in Minas Tirith). Vocative or subject of *lasto*.

nogothrim: 'Dwarf-folk, Dwarves'. A compound composed of *nogoth* 'Dwarf' (< **nukotto*) and -*rim*, a plural affix used for peoples. In genitival position, modifying *fennas*.

beth: lenited form (as object) of *peth* 'word, speech'. Lenited as the direct object of the verb *lasto*.

lammen: 'of (my) tongue', glossal, lingual; an adjectival form (**lambena*), based on Sindarin *lam* 'tongue' (OS **lambe*) with the adjectival suffix -*en* (OS *-*ena*).

Older version:[19]

Annon porennin diragas-venwed
Diragath-telwen porannin nithrad.

[This version cannot be interpreted, except for the word *annon* 'gate'.]

§ A1.14

A word of opening[20]

Edro!: imperative verb, 'Open!'

---

18. *FR*, p. 320.
19. *Return of the Shadow*, p. 394.
20. *FR*, p. 321.

§ A1.15

An Elvish command[21]

Daro!: imperative verb, 'Stop!' from a root √DAR, also seen in the noun *daur* 'stop, halt, pause; league'.

§ A1.16

Samwise's invocation of Elbereth[22]

A Elbereth Gilthoniel
o menel palan-díriel,
le nallon sí di' nguruthos!
A tíro nin, Fanuilos!

[O Queen of the Stars, Kindler of the Stars,
far-watching from heaven,
I cry to you under the horror of death!
O watch over me, Ever-white Veil!]

palan-díriel: adjective, 'gazing afar' with short vowel, a present participle deriving from the verb *palan-dir-* 'look far and wide'.
nallon: first-person present singular verb 'I cry', from a stem *nall-*, root uncertain.
di': preposition, 'beneath', creating soft mutation. Governs *guruthos*. The exact significance of the apostrophe is uncertain.
nguruthos: lenited form of noun *guruthos* 'death-horror', showing the soft mutation of *g* > *ng*. Tatpurusha compound of *guruth* 'death' and *gos* 'horror': horror occasioned by (prospective) death.
tíro: imperative verb 'look!, watch!, guard!', from the verb *tiri-*.
nin: 'me', objective form of *im*, object of *tiro*.

Older version:[23]

O Elbereth Gilthoniel
silevrin pennar óriel
hîr avas-eithen míriel
a tíro 'men Gilthoniel!

Not entirely explicable. *Silevrin* and *pennar* are apparently plural forms, but a noun for them to agree with is not apparent. *A tíro 'men* must mean

21. Ibid., p. 356.
22. *TT*, p. 339; *The Road Goes Ever On*, p. 64.
23. *War of the Ring*, p. 218.

'O watch over us'; *'men* is probably an abbreviated form of *ammen*. The term *óriel* must be derived from an older **auriel*, since the *ó* is not mutated before a following *i* (cf. § 5.9), and is perhaps related to *aur* 'day'.

§ A1.17

People of Gondor to Peregrin Took[24]

Ernil i Pheriannath!

[(There is the) Prince of the Halflings!]

Ernil: noun, 'Prince'. A derivative of *aran* or of the related adjective *arn* 'royal', Q *arna*. The internal affection (§ 5.9) caused by the *-i-* of the ending *-il-* changes **arnil* to *ernil*. It can be construed as definite because it is modified by a definite genitive.

i: plural article 'the', basic form *in*; generating the nasal mutation (see § 5.2; § 12.6). The final *-n* is lost before most following consonants.

Pheriannath: nasal mutation of *Periannath*, the collective-plural of *Perian* 'halfling'; this contains the element *per-* 'half' and a diminutive suffix *-ian(d)*. The double *nn* of *Periannath* comes from the internal consonant mutation of this original *-nd-*. The phrase *i Pheriannath* stands in genitive relationship to *ernil*.

§ A1.18

Praises of Frodo and Samwise[25]

Cuio i Pheriain anann! Aglar 'ni Pheriannath!
Daur a Berhael, Conin en Annûn! Eglerio!

[May the halflings live for long! Glory to the Halflings!
Noble and Half-wise, princes of the West! Glorify!]

cuio: imperative of verb *cuia-* 'live'.

i Pheriain: plural noun, 'the Halflings'; *Pheriain* is the plural by vowel mutation of *Perian*, here showing nasal mutation (*p* > *ph*) after the plural article *in*. Its use here instead of the collective plural *Periannath* is consistent with the use of mutation plurals for definite, limited numbers of persons or things.

anann: adverb, 'long, for a long time'; contains the prefix *an* 'for' and the adjective *and*, *ann* 'long'.

---

24. *Return of the King*, pp. 41, 80.

25. Ibid., p. 231; *Letters of J. R. R. Tolkien*, p. 308.

aglar: noun, 'glory', subject of implied verb *be*.

'ni: elided form of *anin* (or **enin*), a combined form of *an* 'for, to' and the article *in* 'the' (plural), taking nasal mutation.

Pheriannath: collective plural of *perian* 'halfling', showing nasal mutation after **enin*.

Daur: a Sindarin name for Frodo; possibly lenited form of *Taur* 'noble, masterful'. Object of *eglerio*.

a: conjunction, 'and', joining *Taur* and *Perhael*.

Berhael: lenited form of *Perhael*, a Sindarin name for Samwise meaning 'Half-wise': *per-* 'half' + *sael* (lenited to *hael*) 'wise'. This and *Taur* are probably lenited as objects of the verb *eglerio*.

conin: an unusual plural of the noun *caun* 'commander, ruler, governor, prince', in apposition to *Taur* and *Perhael* but not lenited.

en: a particle joining two nouns in quasi compound; usually translatable 'of'.

Annûn: noun, 'West'.

eglerio: imperative verb form of **egleria-* 'praise, glorify'; a *ja*-verb, derivative of *aglar* 'glory', showing *i*-affection throughout.

Older version:[26]

Cuio i Pheriannath anann! Aglar anann!

[May the Halflings [collective plural] live long, glory (be to them) for long.]

§ A1.19

"The King's Letter" (from the third and final tengwar version)[27]

Aragorn Arathornion Edhelharn anglennatha i Varanduiniant erin dolothen Ethuil (egor ben genediad Drannail erin Gwirith edwen) ar ennas aníra i-aran Gondor ar Arnor ar hîr i Mbair Annui, suilannad mhellyn în phain. *Edregol* e aníra tírad i Cherdir *Perhael* (i sennui *Panthael* estathar aen) Condir i Drann; ar *Meril* bess dîn; ar *Elanor*, *Meril*, *Glorfinniel*, *Eirien*, sellath dîn ar *Iorhael*, *Gelir*, *Cordof*, *Baravorn* ionnath dîn. Ar[agorn] El[essar].

A Pherhael ar am Meril suilad uin aran o Minas Tirith nelchaenen ned Echuir.

[Aragorn, son of Arathorn, Elf-stone, will approach the Bridge of Baranduin on the eighth of Spring—or according to the Shire reckoning, on

26. *Sauron Defeated*, pp. 46–47.

27. Ibid., p. 131.

> Gwirith second—and there the king of Gondor and Arnor and Lord of the Westlands desires to greet all his friends. He especially desires to see Master Samwise (who ought to be called Fullwise), Mayor of the Shire; and his wife, Rose; and his daughters, Elanor, Rose, Goldilocks, Daisy; and his sons, Frodo, Merry, Pippin, Hamfast. Aragorn Elessar.

To Samwise and to Rose, greeting from the king from Minas Tirith, thirtieth in Stirring.]

Aragorn: proper name, subject; interpreted as 'royal valor' (see app. 3).

Arathornion: 'son of Arathorn', apposite to *Aragorn*. The suffix *-ion* (< *iôn* 'son') attached to any name means 'son of'. *Arathorn* contains the prefix *Ara-* and a shortened form of the word *thoron* 'eagle'.

Edhelharn: nickname, apposite to *Aragorn*, meaning 'Elf-stone'; contains *edhel* 'Elf' and *sarn* (lenited to *-harn*) 'stone'.

anglennatha: 'will approach', third-person singular future tense of verb *anglenna-*, probably including the prefix *an-* 'to' and a verb stem *gledh-* 'go'; cf. *lend* 'journey', from a root √(G)LED.

i: article. 'the'. Causes soft mutation.

Varanduiniant: lenited form (after *i*) of the name *Baranduiniant* 'Brandywine Bridge'. A tatpurusha compound 'bridge over the Brandywine' composed of *Baranduin* 'Brandywine' and *iant* 'bridge'. *Baranduin* is itself a karmadharaya compound of *baran* 'golden-brown' and *duin* 'river'.

erin: preposition, 'on the'; composed of *or* and a form of the article *i*; takes mixed mutation; modifying *dolothen*.

dolothen: lenited form of *tolothen* 'eighth', mutated by *erin*.

Ethuil: noun, 'spring'; in genitive position following *tolothen*.

egor: conjunction, 'or'.

ben: preposition, 'according to the'; composed of *be* (cf. Q *ve* 'like, as') and a form of the article *i*.

genediad: gerund, 'reckoning', adding the nominalizing suffix *-ad* to the verb *genedi-* from *go* 'together' and *nod-* 'number' (see § 9.7).

Drannail: 'of the Shire'; adjectival derivative of *Trann* 'shire', lenited in adjectival position.

Gwirith: name of the fourth month of the Númenorean calendar, more or less equivalent to our April. In Quenya *Víressë*; from an unknown root, √WIR, with an abstract suffix usually found with verbs; cf. *sirith* 'flowing', *cirith* 'cutting, cleft', *firith* 'fading', *tirith* 'watching, guard'.

edwen: ordinal number, 'second'; perhaps from the root √AT with irregular fronting of the vowel, and an unusual suffix *-wen*.

ar: conjunction, meaning 'and'; the normal form of the word in this text, but elsewhere usually *a* or *ah*.

ennas: adverb, 'there'; probably from **entasse* 'in that (place) yonder', from **enta* 'that over there'; modifying *aníra*.

aníra: verb, third-person singular 'desires'; contains the prefix *an* 'for' and the root √IR 'desire'. Governed by *aran* (see below); governing *suilannad* (see below).

i-aran: noun, 'the king'; *aran* probably originally meant 'high one, noble one', from the root √AR. Subject of *aníra*.

Gondor: proper noun, place-name meaning 'Stone Land', containing the elements *gond* 'stone' and *dôr* 'land'. In genitival position, modifying *aran*.

Arnor: proper noun, place-name, intended to mean 'Royal Land'; *arn* 'royal' and *dôr* 'land' would normally yield *Ardor*, but the name has been influenced by Quenya *Arnórë* 'royal land', *arna* 'royal' + *nórë* 'people, land'. In genitival position, modifying *aran*.

hîr: 'lord'. Secondary subject, coordinate with *aran*.

i-mBair: 'the lands, the homes'. Plural of the noun *bâr* [**mbar*] 'home, house, dwelling-place', taking nasal affection from the preceding plural article *in*.

Annui: plural adjective, 'western', modifying preceding noun *bair*.

suilannad: gerund (in infinitive sense) of a verb *suilanna-*, 'to greet'; perhaps from *suil-* and the verb *anna-* 'give', i.e., 'give greeting'. Governed by *aníra*.

mhellyn: plural noun, 'friends', normal form *mellyn*, singular *mellyn*; *m* lenited to *mh* as direct object of *suilannad*; *mh* is an archaic spelling for a sound that in the Third Age would normally be pronounced, and usually spelled, with *v*: *vellyn*.

în: pronominal adjective or genitive, 'his'; probably 'his own' with reference to the subject (here *aran*).

phain: adjective, 'all', plural of *!pân*, deriving from the root √KWAN 'full, complete'.

edregol: adverb, 'especially, in especial'; cannot be analyzed.

e: personal pronoun, 'he'; of uncertain origin but surely related to the genitive *în*.

tírad: gerund (in infinitive sense) of the verb *tíra-*, 'to see'; a derivative of the verb *tiri-* 'watch over, guard, gaze at'.

i-Cherdir: 'the Master'; the article *i* induces the soft mutation in the following noun *Herdir*, a compound (descriptive determinative) of *Her-* (an early compositive form of *hîr*) 'master' and *dîr* 'man', commonly found as a masculine suffix of agent; probably reflecting an early **kherundiro*.

Perhael: proper noun, 'Samwise, Half-wise'; a dependent determinative compound of the prefix *per-* 'half' and *sael* 'wise'.

i: relative pronoun, 'who, whom'.

sennui: adverb, 'rather, instead'?

Panthael: proper noun, 'Full-wise'; a dependent determinative compound of the adjective *pant* 'full' and *sael* 'wise'.

estathar: third-person plural future tense, 'they shall name' from the verb *esta-* 'name'.

aen: unknown. Possibly a pronoun acting as subject to *estathar* 'people, they'.

Condir: a title, 'Mayor'; a descriptive determinative, composed of the elements *caun*[3] 'ruler, governor' (cf. Q *cáno* 'commander') and *dîr* 'man'.

i-Drann: 'the Shire'; the article should induce soft mutation, so the normal form of the word should be *Trann*; unfortunately, it cannot be analyzed further.

Meril: proper noun, 'Rose'; probably the ordinary name for the flower.

bess: noun 'wife'; from earlier **bessē*; lenited form of *!tîn*, which may relate to the root √T-.

Elanor: proper name and double comparative compound 'like the stars and sun'; the name of a flower, as well as a personal name; combining Sindarin *êl* 'star' and *anor* 'sun'.

Glorfinniel: proper name, 'Goldilocks'; combines the elements *glaur* 'golden in color'; *find* 'hair, lock'; and the feminine termination *-iel*.

Eirien: proper name, 'Daisy'; probably the ordinary name of the flower. Evidently a borrowing from Quenya *Arien(dë)*, 'sunlight-maiden' < CE **asiende* √AS. It cannot be originally Sindarin, since *-s-* became *-h-*, not *-r-*, in Sindarin.

sellath: collective plural noun, 'daughters', from *sell* 'daughter'.

Iorhael: proper name, dvandva compound 'Old and Wise', combining *iaur* 'old' and *sael* 'wise'; a translation of *Frodo*, a name intended to mean 'wise (by experience)'.

Gelir: proper name, 'Merry'; possibly a regular adjective of that meaning. Perhaps to be related to the root √GJEL 'triumph, joy'.

Cordof: proper name, Pippin; uninterpretable. May include the element *corn* 'round'.

Baravorn: proper name, tatpurusha compound, 'Hamfast, stay-at-home'. Containing *bâr* 'home' and *avorn* 'abiding'.

ionnath: collective plural of noun, *iond* 'son' < **jondō*; although the noun is also given as *iôn* < **jonō*. Probably both nouns existed as separate developments from the same root.

El[essar]; Quenya epithet for Aragorn, equivalent to *Edhelharn*.

a Pherhael: 'to Samwise'; *Pherhael* shows the nasal mutation of *Perhael* after the preposition *an* 'to'.

am Meril: 'to Rose'; the preposition *an* here becomes *am* before an initial sound *m*.

suilad: noun, 'greeting'; probably originally a gerund of a verb **suila*- 'greet'.

uin aran: 'from the king'; *uin*, preposition 'from the', a combination of *o* and *in*.

o Minas Tirith: 'from the Tower of Guard'. The preposition *o* 'from' (older **aud*) induces stop mutation (here *m* > *m*).

nelchaenen: adjective, 'thirtieth'; contains the elements *nel*- 'three' *caen*- 'ten' and *-en*, an adjectival ending for ordinals. *Thirty* is three tens. Oddly enough, this adjective is consistently translated 'thirty-first', which appears to be correct with reference to the date.[28] The source for the discrepancy is unclear.

ned: preposition, 'in'; probably altered from original *nedh*, from the root √NED 'middle', which, as a verbal prefix, means 'in'; e.g., *nestegi*- 'stick in'.

Echuir: a seasonal (although here a month) name, 'stirring'; containing the root √KUJ 'come to life'; with prefix *ed*- 'from, out'.

The roman-letter transcription of the third tengwar version put the word *aníra* after the king's titles and before *suilannad*.

The first tengwar version of this text differed in a few small ways: Aragorn's titles *aran Gondor ar Arnor ar hîr i-mBair Annui* followed immediately after the name *Edhelharn*, and the following sentence began *Ar e aníra ennas suilannad* . . . . The final names in the lists of girl children and boy children (*Eirien*, *Baravorn*) were each preceded by *ar*; and *ned Echuir* was *uin Echuir*.

28. See, e.g., *PME*, pp. 133–36.

§ A1.20

Passwords of Minas Tirith[29]

Giron edlothiad na ngalad. melon i ní sero ni edron.

Giron: probably a first-person singular verb but not of *giri* (the form would be *girin*); the implied verb *!gira-* may be related to *aníra-* 'desire'; it is possible that the root, instead of being √IR, is actually √GIR; this would still produce cognate words beginning with *ir-* in Quenya. Possibly 'I desire'.

edlothiad: a gerund derived from a verb *!edlothia-*, probably meaning 'flower' or 'blossom', containing the adverbial prefix *ed-* 'out', often used with reference to changes of state, and *loth* 'flower' (noun) with the verbal ending *-ia*. Possibly 'blossoming'.

na: genitive prefix, 'of'; since the following word takes a form showing the nasal or mixed mutation, the underlying form is probably *nan*, 'of the'; cf. § 12.5.

ngalad: nasal mutation of *galad*, noun; the obvious reading would be 'light', but in context one should probably understand *galað* or *galadh* to be intended: Possibly 'tree'.

The whole phrase could then be read 'I desire the blossoming of the tree'.

melon: possibly a first-person singular form 'I love' of the verb *mela-* 'love'; cf. Quenya *melánë* of like meaning (*The Lost Road*, p. 61) and Sindarin *mellon*, etc.

sero: possibly an infinitive (or an imperative), 'to like' based on a verb *sera-* derived from the root √SER 'like, be friendly to'; cf. Sindarin *seron*.

edron: possibly a first-person singular form 'I open' of the verb *edra-* 'open'. The word may also be read *edran*, which could be an adjectival form 'open, opened'.

The meaning of the second phrase is not clear. It is possible that *melon i ní* represents a first attempt at this sentence, followed at a second attempt in *sero ni edron*.

§ A1.21

Sample sentence 1[30]

Avo garo!

[Don't do it!]

---

29. See *War of the Ring*, p. 293; this reading represents my view of the text.
30. *WJ*, p. 371.

avo: imperative of *ava-*, 'wish not to do', used in expressions of forbidding together with the imperative of the action forbidden.

garo: lenited form of *caro*, imperative of *car-* 'do', lenited because immediately following an imperative verb (and not the subject).

§ A1.22

Sample sentence 2[31]

Guren bêd enni.

[My heart speaks to (or for) me.]

guren (probably for *gúren*): the noun *gûr* 'heart', cognate to Quenya *órë*, followed by the first-person pronominal suffix *-en*.

bêd: the lenited form of the verb *pêd* 'speaks', from OS **petė*, CE **k^{w}eti*. The reason for the lenition is uncertain.

enni: 'for me'; apparently an early coalescence of the preposition *an* 'for' and the pronominal stem *ni*. No other pronoun of similar form is known.

§ A1.23

Translation of the Lord's Prayer[32]

Ae Adar nín i vi Menel, no aer i eneth lín. Tolo i arnad lín; caro den i innas lín bo Geven sui vi Menel. Anno ammen sír imbas ilaurui vín ar diheno ammen i úgerth vín sui mín i gohenam di ai gerir úgerth ammen.

[O my Father who [is] in Heaven, may your name be holy. May your kingdom come; may your will on Earth be done like [your will] in Heaven. Give to us today our daily bread and forgive for us our misdeeds, like us, who forgive those who do misdeeds to us.]

Ae: vocative particle, 'O', introducing *adar*.

adar: 'father', the object of direct address.

nín: 'my', genitive case of the first-person pronoun, modifying *adar*. Perhaps an error for *vín* 'our'.

no: 'be', imperative form of the verb *na-* 'to be'.

aer: lenited form of *gaer* 'dreadful, awful; holy'; lenited because directly following the imperative verb *no*.

31. *Vinyar Tengwar*, no. 41, p. 11.

32. Ibid., no. 44, p. 23.

_i_: 'the', definite article governing _eneth_.

eneth: 'name'; probably arising from OS _*enet_^{h}_ē_ (√ÉNETH), cognate to Quenya _essë_ (< _*eþþe_ < _*enþe_ < _*eneþe_ < _*enet_^{h}_ē_).

lín: 'your', genitive of _le_ 'you', treated as an adjective modifying _eneth_.

tolo: imperative of _tol-_ 'come'.

arnad: 'kingdom'; subject of the verb _tolo_. Related to _aran_ 'king'; perhaps a gerund formed from a verb _arna-_ 'be king, rule'. _arnad_ would then properly mean 'the state or act of being king'.

caro: imperative of _car-_ 'do'.

den: impersonal subject of _caro_, which gives _caro_ a passive sense 'be done'.

i innas lín: 'your will' object of _caro_; an abstract noun (OS _*indasse_) derived from _ind_ 'mind'.

bo Geven: 'on earth'. This phrase actually seems to be written _bo Ceven_ in the text, but since the preposition seems to have originally ended in a vowel (from OS _*pǭ_) a soft mutation _c_ > _g_ is to be expected here. Tolkien's handwritten capital _C_ and capital _G_ are very similar. Like _vi_, the preposition _po_ shows soft mutation to _bo_ here.

sui: 'like, as', a conjunction joining the two prepositional phrases _bo Geven_ and _vi Menel_. Probably from OS _sībe_ (Q _sívë_) joined to the relative pronoun _i_.

vi Menel: 'in heaven'; _vi_ is the lenited form of _min_ 'in'; it takes the nasal mutation _*min menel_ > _*mimmenel_ > _mi menel_. Both _bo Geven_ and _vi Menel_ may be lenited because they function adjectivally to modify _innas_ 'will'; cf. _ben-Adar_ 'fatherless' lenited modifying _Iarwain_ 'Oldest one'.

anno: imperative of _anna-_ 'give'.

ammen: 'for us', composed of _an_ 'to, for', and _men_ 'we'.

sír: 'today, this day'; composed of the near demonstrative element _sí-_ 'this' and an ending _r_ ultimately from CE _*rē_ 'day'.

imbas: 'the bread', a combination of _i_ 'the' and _(m)bas_ 'bread'. The mutation here is unexpected; one would expect instead _*i-mbasse_ > _*immass_ > _i·mas_. Possibly this form either represents an alternative scheme of mutation, or _mb_ here is merely an orthographic sign for _m_ derived from _b_. Compare Noldorin _Cerch i-mBelain_ (from _*in-balani_) next to Sindarin _Taur i-Melegyrn_ (from _*in-belekorni_).

ilaurui: adjective, 'daily'; literally 'all-day-ish', composed of the prefix _il-_ 'all', the noun _aur_ 'day', and the adjectival suffix _-ui_.

vín: 'our', genitive of _men_ 'we', lenited in adjectival position after the noun phrase _imbas ilaurui_, which it modifies.

_ar_: 'and', conjunction joining the two sentences beginning with _anno_ and _diheno_.

diheno: 'forgive, release from obligation'; imperative of _dihena-_, formed by adding a prefix _di-_ to a verb _*sena-_ 'let go'. Since the preposition _di_ means 'under, beneath', it could refer to the action of a superior in forgiving those under him. It could also simply mean 'release from under a yoke of bondage', like Greek _hypolyein_.

úgerth: 'sin, crime, misdeed'; plural of _úgarth_, from the negative prefix _ú-_, indicating something bad, and _carth_ (a form of _cardh_ < _*kard-_) 'deed'. _i úgerth vín_ 'our sins'. Before _r_ followed by a consonant, the plural of words containing _a_ became _e_, not _ai_; cf. _nern_, pl. of _narn_.

sui: 'like, as', here functioning as a preposition instead of a conjunction.

mín: 'us', an object (accusative) form of _men_ 'we'. The object form is selected by the preceding preposition _sui_. _sui mín_ 'like us'.

_i_: relative pronoun, subject of _gohenam_ '(we) who', referring back to _mín_.

gohenam: 'we forgive', a first-person plural present of the _a_-stem verb _gohena-_. Formed by adding the prefix _go-_ 'together' to a verb _*sena-_ 'let go'. It could contrast with _diheno_ above in referring to the actions of equals in forgiving each other, suggesting a collective effort, like Greek _syllyein_. _sui mín i gohenam_ 'like us, who forgive'.

_di_: lenited form of _ti_, a plural demonstrative pronoun, 'them, those', lenited because it is the object of _gohenam_.

_ai_: a relative pronoun whose difference from _i_ is uncertain but that here refers back to _di_.

gerir: lenited form of _cerir_ 'they do' (from the same stem _car-_ as _caro_ but showing _i_-affection of _a_ to _e_), with soft mutation due to the preceding relative pronoun _ai_, which is its subject.

Appendix 2

A Sindarin-English Glossary

The alphabetical order used in appendices 2, 3, 4, and 5 is as follows: A, B, C, ch, D, dh, E, F, G, Gw, H, Hw, I_1, I_2, L, Lh, M, N, O, P, R, Rh, S, T, Th, U, v, w, Y. I_1 represents vocalic *i*, I_2 consonantal *i* (only found initially). They are listed separately, although the letter used to transcribe both is the same. Letters in minuscule are not found initially. The superiors ^{m} and ^{n} mark original nazalized voiced stops.

CONVENTIONS:

All words found in dialectal Sindarin have been given a Classical Sindarin form. Where the CS form shows a divergence from the dialect form (other than the usual *r-*, *l-*, *hw-*, *ae*, and *ai* for Noldorin *rh-*, *lh-*, *chw-*, *oe*, and *ei*), the dialectal form is listed in parentheses following the entry. Evident errors in transcription have been tacitly corrected.

Alternative forms of the same word follow after a comma.

Treatment of final *-nd* has been regularized (*-nd* in monosyllables, *-nn* in bisyllables, *-n* in words of more than two syllables) according to common usage. Final *-m* or *-mb* has been regularized to *-m*; final *-s*, *-ss* to *-s*; and medial *-s-*, *-ss-* to *-ss-*. It has proven impossible, however, to find a regular treatment of medial *-mm-* and *-m-* that would allow the words to continue to be recognizable. The spelling has therefore been left inconsistent.

Single quotes in a definition surround the most literal translation of a word, followed by less literal (but perhaps more explanatory) meanings.

Principal parts of *i*-stem verbs are listed as follows: stem, infinitive, preterite, past participle. When the vowel of the stem and the infinitive are the same, however, only the infinitive is listed. Only irregular forms of *a*-stem verbs are listed after the stem and in such cases are labeled.

Hypothetical Common Eldarin forms are only given when these forms cannot be easily deduced from the Old Sindarin forms; e.g., no notice is taken of the mere shortening of final *ā*, *ē*, *ō*, or of the aspiration of consonant clusters.

Roots are cited for all noncompound words and for compounds when one or more of their elements do not occur separately.

Superscript numbers distinguish words of the same form but of distinct origin and meaning.

GENERAL ABBREVIATIONS AND SYMBOLS

acc.	accusative case
adj.	adjective, adjectival
adv.	adverb, adverbial
art.	article
bv.	bahuvrihi compound
cf.	compare
conj.	conjunction
dat.	dative case
dc.	double comparative compound
dg.	dvigu compound
dim.	diminutive
du.	dual
esp.	especially
f.	feminine
gen.	genitive case
ger.	gerund
impers.	impersonal
impv.	imperative
indef.	indefinite
intj.	interjection
irreg.	irregularly derived from
kd.	karmadharaya compound
late	form dating from after the mid–Second Age
len.	lenited form
m.	masculine
n.	noun
num.	number
pl.	plural
pll.	plurals
pp.	past passive participle
pr. p.	present participle
pref.	prefix
prep.	preposition

pron.	pronoun
pt.	preterite
pth.	prototheme, first element in a compound
sg.	singular
tp.	tatpurusha compound
tth.	telotheme, last element in a compound
v.	verb
1sg.	first-person singular
3sg.	third-person singular
!	unattested or speculative word or form of a word deduced from other words or roots
#	attested word whose form has been significantly altered
*	hypothetical historical form of a word
?	uncertain word, form, or meaning
‡	archaic or poetic word
'	precedes syllable receiving primary stress
´	precedes syllable receiving secondary stress
·	separates syllables
( )	encloses elements that may or may not be part of a word or phrase, also other parenthetical information
-	follows verb stems and elements that are only found attached to other words; also used finally for words whose final vowels cannot be reconstructed
+	joins two or more words that form a compound
[ ]	encloses etymological information
√	root
<	derives from

A

A[1], *intj.*: O! [OS *a √!A]

A[2], **ah**, *conj.*: and [OS *ah < CE *as √AS[2]] *MR*:329 (*ah*)

Ab-, *adv. pref.*: after, later, behind [OS *apa- √AP[2]]

A·'bon·nen, *pl.* **e·'ben·nin**, (1) *adj. pp.*: born after, born later; (2) *n.*: 'one born later (than the Elves)', human being [ab- + onnen, OS *apont^{h}ena √ONO] *WJ*:387

A·charn, *n.*: vengeance [OS *akk^{h}arna < CE *atkarnā 'reaction' √AT[2] √KAR[1]] *WJ*:254

!A·chas, *n.*: dread, fear [OS *ak^{h}asse √!AKH] (perhaps **!ga·chas** √!GAKH; cf. Q *aha* rage) *WJ*:183, 187

Ad, (1) *adj. pref.*: second; (2) *adv. pref.*: back, again, re-; (3) *prep.*: against [OS *ata √AT[2]]

A·da, *n.*: father, daddy (hypocoristic) [shortening of CS adar √AT[1]]

A·dab, *pl.* **e·daib**, *n.*: building, house [OS *atape < CE *atak^{w}ē √A-TAK[1]] (N *pl.* edeb)

A·dan, *pll.* **e·dain**, **'a·da·nath**, *n.*: mortal, man, 'second folk', a member of the Three Houses of the Edain [Q *atan* √AT[2]-AN] *RGEO*:66, *MR*:373, *WJ*:387

A·'da·na·dar, *pl.* **e·'de·ne·dair**, *n. tp.*: one of the 'fathers of men' [adan + adar] *MR*:373

'A·da·neth, *n. f.*: human woman, mortal woman [adan + -eth[2]] *MR*:349

A·dar, *pl.* **e·dair**, *n.*: father [OS *ataro √AT[1]]

A·del, *adv.*, *prep.*: behind, in the rear (of) [OS *atele < CE *atéles √TÉL-ES]

A·'der·tha-, *v.*: reunite [ad + ertha-, OS *atert^{h}a- √ER]

A·'der·thad, *n. ger.*: reunion, reuniting [OS *aterthata √ER]

#Ad·lann, *adj.*: sloping, tilted [OS *atlanda √Á-TALAT] (‡adland)

#Ad·'lan·na-, *v.*: slope, slant [OS *atlant^{h}a- √Á-TALAT]

#Ad·lant, *adj.*: oblique, slanting [OS *atlant^{h}a √Á-TALAT]

‡Ad·leg-, **'ad·le·gi**, *pt.*: **ad·lenc**, *pp.*: **ad·'len·gen**, *v.*: free, release [OS *at(a)lek- √AT[2] √LEK] *VT*45:27

Ad·'lei·tha-, *v.*: free, release [OS *at(a)lekta- √AT[2] √LEK] *VT*45:27

Ad·'lei·thian, *n.*: release [OS *at(a)lekta- √AT[2] √LEK] *VT*45:27

A·'dui·al, *n. kd.*: 'second twilight', evendim, the time of evening when the stars come out [ad + uial, OS *atuiaŋala]

Ae, *intj.*: O [OS *ai]

Ae·ar, *n.*: sea, ocean [OS *aiare √ÁJ-AR] (N oear) *RGEO*:65, *Letters*:386

'Ae·a·ron, *n.*: great ocean [OS *aiarondo √ÁJ-AR] *RGEO*:65

Aeg[1], *adj.*: sharp, pointed, piercing [OS *aika √ÁJAK] (dial. êg, N oeg)

Aeg[2], *n.*: point, peak, thorn [OS *aik- √ÁJAK]

Ae·gas, *pl.* **ae·gais**, *n.*: mountain peak [OS *aikasse √ÁJAK] (N oeg, *pl.* oeges)

Aeg·lir, *n. tp.*: range of mountain peaks [aeg[2] + lîr, OS *aikalīre] (N oeglir)

Aeg·los, *n. impr. tp.*: icicle; 'snow-thorn', a plant similar to gorse, but larger, with white flowers [aeg[2] + los, OS *aikalosse] *UT*:148

Ael, **ae·lin-**, *pl.* **ae·lin**, *n. kd.*: pool, lake, mere [OS *ailin, *pl.* *ailini √AJ √LIN[1]] (N oel, *pl.* oelin)

Aen, *pron. indef.*: ?they [OS *ain-] *SD*:128–31

Aer, *n.*: sea [OS *aire √ÁJ-AR] (N oer)

Aer·linn, *n. tp.*: song about the sea [aer + lind[1], OS *airelinde]

Ae·ruil, *n. tp.*: seaweed [aer + uil, OS *airuile]

Aes, *n.*: cooked food, meat [MS *ais, *axs < OS *apsa √AP[1]]

Aew, *n.*: (small) bird [OS *aiwe √AJW]

Ae·wen, *adj*.: of birds [OS *aiwena or *aiwina √AJW]

A·gar, *n*.: blood [OS *akar- √A-KAR[2]]

A·'gar·waen, *adj. tp*.: bloodstained [agar + gwaen]

Ag·lar, *n*.: brilliance, glitter, glory [OS *aklare √Á-KAL-AR]

'Ag·la·reb, *adj*.: glorious [OS *aklaripa < CE *aklarik^{w}ā √Á-KAL-AR] *WJ*:412

Ag·lonn, *n. kd*.: defile, pass between high walls [OS *aklonde √AK √LON]

A·gor, *adj*.: narrow [MS *agr < OS *akra √AK]

Ai[1], *intj*.: ah! hail!

Ai[2], *pron*.: who, which, that *VT*44:23

Aig, *adj*.: sharp [MS *eig < OS *ekia √EK] *VT*41:14

Aith, *n*.: spear point [OS *ekthė < CE *ekti √EK-ET]

Al-, *adv. pref*.: not [OS *al- < CE *ḷ < *la- √LA]

A·lae, *intj*.: ah! [OS *alaj-]

A·lag, *adj*.: rushing, impetuous [OS *alaka √Á-LAK[1]]

'A·la·gon, *adj*.: rushing [OS *alakǫna √Á-LAK[1]]

'A·la·gos, *n*.: storm of wind [OS *alakosse √Á-LAK[1]]

'Al·fi·rin, (1) *adj*. immortal; (2) *n*.: 'immortal', name of a flower [al- + firin, OS *alp^{h}irinė]

Alph, *pl*. **eilph**, *n*.: swan [OS *alp^{h}a < CE *alk^{w}ā √Á-LAK[1]]

Am, (1) *adj. pref*.: uprising, going up; (2) *adv*.: up, upward (3) *prep*.: upon [OS *amba √AM[1]]

Am·ar, *n*.: the earth [OS *ambar- √A-MBAR]

Am·arth, *n*.: fate, doom [OS *ambart^{h}a < *ṃbartā √MBÁRAT]

Am·ar·than, *adj*.: fated [OS *ambart^{h}ana √MBÁRAT] *VT*41:10

Am·ath, *n*.: shield [OS *ambat^{h}- < CE *ṃbat^{h}- √MBATH] *VT*45:33

Am·benn, *adj. kd. bv*.: uphill, sloping upward [am + pend, OS *ambapenda]

Am·dir, *n. kd*.: 'up-looking', hope based on reason [am + tîr[2], OS *ambatire] *MR*:320

Am·loth, *n. kd*.: 'uprising-flower', crest of a helmet [am + loth, OS *ambalott^{h}e < CE *ambalotsē] (dial. almoth)

Am·lug, *n. kd*.: dragon [OS *ambaḽḽūkė < CE *aŋgwaslōki √AŋGW √S-LOK]

Am·men, *pron*.: to us, for us, of us [an + men √ME]

Am·on, *pl*. **em·yn**, *n*.: hill, steep-sided mount [OS *ambon- √AM[1]]

Am·rûn, *n. kd*.: uprising, sunrise, orient, east [am + rhûn, OS *ambar̭r̭ūna < CE *ambasrōna] *LotR:AppE*

An, (1) *adv. pref*.: for, to, very; (2) *prep*. (with article, **'ni**): for, to [OS *an √ANA]

A·nann, *adv.*: long, for a long time [an + and[1], OS *ananda]
Anc, *n.*: jaw, row of teeth [OS *aŋk^{h}a < CE aŋkā √Á-NAK]
And[1], *adj.*: long [OS *anda √ÁNAD]
!And[2], *n.*: gate, door [OS *ando < CE *adnō √AD]
An·daith, *n. kd.*: 'long mark', a mark, used in writing alphabetic tengwar, over a vowel to indicate that it is lengthened [and[1] + taith] *LotR:AppE*
#An·drann, *n. kd.*: cycle, age [and[1] + *rand < OS randa √RAD] (N anrand)
An·drath, *n. kd.*: 'long climb', a high pass [and[1] + rath, OS *andaratt^{h}a]
An·fang, *pll.* **en·feng, an·'fang·rim**, *n. kd. bv.*: one of the 'Longbeards', a tribe of Dwarves [and[1] + fang] *WJ*:10, 108, 205
Ang, *n.* iron [OS *aŋga √AŋG] *PME*:347
An·'ger·thas, *n. kd.*: 'long rune-row', a system of runes or cirth [and[1] + certhas] *LotR:AppE*
An·'glen·na-, *v.*: approach [an + *glenna-, OS *aŋglenna- < CE *angledna- √G-LED] *SD*:128–31
‡An·gol[1], *n.*: deep lore, magic [OS *ŋgole √ŋGOL]
An·gol[2], *n.*: stench [OS *ŋgol- √ŋOL]
An·gos, *n.*: horror [an + gos, OS *aŋgosse √AN √GOS] *VT*45:15
An·gren, *pl.* **en·grin**, *adj.*: of iron [OS *aŋgrina √AŋG]
An·gwedh, *n. tp.*: 'iron-bond', chain [ang[1] + gwêdh, OS *aŋgaweda]
A·'ní·ra-, *v.*: (to) desire [an + *íra-, OS *anīra- √!IR] *SD*:128–31
Ann, -an, *n.*: gift [OS *anna √AN]
An·na-, *v.*, *pt.* **!aun, o·ne-**: give [OS *ant^{h}a- √AN]
'An·na·bon, 'an·da·bon, *n. kd. bv.*: 'the long-snouted', elephant [and[1] + *bond, MS *annabond *irreg.* < OS *andambunda √MBUD]
!An·neth, *n.*: act or fact of giving [ann + -eth[1], OS *annett^{h}e √AN]
An·non, *pl.* **en·nyn**, *n.*: (great) gate, door [OS *andondo, *ando < CE *adnō √AD]
An·nui, *adj.*: western [OS *anduia < CE *ṇdūjā √NDU] *SD*:128–31
An·nûn, *n.*: sunset, west [OS *andūne < CE *ṇdūnē √NDU] *LotR:AppE*
An·'nú·naid, *n.*: Westron (language) [OS *andūneitė √NDU] *PME*:316
A·nor, *n.*: sun [OS *anǭr < CE *anār √A-NÁR] *SD*:302
Ant, *n.*: gift [OS *ant^{h}a √AN]
A·nu, *adj.*: male [MS *anw < OS *anwa < CE *hanwā √HAN]
An·war, *n.*: awe
'A·pha·da-, *v.*: follow [ab- + pad-, OS *app^{h}ata- √PAT[2]] *WJ*:387
'A·pha·don, *pll.* **'e·phe·dyn, a'phad·rim**, *n.*: 'follower', human being [OS *app^{h}ato(ndo) √PAT[2]] *WJ*:387
Aph·arch, *adj.*: very dry [OS app^{h}ark^{h}a < CE *anparkā √AN √PÁRAK] *VT*45:5, 36

‡**Âr, a·ran-**, *pl.* **e·rain**, *n.*: king [OS *aran √ÁR^{1}-AN]

Ar, *conj.*: and [OS *ar √AR^{2}]

Ar-^{1}, *adj. pref.*: high, noble, royal [OS *ara, *ar- √AR^{1}]

Ar-^{2}, *adv. pref.*: outside, without, not [OS *ar- √AR^{2}]

A·r(a)-, (1) *adj. pref.*, royal, kingly; (2) *n. pref.*: king; element in the names of the kings of Arnor and Arthedain [CS aran]

A·ran, *pll.* **e·rain, 'a·ra·nath**, *n.*: king (of a region), lord [OS *aran √ÁR^{1}-AN, sg. possibly back-formed from erain pl. of âr]

A·ras, *n.*: deer [OS *arasse √A-RAS]

Ardh, *n.*: region, realm [OS *arda √ÁR^{1}-AD]

Ar·dhon, *n.*: great region, great province, world [OS *ardondo √ÁR^{1}-AD]

Arn, *adj.*: royal, noble [OS *arna √ÁR^{1}-AN]

Ar·nad, *n.*: kingdom [OS *arnata √ÁR^{1}-AN] *VT*44:23

Ar·'ne·di·ad, *adj.*: unnumbered, without reckoning, numberless [ar^{2} + nediad, MS *arnödiad < OS *arnotiata]

A·rod, *adj.*: noble [OS *arǭta < CE *arātā √AR^{1}-ÁT] *PME*:363

A·'ro·no·ded, *adj.*: innumerable, countless, endless [ar^{2} + gonoded, OS *arwonodita]

Ar·phen, *pl.* **er·phin**, *n. kd.*: noble [ar^{1} + pen, OS *arp^{h}en- < CE *ark^{w}en- √AR^{1} √KWE-N] *WJ*:376

Arth, *adj.*: noble, lofty, exalted [Q *arta* or OS *art^{h}a < CE *arātā √AR^{1}-ÁT]

Ar·wen, *n. kd.*: noble woman [ar-^{1} + gwên]

As·car, *adj.*: violent, rushing, impetuous [OS *askara √A-SKAR] also spelled asgar

Ast, *n.*: dust [OS *asto √ÁS^{3}-AT]

Ath-, *adv. pref.*: on both sides, across [OS *att^{h}a- √AT^{2}-AT]

A·thar, ath·ra-, (1) *adv. pref.*: across; (2) *prep.*: beyond, across [OS *at^{h}(a)ra √Á-THAR] *SD*:62

'A·the·las, *n.*: a healing plant, brought to Middle-earth by the Númenoreans [Q *aβea + CS las √!ATH]

!Ath·ra-, *v.*: cross [OS *at^{h}ra- < CE *at^{h}ara- √Á-THAR]

'Ath·ra·beth, *n. kd.*: 'cross-talk', debate [athar + peth, OS *at^{h}rapett^{h}a] *MR*:329

Ath·rad, *pl.* **eth·raid**, *n.*: (river-)crossing, ford [OS *at^{h}rata < CE *at^{h}aratā √Á-THAR]

'Ath·ra·da-, *v.*: cross, traverse [ath + rada-, OS *att^{h}arata-]

Aur, or-, *n.*: day, morning [OS *aure √UR^{1}]

Auth^{1}, *n.*: war, battle [MS *ouβ < *oxβa < OS *okt^{h}a √Ó-KOTH]

Auth^{2}, *n.*: dim shape, spectral or vague apparition [OS *aut^{h}a < CE *áwat^{h}ā √Á-WATH]

Av-, *adv. pref.*: don't (with imperative verbs) [OS *aba √ABA] *WJ*:371

A·va-, *v.*: will not [OS *aba- √ABA] *WJ*:371
A·vad, *n. ger.*: refusal, reluctance [OS *abata √ABA] *WJ*:372
A·var, *pl.* **e·vair**, *n.*: non-Eldarin Elf, one of the Avari [OS *abaro √ABA] *WJ*:380
A·vo, *adv.*: don't (before imperative verbs) [OS *aba ǭ √ABA] *WJ*:371
A·vorn, *adj.*: staying, not moving, fast [OS *aborna √BOR^{1}] *SD*:128–31
A·warth, *n.*: abandonment [OS *awart^{h}a √A-WAR]
A·'war·tha-, *v.*: forsake, abandon [OS *awart^{h}a- √A-WAR]

B

^{m}**Bach**, *n.*: article (for exchange), ware, thing [OS *m͡abk^{h}a √MBAKH]
^{m}**Ba·chor**, *n.*: pedlar [MS *baxr < OS *m̃baŋk^{h}ro √MBAKH]
Bad-, **be·di**, **bant**, **ban·nen**, *v.*: go [OS *bati- √BAT]
Bâd, *n.*: beaten track, pathway [OS bata √BAT]
Ba·dhor, *n.*: judge [MS *baðr < OS *badro √BAD]
Badh·ron, *n.* judge [MS *baðrond < OS *badro(ndo) √BAD]
Bain, *adj.*: beautiful, fair [MS *bein < OS *bania √BAN]
Bâl, (1) *adj.*: divine; (2) *n.*: divinity, divine power [OS *bala √BAL]
Ba·lan, *pl.* **be·lain**, *n.*: Vala [OS balano √BAL]
^{m}**Balch**, *adj.*: cruel [OS *m̃balk^{h}a < CE *ŋ^{w}g^{w}alkā √ŋGWAL]
Bal·rog, *pl.* **'bal·ro·gath**, *n. tp.*: 'demon of might', a fire-Maia corrupted by Morgoth and in his service [bâl + raug, OS *balarauko] *MR*:79, *WJ*:415
^{m}**Band**, *n.*: safekeeping, custody, prison, duress, doom, hell [OS *m̃bando √M-BAD] *MR*:350
^{m}**Ban·ga-**, *pt.* **banc**, *pp.* **ban·gen**, *v.*: (to) trade [OS *m̃baŋk^{h}a- √MBAKH]
!**Ban·nen**, *adj. pp.*: gone [OS *bant^{h}ena √BAT]
^{m}**Bâr**, **-bar**, **-mar**, *pl.* **bair**, *n.*: dwelling, house, home; family; land, earth [OS *m̃bar √MBAR]
Ba·ra, *adj.*: fiery, eager [OS baraha < CE *barasā √BARÁS]
Ba·rad^{1}, *pl.* **be·raid**, *n.*: tower, fortress, fort [OS *barata √BAR-AT] *VT*45:7
^{m}**Ba·rad^{2}**, *adj.*: doomed [OS *m̃barata √MBÁRAT]
Ba·radh, *adj.*: steep [OS barada √BAR-ÁD]
Ba·ran, *adj.*: brown, swart, dark brown, yellow brown, golden-brown [OS baranė < CE *barani √BARÁN] *Names*:179, *PME*:54
^{m}**Bar·tha-**, *v.*: (to) doom [OS *m̃bart^{h}a- √MBÁRAT]
^{m}**Bas**, *n.*: bread [OS *m̃bassa √MBAS]
^{m}**Bas·gorn**, *n. impr. kd.*: 'round bread', loaf [bast + corn, OS *m̃bastakorna]
!^{m}**'Bas·so·neth**, *n. f. tp.*: 'bread-giver', Lady [bas + oneth, OS *m̃bassǭnitt^{h}a] *PME*:405

^{m}**Bast**, *n*.: bread [OS *m͡basta √MBAS]

Ba·tha-, *v*.: trample [OS *batt^{h}a- √BAT]

Baudh, *n*.: judgment, sentence [OS *bǭd- < CE *bād- √BAD] *VT*45:33

^{m}**Baug**, *adj*.: tyrannous, cruel, oppressive [OS *m͡bauka √MBAW]

^{m}**Baug·la-**, *v*.: constrain, oppress [OS *m͡baukla- √MBAW]

^{m}**Baug·lir**, *n*.: tyrant, constrainer, oppressor [OS *ma͡bukliro √MBAW]

^{m}**Baug·ron**, *n*.: tyrant, constrainer, oppressor [OS *m͡baukro(ndo) √MBAW]

^{m}**Baul, bol-**, *n*.: torment [OS *m͡bǭl- < CE *ŋ^{w}g͡^{w}āl- √ŋGWAL]

^{m}**Baur**, *n*.: need [OS *m͡baure √MBAW]

Baw, *v. impv*.: no! don't! [OS bǭ < CE *bā √(A)BA] *WJ*:371

Be, *prep*. (with *art*., **ben**): like, as, according to [OS *be √!BE] *SD*:128–131

Be·leg, *adj*.: great, mighty [OS *beleka √BÉL-EK]

Bell, *adj*.: strong in body [OS *belda √BEL] (N belt)

Bel·las, *n*.: bodily strength [OS *beldasse, *belde √BEL]

Benn, *n. m*.: man, ‡husband [OS bḙṋno 'husband' < CE *besnō √BES]

Ben·nas, *n*.: angle [OS *bennass- √BEN √NAS]

Be·reth, *n*.: queen, spouse [OS *barat^{h}il √BARATH] *RGEO*:66

Be·ren, *adj*.: bold [OS berina √BER]

'Be·ri·a-, *v*.: protect [OS *baria- √BAR]

Ber·tha-, *v*.: dare [OS bert^{h}a- √BER]

Bes, *n. f*.: woman, wife [OS besse √BES]

^{m}**Bes·sain**, *n. f. tp*.: 'bread-giver', Lady [OS *m͡bassanie √MBAS √AN] *PME*:404–5

Blab-, ble·bi, blamp, blam·men, *v*.: flap, beat (e. g., a wing) [*irreg*. OS *plapi- < CE *pa 'lapi- √PALÁP]

Bo·da-, *v*.: ban, prohibit [OS *bǭta- < CE *bāta- √(A)BA] *WJ*:372

#^{m}**Boe**, *v. impers*.: it is necessary, one must, one is compelled to [OS *m͡bauia < CE *m͡bauja √MBAW] (N bui)

Bôr, bo·ron-, *pll*. **bŷr, be·ryn**, *n*.: steadfast, trusty man, faithful vassal [OS boron √BOR^{1}]

Born, *adj*.: hot, red [OS *borna √!BOR^{2}]

^{m}**Bôth**, *n*.: puddle, small pool [OS *m͡bot^{h}o √MBOTH]

Bra·gol, *adj*.: sudden [OS *brakǭla < CE *brakālā √BARÁK]

Braig, *adj*.: wild, fierce [OS *brekia < CE *brekjā √BERÉK] *VT*45:34

Brand, *adj*.: high, lofty, noble, fine [OS branda √BAR-ÁD]

Bran·non, *n. m*.: lord [OS *brando(ndo) √BAR-ÁD]

Bras, *n*.: white heat [OS brasse √BARÁS]

Bras·sen, *adj*.: white-hot [OS *brassina √BARÁS]

Brêg, *adj.*: sudden, quick, lively [OS *breka √BERÉK]

Bre·ged, (1) *n.*: violence, suddenness; (2) *adv.*: suddenly [OS *brekete √BERÉK] *VT*35:44

'Bre·ge·dúr, *n. tp.*: wildfire [breged + ûr^{1}]

Bre·gol, *adj.*: violent, sudden, fierce [OS *brekǭla < CE *brekālā √BERÉK]

'Bre·go·las, *n.*: fierceness [OS *brekǭlasse √BERÉK]

Brei·tha-, *v.*: break out suddenly [MS *brexβa- < OS brekt^{h}a- √BERÉK]

'Bre·ni·a-, *v.*: endure [OS broni- √BOR^{1}-ÓN] *VT*45:7

Bren·nil, *n. f.*: lady [OS *brandille √BAR-ÁD]

Bre·thil, *pl.* **bre·thil,** *n.*: birch tree [OS *bret^{h}il- √BERÉTH]

Brith, *n.*: gravel [OS *britt^{h}e √BIRÍT]

Bri·thon, *adj.*: pebbly [OS *britt^{h}ǭna √BIRÍT]

Brôg, *n.*: bear [OS *broko < CE *morokō √MORÓK]

Bro·na-, *v.*: last, survive [OS *brona- < CE *borona- √BOR^{1}-ÓN]

!Bro·nad, *n. ger.*: survival [OS *bronata √BOR^{1}-ÓN]

'Bro·na·dui, *adj.*: enduring, lasting [bronad + -ui OS *bronatuia]

Bron·we, *n. kd.*: endurance [OS *bronwege 'enduring-vigor' √BOR^{1}-ÓN √WEG] *SD*:62

Brui, *adj.*: loud, noisy [OS *bruia √!BUR]

Brûn, *adj.*: old, long endured, long established, long in use [OS brūna < CE *borōnā √BOR^{1}-ÓN]

Bui·a-, *v.*: serve, hold allegiance to [OS *buia- < CE *beuja- √BEW]

^{m}**Bund,** *n.*: snout, nose; cape (of land) [OS *m̑bundȯ < CE *m̑bundu √MBUD]

#Bŷr, *n.*: follower, vassal [OS *biuro < CE *beurō √BEW] (N bior, beor)

C

!Cab-, ce·bi, camp, cam·men, *v.*: leap [OS *kapi- √KAP]

Ca·bed, *n. ger.*: leap [OS *kapita √KAP]

Ca·bor, *n.*: 'leaper' frog [MS *kabr < OS *kapro √KAP]

Ca·du, *adj.*: shaped, formed [MS *kadw < OS *katwe < CE *katwā √KAT]

Cad·wor, cad·war, *adj.*: shapely [MS *kadwaur < OS *katwǭra < CE *katwārā √KAT]

Cae, *n.*: earth [OS *kai(m) < CE *kaem √KEM] (N coe)

Cael, *n.*: lying in bed, sickness [OS *kaila √KAJ^{1}]

Cae·leb, *adj.*: bedridden, sick [OS *kailipa < CE *kailik^{w}ā √KAJ^{1}]

Caer, *num.*: ten [OS *kair- √KÁJ^{2}-AR] *replaced by* **pae**

Caew, *n.*: lair, resting place [MS *kaiṽ < OS *kaima √KAJ^{1}]

Cai, *pl.* **cî,** *n.*: hedge [MS *keiʒ < OS *kegia √KEG]

Cail, *n*.: a fence or palisade of spikes and sharp stakes [MS *keil < OS *kegle √KEG] *UT*:282

Cair, cír-, *pl*. **cîr**, *n*.: ship [MS *keir < OS *kiria √KIR]

Ca·lad, *n*.: light [OS *kalata √KAL-AT]

Ca·lan, *n*.: daytime [OS *kalan- √KAL]

!Ca·lar, *n*.: lamp [OS *kalar- √KAL-ÁR]

Ca'lar·dan, *pl*. **ce·'ler·dain**, *n. tp*.: lampwright [calar + tân] *WR*:287, 388

Cal·ben, *pl*. **cel·bin**, *n. tp*.: 'light-person', Elda, Elf of the great journey [OS *kalapende √KAL √KWE-N] *WJ*:362, 376

Ca·len, *pl*. **ce·lin**, *adj*.: green, bright-colored [OS *kalina √KAL] *Letters*:282

Cal·lon, *n*.: hero [OS *kalro(ndo) √KAL]

Calph, *n*.: water vessel [OS *kalp^{h}a √!KÁLAP]

Cam, *n*.: hand [OS *kambe √KAB]

Cam·lann, *n. tp*.: palm of the hand [cam + land[1]]

Can-, ce·ni, cann, can·nen, *v*.: cry out, shout, call [OS *kani- √KAN[1]] *PME*:362

Ca·nad, *num*.: four [OS *kanata √KÁNAT]

Ca·nath, *n*.: fourth part, farthing (fourth part of a **mirian**) [OS *kanatt^{h}a √KÁNAT] *PME*:45

Cand, *adj*.: bold [OS *kanda √KAN[2]]

Can·nas, *n*.: shaping [OS *kant^{h}asse √KAT]

Can·nui, *num. adj*.: fourth [OS *kant^{h}uia √KÁNAT] (dial. canthui) *VT*42:25

Cant, *pl*. **caint**, *n*.: outline, shape [OS *kant^{h}a √KAT]

Car-, ce·ri, a·gor, ?co·ren, *v*.: do, make, build [OS *kari- √KAR[1]] *WJ*:415

Ca·rab, *n*.: hat [OS *karap- √!KARAP] *WJ*:187

Ca·rach, *n*.: set of jaws [OS *karakk^{h}e or dial. MS *karaxx < OS *karakse √KÁRAK]

Ca·raes, *n*.: hedge of spikes [MS *karais, *karaxs < OS *karakse √KÁRAK]

Ca·rag, *n*.: spike, tooth of rock [OS *karaka √KÁRAK]

Ca·ran, *adj*.: red [OS *karanė < CE *ka 'rani √KAR[2]-ÁN]

Carch, *n*.: tooth, fang [OS *kark^{h}a √KÁRAK]

Car(dh)[1], *n*.: building, house [MS *karð < OS *kard- √KAR[1]]

Cardh[2], *n*.: deed, feat [OS *kard- √KAR[1]] (dial. carth)

!Ca·red, *n. ger*.: doing, making [OS *karita √KAR[1]]

Carn, *adj*.: red [OS *karnė < CE * 'karani √KAR[2]-ÁN]

!Cast, *n*.: cape, headland [OS *kasta √KAS] *VT*42:14

Cath·rae, *n*.: tressure, hairnet [OS *kasraia √KAS √RAJ] (perhaps a dial. form of expected !carrae) *VT*42:12

Caul, *n*.: affliction, heavy burden [OS *kaulo < CE *kaolō √KOL] *VT*39:10

Caun[1], *pl.* **co·nath**, *n*.: outcry, clamor, cry, shout, (in pl.) lamentation [OS *kǭna √KAN[1]] *PME*:345, 362

Caun[2], *n*.: valor [OS *kǭne √KAN[2]]

!**Caun**[3], *pl.* **co·nin**, *n*.: commander, prince [MS *kaun < Q *cáno* √KAN[1]]

Caw, *n*.: top [OS *kǭ < CE *kās √KAS]

Ce·ber, *pl.* **ce·bir**, *n*.: stake, spike, stone ridge [OS *keper- √KEPER]

Cêf, *pl.* **cîf**, *n*.: soil [MS *keṽ < OS *kem- √KEM]

Cefn, *adj*.: earthen [OS *kemna √KEM]

Cef·nas, *n*.: earthenware [OS *kemnasse √KEM] *VT*45:19

Ce·lair, *adj*.: brilliant [OS *kalaria √KAL-ÁR]

Ce·leb, *n*.: silver [OS kelepe < CE *k^{j}elepē √KJELEP] *Letters*:426

Ce·'leb·ren, ce·'leb·rin- *adj*.: of silver, like silver [OS *keleprina √KJELEP] *PME*:179, 318, *VT*45:25

Ce·lefn, *adj*.: of silver [OS *kelemna < CE *k^{j}elepnā √KJELEP]

Ce·leg, *adj*.: swift, agile [OS *keleka < CE *k^{j}elekā √KJELEK] *VT*41:10

Ce·leth, *n*.: stream [OS *kelett^{h}e √KEL] *VT*45:19

Cell, *adj*.: running, flowing (of water) [OS *kella √KEL]

Ce·lon, *n*.: river [OS *keluna √KEL]

Ce·los, *n*.: freshet, water falling swiftly from a spring [OS *kelusse √KEL]

Ce·lu, *n*.: spring, source [MS *kelw < OS *kelwe √KEL]

Cên, *n*.: wedge, gore [OS *kene √KEN[2]] *VT*45:20

!**Ce·ned**, *n. ger*.: seeing, sight [OS *kenita √KEN[1]]

!**Ce·ni, cenn, cen·nen**, *v*.: see [OS *keni- √KEN[1]]

Ce·'ned·ril, *n. tp*.: mirror [cened + rill] *RS*:466

Cen·nan, *n. tp*.: potter [cêf + tân, OS *kent^{h}ano < CE *kemtanō]

Cerch, *n*.: sickle [OS *kirk^{h}a √KÍR-IK]

'Ce·re·dir, *n. tp*.: doer, maker [cared + dîr]

Ce·rin, *n*.: circular raised mound, circular enclosure [OS *korin- √KOR]

Certh, *pl.* **cirth**, *n*.: rune [OS *kirt^{h}a *irreg*. < CE *kirtē √KIR] *LotR:AppE*

Cer·thas, *n*.: rune-row, collection of runes, alphabet [certh + -as] *LotR:AppE*

Ce·ven, *n*.: earth [OS *kemen- √KEM] *VT*44:23

Cîl, *n*.: cleft, pass between hills, gorge [OS *kil- √KIL]

Cîn, *n*.: wedge, gore [OS *kēne √KEN[2]] *VT*45:20

Cír·bann, *n. tp*.: haven [cair + pand OS *kiriapanda]

Cír·dan, *n. tp*.: shipbuilder, shipwright [cair + tân OS *kiriatano]

'Ci·ri·on, *n*.: shipman, sailor [OS *kirio(ndo) √KIR]

Ci·rith, *n*.: cleft, cutting, pass [OS *kiritt^{h}e √KIR] *Names*:181

‡**Claur**, *n.*: splendor, glory [OS *klǫre < CE *kalārē √KAL-ÁR]
Côf, *n.*: bay [OS *koba √KOB] *VT*42:15
Cofn, *adj.*: empty, void [OS *kumna √KUM] (dial. caun)
Coll[1], *adj.*: hollow [OS *kulda √KUL[1]] *WJ*:414
Coll[2], *adj.*: red, scarlet [OS *kulda √KUL[2]] *VT*45:15, 24
Coll[3], *n.*: cloak [OS *kolla < CE *kolnā √KOL]
Con·dir, *n. kd.*: mayor [caun[3] + dîr] *SD*:128–31
!**Co·nui**, *adj.*: ?commanding [caun[3] + -ui]
Corch, *n.*: crow [OS *kork^{h}- √KÓROK]
Cor·dof, *n.*: a small red apple, pippin *SD*:128–31
Corn[1], *adj.*: circular, round, globed [OS *korna √KOR]
Corn[2], *n.*: circle [OS *korne < CE *koronē √KOR]
Co·ron, *n.*: mound; globe, ball [OS *korone √KOR]
Co·ru, *adj.*: cunning, wily [MS *korw < OS *kurwa √KUR]
Cost, *n.*: quarrel [OS *kosta < CE *kot^{h}tā √KOTH]
Coth[1], *n.*: enmity [OS *kott^{h}e < CE *kotsē √KOTH] *VT*45:23
Coth[2], *n.*: enemy [OS *kott^{h}o √KOTH]
!**Cra·ban**, *pl.* **cre·bain**, *n.*: crow [OS *krapan- < CE *karak^{w}an- √!KARÁKW]
Cram, *n.*: cake of compressed flour or meal (often containing honey and milk) used on long journeys [OS *kramb- √!KARÁB] *Hobbit*
Crann, *adj.*: ruddy (of face) [OS *kranna √KAR[2]-ÁN]
Cris, **criss-**, *n.*: cleft, cut, slash [OS *krisse √KIR-ÍS] *VT*45:23
Crist, *n.*: cleaver, sword [OS *kristo √KIR-ÍS]
Cri·tha-, *v.*: reap [MS *krixβa- < OS *krikt^{h}a- √KÍR-IK]
Crom, *adj.*: left [OS *krumba √KURÚM]
Crûm, *n.*: the left hand [OS *krumbe √KURÚM]
'**Crum·gu·ru**, *adj. kd. bv.*: having a cunning left hand, wily, sinister, guilty [crûm + curu √KURÚM √KUR] *VT*45:24
Crum·ui, *adj.*: left-handed [crûm + -ui √KURÚM]
Cû, *n.*: bow; arch, crescent [OS *kū √KUH]
Cu·en, *n.*: small gull, petrel [Oss. cwén < CE *kwainē √KWAJ] *VT*45:24
Cu·gu, *n.*: dove [OS *kukūwa √KU]
Cui·a-, *v.*: live [OS *kuia- √KOJ]
Cuil, *n.*: life [OS *kuile √KOJ]
Cuin, *adj.*: alive [OS *kuina √KOJ]
Cui·na-, *v.*: be alive [OS *kuina- √KOJ]
Cûm, *n.*: mound, heap [OS *kumbe √KUB]
Cûn, *adj.*: bowed, bow-shaped, bent [OS *kugna < CE *kuhnā √KUH]
‡**Cund**, *n.*: prince [OS *kundu √KUND] *VT*45:24

#Cú·ron, *n. kd.*: the crescent moon [cû + raun^{2}, OS *kūrǭna] (N cúran)
Cu·ru, *pl.* **cy·ry**, *n.*: skill, cunning, cunning device, craft [MS *kurw < OS *kurwe √KUR] *VT*45:24
'Cu·ru·nír, *n. tp.*: man of craft, wizard [curu + dîr] *VT*45:24
Cyll, *n.*: bearer [OS *kolli √KOL] *MR*:385

D

Dad, *adv.*: down, downward [OS *dat(a) √DAT]
Dad·benn, *adj. kd. bv.*: downhill, sloping down, inclined, prone [dad + pend, OS *datapenda]
^{n}**Dae**^{1}, *adj.*: great [OS *ñdaia √N-DAJ^{1}]
Dae^{2}, *n.*: shadow, shade [OS *daio < CE *dajō √DAJ^{2}] *VT*45:8
Dae^{3}, *adv.*: very, exceedingly [OS *dai √DAJ^{1}] *VT*45:8
^{n}**'Dae·dhe·los, -oth**, *n. kd.*: great fear, great dread [dae^{1} + delos]
'Dae·de·lu, *n. tp.*: canopy [dae^{2} + telu OS *daiotelume]
^{n}**Daen**, *n.*: corpse [OS ñdagno √NDAK]
Daer^{1}, *adj.*: great, large [OS *daira √DAJ^{1}]
^{n}**Daer**^{2}, *n.*: bridegroom [OS ñdair < CE *ñdaer √NDER] (N doer)
Daew, *n.*: shadow [OS *daimē √DAJ^{2}] *VT*45:8
Dâf, *n.*: permission [OS *dab- √DAB]
^{n}**Dag-, de·gi**, *pt.* **danc** or **da·gant**, *pp.* **dan·gen**, *v.*: slay [OS ñdaki- √NDAK] *VT*45:37
^{n}**Dag·nir**, *n. tp.*: bane, killer [dag- + dîr]
^{n}**Da·gor**, *pl.* **'da·go·rath**, *n.*: battle [MS *dagr < OS *ñdakro √NDAK]
^{n}**Dag·ra-**, *v.*: do battle, make war [OS *ñdakra- √NDAK]
^{n}**'Dag·ra·da-**, *v.*: (to) battle, make war [OS *ñdakrata- √NDAK] *VT*45:37
^{n}**Dam**, *n.*: hammer [OS *ñdamba √NDAM]
^{n}**Dam·beth**, *n. kd.*: answer, response [dan + peth, OS *ñdanapett^{h}a √NDAN √KWE-T] *PME*:395
^{n}**Dam·ma-**, *pt.* **dam·mant**, *v.*: (to) hammer [OS *ñdamba- √NDAM] *VT*45:37
^{n}**Dan**, *prep.*: back, again, against [OS *ñdana √NDAN]
^{n}**Dan·gen**, *pl.* **den·gin**, *adj. pp.*: slain [OS *ñdaŋk^{h}ena √NDAK]
^{n}**Dan·gweth**, *n. kd.*: answer, reply giving new information [OS *ñdan-gwet^{h}a √NDAN √GWETH] *PME*:395
Dan·na-, *pt.* **dant**, *pp.* **dan·nen**, *v.*: fall [OS *dant^{h}a- √DAT]
Dan·nas, *n.*: falling, fall; autumn [OS *dant^{h}asse √DAT] *PME*:135
Dan·nen, *adj. pp.*: fallen [OS *dant^{h}ena √DAT]
Dant, *n.*: falling, fall; autumn [OS *dant^{h}a √DAT] *MR*:373, *PME*:135
^{n}**Dan·waith**, *n. kd.*: the Nandor [dan + gwaith] *WJ*:385

^{n}**Dan·wedh**, *n. kd.*: ransom [dan + gwêdh]
Dar-, de·ri, darn, dar·nen, *v.*: stop, halt [OS *dari- √DAR]
Dar·tha-, *v.*: wait, stay, remain, last, endure [OS *dart^{h}a- √DAR] *VT*45:8
Dath, *n.*: hole, pit, steep fall, abyss [OS *datt^{h}a √DAT] *VT*45:8
^{n}**Daug, -dog**, *n.*: warrior, soldier (of Orcs) [OS n͠dǭko < CE *n͠dākō √NDAK]
Daur, *n.*: 'pause, stop', league (about three miles) [OS *dǭr < CE *dār √DAR] *UT*:279
Daw, *n.*: nighttime, gloom [MS *douṽ < OS dogme < CE *dohmē √DO-H]
Dêl, *n.*: fear, disgust, loathing, horror [OS *del- √DJEL]
De·leb, *adj.*: horrible, abominable, loathsome [OS *delipa < CE *d^{j}elik^{w}ā √DJEL]
'De·li·a-, *pt.* ‡**daul** or **'de·li·ant**, *pp.* **do·len**, *v.*: conceal [OS *dulia- √DUL] *VT*45:11
De·los, de·loth, *n. kd.*: fear, horror, abhorrence, dread, detestation, loathing [dêl + gos, MS *delʒoss, *delʒoββ< OS *delegosse, *delegott^{h}e]
De·lu, *adj.*: hateful, deadly, fell [MS *delw < OS *delwa √DJEL]
Dem, *adj.*: sad, gloomy [OS *dimba √DIM]
Den·waith, *n. tp.*: people of Denwe, Nandor [Den(we) + gwaith] *WJ*:385
‡^{n}**Des**, *n.*: young woman [OS *n͠dissa √NDIS]
^{n}**Dî^{1}**, unstressed **di**, *prep.*: in; (submerged?) beneath, under [OS n͠di < CE n͠di √NDI] *VT*45:37
‡^{n}**Dî^{2}**, *n. f.*: bride, lady [OS *n͠dihė < CE *n͠disi √NDIS and OS nī √(I)NI (altered by influence of dîr, dîs)]
'Di·he·na-, *v.*: forgive, release from obligation (of a superior to an inferior) [OS *n͠dihen- < CE *n͠disen- √NDI √SEN] *VT*44:23
Dîl, *n.*: stopper, stopping, stuffing [OS *dil- √DIL]
'Di·li·a-, *pt.* **'di·li·ant**, *v.*: stop up [OS *dilia- √DIL] *VT*45:9
Dim^{1}, *n.*: stair [OS *dimb- √!DIB]
Dim^{2}, *n.*: gloom, sadness [OS *dimbe √DIM]
Dîn^{1}, *n.*: opening, gap, mountain pass [OS *dīn- < CE *dēn- √DEN]
Dîn^{2}, *n.*: silence [OS *dīn- √!DIN]
Dí·nen, *adj.*: silent [OS *dīnina √!DIN]
^{n}**Dí·neth**, *n. impr. kd.*: bride [dî + neth]
‡^{n}**Dîr, dír-, -dir, -nir**, *n. m.*: man, adult male; agental ending [OS *n͠dīr < CE *n͠dēr √NDER]
^{n}**Dír·naith**, *n. tp.*: 'spearhead of men', wedge formation in battle [dîr + naith, OS*n͠dīrnekt^{h}a] *UT*:282
^{n}**Dîs, -dis**, *n. f.*: bride, young woman [blend of ‡dî and ‡des]
Dofn, *adj.*: gloomy [OS *dumna < CE *dubnā √DUB]

Dôl, *n.*: head; hill [OS *dolo √DOL]

Do·len, *pl.* **do·lin**, *adj. pp.*: hidden, secret [OS *daulena √DUL]

^{n}**Doll**, *adj.*: dark, dusky, misty, obscure [OS *n͡dulla, *n͡dulda < CE *n͡dulnā, *n͡duldā √N-DUL] (N doll, dolt) *VT*45:11

Dolt, *pl.* **dylt**, *n.*: round knob, boss [OS *dolt^{h}- √DOL]

Dol·tha-, *pt.* ‡**daul**, *pp.* **do·len**, *v.*: conceal [OS *dult^{h}a- √DUL]

Donn, **dunn-**, *adj.*: black, swart, swarthy; shady, shadowy [OS *dunna √DUN] *VT*45:11

^{n}**Dôr**, *n.*: land, dwelling place, region [OS *n͡dore √N-DOR] *WJ*:413

Dorn, *adj.*: stiff, tough [OS *dorna √DOR] *WJ*:413

Dorn·hoth, *n. kd.*: 'thrawn folk', Dwarves [dorn + hoth] *WJ*:388, 408

Do·ron, *pl.* **de·ryn**, *n.*: oak tree [OS *dorono √DÓRON] (N *pl.* döröin, deren) *VT*45:11

^{n}**Dor·tha-**, *v.*: dwell, stay [OS *n͡dort^{h}a- √N-DOR]

Dos·ta-, *v.*: burn [OS *dusta- √DUS] *VT*45:10–11

Drafn, *pl.* **drefn**, (1) *adj.*: ‡hewn; (2) *n.*: hewn log, hewn stone [OS *dramna √DARÁM] *VT*45:8

Dram, *n.*: a heavy stroke, blow [OS *dramb- √DARÁM]

Dram·bor, *n. impr. tp.*: clenched fist, blow with fist [dram + paur]

Draug, *n.*: wolf [OS *drǭk- √DARÁK]

Dra·va-, *pt.* ‡**dramp** or **dra·vant**, *pp.* **dram·men**, *v.*: hew [OS *drama- √DARÁM] *VT*45:8

Dre·ga-, *v.*: flee [OS *drek- √!DERÉK]

Dring, *n.*: hammer [OS *driŋg- √!DIRÍG]

Drin·ga-, *v.*: beat [OS *driŋga- √!DIRÍG]

Drû, *pll.* **drú·in**, **drú·ath**, *n.*: wild man, one of the small humans who lived among the Haladin in the First Age and in the White Mountains in the Second and Third Ages [MS *druʒ < Dr druʒu]

'Drú·a·dan, *pl.* **'drú·e·dain**, *n. kd.*: 'Drû-man', wild man [drû + adan]

Drú·nos, *n. tp.*: family of the Drû-folk [drû + nos]

Dû, *n.*: night, nightfall, dusk, late evening, darkness [OS *dūmė < CE dōmi √DO] *SD*:302

Dú·ath, *n. kd.*: nightshade, dark shadow [dû + gwâth]

Duin, *pl.* **dui·nath**, *n.*: large river [OS *duine √DUJ] *Names*:179, *PME*:54

Dú·linn, *n. tp.*: 'dusk-singer', nightingale [dû + lind^{2} OS *dūmelinde] *SD*:302

^{n}**Dûn**, *n.*: west [OS *n͡dūne √NDU] *LotR:AppE*

^{n}**'Dú·na·dan**, *pl.* **'dú·ne·dain**, *n. tp.*: man of the west, Númenórean [dûn + adan] *LotR*, *WJ*:378, 386

^{n}**'Dú·ne·dhel**, *pl.* **'dú·ne·dhil**, *n. tp.*: Elf of Beleriand (including Noldor and Sindar) [dûn + edhel OS *n͡dūnedelo] *WJ*:378, 386

Dûr, *pl.* **duir**, *adj.*: dark, sombre [OS *dūra < CE *dōrā < *dohrā √DO-H]
'Dú·re·dhel, *n. kd.*: dark Elf [dûr + edhel OS *dūredelo]
Dur·gul, *n. kd.*: sorcery [dûr + gûl, OS *dūraŋgūle]
'Dú·ri·on, *n. kd.*: 'dark son', dark Elf [dûr + iôn, OS *dūriono]
^{n}**Dú·ven**, *pl.* **dú·vin**, *n. kd*: west [OS *n̄dūmen √NDU √MEN] *VT*45:38
Du·vui, *adj.*: gloomy [OS *dubuia √DUB] *VT*45:11
#^{n}**Dŷr**, *n.*: successor [OS *n̄diuro < CE *n̄deurō √NDEW] (DorS dior)

E

E^{1}, **ed**, (1) *adv. pref.*: out, away, forth; (2) *adj. pref.*: outer; (3) *prep.*: out from, out of [OS *et √ET] *WJ*:367
E^{2}, *pron.*: he [OS *e √!E] *SD*:128–31
Ec·thel, *n. kd.*: 'thorn-point', spear point [êg + thela]
Ech, *n.*: spine (i.e., prickle or thorn) [OS *ekk^{h}o √EK] *VT*45:12
E·chad, *n.*: camp [OS *ekk^{h}at-]
E·chad-, **'e·che·di**, **e·chant**, **e·'chan·nen**, *v.*: make, fashion, shape [OS *ekk^{h}ati- < CE *etkati- √ET √KAT] *VT*45:19
E·chil, *pl.* **e·chil**, *n.*: 'follower', human being [OS *ekk^{h}ildo √ET √KHIL] *WJ*:219
E·chor, *n.*: outer ring, outer circle [OS *ekk^{h}oro < CE *etkoro √ET √KOR]
E·chui(w), *n.*: awakening [OS *ekk^{h}uiwe < CE *etkuiwē √ET √KUJ]
E·chuir, *n.*: season of stirring [OS *ekk^{h}uire < CE *etkoirē √ET √KOJ]
E·daid, *adj.*: double [OS *atatia √AT^{2}-AT]
E·den, *adj.*: new, begun again [?OS *etina √AT^{2}]
#**'E·di·nor**, *n. tp.*: anniversary day [ad + în + aur, OS *atīnaure]
#**'Ed·le·dhi-**, *pt.* **ed·lent** or **'ed·le·dhas**, *pp.* **ed·'len·nen**, *v.*: go into exile [OS *etledi- √ET √LED] (N egledhi-) *VT*45:27
#**Ed·'le·dhi·a-**, *v.*: go into exile [OS *etledi- √ET √LED] (N egledhia-)
#**Ed·'ledh·ron**, *pl.* **ed·'ledh·ryn**, *n.*: exile, person who is exiled [OS etledro(ndo) √ET √LED] (N egledhron)
#**Ed·lenn**, *adj.*: exiled [OS etlenna < CE *etlednā √ET √LED] (N eglenn)
!**Ed·'lo·thi·a-**, *v.*: flower, blossom [OS *etlotsja- √ET √LOT]
Ed·'lo·thi·ad, *n.*: flowering, blossoming [OS *etlotsjata √ET √LOT] misread edlothiand *WR*:293
Ed·'on·na-, *pp.* !**ed·'on·nen**, *v.*: beget [ed + *onna-, OS *etont^{h}a-]
Ed·ra-, *v.*: open [OS *etra- √ÉT-ER]
Ed·rain, *n.*: border [ed + rain^{2}, OS *etregna]
Ed·raith, *n.*: saving, salvation [MS *edreiβ]
'Ed·re·gol, *adv.*: especially [?OS *etrekl-] *SD*:128–31
Ed·wen, *num. adj.*: second [?OS *atwina √AT^{2}] *SD*:128–31

E·dhel, *pl.* **e·dhil**, *n.*: Elf [OS *edelo √É-DEL] *WJ*:364, 377

E·'dhel·harn, *n. tp.*: Elf-stone or beryl, a jewel thought of as particularly related to Elves [edhel + sarn[2]] *SD*:128–31

E·'dhel·len, *pl.* **e·'dhel·lin**, *adj.*: Elvish [edhel + -ren]

E·'dhel·rim, e·'dhel·lim, *pl. n. kd.*: Elves [edhel + rim] *UT*:318

Êg, *n.*: thorn [OS *ek- √EK]

Eg·lan, (1) *pl.* **eg·lain**, *adj.*: forsaken; (2) *pll.* **eg·lain, eg·'ladh·rim**, *n.*: 'the forsaken' Elves, Sindar, Falathrim [OS *eklana < CE *heklanā √HEK] *WJ*:365, 379

Eg·'le·ri·a-, *v.*: glorify, praise [OS *aklaria- √Á-KAL-AR]

Eg·nas, *n. kd*: 'point like a thorn', sharp point, peak [êg+nass √EK √NAS] *VT*45:12

E·go, *v. impv.*: be off! [OS *ek(e) ǭ √HEK] *WJ*:365

!E·gol, eg·la-, *pl.* **eg·lath**, *n.*: 'one forsaken', an Elf of the Falathrim (**egol** is not found; **egla-** is only used as *pth.*) [OS *ekla √HEK] *MR*:164

E·gor, *conj.*: or [?OS *ekr-] *SD*:128–31

'Ei·li·an, *n. tp.*: 'sky-bridge', rainbow [ell-[2] + ianu, MS *elianw < OS *elianwe < CE *heljatmē √HEL √JAT]

'Ei·ni·or, *adj.*: elder [an + iaur, MS *eniaur < OS *aniǭra < CE *anjāra] *PME*:358

'Ei·ri·en, *n.*: 'day-maiden', daisy [MS *eriend < Q *arien(de)* √AS[1]] *SD*:128–31

Ei·tha-, *v.*: prick with a sharp point, stab; treat with scorn, insult [OS *ekt^{h}a- < CE *ektā, *hektā √EK √HEK] *WJ*:365

Ei·thad, *n. ger.*: an insult [OS *ekt^{h}ata √EK √HEK] *WJ*:365

Ei·thel, *pl.* **ei·thil**, *n.*: spring, source, 'well', issue of water [OS *ekt^{h}ele < CE *etkelē √ET √KEL]

‡Êl, e·len-, *pll.* **e·lin, 'e·le·nath**, *n.*: star [OS *elen √EL-EN] *RGEO*, *Letters*:281, *WJ*:363

'E·la·nor, *n. dc.*: 'star-sun', a kind of *Anagallis* (pimpernel) bearing golden and silver flowers [êl + anor]

‡E·ledh, *pl.* **e·lidh**, *n.*: Elf [OS *eleda √EL-ED] *Letters*:281

E·'ledh·rim, *pl. n. kd.*: Elves [elen + rim or eledh + rim] *UT*:318, *WJ*:363, 377–78,

E·len, *pll.* **e·lin, e·'ledh·rim**, *n.*: Elf [OS *elena √EL-EN] *WJ*:363, 377–78

'E·li·a-, *impers.* **uil**, *v.*: rain [OS *ulia- √UL[1]] (N impers. öil)

Ell-[1], *n. pref.*: Elf [OS *elda √EL] *WJ*:364, 378

Ell-[2], *n. pref.*: sky (only found as *pth.* in names) [OS *elle < CE *helle √HEL]

El·leth, *n. f.*: Elf-woman [OS *eldittʰa < CE *eldē √EL] *WJ*:363–4, 377

El·lon, *pl.* **el·lyn**, *n. m.*: Elf-man [OS *eldo(ndo) < CE *eldō √EL] *WJ*:363–64, 377

El·loth, *n.*: single flower [er- + loth] *VT*42:18
E·lo, *intj.*: an exclamation of wonder, admiration, delight [OS *el ǭ √EL]
El·rim, *pl. n. kd.*: Elves [ell-[1] + rim, OS *eldarimbe] (earlier eldrim) *WJ*:363–64, 377
E·lu, *adj.*: pale blue [MS *elw < OS *elwa < CE *helwā √HEL]
'E·lu·waith, *n. tp.*: the Sindar, the subjects of King Thingol [Elu (name) + gwaith] *WJ*:378
El·'vel·lon, *pl.* **el·'vel·lyn**, *n. tp.*: Elf-friend [ell-[1] + mellon, OS *eldameldo(ndo)] *WJ*:412
'Em·e·rain, *n. impr. kd.*: Middle-earth [MS *emmereind < OS *ambarendia √A-MBAR √É-NED]
‡**Em·il**, *n.*: mother [OS *ammille √AM[2]] *VT*45:5
Em·linn, **'em·e·lin**, *n. kd.*: 'yellow singer', yellow bird, yellowhammer [OS *am̭m̭alinde < CE *asmalindē √S-MAL √LIN[2]]
En, **e-**, *art.*: of the [i + na, OS *ina] see **I**
E·naith, *n.*: sixth part [OS *enekt^{h}e √ÉNEK] (N eneith)
E·'nec·thui, *num. adj.*: sixth [OS *enekt^{h}uia √ÉNEK] *VT*42:25
E·nedh, *n.*: middle, core, center [OS *enede √É-NED]
'E·ne·dhin, *n. impr. tp.*: midyear [enedh + în] *VT*45:27
E·neg, *num.*: six [OS *eneke √ÉNEK]
E·neth, *n.*: name [OS *enet^{h}e √ÉNETH]
En·gui, *num. adj.*: sixth [OS *eŋk^{h}uia √ÉNEK] (Dial. enchui) *VT*42:25
En·nas, *pron.*: there, in that place [OS *ent^{h}asse √EN] *SD*:128–31
En·nin, *n. kd.*: 'long year', Valian year [and[1] + în, OS *andīn]
En·nor, *pl.* **'en·no·rath**, *n. kd.*: central lands, Middle-earth [OS *endore < CE *endandorē √É-NED √N-DOR] *RGEO*, *Letters*:384
E·phel, *n.*: outer fence, encircling fence [ed + pêl, OS *epp^{h}ele < CE *etpeles]
Êr, *num.*: one [OS *er √ER]
Er-, *adj. pref.*: one, alone, lone [OS *er √ER]
Erch, *n.*: a prickle [OS *erk^{h}a √E-RÉK]
Er·cha-, *v.*: prick [OS *erk^{h}a- √E-RÉK]
Er·'cham·i·on, *adj.*: one-handed [OS *erk^{h}ambiǭna < CE *erkambjānā √ER √KAB]
Er·'cham·ui, *adj.*: one-handed [er- + cam + -ui, OS *erk^{h}ambuia √ER √KAB]
!**'Er·chi·on**, *adj.*: orkish, of or related to orcs [MS *örxiaun < OS *urk^{h}iǭna √U-RUK]
E·reb, *pl.* **e·rib**, *adj.*: isolated, lonely [OS *erepa < CE *erek^{w}ā √ER]
E·redh, *n.*: seed, germ [OS *erede √E-RÉD]
E·reg, *pl.* **e·rig**, *n.*: holly tree [OS *ereka √E-RÉK]
E·'reg·dos, *n. kd.*: holly tree [ereg + toss]

'E·ri·a-, *pt.* **'e·ri·ant**, *v.*: rise, arise [OS ori-, *pt.* oront^{h}e √ORO]

E·'ri·a·dor, *n.*: wilderness [OS *eria 'isolated, lonely' + dôr, modified from earlier *eriannor < OS *eriandore < CE *erjandorē √ER √NDOR] *VT*42:4

E·rin, *prep.*: on the [or + i MS *örin]

'E·ri·ol, *adj.*: alone, single [OS *eriǭla < CE *erjālā √ER]

Er·nil, *n.*: prince [OS *arnilo √ÁR^{1}-AN]

!Er·tha-, *v.*: unite [OS *ert^{h}a- √ER]

!Er·thad, *n. ger.*: union, uniting [OS *ert^{h}ata √ER]

E·ru^{1}, *n.*: waste, desert [MS *eruṽ < OS *erume √ER]

E·ru^{2}, *n.*: the One [Q *Eru* √ER]

'E·ru·chen, *pl.* **'e·ru·chín**, *n. tp.*: 'child of the One', Elf or human [eru^{2} + hên]

E·rui, *adj.*: first; single, alone [êr + -ui, OS *eruia √ER]

E·ryn, *n.*: wood [OS *oroni- √ÓR-ON]

Es·cal, *n.*: veil, screen, cover that hides [OS *eskal- √SKAL^{1}] also spelled esgal

Es·ta-, *v.*: name, call; **esta aen**: is called [OS *esta- √ES] *SD*:128–31

Es·tel, *n.*: trust, faith, hope, steady purpose [OS *estel- √E-STEL] *MR*:320

Es·tent, *adj.*: ?short [OS *estinta √STINT]

'Es·to·lad, *n.*: encampment

E·thir^{1}, *n.*: mouth or outflow of a river, estuary [ed + sîr, OS *ett^{h}irė < CE *etsiri]

E·thir^{2}, *pl.* **e·thir**, *n.*: 'out-watcher', spy [ed + tirn, OS *ett^{h}irno]

E·thuil, *n.*: season of spring [OS *ett^{h}uile √ET √TUJ]

F

Fae, *n.*: spirit, soul, radiance [OS *p^{h}aia √PHAJ] *MR*:165

Faeg, *adj.*: mean, poor, bad [OS *sp^{h}aika √SPAJ] (N foeg)

Fael^{1}, *adj.*: fair-minded, just, generous [OS *p^{h}aila √PHAJ] *PME*:352

Fael^{2}, *n.*: gleaming brilliance [OS *p^{h}aile √PHAJ]

Faen, *adj.*: radiant, white [OS *p^{h}aina √PHAJ] (N foen)

Faer, *n.*: spirit, radiance [OS p^{h}aire √PHAJ] *MR*:349

Fain, *adj.*: white [OS *sp^{h}ania √SPAN]

Fair, fír-, fir-, *pll.* **fîr, 'fi·ri·ath**, *n.*: mortal man [Q *firya* √PHIR] (‡feir) *WJ*:387

Fa·las, *pl.* **fe·lais**, *n.*: beach, shore, coast, strand, line of surf, foaming shore; *esp.* the western seaboard of Beleriand [OS *p^{h}alasse √PHÁL-AS] *VT*42:15

Fa·'lath·ren, *adj.*: of the shore, of the Falas [falas + -ren] *PME*:55

Fa·'lath·rim, *pl. n. tp.*: people of the Falas [falas + rim] *WJ*:378, *PME*:386

Falch, *n.*: deep cleft, ravine?

Falf, *n.*: foam, breaker [OS *p^{h}alma √PHAL]

Fal·tha-, *v.*: (to) foam [OS *p^{h}alsa- √PHÁL-AS]

Fân, *n.*: cloud, veil, manifested body of a Vala [OS *sp^{h}ana and Q *fana* √SPAN] *RGEO*:66, *Letters*:278

Fang, *pl.* **feng**, *n.*: beard [OS sp^{h}aŋga √SPÁNAG]

Fa·nui, *adj.*: cloudy [fân + -ui, OS *sp^{h}anuia < CE *spanājā √SPAN]

Far, *adv.*: sufficient, enough, quite [OS *p^{h}ar- √PHAR]

Fa·ra-, *v.*: (to) hunt [OS *sp^{h}ara- √SPAR]

!Fa·rad, *n. ger.*: hunting [OS *sp^{h}arata √SPAR]

Fa·'rad·rim, *pl. n. tp.*: hunters [farad + rim]

Fa·ras, *n.*: hunt, hunting [OS sp^{h}arasse √SPAR]

Farn, *adj.*: enough [OS *p^{h}arna √PHAR]

Fa·ron, *n.*: hunter [OS *sp^{h}aro(ndo) √SPAR]

Fa·roth, *n.*: ?group of hunters [OS *sp^{h}arott^h- √SPAR]

Fast, *n.*: shaggy hair [OS *p^{h}asta √PHAS]

Faug, *adj.*: thirsty, gasping, choking [OS p^{h}auka √PHAW]

Faun, *n.*: cloud [OS sp^{h}ǭna < CE *spānā √SPAN]

Fe·la, *pl.* **fi·li**, *n.*: cave [MS *ϕelʒ, *pl.* *ϕilʒ, OS p^{h}elga, *pl.* *p^{h}elgi √PHÉLEG]

Fen(d), *n.*: door, threshold [OS p^{h}enda √PHEN]

Fen·nas, *n.*: gateway, door [OS *p^{h}endasse √PHEN]

‡Fêr, **fe·ren-**, *pl.* **fe·rin**, *n.*: beech, mast [OS p^{h}eren, *pl.* p^{h}ereni √PHÉREN]

'Fe·re·dir, *pl.* **fa·'rad·rim**, *n. tp.*: hunter [farad + dîr]

Fern, *pl.* **firn**, (1) *adj.*: dead (of mortals); (2) *n.*: a dead person [OS *p^{h}irna √PHIR]

Fi·leg, *pl.* **fi·lig**, *n.*: small bird (*sg.* formed by analogy) [OS *p^{h}ilika √PHILIK]

'Fi·li·god, *pl.* **fi·lig**, *n.*: small bird [OS *p^{h}ilikot- √PHILIK]

Fim, *adj.*: slim, slender *LotR:AppF*

Fîn, *n.*: a single hair [OS *p^{h}inė < CE *p^{h}ini √PHIN] *PME*:362

Find, *n.*: hair, lock of hair, tress [OS *p^{h}inde √PHIN]

Fin·nel, **fin·del**, *n.*: braided tress of hair [OS p^{h}indele √PHIN]

Fí·reb, (1) *pl.* **fí·rib**, *adj.*: mortal, apt to die; (2) *pll.* **fí·rib**, **fi·'reb·rim**, *n.*: a mortal [fair[1] + -eb] *WJ*:387

Fi·ren, *adj.*: human [fair[1] + -en[4] √PHIR]

Fi·ri, **firn**, **fir·nen**, *v.*: fade, die [OS *p^{h}iri- √PHIR]

'Fi·ri·ath, *pl. n.*: mortal humans [fair[1] + -ath √PHIR] *WJ*:219, 387

'Fi·ri·eth, *n.*: mortal woman [fair[1] + -eth[2] √PHIR] *WJ*:387

!Fi·rin, *adj.*: mortal [OS *p^{h}irin" < CE *p^{h}irini √PHIR]

'Fi·ri·on, *n. m.*: mortal man [fair[1] + -on[1] √PHIR] *WJ*:387

Fi·rith, *n.*: season of fading [OS *p^{h}iritt^{h}e √PHIR]

Flâd, *n.*: skin

Fôr, *adj.*: right, north [OS *p^{h}ora √PHOR]

For·gam, *adj. kd. bv.*: right-handed [fôr + cam, OS *p^{h}orokamba]

Forn, *adj.*: northern, north, right [OS *p^{h}orna √PHOR]

Fo·rod, *n.*: north [OS *p^{h}orotė < CE *p^{h}oroti √PHOR] *LotR:AppE*

Fo·'rod·ren, *adj.*: northern [forod + -ren]

Fo·'rod·rim, *pl. n. tp.*: northmen [forod + rim]

Fo·'rod·waith, *n. tp.*: northmen, north-folk, northerland [forod + gwaith] *UT*:14

For·ven, *n. kd.*: north [fôr + mên]

Fui·a-, *v.*: feel disgust at, abhor [OS *p^{h}uia- < CE *p^{h}euja- √PHEW]

Fuin, *n.*: night, gloom, darkness, dead of night, nightshade [OS p^{h}uine √PHUJ]

Fuir, *pl.* **fŷr,** (1) *adj.*: right, north; (2) *n.*: right hand [OS *p^{h}oria √PHOR] (N föir) *VT*42:20

G

Gad-, ge·di, gant, gan·nen, *v.*: catch [OS *gati- √GAT^{1}]

Ga·dor, *n.*: prison, dungeon [MS *gadr < OS *gatr- √GAT^{2}]

Gae, *n.*: dread [OS *gaia √GAJ^{1}]

Gael, *adj.*: pale, glimmering [OS *ŋ͡g aila √ŋIL]

Gae·ar, *n.*: sea, ocean [OS *gaiar- < CE *gajār √GAJ^{1}] *PME*:363

'Gae·a·ron, *n.*: great ocean [OS *gaiarond- √GAJ^{1}] *PME*:363

Gaer^{1}, *adj.*: dreadful, awful, fearful; holy [OS *gaira √GAJ^{1}]

Gaer^{2}, *adj.*: red, reddish, copper-colored, ruddy [OS *gaira √GAJ^{2}] (N goer)

Gaer^{3}, *n.*: sea [OS *gair- √GAJ^{1}]

Gae·ron, *n.*: great ocean [OS *gairond- √GAJ^{1}] *PME*:363

Gail, *adj.*: bright, light [OS *ŋ͡g alia √ŋAL] *VT*45:18

Gâl, gal-, -al, *n.*: light [OS *ŋ͡g ala √ŋAL]

Ga·la-, *v.*: grow [OS *gala- √GAL]

Ga·lad, *n.*: light, bright light, sunlight, brilliance, radiance, glittering reflection [OS *ŋ͡g alata < CE *ŋalatā √ŋAL-AT]

Ga·ladh, *n.*: tree [OS *galada √GÁL-AD] *Letters*:426, *SD*:302

'Ga·la·dhon, *adj.*: of or related to trees [OS *galadǫna √GÁL-AD]

´Ga·ladh·'rem·men, *pl.* **-'rem·min,** *adj. tp.*: tangled with trees, a poetic word used to describe the woodlands of Middle-earth [galadh + remmen]

Ga·'ladh·rim, *pl. n. tp.*: 'people of the trees', Elves of Lórien [galadh + rim] *Letters*:426

Ga·las, *n.*: growth, plant [OS *galasse √GAL]

'**Ga·le·nas**, *n.*: pipe-weed, tobacco
Ga·lu, *n.*: good fortune, weal, wealth [OS *galw- √GAL]
Gal·vorn, *n. impr. kd.*: a black metal made by the Dark Elf Eöl [gâl + morn] *Silm*, *WJ*:322
Gam·mas, *n.*: a hook-shaped addition to a letter to indicate following *s* [OS *gamp^{h}asse √GAP] *VT*45:14
Gamp, *n.*: hook, claw [OS *gamp^{h}a √GAP]
^{n}**Gan·nel, gan·del**, *n.*: a harp [OS *ŋ͡gandelle √ŋGÁNAD]
^{n}**Gan·na-**, *v.*: play a harp [OS *ŋ͡ganda- √ŋGÁNAD]
^{n}'**Gan·na·da-**, *v.*: harp, play a harp [OS *ŋ͡gandata- √ŋGÁNAD]
Ga·r-, ge·ri, *pt.* **garn** or **ga·rant**, *pp.* **garnen**, *v.*: hold, have, possess; be able, can [OS *gari- √GAR] *AI*:92, *VT*45:14
^{n}**Ga·raf**, *n.*: wolf [OS *ŋ͡garam- √ŋGÁRAM]
Gardh, *n.*: bounded or defined place, region [OS *garda √GAR] *WJ*:402
Garn, (1) *adj.*: own, (2) *n.*: one's 'own', property [OS *garna √GAR]
Garth, *n.*: fort, fortress, stronghold [OS *gart^{h}a √GÁR-AT] *VT*45:14
Gar·tha-, *v.*: keep, defend [OS *gart^{h}a- √GÁR-AT] *VT*45:14
Gas, *n.*: hole, gap [OS *gassa √GAS]
Gas·dil, *n. tp.*: stopgap; in writing, a sign for the hiatus where MS *ʒ had disappeared [gas + dîl OS *gassadil-]
Gast, *n.*: the Void [OS *gast- √GAS]
Gath, *n.*: cavern [OS *gatt^{h}a √GAT^{2}]
Gath·rod, *n. kd.*: cave [gath + grôd]
Gaud, *n.*: device, contrivance, machine [OS *gauta √GAW]
Gaul^{1}, *n.*: light [OS *ŋ͡gǭla < CE *ŋālā √ŋAL] *VT*45:13
^{n}**Gaul**^{2}, *n.*: wolf-howl [OS *ŋ͡gaule √ŋGAW]
^{n}**Gaur**, *n.*: wolf, werewolf [OS *ŋ͡gauro √ŋGAW]
^{n}**Gaur·hoth**, *n. kd.*: group of werewolves, wolf-host [gaur + hoth]
^{n}**Gaur·waith**, *n. kd.*: outlaws, wolf-men [gaur + gwaith] *UT*:85
Gaw, *n.*: void [OS *gǭha < CE *gāsā √GAS]
^{n}**Ga·wa-**, *v.*: howl [OS *ŋ͡gawa- √ŋGAW]
^{n}**Ga·wad**, *n. ger.*: howling [OS *ŋ͡gawata √ŋGAW]
Ge·lir, *adj.*: merry [√GAL or √GJEL?] *SD*:128–31
Gell, *n.*: joy, triumph [OS *gello < CE *g^{j}ellō √GJEL]
Gel·lam, *n. kd.*: jubilation [gell + glam]
Gel·lui, *adj.*: triumphant [gell + -ui, OS *gelluia √GJEL]
Gem, *adj.*: sickly [OS *gemba < CE *geŋ^{w}g^{w}ā < *geŋgwā √GEŋG]
!**Ge·'ne·di·a-**, *v.*: reckon [OS *wonotia- √NOT]
Ge·'ne·di·ad, *n. ger.*: reckoning, count [OS *wonotiata √NOT] *SD*:128–31
Gern, *adj.*: worn, old (of things) [OS *gerna < CE *g^{j}ernā √GJER]

Gîl, *pl.* **'gi·li·ath**, *n.*: bright spark, star, silver glint [OS *ŋ͡gile < CE *ŋile √ŋIL] *RGEO*, *MR*:388

Gil·din, *n. kd.*: silver spark [gîl + tinu]

'Gil·ga·lad, *n. tp.*: starlight [gîl + calad]

'Gi·li·on, *adj.*: of stars [OS *ŋ͡giliǫna √ŋIL]

Gi·lith, *n.*: starlight; region of stars (Q *Ilmen*) [OS *ŋ͡gilitt^{h}e √ŋIL]

Gil·wen, *n. tp.*: region of stars (Q *Ilmen*) [gîl + mên]

Gi·ri, girn, gir·nen, *v.*: shudder [OS *giri- √GIR]

Gi·rith, *n.*: shuddering, horror [OS *giritt^{h}e √GIR]

Glâd, *n.*: wood, (small) forest [OS *glata < CE *galatā √GAL-ÁT]

Gla·dha-, *v.*: laugh [OS *glada- √G-LAD^{2}] *PME*:359

Glae, *n.*: grass [OS *glai or *glaj- √G-LAJ]

Glaer, *n.*: long lay, narrative poem [OS *glaire √G-LIR^{1}]

Glaew, *n.*: salve [OS *glaibe √G-LIB]

Glam, *n.*: a body of orcs; din, uproar, tumult, the confused yelling of beasts; shouting, confused noise [OS *glamb- √G-LAM] *WJ*:416

Glam·hoth, *n. tp.*: 'host of tumult', Orcs [glam + hoth] *UT*:54; *MR*:109, 195; *WJ*:391

Glam·og, *n.*: an Orc [OS *glambuk- √G-LAM] *WJ*:391

Glam·or, *n.*: echo [MS *glamr < OS *glambr- √G-LAM] (dial. glambr)

Glam·ren, *pl.* **glem·rin**, *adj.*: echoing [OS *glambrina √G-LAM]

Glân^{1}, *adj.*: white, clear [OS *ŋ͡glan- < ?CE *ŋalan- √ŋAL-ÁN] *UT*:390, *VT*45:13

Glân^{2}, *n.*: hem, border [OS *glana √G-LAN^{2}] *VT*42:8

'Glan·da·gol, *n.*: boundary marker [gland + tagol √G-LAN^{2} √TAK] *VT*42:8

Gland, *n.*: boundary [OS *glanda √G-LAN^{2}] *VT*42:8

!Glan·na-, *v.*: clear, make clear [OS *ŋ͡glant^{h}a- √ŋAL-ÁN] *VT*45:13 (dial. glantha-)

Glas, *n.*: joy [OS *glasse √GAL-ÁS]

Glaur, *n.*: golden light [OS *glaure √G-LÁWAR] *VT*41:10

Glav·ra-, *v.*: babble [OS *glamra- √G-LAM]

Glav·rol, *adj. pr. p.*: babbling [OS *glamrǫla < CE *glamrālā √G-LAM]

Glaw, *n.*: radiance [OS *ŋ͡glǫ < CE *ŋalā √ŋAL]

Gla·war, *n.*: sunlight, gold, radiance of Laurelin [OS *glaware √G-LÁWAR] *VT*41:10

#'Glei·ni·a-, *v.*: bound, enclose, limit [OS *glania- √G-LAN^{2}] spelled gleina- *VT*42:8

Glî, *n.*: honey [OS *glihė < CE *glisi √G-LIS]

#Glind, *n.*: glance [OS *glind- < CE *glimd- √GLIM] spelled glînn *WJ*:337

Gling, *adj.*: hanging [OS *gliŋgė < CE *liŋgi √G-LIŋG]

Glin·ga-, *v.*: hang, dangle [OS *gliŋg- √G-LIŋG]

Glin·na-, *v.*: glance at [OS *glint^{h}a- < CE *glimta- √GLIM] spelled glintha- *WJ*:337

Glin·nel, *pl.* **glin·nil**, *n. kd.*: one of the Teleri [‡Glind 'Teler' + -el^{1}, OS *glindelda √G-LIN^{2} √EL] *WJ*:378, 385

Glîr, *n.*: song, poem, lay [OS *glir- √G-LIR^{1}]

Gli·ri, glirn, glir·nen, *v.*: sing, recite poem [OS *gliri- √G-LIR^{1}]

Gló·ren, gló·rin-, *adj.*: golden [OS *glaurina < CE *laurinā √G-LÁWAR]

'Gló·ri·el, *adj.*: golden, shining with golden light [OS *glauriela < CE *laurejelā √G-LÁWAR]

Glos, -los, *adj.*: dazzling white, white as snow [OS *glossa √G-LOS] *RGEO*:62

Glûdh, *n.*: soap [OS *glūda < gljūdā < *gliudā < CE *glibdā √G-LIB]

Go-, *adv. pref.*: together [MS *gwo-, *gwa- < OS *wo- √WO]

Go·bel, *n.*: enclosed dwelling, walled house or village, town (in an archaic sense) [OS *wopele √PEL-ES]

Go·'ben·nas, *n.*: history [go- + pennas, OS *wopent^{h}asse √KWE-T]

ˌGo·ben·'nath·ren, *adj.*: historical [gobennas + -ren]

Go·chel, *n.*: ice, mass of ice [OS *wok^{h}elle √KHEL]

God·ref, *adv.*: through together [go- + tre- + be, OS *wotrebe, CE *wo-tere-be] *AI*:92

Gó·dhel, *pll.* **gó·dhil, gó·'dhel·lim**, *n.*: Noldo Elf [go(lodh) + ódhel or OS *wǭdelo √(A)WA √DEL] *WJ*:364

Goe^{1}, *n.*: terror, great fear [MS *goi < OS *gǭia < CE *gājā √GAJ^{1}] *PME*:363

#Goe^{2}, *n.*: envelope of the Outer Sea and Air [MS *gwoi < OS *wǭia < CE *wājā √WAJ] (N ui)

Goe·ol, *adj.*: fell, terrible, dire [OS *gǭiǭla < CE *gājālā √GAJ^{1}] *PME*:363

'Go·he·na-, *v.*: forgive, release from obligation (between equals) [OS *wohena-, CE *wosena- √SEN] *VT*44:23

Go·las, *n.*: collection of leaves, foliage [OS *wolasse √LAS^{1}] *Letters*:282, 297 *p.* 386

^{n}**Goll**, *adj.*: wise [OS ŋ̃golda √ŋGOL]

nGol·lor, *n.*: magician [MS *gollr < OS *ŋ̃goldro √ŋGOL]

^{n}**Go·lodh**, *pll.* **ge·lydh, go·'lodh·rim**, *n.*: one of the Noldor [OS ŋ̃golodo √ŋGOL-OD] (N *pl.* gölöidh) *WJ*:364, 379, 383, *PME*:360

!^{n}**Go·'lodh·ren**, *adj.*: Noldorin, of the Noldor [OS ŋ̃golodorina √ŋGOL-OD] *WJ*:318

Go·loth: see **gwaloth** *VT*42:18

^{n}**'Go·lo·vir,** *n. tp.*: 'jewel of the Noldor', Silmaril [golodh + mîr]
‡^{n}**Go·lu,** *n.*: wisdom, secret lore [MS *golw < OS *ŋ͡golwe √ŋGOL]
^{n}**Gol·wen,** *adj.*: wise, learned in deep arts [OS ŋ͡golwina √ŋGOL]
Gôn, *pl.* **go·nath,** *n.*: stone [OS *gono √GON]
Go·'nath·ra-, *v.*: entangle, enmesh [OS *wonat^{h}ra- < CE *wonatsra- √NAT]
Go·'nath·ras, *n.*: entanglement [OS *wonat^{h}rasse < CE *wonatsrassē √NAT]
Gond, *n.*: stone, great stone or rock [OS *gondo √GON] *Letters*:410
ˌ**Gon·do·'lin·dren,** *adj.*: of or related to Gondolin [Gondolin(d) + -ren]
ˌ**Gon·do·'lin·drim,** *pl. n. tp.*: people of Gondolin [Gondolin(d) + rim]
Gon·drafn, gon·dram, *n. impr. kd.*: hewn stone [gond + drafn]
Gon·drath, *n. tp.*: 'street of stone', causeway, raised stone highway [gond + rath] *WR*:340
Gon·dren, *adj.*: stony, made of stone [OS *gondrina √GON] *TI*:270
#**Gon·hir,** *pl.* **gon·'hir·rim,** *n. tp.*: 'master of stone', Dwarf [gond + hîr] spelled **Gonnhirrim** *WJ*:205
Go·nod-, 'ge·ne·di, go·nont, go·'non·nen, *v.*: count up, reckon, sum up [OS *wonoti- √NOT]
!**'Go·no·ded,** *n. ger.*: reckoning [OS *wonotita √NOT]
Gôr^{1}, *n.*: vigor [OS *gore √GOR]
!^{n}**Gôr^{2},** *n.*: horror, fear, dread [OS *ŋ͡gur √ŋGUR^{2}]
Gor-, ge·ri, gorn, gor·nen, *v.*: warn, counsel [OS *gori- √GOR] *VT*41:11
Gorf, *n.*: impetus, vigor [OS *gorme √GOR]
^{n}**Gor·gor,** *pl.* **'gor·go·rath,** *n. kd.*: extreme horror, deadly fear [gôr^{2} + gôr^{2}] *WJ*:415
^{n}**'Gor·go·roth,** *n. kd.*: terror, deadly fear [gôr^{2} + goroth]
Gorn^{1}, *adj.*: impetuous, vigorous, hasty [OS *gorna √GOR]
Gorn^{2}, *n.*: valor [OS *gorne √GOR]
^{n}**Go·rog,** *n.*: horror [OS *ŋ͡guruka √ŋGUR^{2}-UK] *WJ*:415
^{n}**Go·roth,** *n.*: horror, dread [OS ŋ͡gorot^{h}- √ŋGOROTH]
!^{n}**Gorth^{1},** *pl.* **gyrth,** (1) *adj.*: dead; (2) *n.* a dead person [OS *ŋ͡gurt^{h}a √ŋGUR^{1}]
^{n}**Gorth^{2},** *n.*: dread, horror [OS *ŋ͡gurt^{h}- √ŋGUR^{2}] *WJ*:415
^{n}**Gor·thad,** *pl.* **ger·thaid,** *n. tp.*: 'place of the dead', barrow [gorth^{1} + sâd OS *ŋ͡gurt^{h}ahata]
^{n}**Gor·theb,** *adj.*: horrible [OS *ŋ͡gurt^{h}ipa √ŋGUR^{2}]
^{n}**Gor·thob,** *adj.*: horrible [OS *ŋ͡gurt^{h}upa √ŋGUR^{2}] *WJ*:415
Gos, *n.*: dread, horror [OS *gosse √GOS]
Gost, *n.*: dread, terror [OS *gost- √GOS]
Gos·ta-, *v.*: fear exceedingly [OS *gosta- √GOS]
^{n}**Goth,** *n.*: enemy [OS *ŋ͡got^{h}o √ŋGOTH]

!Go·vad-, 'ge·ve·di, go·vant, go·'van·nen, *v.*: meet, come together [OS *wobati- √BAT]

Go·'van·nen, *adj. pp.*: met [OS *wobant^{h}ena < CE *wobantā √BAT]

Go·west, *n.*: contract, compact, treaty [go- + gwest]

Graug, *n.*: a powerful, hostile, and terrible creature [OS *grauko √G-RUK] *WJ*:415

Grau·rim, *pl. n. kd.*: dark people [graw + rim] *VT*45:16

Graw, *adj.*: dark, swart [OS *grawa √GRAW] *VT*45:16

Grôd, *n.*: cave, delving, excavation, underground dwelling [OS *grota √G-ROT] *WJ*:414

Gro·ga-, *v.*: feel terror [OS *gruka- √G-RUK] *WJ*:415

Grond, *n.*: club [OS runda √G-RUD[1]]

Groth, -roth, *n.*: cave, delving, large excavation [OS *grott^{h}a √G-ROT] *WJ*:415

Gruin, *adj.*: ruddy [OS *gruina < CE *roinā √G-ROJ[2]]

Grui·tha-, *v.*: terrify [OS *grukt^{h}a- √G-RUK] *WJ*:415

Gû-, *adv. pref.*: no, not [OS *gū- √GU]

^{n}**Gûd,** *n.*: enemy, foe [OS *ŋ͡gūt < CE *ŋ͡gōt^h √ŋGOTH]

^{n}**Gûl,** *n.*: magic, sorcery, necromancy, evil knowledge [OS *ŋ͡gūle < CE *ŋ͡gōlē √ŋGOL] *Silm:App*, *MR*:350, *WJ*:383

^{n}**Gul·dur,** *n. impr. kd.*: dark sorcery [gûl + dûr]

Gûr[1], *n.*: heart, inner mind [OS *gūre < CE *gōrē √GOR] *VT*41:11

^{n}**Gûr[2],** *n.*: death [OS ŋ͡guru √ŋGUR[1]]

^{n}**Gurth,** *n.*: death [OS ŋ͡gurt^{h}u √ŋGUR[1]]

^{n}**Gu·ruth,** *n.*: death [OS ŋ͡gurutt^{h}e √ŋGUR[1]]

^{n}**'Gu·ru·thos,** *n.tp.*: death-horror, dread of death [guruth + gos]

Gw

Gwa-, *adv. pref.*: together, co-, com- [OS *wa- < CE *wo √WO]

Gwa·chae, *adj.*: far away, remote [OS *wak^{h}aja √(A)WA √KHAJ] (late gwahae) *VT*45:21

Gwa·'chae·dir, *pl.* **gwa·'chae·dir,** *n. tp.*: palantír, seeing-stone [gwachae + tirn] (late gwahaedir) *PME*:186

Gwa·dor, *pl.* **gwe·dyr,** *n. m.*: sworn brother [OS *wator- √TOR]

Gwaedh, *n.*: bond, troth, compact, oath [OS waide < CE *waedē √WED]

Gwael, *n.*: gull [OS *wail-]

Gwaen, *adj.*: stained [OS *wagna < CE *wahnā √WAH]

Gwae·ren, *adj.*: windy [OS *waiwarina √WAJW] *VT*42:15

Gwaew, *n.*: wind, storm [OS *waiwa √WAJW]

Gwain, gwin-, *pl.* **gwîn,** *adj.*: new [OS *winia √WIN]

Gwaith, *n.*: manhood, manpower, troop of able-bodied men, host, regiment; people; region; wilderness [OS *wekt^{h}e < CE *wegtē √WEG] *PME*:330

Gwa·loth, *n.*: blossom, collection of flowers [gwa- + loth, OS *walott^{h}e < CE *woloth^{h}sē √LOTH] also **goloth**

Gwa·nath, *n.*: death (act of dying) [OS *wanatt^{h}e √(A)WA-N]

Gwann, *adj.*: departed, dead [OS *wanna √(A)WA-N]

Gwan·na-, *v.*: depart, die [OS *want^{h}a- √(A)WA-N]

Gwa·nod, *n.*: tale, number [OS *wanot- < CE *wonot- √NOT]

Gwa·nu, *n.*: death (act of dying); *esp.* the death of Elves by fading or weariness [MS *gwanw < OS *wanwe √(A)WA-N]

Gwa·nûn, *du. n.*: a pair of twins [OS *wanūn- < CE *wonōn- √(O)NO] *WJ*:367

'Gwa·nu·nig, *n.*: a twin [OS *wanūniko √(O)NO] *WJ*:367

Gwa·nur[1], *n.*: brother, kinsman or kinswoman [OS *wanūr- < CE *wonōr- √(O)NO]

Gwa·nur[2], *du. n.*: a pair of twins [OS *wanūr- < CE *wonōr- √(O)NO]

Gwan·wel, *pl.* **gwen·wil**, *n. kd.*: 'the departed', an Elf of Aman [gwanw(en) + -el[1], OS *wanwelda] *WJ*:378

Gwan·wen, *pl.* **gwen·win**, (1) *adj. pp.*: departed (2) *n.*: 'the departed', an Elf of Aman [OS *wanwena, *wanwa √(A)WA] *WJ*:378

Gwarth, *n.*: betrayer [OS *wart^{h}o √WAR]

Gwas, *n.*: stain [OS wasse < CE *wahsē √WAH]

Gwas·tar, *n.*: hummock [gwa- + thâr, OS *wastara √STAR]

Gwath, *n.*: stain [OS *watt^{h}e < CE *wahtē √WAH]

Gwâth, *n.*: shade, shadow, dim light [OS *wat^{h}a √WATH] *UT*:261

Gwa·tha-, *v.*: (to) soil, stain [OS *watt^{h}a- < CE *wahta- √WAH]

Gwa·thel, *pl.* **gwe·thil**, *n. f.*: sister [OS *wat^{h}el- √THEL]

Gwath·ra-, *v.*: overshadow, dim, veil, obscure [OS *wat^{h}ra- √WATH] *VT*42:9

Gwath·ren, *pl.* **gweth·rin**, *adj.*: shadowy, dim [OS *wat^{h}rina √WATH]

Gwa·thui, *adj.*: shadowy [gwâth + -ui, OS *wat^{h}uia √WATH]

Gwa·'thui·rim, *n. pl. kd.*: 'shadowy people', people of Dunland [gwathui + rim[1]] *PME*:330

Gwaun, *pl.* **goen**, *n.*: goose [OS *wǭn < CE *wān √WA-N] (N *pl.* guin)

Gwaur, *adj.*: soiled, dirty [OS wǭra < CE *wahrā √WAH]

‡Gwê, *n.*: man; (only found as *tth.* **-we** in names) [OS wega √WEG]

Gwêdh, *n.*: bond [OS weda √WED]

Gwe·dhi, gwe·dhant (**‡gwend**), **gwen·nen**, *v.*: bind [OS *wedi- √WED]

Gwe·lu, *n.*: air, as a substance [MS *gwelw < OS *wilwa √WIL]

Gwel·wen, *n. kd.*: 'way of air', air, as a region [gwelu + mên]
‡**Gwên**, *n.*: girl, maiden, virgin (only found as *tth.* **-wen** in names) [OS *wene √WEN]
Gwend[1], *n.*: bond, friendship [OS *wend- √WED]
Gwend[2], *n.*: maiden [OS *wende √WÉN-ED]
Gwe·neth, *n.*: virginity [OS *wenett^he √WEN]
Gwe·nyn, *du. n.*: a pair of twins [OS *wanoni √(O)NO] *PME*:353, 365
'Gwe·ri·a-, *v.*: betray, cheat [OS *wari- √WAR]
Gwest, *n.*: oath [OS *westa < CE *wedtā √WED]
Gwes·ta-, *v.*: swear [OS *westa- < CE *wedta- √WED]
Gwî, *n.*: net, web [OS *wī < CE *wei √WEJ]
Gwi·lith, *n.*: air, as a region [OS *wilitt^he √WIL]
'Gwil·wi·leth, *n.*: butterfly [OS *wilwilitt^ha √WIL]
Gwind, *adj.*: pale blue [OS *windė < CE *windi √WIND]
Gwing, *n.*: foam, spindrift, spume, (flying) spray blown off wave-tops [OS *wiŋge √!WIŋ] *PME*:376,392

H

Ha, han, ha·na, *pl.* **hain**, *pron.*: it [OS *sa(na) √S]
Hab-, he·bi, hamp, ham·men, *v.*: clothe [OS *k^hap- √KHAP]
Ha·bad, *pl.* **he·baid**, *n.*: shore [backformed from OS sk^hapati, *pl.* of sk^hapa < CE *sk^japat √SKJAP]
Ha·bar (?**sa·bar**), *n.*: delved mine
Had-, he·di, hant (1*sg.* **hen·nin**), **han·nen**, *v.*: hurl [OS *k^hati- √KHAT]
Had·lath, *n. tp.*: sling [OS *k^hatalatt^ha √KHAT √LATH] (N haglath)
Ha·dor, *n.*: warrior, thrower, hurler (of spears and darts) [MS *xadr < OS *k^hatro √KHAT]
Had·ron, *n.*: warrior, thrower, hurler (of spears and darts) [OS *k^hatro(ndo) √KHAT]
‡**Hâdh**, *n.*: cleaver [OS *çada < CE *sjadā √SJAD]
Ha·dhod, *pl.* **ha·'dhod·rim**, *n.*: Dwarf [MS *xaðaud < Kh khazâd] *WJ*:388
Hae, *adj.*: remote, far, distant, on the other side, further [OS *k^haia √KHAJ]
#**Haer**, *adj.*: remote, far, distant [OS *k^haira √KHAJ] (spelled *haen*) *VT*45:21
Hae·red, *n.*: far away, remote distance [OS *k^hairet- √KHAJ]
Hae·ron, *adj.*: far, distant, remote [OS *k^hairǫna √KHAJ]
Haew, *n.*: custom, habit [MS *xaiṽ < OS *k^haime √KHIM]
Hair, (1) *adj.*: left; (2) *n.*: left hand [OS *k^haria < CE *k^h^jarjā √KHJAR]
Hal-, he·li, *pt.* **haul, hol-**, *pp.* **ho·len**, *v.*: lift [OS *k^hal- √KHAL] *VT*45:20
Hâl, *n.*: fish [OS *skala √SKAL[2]] *VT*45:20
Half, *n.*: seashell [OS *çalma < CE *sjalmā √SJAL]

Hall[1], *adj.*: exalted, high [OS kʰalla < CE *kʰalnā √KHAL]
Hall[2], *adj.*: veiled, hidden, shadowed, shady [OS skʰalla < CE *skalnā √SKAL[1]]
Hal·tha-, *v.*: (to) screen [OS *skʰaltʰa-, *skʰalia- √SKAL[1]]
Ham, *n.*: chair [MS *xamm < OS *kʰamma √KHAM] *VT*45:20
Ham·ma-, *v.*: clothe [OS *kʰampʰa- √KHAP]
Ham·mad, *n. ger.*: clothing [OS *kʰampʰata √KHAP]
Hamp, *n.*: garment [OS *kʰampʰ- √KHAP]
Hand, *adj.*: intelligent [OS *kʰanda √KHAN]
Han·nas, *n.*: understanding [OS *kʰandasse √KHAN]
Ha·nu, *n.*: chair [MS *xanw < OS *kʰanwa < CE *kʰamwā √KHAM] *VT*45:20
Hâr, *adj.*: south, left [OS *kʰara < CE *kʰʲarā √KHJAR]
Ha·rad, *n.*: south, the South [OS *kʰaratė < CE *kʰʲarati √KHJAR] *LotR:AppE*
Ha·'rad·ren, *adj.*: southern [OS *kʰaratrina √KHJAR]
Ha·'rad·rim, *pl. n. tp.*: Southerners, Southrons, people of Harad [harad + rim] *Letters*:178
Har·gam, *adj. kd. bv.*: left-handed [hâr + cam, OS *kʰarakamba]
Harn[1], *adj.*: south, southern [OS *kʰarna < CE *kʰʲarnā √KHJAR]
Harn[2], *adj.*: wounded [OS *skʰarna √SKAR]
Harn[3], *n.*: helmet [OS *kʰarna √KHAR[1]] *VT*45:21
Har·na-, *v.*: wound [OS *skʰarna- √SKAR]
!Har·tha-, *v.*: hope [OS *kʰartʰa- √!KHAR[2]]
Har·thad, *n. ger.*: hope [OS *kʰartʰata √!KHAR[2]] *SD*:62
Ha·ru, *n.*: wound [MS *xarw < OS *skʰarwe √SKAR]
Har·ven, *pl.* **her·vin**, *n. kd.*: south [hâr + mên] *VT*45:23
Hast, *n.*: axe-stroke [OS *çasta < CE *sjadtā √SJAD]
Has·ta-, *v.*: hack through [OS *çasta- < CE *sjadta- √SJAD]
Ha·thel, *n.*: broadsword blade or axe blade [OS *çattʰela < CE *sjatselā, *sjadselā √SJAD]
Ha·thol, *n.*: axe [MS *haβl < OS *çatʰla < CE *sjatslā, *sjadslā √SJAD]
Haudh, *n.*: (burial) mound, barrow, grave, tomb [OS *kʰauda √KHAG √KHAW]
Haust, *n.*: 'resting', bed [OS *kʰausta √KHAW]
Hav-, **he·vi**, *pt. 1s.* **hem·min**, *pt. 3s.* **hamp** or **ha·vant**, *v.*: sit [MS *xaṽ- < OS *kʰam- √KHAM] *VT*45:20
He, **hen**, **he·ne**, *pl.* **hîn**, *pron.*: she [OS *se(ne) √S]
Heb-, **he·bi**, *v.*: keep, retain [OS *kʰep- √KHEP] *VT*41:6
Helch, *adj.*: bitter cold [OS *kʰelkʰa √KHEL-EK]

'He·le·dir(*n.*), n *tp.*: 'fish-watcher', kingfisher [*irreg.* OS *sk^{h}alatirno √SKAL^{2} √TIR]
He·ledh, *n.*: glass [MS *xeleð < Kh kheled]
He·leg, *n.*: ice [OS *k^{h}elek- √KHEL-EK]
He·leth, *n.*: fur, fur coat [OS *sk^{h}elett^{h}e √SKEL]
Helf, *n.*: fur [OS *sk^{h}elma √SKEL]
Hell, *adj.*: naked [OS sk^{h}ella < CE *skelnā √SKEL]
#Hel·tha-, *v.*: (to) strip [OS *sk^{h}elt^{h}a- √SKEL]
Hên, -chen, *pl.* **hîn, -chín**, *n.*: child [OS *k^{h}ina √KHIN] *WJ*:403
Hen(d), *pl.* **hin(d)**, *du.* **hent**, *n.*: eye [OS *k^{h}ende √KHEN] *VT*45:22
He·neb, *adj.*: eyed, having eyes [OS *k^{h}enipa √KHEN] *WJ*:337
'He·ni·a-, *v.*: understand [OS *k^{h}ania- √KHAN]
Hen·neth, *n.*: window [OS *k^{h}endett^{h}e √KHEN]
Her·dir, *n. m. kd.*: master, Mr. [hîr + dîr, OS *k^{h}erundīro] *SD*:128–31
'He·ri·a-, *v.*: have an impulse, be compelled to do something, begin suddenly and vigorously, set vigorously out to do [MS *xöria- < OS *k^{h}oria- √KHOR] *VT*45:22
He·ron, *n. m.*: lord, master [OS *k^{h}erondo √KHER] *VT*45:22
Herth, *n.*: household, troop under a hîr [OS *k^{h}ert^{h}- √KHER]
Her·venn, *n. m. kd.*: husband [hîr + benn, OS *k^{h}erubenno]
Her·ves, *n. f. kd.*: wife [hîr + bess, OS *k^{h}erubesse]
He·ryn, *n. f. kd.*: lady [hîr + dî, OS *k^{h}eruni]
Hest, *n.*: captain [OS *k^{h}estō √KHES] *VT*45:22
He·thu, *adj.*: foggy, obscure, vague [MS *xeβw < OS *k^{h}it^{h}wa √KHITH]
Hîl, *n.*: heir [OS *k^{h}ilo √KHIL]
Him^{1}, *adj.*: cool [OS *k^{h}imbė √!KHIB]
Him^{2}, (1) *adj.*: steadfast, abiding; (2) *adv.*: continually [OS *k^{h}imbė √KHIM]
Hîr, hir-, her-, *n. m.*: master, lord [OS k^{h}īr, *k^{h}eru < CE *k^{h}ēr, *k^{h}erū √KHER] *Letters*:282, 386; *VT*41:9
Hí·ril, *n.*: lady [OS k^{h}īrille √KHER]
Hîth, *n.*: mist, fog [OS *k^{h}īt^{h}ė < CE *k^{h}īt^{h}i √KHITH]
Hith·lain, *n. kd.*: 'mist-thread', a fiber made in Lórien [hîth + lain^{2}, OS *k^{h}īt^{h}ilania]
Hi·thu, *n.*: fog [MS *xiβw < OS *k^{h}it^{h}we < CE *k^{h}it^{h}mē √KHITH]
Hi·thui, *adj.*: misty, foggy [hîth + -ui, OS *k^{h}it^{h}uia √KHITH]
Hîw, *adj.*: sticky, viscous [MS *xiṽ < OS *k^{h}īma √KHIM]
Ho, hon, ho·no, *pl.* **hyn**, *pron.*: he [OS *so √S]
Ho·bas, *n.*: harborage [OS *k^{h}opasse √KHOP]
!Hol-, he·li, holl, hol·len, *v.*: close

Hol·len, *adj. pp.*: closed

Horn, *adj.*: driven under compulsion, impelled [OS *k^{h}orna √KHOR]

Hor·tha-, *v.*: urge on, speed [OS *k^{h}ort^{h}a- √KHOR]

Host, *num.*: one hundred forty-four, a gross [OS *k^{h}osta < CE *k^{h}ot^{h}tā √KHOTH]

Hoth, *n.*: crowd, host, horde [OS *k^{h}ott^{h}e < CE *k^{h}ot^{h}sē √KHOTH]

Hû, *n.*: dog [OS *k^{h}ugo √KHUG]

Hû-, *n. pref.*: heart [OS *k^{h}ū- < CE *k^{h}ō √KHO]

Hûb, *n.*: haven, harbor, small landlocked bay [OS *k^{h}ūpa < CE *k^{h}ōpā √KHOP]

Hûd, *n.*: assembly [OS *k^{h}ūt < CE *k^{h}ōt^{h} √KHOTH]

Hûl, *n.*: cry of encouragement in battle [OS çūle < CE *siulē √SIW]

Hûn, *n.*: physical heart [OS *k^{h}ūn < CE *k^{h}ōn √KHO-N]

Hu·orn, *n. tp.*: one of the walking trees of Fangorn [?hû- + orn^{2}]

Hûr, *n.*: readiness for action, vigor, fiery spirit [OS *k^{h}ūre < CE *k^{h}ōrē √KHOR]

Hw

Hwand, *n.*: sponge, fungus [OS *ƕanda < CE *swandā √SWAD]

Hwest, *n.*: puff, breath, breeze [OS *ƕesta < CE *swestā √SWES]

Hwîn, *n.*: giddiness, faintness [OS *ƕin- √SWIN]

Hwind, *adj.*: whirling [OS *ƕindė < CE *swindi √SWIN]

'Hwi·ni·a-, *v.*: twirl, whirl, eddy [OS *ƕinia- < CE *swinja- √SWIN]

'Hwi·ni·ol, *adj. pr. p.*: whirling, giddy, fantastic [OS *ƕiniǫla < CE *swinjālā √SWIN]

I

I, *gen. sg.* **en**, **e-**, *pl.* **in**, **i-**, (1) *art.*: the; (2) *rel. pron.*: who, which, that [OS *i, *gen. sg.* *ina, *pl.* *in √I]

Îdh, *n.*: rest, repose [OS īde < *eide < CE *ezdē < *esdē √É-SED] *WJ*:403–4

#I·dhor, *n.*: thoughtfulness [MS *iðr < OS *inre √I-NIR]

Idh·ren, *adj.*: pondering, wise, thoughtful [OS *inrina √I-NIR]

Idh·rinn, *n. kd.*: year [în + rind^{2} OS *jīnrinde]

I·'lau·rui, *adj.*: daily [OS *ilauruia < CE *ilaurējā] √IL √UR^{1}] *VT*44:23

Im^{1}, (1) *adv. pref.*: between, inter-; (2) *prep.*: between, within [OS *imbė < CE *imbi √IMBI]

Im^{2}, *pron.*: I (*gen.* **nîn**, *dat.* **a·nim**, *acc.* **nin**) [OS *imbė < CE *iŋgwi, *iŋwi √!I-ŋWI √NI]

Im^{3}, *n.*: dell, deep vale [OS *imbe √IMB] *VT*45:18

Im·lad, *n. impr. tp.*: deep valley, glen, narrow valley with steep sides [im[3] + lâd, OS *imbelat-]

Im·loth, *n. impr. tp.*: flowering valley [im[3] + loth, OS *imbelott^{h}e] *VT*42:18

Im·rath, *n. impr. tp.*: a long narrow valley with a road or watercourse running through it lengthwise [im[3] + rath, OS *imberatt^{h}-] *UT*:465

În[1], *n.*: year [OS *jīn < CE *jēn √JEN]

În[2], *pron.*: his, referring to the subject [OS *īn < CE *ēn- √!E]

Inc, *n.*: guess, idea, notion [OS *iŋk^{h}i- < CE *iŋkj- √IŋK]

Ind, *n.*: inner thought, mind, meaning, heart [OS *indo √Í-NID[2]] *VT*41:17

In·gem, *adj. tp.*: suffering from old age [în + gem]

'Í·ni·as, *n.*: annals [OS *jīniasse, *jīnie √JEN]

In·nas, *n.*: will [OS *indasse √Í-NID[2]] *VT*44:23

I·nu, *adj.*: female [MS *inw (reformed after CS anu, MS *anw) < OS *inia √INI]

I·phant, **i·fant**, *adj. tp.*: 'full of years', aged, long-lived [în + pant OS *jīnp^{h}anta]

Ir, *art.?*: ?form of *i* used before words beginning in *i-*

Ist, *n.*: lore, knowledge [OS *ist- < CE *it^{h}t- √ITH]

Is·ta-, *pt.* **sint** or **istas**, *v.*: have knowledge [OS *ista- < CE *it^{h}ta- √ITH] *VT*45:18

Is·tui, *adj.*: learned [ist + -ui, OS *istuia √ITH]

I·thil, *n.*: 'the sheen', moon [OS *it^{h}īl √I-THÍL] *SD*:302

I·'thil·din, *n.dc.*: 'moon-star' a silver-colored metallic material, refined from mithril, which 'mirrors only starlight and moonlight' [ithil + tinu] *LotR*

Ith·ron, *pl.* **ith·ryn**, *n.*: wizard; a member of the Order of Wizards [OS *istro(ndo) < CE *it^{h}trō √ITH] *UT*:388

I·'von·wen, *pl.* **i·'von·win**, *n. tp.*: maiden of Yavanna [Ivon 'Yavanna' + gwên, OS *jabǭnawene] *PME*:404

I·vor, *n.*: ?crystal [MS *iṽr < OS *imre √!Í-MIR]

Iv·rin, *adj.*: ?crystalline [OS *imrinė √!Í-MIR]

J (consonantal I)

Ia, **io**, *adv.*: ago [OS *ja, *jǭ < CE *ja, *jā √JA]

Iâ, *n.*: gulf, chasm, void, abyss [MS *jaʒ < OS *jaga √JAG] *LR*:400, *RS*:437, *Letters*:383

Iach, *n.*: crossing, ford [OS *ja(k)k^{h}-]

!Iâd, *n.*: fence [OS *jat^{h} √JATH]

Iaeth, *n.*: neck [OS *jakt^{h}a √JAK]

Iaew, *n.*: mocking, scorn [OS *jaiwe √JAJ]

Iant, *n.*: bridge, yoke [OS *jantʰa √JAT]
Ia·nu, *n.*: bridge [MS *janw < OS *janwe < CE *jatmā √JAT]
Iâr, *n.*: blood [OS *jar √JAR]
Iar·wain, *adj.*: eldest [iaur + -wain √JA]
Iâth, *n.*: fence [OS *jatʰ- √JATH] *WJ*:370,378
Iath·rim, *pl. n. tp.*: people of Doriath [iâth + rim] *WJ*:378
Iaun, *n.*: holy place, fane, sanctuary [Q *yána* √(A)JAN]
Iaur, **ior-**, **iar-**, *adj.*: old, ancient, former [OS *jǭra < CE *jārā √JA]
Ia·vas, *n.*: season of autumn [OS *jabasse √JAB]
Iaw[1], *n.*: corn [MS *jauƀ < OS *jǭbe < CE *jābē √JAB]
Iaw[2], *n.*: ravine, cleft, gulf [MS *jaʒw < OS *jagwe √JAG]
Iell, **-iel**, *n.*: girl, daughter, maid; feminine ending [OS *jelle √JEL]
Iest, *pl.* **ist**, *n.*: wish [OS *jesta √JES]
Iôn, **-i·on**, *pl.* **io·nath**, *n.*: son, descendant [OS *jono √JON] *MR*:373, *WJ*:337, *PME*:202–3, 218
Iond, *pl.* **ion·nath**, *n.*: son [OS *jondo √JON] *SD*:128–31
Iuith, *n.*: use [OS *juktʰ- √JUK]
Iui·tha-, *v.*: use, employ [OS *juktʰa- √JUK]
Iûl, *n.*: embers [OS *jūla √JUL[2]]

L

La·ba-, *v.*: hop [OS *lapa- √!LAP[2]]
Lach, *n.*: flame, leaping flame [OS *lakkʰ- √!LAK[2]]
La·cha-, *v.*: (to) flame [OS *lakkʰ- √!LAK[2]]
La·chenn, *pl.* **le·chinn**, *n. kd. bv.*: 'flame-eyed,' Noldo [lach + hend] (‡lachend) *WJ*:384
Lâd, *n.*: plain, valley, lowland [OS *lat- √LAT]
La·den, *pl.* **le·din**, *adj.*: flat, plain, wide; open, cleared [OS *latina √LAT]
Lae, *n.*: great number [OS *lai √LI] *VT*45:27
Laeb, *adj.*: fresh [OS *laipa < CE *laikʷā √LÁJ-AK] (N lhoeb)
Laeg[1], *adj.*: green, fresh [OS *laika √LÁJ-AK] (dial. lêg) *Letters*:282, 386
Laeg[2], *adj.*: keen, sharp, acute [OS *laika √LAJK]
Lae·gel, *pll.* **lae·gil**, **laeg·rim**, **lae·'gel·rim**, *n. kd.*: one of the Green-Elves [laeg[1] + -el[1], OS *laikelda] *WJ*:385
Laer[1], *n.*: season of summer [OS *laire √LAJ]
Laer[2], *n.*: song [OS *lair- √LIR[1]]
Laes, *n.*: babe [MS *lais, *laxs < OS *lapse √LAP[1]]
Laew, *adj.*: frequent, many [OS *laiw- √LI] *VT*45:27
La·gor, *adj.*: swift [MS *lagr < OS *lakra √LAK[1]]
Lain[1], *adj.*: free, freed [OS *legna < CE *leknā √LEK]

Lain[2], *n.*: thread [OS *lania √LAN[1]]

La·laith, *n.*: laughter [MS *laleiþ < Q *lala-* laugh √G-LAD[2]]

Lalf, *pl.* **leilf,** *n.*: elm tree [OS *lalme √LÁLAM]

La·lorn, *n. kd.*: elm tree [lalf + orn[2], MS *lalworn, *lalṽorn < OS *lalmorne]

Lal·ven, lal·wen, *pl.* **lel·vin, lel·win,** *n.*: elm tree [OS *lalmen- or lalmina √LÁLAM]

Lam[1], *n.*: (physical) tongue; dialect, language [OS *lambe, *lamba √LAB] *WJ*:394, 416

Lam[2], *pl.* **lam·ath,** *n.*: echo, voice, echoing voice [OS *lamma √LAM]

Lam·mad, lam·ad, *n.*: echo, sound of voices [OS *lammata √LAM]

Lam·mas, *n.*: account of tongues [OS *lambasse √LAB]

Lam·men, *adj.*: of or related to the tongue or speech, spoken [OS *lambena √LAB]

Lanc[1], *adj.*: naked [OS *laŋk^{h}a]

Lanc[2], **lang,** *n.*: neck, throat [OS *laŋk^{h}o √LAŋK]

Lanc[3], *n.*: sharp edge, sudden end, brink [OS *laŋka √LAN[2]] *VT*42:8

Land[1], *adj.*: wide, plain [OS *landa √LAD[1]]

Land[2], *n.*: open space, level [OS *land- √LAT]

Lang, *n.*: cutlass, sword [OS *laŋgo √LAŋG]

!Lant[1], *n.*: fall [Q *lanta* √DAT]

Lant[2], *n.*: clearing in forest [OS *lant^{h}a √LAT]

Lant·hir, *n. kd.*: 'falling stream', waterfall [lant[1] + sîr]

Las, *n.*: leaf [OS *lasse √LAS[1]] *Letters*:282, *PME*:135

'Las·be·lin, *n. tp.*: 'leaf-withering', autumn [las + pelin, OS *lassepelīn] *PME*:136

'Las·ga·len, *adj. impr. kd. bv.*: green of leaf, having green leaves [las + calen]

Las·ta-, *v.*: listen [OS *lasta- √LAS[2]]

Lath, *n.*: thong [OS *latt^{h}a √LATH]

Lath·ra-, *v.*: listen in, eavesdrop [OS *lansr̯a- < CE *lansra- √LAS[2]]

'Lath·ra·da-, *v.*: listen in, eavesdrop [OS *lansr̯ata- √LAS[2]]

Lath·ron, *n. m.*: hearer, listener, eavesdropper [OS *lansr̯o(ndo) < CE *lansrō √LAS[2]]

Laug, *adj.*: warm [OS *lauka √LAW]

Laus, *n.*: ringlet [MS *lous < OS *lokse √LOKH]

Lav- (3*sg.* **lâf**), **le·vi, lam, lam·men,** *v.*: lick [OS *labi- √LAB]

La·van, *pl.* **le·vain,** *n.*: animal, quadrupedal mammal [OS *lamana √LAM] *WJ*:416

Le, *pron.*: thee, to thee (reverential form)(*gen.* **lín,** *dat./acc.* **le**) [Q *(e)lje < CE *(e)de, *(e)dje √DE]

Le·bed, *n.*: finger [OS *lepet- √LEP-ET]
Le·ben, *num.*: five [OS *lepene √LÉP-EN]
Le'beth·ron, *n.*: a kind of tree and its wood
Lefn, (1) *adj.*: left behind; (2) *n.*: Elf left behind, Avar [OS *lemna < CE lebnā √LEB]
#Lef·nir, *n. kd.*: Elf 'left behind', Avar [lefn + dîr, OS *lemnandīro]
#Lef·nor, *n. dg.*: week (of five days) [leben + aur, OS *lemnaure]
Lef·nui, *num. adj.*: fifth [OS *lemnuia < CE *lepnējā √LÉP-EN]
Leg·rin, *adj.*: swift, rapid [OS *lakrinė < CE *lakrini √LAK^{1}] *VT*45:25
Lei·tha-, *v.*: set free [OS *lekt^{h}a- √LEK]
'Lei·thi·an, *n.*: release, freeing [OS *lekt^{h}ian- < CE *lektjan- √LEK]
Lem·bas, *n. tp.*: 'journey-bread', way-bread [lend + bas, OS *lendembassa] *PME*:404
Lend^{1}, *adj.*: tuneful, sweet [OS *linda √LIN^{2}]
Lend^{2}, *n.*: way, journey [OS *lende √LED]
Lest, *n.*: girdle, boundary, fence [OS *lesta √!LES]
Leth·ril, *n. f.*: hearer, listener, eavesdropper [OS *lansr̭ille √LAS^{2}] *VT*45:26
Lim^{1}, *adj*: clear, sparkling, light *WJ*:337
Lim^{2}, *n.*: fish [OS *limbė < CE *liŋgwi, liŋwi √LIW]
Lim·lug, *n. kd.*: fish-dragon, sea serpent [lim^{2} + lhûg, OS*limbiḽḽūke]
'Lim·mi·da-, *pt.* **lim·mint**, *v.*: moisten [OS *limp^{h}it- < CE *liŋk^{w}it- √LIŋKW]
Limp, *adj.*: wet [OS *limp^{h}ė < CE *liŋk^{w}i √LIŋKW]
Lîn, *pl.* **'li·ni·ath**, *n.*: lake, pool [OS *lini- √LIN^{1}]
Lind^{1}, *n.*: song, air, tune [OS *linde √LIN^{2}]
Lind^{2}, *n.*: singer (also used of rivers) [OS *lindo, *linde √LIN^{2}] *WJ*:309
Lin·del, *pl.* **lin·dil**, *n. kd.*: one of the Green-Elves [Oss lind 'Green-Elf' + -el^{1} √LIN^{2} √EL] *WJ*:385
'Lin·de·dhel, *pl.* **'lin·de·dhil**, *n. kd.*: one of the Green-Elves [Oss lind 'Green-Elf' + edhel √LIN^{2}] *WJ*:385
Lin·na-, *v.*: sing, chant [OS *linda- √LIN^{2}]
Lin·nod, *n.*: verse couplet [?OS *lindot- √LIN^{2}] *LotR:AppA*
Lint, *adj.*: swift [OS *lint^{h}ė < CE *linti √!LINT]
Lîr, *n.*: line, row [OS līre √LIR^{2}]
Lisc, *n.*: reed [OS *lisk- √!LÍSIK]
Lith, *n.*: dust, sand, ash [OS litt^{h}e < CE *litsē √LIT] *Names*:178
Li·thui, *adj.*: ashen, ashy [lith + -ui, OS *litt^{h}uia √LIT]
Lô, *n.*: shallow lake, fenland [OS *loga √LOG] *UT*:263
Lo·bor, *n.*: horse [OS *lopro √LOP] *VT*45:28
Loch, *n.*: ringlet [OS *lokk^{h}o √LOKH]

Lo·da-, *3s.* **lôd**, *v.*: float [OS *luta- √LUT] *VT*45:29
Loeg, *pl.* **loeg**, *n.*: pool [MS *loʒeg < OS *logika or *logek- √LOG]
Loen, *adj.*: soaking wet, swamped [OS *logna √LOG] *VT*42:10
Lom, *adj.*: weary [OS *lumba √LUB] *VT*45:29
Lond, *pl.* **lon·nath**, *n.*: harbor, haven; pass, strait; narrow path [OS *londe √LON]
Long, *adj.*: heavy [OS *luŋga √LUG] (DorS lung)
Lorn, *n.*: quiet water, anchorage, haven, harbor [OS *lurna √LUR] *VT*45:29
Los[1], *n.*: fallen snow [OS *losse √LOS] *RGEO*:61–62, *Letters*:278, *VT*42:18
Los[2], *n.*: flower [OS *losse var. of *lott^{h}e < CE *lott^{h}ē √LOTH]
Los[3], *n.*: wilderness [OS *lussa √LUS] *VT*45:29
Los·sen, *adj.*: snowy [OS *lossena √LOS] *RGEO*:62
Los·soth, *n. tp.*: 'snow-men,' a northern people living near the bay of Forochel [los + hoth] *RGEO*:62
Lost, *adj.*: empty [OS *lusta √LUS]
Loth, *n.*: flower, blossom [OS *lott^{h}e < CE *lot^{h}sē √LOTH]
Lo·theg, *n.*: single flower [OS *lott^{h}ika √LOTH] *VT*42:18
Lo·thod, *n.*: single flower [OS *lott^{h}ota √LOTH] *VT*45:29
Loth·ren, *adj.*: wild, waste [OS *lus(t)rina √LUS] *VT*45:29
#‡Lo·ven, *pl.* **lo·vin**, *adj.*: echoing [MS *lauṽen < OS *lǭmina < CE *lāminā √LAM] (NS lǭmin)
Lû, *n.*: a time, occasion [OS *lūme √LU]
Luin, *adj.*: blue [OS *luinė √LUJ]
#Luith, *n.*: spell, charm [OS *lukt^{h}- √LUK] (DorS lûth)
#Lui·tha-, *v.*: enchant [OS *lukt^{h}a- √LUK] (DorS lútha-)
!'Lui·thi·a-, *v.*: quench [OS *lukt^{h}ia-]
#'Lui·thi·en, *n. f.*: enchantress [OS *lukt^{h}iene < CE *luktiēnē √LUK] (DorS lúthien)
Lûm, *n.*: shade [OS *lumbe √LUM]
Lum·ren, *adj.*: shady [OS *lumbrina √LUM]
Lunt, *n.*: boat [OS *lunt^{h}e √LUT]
Lŷg, *n.*: snake [OS *liuka < CE *leukā √!LEW]

Lh

Lhaew, *adj.*: sickly, sick, ill [OS *ḽaiwa √SLIW] (N thloew, flaew)
Lhain, *pl.* **lhîn**, *adj.*: lean, thin, meager [OS *ḽinia √SLIN] (N thlein)
Lhaw, *du. n.*: ears, group of two ears [OS *ḽǭhu < CE *slāsū √S-LAS[2]]
Lhê, *n.*: fine thread, spider filament [OS *ḽiga √SLIG] (N thlê)

Lhe·wig, *n.*: ear [lhaw + -ig √S-LAS[2]]
Lhind, *adj.*: fine, slender [OS *ḽindė < CE *slindi √SLIN] (N thlind)
Lhing, *n.*: spider, spider's web, cobweb [OS *ḽiŋge √SLIG] (N thling)
Lhin·gril, *n.*: spider [OS *ḽiŋgrille √SLIG] (N thlingril)
Lhîw, *n.*: sickness, disease [OS *ḽīwe √SLIW] (N thliw, fliw)
Lhos, *n.*: whisper or rustling sound [OS *ḽusse √SLUS] (N thloss, floss)
Lhûg, *n.*: dragon, snake, serpent [OS *ḽūkė < CE *slōki √S-LOK]
Lhûn, *pl.* **lhuin**, *adj.*: ?making sound [OS *ḽūna < CE *slōnā √SLON]

M

Mâb, *n.*: hand [OS map- √MAP]
!Mab-, me·bi, mamp, mam·men, *v.*: grasp, seize [OS *mapa √MAP]
Mad-, me·di, mant, man·nen, *v.*: eat [OS *mati- √MAT]
Mae[1], *adj.*: soft [MS *maiʒ < OS *maiga < CE *mazgā < *masgā √MÁSAG] (N moe)
Mae[2], *adv.*: well [MS *mai √MAJ]
Mae·as, *n.*: dough [MS *maiʒass < OS *maigasse < CE *mazgassē √MÁSAG] (N moeas)
'Mae·che·neb, *adj. kd.*: sharp-eyed [maeg + heneb, OS *maik^{h}enipa, *maikak^{h}enipa] *WJ*:337
Maed[1], *adj.*: handy, skilled [MS *maid < OS maitė < CE *mahiti √MAH] (N moed)
Maed[2], *adj.*: shapely [MS *maʒid < OS *magitė < CE *magiti √MAG] *PME*:366, *VT*41:10
Maeg, *adj.*: sharp, penetrating, going deep in [OS *maika √MIK] *WJ*:337
Mael[1], (1) *adj.*: stained; (2) *n.*: stain [OS *m̭agla < CE *smaglā √SMAG]
Mael[2], *n.*: lust [OS *maile √MIL]
Mae·lui, *adj.*: lustful [mael[2] + -ui, OS *mailuia √MIL]
Maen, *adj.*: skilled, clever [OS *magna √MAG]
Mae·nas, *n.*: craft, handicraft, art [OS *magnasse √MAG]
Maer, *adj.*: useful, fit, good (of things) [OS *magra √MAG]
Maeth, *n.*: battle, fight (not of general host but of two or a few) [OS *makt^{h}a √MAK]
Mae·tha-, *v.*: fight [OS *makt^{h}a- √MAK]
Mae·thor, *n.*: warrior [MS *maiβr, *maxβr < OS *makt^{h}ro √MAK]
Maew, *pl.* **maew·rim**, *n.*: gull [OS *maiwe √MIW[1]]
Ma·gol, *n.*: sword [MS *magl < OS *makla √MAK]
Ma·gor, *n.*: swordsman [MS *magr < OS *makro √MAK]
Maidh, *adj.*: pale, fallow, fawn [OS *madia √MAD]
Mail, me·li-, *pl.* **mîl**, *adj.*: dear [OS *melia √MEL]

Main, *adj.*: prime, chief, preeminent [MS mein < OS *minia √MIN] *VT*42:15

Mâl, *pll.* **mail, me·ly**, *n.*: pollen, yellow powder [OS *m̭alȯ e*pl.* *m̭alui < CE *smalu √S-MAL]

Ma·lad, *n.*: the metal gold [OS *malata √MÁL-AT]

Ma·len, *pl.* **me·lin**, *adj.*: yellow [OS *m̭alina √S-MAL]

Mall, *n.*: gold color [OS *m̭alda < CE *smaldā √S-MAL] (N malt)

Mal·len, *adj.*: golden [OS *m̭aldina < CE *smaldinā √S-MAL]

Mal·lorn, *pl.* **mel·lyrn**, *n. tp.*: 'tree of gold', a beechlike tree found in Lórien [mall + orn[2], OS *m̭aldorne]

Mal·los, *n. tp.*: 'flower of gold', a flower growing in Lebennin [mall + los[2], OS *m̭aldalosse]

Malt, *n.*: gold [OS *malta √MÁL-AT] *VT*42:27

Mal·then, mel·thin- *adj.*,: golden, of gold [OS *malt^{h}ina √MÁL-AT]

Ma·lu, *adj.*: fallow, pale [MS *malw < OS *m̭alwa √S-MAL]

Mân, *n.*: departed spirit [OS *manu √MAN]

Ma·nadh, *n.*: doom, final end, fate, fortune [OS *manad- √MAN-AD]

Mann, *n.*: food [OS *manna < CE *matnā √MAT] *VT*45:32

Ma·tha-, *v.*: stroke, feel, handle; wield [OS *matt^{h}a- < CE *mahta- √MAH]

Maur, *n.*: gloom [OS *maurė < CE *maori √MOR] *VT*45:35

‡**Maw[1]**, *pl.* **mae**, *n.*: hand [OS mǭ, *pl.* mai < CE *mā < *mah, *pl.* mahi √MAH]

Maw[2], *n.*: soil, stain [MS *mauʒ < OS *m̭ǭga < CE *smāgā √SMAG]

Med·li, *n. impr. tp.*: 'honey-eater', bear [mad- + glî, OS *matiglihė] (N megli)

Med·lin, *adj.*: ?bearish, of bears [medli + -in[3]] (N meglin)

Me·dui, *adj.*: last [OS *metuia √MET]

Me·gil, *n.*: sword [OS *makilė < CE *makili √MAK] *VT*45:32

Me·gor, *adj.*: sharp-pointed [MS *megr < OS *mikra √MIK] spelled megr *WJ*:337

Mela-, *pt.* **me·lant**, *v.*: love [OS *mela- √MEL] *VT*45:34

Melch, *adj.*: greedy [OS *milk^{h}a √MÍL-IK]

Mel·dir, *n. m. kd.*: friend [mell + dîr]

Mel·dis, *n. f. kd.*: friend [mell + dîs]

Me·leth, *n.*: love [OS *melett^{h}e √MEL]

Me·'leth·ril, *n. f.*: lover [OS *melet^{h}rille √MEL]

Me·'leth·ron, *n. m.*: lover [OS *melet^{h}ro(ndo) √MEL]

Mell, *adj.*: dear [OS *melda √MEL]

Mel·lon, *pl.* **mel·lyn**, *n. m.*: friend, lover [OS *meldo(ndo) < CE *meldō √MEL] *WJ*:412

Me·lui, *adj.*: sweet [OS *meluia √MEL] *VT*42:18

Men, _pron._: we (_gen._ **vín**; _acc._ **mín** see also **ammen**) [OS *men < CE *men √ME]

Mên, men-, -ven, _n._: way, road [OS *men √MEN]

Me·neg, _num._: thousand [OS *meneke √MENEK]

Me·nel, _n._: heaven [Q _menel_ √MEN √EL] _MR_:387

Ment, _n._: point (at the end of a thing) [OS *ment^{h}e √MET]

Me·ren, _adj._: festive, gay, joyous [OS *merina √MER]

Me·reth, _n._: feast, festival [OS *merett^{h}e √MER]

Me·ril, _n._: rose _SD_:128–31

'Me·ri·lin, _n. kd._: nightingale [môr + lind^{2} _irreg._ OS *morilinde] (N mörilind)

Mesc, _adj._: wet [OS *miska √!MÍS^{2}-IK] also spelled mesg

Meth, (1) _adj._: last; (2) _n._: end [OS *mett^{h}a √MET]

Me·thed, _n._: end, last point in a line [OS *mett^{h}ete √MET]

Me·then, _adj._: end, final [?OS *mett^{h}ina √MET] _VT_45:34

Mi, _prep._ (with _art._, **min**): between [OS *mi √MI]

Mîdh, _n._: dew [OS *mīde < CE *mizdē √!MÍS^{2}-ID]

Mîl, _n._: love, affection, kindness [OS *mīl- < CE *mēl- √MEL] _VT_45:34

Mi·lui, _adj._: friendly, loving, kind [mîl + -ui, OS *mīluia √MEL]

Min, _len._ **vi(n)**, _prep._: in [OS *min √MI-N]

Mîn, (1) _adj._: first; isolated; towering; (2) _n._: peak (3) _num._: one [OS *minė < CE *mini √MIN]

Mi·nai, _pl._ **mi·ni**, _adj._: single, distinct, unique [MS *minei < OS *miniia √MIN]

Mi·nas, _n._: tower, fort, city with citadel and central watchtower [OS *minasse √MIN]

'Mi·ni·el, _pl._ **mí·nil**, _n. kd._: 'first Elf', one of the Vanyar [mîn + -el^{1} OS *minielda] _WJ_:383

Min·na-, _v._: enter [OS *mint^{h}a- or *minna- √MI-N]

Mi·nui, _adj._: first [OS *minuia √MIN] _VT_42:15

Mi·'nui·al, _n. kd._: 'first twilight', morning twilight, dawn, morrowdim [mîn + uial, OS *minuiaŋala]

Mîr, _n._: jewel, precious thing, treasure [OS mīre √MIR]

Mír·dan, _pl._ **mír·dain**, _n. tp._: jewel-smith [mîr + tân OS *mīretano]

'Mi·ri·an, _n._: penny, name of a coin [OS *mīrian- √MIR] _PME_:45

'Mí·ri·el, _adj._: jewel-like, sparkling like a jewel [OS *mīriela √MIR]

'Mi·ri·on, _pl._ **mí·ryn**, _n._: 'great jewel', Silmaril [mîr + -on^{2} √MIR]

Mist, _n._: error [OS *mist- √MIS^{1}]

Mis·ta-, _v._: (to) stray [OS *mista- √MIS^{1}]

#Mis·tad, _n. ger._: straying, error [OS *mistata √MIS^{1}]

Mîth^{1}, *adj.*: (pale) grey [OS *mit^{h}ė < CE *mit^{h}i √MITH]
Mîth^{2}, *n.*: white fog, wet mist [OS *mit^{h}- √MITH]
Mith·ren, *pl.* **mith·rin**, *adj.*: grey [OS *mit^{h}rina √MITH]
Mith·ril, *n. kd.*: 'grey brilliance', true-silver; a remarkably hard but malleable metal, found principally in Moria [mîth^{1} + rill, OS *mit^{h}irilde]
Mîw, *adj.*: small, tiny, frail [OS *mīwa √MIW^{2}] *VT*45:35
‡**Môr**^{1}, *adj.*: black, dark [OS *morė < CE *mori √MOR] *Letters*:386
Môr^{2}, *n.*: darkness [OS *morė < CE *mori √MOR] *Letters*:386
Mor·ben, *pll.* **mer·bin**, **mor·bin**, *n. kd.*: one of the Avari or Easterlings in Beleriand [morn + pen, altered from OS *moripende] *WJ*:362, 376
Mor·chant, *pl.* **mor·chaint**, *n. kd.*: 'dark shape', shadow [OS *morcant^{h}a √MOR √KAT] *Silm:App gwath*
Mor·gul, *n. kd.*: 'dark magic', sorcery [morn + gûl] *WJ*:383, 409
Morn, *pl.* **myrn**, (1) *adj.*: black, dark; (2) *n.*: darkness, night [OS *morna √MOR] *Letters*:386
'Mor·ne·dhel, *n. kd.*: dark Elf [morn + edhel OS *mornedelo] *WJ*:409
Môth, *n.*: dusk [OS *moth- √!MOTH] *Silm:App moth*
Mu·da-, *pt.* **mu·das**, *v.*: labor, toil [OS *mūta- < CE *mōta- √MO]
Muil, *n.*: dreariness, twilight, shadow, vagueness [OS *muile √MUJ]
Muin, *adj.*: dear [OS muina < CE *moinā √MOJ]
Muin·dor, *pl.* **muin·dyr**, *n. m. kd.*: brother [muin + tôr]
Muin·thel, *pl.* **muin·thil**, *n. f. kd.*: sister [muin + thêl]
Mûl, *n.*: slave, thrall [OS *mūl < CE *mōl- √MO]
Mund, *n.*: bull [OS *mundo √!MUND] *Letters*:422–23
Mŷl, *n.*: gull [OS *miule √MIW^{1}]

N

Na, *prep.* (with *art.*, **nan**): with, by, near; to, toward, at; of [OS *na √(A)NA]
Na-, *v.*: be [OS *na- √NA]
Nad, *n.*: thing [OS *nata √NA]
Na·dhor, *n.*: pasture [MS *naðr < OS *nadr- √NAD]
Nadh·ras, *n.*: pasture [OS *nadrasse √NAD]
Nae, *intj.*: alas [OS *nai √NAJ]
Naeg, *n.*: pain [OS *naike √NÁJAK]
#**Naeg·ra-**, *v.*: cause pain [OS *naikra- √NÁJAK]
Naer, *adj.*: sad, dreadful, lamentable, woeful [OS *naira √NAJ]
Naer·gon, *n. kd.*: woeful lament [naer + caun^{1}, OS *nairakǭna √NAJ √KAN] *PME*:362
Naes, *n.*: tooth [MS *nais, *naxs < OS *nakse √NAK] *VT*45:36

Naeth, *n.*: biting, gnashing of teeth (in grief), woe [OS *nakt^{h}a √NAK]
Naew, *n.*: jaw [OS *nagma < CE *nakmā √NAK]
Nag-, ne·gi, nanc, nan·gen, *v.*: bite [OS *nak- √NAK]
!Na·gol, *pl.* **nag·lath**, *n.*: tooth [OS *nakla √NAK]
Nail, *num. adj.*: third [MS neil < OS *nelia √NEL^{1}]
Naith, *n.*: spearhead, gore, wedge, point, promontory [OS *nekt^{h}e √NEK] *UT*:282
Nal·la-, *v.*: cry, cry out [OS *nalla- √!NAL]
Na·na, *n. f.*: mother, mama (hypocoristic) [OS *nana √NAN]
Nan(d), *n.*: valley, wide grassland, land at the foot of hills with many streams [OS *nanda, *nande √NAD] *VT*45:36
Na·neth, *n. f.*: mother [OS *nanitt^{h}a √NAN]
Nâr, *n.*: rat [*irreg.* MS *naðr < OS *nadro < CE *n^{j}adrō √NJAD]
‡Na·ra-, *v.*: tell (a story) [OS *nara-, *pt.* *narne √NJAR]
Nar·cha-, *v.*: rend [OS *nark^{h}a- √NÁRAK]
Nardh, *n.*: knot [OS *ṋarda √SNAR]
Narn, *pl.* **nern**, *n.*: tale, saga; versified tale to be spoken, not sung [OS *narna < CE *n^{j}arnā 'told' √NJAR] *MR*:373
Na·rtha-, *v.*: kindle [OS *nart^{h}a- √NAR] *VT*45:37
Nar·than, *n.*: 'fire-sign', beacon [OS *nartanna √NAR √TA-N] *VT*14:20
Na·ru, *adj.*: red [MS *narw < OS *narwa √NAR]
Nas, *n.*: point, sharp end, angle, corner [OS *nasse √NAS]
Nas·ta-, *v.*: prick, point, stick, thrust [OS *nasta- √NAS]
Nath, *n.*: web [OS *natt^{h}e < CE *natsē √NAT]
Nath·ron, *n.*: weaver, webster [OS *nat^{h}ro(ndo) < CE *natsrō √NAT]
Naud, *adj.*: bound [OS *nauta √NUT]
Naug^{1}, *adj.*: stunted, dwarfed [OS *nauka √NUK]
‡Naug^{2}, -nog, *pll.* **noeg, naug·rim, -nog·rim**, *n.*: Dwarf [OS *nauko, *nauka √NUK] (N *pl.* nuig) *WJ*:388, 408, 413; *VT*45:3
Nau·gol, naug·la-, *pl.* **naug·lath**, *n.*: Dwarf (dim. of **naug^{2}**) [MS *naugl < OS *nauklo √NUK]
Naur, nar-, nór-, -nor, *n.*: fire, flame, sun [OS nǭr, nǭre, nar- < CE *nār, nāre √NAR]
Nauth, *n.*: thought [OS *nout^{h}e √NOW]
Nau·tha-, *v.*: conceive [OS *nout^{h}a- √NOW]
‡Naw^{1}, nov-, *adj.*: hollow [MS *nauƀ < OS *nǭba < CE *nābā √NAB] (NS noṽ) *WJ*:414
Naw^{2}, *pl.* **noe**, *n.*: idea [OS *nou, *nowa < CE *now, nowā √NOW] (N *pl.* nui)
Ne-, *adv. pref.*: in, inside, mid- [OS *ne- √NE]

Ne, ned, *prep.*: in, of (time) [MS *neð < OS *ned- √NED]
Ne·der, *num.*: nine [OS *netere √NÉTER]
Ne·dhu, *n.*: bolster, cushion [MS *neðw < OS nidwa < CE *nidwō √NID[1]]
'Ne·di·a-, *v.*: count, reckon, number [MS *nödia- < OS *notia- √NOT] (N nödia-)
!'Ne·di·ad, *n. ger.*: reckoning [MS *nödiad < OS *notiata √NOT]
Ned·rui, *num. adj.*: ninth [OS *netruia √NÉTER] *VT*42:25
Nef, nev-, (1) *prep.*: on this side of; (2) *adj. pref.*: hither, near, on this side
!Nei·tha-, *v.*: deprive [OS *nekt^{h}a-]
Nei·than, (1) *adj.*: deprived, wronged; (2) *n.*: one who is deprived [OS *nekt^{h}ana] *Silm*, *UT*:86
Nêl[1], nel-, *num.*: three, tri- [OS *nele √NEL[1]]
Nêl[2], ne·leg-, *pl.* **ne·lig,** *n.*: tooth [OS nele, *pl.* *neleki < CE *nelek √NEL[2]-EK]
Nel·'chae·nen, *adj.*: ?thirtieth [OS *nelk^{h}ainina √NEL[1] √KÁJ[2]-AN]
Nel·dor, *n. dg.*: beech tree [neled + orn[2], MS *neldorn < * nelðorn < OS *neledorne]
Ne·led, ‡ne·ledh, *num.*: three [OS *nelede √NEL[1] -ED]
'Ne·le·dhi, ne·lenn, ne·'len·nen, *v.*: go in, enter [OS *neledi- < CE *neledi- √NE √LED] *AI*:92
Ne·leg, *n.*: tooth [OS *neleke √NEL[2]-EK]
Nell, *n.*: bell [OS *nelle < CE *n^{j}ellē √NJEL]
Nel·la-, *v.*: sound bells [OS *nella- < CE *n^{j}ella- √NJEL]
!Nel·lad, *n. ger.*: sound of bells [OS *nellata √NJEL]
'Nel·la·del, *n.*: ringing of bells [nellad + -el[2] OS *nellatelle √NJEL]
Nel·thil, *n. dg.*: triangle [nel + till OS *nelt^{h}ilde]
Ne·lui, *num. adj.*: third [OS *neluia √NEL[1]]
Nem, *n.*: nose [OS *nembė < CE *neŋgwi, neŋwi √NEŋ]
Nên, *pl.* **nîn,** *n.*: water, lake, pool, stream, waterland [OS *nen- √NEN]
Nend, *adj.*: watery [OS *nenda √NEN]
Nest, *n.*: heart, core, center [OS *nest- < CE *nedt- √NED]
!Nes·ta-, *v.*: heal [OS *nesta- < CE *net^{h}ta- √NETH]
Nes·tad, *n. ger.*: healing [OS *nestata √NETH]
Nes·'tad·ren, *pl.* **nes·'ted·rin,** *adj.*: of or related to healing [nestad + -ren]
Nes·tag-, 'nes·te·gi, nes·tanc, nes·'tan·gen, *v.*: insert, stick in [OS *nestaki- < CE *nestaki- √NE √STAK]
Neth, *adj.*: young [*irreg.* MS *neþr < OS *net^{h}ra √NETH]
'ni, *prep.*: for the, to the [an + i]
Ni·ben, *pl.* **ni·bin,** *adj.*: small, petty [OS *nipina √!NIP]
'Ni·bin- 'noeg, 'ni·bin- 'nog·rim, *pl. n. kd.*: 'petty Dwarves' [niben, naug] *UT*:148

Nîd, *adj.*: damp, wet; tearful [OS *nītė < CE *neiti √NEJ]
Nîdh, *n.*: honeycomb [OS *neide < CE *negdē √NEG] *VT*45:38
Nîf, *n.*: front, face [OS *nībe √NIB]
'Nim·mi·da-, *pt.* **nim·mint**, *v.*: whiten [OS *nimp^{h}it- √NIKW]
Nimp, nim- *adj.*: pale, white [OS *nimp^{h}ė < CE *niŋk^{w}i √NIKW]
Nîn^1, *adj.*: wet, watery [OS *nīna < CE nēnā √NEN] *Names*:195
Nîn^2, *n.*: tear [OS *nīne < CE *neinē √NEJ]
Nind, *adj.*: fragile, thin, slender [OS *nindė < CE *nindi √NIN]
Nin·glor, *n. kd.*: 'water-gold', golden water-flower, yellow-flag, gladden (*Iris pseudacorus*) [nîn^1 + glaur, OS *nīnaglaure]
'Nin·glo·ron, *adj.*: having gladden-flowers, full of gladdens [ninglor + -on^3]
'Ní·ni·el, *adj.*: tearful [OS *nīniela < CE *neinielā √NEJ]
Ní·nim, *n. impr. kd.*: 'white tear', snowdrop [nîn + nimp]
'Nin·ni·ach, *n. kd.*: 'slender-crossing', rainbow [nind + iach]
Ní·nui^1, *adj.*: tearful [nîn^2 + -ui, OS *nīnuia √NEJ]
Ní·nui^2, *adj.*: watery [OS *nīnuia √NEN]
Niph·red, *n.*: pallor, fear [OS *nimp^{h}ret- √NIKW]
'Niph·re·dil, *n.*: 'little pallor', name of a flower similar to the snowdrop [niphred + -il^2]
Nîr, *n.*: tear, weeping [OS *nīre < CE *neirē √NEJ]
Nír·naeth, *n. tp.*: 'tear-gnashing', lamentation [nîr + naeth]
Nîth, *n.*: youth [OS *nīt^{h}e < CE *nēt^{h}ē √NETH]
Nod-, ne·di, nunt, nun·nen (**?no·den**), *v.*: tie, bind [OS *nuti- √NUT]
#**Noe**, *n.*: lament [OS *nǭie < CE *nājē √NAJ] (N nui)
No·goth, *pll.* **ne·gyth, no·'goth·rim**, *n.*: Dwarf [OS *nukott^{h}o √NUK] (‡ *pl.* nögyth) *WJ*:388, 413
No·goth ni·ben, *pl.* **ne·gyth ni·bin**, *n.*: petty-Dwarf [nogoth, niben] (‡ *pl.* nögyth nibin) *WJ*:388, 408
'No·go·theg, *pl.* **'ne·ge·thig**, *n.*: Dwarflet, petty Dwarf [nogoth + -eg] *WJ*:388
Nor-, ne·ri, norn, nor·nen, *v.*: run [OS *nori- √!NOR]
Nordh, *n.*: cord [OS *ṋurda < CE *snurdā √SNUR]
Norn, (1) *pl.* **nyrn**, *adj.*: twisted, knotted, crabbed, contorted, hard; (2) *pll.* **nyrn, norn·waith**, *n.*: Dwarf [OS *ṋurna < CE *snurnā √SNUR] *MR*:93, *WJ*:205
Nó·rui, *adj.*: sunny, fiery [naur + -ui, OS *nǭruia]
Nos, *n.*: clan, family, house [OS *nosse √(O)NO-S]
Nost, *n.*: house, family [OS *nost- √(O)NO-S] *PME*:360
Noth·lir, *n. tp.*: family line, family tree [nos + lîr, OS *nosselīre] *WJ*:237, 309
Noth·rim, *n. tp.*: house, family [nos + rim, OS *nosserimbe] *PME*:360
Nu, *prep.* (with *art.*, **nuin**): under [OS *nu √NU]
Nûd, *n.*: bond [OS *nūte √NUT]

Nui·tha-, *v.*: stunt, prevent from coming to completion, stop short, not allow to continue [OS *nuktʰa- √NUK] *WJ*:413
Nûr[1], *adj.*: deep [OS *nūra √NU or √NU-R]
Nûr[2], *adj.*: sad [OS *nūra √NU-R]
Nûr[3], *n.*: race (group of related people) [OS *nūre < CE *nōrē √(O)NO]
#Nŷw, *n.*: noose [OS *n̯iuma < CE *sneumā √SNEW] (N hniof)

O

O[1], **od**, *prep.* (with *art.*, **uin**): from, of [OS *aud √AWA] *WJ*:366
O[2], **o h-**, *prep.*: about, concerning; becomes *o h* before a vowel, thus o[2] + Edain = o hEdain 'about humans' [OS *o, *oh < CE *os √OS]
O·do, *num.*: seven [OS *otoho < CE *otosō √OT-OS]
O·dog, *num.*: seven [OS *otoko √OT-OK]
'O·do·thui, *num. adj.*: seventh [OS *ototʰuia √OT-OTH]
Ó·dhel, *pll.* **ó·dhil**, **ó·'dhel·lim**, *n.*: Noldo Elf [OS *audelo √AWA √DEL] *WJ*:364, 378-9
Odh·ril, *n. f.*: female parent [OS *onrille √ONO]
Odh·ron, *n.*: parent [OS *onro(ndo) < CE *onrō √ONO]
Ôl, **o·lo-**, *pl.* **e·ly**, *n.*: dream [OS *olo, *pl.* *olohi < CE *olos, *pl.* olosī √ÓL-OS]
Olf, *n.*: branch, wand [OS *olba √ÓLOB]
Oll, *n.*: torrent, mountain stream [OS *ulda √UL[1]]
Ol·tha-, *v.*: dream [OS *olsa- < CE *olosa- √ÓL-OS]
!O·neth, *pl.* **o·nith**, *n. f.*: giver [OS *ǫnittʰa < CE *ānittā √AN]
On·na-, *pp.* **!on·nen**, *v.*: beget [OS *ontʰa- √ONO]
!On·nen, *pl.* **en·nin**, *adj. pp.*: born [OS *ontʰena √ONO]
O·nod, *pll.* **e·nyd**, **o'nod·rim**, *n.*: Ent [OS *onoto √!ONOT] *Names*:165, *Letters*:178
Or, (1) *adv. pref.*: above, over, high; (2) *prep.* (with *art.*, **erin**): above, on [OS *or √ORO] *SD*:128–31
Ôr, **o·rod-**, *pll.* **e·ryd**, **e·red**, *n.*: mountain [OS oro, *pl.* oroti < CE *orot √ÓR-OT] *Names*:178
Orch, *pll.* **yrch**, **or·choth**, *n.*: Orc [OS *urkʰo, *urkʰa √Ú-RUK] *RGEO*:66, *Names*:171, *Letters*:178, *MR*:195, *WJ*:390–91
Or·chall, *adj.*: superior, lofty, eminent [or + hall OS orkʰalla] *WJ*:305
‡Orn[1], *adj.*: tall [OS *orna √ORO] *Letters*:426
Orn[2], *pl.* **yrn**, *n.*: tree [OS *orne √ÓR-ON] *SD*:302
O·rod, *pll.* **e·red**, **e·ryd**, **o·'rod·rim**, *n.*: mountain [OS oroto, *pl.* oroti √ÓR-OT]
O·'rod·ben, *pll.* **e·'ryd·bin**, **o·'rod·bin**, *n. tp.*: one living in the mountains, mountaineer [orod + pen] *WJ*:376

O·'rod·rim, *n. kd.*: range of mountains [orod + rim]
Or·tha-, *v.*: raise [OS *ort^{h}a- √ORO]
Or·thad, *n. ger.*: raising [OS *ort^{h}ata √ORO] *MR*:373
'Or·the·li, or·thell, or·'thel·len, *v.*: roof, screen above [OS *ort^{h}eli- √ORO √TEL]
Or·'the·li·an, *n.*: canopy [OS *ort^{h}elian- √TEL]
Or·thor-,·'or·the·ri, or·thorn, or·'thor·nen, *v.*: master, conquer [OS *ort^{h}uri- √ORO √TUR]
Os-, *adv. pref.*: about, around [OS *os- √OS]
Os·car-,·'es·ce·ri, os·carn, os·'car·nen, *v.*: cut round, amputate [OS *osskari- √OS √SKAR] also spelled osgar
Osp, *n.*: reek, smoke [OS *uspe < CE *usuk^{w}ē √ÚSUK]
Ost, oth-, *n.*: fortress, stronghold [OS *osto < CE *osotō √Ó-SOT] *WJ*:414
Os·'ti·ri·on, *n. impr. tp.*: fortress with a watchtower [ost + tirion]
Oth·lonn, *n. tp.*: paved way [ost + lond, OS *ostolonde]
#Oth·rad, *n. tp.*: street [ost + râd, OS *ostorata]
Oth·ronn, *n. kd.*: underground stronghold, fortress in cave(s) [ost + rond OS *ostrondo] (‡othrond) *WJ*:414
O·thui, *num. adj.*: seventh [OS *ott^{h}ūia < CE *otsōjā √OT-OS] *VT*42:25
O·vor, *adj.*: abundant [MS *ovr < OS *ubra √UB]
Ov·ra-, *v.*: abound [OS *ubra- √UB]
Ov·ras, *n.*: crowd, heap [OS *ubrasse √UB]

P

Pa·da-, *v.*: walk on a track or path [OS *pata- √PAT^{2}]
!Pâd, -bad, *n.*: way [OS *pata √PAT^{2}]
Pae, *num.*: ten [OS *paia < CE *k^{w}aja √KWA-J] *VT*42:25
‡Paen, *n.*: small gull, petrel [OS *paine √KWAJ] (N poen) *VT*45:24
Paenui, *num. adj.*: tenth [OS *painuia < CE *k^{w}ainajā √KWA-J] *VT*42:25
Paich, *pl.* **pîch,** *n.*: juice, syrup [OS *pihia < CE *pisjā √PIS]
Pa·lan-, *adv. pref.*: far off, over a wide area [Q *palan* √PAL]
ˌPa·lan-·'di·ri, ·'palan-dirn, ˌpa·lan-·'dir·nen, *v.*: view far and wide [palan + tiri-]
Pa·lath, *n.*: surface [OS *palatt^{h}e √PAL]
Pân^{1}, *pl.* **pain,** *adj.*: all [OS *pana < CE *k^{w}anā √KWA-N] *SD*:128–31
Pân^{2}, *pl.* **pain,** *n.*: plank, fixed board in a floor [OS pano √PAN]
Pa·nas, *n.*: floor [OS *panasse √PAN]
Pand, *n.*: courtyard [OS *panda √PAD]
Pann, *adj.*: wide [OS *panna < CE *patnā √PAT^{1}]
Pan·na-^{1}, *v.*: open, enlarge [OS *pant^{h}a- √PAT^{1}]
Pan·na-^{2}, *v.*: fill [OS *pant^{h}a- < CE k^{w}anta- √KWA-T]

Pant, *adj.*: full, complete, whole [OS *pant^{h}a < CE *k^{w}antā √KWA-T]
Parch, *adj.*: dry [OS park^{h}a √PÁRAK]
Parf, *pl.* **perf,** *n.*: book [OS parma √PAR]
Parth, *n.*: field, sward, (enclosed) grassland [OS *parth^{h}-]
!Par·tha-, *v.*: arrange, compose [OS *part^{h}a- √PAR]
Path, *adj.*: smooth [OS patt^{h}a < CE *pat^{h}nā √PATH]
Path·ra-, *v.*: fill [OS *pant^{h}ra- < CE *k^{w}antra- √KWA-T]
Path·red, *n.*: fullness [OS *pant^{h}ret- < CE *k^{w}antret- √KWA-T]
Pa·thu, *n.*: level space, sward [MS *paβw < OS pat^{h}wa < CE *pat^{h}mā √PATH]
Paur, -bor, *n.*: fist, tightly closed hand [OS pǭra < CE *k^{w}ārā √KWAR] *PME*:179, 318
Paw, *n.*: sickness [MS *pauṽ < OS *pǭme < CE *k^{w}āmē √KWAM]
Pe·di, pent, pen·nen, *v.*: say, speak [OS *pet- < CE *k^{w}et- √KWE-T]
Pêg, *n.*: small spot, dot [OS pika √PIK]
Pêl, pe·le-, *pl.* **pe·li,** *n.*: fence, fenced field, enclosure, garth [OS pele, *pl.* *pelehi < CE *peles, *pl.* pelesī √PEL-ES]
Pe·leth, *n.*: fading, withering [OS *pelett^{h}e < CE *k^{w}elettē √KWEL]
Pe·li, pell, pel·len, *v.*: fade, wither [OS *pel- < CE *k^{w}el- √KWEL]
'Pe·li·a-, *v.*: spread [OS *palia- √PAL]
!Pe·lin, *n.*: fading, withering [OS *pelīne < CE *k^{w}elēne √KWEL]
Pel·thaes, *n.*: pivot [MS *pelβais, *pelβaxs < OS pelt^{h}aksa √PEL √TAK^{1}]
Pen^{1}, *prep.*: without, lacking, -less [OS *pen √PEN] *WJ*:375
Pen^{2}, *len.* **ben,** *pron. indef. enclitic*: one, somebody, anybody [OS *pen < CE *k^{w}en √KWE-N] *WJ*:376
Pend, *n.*: declivity, fall [OS *pende √PED]
Pen·drad, *n. tp.*: passage up or down slope, stairway [pend + râd]
Pen·drath, *n. tp.*: passage up or down slope, stairway [pend + rath]
Peng, *n.*: bow (for shooting) [OS *piŋga < CE *k^{w}iŋgā √KWIG]
'Pe·ni·a-, *v.*: fix, set [OS *pania- √PAN]
Pen·na-, *v.*: slant down [OS *penda- √PED]
Pen·nas, *n.*: history, account [OS *pent^{h}asse √KWE-T]
#'Pen·ni·nor, *n. tp.*: last day of the year [pant + în + aur, OS *pant^{h}īnaure]
Pent, *n.*: story, tale [OS *pent^{h}a < CE *k^{w}entā √KWE-T]
Per-, *adj. pref.*: half [OS *per √PER]
'Pe·re·dhel, *pl.* **'pe·re·dhil,** *n. kd.*: half-Elf [per- + edhel, OS *peredelo] *PME*:256, 348
'Pe·ri·an, *pll.* **'pe·ri·ain, ˊpe·ri·'an·nath,** *n.*: halfling [per + -ian^{2} √PER] *RGEO*, *Letters*:426
Pe·rin, *adj.*: half [OS *perinė < CE *perini √PER]

Pe·'rin·gol, *pl.* **pe·'rin·gyl**, *n. kd.*: half-Elf, half-Noldo [perin + gol(odh)]
Pes·seg, *n.*: pillow [OS *pessek- √KWES]
Peth, *n.*: word [OS *pett^{h}a < CE *k^{w}ettā √KWE-T]
Peth·ron, *n.*: narrator [OS *pent^{h}ro < CE *k^{w}entrō √KWE-T]
Pi·gen, *adj.*: tiny [OS pikina √PIK]
#Pi·hen, *adj.*: juicy [OS *pihina < CE *pisinā √PIS]
Pin·nath, *pl. n.*: ridges [OS *pinnatt^{h}e or *pindatt^{h}e]
Po, *len.* **bo**, *prep.*: on [OS *pǭ < CE *pā √PA] *VT*44:23
Pôd, *pl.* **pŷd**, *n.*: animal's foot [OS poto √POT]
Post, *n.*: pause, halt, rest, cessation, respite [OS *pusta √PUT]
Pres·ta-, *v.*: affect, trouble, disturb [OS *presta- √PÉRES]
Pres·'tan·nen, *adj.* pp.: 'affected', referring to a mutated vowel [OS *prestant^{h}ena √PÉRES]
Pres·'tan·neth, *n.*: 'affection' of vowels [OS *prestant^{h}ett^{h}e √PÉRES]
Pui·a-, *v.*: spit [OS *puia- < CE *piuja- √PIW]
Puig, *adj.*: clean, tidy, neat [OS *puika < CE *poikā √POJ]

R

!Rach, *pl.* **raich**, *n.*: wagon, wain *UT*:465
Râd, *n.*: path, track [OS *rata √RAT]
Ra·da-, *v.*: make a way, find a way [OS *rata- √RAT]
Rae·da-, *v.*: catch in a net [OS *raita- √RAJ] *VT*42:12
Raef, *n.*: net [OS *raima √RAJ] *also* **raew** *VT*42:12
Raeg, *adj.*: wrong [OS *raika √RÁJAK] (N rhoeg)
Raen[1], *adj.*: crooked [OS ragna √RAG]
Raen[2], *adj.*: netted, enlaced [OS raina √RAJ] *VT*42:12
Raew[1], *n.*: fathom [OS ragme < CE *rakmē √RAK]
Raew[2], *n.*: net [OS *raiwe √RAJ] *VT*42:12
Rafn, *n.*: wing, horn, extended point at the side [OS *ramna √RAM]
Rain[1], *adj.*: erratic, wandering [OS *ranja √RAN] *UT*:242, *VT*42:12
Rain[2], *n.*: border [OS *regna √REG]
Ram, *n.*: wall [OS *ramba √RAB]
Ram·mas, *n.*: wall [OS *rambasse √RAB]
Ranc, *pll.* **ren·gy**, **rainc**, *n.*: arm [OS *raŋk^{h}ȯ < CE *raŋku √RAK]
Ran·dir, *n. tp.*: wanderer, pilgrim [OS *ranandīro √RAN √NDER]
Rant, *n.*: course, watercourse, water-channel, stream; lode, vein [OS *rant^{h}- √RAT]
!Raph, *n.*: strap, rope [OS *rapp^{h}- < CE *rapp- √!RAP]
Ras, *pl.* **rais**, *n.*: horn, mountain peak [OS *rasse √RAS]
Rasc, *n.*: horn, mountain peak [OS *rask- √RAS] also spelled rhasg

Rast, ras, *n.*: cape [OS *rast- √RAS]
Rath, *n.*: climb, climbing path, street; course, riverbed [OS *ratt^{h}a √RAT] *UT*:255
Raud[1]**, rod-,** *adj.*: high, eminent, noble [OS *(a)rǭta < CE *arātā √(A)R[1]-AT]
Raud[2]**, -rod,** *n.*: champion, eminent man, noble [OS *(a)rǭto < CE *arātō √(A)R[1]-AT]
Raud[3]**,** *n.*: metal [OS *rauta √RAWT]
Raudh, *adj.*: hollow, cavernous [OS *rauda < CE *raoda √ROD]
Raug, *n.*: a powerful, hostile, and terrible creature, demon [OS *rauko √RUK] *WJ*:415
Raun, -ron, (1) *adj.*: straying, wandering; (2) *n.*: 'the Wanderer', moon, month [OS *rǭna < CE *rānā √RAN] (N rhân)
Raw[1]**,** *n.*: bank, especially of a river [MS *rauƀ < OS *rǭba < CE *rābā √RAB]
Raw[2]**,** *pl.* **roe,** *n.*: lion [OS rǭ, *pl.* rǭwi < CE *rāu, *pl.* rāwi √RAW] (N *pl.* rui)
Raw[3]**,** *n.*: rush, roaring noise [OS *rǭwe < CE *rāwe √RAW]
Rêd, *n.*: heir [Be rēda]
Re·dhi, rend, ren·nen, *v.*: sow [OS *redi- √RED]
Rêg, *n.*: holly, thorn [OS *rek- √REK]
Rem[1]**,** *adj.*: frequent, numerous [OS rimba √RIM]
Rem[2]**,** *n.*: mesh, net [OS *rembe √!REM]
Rem·men, *pl.* **rem·min,** *adj.*: tangled, woven, netted [OS *rembina √!REM]
'Re·ni·a-, *v.*: fly, sail; wander, stray [OS *ramia- √RAM and *rania- √RAN]
Res, *n.*: ravine [OS *rissa √RIS]
Rest, *n.*: ravine, cleft, cut [OS *rista √RIS]
Rî, *n.*: crown, wreath, garland [OS rīge, *rīga √RIG] *PME*:347
Rí·an, *n. tp.*: 'crown-gift', queen [rî + ann OS *rīganna]
Ri·bi, rimp, rim·men, *v.*: rush, fly, fling [OS *rip- √RIP]
Ri·el, *n.*: garlanded maiden, princess [rî + -el[3] OS *rīgelle √RIG]
Ri·en, *n.*: queen, crowned lady [OS *rigende √RIG] (N rhien) *TI*:429
Rîf, *n.*: bark [OS *rib- √!RIB]
Rill, *n.*: brilliance, flame, glittering (reflected) light [OS *rilde √RIL]
Rim[1]**,** *n.*: crowd, great number, host; plural marker [OS rimbe √RIM] *UT*:318, *Letters*:386
Rim[2]**,** *n.*: cold pool or lake [OS *rimbe < CE *riŋ^{w}g^{w}ē < *riŋgwē √RIŋG]
Rimp, *adj.*: rushing, flying [OS *rimp^{h}ė < CE *rimpi √RIP]
Rim·ma-, *v.*: flow like a torrent [OS *rimp^{h}a- √RIP]
Rîn[1]**,** (1) *adj.*: crowned; (2) *n.*: crowned (woman), queen [MS *riʒn < OS *rigna √RIG]
Rîn[2]**,** *n.*: remembrance [OS *rīne < CE *rēnē √REN] *PME*:372

Rinc, *n.*: twitch, jerk, trick, sudden move [OS *riŋk^{h}ė < CE *riŋk^{h}i √RIKH]

Rind[1], *adj.*: circular [OS *rindė < CE *rindi √RIN]

Rind[2], *n.*: circle [OS *rinde √RIN]

Ring, *adj.*: cold [OS *riŋgė < CE *riŋgi √RIŋG]

Rin·gorn, *n. impr. kd.*: circle [rind[2] + corn[1]]

Ris, *n.*: a ravine [OS *risse √RIS]

Rîs, *n.*: queen [OS *rīgisse √RIG]

Rist[1], **-ris**, *n.*: cleft [OS *riste √RIS]

Rist[2], *n.*: cleaver, cutter [OS *risto √RIS]

Ris·ta-, *v.*: rend, rip, cut, cleave [OS *rista- √RIS]

Ri·tha-, *v.*: jerk, twitch, snatch [OS *rikt^{h}a- √RIKH]

#Rîw, *n.*: edge, hem, border [MS *riṽ < OS *rīma √RI] (N rhîf)

Roch, *n.*: horse, swift horse for riding [OS *rokk^{h}o √ROK] *Letters*:282, 386

Roch·ben, *pll.* **roch·bin, rech·bin**, *n. tp.*: rider [roch + pen] *WJ*:376

Ro·chir, *pl.* **ro·'chir·rim**, *n. m. tp.*: knight, rider, horse-lord [roch + hîr OS *rokk^{h}īro, *rokk^{h}okh^{h}īro] *UT*:318; *Letters*:178, 282

Ro·chon, *n.*: rider [OS *rokk^{h}ondo √ROK] *UT*:313

Ro·don, *pl.* **ro·dyn**, *n.*: a Vala [OS *(a)rǭto(ndo) < CE *arātō √(A)R[1]-AT] *LotR*

Ro·'hir·rim, *n. pl. kd.*: horse-riders, people of Rohan [rochir + rim[1]] *Letters*:178

Rom, *n.*: horn, trumpet [OS romba √ROM]

Rom·loth, *n. kd. bv.*: '(plant) having a flower like a horn', descriptive name of tobacco (**galenas**) [rom + loth]

Rom·ru, *n. tp.*: sound of horns [rom + rû MS *rommruṽ < OS *rombarūma]

Rond, *n.*: cave, cavern, vault, vaulted ceiling, hall with vaulted roof [OS *rondo √RON] *Letters*:282, *WJ*:414

Ros[1], *adj.*: reddish, russet, copper-colored; red-haired [OS *russa √RUS] *PME*:366, *VT*41:9

Ros[2], *n.*: foam, rain, dew, spray (of fall or fountain) [OS *rosse √ROS] *Letters*:282

‡Ros[3], *n.*: polished metal, glitter [OS *russe √RUS]

Rost, *adj.*: rainy [OS *rosta √ROS]

Ros·ta-, *v.*: hollow out, excavate [OS *rosta- < CE *rodta- √ROD]

Ro·val, *pl.* **ro·vail**, *n.*: pinion, wing, great wing (of eagle) [OS *rǭmale < CE *rāmalē √RAM] (N rhoval, pl. rhovel)

‡Rû, *n.*: sound (of horns) [OS rūma < CE *rōmā √ROM]

Rûdh, *adj.*: bald [OS *rūda √!RUD[2]]

Ruin[1], (1) *adj.*: burning, fiery red; (2) *n.*: red flame, blazing fire [OS *runia √RUN[2]] *Silm:App ruin*, *PME*:366
#Ruin[2], *pl.* **rŷn**, *n.*: slot, spoor, track, footprint [MS *röin < OS *runia √RUN[1]] (N rhöin)
Rui(w), *n.*: hunt, hunting [OS *ruime < CE *roimē √ROJ[1]]
#Ruith, *n.*: anger, ire [OS *rukt^h- √RUK] (DorS rûth) *Silm:App rûth*
Rusc, *n.*: fox [OS *ruskė < CE *rusku √RUS-UK] *VT*41:10
Rust, *n.*: copper [OS *rustė < CE *rustu √RUS] *VT*41:10
Rus·tui, *adj.*: of copper [OS *rustuia < CE* rustujā √RUS] *VT*41:10
Rŷn, *n.*: hound of chase [OS *ronio √ROJ[1]]

Rh

!Rhach, *n.*: curse (appears as **'rach**) *MR*:373
Rhas, *n.*: precipice [MS *xrass < OS *k^hrasse √KHARÁS]
Rhast, *n.*: shore [OS *r̯asta < CE *srastā]
Rha·van, *pl.* **rhe·vain**, *n.*: wild man, man not of the Edain [OS *r̯abano < CE *srabanō √SRAB] *WJ*:219
Rhaw[1], *n.*: wilderness [MS *r̯auƀ < OS *r̯ǭba < CE *srābā √SRAB]
Rhaw[2], *n.*: flesh, body [MS *r̯au < OS *r̯awa, r̯ǭwe < CE *srawā, srāwē √SRAW] *MR*:350
Rhi·bi, rhimp, rhim·men, *v.*: scratch [OS *r̯ipi- √SRIP] (N thribi)
Rhîw, *n.*: winter [OS *r̯īwe < CE *srīwē √SRIW]
Rhos, *n.*: a whisper or rustling sound [OS *r̯ussa √SRUS] (N thross)
Rhosc, *adj.*: red, russet, brown [OS *r̯uska < CE *sruskā √S-RÚS-UK]
Rho·van, *adj.*: wild [OS *r̯ǭbana < CE *srābanā √SRAB]
Rhu-, *adj. pref.*: east [OS *r̯ū-, r̯ūme < CE *(s)rō-, *(s)rōmē √(O)S-RO]
!Rhûd, *n.*: dwelling underground, artificial cave, rockhewn hall, mine [OS *r̯ūta < CE *srōtā √S-ROT] *PME*:365
Rhûn, *n.*: east, the East [OS *r̯ūna < CE *(s)rōna √(O)S-RO]
Rhú·nen, *adj.*: eastern [OS *r̯ūnina √(O)S-RO]
‡Rhu·ven, *n. kd.*: east [rhu- + mên OS *r̯ūmen]

S

Sâd, -had, *n.*: place, spot, a limited area naturally or artificially defined [OS *sat- √SAT] *UT*:314, *VT*42:20
Sâdh, *n.*: sward, turf [OS *sad- √SAD] *VT*42:20
Sael, *adj.*: wise [OS *saila √SAJ]
Saer, *adj.*: bitter [OS *sagra √SAG]
Saew, *n.*: poison [OS *sagma √SAG]
Said, *adj.*: private, separate, not common, excluded [MS *seid < OS *satia √SAT] *VT*42:20

Sain, sin-, *pl.* **sîn**, *adj.*: new [OS *sinia √SI-N]

Sa·lab, *pl.* **se·laib**, *n.*: herb [OS salape < CE *salak^{w}ē √SALÁK]

Salph, *n.*: liquid food, soup, broth [OS salp^{h}a √SÁLAP]

Sam, *pl.* **sam·math**, *n.*: chamber [Q **sambë* √STAB]

Sant, *n.*: garden, field, yard, or other place in private ownership [OS *sant^{h}a √SAT] *VT*42:20

Sarch, *n.*: grave [OS *sark^{h}-]

Sarn[1], *adj.*: stony, made of stone [OS *sarna √SAR]

Sarn[2], *pl.* **sern**, *n.*: small stone, pebble, stone (as a material) [OS *sarn- √SAR]

Sar·nas, *n.*: cairn, pile of stones [OS *sarnasse √SAR] *LR*

Sau·tha-, *v.*: (to) drain [MS *souβa-, *soxβa- *irreg.* < OS *sukt^{h}a- √SUK]

Saw, *pl.* **soe**, *n.*: juice [MS *sauƀ < OS sǭba < CE *sābā √SAB] (N *pl.* sui)

Sed·ryn, *pl. n.*: faithful ones [?OS *satrondi]

'Sei·di·a-, *v.*: set aside, appropriate to special purpose or owner [OS *satia- √SAT] *VT*42:20

Sell, *pl.* **sel·lath**, *n.*: daughter; girl, maid [OS *selde √SEL] *SD*:128–31

Sen, *len.* **hen**, *pl.* **sin**, *len.* **hin**, *adj.*: this, these [OS *sina *pl.* *sini √SI]

Send, *pl.* **Sen·drim**, *n.*: Grey-Elf, one of the Sindar (probably only used by the Noldor) [Q *Sinda*]

Sen·nui, *adv.*: rather, instead *SD*:128–31

Se·reg, *n.*: blood [OS *sereke √SEREK] *Silm:App sereg*

'Se·re·gon, *n. impr. tp.*: 'blood of stone', name of a stonecrop with deep red flowers [sereg + gond] *UT*:148

Ser·ni, *n.*: shingle, pebble-bank [OS *sarniie √SAR]

Se·ron, *n.*: friend [OS *sero(ndo) √SER]

Si, *len.* **hi**, *adv.*: now [OS *si √SI]

Sí, *adv.*: here [OS *sī < CE ?*sis(e) √SI]

Sîdh, *n.*: peace [OS *sīde < CE *sēdē √SED]

Si·gil[1], *n.*: dagger, knife [Q **sicil* √SIK]

Si·gil[2], *n.*: necklace *WJ*:258

Sí·la-, *v.*: shine white [OS *sīla- √SIL]

‡**Si·lef**[1], *adj.*: silver, shining white [OS *silima √SIL]

Si·lef[2], *n.*: silima, the crystal substance of the silmarils [Q *silima* √SIL]

Si·'lev·ril, *pl.* **si·'lev·ril**, *n. tp.*: silmaril [silef[2] + rill]

‡**Si·lif**, *n.*: silver light [OS *silime √SIL]

Si·lith, *n.*: silver light [CS silif]

Si·'liv·ren, *pl.* **si·'liv·rin**, *adj.*: glittering white (like a silmaril), of silima [silif + -ren]

'Si·ni·ath, *pl. n.*: news, tidings [OS *siniatt^{h}e √SI-N]

Sin·narn, *n. kd.*: novel tale [sain + narn, OS *sinianarna]

Sîr^1, **-hir, -hír,** *pl.* **'si·ri·ath,** *n.*: river, rill [OS sīrė < CE *sīri √SIR] *Silm:App sîr*

Sîr^2, *adv.*: today [OS sīre √SI √RE] *VT*44:23

'Si·ri·a-, *v.*: flow [OS siria- √SIR]

'Si·ri·on, *n.*: great river [OS *siriondo √SIR]

Si·rith, *n.*: flowing, stream [OS *siritt^{h}e √SIR]

So·ga-, *3sg.* **sôg,** *pt.* **sunc** or **so·gant,** *pp.* **so·'gan·nen,** *v.*: drink [OS *suka- √SUK]

Solch, *n.*: root, especially an edible root [OS sulk^{h}a √SÚLUK]

Sui, *cj.* and *prep.*: like, as [OS *siui < CE *sībe i *like this which* √SI √BE √I] *VT*44:23

Sui·lad, *n.*: greeting [OS *suilata √!SUJ] *SD*:128–31

Sui·'lan·na-, *v.*: greet [OS *suilant^{h}a- √!SUJ √AN] *SD*:128–31

Sûl^1, *n.*: goblet [OS *suglė < CE *suglu √SUG]

Sûl^2, *n.*: wind [Q *súlë* √THU]

#Suith, *n.*: draught [OS *sukt^{h}o √SUK] (N sûth)

T

Ta·chol, *n.*: pin, brooch [OS *taŋk^{h}la √TAK^1]

Tâd, tad-, *num.*: two [OS *tata < CE *atata √(A)T^2-AT]

Tad-dal, *pl.* **tad-dail,** (1) *adj. dg.*: two-legged; (2)*n. dg.*: biped [tâd + tâl] *WJ*:388

Ta·dol, *adj.*: double [OS *tatla or *tatǭla √(A)T^2-AT]

Ta·dui, *num. adj.*: second [OS *tatuia √(A)T^2-AT] *VT*42:15

Taeg, *n.*: boundary, limit, boundary line [OS *taika √TÁJ^2-AK] *WJ*:309

Taen^1, *adj.*: long (and thin) [OS *taina √TAJ^1]

Taen^2, *n.*: height, summit of high mountain [OS *tagna < CE *tahnā √TAH]

Taes, *n.*: nail [OS *takse √TAK^1]

Tae·tha-, *v.*: fasten, tie [OS *takt^{h}a- √TAK^1]

Taew, *n.*: holder, socket, hasp, clasp, staple [OS *tagma < CE *takmā √TAK^1]

Taf·nen, *adj.*: closed, stopped, blocked [OS *tamnina < CE *tapnā √TAP] *WR*:341

!Ta·gol, *n.*: marker [OS *takla √TAK^2]

Taid, *adj.*: supporting, second-in-command [OS *tatia √(A)T^2-AT]

!Taig, *adj.*: marking (a boundary) [OS *takia √TAK^2]

Taith, *n.*: mark [OS *tekt^{h}a √TEK]

Tâl, -dal, *pl.* **tail,** *n.*: foot, both of the body and a unit of measurement; in composition 'end, lower end' [OS *tal √TAL^1] *AI*:92

Ta·lad, *n.*: incline, slope [OS *talata √TALÁT]

Ta·laf, *pl.* **te·laif,** *n.*: ground, floor [OS *talam- √TAL^{1}-AM]

'Ta·la·gan, *n. impr. tp.*: harp player [*irreg.* OS *talaŋgando < CE *tjala ŋgandō √TJAL √ŋGÁNAD] (‡talagand)

Ta·lan, *pl.* **te·lain,** *n.*: 'flat surface', platform, flet (high platform used in trees in Lothlórien) [OS *talan- √TAL^{2}] *UT*:245

Ta·lath, *n.*: flat surface, plane; flatlands, plain, (wide) valley [OS *talatt^{h}e √TAL^{2}]

Talf^{1}, *n.*: low, flat field or wetland [OS *talma √TAL^{2}] *Names*:195

#Talf^{2}, *n. impr. tp.*: 'flat of the hand', palm [tal(u) + maw^{1}, OS *talma √TAL^{2} √MAH]

Tal·raph, *n. tp.*: 'foot-rope', stirrup [tâl + raph]

Talt, *adj.*: slipping, falling, insecure [OS *talt^{h}a √TALÁT]

#Ta·lu, *adj.*: flat [MS *talw < OS *talwa √TAL^{2}]

Tam·ma-, *v.*: knock [OS *tamba- √TAM]

!Tân, -tan, *n.*: maker, wright, craftsman, smith [OS *tano √TAN]

Tanc, *adj.*: firm [OS *taŋk^{h}a √TAK^{1}]

Tang, *n.*: bowstring [OS *taŋg- TAŋG]

'Tan·ga·da-, *v.*: make firm, confirm, establish [OS *taŋk^{h}ata- √TAK^{1}]

Tann, *n.*: sign, something shown or indicated [OS *tanna √TA-N] *MR*:385

Ta·ra, tar-, *pl.* **!tei·ri,** *adj.*: tough, stiff [MS *tarʒ < OS targa √TÁRAG]

Ta·rag, *n.*: horn, steep mountain peak [OS *tarak- √TARÁK]

'Ta·ri·as, *pl.* **'te·ri·ais,** *n.*: stiffness, toughness, difficulty [MS *tarʒass < OS *targasse √TÁRAG]

Tar·lanc, *adj. kd. bv.*: stiff-necked, obstinate [tara + lanc^{2}, OS *targalaŋk^{h}o]

Tas, *n.*: trouble [MS *tass, *tars < OS tarsa √TÁRAS]

Ta·thar, *n.*: willow [OS *tat^{h}are √TÁTHAR]

Ta·thor, *n.*: willow [MS *taβr < OS *tat^{h}re √TÁTHAR]

Tath·ren, *adj.*: of willow, having willows [OS *tat^{h}rina √TÁTHAR]

Taur^{1}, tor-, tar-, *adj.*: lofty, high, sublime, noble; vast, masterful, mighty, overwhelming, huge, awful [OS *tǫra < CE *tārā √TAR and OS *taura √TUR]

‡Taur^{2}, -dor, *pll.* **toer, to·rath,** *n.*: king (of a people) [OS *tǫro < CE *tārō √TAR]

Taur^{3}, *n.*: great wood, forest [OS *taure √TÁWAR]

Tau·ron, *n.*: forester [OS *tauro(ndo) √TÁWAR]

Taus, *n.*: thatch [MS *tous *irreg.* < OS *tupse √TUP]

Ta·vor, tav·r(a)-, *n.*: 'knocker', woodpecker [MS *taṽr < OS *tamro √TAM]

Taw^{1}, *adj.*: woollen, of wool [MS *tau, *tou < OS *towa √TOW]

Taw^{2}, *n.*: wool [OS *tou < CE *tow √TOW]

!**Taw**[3], *pron.*: that [OS *tǭ √TA]

Ta·war, *n.*: forest; wood (material) [OS *taware √TÁWAR]

'Ta·wa·ren, *pl.* **'te·we·rin**, *adj.*: wooden [OS *tawarina √TÁWAR]

Ta·'war·waith, *n. tp.*: forest-people, Silvan Elves [tawar + gwaith] *UT*:256

Tê, *pl.* **tî**, *n.*: line, way [OS *te, *pl.* tī < *tee, *pl.* *tei < CE *tehe, *pl.* tehi √TEH]

Te·gil, *n.*: pen [Q *tecil* √TEK] *PME*:318

Te·'gil·bor, *n. kd. bv.*: one skilled in calligraphy [tegil + paur] *PME*:318

Te·gol, *n.*: pen [MS *tegl < OS *tekla, or a modification of Q *tecil* √TEK]

'Tei·li·a- or **'te·li·a-**, *v.*: play [MS *telia- < OS *talia- < CE *t^{j}alja- √TJAL]

'Tei·li·en or **'te·li·en**, *n.*: sport, play [MS *telien- < OS *talien- √TJAL]

Tei·tha-, *v.*: draw, write [OS *tekt^{h}a- √TEK]

Telch, *pl.* **tilch**, *n.*: stem [OS *telk^{h}o √TÉLEK]

Te·le, *pl.* **te·li**, *n.*: end, rear, hindmost part [OS *telehe, *pl.* *telehi √TÉL-ES]

Te·ler, *pll.* **te·lir**, **te·'ler·rim**, *n.*: person or thing at the rear, one of the Teleri [OS *telero √TEL] *PME*:385

#**Tel·luin**, *pl.* **tel·lyn**, *n.tp.*: sole of the foot [tâl + ruin[2] OS *talrunia] (N tellöin)

Te·lu, *n.*: dome, high roof [MS *teluṽ < OS *telume √TEL]

Ten, *len.* **den**, *pron. indef.*: one [OS *ten-] *VT*44:23

Têw, *pl.* **tîw**, *n.*: letter, sign [OS *teŋwe < CE *teŋmē √TEŋ] *LotR:AppE*

Ti, *len.* **di**, *pron.*: those, them [OS *tei √TE] *VT*44:23

Tî, *n.*: line, row [OS *tīe < CE *tēhe √TEH]

Till, **-dil**, **-thil**, *n.*: tine, spike, point, (sharp) horn, sharp-pointed peak [OS *tilde √TIL]

'Ti·li·as, *n.*: line of peaks [OS *tiliasse √TIL]

Tim: see **tinu** *MR*:388

!**Tîn**, *len.* **dîn**, *pron.*: his, ?her, ?its (of a person not the subject) [OS *tīn- < CE *tēn- √T] *SD*:128–31

Tinc, *n.*: metal [OS *tiŋk^{h}o √TIŋK]

Tin·na-, *v.*: glint [OS *tint^{h}a- √TIN]

Tin·nu, *n. tp.*: dusk, twilight, starlit evening, early night without a moon, starry twilight [tinu + dû, MS *tinnūṽ < OS *tindūmė < CE *tindōmi]

Tint, *n.*: spark [OS *tint^{h}- √TIN]

Ti·nu, **-din**, *n.*: spark, small star [MS *tinw < OS *tinwe < CE *tinmē √TIN] (NS tim 'spark')

‡**Ti·'nú·vi·el**, *n. tp.*: 'daughter of twilight', nightingale [tinnu + iell, MS *tinnūṽiell < OS *tindūmielle] *MR*:373, *WJ*:62

Tîr[1], *adj.*: straight, right [OS *tīra < CE *tēra < *tehrā √TEH]

Tîr[2], **-dir**, *n.*: looking, view, glance [OS *tire √TIR]

Tí·ra-, *v.*: see [OS *tīra- √TIR] *SD*:128–31

Ti·ri, tirn, tir·nen, *v.*: watch, watch over, guard, gaze, look at, look towards [OS *tiri- √TIR]

'Ti·ri·a-, *v.*: watch, guard, gaze, look toward [OS *tiria- √TIR]

'Ti·ri·on, *n.*: great watchtower [OS *tiriond- √TIR]

Ti·rith, *n.*: watch, watching, guard, guarding, vigilance [OS *tiritt^{h}e √TIR]

Tirn, -dir, -thir, *n.*: watcher [OS *tirno √TIR]

Tir·nen, *adj. pp.*: guarded [OS *tirnena √TIR]

Ti·then, *pl.* **ti·thin**, *adj.*: little, tiny [OS *titt^{h}ina √TIT]

To·ba-, *v.*: cover, roof over [OS *tupa- √TUP]

To·bas, *n.*: roofing [OS *tupasse √TUP]

Tofn, *adj.*: deep, low, low-lying [OS *tumna < CE *tubnā √TUB]

Tog-, te·gi, tunc, tun·gen, *v.*: lead, bring [OS *tuki- √TUK]

Tol-, te·li, toll, tol·len, *v.*: come [OS *tuli- √TUL]

Toll, *pl.* **tyll**, *n.*: island [OS *tollo √TOL^{2}]

Tol·lui, *num. adj.*: eighth [OS *tolduia √TOL^{1}-OD] *VT*42:15

To·log, *adj.*: stalwart, trusty [OS *tuluka √TULUK]

To·lodh, *num.*: eight [OS *tolodo √TOL^{1}-OD] *VT*42:15

To·loth, *num.*: eight [OS *tolot^{h}o √TOL^{1}-OTH]

To·lo·then, *num. adj.*: eighth [OS *tolot^{h}ina √TOL^{1}-OTH]

Tol·tha-, *v.*: fetch, make come [OS *tult^{h}a- √TUL]

Tond, *adj.*: tall [OS *tunda √TUN]

Tong, *adj.*: taut, tight, resonant (of strings) [OS *tuŋga √TUG]

‡**Tôr**, *pl.* **te·ryn**, *n. m.*: brother [OS toron, *pl.* toroni √TOR-ON]

To·rech, *n.*: lair, hole

!**Torn**, *pl.* **tyrn**, *n.*: down

To·rog, *n.*: troll [OS *turuka √TUR-UK]

Tor·tha-, *v.*: wield, control [OS *turt^{h}a- √TUR]

Tos, *n.*: bush, low-growing tree (maple, hawthorn, blackthorn, holly, etc.) [OS *tussa √TUS]

Trann, *n.*: administrative district, shire, division of a realm *SD*:128–31

Tran·nail, *adj.*: of a shire *SD*:128–31

Tras·ta-, *v.*: harass, trouble [OS *trasta- < CE *tarasta- √TÁRAS]

Tre-, tri-, *adv. pref.*: through, completely [OS tre < CE *tere √TER]

Tre·nar-, 'tre·ne·ri, tre·nor, ?'tre·no·ren, *v.*: recount, tell to the end [tre- + nara-, OS trenari-]

Tre·narn, *n.*: account, tale [tre- + narn, OS trenarna]

Tre·vad-, 'tre·ve·di, tre·vant, tre·'van·nen, *v.*: traverse [OS trebati- √BAT]

Trî, *prep.*: through [OS trī < CE *terē √TER]

Trîw, *adj.*: fine, slender [OS *trīwa < CE *terēwā √TER]

Tû, *n*.: muscle, sinew; vigor, physical strength [OS tūgė < CE *tūgu √TUG]
Tûg, *adj*.: thick, fat [OS tūka < *t^{j}ūkā < CE *tiukā √TIW]
Tui·a-, *v*.: swell; spring, sprout [OS *tuia- < CE *tiuja- √TIW and CE *tuja- √TUJ]
Tui·linn, *n. tp*.: 'spring-singer', swallow [OS *tuilindo, *tuilelindo √TUJ √LIN[2]]
Tui(w), *n*.: sprout, bud [OS *tuima √TUJ]
Tu·lu, *n*.: support, prop [MS *tulūṽ < OS tulugme < CE *tulukmē √TULUK]
Tu·lus, *pl.* **ty·lys**, *n*.: poplar tree [OS *tulusse < CE *t^{j}ulussē √TJUL]
Tûm, tum-, *n*.: deep valley, under or among hills [OS *tumbė < CE *tumbu √TUB]
Tump, *n*.: hump [OS *tump^{h}ė < CE *tumpu √TUMP]
Tund, *n*.: hill, mound [OS *tundė < CE *tundu √TUN]
Tûr[1], *n*.: victory, mastery, power, control [OS *tūre √TUR]
Tûr[2], *n*.: master, victor, lord [OS *tūro √TUR]

Th

Thafn, *n*.: post, wooden pillar [OS st^{h}amne < CE *stabnē √STAB]
Tha·la, *pl.* **!thei·li**, *adj*.: stalwart, steady, firm [MS *βalʒ < OS st^{h}alga √STÁL-AG]
'Tha·li·on[1], *adj*.: strong, steadfast, dauntless [OS *st^{h}algǫna √STÁL-AG]
'Tha·li·on[2], *pl.* **the·lyn**, *n*.: hero, dauntless man [OS *st^{h}algo(ndō) √STÁL-AG]
Tham, *n*.: hall [OS *st^{h}ambe √STAB]
Tham·as, *n*.: great hall [OS *st^{h}ambasse √STAB]
Thanc, *adj*.: forked, cleft, split [OS st^{h}aŋk^{h}a √STAK]
Thand, *n*.: shield [OS *t^{h}anda]
Thang, *n*.: compulsion, duress, need, oppression, tyranny [OS *t^{h}aŋga √THAG]
Than·gail, *n. tp*.: shield fence, shield wall [thand + cail, OS *t^{h}andakegle] *UT*:281
Thar-, *adv. pref*.: across, athwart, over, beyond [OS *t^{h}ara √THAR]
Thâr, *n*.: stiff grass [OS *st^{h}ara √STAR]
Tha·ras, *n*.: hassock, footstool [OS *st^{h}arasse √STAR]
Thar·bad, *n. kd*.: crossway [thar + pâd, OS *t^{h}arapata]
Tharn, *adj*.: sapless, stiff, rigid, withered [OS st^{h}arna √STAR]
Thaur[1], *adj*.: detestable, abhorrent, abominable, foul [OS *t^{h}aura √THAW]
Thaur[2], *adj*.: fenced [OS *t^{h}aura √THUR]
Thav·ron, *n*.: carpenter, wright, builder [OS st^{h}abro(ndo) √STAB]

Thaw, *adj.*: corrupt, rotten [OS *t^{h}auha < CE *t^{h}ausā √THU-S]
Thêl, the·le-, *pl.* **the·li,** *n. f.*: sister [OS t^{h}ele, *pl.* t^{h}elehi √THEL-ES]
The·la, -thel, *pl.* **!thi·li,** *n.*: point (of spear) [MS *þelʒ < OS *st^{h}elga √STÉLEG]
!The·li, thell, thel·len, *v.*: intend, mean, purpose, resolve, will [OS *st^{h}eli- √STEL]
'The·li·on, *n. m.*: one who purposes or has purpose [OS *st^{h}elio(ndo) √STEL]
The·nid, *adj.*: firm, true, abiding [OS *st^{h}anitė < CE *staniti √STAN]
The·nin, *adj.*: firm, true, abiding [OS *st^{h}aninė √STAN]
Thent, *adj.*: short [OS st^{h}int^{h}a √STINT]
Thi·a-, *v.*: appear, seem [OS *t^{h}īa- < *t^{h}eia < CE *t^{h}eja- √THE]
Thîl, *n.*: radiance [OS *t^{h}il- √THIL]
'Thi·li·a-, *v.*: glister, glisten [OS *t^{h}ilia- √THIL]
'Thi·li·on, *adj.*: glistening silver [OS *t^{h}iliǭna √THIL]
‡**Thîn,** *n.*: evening [OS *t^{h}inie √THIN]
Thind, *adj.*: grey, pale [OS *t^{h}indė < CE *t^{h}indi √THIN]
Thin·drim, *n. pl.*: Sindar [thind + rim] *VT*41:9
Thin·na-, *v.*: fade, grow toward evening [OS *t^{h}int^{h}a- √THIN]
Thin·nas, *n.*: shortness; 'breve' (a mark indicating that a vowel is short) [OS *st^{h}int^{h}asse √STINT]
Thîr, *n.*: look, face, expression, countenance [OS *st^{h}ir- < CE *stir- √STIR] *VT*41:10
Thôl, *n.*: helm
Thôn, *pl.* **thŷn,** *n.*: pine-tree [OS *t^{h}on- √THON]
Thond, *n.*: root [OS *t^{h}unda √THUD]
'Tho·ni·el, *n. f.*: kindler [OS *t^{h}ǭnielle < CE *t^{h}ānjellē √THAN] *MR*:388
'Tho·ni·on, *adj.*: having pine trees [OS *t^{h}oniǭna < CE *t^{h}onjānā √THON]
Thôr[1], *adj.*: swooping, leaping down [OS *t^{h}ora √THOR]
Thôr[2], *pl.* **the·ryn,** *n.*: eagle [OS *t^{h}oron √THOR-ON]
Tho·ra-, *pp.* **tho·ren,** *v.*: fence [OS *t^{h}ura- √THUR]
Tho·ren, *adj. pp.*: fenced, guarded, hidden [OS *t^{h}aurena < CE *'t^{h}aurēnā √THUR]
Tho·rod, *n.*: torrent [OS *t^{h}orot- √THOR]
Tho·ron, -thorn, *pll.* **the·ryn,·'tho·ro·nath,** *n.*: eagle [back formation from **theryn**; cf. **thôr**[2]]
Thû, *n.*: stench [OS *t^{h}ūh- < CE *t^{h}ūs- √THU-S]
Thui·a-, *v.*: breathe [OS *t^{h}uia- < CE *t^{h}ūja- √THU]
Thûl, *n.*: breath [OS *t^{h}ūle √THU]
Thu·rin, *adj.*: secret, hidden [OS *t^{h}ūrinė < CE *t^{h}ūrini √THUR] *UT*

U

Ú-, u-, *adv. pref.*: not, without [OS *ū, *ugu √U] *WJ*:369
Ú·an, *n. kd.*: monster [MS *ūƀan < OS *ūbano √U √BAN]
'U·a·nui, *adj.*: monstrous, hideous [úan + -ui, OS *ūbanuia √U √BAN]
U·bed, *n. kd.*: denial [OS *ūpet- √U √KWE-T] *WR*:132, 137
U·dûn, *n.*: hell [MS *uduṽn < OS *utumnė < CE *utupnu √U-TUP]
Ú·garth, *pl.* **ú·gerth**, *n.*: ill deed, sin [ú + cardh[2], OS ūkard- √U √KAR[1]] *VT*44:23
Ui-, *adj. pref.*: both, two, twi- [OS *uia < CE *jūjā √JU]
Ui[1], *adj.*: everlasting, eternal [OS *uia < CE ojā √OJ]
Ui[2], *adv.*: ever, always [OS *uio < CE *ojo √OJ]
Ui·al, *n. dg.*: 'both-light', twilight [ui- + gal OS *uiaŋala]
Ui·'daf·nen, *adj.*: ever-closed [ui[2] + tafnen] spelt Uidavnen *WR*:341
Uil, *n.*: seaweed [OS *uile √UJ]
Ui·los[1], *adj. kd.*: always snow-white [ui[2] + glos OS *uioglossa] *RGEO*:62, 66; *Letters*:278
Ui·los[2], *n. kd.*: everlasting flower; the flower called by the Rohirrim *simbelmynë*, or 'evermind', a kind of *Anemone* growing in turf [ui[1] + los[2], OS *uialosse] *UT*:55
Uin, *prep.*: from the, of the [o[1] + i] *SD*:128–31
Uir, *n.*: eternity [OS *uire < CE *oirē √OJ]
Ui·reb, *adj.*: eternal [OS *uiripa < CE *oirik^{w}ā√OJ]
Ul-, *adj. pref.*: hideous, horrible (only found as *pth.* in names) [MS *ulʒ- < OS *ulgu- √ÚL[2]-UG]
Ûl, *n.*: odor [OS *ūle *irreg.* < CE *ŋōle √ŋOL]
U·'lui·thi·ad, *adj.*: without quenching, unquenchable [ú- + luithia-, OS *ūlukt^{h}iata] *SD*:62
U·lunn, *n.*: monster, deformed and hideous creature [OS *ulgundo √ÚL[2]-UG]
Ûm, *adj.*: bad, evil [OS *umb- √UM]
Úm·arth, *n. kd.*: evil fate [OS *umbart^{h}a √U √MBÁRAT]
Ûn, *n.*: creature [OS *ūno < CE *ōno √ONO]
Un·gol, *n.*: spider [MS *uŋgl < OS *uŋgl- √!UŋG]
Ûr[1], *n.*: fire, heat [OS *ūre √UR[1]]
Ûr[2], *adj.*: wide [OS *ūra √UR[2]]
U·rug, *pl.* **y·ryg**, *n.*: bogey, monster, orc [OS *urukė < CE *uruku √Ú-RUK]
Ú·rui, *adj.*: hot [ûr[1] + -ui, OS *ūruia √UR[1]]
!U·run, *n.*: copper [OS *urunė < CE *urunu √U-RUN[2]]
Ú·thaes, *n.*: temptation [MS *úβaiβ, *úβaxβ < OS *ūt^{h}akte √U √THAG] *VT*44:23

Y

Ylf[1], *n.*: drinking vessel [OS *julma √JUL[1]] *WJ*:416
#Ylf[2], *n.*: brand [OS *julma √JUL[2]] (N iolf)
#Ŷr, *n.*: course [OS *jura √JUR] (N iôr)
#Y·ri, yrn, yr·nen, *v.*: run [OS *juri- √JUR] (N ior-, ieri)

Appendix 3

Eldarin Roots

This list of roots will allow the reader to perceive at a glance some of the relationships among words in Appendix 2, which should be consulted for more information about each specific word. The roots are arranged alphabetically, but roots bearing an obvious relationship to each other are arranged together. In order to find a root in this list, ignore any prefix or ending separated from the rest of the root by a hyphen, and look under the main part of the root; but do not ignore any part of the root within parentheses. For example, to find (A)BA, look under ABA; to find ÁJ-AR look under AJ; but to find Á-KAL-AR look under KAL.

Roots of non-Eldarin origin will be indicated as such. Where two or more roots appear to be related, but the relationship is a distant one, it will be indicated in parentheses following the root.

It should be understood that the "definitions" of the roots are very general and do not cover all of the meanings of the derived words.

Primary derivatives of a root are given after the root; compounded derivatives are given after the primary derivatives and are separated from them by a semicolon.

A

√A O!: a[1], ai, alae
√ABA refuse, prohibit: av-, ava-, avad, avar, avo
  √(A)BA no: baw, boda-
√AD entrance, gate: and[2], annon
√AJ pool, lake: ael
  √ÁJ-AR sea: aear, aearon, aer; aerlinn, aeruil
√ÁJAK sharp, pointed: aeg[1], aeg[2], aegas; aeglir, aeglos
√(A)JAN holy (borrowed from Valarin ayanûz): iaun
√AJW bird: aew, aewen
√AK narrow, confined: agor; aglonn
√!AKH anger, fear: achas
√AM[1] up: am, amon; ambenn, amdir, amloth, amrûn

√AM[2] mother: emil
√AN give (cf. √ANA): ann, anna-, anneth, ant, oneth; rían, suilanna-, bessain, bassoneth, ivonwen
√ANA to, toward (cf. √AN): an, an-; ammen, anann, aníra-, anwar, anglenna-, angos, apharch, einior
√(A)NA: na, en, 'ni
√ÁNAD long: and[1]; anann, andaith, annabon, andrath, anfang, angerthas, ennin
√AŋG iron: ang, angren; angwedh
√AŋGW snake: amlug
√AP[1] food: aes
√AP[2] after: ab-, abonnen, aphada-, aphadon
√AR[1] lofty, noble: ar-[1]; arphen, arwen
√ÁR[1]-AD realm: ardh, ardhon
√ÁR[1]-AN king: âr, ar(a)-, aran, arn, arnad, ernil
√AR[1]-ÁT noble: arod, arth
√(A)R[1]-AT noble: raud[1], raud[2], rodon
√AR[2] outside, beside: ar, ar-[2]; arnediad, aronoded
√AS[1] daylight, warmth: eirien
√AS[2] and: a[2]
√ÁS[3]-AT dust: ast
√AT[1] father: adar, ada; adanadar
√AT[2] again, back: ad, eden, edwen; aduial, adertha-, aderthad, adleg-, adleitha-, adleithian, acharn; edinor
√AT[2]-AN*: adan; adanadar, adaneth, drúadan, dúnadan
√AT[2]-AT two, both: ath-, edaid; athrada-
√(A)T[2]-AT two, both: tâd, tadol, tadui, taid; tad-dal
√!ATH: athelas
√AWA move away from: o[1], ódhel, uin
√(A)WA depart: gwanwel, gwanwen, gódhel; gwachaedir
√(A)WA-N depart, go away, disappear, vanish: gwanath, gwann, gwanna-, gwanu

B

√BAD judge: badhor, badhron, baudh
√M-BAD duress, prison, doom, hell: band
√BAL power (cf. √BEL): bâl, balan; balrog

---

*This root is also said to be borrowed from a word *atan* in the human language of the people of Bëor (*PME*, p. 324).

√BAN fair: bain; úan, uanui
√BAR raise: beria-
  √BAR-AT tower: barad
  √BAR-ÁD lofty: brand, baradh, brannon, brennil
√BARÁK sudden (cf. √BERÉK): bragol
√BARÁN brown: baran
√BARÁS hot, burning: bara, bras, brassen
√BARATH spouse: bereth
√BAT tread (cf. √PAT[2], √RAT): bad-, bâd, bannen, batha-, govad-, govannen, trevad-
√BE like, as: be, godref, sui
√BEL strong (cf. √BAL): bell, bellas
  √BÉL-EK mighty: beleg
√BEN corner: bennas
√BER valiant: beren, bertha-
√BERÉK wild, violent, sudden: braig, brêg, breged, bregol, bregolas, breitha-; bregedur
√BERÉTH birch tree: brethil
√BES (or √BED) wed: benn, bes; hervenn, herves
√BEW follow, serve: buia-, bŷr
√BIRÍT broken stones: brith, brithon
√BOR[1] endure: avorn, bôr
√BOR[1] -ÓN enduring: brona-, bronad, bronadui, brenia-, brûn; bronwe
√!BOR[2] hot, red: born
√!BUR loud: brui

D

√DAB give way, make room, permit, allow: dâf
√DAJ[1] great: dae[3], daer[1]
  √N-DAJ[1] great: dae[1]; daedhelos
√DAJ[2] shadow: dae[2], daew; daedelu
√DAR stay, wait, stop, remain: dar-, dartha-, daur
√DARÁK wolf: draug
√DARÁM beat, hew: drafn, dram, drava-; drambor, gondrafn
√DAT fall down (cf. √TALÁT): dad, danna-, dannas, dannen, dant, dath, lant[1]; dadbenn, lanthir
√DE thou, second-person familiar pronominal: le
√DEL walk, go, proceed, travel (cf. √LED): ódhel, gódhel
  √É-DEL traveler, migrant: edhel, edhellen; dúredhel, lindedhel, mornedhel, peredhel, edhelrim, edhelharn

√DEN hole, gap, passage: dîn[1]
√!DERÉK flee: drega-
√DIB stair: dim[1]
√DIL stop up, fill up hole: dîl, dilia-, gasdil
√DIM sad, gloomy: dem, dim[2]
√!DIN silent: dîn[2], dínen
√!DIRÍG beat, strike: dring, dringa-
√DO night: dû, dúath, dúlinn, tinnu, tinúviel
  √DO-H night: daw, dûr; dúredhel, durgul, dúrion, guldur
√DOL head: dôl, dolt
√DOR dried up, hard, yielding: dorn; dornhoth
  √N-DOR dry land: dôr, dortha-; ennor
√DÓRON oak tree: doron
√DRUG (borrowing): drû; drúadan, drúnos
√DUB lie, lie heavy, loom, hang over oppressively (of clouds) (cf. √LUM): dofn, duvui
√DUJ flow (in volume): duin
√DUL hide, conceal: delia-, dolen, doltha-
  √N-DUL hide, conceal: doll
√DUN dark (of color): donn
√DUS burn: dosta-

DJ

√DJEL feel fear and disgust; abhor: dêl, deleb, delu; delos, daedhelos

E

√!E third-person pronominal: e[2], în[2]
√EK sharp point: aig, êg, ech, eitha-, eithad; ecthel, egnas
  √EK-ET sharp weapon: aith
√EL behold, star: elo, ell-[1], elleth, ellon; elrim, elvellon, glinnel, laegel, lindel, menel, miniel
  √EL-ED Elf: eledh
  √EL-EN star: êl, elen, elanor, eledhrim
√EN over there, yonder: ennas
√ÉNEK six: eneg, enaith, enecthui, engui
√ÉNETH name: eneth
√ER one, alone: êr, er-, ereb, eriol, ertha-, erthad, eru[1], eru[2], erui; adertha-, aderthad, elloth, erchamion, erchamui, eruchen
√ES indicate, name: esta-
√ET forth, out: e[1]; echad-, echil, echor, echui(w), echuir, edrain, edledhi,

edledhia-, edledhron, edlenn, edonna-, eithel, ephel, ethir[1], ethir[2], ethuil
√ÉT-ER open: edra-

G

√GAJ[1] awe, dread, astound, make aghast: gae, gaear, gaearon, gaer[1], gaer[3], gaeron, goe[1], goeol
√GAJ[2] red: gaer[2]
√GAL grow, thrive: gala-, galas, galu, glad
√GÁL-AD tree: galadh, galadhon; galadhrim
√GAL-ÁS joy, be glad: glas
√GAL-ÁT wood: glâd
√GAP hook: gamp, gammas
√GAR hold, possess: gar-, gardh, garn
√GÁR-AT fort: garth, gartha-
√GAS yawn, gape: gas, gast, gaw; gasdil
√GAT[1] catch: gad-
√GAT[2] cave: gador, gath, gathrod
√GAW think out, devise, contrive: gaud
√GEŋG sick: gem, ingem
√GIR quiver, shudder: giri, girith
√GLIM gleam, glint: glind, glinna-
√GON stone: gôn, gond, gondren; gondolindren, gondolindrim, gondrafn, gondrath, gonhir, seregon
√GOR warn, counsel, urge, impel, move: gôr[1], gor-, gorf, gorn[1], gorn[2], gûr[1]
√GOS dread (cf. **√KOTH, √ŋGOROTH, √ŋGOTH, √ŋGUR**): gos, gost, gosta-; angos, delos, daedhelos, guruthos
√GRAW dark, swart: graw; graurim
√GU not: gû-

GJ

√GJEL triumph, joy: gell, gellui; gellam
√GJER wear out: gern

GW

√GWETH report, give account of, inform of things unknown or wished to be known: dangweth

H

√HAN male: anu
√HEK aside, apart, separate: eglan, eglan, ego, egol, eitha-, eithad
√HEL sky: ell-[2], elu; eilian

I

√I that: i; en, erin, uin, 'ni , sui
√IL all, every: ilaurui
√IMB dale, deep vale: im[3], imlad, imloth, imrach
√IMBI between (cf. **√MI**): im[1]; imlad, imloth, imrath
√INI: inu
  √(I)NI: dî[2]; heryn
√IŋK guess: inc
√!IR desire: aníra-
√ITH know: ist, ista-, istui, ithron

J

√JA ago, in the past: ia, iaur; einior, iarwain
√JAB fruit: iavas, iaw[1], ivonwen
√JAG yawn, gape: iâ, iaw[2]
√JAJ mock: iaew
√JAK neck: iaeth
√JAR blood: iâr
√JAT join: iant, ianu, eilian
√!JATH fence: iâd, iâth, eriad, iathrim
√JEL daughter, girl: iell, tinúviel
√JEN year: în[1], ínias, idhrinn, ingem, iphant, edinor, enedhin, ennin, penninor
√JES desire: iest
√JON son: iôn, iond, dúrion
√JU two, both: ui-, uial, aduial, minuial
√JUK employ, use: iuith, iuitha-
√JUL[1] drink: ylf[1]
√JUL[2] smolder: iûl, ylf[2]
√JUR run: ŷr, yri

K

√KAB hollow: cam; camlann, erchamion, erchamui, forgam, hargam
√KAJ[1] lie down: cael, caeleb, caew
√KAJ[2] ten

√KÁJ[2]-AR ten: caer

√KÁJ[2]-AN ten: nelchaenen

√KAL shine: calan, calen, callon, calben, lasgalen

√KAL-ÁR brilliance: calar, claur, celair; calardan

√Á-KAL-AR glory: aglar, aglareb, egleria-

√KAL-AT light: calad; gilgalad

√!KÁLAP water vessel: calph

√KAN[1] cry, call aloud: can-, caun[1], caun[3], conui; naergon, condir

√KAN[2] dare: cand, caun[2]

√KÁNAT four: canad, canath, cannui

√KAP leap: cab-, cabed, cabor

√KAR[1] make, do, build: car-, car(dh)[1], cardh[2], cared; acharn, ceredir, úgarth

√KAR[2] red

√A-KAR[2] blood: agar; agarwaen

√KAR[2]-ÁN red: caran, carn, crann

√!KARÁB press: cram

√KÁRAK sharp fang, spike, tooth: carach, caraes, carag, carch

√!KARÁKW crow (cf. √KOROK): craban

√!KARAP hat: carab

√KAS head: cast, caw; cathrae

√KAT shape: cadu, cadwor, cannas, cant; echad-, morchant

√KEG snag, barb: cai, cail; thangail

√KEL flow away, flow down, flow out swiftly (cf. √KWEL, √TEL): celeth, cell, celon, celos, celu; eithel

√KEM soil, earth: cae, cêf, cefn, cefnas, ceven; cennan

√KEN[1] see (cf. √KHEN): ceni, cened, cenedril

√KEN[2] spearhead, gore: cên, cîn

√KEPER spike: ceber

√KIL divide, choose (cf. √KIR): cîl

√KIR cut, cleave: cair, cirion, cirith, certh, certhas; círbann, círdan, angerthas

√KÍR-IK sickle: cerch, critha-

√KIR-ÍS cut (cf. √RIS): cris, crist

√KOB bay (cf. √KHOP): côf

√KOJ live (cf. √KUJ): cuia-, cuil, cuin, cuina-; echuir

√KOL bear, carry, wear: caul, coll[3], cyll

√KOR round: cerin, corn[1], corn[2], coron, echor; basgorn, ringorn

√KÓROK crow (cf. √KARÁKW): corch

√KOTH strive, quarrel (cf. √ŋGOTH, √GOS): cost, coth[1], coth[2]

√Ó-KOTH **war**: auth[1]
√KU dove: cugu
√KUB mound: cûm
√KUH bow, bend: cû, cûn; cúron
√KUJ wake (cf. √KOJ): echui(w)
√KUL[1] hollow: coll[1]
√KUL[2] golden-red: coll[2]
√KUM void: cofn
√KUND guardian, prince: cund
√KUR craft: coru, curu, curunír, crumguru
√KURÚM left: crom, crûm, crumui; crumguru

KH

√KHAG pile, mound: haudh
√KHAJ far, distant: hae, haer, haered, haeron, gwachaedir
√KHAL uplift: hal-, hall[1], orchall
√KHAM sit: ham, hanu, hav-
√KHAN understand, comprehend: hand, hannas, henia-
√KHAP enfold: hab-, hamma-, hammad, hamp
√KHAR[1] helmet: harn[3]
√!KHAR[2] hope: hartha-, harthad
√KHARÁS precipice (cf. √KÁRAK, √RAS): rhass
√KHAT hurl: had-, hador, hadron; hadlath
√KHAW rest, lie at ease (cf. √KAJ): haudh, haust
√!KHAZAD Dwarf (borrowing from Khuzdul): hadhod
√KHEL freeze: gochel
√KHEL-EK ice: helch, heleg
√KHELED glass (borrowing from Khuzdul): heledh
√KHEN eye (cf. √KEN): hen(d), heneb, henneth; lachenn, maecheneb
√KHEP retain, keep, do not give away or release, keep hold of: hebi
√KHER rule, govern, possess: heron, herth, hîr, híril; herdir, hervenn, herves, heryn, rochir, gonhir
√KHES command: hest
√KHIL follow: hîl; echil
√!KHIB cool: him[1]
√KHIM stick, cleave, adhere: haew, him[2], hîw
√KHIN child: hên; eruchen
√KHITH mist, fog: hethu, hîth, hithu, hithui; hithlain
√KHO heart: hû-, huorn
√KHO-N: hûn

√KHOP haven, harbor (cf. √KOB): hobas, hûb
√KHOR set going, put in motion, urge on: heria-, horn, hortha-, hûr
√KHOTH gather: hûd, host, hoth; dornhoth, gaurhoth, glamhoth, lossoth
√KHUG bark, bay: hû

KHJ

√KHJAR left: hair, hâr, harad, haradren, harn[1]; hargam, harven, haradrim

KJ

√KJELEK swift, agile: celeg
√KJELEP silver: celeb, celebren, celefn

KW

√KWA complete
  √KWA-J ten: pae, paenui
  √KWA-N whole, all: pân[1]
  √KWA-T fill: panna-[2], pathra-, pathred, pant; iphant, penninor
√KWAJ (sound of) gull: poen, cuen
√KWAM sick: paw
√KWAR press together, squeeze, wring: paur, drambor, tegilbor
√KWE say, speak
  √KWE-N person: pen[2], calben, morben, orodben, rochben
  √KWE-T speak, utter words, say: pedi, pennas, pent, peth, pethron; athrabeth, dambeth, gobennas, gobennathren, ubed
√KWEL fade, wither (cf. √KEL, √TEL, √ŋGWAL): peli, peleth, pelin; lasbelin
√KWES feather: pesseg
√KWIG bow (cf. √KUH): peng

L

√LA no, not: al-, alfirin
√LAB move the tongue, lick: lam[1], lammas, lammen, lav-
√LAD[1] wide: land[1], camlann
√LAD[2] laugh: lalaith
  √G-LAD[2] laugh: gladha-
√LAG sword: lang
√LAJ grow green: laer[1]
  √LÁJ-AK green: laeg[1], laeb; laegel
  √G-LAJ grass: glae

√LAJK keen, sharp, acute: laeg[2]
√LAK[1] swift: lagor, legrin
√Á-LAK[1] rushing: alag, alagon, alagos, alph
√!LAK[2] flame: lach, lacha-; lachenn
√LÁLAM elm tree: lalf, lalven; lalorn
√LAM make a vocal sound, cry out: lam[2], lammad, lavan, lóven
√G-LAM inarticulate sound: glam, glamog, glamor, glamren, glavra-, glavrol; gellam, glamhoth
√LAN[1] weave: lain[2]; hithlain
√LAN[2] rim, edge, border, boundary, limit: lanc[3]
√G-LAN[2]: glân[2], gland, gleinia-; glandagol
√LAŋK throat: lanc[2]; tarlanc
√**LAP[1] baby**: laes
√LAP[2] hop: laba-
√LAS[1] leaf: las; athelas, lasbelin, lasgalen, golas
√LAS[2] hear: lasta-, lathra-, lathrada-, lathron, lethril
√S-LAS[2] ear: lhaw, lhewig
√LAT lie open (cf. **√LAD**): lâd, laden, land[2], lant[2]; imlad
√LATH string, thong: lath; hadlath
√LAW warm: laug
√G-LÁWAR golden light: glaur, glawar, glóren, glóriel; ninglor
√LEB stay, stick, adhere, remain, tarry: lefn; lefnir
√LED go, fare, travel (cf. **√DEL**): lend[2]; edledhi, edledhia-, edledhron, edlenn, lembas, neledhi
√G-LED go: anglenna-
√LEK loose, let loose, release: lain[1], leitha-, leithian; adleg-, adleitha-, adleithien
√LEP finger
√LEP-ET finger: lebed
√LÉP-EN five: leben, lefnui, lefnor
√!LES measure: lest
√!LEW snake: lŷg
√LI many: lae, laew
√G-LIB slippery substance: glaew, glûdh
√**!LIŋKW wet**: limmid-, limp
√LIN[1] water, pool (said to be related to √LIN[2]): lîn, ael
√LIN[2] sing: lend[1], lind[1], lind[2], linna-, linnod; aerlinn, dúlinn, emelin, tu-ilinn, gondolindren, gondolindrim, lindel, lindedhel, merilin
√G-LIN[2] sing: glinnel
√LINT swift: lint

√G-LIŋG hang: gling, glinga-
√LIR[1] sing, trill (cf. √LIN[2]): laer[2]
  √G-LIR[1] sing, trill: glîr, gliri, glaer
√LIR[2] row: lîr; aeglir, nothlir
√G-LIS honey: glî; medli, medlin
√!LÍSIK reed: lisc
√LIT sand: lith, lithui
√LIW fish: lim[2]; limlug
√LOG wet, soaked, swampy: lô, loeg, loen
√S-LOK bend, loop: lhûg; amlug, limlug
√LOKH hair: laus, loch
√LON haven: lond; aglonn, othlonn
√LOP horse: lobor
√LOS fallen snow: los[1], lossen; aeglos, lossoth
  √G-LOS snow-white: glos; uilos[1]
√LOTH flower: los[2], loth, lotheg; amloth, elloth, goloth, gwaloth, imloth, romloth, mallos, uilos[2]
√LU time: lû
√LUB weary: lom
√LUG heavy: long
√LUJ blue: luin
√LUK magic, enchantment: luith, luitha-, luithien
√LUM gloom, shade (cf. √DUB): lûm, lumren
√LUR be quiet, still, calm: lorn
√LUS empty: los[3], lost, lothren
√LUT float, swim: loda-, lunt

M

√MAD pale: maidh
√MAG use, handle (cf. √MAH): maed[2], maen, maenas, maer
√MAH hand (cf. √MAG): maed[1], matha-, maw[1], talf[2]
√MAJ good: mae
√MAK sword, fight with a sword, cleave: maeth, maetha-, maethor, magol, magor, megil
√MAL yellow
  √S-MAL yellow: mâl, malen, mall, mallen, malu; emelin, mallorn, mallos
  √MÁL-AT gold: malad, malt, malthen
√MAN holy spirit: mân
  √MAN-AD doom, final end, fate, fortune: manadh

√MAP lay hold of with hand, seize: mâb, mab-
√MÁSAG knead, soften by rubbing: mae[1], maeas
√MAT eat: mad-, mann; medli, medlin
√ME we (first-person plural pronominal): men, ammen
√MEL love as a friend: mela-, mail, meleth, melethril, melethron, mell, mellon, melui, mîl, milui, meldir, meldis, elvellon
√MEN way, region: mên; menel, forven, gilwen, gwelwen, rhuven, dúven, harven
√MENEK thousand: meneg
√MER feast, festive: meren, mereth
√MET end: medui, ment, meth, methed, methen
√MI inside (cf. √IMBI): mi
  √MI-N: min, minna-
√MIK pierce (cf. √MI): maeg, megor, maecheneb
√MIL desire, lust: mael[2], maelui
  √MÍL-IK greed: melch
√MIN stand alone, stick out: main, mîn, minai, minas, minui; miniel, minuial
√MIR jewel: mîr, mirian, míriel, mirion; mírdan, golovir
  √!Í-MIR crystal: ivor, ivrin
√MIS[1] go free, stray, wander: mist, mista-, mistad
√MIS[2] moist (cf. √MITH)
  √!MÍS[2]-ID fine rain: mîdh
  √!MÍS[2]-IK wet: mesc
√MITH grey, foggy (cf. √MIS[2]): mîth[1], mîth[2], mithren; mithril
√MIW[1] whine: maew, mŷl
√MIW[2] small, tiny, frail: mîw
√MO serve by labor: muda-, mûl
√MOJ dear: muin, muindor, muinthel
√MOR black, dark: maur, môr[1], môr[2], morn; galvorn, morben, morchant, morgul, mornedhel, merilin
√MORÓK bear: brôg
√!MOTH dusk: môth
√MUJ hidden: muil
√!MUND bull: mund

MB

√MBAKH exchange: bach, bachor, banga-
√MBAR dwell, inhabit: bâr
  √A-MBAR earth: amar; emerain

√MBÁRAT doom: barad, bartha-, amarth; úmarth
√MBAS knead: bas, bast; lembas, basgorn, bassoneth, bessain
√MBATH screen, shield: amath
√MBAW compel, force, subject, oppress: baug, baugla-, bauglir, baugron, baur, boe
√MBOTH pool: bôth
√MBUD project: bund; annabon

N

√NA: na-, nad
√NAB hollow: naw[1]
√NAD valley, wide plain (cf. √LAT): nadhor, nadhras, nan(d)
√NAJ lament: nae, naer, noe; naergon
√NÁJAK (cf. √NAJ, √NAK) pain: naeg, naegra-
√NAK bite: naes, naeth, naew, nag-, nagol; nírnaeth
  √Á-NAK jaw: anc
√!NAL, √!NJAL call out: nalla-
√NAN mother: nana, naneth
√NAR flame, fire: naru, naur, nórui; nartha-, narthan
  √A-NÁR sun: anor; elanor
√NÁRAK tear, rend: narcha-
√NAS point, sharp end: nas, nasta-; bennas, egnas
√NAT lace, weave, tie (cf. √NUT): nath, nathron; gonathra-, gonathras
√NE in, inside (cf. √NED) : ne-, nestag, neledhi
√NED middle: ned, nedh-, nest
  √É-NED center: enedh; ennor, emerain, enedhin
√NEG honeycomb: nîdh
√NEJ tear: nîd, nîn[2], níniel, nínui[1], nîr; nínim, nírnaeth
√NEK narrow: naith, dírnaith
√NEL[1] three: nêl[1], nel-, nelui; nelchaenen
  √NÉL[1]-ED three: neled; neldor
√NÉL[2]-EK tooth: nêl[2], neleg
√NEN water: nên, nend, nîn[1], nínui[2]; ninglor
√NEŋ nose: nem
√NÉTER nine: neder, nedrui
√NETH young, healthy: nesta-, nestad, nestadren, neth, nîth; díneth
√NI I (first person singular pronominal): im (acc. nin)
√NIB face, front: nîf
√NID[1] lean against: nedhu
√NID[2] force, pressure, thrust

√Í-NID[2] mind: ind, innas
√NIKW chill, cold: nimmid-, nimp, niphred; nínim, niphredil
√NIN fragile, thin: nind; ninniach
√!NIP small: niben; nibin-noeg
√NIR will, intention, conscious resolve to move or do
√I-NIR: idhor, idhren
√!NOR run: nor-
√NOT count, reckon: nedia-, nediad; arnediad, aronoded, genedia-, genediad, gonod-, gonoded, gwanod
√NOW think, form idea, imagine: nauth, nautha-, naw[2]
√NU under (cf. **√NDU**): nu, nûr[1]
√NU-R: nûr[1], nûr[2]
√NUK Dwarf, stunted, not reaching full growth or achievement, failing of some mark or standard: naug[1], naug[2], naugol, nogoth, nogotheg, nuitha-; nibin-noeg
√NUT tie, bind (cf. **√NAT**): nod-, naud, nûd

ND

√NDAK slay: daen, dag-, dagor, dagra-, dagrada-, dangen, daug; dagnir
√NDAM hammer, beat (cf. **√TAM**): dam, damma-
√NDAN back: dân; dambeth, danwaith, danwedh
√NDER man, adult male (<**√NER**): daer[2], dîr; ceredir, condir, curunír, dírnaith, dagnir, feredir, herdir, lefnir, meldir, randir
√NDEW follow, come after: dŷr
√NDI in: dî[1], dihena-
√NDIS woman (cf. **√INI**): dess, dî[2], dîs; díneth, meldis
√NDU go down, sink, set (cf. **√NU**): annui, annûn, annúnaid, dûn; dúnadan, dúnedhel, dúven

NJ

√NJAD gnaw: nâr
√NJAR tell, relate: ‡nara-, narn; trenar, trenarn
√NJEL ring, sing, give out a sweet sound: nell, nella-, nellad, nelladel

ŋ

√ŋAL shine by reflection: gâl, gail, gaul[1], glaw; uial, aduial, minuial, galvorn
√ŋAL-ÁN: glân[1], glanna-
√ŋAL-AT: galad

√ŋIL spark, silver glint: gael, gîl, gilion, gilith; gildin, gilgalad
√ŋOL smell: ûl, angol[2]

ŋG

√ŋGÁNAD play on a stringed instrument: gannel, gannada-, ganna-; talagan
√ŋGÁRAM wolf (cf. √ŋGAW): garaf
√ŋGAW howl (cf. √ŋGÁRAM): gaul, gaur, gawa-, gawad; gaurhoth, gaurwaith
√ŋGOL knowledge, wisdom, lore: goll, gollor, golu, golwen, gûl, angol[1]; morgul, guldur, durgul, peringol
  √ŋGOL-OD Noldo: golodh, golovir
√ŋGOROTH horror (cf. √ŋGUR[2]): goroth; gorgoroth
√ŋGOTH foe, enemy (cf. √KOTH, √GOS): goth, gûd
√ŋGUR[1] death: gorth[1], gûr, gurth, guruth; gorthad, guruthos
√ŋGUR[2] horror (probably related to √ŋGUR[1]): gôr[2], gorth[2], gortheb, gorthob, gorog; gorgor, gorgoroth
  √ŋGUR[2] -UK (cf. √RUK): gorog

ŋGW

√ŋGWAL torment (cf. √KWEL): balch, baul

ŋW

√!ŋWI first-person singular pronominal
  √!I-ŋWI: im[2]

O

√OJ ever, eternal: ui[1], ui[2], uir, uireb; uilos[1], uilos[2]
√ÓLOB branch: olf
√ÓL-OS dream, imagination: ôl, oltha-
√ONO beget, give birth to: onna-, onnen, odhril, odhron, ûn; abonnen, edonna-
  √(O)NO beget: nûr[3]; gwanûn, gwanunig, gwanur[1], gwanur[2], gwenyn
  √(O)NO-S family: nos, nost; nothlir, nothrim, drúnos
√!ONOT ent: onod
√ORO rise up, go high; up, high: or, or-, orn[1], eria-, ortha-, orthad; erin, orchall, ortheli, orthelian, orthor-
  √ÓR-ON (tall) tree: orn[2], eryn; huorn, lalorn, mallorn, neldor
  √ÓR-OT height, mountain: ôr, orod; orodben, orodrim
  √(O)S-RO east (arising, orient): rhu-, rhûn, rhúnen, rhuven; amrûn

√OS round, about: o[2], os-, osgar-
√OT seven
√OT-OK: odog
√OT-OS: odo, othui
√OT-OTH: odothui

P

√PA on: po
√PAD enclosure: pand; círbann
√PAL wide open (cf. √PAT[1]): palan-, palath, pelia-; palandiri
√PALÁP beat: blab-
√PAN place, set, fix in place: pân[2], panas, penia-
√PAR compose, put together: parf, partha-
√PÁRAK dry: parch
√PAT[1] wide open (cf. √PAL): pann, panna-[1]
√PAT[2] walk (cf. √BAT, √RAT): pâd, pada-; tharbad, aphada-, aphadon
√PATH smooth, level: path, pathu
√PED slope, slant down: pend, penna-; ambenn, dadbenn, pendrad, pendrath
√PEL revolve on a fixed point, go around, encircle: pelthaes
√PEL-ES encircled enclosure: pêl; gobel, ephel
√PEN lack, be without: pen[1]
√PER half: per-, perian, perin; peredhel, peringol
√PÉRES affect, disturb, alter: presta-, prestannen; prestanneth
√PIK small: pêg, pigen
√PIS juice: paich, pihen
√PIW spit (cf. √PHEW): puia-
√POJ clean, pure: puig
√POT animal's foot: pôd
√PUT stop, halt, pause: post

PH

√PHAJ radiate: fae, fael[1], fael[2], faen, faer
√PHAL foam: falf
√PHÁL-AS shore, beach: falas, faltha-, falathren, falathrim
√PHAR reach, go all the way, suffice: far, farn
√PHAS tangled hair: fast
√PHAW gape: faug
√PHÉLEG cave: fela
√PHEN door: fen(d), fennas

√PHÉREN beech tree: ‡fêr
√PHEW feel disgust at, abhor (cf. √PIW): fuia-
√PHILIK small bird: fileg, filigod
√PHIN hair: fîn, find, finnel
√PHIR exhale, expire, breathe out: fair, fern, físeb, firen, firi, firiath, firieth, firin, firion, firith; alfirin
√PHOR right: fôr, forn, forod, forodren, fuir; forgam, forven, forodrim, forodwaith
√PHUJ deep shadow of night: fuin

R

√RAB wall: ram, rammas, raw[1]
√RAD back, return: andrann
√RAG crooked (cf. √RÁJAK): raen[1]
√RAJ catch with a net: raeda-, raef, raen[2], raew[2]; cathrae
√RÁJAK crooked, wrong (cf. √RAG): raeg
√RAK stretch out, reach: raew[1], ranc
√RAM wing: rafn, renia-, roval
√RAN wander, stray, go on uncertain course: rain[1], raun, renia-; randir, cúron
√!RAP strap, rope: raph; talraph
√RAS stick up: ras, rasc, rast
  √A-RAS horned beast, deer: aras
√RAT(H) walk, climb (cf. √BAT, √PAT[2]): râd, rada-, rant, rath; athrada-, othrad, pendrad, andrath, gondrath, imrath, pendrath
√RAW roar: raw[2], raw[3]
√RAWT metal: raud[3]
√RE day: sîr[2]
√RED scatter, sow: redhi
  √E-RÉD seed: eredh
√REG edge, border, margin (cf. √RI): rain[2], edrain
√REK prick: rêg
  √E-RÉK thorn: erch, ercha-, ereg; eregdos
√!REM or √!REB mesh, net: rem[2], remmen
√REN recall, have in mind: rîn[2]
√!RET (Be): rêd
√RI edge (cf. √REG): rîw
√!RIB: rîf
√RIG twine, wreathe: rî, rîn[1], rîs; rían, riel, rien
√RIKH jerk, sudden move: rinc, ritha-

√RIL glitter, shine (of reflected light): rill; cenedril, mithril, silevril
√RIM many, numerous: rem[1], rim[1]; edhelrim, elrim, eledhrim, falathrim, faradrim, forodrim, galadhrim, gondolindrim, graurim, gwathuirim, haradrim, iathrim, nothrim, orodrim, rohirrim
√RIN circle: rind[1], rind[2]; ringorn, idhrinn
√RIŋG cold: rim[2], ring
√RIP rush, fly, fling: ribi, rimp, rimma-
√RIS cut, cleave (cf. √KIR-ÍS): ress, rest, ris, rist[1], rist[2], rista-
√ROD cave: raudh, rosta-
√ROJ[1] chase: rui(w), rŷn
√G-ROJ[2] ruddy, red: gruin
√ROK horse: roch, rochon; rochben, rochir, rohirrim
√ROM loud noise, horn-blast: rom, rû; romru, romloth
√RON arch over, roof in: rond, othronn
√ROS drip, spray of water (in fine droplets): ros[2], rost
√ROT
  √G-ROT dig, excavate, tunnel: grôd, groth, gathrod
  √S-ROT delve underground, excavate, tunnel: rhûd
√G-RUD[1] unshaped wood: grond
√!RUD[2] bald: rûdh
√RUK terrible shape: raug, ruith, balrog
  √G-RUK terror: graug, groga-, gruitha-
  √Ú-RUK bogey, orc: orch, urug, erchion
√RUN[1] flat of hand or foot: ruin[2], telluin
√RUN[2] red, glowing: ruin[1]
  √U-RUN[2] copper: urun
√RUS reddish-brown: ros[1], ros[3], rust, rustui
  √RÚS-UK fox: rusc
  √S-RÚS-UK russet: rhosc

S

√S- he, she, it (demonstrative stem) (cf. √SI): ha, he, ho
√SAB juice: saw
√SAD strip, flay, peel off: sâdh
√SAG bitter: saer, saew
√SAJ know, understand: sael
√SALÁK grass: salab
√SÁLAP lick up (cf. √LAB): salph
√SAR hard (cf. √STAR): sarn[1], sarn[2], sarnas, serni; edhelharn
√SAT limit, set apart: sâd, said, sant, seidia-; gorthad

√SED rest, peace: sîdh
  √É-SED repose: îdh
√SEL daughter (cf. √JEL): sell
√SEN let go, let loose, free: dihena-, gohena-
√SER love, be fond of: seron
√!SEREK blood: sereg; seregon
√SI this, here, now (cf. √S-): si, sí, sen,sîr[2], sui
  √SI-N new: sain, siniath; sinnarn
√SIK dagger, knife: sigil[1]
√SIL shine silver (cf. √THIL): síla-, silef[1], silef[2], silif, silith, silivren, silevril
√SIR flow: sîr[1], siria-, sirion, sirith; ethir[1], lanthir
√SIW excite, egg on, urge: hûl
√SJAD shear through, cleave: hâdh, hast, hasta-, hathel, hathol
√SJAL shell: half
√SKAL[1] screen, hide from light: escal, hall[2], haltha-
√SKAL[2] small fish: hâl, heledir(n)
√SKAR tear, rend: harn[2], harna-, haru, oscar-
  √A-SKAR tearing, hastening: ascar
√SKEL skin: heleth, helf, hell, heltha-
√SKJAP shore: habad
√SLIG web, thread: lhê, lhing, lhingril
√SLIN fine, delicate: lhain, lhind
√SLIW sickly: lhaew, lhîw
√SLON sound: lhûn
√SLUS whisper (cf. √SRUS): lhoss
√SMAG soil, stain: mael[1], maw[2]
√SNAR tie (cf. √SNUR): nardh
√SNEW entangle: nŷw
√SNUR twist (cf. √SNAR): nordh, norn
√SOT shelter, protect, defend
  √Ó-SOT fortress: ost; ostirion, othlonn, othrad, othronn
√SPAJ despise, contemn: faeg
√SPAN white: fain, fân, fanui, faun
√SPÁNAG beard: fang; anfang
√SPAR hunt, pursue: fara-, farad, faradrim, feredir, faras, faron, faroth
√SRAB wild, untamed: rhavan, rhaw[1], rhovan
√SRAW flesh, body: rhaw[2]
√SRIP scratch: rhibi
√SRIW winter: rhîw
√SRUS whisper (cf. √SLUS): rhoss

√STAB build (of wood): thafn, tham, thamas, thavron; sam
√STAK split, insert: thanc
√STÁL-AG valiant, firm (cf. √STEL): thala, thalion[1], thalion[2]
√STAN fix, decide: thenid, thenin
√STAR (cf. **√SAR**) **stiff:** thâr, tharas, tharn, gwastar
√STEL remain firm (cf. **√STAL**): theli, thelion
  √E-STEL hope: estel
√STÉLEG spear point: thela, ecthel
√STINT short (cf. **√TIT**): thent, thinnas, estent
√STIR face (cf. **√TIR**): thîr
√SUG drink (cf. **√SUK**): sûl[1]
√!SUJ or **√!SOJ greet:** suilanna-, suilad
√SUK drink (cf. **√SUG**): sautha-, soga-, suith
√SÚLUK edible root: solch
√SWAD fungus: hwand
√SWES noise of blowing or breathing: hwest
√SWIN whirl, eddy: hwîn, hwind, hwinia-, hwiniol

T

√T- he, she, it (demonstrative stem) (cf. √TA): tîn
√TA that, there, then (cf. **√T-**): taw[3]
  √TA-N show, indicate: tann; narthan
√TAH high, lofty (cf. **√TAR**): taen[2]
√TAJ[1] extend, lengthen: taen[1]
√TÁJ[2]-AK mark, line, limit: taeg
√TAK[1] fix, make fast: tachol, taes, taetha-, taew, tanc, tangada-; pelthaes
  √A-TAK[1] construction: adab
√TAK[2] mark (a boundary): taig, tagol
√TAL[1] foot: tâl; tad-dal, talraph, telluin
  √TAL[1]-AM floor, base, ground: talaf
√TAL[2] flat (cf. √LAT): talan, talath, talf[1], talu; talf[2]
√TALÁT slip, slide, fall down (cf. √DAT): talad, talt
  √Á-TALAT fall down: adlann, adlanna-, adlant
√TAM knock (cf. √NDAM): tamma-, tavor
√TAN make, fashion: tân; calardan, cennan, círdan, mírdan
√TAŋG twang: tang
√TAP stop, block: tafnen, uidafnen
√TAR high (cf. √TAH): taur[1], taur[2]
√TÁRAG tough, stiff: tara, tarias; tarlanc
√TARÁK animal horn: tarag

√TÁRAS trouble: tas, trasta-
√TÁTHAR willow tree: tathar, tathor, tathren
√TÁWAR wood, forest: taur[3], tauron, tawar, tawaren; tawarwaith
√TEH line, direction: tê, tî, tîr[1]
√TEK make a mark, write, draw (cf. √TEŋ): taith, tegil, tegol, teitha-; andaith, tegilbor
√TEL close, end, come at the end (cf. √KEL, √KWEL): telu, teler; daedelu, orthel-, orthelian
  √TÉL-ES rear: adel, tele
√TÉLEK stalk, stem, leg: telch
√TEŋ indicate, signify (cf. √TEK): têw
√TER pierce: tre-, trî, trîw; trenar-, trenarn, trevad-, godref
√TIL point: till, tilias; niphredil, nelthil
√TIN spark, sparkle, glint: tinna-, tinnu, tint, tinu; gildin, ithildin, tinúviel
√TIŋK metal: tinc
√TIR look, watch, guard, gaze (cf. √STIR): tîr[2], tíra-, tiri, tiria-, tirion, tirith, tirn, tirnen; amdir, ethir[2], gwachaedir, heledir(n), ostirion, palandiri
√TIT little (cf. √STINT): tithen
√TIW fat, thick: tuia-, tûg
√TOL[1] eight:
  √TOL[1]-OD eight: tolodh, tollui
  √TOL[1]-OTH eight: toloth, tolothen
√TOL[2] island: toll
√TOR brother: gwador
  √TOR-ON brother: tôr; muindor
√TOW wool: taw[1], taw[2]
√TUB deep: tofn, tûm
√TUG muscle: tû, tong
√TUJ spring, sprout: tuia-, tui(w), ethuil; tuilinn
√TUK draw, bring: tog-
√TUL come, approach, move towards: tol-, toltha-
√TULUK firm, strong: tolog, tulu
√TUMP hump: tump
√TUN high hill: tond, tund
√TUP roof over, cover over, hide: taus, toba-, tobas
  √U-TUP cover: udûn
√TUR power, control, mastery, victory: taur[1], tortha-, tûr[1], tûr[2], orthor-
  √TUR-UK strong: torog
√TUS bush: toss; eregdos

TH

√THAG press: thang, úthaes, úthaeth
√THAN kindle, set light to: thoniel
√THAR across, beyond: thar-; tharbad
  √Á-THAR beyond: athar, athra-, athrad; athrabeth
√THAW detestable: thaur[1]
√THE look, see, seem: thia-
√THEL sister: gwathel
  √THEL-ES sister: thêl; muinthel
√THIL shine with white light (cf. **√SIL**): thîl, thilia-, thilion
  √I-THÍL moon: ithil; ithildin
√THIN grey: thin, thind, thinna-
√THON pine tree: thôn, thonion
√THOR swoop down: thôr[1], thorod
  √THOR-ON eagle: thôr[2], thoron
√THU puff, blow: thuia-, thûl, sûl[2]
  √THU-S foul, putrid: thaw, thû
√THUD base, ground: thond
√THUR surround, fence, ward, hedge in, make secret: thaur[2], thora-, thoren, thurin

TJ

√TJAL play: teilia-, teilien; talagan
√TJUL stand up straight: tulus

U

√U not, ill (cf. **√GU**, **√UM**): ú-, úan, uanui, ubed, úgarth, uluithiad, úmarth
√UB abound: ovor, ovra-, ovras
√UJ seaweed: uil, aeruil
√UL[1] pour out: elia-, oll
√ÚL[2]-UG horrible: ul-, ulunn
√UM evil (cf. **√U**): ûm
√!UŋG spider: ungol
√UR[1] hot: ûr[1], úrui, aur; bregedur; edinor, ilaurui, lefnor, penninor
√UR[2] wide, large: ûr[2]
√ÚSUK smoke: osp

W

√WA-N goose: gwaun
√WAH stain, soil: gwaen, gwass, gwath, gwatha-, gwaur; agarwaen

√WAJ enfold: goe[2]
√WAJW blow: gwaeren, gwaew
√WAR give way, yield, not endure, let down, betray: gweria-, gwarth
√A-WAR forsake: awarth, awartha-
√WATH shade: gwâth, gwathra-, gwathren, gwathui; gwathuirim, dúath
√Á-WATH shade: auth[2]
√WED bind: gwaedh, gwêdh, gwedhi, gwend[1], gwest, gwesta-, gowest; angwedh, danwedh
√WEJ wind, weave: gwî
√WEG vigor, manliness: gwê, gwaith; danwaith, denwaith, eluwaith, forodwaith, gaurwaith, tawarwaith
√WEN maiden: gwên, gweneth; arwen, ivonwen
√WÉN-ED maiden: gwend[2]
√WIL fly, float in the air: gwelu, gwelwen, gwilith, gwilwileth
√WIN new: gwain
√!WIŋ scatter, blow about: gwing
√WIND pale blue: gwind
√WO together: go-, gwa-; genedia-, genediad, gobel, gobennas, gobennathren, gochel, godref, gohena-, golas, gonathra-, gonathras, gonod-, gonoded, govad-, govannen, gowest, gwador, gwaloth, gwanod, gwanûn, gwanunig, gwanur[1], gwanur[2], gwastar, gwenyn

Words of Uncertain Derivation

aen, cordof, echad, edraith, edregol, egor, eneth, estolad, falch, fim, flâd, galenas, gelir, gwael, habar, hol-, hollen, iach, lanc[1], lebethron, lim[1], luithia-, meril, nef, neitha-, neithan, ninniach, parth, pind, rach, rhast, rhach, sarch, sedryn, sennui, sigil[2], torech, torn, trann, trannail, thand, thôl, uluithiad

Appendix 4

An English-Sindarin Glossary

A

abandon: awartha-
abandonment: awarth
abhor: fuia-
abhorrence: delos, deloth
abhorrent: thaur[1]
abiding: him[2], thenid, thenin
able, be: gar-
abominable: deleb, thaur[1]
abound: ovra-
about: o[2], os-
above: or
abundant: ovor
abyss: iâ, dath
according to: be
account: pennas, trenarn
across: ath-, athar, thar-
action, readiness for: hûr
acute: laeg[2]
administrative district: trann
affect: presta-
affected: prestannen
affection (alteration): prestanneth
affection (love): mîl
affliction: caul
after: ab-
again: ad-, dan
against: ad-, dan
age (era): andrann
age, old, suffering from: ingem
aged: iphant
agile: celeg
ago: ia, io
ah!: ai[1], alae
air (musical): lind[1]
air (region): gwelwen, gwilith
air (substance): gwelu
alas: nae
alive: cuin
alive, be: cuina-
all: pân[1]
allegiance, hold (to): buia-
alone: er-, eriol, erui
alphabet: angerthas, certhas
always: ui[2]
always snow-white: uilos[1]
amputate: oscar-
anchorage: lorn
ancient: iaur
and: a[2]
anemone, a kind of: uilos[2]
anger: ruith
angle: bennas, nas
animal: lavan
animal's foot: pôd
annals: ínias
anniversary day: edinor
answer: dambeth, dangweth
anybody: pen[2]
apparition, spectral or vague: auth[2]
appear: thia-
apple, small red: cordof
approach: anglenna-
appropriate (to special purpose or owner): seidia-
apt to die: fíreb
arch: cû
area, limited (naturally or artificially defined): sâd
arise: eria-
arm: ranc
around: os-
arrange: partha-
art: maenas
article (for exchange): bach
artificial cave: rhûd
as: be
ash: lith
ashen: lithui
ashy: lithui
assembly: hûd
at: na
athwart: thar-
autumn: dannas, dant, iavas, lasbelin
Avar: lefn, lefnir, morben
awakening: echui(w)
away: e[1]
awe: anwar
awful: gaer[1], taur[1]
axe: hathol
axe-blade: hathel
axe-stroke: hast

B

babble: glavra-
babbling: glavrol
babe: laes
back: ad, dan
bad: faeg, ûm
bald: rûdh
ball: coron
ban: boda-
bane: dagnir
bank (e.g., of river): raw[1]
bark: rîf
barrow: gorthad, haudh

battle: auth, dagor, maeth
battle, do: dagra-, dagrada-
bay: côf
bay, small landlocked: hûb
be: na-
be able: gar-
be compelled: heria-
be off!: ego
beach: falas
beacon: narthan
bear (*n.*): brôg, medli
beard: fang
bearer: cyll
bearish: medlin
bears, of: medlin
beat: dringa-
beat (wing): blab-
beaten track: bâd
beautiful: bain
bed: haust
bed, lying in: cael
bedridden: caeleb
beech tree: fêr, neldor
beech, tree resembling: mallorn
beget: edonna-, onna-
begin suddenly and vigorously: heria-
begun again: eden
behind: ab-, adel
bell: nell
bells, ringing of: nelladel
bells, sound: nella-
bells, sound of: nellad
beneath: dî, dî[1]
bent: cûn
beryl: edhelharn
betray: gweria-
betrayer: gwarth
between: im[1], mi
beyond: athar, thar-
bind: gwedhi, nod-
biped: tad-dal
birch tree: brethil
bird, small: aew, fileg, filigod
bird, yellow: emelin
birds, of: aewen
bite: nag-
biting: naeth
bitter: saer
bitter cold: helch
black: donn, môr[1], morn
blade (of broadsword or axe): hathel
blazing fire: ruin[1]
blood: agar, iâr, sereg
bloodstained: agarwaen
blossom: gwaloth, loth
blow: dram
blow with fist: drambor
blue: luin
blue, pale: elu, gwind
board, fixed in floor: pân[2]
boat: lunt
bodily strength: bellas
body: rhaw[2]
body, strong in: bell
bogey: urug
bold: beren, cand
bolster: nedhu
bond: gwaedh, gwêdh, gwend[1], nûd
book: parf
border: edrain, glân[2], rain[2], rîw
born: onnen
born after or later: abonnen
boss (e.g., of shield): dolt
both: ui-
bound (*adj.*): naud
bound (*v.*): gleinia-
boundary: gland, lest, taeg
boundary line: taeg
boundary marker: glandagol
bounded place: gardh
bow (bent shape, weapon): cû
bow (weapon): peng
bowed: cûn
bow-shaped: cûn
bowstring: tang
braided tress of hair: finnel
branch: olf
brand: ylf[2]
bread: bas, bast
'bread-giver': bassoneth, bessain
breaker (wave): falf
break out suddenly: breitha-
breath: hwest, thûl
breathe: thuia-
breeze: hwest
breve: thinnas
bride: dî[2], díneth, dîs
bridge: iant, ianu
bright-colored: calen
bright light: gail, galad
bright spark: gîl
brilliance: aglar, galad, rill
brilliance, gleaming: fael[2]
brilliant: celair
bring: tog-
brink: lanc[3]
broadsword blade: hathel
brooch: tachol
broth: salph
brother: gwanur[1], muindor, tôr
brother, sworn: gwador
brown: baran, rhosc
bud: tui(w)
build: car-
builder: thavron
building: adab, car(dh)[1]
bull: mund
burden, heavy: caul
burial mound: haudh
burn: dosta-
burning: ruin[1]
bush: tos
butterfly: gwilwileth
by: na

C

cairn: sarnas
cake of meal: cram
call: can-, esta-
calligraphy, one skilled in: tegilbor
camp: echad
can (*v.*): gar-

canopy: daedelu, orthelian
cape (of land): bund, cast, rast
captain: hest
carpenter: thavron
catch: gad-
catch in a net: raeda-
cause pain: naegra-
causeway: gondrath
cave: fela, gathrod, grôd, groth, rond
cave, artificial: rhûd
cave, fortress in: othronn
cavern: gath, rond
cavernous: raudh
ceiling, vaulted: rond
center: enedh
central lands: Ennor
cessation: post
chain: angwedh
chair: ham, hanu
chamber: sam
champion: raud[2]
chant: linna-
charm: luith
chase, hound of: rŷn
chasm: iâ
cheat: gweria
chief (*adj.*): main
child: hên
choking: faug
circle: corn[2], rind[2], ringorn
circle, outer: echor
circular: corn[1], rind[1]
circular enclosure: cerin
city: minas
clamor: caun[1]
clan: nos
clasp (*n.*): taew
claw: gamp
clean: puig
clear (*adj.*): lim[1], glân[1]
clear (*v.*): glanna-
cleared: laden
clearing in forest: lant[2]
cleave: rista-
cleaver: crist, hâdh, rist[2]
cleft (*adj.*): thanc
cleft (*n.*): cîl, cirith, cris, iaw[2], rest, rist[1]
cleft, deep: falch
clenched fist: drambor
clever: maen
climb (*n.*): rath
climb, long: andrath
climbing path: rath
cloak: coll[3]
close: hol-
closed: hollen, tafnen
clothe: hab-, hamma-
clothing: hammad
cloud: fân, faun
cloudy: fanui
club: grond
co-: gwa-
coast: falas
cobweb: lhing
coin, kind of: mirian
cold: ring
cold, bitter: helch
cold pool or lake: rim[2]
collection of flowers: gwaloth
collection of leaves: golas
com-: gwa-
come: tol-
come together: govad-
commander: caun[3]
commanding: conui
compact (*n.*): gowest, gwaedh
compelled, be: heria-
compelled to, one is: boe
complete: pant
completely: tre-
compose: partha-
compulsion: thang
conceal: delia-, doltha-
conceive (in mind): nautha-
concerning: o[2]
confirm: tangada-
confused noise: glam
confused yelling of beasts: glam
conquer: orthor-
constrain: baugla-
constrainer: bauglir, baugron
continually: him[2]
contorted: norn
contract: gowest
contrivance: gaud
control (*n.*): tûr[1]
control (*v.*): tortha-
cooked food: aes
cool: him[1]
copper (*adj.*): rustui
copper (*n.*): urun, rust
copper-colored: gaer[2], ros[1]
cord: nordh
core: enedh
corn (grain, not maize): iaw[1]
corner: nas
corpse: daen
corrupt: thaw
counsel (*v.*): gor-
count (*n.*): genediad
count (*v.*): nedia-
countenance: thîr
countless: aronoded
count up: gonod-
course: rant, rath, ŷr
courtyard: pand
cover (*v.*): toba-
cover that hides: escal
crabbed: norn
craft: curu, maenas
craft, man of: curunír
craftsman: tân
creature: ûn
creature, deformed and hideous: ulunn
crescent: cû
crescent moon: cúron
crest of helmet: amloth
crooked: raen
cross (*v.*): athra-, athrada-
crossing: athrad, iach
crossway: tharbad
crow: corch, craban
crowd: hoth, ovras, rim[1]
crown: rî

crowned: rîn[1]
crowned lady: rien, rîn[1]
cruel: balch, baug
cry (*n.*): caun[1]
cry (*v.*): nalla-
cry of encouragement in battle: hûl
cry out: can-, nalla-
crystal: ivor
crystalline: ivrin
cunning (*adj.*): coru
cunning (*n.*): curu
cunning device: curu
curse: rhach
cushion: nedhu
custody: band
custom: haew
cut (*n.*): cris, rest
cut (*v.*): rista-
cutlass: lang
cut round: oscar-
cutter: rist[2]
cutting: cirith
cycle (of time): andrann

D

daddy: ada
dagger: sigil[1]
daily: ilaurui
daisy: eirien
damp: nîd
dangle: glinga-
dare: bertha-
dark: doll, dûr, graw, môr[1], morn
dark brown: baran
dark Elf: dúredhel, dúrion, mornedhel
dark magic: morgul
darkness: dû, fuin, môr[2], morn
dark people: graurim
dark shadow: dúath
dark sorcery: guldur
daughter: iell, sell
dauntless: thalion[1]
dauntless man: thalion[2]
dawn: minuial
day: aur
day, last (of the year): penninor
daytime: calan
dazzling white: glos
dead: fern, gorth[1], gwann
dead of night: fuin
dead person: fern, gorth[1]
dead, place of the: gorthad
deadly: delu
deadly fear: gorgor, gorgoroth
dear: mail, mell, muin
death: gûr[2], gurth, guruth
death, act of: gwanath, gwanu
death, dread of: guruthos
death of Elves by fading or weariness: gwanu
declivity: pend
deed: cardh[2]
deep: nûr[1], tofn
deep, going in: maeg
deep cleft: falch
deep lore: angol[1]
deep vale: im[3]
deep valley: imlad
deep valley among hills: tûm
deer: aras
debate: athrabeth
defend: gartha-
defile: aglonn
defined place: gardh
deformed creature: ulunn
dell: im[3]
delved mine: habar
delving: grôd, groth
demon: raug
denial: ubed
depart: gwanna-
departed: gwann, gwanwen
departed spirit: mân
deprive: neitha-
deprived: neithan
descendant: iôn
desert: eru
desire (*v.*): aníra-
detestable: thaur[1]
detestation: delos, deloth
device: gaud
dew: mîdh, ros[2]
dialect: lam[1]
die: firi, gwanna-
difficulty: tarias
dim (*adj.*): gwathren
dim (*v.*): gwathra-
dim light: gwâth
dim shape: auth[2]
din: glam
dire: goeol
dirty: gwaur
disease: lhîw
disgust: dêl
disgust (i.e., feel d. at): fuia-
distance, remote: haered
distant: hae, haer, haeron
distinct: minai
district, administrative: trann
disturb: presta-
divine: bâl
divine power: bâl
divinity: bâl
division of realm: trann
do: car-
doer: ceredir
dog: hû
doing: cared
dome: telu
don't: av-, avo, baw
doom (*n.*): amarth, band, manadh
doom (*v.*): bartha
doomed: barad[2]
door: and[2], annon, fen(d), fennas
dot: pêg
double: edaid, tadol
dough: maeas
dove: cugu
down (*adv*): dad
down (*n.*): torn
downhill: dadbenn

downward: dad
dragon: amlug, lhûg
drain (*v.*): sautha-
draught: suith
draw: teitha-
dread: achas, delos, deloth, gae, gôr[2], goroth, gorth[2], gos, gost
dread, great: daedhelos, daedheloth
dreadful: gaer[1], naer
dread of death: guruthos
dream (*n.*): ôl
dream (*v.*): oltha-
dreariness: muil
drink: soga-
drinking vessel: ylf[1]
driven under compulsion: horn
dry: parch
dry, very: apharch
dungeon: gador
Dunlendings: Gwathuirim
duress: band, thang
dusk: dû, môth, tinnu
dusky: doll
dust: ast, lith
Dwarf: gonhir, hadhod, naug[2], naugol, nogoth, norn
dwarfed: naug[1]
Dwarflet: nogotheg
Dwarves: dornhoth
dwell: dortha-
dwelling: bâr
dwelling, enclosed: gobel
dwelling, underground: grôd, rhûd
dwelling place: dôr
dying, act of: gwanath, gwanu

E

eager: bara
eagle: thôr[2], thoron
ear: lhewig
early night (moonless): tinnu
ears (two): lhaw
earth: amar, bâr, cae, ceven
earthen: cefn
earthenware: cefnas
east: amrûn, rhu-, rhûn, rhuven
eastern: rhúnen
eat: mad-
eavesdrop: lathra-, lathrada-
eavesdropper: lathron, lethril
echo: glamor, lam[2], lamed, lammad
echoing: glamren, loven
echoing voice: lam[2]
edible root: solch
eddy (*v.*): hwinia-
edge: rîw
edge, sharp: lanc[3]
eight: tolodh, toloth
eighth: tollui, tolothen
elder: einior
eldest: iarwain
elephant: annabon
Elf: edhel, eledh, elen, ell-[1]
Elf, dark: dúredhel, dúrion
Elf, Grey-: Send
Elf-friend: elvellon
Elf-man: ellon
Elf of Aman: gwanwen, gwanwel
Elf of Beleriand: dúnedhel
Elf of light: calben
Elf of the Falathrim: egol
Elf or human: eruchen
Elf-stone: edhelharn
Elf-woman: elleth
elm-tree: lalf, lalorn, lalven, lalwen
Elves: edhelrim, eledhrim, elrim
Elves, silvan: tawarwaith
Elvish: edhellen
embers: iûl
eminent: orchall, raud[1]
eminent man: raud[2]
employ (*v.*): iuitha-
empty: cofn, lost
encampment: estolad
enchant: luitha-
enchantress: luithien
encircling fence: ephel
enclose: gleinia-
enclosed dwelling: gobel
enclosure: pêl
end (*adj.*): methen
end (*n.*): meth, methed, tele
end, final: manadh
end, lower: tâl
end, sharp: nas
end, sudden: lanc[3]
endless: aronoded
endurance: bronwe
endure: brenia-, dartha-
endured, long: brûn
enduring: bronadui
enemy: coth[2], goth, gûd
enlaced: raen[2]
enlarge: panna-[1]
enmesh: gonathra-
enmity: coth[1]
enough (*adj.*): far
enough (*adv.*): farn
ent: onod
entangle: gonathra-
entanglement: gonathras
enter: minna-, neledhi
envelope of Outer Sea and Air: goe[2]
error: mist, mistad
especially: edregol
establish: tangada-
established, long: brûn
estuary: ethir[1]
eternal: ui[1], uireb
eternity: uir
evendim: aduial
evening: aduial, thîn
evening, grow toward: thinna-
evening, late: dû
evening, starlit: tinnu
ever: ui[2]

ever-closed: uidafnen
everlasting: ui[1]
'evermind': uilos[2]
evil (*adj.*): ûm
evil fate: úmarth
evil knowledge: gûl
exalted: arth, hall[1]
excavate: rosta-
excavation: grôd
excavation, large: groth
exceedingly: dae[3]
exclamation of wonder: elo
excluded: said
exile (person): edledhron
exile, go into: edledhi, edledhia
exiled: edlenn
expression: thîr
extended point at side: rafn
extreme horror: gorgor
eye: hend
eyed: heneb

F

fabric made in Lórien: hithlain
face: nîf, thîr
fade: firi, peli, thinna-
fading: firith, peleth
faintness: hwîn
fair (beautiful): bain
fair-minded: fael[1]
faith: estel
faithful ones: sedryn
Falathrim: Eglain
fall (*n.*): dannas, dant, lant[1], pend
fall (*v.*): danna-
fall, steep: dath
fallen: dannen
falling (*adj.*): talt
falling (*n.*): dannas, dant
fallow: maidh, malu
family: bâr, nos, nost, nothrim
family line: nothlir
family of wild men: drúnos
family tree: nothlir
fane: iaun
fang: carch
fantastic: hwiniol
far: hae, haer, haeron
far away (*n.*): haered
far off: palan
farthing: canath
fashion: echad-
fast: avorn
fasten: taetha-
fat: tûg
fate: amarth, manadh
fated: amarthan
father: ada, adar
'father of men': adanadar
fathom: raew[1]
fawn (*adj.*): maidh
fear: achas, dêl, delos, deloth, gôr[2], niphred
fear, deadly: gorgor, gorgoroth
fear exceedingly: gosta-
fear, great: daedhelos, daedheloth, goe[1]
fearful: gaer[1]
feast: mereth
feat: cardh[2]
feel: matha-
feel disgust at: fuia-
feel terror: groga-
fell (*adj.*): delu, goeol
female (*adj.*): inu
fence (*n.*): iâd, iâth, lest, pêl
fence (*v.*): thora-
fence, encircling: ephel
fence (of stakes): cail
fence, outer: ephel
fenced: thaur[2], thoren
fenced field: pêl
fenland: lô
festival: mereth
festive: meren
fetch: toltha-
field: parth, sant
field, low and flat: talf[1]
fierce: braig, bregol
fierceness: bregolas
fiery: bara, nórui
fiery red: ruin[1]
fiery spirit: hûr
fifth: lefnui
fight (*n.*) (of two or a few): maeth
fight (*v.*): maetha-
filament, spider: lhê
fill: panna-[2], pathra-
final: methen
final end: manadh
find a way: rada-
fine (excellent): brand
fine (very slender): lhind, trîw
fine thread: lhê
finger: lebed
fire: naur, ûr[1]
fire, blazing: ruin[1]
'fire-sign': narthan
firm: tanc, thala, thenid, thenin
firm, make: tangada-
first: erui, main, mîn, minui
fish: lim[2], hâl
fish-dragon: limlug
fist: paur
fist, blow with: drambor
fist, clenched: drambor
fit (*adj.*): maer
five: leben
fix: penia-
fixed board in floor: pân[2]
flag, yellow (flower): ninglor
flame (*n.*): naur, rill
flame (*v.*): lacha-
flame (leaping): lach
flame, red: ruin[1]
flap: blab-
flat: laden, talu
flat field: talf[1]
flatlands: talath
flat of hand: talf[2]
flat surface: talath
flee: drega-
flesh: rhaw[2]

flet: talan
fling: ribi
float: loda-
floor: panas, talaf
floor, fixed board in: pân[2]
flow: siria-
flow like a torrent: rimma-
flower: los[2], loth
flower, like pimpernel: elanor
flower, single: elloth, lotheg, lothod
flowering valley: imloth
flowers, collection of: gwaloth
flowing (*adj.*): cell
flowing (*n.*): sirith
fly: renia-, ribi
flying: rimp
flying spray: gwing
foam (*n.*): falf, gwing, ros[2]
foam (*v.*): faltha-
foe: gûd
fog: hîth, hithu
fog, white: mîth[2]
foggy: hethu, hithui
foliage: golas
follow: aphada
follower: aphadon, bŷr, echil
food: mann
food, cooked: aes
food, liquid: salph
foot: tâl
foot, animal's: pôd
foot, sole of: telluin
footprint: ruin[2]
for: an
ford: athrad, iach
forest: glâd, taur[3], tawar
forest, clearing in: lant[2]
forester: tauron
forest-people: tawarwaith
forgive: dihena-, gohena-
forked: thanc
formed: cadu
former: iaur
forsake: awartha-
forsaken: eglan
fort: barad[1], garth, minas
forth: e[1]
for the: 'ni
fortress: barad[1], garth, ost
fortress in cave: othronn
fortress with a watchtower: ostirion
fortune: manadh
fortune, good: galu
foul: thaur[1]
four: canad
fourth: cannui
fourth part: canath
fox: rusc
fragile: nind
frail: mîw
free: lain[1]
free, set: leitha-, adleg-, adleitha-
freed: lain[1]
freeing: leithian
frequent: rem[1], laew
fresh: laeb, laeg[1]
freshet: celos
friend: meldir, meldis, mellon, seron
friendly: milui
friendship: gwend[1]
frog: cabor
from: o[1]
from the: uin
front: nîf
full: pant
fullness: pathred
fungus: hwand
fur: heleth, helf
fur coat: heleth
further: hae

G

gap: dîn[1], gas
garden: sant
garland: rî
garlanded maiden: riel
garment: hamp
garth: pêl
gasping: faug
gate: and[2], annon
gateway: fennas
gay: meren
gaze: tiri, tiria-
generous: fael[1]
germ: eredh
giddiness: hwîn
giddy: hwiniol
gift: ann, ant
girdle: lest
girl: gwên, iell, sell
give: anna-
giver (*f.*): oneth
giving (*n.*): anneth
gladden (flower): ninglor
gladdens, (full) of: ningloron
glance (*n.*): glind, tîr[2]
glance at: glinna-
glass: heledh
gleaming brilliance: fael[2]
glen: imlad
glimmering: gael
glint (*v.*): tinna-
glint, silver: gîl
glisten: thilia-
glister: thilia-
glitter: aglar, ros[3]
glittering (reflected) light: rill
glittering reflection: galad
glittering white: silivren
globe: coron
globed: corn[1]
gloom: daw, dim[2], fuin, maur
gloomy: dem, dofn, duvui
glorify: egleria-
glorious: aglar
glory: aglar, claur
gnashing of teeth (in grief): naeth
go: bad-
goblet: sûl[1]
go in: neledhi
going deep in: maeg
going up: am
go into exile: edledhi, edledhia-

gold (color): mall
gold (light): glawar
gold (metal): malad, malt
gold, of: malthen
golden: glóren, glóriel, mallen, malthen
golden brown: baran
golden light: glaur
golden light, shining with: glóriel
gone: bannen
good (of things): maer
good fortune: galu
goose: gwaun
gore (point): naith, cên, cîn
gorge: cîl
grasp: mab-
grass: glae
grass, stiff: thâr
grassland: nan(d)
grassland (enclosed): parth
grave: haudh, sarch
gravel: brith
great: beleg, dae[1], daer[1]
great door: annon
great dread: daedhelos, daedheloth
great fear: daedhelos, daedheloth, goe[1]
great gate: annon
great hall: thamas
great jewel: mirion
great number: rim[1], lae
great ocean: aearon, gaearon, gaeron
great province: ardhon
great region: ardhon
great stone: gond
great watchtower: tirion
great wing: roval
great wood: taur[3]
greedy: melch
green: calen, laeg[1]
Green-Elf: Laegel, Lindel, Lindedhel
green leaves, having: lasgalen
green of leaf: lasgalen
greet: suilanna-
greeting: suilad
grey: mithren, thind
grey (pale): mîth[1]
Grey-Elf: Send
gross (144): host
ground: talaf
grow: gala-
growth: galas
grow toward evening: thinna-
guard (*n.*): tirith
guard (*v.*): tiri, tiria-
guarded: tirnen, thoren
guarding: tirith
guess: inc
guilty: crumguru
gulf: iâ, iaw[2]
gull: gwael, maew, mŷl
gull, small: cuen, paen

H

habit: haew
hack through: hasta-
hail!: ai[1]
hair, braided tress of: finnel
hair (general): find
hair, lock of: find
hair, shaggy: fast
hair (single): fîn
hairnet: cathrae
half: per-, perin
half-Elf: peredhel, peringol
halfling: perian
half-Noldor: peringol
hall: tham
hall, great: thamas
hall, rockhewn: rhûd
hall with vaulted roof: rond
halt (*n.*): post
halt (*v.*): dar-
hammer (*n.*): dam, dring
hammer (*v.*): damma-
hand: cam, mâb, maw[1]
hand, flat of: talf[2]
hand, left: crûm
hand, palm of: camlann
hand, right: fuir
hand, tightly closed: paur
handicraft: maenas
handle: matha-
handy: maed[1]
hang: glinga-
hanging: gling
Harad, people of: Haradrim
harass: trasta-
harbor: hûb, lond, lorn
harborage: hobas
hard: norn
harp (*n.*): gannel
harp (*v.*): ganna-, gannada-
harp player: talagan
hasp: taew
hasty: gorn[1]
hat: carab
hateful: delu
have: gar-
have an impulse: heria-
haven: círbann, hûb, lond, lorn
having eyes: heneb
he: e[2], ho
head: dôl
headland: cast
heal: nesta-
healing: nestad
healing, of: nestadren
heap: cûm, ovras
hearer: lathron, lethril
heart: gûr[1], hû-, hûn, ind
heat: ûr[1]
heat, white: bras
heaven: menel
heavy: long
heavy burden: caul
heavy stroke: dram
hedge: cai
hedge of spikes: caraes
height (summit): taen[2]
heir: hîl, rêd
hell: band, udûn
helm: thôl
helmet: harn[3]

hem: glân[2], rîw
herb: salab
here: sí
hero: callon, thalion[2]
hew: drava-
hewn: drafn
hewn log: drafn
hewn stone: drafn, gondrafn
hidden: dolen, hall[2], thoren, thurin
hideous: uanui, ul-
hideous creature: ulunn
high: ar-[1], brand, hall[1], or, raud[1], taur[1]
high roof: telu
highway, raised stone: gondrath
hill: amon, dôl, tund
hindmost part: tele
his (of nonsubject): tîn
his (of subject): în[2]
historical: gobennathren
history: gobennas, pennas
hither (*adj.*): nef
hold: gar-
hold allegiance to: buia-
holder: taew
hole: dath, gas, torech
hollow: coll[1], naw[1], raudh
hollow out: rosta-
holly tree: ereg, eregdos, rêg
home: bâr
honey: glî
honeycomb: nîdh
hook: gamp
hop: laba-
hope (*n.*): amdir (based on reason), estel (faith), harthad
hope (*v.*): hartha-
horde: hoth
horn: rafn, ras, rasc, tarag, till
horn (musical): rom
horn, sharp: till
horns, sound of: romru, rû
horrible: deleb, gortheb, gorthob, ul-
horror: angos, dêl, delos, deloth, girith, gôr[2], gorog, goroth, gorth[2], gos
horror, extreme: gorgor
horror of death: guruthos
horse: roch, lobor
horse, swift for riding: roch
horse-riders: Rohirrim
host: gwaith, hoth, rim[1]
hostile creature: graug, raug
hot: born, úrui
hound of chase: rŷn
house: adab, bâr, car(dh)[1], nos, nost, nothrim
house, walled: gobel
household: herth
howl (*v.*): gawa-
howl, wolf-: gaul[2]
howling: gawad
huge: taur[1]
human: firen
human being: abonnen, adan, aphadon, echil
humans, mortal: firiath
hummock: gwastar
hump: tump
hunt (*n.*): faras, rui(w)
hunt (*v.*): fara-
hunter: faron, feredir
hunters: faradrim, faroth
hunting: farad, faras, rui(w)
hurl: had-
hurler (of spears and darts): hador, hadron
husband: benn, hervenn

I

I: im[2]
ice: heleg, gochel
ice, mass of: gochel
icicle: aeglos
idea: inc, naw[2]
ill: lhaew
immortal: alfirin
impelled: horn
impetuous: alag, ascar, gorn[1]
impetus: gorf
impulse, have: heria-
in: min, ne, ne-, dî[1]
in, go: neledhi
incline (*n.*): talad
inclined: dadbenn
indicated, thing: tann
inner mind: gûr[1]
inner thought: ind
innumerable: aronoded
insecure: talt
insert: nestag-
inside: ne-
instead: sennui
insult (*n.*): eithad
insult (*v.*): eitha-
intelligent: hand
intend: theli
inter-: im[1]
in that place: ennas
in the rear of: adel
ire: ruith
iron: ang
iron, of: angren
island: toll
isolated: ereb, mîn
issue of water: eithel
it: ha

J

jaw: anc, naew
jaws, set of: carach
jerk (sudden move): rinc
jerk (*v.*): ritha-
jewel: mîr
jewel, great: mirion
jewel, sparkling like: míriel
jewel-like: míriel
jewel of the Noldor: Golovir
jewel-smith: mírdan
journey: lend[2]
joy: gell, glas
joyous: meren
jubilation: gellam
judge: badhor, badhron
judgment: baudh
juice: paich, saw

juicy: pihen
just: fael[1]

K

keep: heb-, gartha-
keen: laeg[2]
killer: dagnir
kind: milui
kindle: nartha-
kindler (*f.*): thoniel
kindness: mîl
king (of region): âr, ar(a)-, aran
king (of tribe): taur[2]
kingdom: arnad
kingfisher: heledir
kingly: ar(a)-
kinsman or kinswoman: gwanur[1]
knife: sigil[1]
knight: rochir
knob, round: dolt
knock (*v.*): tamma-
knot: nardh
knotted: norn
knowledge: ist
knowledge, evil: gûl
knowledge, have: ista-

L

labor (*v.*): muda-
lacking: pen[1]
lady: bassoneth, bessain, brennil, dî[2], heryn, híril
lady, crowned: rien
lair: caew, torech
lake: ael, lîn, nên
lake, cold: rim[2]
lake, shallow: lô
lament (*n.*): noe
lament, woeful: naergon
lamentable: naer
lamentation: conath (*see* caun[1]), nírnaeth
lamp: calar
lampwright: calardan
land: bâr, dôr
land at foot of hills: nand
lands, central: Ennor
lands, flat: talath
language: lam[1]
large: daer[1]
large river: duin
last (*adj.*): medui, meth
last (*v.*): brona-, dartha-
last day of the year: penninor
lasting: bronadui
last point in line: methed
late evening: dû
later: ab-
laugh (*v.*): gladha-
laughter: lalaith
lay: glîr
lay, long: glaer
lead (*v.*): tog-
leaf: las
leaf, green of: lasgalen
league: daur
lean: lhain
leap (*n.*): cabed
leap (*v.*): cab-
leaping down: thôr[1]
leaping flame: lach
learned: istui
learned in deep arts: golwen
leaves, collection of: golas
leaves, having green: lasgalen
left: crom, hair, hâr
left behind: lefn
left hand: crûm, hair
left-handed: crumui, hargam
-less: pen[1]
letter: têw
level (land): land[2]
level space: pathu
lick: lav-
life: cuil
lift: hal-
light (*adj.*): lim[1]
light (*n.*): calad, gâl, galad, gaul[1]
light, bright: gail, galad
light, glittering (reflected): rill
light, golden: glaur
light, golden, shining with: glóriel
light, silver: silif, silith
like: be
like silver: celebren
limit (*n.*): taeg
limit (*v.*): gleinia-
limited area (artificially or naturally defined): sâd
line: lîr, tê, tî
line, boundary: taeg
line, family: nothlir
line of peaks: tilias
line of surf: falas
lion: raw[2]
liquid food: salph
listen: lasta-
listener: lathron, lethril
listen in: lathra-, lathrada-
little: tithen
live (*v.*): cuia
lively: brêg
loaf: basgorn
loathing: dêl, delos, deloth
loathsome: deleb
lode: rant
lofty: arth, brand, orchall, taur[1]
lone: er-
lonely: ereb
long (*adj.*): and[1]
long (*adv.*): anann
long (and thin): taen[1]
Longbeard (Dwarf): Anfang
long climb: andrath
long endured: brûn
long established: brûn
long in use: brûn
long lay: glaer
long-lived: iphant
long mark: andaith
long rune-row: angerthas
look (*n.*): thîr
look at: tiri

looking: tîr[2]
look toward: tiri, tiria-
lord: aran, brannon, heron, hîr, tûr[2]
lore: ist
lore, deep: angol[1]
loud: brui
love (*n.*): meleth, mîl
love (*v.*): mela-
lover: melethril, melethron, mellon
loving: milui
low: tofn
lower end: tâl
low field: talf[1]
low-growing tree: tos
lowland: lâd
low-lying: tofn
lust: mael[2]
lustful: maelui
lying in bed: cael

M

machine: gaud
magic: angol[1], gûl
magic, dark: morgul
magician: gollor
maid: iell, sell
maiden: gwên, gwend[2]
maiden, garlanded: riel
maiden of Yavanna: Ivonwen
make: car-, echad-
make a way: rada-
make clear: glanna-
make come: toltha-
make firm: tangada-
make war: dagra-, dagrada-
maker: ceredir, tân
making: cared
male (*adj.*): anu
male, adult: dîr
mama: nana
mammal, quadrupedal: lavan
man (mortal): adan, fair, firion
man (male): benn, dîr, -we (gwê)
man of craft: curunír
man of the West: dúnadan
man, wild (not of Edain): rhavan
manhood: gwaith
manifestation of Vala: fân
manpower: gwaith
many: laew
mark: taith
mark, long: andaith
mark, short: thinnas
mass of ice: gochel
mast (beechnuts): fêr
master (*n.*): herdir, heron, hîr, tûr[1]
master (*v.*): orthor-
masterful: taur[1]
mastery: tûr[1]
mayor: condir
meager: lhain
mean (*adj.*): faeg
mean (*v.*): theli
meaning: ind
meat: aes
meet: govad-
mere (pool): ael
merry: gelir
mesh: rem[2]
met: govannen
metal: raud[3], tinc
metal, polished: ros[3]
mid-: ne-
middle (*n.*): enedh
Middle-earth: Emerain, Ennor
midyear: enedhin
mighty: beleg, taur[1]
mind: ind
mind, inner: gûr[1]
mine, delved: habar, rhûd
mirror: cenedril
misdeed: úgarth
mist: hîth
mist, wet: mîth[2]
'mist-thread' (kind of fiber): hithlain
misty: hithui, doll
mocking: iaew
moisten: limmid-
monster: úan, ulunn, urug
monstrous: uanui
month: raun
moon: ithil, raun
moon, crescent: cúron
'moon-star': ithildin
morning: aur
morning twilight: minuial
morrowdim: minuial
mortal (*adj.*): fíreb, firin
mortal (*n.*): adan, fair, fíreb
mortal humans: firiath
mortal man: firion
mortal woman: adaneth, firieth
mother: nana, naneth, emil
mound: cerin, coron, cûm, tund
mound (burial): haudh
mount, steep-sided: amon
mountain: ôr, orod
mountaineer: orodben
mountains, one living in: orodben
mountain pass: dîn[1]
mountain peak: aegas, ras, rasc
mountain peak, steep: tarag
mountain range: aeglir
mountains, range of: orodrim
mountain stream: oll
mountain, summit of high: taen[2]
move, sudden: rinc
muscle: tû
must, one: boe

N

nail: taes
naked: hell, lanc[1]
name (*n.*): eneth
name (*v.*): esta-

Nandor: Danwaith, Denwaith
narrative poem: glaer
narrator: pethron
narrow: agor
narrow path: lond
narrow valley with steep sides: imlad
near (*adj.*): nef
near (*prep.*): na
neat: puig
necessary, it is: boe
neck: iaeth, lanc[2]
necklace: sigil[2]
necromancy: gûl
need: baur, thang
net: gwî, raef, raew[2], rem[2]
net, catch in a: raeda-
netted: raen[2], remmen
new: eden, gwain, sain
news: siniath
night: dû, fuin, morn
night, dead of: fuin
night, early (moonless): tinnu
nightfall: dû
nightingale: dúlinn, merilin, tinúviel
nightshade: dúath, fuin
nighttime: daw
nine: neder
ninth: nedrui
no: gû-
no!: baw
noble (*adj.*): ar-[1], arn, arod, arth, brand, raud[1], taur[1]
noble (*n.*): arphen
noble woman: arwen
noise, confused: glam
noisy: brui
Noldo: Gódhel, Golodh, Lachenn, Ódhel
Noldor, jewel of: Golovir
noose: nŷw
north (*adj.*): fôr, forn, fuir
north (*n.*): forod, forven
northerland: forodwaith
northern: forn, forodren
north-folk: forodwaith
northmen: forodrim, forodwaith
nose: bund, nem
not: ú
not: al-, ar-[2], gû-
not common: said
notion: inc
not moving: avorn
novel tale: sinnarn
now: si
number (*n.*): gwanod
number (*v.*): nedia-
number, great: rim[1], lae
numberless: arnediad
Númenórean: dúnadan
numerous: rem[1]

O

O!: a[1]
oak tree: doron
oath: gwaedh, gwest
oblique: adlant
obscure (*adj.*): doll, hethu
obscure (*v.*): gwathra-
obstinate: tarlanc
occasion: lû
ocean: aear, aearon, gaear, gaearon, gaeron
ocean, great: aearon, gaearon, gaeron
odor: ûl
of: na
of (place): o[1]
of (time): ne
of the: en, uin
old: brûn, iaur
old (of things): gern
on: or
on both sides: ath-
on the: erin
on the other side: hae
on this side (of): nef
one: êr, er-, mîn
one (*pron.*): pen[2], ten
One, the: Eru
one-handed: erchamion, erchamui
one hundred forty-four: host
open (*adj.*): laden
open (*v.*): edra-, panna-[1]
opening: dîn[1]
open space: land[2]
oppress: baugla-
oppression: thang
oppressive: baug
oppressor: bauglir, baugron
or: egor
orc: glamog, orch, urug
orcs, body of: glam
orcs: glamhoth
orient: amrûn
orkish: erchion
out: e[1]
outcry: caun[1]
outer: e[1]
outer circle: echor
outer fence: ephel
outer ring: echor
out from: e[1]
outlaws: gaurwaith
outline: cant
out of: e[1]
outside (*adv.*): ar-[2]
over: or
over (across): thar-
over a wide area: palan
overshadow: gwathra-
overwhelming: taur[1]
own (*adj.*): garn

P

pain: naeg
pain, cause: naegra-
palantír: gwachaedir
pale: gael, maidh, malu, nimp, thind
pale blue: elu, gwind
pale grey: mîth[1]
palisade (of stakes): cail
pallor: niphred
palm of hand: camlann, talf[2]

parent (female): odhril
parent: odhron
pass: cirith, lond
pass, between high walls: aglonn
pass, between hills: cîl
pass, long and climbing: andrath
pass, mountain: dîn[1]
passage up or down slope: pendrad, pendrath
pasture: nadhor, nadhras
path: râd
path, climbing: rath
pathway: bâd
pause: daur, post
paved way: othlonn
peace: sîdh
peak: aeg[2], aegas, egnas, mîn, ras, rasc
peak, sharp pointed: till
peak of steep mountain: tarag
peaks, line of: tilias
peaks, range of: aeglir
pebble: sarn
pebble bank: serni
pebbly: brithon
pedlar: bachor
pen: tegil, tegol
penetration: maeg
penny: mirian
people: gwaith
people, dark: graurim
people of Doriath: Iathrim
people of Harad: Haradrim
people of Rohan: Rohirrim
people of the shore: Falathrim
people of the trees: Galadhrim
permission: dâf
petrel: cuen, paen
petty: niben
petty-Dwarf: nogotheg
petty-Dwarves: nibin-noeg
physical strength: tû
piercing: aeg[1]
pile of stones: sarnas
pilgrim: randir
pillar, wooden: thafn
pillow: pesseg
pin: tachol
pine tree: thôn
pine trees, having: thonion
pinion: roval
pipe-weed: galenas
pippin (apple): cordof
pit: dath
pivot: pelthaes
place: sâd
place, bounded or defined: gardh
place, holy: iaun
place of the dead: gorthad
plain (*adj.*): laden, land[1]
plain (*n.*): lâd, talath
plane: talath
plank: pân[2]
plant: galas
platform: talan
play (*n.*): teilien
play (*v.*): teilia-
play a harp: ganna-, gannada-
poem: glîr
poem, narrative: glaer
poem, recite: gliri
point (*n.*): aeg[2], nas, naith, till
point (*v.*): nasta-
point (at the end of a thing): ment
point at side, extended: rafn
point, sharp: egnas
pointed: aeg[1]
pointed, sharp: megor
pointed peak, sharp: till
point of spear: aith, ecthel
poison: saew
polished metal: ros[3]
pollen: mâl
pondering: idhren
pool: ael, lîn, loeg, nên
pool, cold: rim[2]
pool, small: bôth
poor: faeg
poplar tree: tulus
possess: gar-
post: thafn
potter: cennan
powder, yellow: mâl
power: tûr[1]
powerful creature: graug, raug
praise: egleria-
precious thing: mîr
precipice: rhas
preeminent: main
prevent from completing or continuing: nuitha-
prick: ercha-, nasta-
prick with a sharp point: eitha-
prickle: erch
prime: main
prince: caun[3], cund, ernil
princess: riel
prison: band, gador
private: said
prohibit: boda-
promontory: naith
prone: dadbenn
prop: tulu
property: garn
protect: beria-
province, great: ardhon
puddle: bôth
puff: hwest
purpose (*v.*): theli
purpose, one with: thelion
purpose, steady: estel

Q

quadrupedal mammal: lavan
quarrel: cost
queen: bereth, rían, rien, rîn[1], rîs
quench: luithia-
quenching, without: uluithiad

quick: brêg
quiet water: lorn
quite: far

R

race (related group): nûr[3]
radiance: fae, faer, galad, glaw, thîl
radiance of Laurelin: glawar
radiant: faen
rain (*n.*): ros[2]
rain (*v.*): elia-
rainbow: eilian, ninniach
rainy: rost
raise: ortha-
raised stone highway: gondrath
raising: orthad
range of mountains: orodrim
range of peaks: aeglir
ransom: danwedh
rapid: legin
rat: nâr
rather: sennui
ravine: falch, iaw[2], res, rest, ris
re-: ad
readiness for action: hûr
realm: ardh
realm, division of: trann
reap: critha-
rear: tele
rear, person or thing at: teler
recite poem: gliri
reckon: genedia-, gonod-, nedia-
reckoning: genediad, gonoded, nediad
recount: trenar-
red: born, caran, carn, coll[2], gaer[2], naru, rhosc
reddish: ros[1], gaer[2]
red, fiery: ruin[1]
red flame: ruin[1]
reed: lisc
reek: osp
reflection, glittering: galad
refusal: avad
regiment: gwaith
region: ardh, dôr, gardh, gwaith
region, great: ardhon
region, king of: aran
region of stars: gilith, gilwen
release (*n.*): leithian, adleithian
release (*v.*): adleg-, adleitha-
reluctance: avad
remembrance: rîn[2]
remain: dartha-
remote: hae, haer, haeron
remote distance: haered
rend: narcha-, rista-
repose: îdh
resolve (*v.*): theli
resonant (of strings): tong
respite: post
response: dambeth
rest (abstract): îdh
rest (pause): post
resting place: caew
reunion: aderthad
reunite: adertha-
reuniting: aderthad
rider: rochben, rochir, rochon
ridge, stone: ceber
ridges: pinnath
right (*adj.*): fôr, forn, fuir
right (straight): tîr[1]
right hand: fuir
right-handed: forgam
rigid: tharn
rill: sîr[1]
ring, outer: echor
ringing of bells: nelladel
ringlet: laus, loch
rip: rista-
rise: eria-
river: celon, sîr[1]
river, great: sirion
river, large: duin
river, mouth of: ethir[1]
river, outflow of: ethir[1]
riverbed: rath
road: mên
roar: raw[3]
roaring noise: raw[3]
rock: gond
rockhewn hall: rhûd
Rohan, people of: Rohirrim
roof (*v.*): ortheli
roof, hall with vaulted: rond
roof, high: telu
roofing: tobas
roof over: toba-
root: thond
root (edible): solch
rope: raph
rose: meril
rotten: thaw
round: corn[1]
round knob: dolt
row: lîr, tî
row of teeth: anc
royal: ar-[1], ar(a)-, arn
ruddy: gaer[2], gruin
ruddy (of face): crann
run: nor-, yri
rune: certh
rune-row: certhas
rune-row, long: angerthas
runes, collection of: certhas
running (of water): cell
rush (*n.*): raw[3]
rush (*v.*): ribi
rushing: alag, alagon, ascar, rimp
russet: ros[1], rhosc
rustling sound: lhos, rhos

S

sad: dem, naer, nûr[2]
safekeeping: band
saga: narn
sail: renia-
sailor: cirion
salvation: edraith
salve: glaew
sanctuary: iaun
sand: lith
sapless: tharn

saving: edraith
say: pedi
scarlet: coll[2]
scorn: iaew
scorn, treat with: eitha-
scratch: rhibi
screen (*n.*): escal
screen (*v.*): haltha-
screen above (*v.*): ortheli
sea: aear, aer, gaear, gaer[3]
sea serpent: limlug
seashell: half
sea-song: aerlinn
seaweed: aeruil, uil
second: ad, edwen, tadui
'second folk': adan
second-in-command (*adj.*): taid
'second twilight': aduial
secret: dolen, thurin
secret lore: golu
see: ceni, tíra-
seed: eredh
seeing: cened
seeing-stone: gwachaedir
seem: thia-
seize: mab-
sentence (judicial): baudh
separate: said
serpent: lhûg
serpent, sea: limlug
serve: buia-
set: penia-
set aside: seidia-
set free: leitha-
set out to do: heria-
seven: odo, odog
seventh: odothui, othui
shade: gwâth, lûm, dae[2]
shadow (cast by sunlight): morchant
shadow, dark: dúath
shadow (dim light): dae[2], daew, gwâth, muil
shadowed: hall[2],
shadowy: gwathren, gwathui, donn
shady: hall[2], lumren, donn
shaggy hair: fast
shallow lake: lô
shape (*n.*): cant
shape (*v.*): echad
shape, dim: auth[2]
shaped: cadu
shapely: cadwor, cadwar, maed[2]
shaping: cannas
sharp: aeg[1], aig, laeg[2], maeg
sharp edge: lanc[3]
sharp end: nas
sharp-eyed: maecheneb
sharp horn: till
sharp point: egnas
sharp-pointed: megor
sharp-pointed peak: till
she: he
shield: thand, amath
shield fence: thangail
shield wall: thangail
shine (white): síla-
shingle (coarse gravel-bank): serni
shining with golden light: glóriel
ship: cair
shipbuilder: círdan
shipman: cirion
shipwright: círdan
shire: trann
shire, of: trannail
shore: falas, habad, rhast
shore, of the: falathren
shore, people of the: Falathrim
short: estent, thent
short mark: thinnas
shortness: thinnas
shout (*n.*): caun[1]
shout (*v.*): can-
shouting: glam
shown, thing: tann
shudder: giri
shuddering: girith
sick: caeleb, lhaew
sickle: cerch
sickly: gem, lhaew
sickness: cael, lhîw, paw
sight: cened
sign: tann, têw
silence: dîn[2]
silent: dínen
silima: silef[2]
silima, of: silivren
Silmaril: Golovir, Mirion, Silevril
Silvan Elves: tawarwaith
silver: celeb
silver, glistening: thilion
silver (in color): silef[1]
silver, like: celebren
silver, of: celebren, celefn
silver glint: gîl
silver light: silif, silith
silver spark: gildin
simbelmynë: uilos[2]
sin: úgarth
Sinda: Send
sinew: tû
sing: gliri, linna-
singer: lind[2]
single: eriol, erui, minai
single flower: elloth, lotheg, lothod
sinister: crumguru
sister: gwathel, muinthel, thêl
sit: hav-
six: eneg
sixth: engui, enecthui
sixth part: enaith
skill: curu
skilled: maed[1], maen
skin: flâd
sky: ell-[2]
slain: dangen
slant: adlanna-
slant down: penna-
slanting: adlant
slash: cris
slave: mûl
slay: dag-

slender: fim, lhind, nind, trîw
slim: fim
sling: hadlath
slipping: talt
slope (*n.*): talad
slope (*v.*): adlanna-
sloping: adlann
sloping down: dadbenn
slot: ruin[2]
small: niben, mîw
small bird: aew, fileg, filigod
small gull: cuen, paen
small landlocked bay: hûb
small pool: bôth
small spot: pêg
small star: tinu
small stone: sarn[2]
smith: tân
smith, jewel-: mírdan
smoke: osp
smooth: path
snake: lŷg, lhûg
snatch: ritha-
snout: bund
snow: los[1]
snowdrop: nínim
snowdrop, flower similar to: niphredil
'snow-men' (tribe): Lossoth
'snow-thorn': aeglos
snow-white: glos
snow-white, always: uilos[1]
snowy: lossen
soaking wet: loen
soap: glûdh
socket: taew
soft: mae[1]
soil (*n.*): cêf, maw[2]
soil (*v.*): gwatha-
soiled: gwaur
soldier (of Orcs): daug
sole of the foot: telluin
somber: dûr
somebody: pen[2]
son: iôn, iond
song: glîr, laer[2], lind[1]
song of the sea: aerlinn
sorcery: durgul, gûl, morgul
sorcery, dark: guldur
soul: fae
sound, making: lhûn
sound, rustling: lhos, rhos
sound bells: nella-
sound of bells: nellad
sound of horns: romru, rû
sound of voices: lammad
soup: salph
source: celu, eithel
south (*adj.*): hâr, harn[1]
south (*n.*): harad, harven
southern: haradren, harn[1]
southerners: Haradrim
Southrons: Haradrim
sow: redhi
space, level: pathu
spark: tint, tinu
spark, bright: gîl
spark, silver: gildin
sparkling: lim[1]
sparkling like a jewel: míriel
speak: pedi
spearhead: naith
spear point: aith, ecthel, thela
spectral apparition: auth[2]
speech, of or related to: lammen
speed (*v.*): hortha-
spell: luith
spider: lhing, lhingril, ungol
spider filament: lhê
spider's web: lhing
spike: till
spike (of rock): carag, ceber
spikes, hedge of: caraes
spindrift: gwing
spine: ech
spirit: fae, faer
spirit, departed: mân
spirit, fiery: hûr
spit: puia-
splendor: claur
split: thanc
spoken: lammen
sponge: hwand
spoor: ruin[2]
sport: teilien
spot (place): sâd
spot, small: pêg
spouse: bereth
spray (of fall or fountain): ros[2]
spray, flying (blown off wave-tops): gwing
spread: pelia-
spring (season): ethuil
spring (source): celu, eithel
spring (*v.*): tuia-
sprout (*n.*): tui(w)
sprout (*v.*): tuia-
spume: gwing
spy: ethir[2]
stab: eitha-
stain (*n.*): gwas, gwath, mael[1], maw[2]
stain (*v.*): gwatha-
stained: gwaen, mael[1]
stair: dim[1]
stairway: pendrad, pendrath
stake: ceber
stalwart: tolog, thala
staple: taew
star: êl, gîl
star, small: tinu
starlight: gilgalad, gilith
starlit evening: tinnu
starry twilight: tinnu
stars, of: gilion
stars, region of: gilith, gilwen
stay: dartha-, dortha-
staying: avorn
steadfast: him[2], thalion[1]
steadfast man: bôr
steady: thala
steady purpose: estel
steep: baradh
steep fall: dath
steep mountain peak: tarag
steep-sided mount: amon

stem: telch
stench: angol[2], thû
stick (*v.*): nasta-
stick in: nestag-
sticky: hîw
stiff: dorn, tara, tharn
stiff grass: thâr
stiff-necked: tarlanc
stiffness: tarias
stirring: echuir
stirrup: talraph
stone: gôn, gond
stone (material): sarn[2]
stone, great: gond
stone, hewn: gondrafn, drafn
stone, made of: gondren, sarn[1]
stone, master of: gonhir
stone, pile of: sarnas
stone ridge: ceber
stonecrop, a kind of: seregon
stone, small: sarn[2]
stony: gondren, sarn[1]
stop (*n.*): daur
stop (*v.*): dar-
stopgap: gasdil
stopper: dîl
stopping: dîl
stop short: nuitha-
stop up: dîl
storm (of wind): alagos
story: pent
story, tell a: nara-
straight: tîr[1]
strait: lond
strand: falas
strap: raph
stray (*v.*): mista-, renia-
straying (*adj.*): raun
straying (*n.*): mistad
stream: nên, rant, sirith, celeth
stream, mountain: oll
street: othrad, rath
strength, bodily: bellas
strength, physical: tû
strip: heltha-
stroke (*v.*): matha-
stroke, axe-: hast
stroke, heavy: dram
strong: thalion[1]
stronghold: ost, garth
stronghold, underground: othronn
strong in body: bell
stuffing: dîl
stunt: nuitha-
stunted: naug[1]
subjects of Thingol: Eluwaith
sublime: taur[1]
successor: dŷr
sudden: bragol, brêg, bregol
sudden end: lanc[3]
sudden move: rinc
suddenly: breged
suddenness: breged
suffering from old age: ingem
sufficient: far
summer: laer[1]
summit of high mountain: taen[2]
sum up: gonod-
sun: anor, naur
sunlight: galad, glawar
sunny: nórui
sunrise: amrûn
sunset: annûn
superior: orchall
support: tulu
supporting: taid
surface: palath
surface, flat: talath
surf, line of: falas
survival: bronad
survive: brona-
swallow (bird): tuilinn
swampy: loen
swan: alph
sward: parth, pathu, sâdh
swart: baran, donn, graw
swarthy: donn
swear: gwesta-
sweet: lend[1], melui
swell (*v.*): tuia-
swift: celeg, lagor, legin, lint
swift horse for riding: roch
swooping: thôr[1]
sword: crist, lang, magol, megil
swordsman: magor
sworn brother: gwador
syrup: paich

T

tale (count): gwanod
tale (story): pent, trenarn
tale, novel: sinnarn
tale, versified: narn
tall: orn[1], tond
tangled: remmen
tangled with trees: galadhremmen
taut: tong
tear: nîn[2], nîr
tearful: nîd, níniel, nínui[1]
teeth, gnashing of (in grief): naeth
teeth, row of: anc
Teleri, one of: Glinnel
tell (a story): nara-
tell to the end: trenar-
ten: caer, pae
tenth: paenui
terrible: goeol
terrible creature: graug, raug
terrify: gruitha-
terror: goe[1], gorgoroth, gost
terror, feel: groga-
that (*dem.*): taw[3]
that (*rel.*): i, ai
thatch: taus
the: i
thee (reverential you): le
them: ti
there: ennas
they: ?aen
thick: tûg
thin: lhain, nind
thin (and long): taen[1]

thing: bach, nad
third: nail, nelui
thirsty: faug
thirtieth: nelchaenen
this: sen
thong: lath
thorn: aeg[2], êg, rêg
those: ti
thought: ind, nauth
thoughtful: idhren
thoughtfulness: idhor
thousand: meneg
thrall: mûl
'thrawn folk': Dornhoth
thread: lain[2]
thread, fine: lhê
three: nêl[1], nel-, neled
threshold: fen(d)
throat: lanc[2]
through: tre-, trî
through together: godref
thrower: hador, hadron
thrust: nasta-
tidings: siniath
tidy: puig
tie: nod-, taetha-
tight: tong
tightly closed hand: paur
tilted: adlann
time: lû
tine: till
tiny: pigen, tithen, mîw
to: an, na
tobacco: galenas, romloth
today: sîr[2]
together: go-, gwa-
toil (*v.*): muda-
tomb: haudh
tongue: lam[1]
tongue, of or related to: lammen
tongues, account of: lammas
tooth: carch, nagol, naes, nêl[2], neleg
tooth of rock: carag
top: caw
torment: baul
torrent: oll, thorod
torrent, flow like a: rimma-
to the: 'ni
tough: dorn, tara
toughness: tarias
toward: na
tower: barad[1], minas
towering: mîn
town (walled village): gobel
track: râd, ruin[2]
track, beaten: bâd
trade: banga-
trample: batha-
traverse: athrada-, trevad-
treasure: mîr
treat with scorn: eitha-
treaty: gowest
tree: galadh, orn[2]
tree, family: nothlir
tree, low-growing: tos
tree, walking: huorn
tree-folk: Galadhrim
trees, of: galadhon
tree-tangled; galadhremmin
tress: find
tress, braided: finnel
tressure: cathrae
tri-: nel-
triangle: nelthil
tribe, king of: taur[2]
trick: rinc
triumph: gell
triumphant: gellui
troll: torog
troop of able-bodied men: gwaith
troop under a *hîr*: herth
troth: gwaedh
trouble (*n.*): tas
trouble (*v.*): presta-, trasta-
true: thenid, thenin
true-silver: mithril
trumpet: rom
trust: estel
trusty: tolog
trusty man: bôr
tumult: glam
tune: lind[1]
tuneful: lend[1]
turf: sâdh
twi-: ui-
twilight: aduial, muil, tinnu, uial
twilight, evening: aduial
twilight, morning: minuial
twilight, starry: tinnu
twin: gwanunig
twins, pair of: gwanûn, gwanur, gwenyn
twirl: hwinia-
twisted: norn
twitch (*n.*): rinc
twitch (*v.*): ritha-
two: tâd, ui-
two-legged: tad-dal
tyrannous: baug
tyrant: bauglir, baugron

U

under: dî[1], nu
underground dwelling: grôd, rhûd
underground stronghold: othronn
understand: henia-
understanding: hannas
union: erthad
unique: minai
unite: ertha
uniting: erthad
unnumbered: arnediad
unquenchable: uluithiad
up: am
upon: am
uprising (*adj.*): am
uprising (*n.*): amrûn
uproar: glam
upward: am
urge on: hortha-
us, to, for, of: ammen
use (*n.*): iuith

use (*v.*): iuitha-
use, long in: brûn
useful: maer

V

vague: hethu
vague apparition: auth[2]
vagueness: muil
Vala: Balan, Rodon
vale, deep: im[3]
Valian year: ennin
valley: lâd, nan(d)
valley, deep amid hills: tûm
valley, deep and narrow with steep sides: imlad
valley, flowering: imloth
valley, long and narrow with watercourse: imrath
valley, wide: talath
valor: caun[2], gorn[2]
Vanya: miniel
vassal: bŷr
vast: taur[1]
vault: rond
vaulted ceiling: rond
vaulted roof, hall with: rond
veil (*n.*): escal, fân
veil (*v.*): gwathra-
vein (e.g., in rock): rant
vengeance: acharn
verse couplet: linnod
very (*adv.*): dae[3]
very (*pref.*): an-
very dry: apharch
vessel, drinking: ylf[1]
vessel, water: calph
victor: tûr[2]
victory: tûr[1]
view: tîr[2]
view far and wide: palandiri
vigilance: tirith
vigor: gôr[1], gorf, hûr, tû
vigorous: gorn[1]
village, walled: gobel
violence: breged
violent: ascar, bregol
virgin: gwên
virginity: gweneth
viscous: hîw
voice, echoing: lam[2]
voice, sound of: lammad
void: cofn, gast, gaw, iâ

W

wagon: rach
wain: rach
wait: dartha-
walk (on track or path): pada-
walking tree: huorn
wall: ram, rammas
walled house: gobel
walled village: gobel
wand: olf
wander: renia-
wanderer: randir
wandering: rain[1], raun
war: auth
war, make: dagra-, dagrada-
ware: bach
warrior: hador, hadron, maethor
warrior (orc): daug
warm: laug
warn: gor-
waste (*adj.*): lothren
waste (*n.*): eru
watch (*n.*): tirith
watch (*v.*): tiri, tiria-
watcher: tirn
watching: tirith
watch over: tiri, tiria-
watchtower, fortress with a: ostirion
watchtower, great: tirion
water: nên
water, quiet: lorn
water-channel: rant
watercourse: rant
waterfall: lanthir
water falling swiftly from spring: celos
waterland: nên
water vessel: calph
watery: nend, nîn[1], nínui[2]
way: lend[2], mên, pâd, tê
way, find a: rada-
way, make a: rada-
way, paved: othlonn
way-bread: lembas
we: men
weal: galu
wealth: galu
weary: lom
weaver: nathron
web: gwî, nath
web, spider's: lhing
webster: nathron
wedge: naith, cên, cîn
wedge formation: dírnaith
week (of five days): lefnor
weeping: nîr
well (*adv.*): mae[2]
well (*n.*): eithel
werewolf: gaur
werewolves: gaurhoth
west: annûn, dûn, dúven
western: annui
Westron: Annúnaid
wet: limp, mesc, nîd, nîn[1],
wet, soaking: loen
wetland: talf[1]
wet mist: mîth[2]
which (*rel.*): i, ai[2]
whirl: hwinia-
whirling: hwind, hwiniol
whisper: lhos, rhos
white: faen, fain, glân[1], nimp
white, dazzling (as snow): glos
white, glittering: silivren
white fog: mîth[2]
white heat: bras
white-hot: brassen
whiten: nimmid-
who (*rel.*): i, ai[2]
whole: pant
wide: laden, land[1], pann, ûr[2]

wide grassland: nan(d)
wide valley: talath
wield: matha-, tortha-
wife: bes, herves
wild: braig, rhovan, lothren
wilderness: gwaith, rhaw[1], los[3]
wildfire: bregedúr
wild man: drû, drúadan
wild man (not of Edain): rhavan
will (*n.*): innas
will (*v.*): theli
will not: ava-
willow: tathar, tathor
willow, of: tathren
willows, having: tathren
wily: coru, crumguru
wind: gwaew, sûl[2]
wind, storm of: alagos
window: henneth
windy: gwaeren
wing: roval
wing, great: roval
winter: rhîw
wisdom: golu
wise: goll, golwen, idhren, sael
wish: iest
with: na
wither: peli
withered: tharn
withering: peleth, pelin
within: im[1]
without: ar-[2], pen[1], ú
without quenching: uluithiad
without reckoning: arnediad
wizard: curunír, ithron
woe: naeth
woeful: naer
woeful lament: naergon
wolf: draug, garaf, gaur
wolf-host: gaurhoth
wolf-howl: gaul
wolf-men: gaurwaith
woman: bes
woman, crowned: rîn[1]
woman, mortal: adaneth, firieth
woman, young: des, dîs
wood, great: taur[3]
wood (material): tawar
wood (of trees): eryn, glâd
wooden: tawaren
wooden pillar: thafn
woodpecker: tavor
wool: taw[2]
wool, of: taw[1]
woollen: taw[1]
word: peth
world: ardhon
worn: gern
wound (*n.*): haru
wound (*v.*): harna-
wounded: harn[2]
woven: remmen
wreath: rî
wright: tân, thavron
write: teitha-
wrong: raeg
wronged: neithan

Y

yard: sant
Yavanna, maiden of: ivonwen
year: idhrinn, în[1]
year, last day of: penninor
year, Valian: ennin
yelling (of beasts), confused: glam
yellow: malen
yellow brown: baran
yellow flag (flower): ninglor
yellowhammer: emelin
yellow powder: mâl
yoke: iant
young: neth
young woman: des, dîs
youth: nîth

Appendix 5

Sindarin Names

ABBREVIATIONS

ajph.	adjectival phrase (noun modified by adjective)
alt.	alternative (rejected) name
bv.	bahuvrihi compound
dc.	double comparative
dg.	dvigu compound
dv.	dvandva compound
fn.	father-name
gph.	genitive phrase (noun modified by noun)
impr.	improper compound
kd.	karmadharaya compound
pc.	prepositional compound
prph.	prepositional phrase (noun modified by prepositional clause)
tp.	tatpurusha compound
#	attested name whose form has been significantly altered

This appendix offers a listing of the Sindarin names of persons, things, and places from *The Lord of the Rings*, *The Silmarillion*, *Unfinished Tales*, and related texts of contemporary or later date (e.g., those found in *The History of Middle-earth*, vols. 9–12). The list intends to be complete with respect to these primary sources, including even some names that are not altogether intelligible. A selection is given of "alternate" names found in earlier draft texts, names that were replaced or not used; the selection is usually based on intelligibility combined with textual or linguistic significance, e.g., the use of word forms that are readily interpreted but not found elsewhere. The references provided are by no means exhaustive but are intended to point to glosses, etymological information, or novel forms found in the texts, or at least suggest where to look for the name.

The spelling of Sindarin names is, with few exceptions, the same as that for ordinary words. The chief exception involves the use of *d* and *dh*. In a letter written in 1972, J. R. R. Tolkien explained to Richard Jeffery that he had written *d* for *ð* or *dh* because he thought people would find the spelling *dh* "uncouth" (see *Letters*, p. 426n); but in later editions he changed the names (*Caras*) *Galadon* and *Galadrim* to *Galadhon* and *Galadhrim*.

Caras Galadhon and *Galadhrim* were not, however, the only words in which *dh* was spelled *d*, and many of these were never replaced; even in unpublished papers the spellings *dh* and *d* alternate bewilderingly. The actual Sindarin pronunciation of any given *d* can only be established—not always firmly—on a combination of textual and philological evidence. Thus it seems that the actual spellings for such names as *Bregalad*, *Enedwaith*, and *Nardol* should have been *Bregaladh*, *Enedhwaith*, and *Nardhol*. In the following index the spelling with *dh* will be used in the main entry, with any alternate spelling in *d* noted after the entry. This orthographic confusion of *d* and *dh* is distinct from the grammatical uncertainty regarding the lenition (or its absence) of *d* to *dh* in adjectival position, which produces such double forms as *Athrad Daer* and *Athrad Dhaer* (see § 7.5).

Another exception is in the use of final *-nd*, which is preserved in many cases where it would have been reduced to *-nn* or *-n* in ordinary CS words.

Use of hyphens, which were irregularly transcribed in names containing articles or prepositions, has been standardized, hyphens being used only following a preposition or article.

Many of the names given to the Edain in the First Age are entirely acceptable as CS in phonetic form but have no ready interpretation in CS. These names may be derived from the languages of the Edain but adapted in form to CS. They include the names of outlaws Algund, Andróg, Andvír, Forweg, Orleg, Ragnir, Ulrad; the names of Hadorians Aerin, Amlach, Arachon, Asgon, Dírhaval, Gethron, Grithnir, Imlach, Imrach, Indor, Malach, Marach, Sador; the names of Bëorians Angrim, Arthad, Balan, Baran, Belen, Dairuin, Eilinel, Gorlim, Radhruin, Ragnor, Urthel (Huor and Tuor are also said to be Mannish names); the names of Haladic-speaking persons such as Agathor, Avranc, Brandir, Dorlas, Ebor, Enthor, Forhend, Glirhuin, Haldad, Haldar, Haldir, Haleth, Halmir, Handir, Harathor, Hardang, Hareth, Hundad, Hunthor, Larnach, Manthor, Sagroth, and the place-name Tûr Haretha (of the Haudh en-Arwen). Such names continued to be used in the Third Age and include Forlong, Adrahil, Imrahil, and the place-names Adorn, Arnach, Eilenaer, Eilenach, Erech, Lamedon, Rimmon, and Umbar. The possibility cannot be excluded that some of these names are CS, or at least contain CS elements, or that other apparently CS names, especially of the Edain, include non-CS elements.

There are also several Elvish names of CS appearance that are perhaps not CS but Ossiriandic Nandorin or Avarin in origin. These include the personal names Denethor, Denwë, Eöl and Saeros, and the place-names Adurant, Aros, Ascar, Brilthor, Dolmed, Duilwen, Legolin, Lindon, Thalos, Rerir. In the Third Age the names Amroth, Esgaroth, Nimrodel, Rúmil, and Thranduil may be of the same sort, of Silvan (Nandorin) origin.

NAMES OF PERSONS AND CREATURES

Note on Elvish personal names. The Eldar (especially the Noldor), and others who took names in the Elvish languages, customarily used several different kinds of names. These included the following:

1. The Father-name, a name chosen for a child at birth by his or her father and whose owner could not alter it. It often resembled the father's name.
2. The Chosen Name, a name chosen (usually newly invented) by a child at about the age of ten, expressing his or her own preferences in language. Other chosen names might be added later in life.
3. 'Given' or Added Names (Q *anessi*, sg. *anessë*), which included:
   - A. The Mother-name (Q *amilessë*), a special name given by a mother to her child, often expressing a special insight into the child's nature or foresight of its fate.
   - B. Nicknames (Q *epessi*, sg. *epessë*), names by which a person was commonly known, but not his or her true name. These included (1) names given by others, like *Mormegil Blacksword* or *Thingol Greycloak* and (2) names of personal choice (Q *cilmessi*, sg. *cilmessë*), chosen by a person either as a disguise or in reference to his or her own history.

A

A·'da·ne·dhel, *impr. kd.*: man like an Elf; an *epessë* given to Túrin in Nargothrond [adan + edhel] *Silm*

'A·da·nel: maiden of the Edain; a woman of the tribe of Marach [adan + -el[3]] *MR*, *WJ*

'A·da·neth: woman of the Edain; *epessë* given to *Andreth* by Finrod [adan + -eth[2]] *MR*

Aec·'the·li·on, *kd.*: one with sharp will; a Noldo of Gondolin [aeg[1] + thelion] late popular form *Ecthelion* *WJ*:318

Ae·'gam·loth, *kd. bv.*: one with a pointed crest; a Noldo of Gondolin [aeg + amloth] late popular form *Egalmoth WJ*:318

Aeg·nor, *kd.*: fell fire; *amilessë* of the youngest son of Finarfin [a Sindarized form of Q *Aicanár* < CE *gaika-nār √GAJ √NAR] called *Amrod*, also *Eignor Silm*, *MR*:323–24, *PME*:347

Ae·'ran·dir, *tp.*: wanderer on the sea; a mariner, companion of Eärendil [aer + randir] *Silm*

Ae·'ren·dil, *tp.*: one devoted to the sea; Eärendil the mariner [from Q *Eärendil*] also *Ae·'ren·nel PME*:364

A·'gar·waen, *tp.*: stained with blood; *cilmessë* taken by *Túrin* in Nargothrond [agar + gwaen] *Silm*, *WJ*:142

'Ag·la·had, *tp.*: ?warrior of light; a prince of Dol Amroth [the meaning of this name is uncertain; it is probably a compound of two otherwise unknown elements !agol < OS *akla √KAL, which should mean either 'light' or 'fame' (cf. *aglar* and Q *alca* 'ray of light') and !hâd < OS *k^{h}ato √KHAT, which could mean 'warrior' (cf. *hador*). *PME*:223

Al·phros, *tp.*: foam of swans; a prince of Dol Amroth [alph + ros^{2}] *PME*:221

Am·'ar·than, *adj.*: fated (one); *Amrod* [amarthan] *VT*41:10

Am·dír, *kd.*: uprising man; king of Lórien before Amroth [am + dîr] *UT*

Am·laith: meaning uncertain; a king of Arthedain [probably contains *am* 'uprising'] *LotR:AppA*

Am·ras, *kd.*: uprising horn; one of several names given to one of the youngest sons of Fëanor [am + ras] *MR*:177

Am·rod, *kd.*: uprising champion; *fn.* of *Aegnor*, also one of several names given to one of the youngest sons of Fëanor [am + raud^{2}; from Q *Ambaráto*] also *Amarthan PME*:347

Am·ros, *kd. bv.*: having a russet (head) above; the name of the youngest surviving son of Fëanor, who had reddish-brown hair [am + ros^{1}; from Q *Ambarussa*] *VT*41:10

'Am·ro·thos, *tp.*: ?terror of Amroth; son of a prince of Dol Amroth [?Amroth (name) + gos] *PME*:221

An·born, *kd.*: ?very steadfast; a Ranger of Ithilien [an + ?bor(o)n (or cf. *avorn*)] *LotR*

An·'ca·la·gon, *impr. kd.*: rushing jaw; the greatest of the winged dragons [anc + alagon] *LotR*

An·dreth: meaning uncertain; a wisewoman of the house of Bëor [perhaps contains *and*^{1} 'long' and the *-reth* also seen in Orodreth] called *Saelind*, *Adaneth MR*:329, *WJ*:231

An·'faug·lir, *kd.*: very thirsty row (?of teeth); the wolf *Carcharoth* [an +

faug + lîr] *Silm*

Ang·bor, *tp.*: fist of iron; lord of Lamedon [ang + paur] *LotR*

An·'ge·li·mir, *kd.*: very brilliant jewel; a prince of Dol Amroth [from Q *Ancalimir* = *ancalima* + *mírë*, cf. √KAL, √MIR] misspelled Angelimar in *UT PME*:221

'An·go·lodh: the (eminent) Noldo; a possible CS form of Q *Ingoldo*, the *amilessë* of both Finarfin and Finrod [CE *ŋgolodō] *PME*:360

An·grod, *tp.*: champion of iron; *fn.* of Finarfin's second son [ang + raud[2]; from Q *Angaráto*; named for his strong hands 'like iron'] *PME*:346

An·nael, *kd.*: ?very wise; a Sinda of Mithrim [?an + sael] *Silm*, *UT*

A·'rach·ír, *kd.*: noble lord [MS *araxxīr < OS *arakk^{h}īr < CE *aratk^{h}ēr √AR[1]-ÁT √KHER] *VT*41:9

'A·ra·dan, *kd.*: noble man; *epessë* of Malach, chief of the house of Marach [ar-[1] + adan] *Silm*

'A·ra·dor, *kd.*: royal king; chieftain of the Dúnedain of Eriador [ar(a)- + taur[2]] *LotR:AppA*

A·'rag·las, *kd.*: having royal joy; chieftain of the Dúnedain of Eriador [ar(a)- + glas] *LotR:AppA*

'A·ra·gorn, *kd. bv.*: having royal valor; two chieftains of the Dúnedain of Eriador, the last becoming King of Gondor and Arnor [ar(a)- + gorn[2]] called *Dúnadan*, *Edhelharn*, *Thorongil LotR*, *PME:xii*

'A·ra·gost, *kd.*: ?royal terror; chieftain of the Dúnedain of Eriador [ar(a)- + gost] *LotR:AppA*

'A·ra·had, *kd.*: ?royal warrior; two chieftains of the Dúnedain of Eriador [ar(a)- + *hâd; cf. Aglahad] *LotR:AppA*

'A·ra·hael, *impr. kd.*: wise king; chieftain of the Dúnedain of Eriador [ar(a) + sael] *LotR:AppA*

A·'ram·und, *kd.*: bull like a king; a bull [aran + mund] *Letters*:423

'A·ra·narth, *impr. kd.*: noble king; chieftain of the Dúnedain of Eriador [aran + arth] *LotR:AppA*

A·ran 'Ei·ni·or, *ajph.*: elder king; the Vala Manwë [aran, einior] *PME*:358

'A·ra·nel, *kd.*: royal Elf; *anessë* of *Dior* of Doriath [aran + -el[1]] *Silm*

A·ran Hith·lum, *gph.*: king of Hithlum; title of *Fingolfin* [aran, Hithlum] (N Aran Chithlum) *LR*:389 *TA-*

A·ran Tin·nu, *gph.*: king of twilight; title of *Thingol* [aran, tinnu] (N Aran Dinnu) *LR*:393 *TIN-*

'A·ra·nuir: *impr. tp.*: ?king for ever; a chieftain of the Dúnedain of Eriador [aran + uir] *LotR:AppA*

'A·ra·phant: *impr. kd.*: complete king; king of Arthedain [aran + pant as if from OS *aranp^{h}anta] *LotR:AppA*

'A·ra·phor: *impr. tp.*: king of the fist; king of Arthedain [aran + paur, as if from OS *aranphǭra] *LotR:AppA*

A·'ras·suil: meaning obscure; chieftain of the Dúnedain of Eriador [contains ar(a)-] *LotR:AppA*

'A·ra·thorn, *kd.*: (like a) royal eagle; two chieftains of the Dúnedain of Eriador [ar(a)- + thor(o)n] *LotR*, *Letters*:427

ˊA·ra·'thor·ni·on, *tp.*: son of Arathor; patronymic of *Aragorn* II [Arathorn + iôn] *SD*:128–31

'A·ra·val, *impr. tp.*: king of gold; king of Arthedain [ar(a)- + mall] *LotR:AppA*

'A·ra·vir, *kd.*: (like a) royal jewel; chieftain of the Dúnedain of Eriador [ar(a)- + mîr] *LotR:AppA*

'A·ra·vorn, *impr. kd.*: steadfast king or black king; chieftain of the Dúnedain of Eriador [ar(a)- + avorn or ar(a)- + morn] *LotR:AppA*

A·raw: original meaning unknown; Oromë, one of the Valar [MS *Arauṽ < OS *Arǭme < V Arǭmēz; NS Arum] called *Tauron LotR*, *WJ*:400

'A·re·dhel, *kd.*: noble Elf; *anessë* of *Írith* [ar-[1] + edhel] *Silm*, *WJ*:318

Ar-·'Fei·ni·el, *kd.*: noble white lady; *anessë* of *Írith* [ar + fain + -iel[1]] *Silm*, *WJ*:318

Ar·fin, *kd.*: noble Finu; *Finarfin* [ar-[1] + Finu; from Q *Arafinwë*]

'Ar·ge·leb, *impr. tp.*: king of silver; two kings of Arthedain [ar(a)- + celeb] *LotR*

Ar·gon, *kd.*: high chieftain; *amilessë* of *Fingolfin* and *fn.* of one of his sons [ar-[1] + caun[3]; from Q *Aracáno*] *PME*:345

'Ar·go·nui, *impr. kd.*: ?commanding king; chieftain of the Dúnedain of Arnor [ar(a)- + conui] *LotR:AppA*

'Ar·mi·nas, *kd.*: (like a) royal tower; a Noldo Elf of the people of Angrod [arn + minas] *Silm*

'A·ro·thir, *kd.*: noble lord; son of Angrod and king of Nargothrond [arod + hîr] also called *Orodreth PME*:346, *VT*41:9

Ar·roch, *kd.*: noble horse; a horse belonging to Húrin [ar-[1] + roch] *UT*

Ar·thael, *dv.*: noble and wise; alt. to *Saelon* [arth + sael] *PME*:409

'Ar·ve·dui, *impr. kd.*: last king; the last king of Arthedain [ar(a)- + medui] *LotR*

'Ar·ve·gil, *kd. bv.*: having a royal sword; king of Arthedain [ar(a)- + megil] *LotR:AppA*

'Ar·ve·leg, *impr. kd.*: mighty king; king of Arthedain [ar(a)- + beleg] *LotR:AppA*

Ar·wen, *kd.*: noble maiden; daughter of Elrond, later queen of Gondor [ar-[1] + gwên] *LotR*

'As·fa·loth, *tp.*: ?flower of the foam; the horse of Glorfindel [!asfal + loth, the first element possibly being a word meaning 'foam, froth' < OS *asp^{h}al- √SPAL] *LotR*

B

Ba·lar: meaning uncertain; a name given to Ossë (*Yssion*) by the Sindar [OS *balare < PQ *'balāre √BAL] *WJ*:5

'Ba·ra·chir, *kd.*: eager lord; a man of the house of Bëor, father of Beren [bara + hîr] usually spelled *'Ba·ra·hir LotR*, *Silm*

'Ba·ra·gund, *kd.*: eager prince; a man of the house of Bëor [bara + cund] *Silm*

'Ba·ra·nor, *kd.*: (like an) eager flame; a man of Gondor [bara + naur] *LotR*

'Ba·ra·vorn, *tp.*: staying at home; a *perian*, son of Perhael and Meril [bâr + avorn] translation of Hamfast *SD*:128–31

Baug·lir, *n.*: constrainer; *Morgoth* [bauglir] *Silm*

Baug·ron, *n.*: constrainer; a late alteration of *Bauglir* [baugron] *MR*:149

Bel·dir: meaning uncertain; a man of the house of Bëor [contains *dîr* 'man'] *WJ*:231

Bel·dis: meaning uncertain; a woman of the house of Bëor [contains *dîs* 'woman'] *WJ*:231

Be·'lec·thor, *kd.*: (like a) mighty eagle; two stewards of Gondor [beleg + thôr[2]] *LotR:AppA*

Be·leg, *adj.*: mighty; a Sinda of Doriath [beleg] called *Cúthalion Silm*

'Be·le·gor, *kd. bv.*: ?having mighty vigor; a man of the house of Bëor [beleg + gôr] *WJ*:231

'Be·le·gorn, *kd. bv.*: having mighty valor; a steward of Gondor [beleg + gorn[2]] *LotR:AppA*

'Be·le·gund, *kd.*: mighty prince; a man of the house of Bëor [beleg + cund] *Silm*

'Be·le·gúr, *tp.*: ariser in might; *Morgoth* [disused CS form of the ancient name of the Vala Melkor, OS *belekūro, CE *(m)belekōrō; the element *beleg* in this name was a nominal form (*[m]belekē) meaning 'might', derived from the same root √BELEK or √M-BELEK as the adjective *beleg* (CE *belekā) 'mighty', but distinct in formation; it does not seem to have occurred elsewhere in CS] *PME*:358

'Be·le·gurth, *kd.*: great death, *epessë* of Morgoth [beleg + gurth; an intentionally altered form of *Belegúr*] *PME*:358

'Be·le·mir, *tp.*: meaning uncertain; a man of the house of Bëor [possibly from Q *Valamirë* 'jewel of the Valar'] *WJ*:231

Be·leth: meaning uncertain; a woman of the house of Bëor [contains *-eth*[2]] *WJ*:231

Ben-adar: lenited form of *Pen-adar* (q.v.) *LotR*

Bë·or, *n.*: vassal; *epessë* of the first chief of the house of Bëor [either from a word in his native language, or a dialectal variant of *bŷr* 'follower'] *Silm*

Be·reg, *adj.*: ?fierce; a man of the house of Bëor [perhaps from the root √BERÉK wild, violent] *Silm*

'Be·re·gar: meaning uncertain; a man of Númenor, father of Erendis [probably contains !bereg] *UT*

'Be·re·gond, *kd.*: ?fierce stone; a man of Gondor [!bereg + gond] *LotR*

'Be·re·lach: meaning uncertain; a man of Gondor [contains *lach* 'flame'] *PME*:416

Be·ren, *adj.*: bold; a man of the house of Bëor, husband of Lúthien [beren] called *Erchamion*, *Camlost LotR*, *Silm*

Ber·gil: meaning uncertain; a boy of Gondor [probably contains *gîl* 'star'] *LotR*

Be·ril: meaning uncertain; a woman of the house of Bëor [probably contains *-il*[1]] *WJ*:231

Be·'rú·thi·el: meaning uncertain; a queen of Gondor [contains *-iel*[1] 'maiden'] *LotR*

Bla·'dor·thin: meaning uncertain; possibly an ancient king of Dale [may contain *thind* 'grey'] *Hobbit*

Bol·dog, *tp.*: soldier of torment; name given to certain orcs [baul + daug] *LR*:375 *NDAK-*, 377 *ÑGWAL-*

Bôr, *n.*: trusty man; chieftain of Easterlings in Beleriand [bôr] *Silm*

Bor·lach, *impr. kd.*: trusty man like a flame; an Easterling in Beleriand [bôr + lach] *Silm*

Bor·lad: meaning uncertain; an Easterling in Beleriand [contains *bôr*] *Silm*

Bor·las, *impr. tp.*: trusty man (full) of joy; an Easterling in Beleriand [bôr + glas] *LR*:353 *BOR-*

'Bo·ro·mir, *kd.*: enduring jewel; a man of the house of Bëor and others later named for him [from Q **Voromir* or *Voromírë* √BOR[1] √MIR] *LotR*, *Silm*

Bo·ron: ?steadfast one; a man of the house of Bëor [bôr + -on[1]] *Silm*

Bo·'ron·dir, *kd.*: man who is trusty; a rider of Gondor [bôr + dîr] called *Udalraph UT*:313

Bran·dir, *kd.*: ?high man; a man of the house of Haleth [the name is probably in the language of the Haladin, but it is interpretable in CS as *brand* + *dîr*] *Silm*

#'**Bre·ga·ladh**, *kd.*: quick tree; an ent [brêg + galadh] spelled *Bregalad* *LotR*, *Names*:172

Bre·gil, *kd.*: ?quick star; a woman of the house of Bëor [brêg + gîl] *WJ*:231

'**Bre·go·las**, *n.*: fierceness; a man of the house of Bëor [bregolas] *Silm*

Bre·gor, *kd. bv.*: ?having quick vigor; a man of the house of Beör [brêg + gôr] *Silm*

Bron·we, *kd.*: steadfast man; CS name of the Noldo Voronwë [b(o)ron + gwê] *LR*:353 *BORÓN*

Bron·we a·thar Har·thad, *prph.*: endurance beyond hope; *epessë* given to Frodo Baggins [bronwe, athar, harthad]; spelled *Bronwe athan Harthad* *SD*:62

C

Cam·bant, *impr. kd. bv.*: he whose hand is full; probably an *epessë* of *Beren* [cam + pant] *LR*:366 *KWAT-*

Cam·lost, *impr. kd. bv.*: he whose hand is empty; *cilmessë* of *Beren*, after he lost the Silmaril to Carcharoth [cam + lost] *WJ*:69

Ca·'ran·thir, *kd. bv.*: he whose face is red; fifth son of Fëanor, named for a personal characteristic [caran + thîr; from Q *Carnistir*] *Silm*, *VT*41:10

'**Car·cha·roth**: said to mean 'red maw'; the wolf of Angband [possibly contains *carch* 'fang' or *carn* 'red'; second element obscure] called *Anfauglir Silm*

'**Ce·le·born**, *tp. bv.*: tall one of silver (-colored hair); lord of Lórien [celeb + orn[1]] also *Galathir LotR*, *UT*:266

ˊ**Ce·leb·'rí·an**, *tp.*: queen of silver; wife of Elrond [celeb + rían] *LotR*, *Letters*:423

ˊ**Ce·leb·'rim·bor**, *kd. bv.*: he whose clenched hand is of silver; a Noldo, ruler of Eregion [celebren + paur; Q *Telperinquar*] *LotR*; *Silm:App*, s.v. "celeb"; *PME*:179, 318

ˊ**Ce·leb·'rin·dal**, *kd. bv.*: she whose feet are like silver, *anessë* of *Idril* [celebren + tâl] (also *Celebrendal*) *Silm*

ˊ**Ce·leb·'rin·dor**, *kd.*: silver king; king of Arthedain [celebren + taur[2]] *LotR:AppA*

'**Ce·le·gorm**, *kd.*: swift riser; third son of Fëanor, said to leap up hastily when angered [celeg + !orm(√ORO); from Q *Tyelcormo* < CE *Kʲelekormō; a NS form, whose normal S form would be '*Ce·le·gorf*] *Silm*, *VT*41:10

'**Ce·le·gorn**, *dv.*: swift and hasty; alt. to *Celegorm* [celeg + gorn[1]] *TI*

?**Ce·'lem·me·gil**, *tp.*: sword of silver; alt. to *Celebrindor* [celeb + megil;

perhaps from a Q **Telemmacil*]. The spelling of this name is uncertain. *PME*:208

'Ce·le·pharn, *tp.*: stone of silver; king of Arthedain [celeb + sarn²] *LotR:AppA*

Cír·dan, *tp.*: maker of ships; lord of the Falas and of Mithlond [cair + tân, OS *kiriatano] *LotR*, *Silm*, *PME*:385

'Ci·ri·on, *n.*: shipman; a steward of Gondor [cirion] *LotR:AppA*

Cor·dof, *n.*: small red apple; a son of Samwise (Perhael), called Pippin [cordof] *SD*:128–31

Cran·thir, *kd. bv.*: having a ruddy face; alt. to *Caranthir* [crann + thîr] *LR*:362 *KARÁN-*, 392 *THE-*

'Cu·ru·fin, *tp.*: Finu of skill; fourth son of Fëanor [curu + Finu] (NS Curufim) *Silm*, *PME*:344, *VT*41:10

'Cu·ru·nír, *tp.*: man of skill; the wizard called Saruman [curu + dîr] called *Glân* (lenited *'Lân*) 'the White'; *LotR*, *Silm*, *UT*:390

Cú·'tha·li·on, *impr. kd. bv.*: having a strong bow; *anessë* of *Beleg* [cû + thalion] *Silm*

D

Dae·ron: ?great man; a Sinda of Doriath, minstrel and loremaster of Thingol [daer¹ + -on¹] *LotR*

Dag·nir, *n.*: slayer; a man loyal to the house of Bëor [dagnir] *Silm*

Dag·nir Glau·'run·ga, *gph.*: slayer of Glaurung; *epessë* of *Túrin* [dagnir, Glaurung (see § 6.1)] *Silm*

Da·'gor·lind, *tp.*: singer in battle; *anessë* of *Magor* [dagor + lind²] *UT*:235

Dam·rod, *tp.*: champion with a hammer; a ranger of Gondor [dam + raud²] *LotR*

Del·'duth·ling, *tp.*: spider of the horror of night; *Ungoliant* [dêl + dû + lhing] *LR*:354 *DOȜ-*, 355 *DYEL-*, 386 *SLIG-*

'De·ru·fin, *kd.*: ?manly hair; a man of the Morthond Vale in Gondor [!deru + find, the first element possibly being from CE *nderwā √NDER 'manly'] *LotR*

'Der·vo·rin: meaning uncertain; lord of Ringló Vale in Gondor [may contain !deru; cf. Derufin] *LotR*

Di·or, *n.*: successor; son of Lúthien and Beren and last king of Doriath [dialectal form of *dŷr*] called *Eluchíl*, *Aranel LotR*, *Silm*

Dír·hael, *impr. kd.*: wise man; grandfather of Aragorn II [dîr + sael] *LotR:AppA*

'Dí·ri·el, *impr. tp.*: man of joy; rejected name of the youngest son of Fëanor [dîr + gell]

'Dol·we·thil, *kd.*: dark shadow-woman; a vampire [doll + gwâth + -il[1]], also called *Thuringwethil LR*:393 *THUR-*

Draug·luin, *impr. kd.*: blue wolf; a werewolf of Tol in-Gaurhoth [draug + luin] *Silm*

Dui·lin, *tp.*: ?singer by the river; a man of the Morthond Vale in Gondor [duin + lind[2]] *LotR*

Duin·hir, *tp.*: lord of the river; lord of Morthond Vale in Gondor [duin + hîr] *LotR*

'Dú·na·dan, *tp.*: man of the West (Númenórean); *epessë* of *Aragorn* II [dûn + adan] *LotR*:245

E

Ec·'the·li·on: see *Aecthelion LotR*

E·'den·nil, *tp.*: friend of the Edain; *epessë* given to *Finrod* [from Q *Atandil*] *MR*:305

E·'dhel·harn *tp. bv.*: having an Elf-stone (beryl); *epessë* of *Aragorn* II [edhel + sarn, given on account of the precious jewel called *Elessar*, which was given to Aragorn by Galadriel] *SD*:128–31

E·'dhel·los, *tp.*: flower of the Elves; wife of Angrod [edhel + los[2], from Q *Eldalótë*] *PME*:346

E·'dhel·wen, *kd.*: maiden like an Elf; *epessë* of *Morwen* [edhel + gwên] alt. from *Eledhwen WJ*

'Ed·ra·hil: meaning obscure; an Elf of Nargothrond *Silm*, *WJ*:66

E·'gal·moth: see *Aegamloth LotR:AppA*

Eig·nor, *kd.*: sharp flame; alt. from *Aegnor* [aig + naur, a Sindarized form of Q Ekyanáro] *VT*41:14

'Ei·ri·en, *n.*: daisy; a *perian*, daughter of Perhael and Meril [eirien] *SD*:128–31

'El·a·dar, *tp.*: father of the star; *epessë* of *Tuor* [êl + adar; the 'star' of the name refers to Tuor's son Eärendil] *WJ*:235

'El·a·nor, *dc.*: *elanor* 'flower'; a *perian*, daughter of Perhael and Meril [êl + anor] *LotR*, *SD*:128–31

'El·be·reth, *tp.*: queen of stars; the Valië Varda [êl + bereth, OS *elembarat[h]il] called *Gilbrennil*, *Gilthoniel*, *Fanuilos LotR*, *RGEO*, *MR*:387

'El·bo·ron, *kd.*: trusty man like a star; son of Faramir [êl + bôr + -on[1]] *PME*:221

El·dûn, *impr. tp.*: star of the West; alt. to *Eluréd* [êl + dûn] *PME*:372

E·'ledh·wen, *kd.*: maiden like an Elf; *epessë* of *Morwen* [eledh + gwên] alt. to *Edhelwen Letters*:281

'El·la·dan, *dc.*: like both Elves and men; a son of Elrond [ell-[1] + adan] *LotR*, *Letters*:282

El·phir, *tp.*: lord of swans; a prince of Dol Amroth, of which city the swan was the emblem [alph + hîr] *PME*:221

'El·ro·hir, *kd.*: knight who is an Elf; a son of Elrond [ell-[1] + rochir] *LotR*, *Letters*:282

El·rond, *tp.*: dome of stars; the half-Elven sage of Imladris [êl + rond, named after the hall of Menelrond in Menegroth] *Hobbit*, *LotR*, *Letters*:282, *WJ*:414, *PME*:371

El·ros, *tp.*: foam of stars or glitter of stars; the first king of Númenor, brother of Elrond [êl + ros[2] or êl + ros[3]] *LotR*, *UT*, *Letters*:282, *WJ*:414

El·rûn, *impr. tp.*: star of the East; alt. to *Elurín* [êl + rhûn] *PME*:372

El·thorn or **'El·tho·ron**, *tp.*: eagle of the sky; an unknown person [ell-[2] + thoron] *LR*:392 *THOR-*

E·lu: meaning obscure; original name of *Thingol* [OS *Elwe] *Silm*, *MR*:217

'E·lu·chîl, *tp.*: heir of Elu; *cilmessë* of *Dior* [Elu + hîl] *Silm*, *WJ*:350

'E·lu·réd, *tp.*: heir of Elu; a son of Dior [Elu + rêd] *Silm*

'E·lu·rín, *tp.*: remembrance of Elu; a son of Dior [Elu + rîn] *Silm*, *PME*:372

'El·wing, *tp.*: foam of stars; daughter of Dior [êl + gwing, named for the waterfall of Lanthir Lamath in Ossiriand] *LotR*, *Letters*:282, *PME*:371, 376

E·'mel·dir: meaning uncertain; a woman of the house of Bëor [probably contains *dîr* 'man'; she was called 'the Manhearted'] *Silm*

E·'ner·dhil, *tp.*: friend of the sun; a Noldo of Gondolin [from Q *Anardil*] *UT*

'E·ra·dan, *kd.*: single man; a steward of Gondor [er- + adan] *LotR:AppA*

Er·'cham·i·on, *kd.*: having one hand; *epessë* of *Beren* [er- + cam + -ion[2]] *Silm*

Er·'chi·ri·on, *tp.*: son of a noble lord; a son of Imrahil [ar-[1] + hîr + iôn] *PME*:221

E·'rei·ni·on, *tp.*: son of kings; *Gil-galad* [aran + iôn] *Silm*

E·'rel·lont: meaning uncertain; a mariner who accompanied Eärendil [possibly contains a derivative of the root √LUT 'float'] *Silm*

E·'res·tor: meaning uncertain; a counselor of Elrond in Imladris *LotR*

Er·nil i-ˌPhe·ri·'an·nath, *gph.*: prince of the halflings; *epessë* given to Peregrin Took in Gondor *LotR*

Er·nis, *kd.*: single woman; rejected name for a daughter of Fingon [er- + dîs] *PME*:361

Es·tel, *n.*: hope; original name of *Aragorn* II [estel] *LotR*

F

Fae·'liv·rin, *impr. tp.*: gleam on Ivrin; *epessë* of *Finduilas* [fael + Ivrin] *Silm*

Fae·nor, *impr. tp.*: "correct" CS form of *Fëanor* [fae + naur] *PME*:343

'Fa·la·thar: meaning obscure; a mariner, companion of Eärendil [may contain *falas* 'shore'] *Silm*

Fan·gorn, *impr. tp. bv.*: having the beard of a tree; the ent Treebeard [fang + orn[2]] *LotR:AppF*, *Names*:175

Fa·'nui·los, *impr. kd. bv.*: having an eternally white *fana* (apparition form); *Elbereth*, when seen as a shining white figure standing on Oiolossë (Amon Uilos) [fân + uilos[1]] *RGEO*:66, *Letters*:278

'Fë·a·nor, *impr. tp.*: spirit of fire; *amilessë* of a Noldo, son of Finu, maker of the Silmarils [Q *fëa* 'spirit' + naur] *fn. Curufin Silm*

'Fe·la·gon, *kd.*: just commander; *Finrod* [an alteration of Kh Felakgundu, as if somehow derived from fael[1] + caun[3]] *PME*:352

'Fe·la·gund: hewer of caves; *epessë* of *Finrod* [from Khuzdul *felakgundu*, but interpretable as *tp. fela* + *cund* 'prince of caves', although such a name would have the proper form !Felgund. This name was given on account of Finrod's skill in stone-carving] *Silm:Index*, *PME*:352

'Fim·bre·thil, *kd.*: slender birch; an Entwife [fim + brethil] *LotR:AppF*

Fi·'nar·fin, *kd.*: noble Finu; *fn.* of a son of Finu, king of the Noldor in Aman [Finu + ar-[1] + Finu; based on Q *Arafinwë*] also *Arfin Silm*

Fin·bor, *dv. bv.*: having hair and fist; rejected name for a son of Fingon [find + paur] *PME*:361

'Fin·de·gil, *dv. bv.*: having hair and pen [find + tegil] *LotR*

Fin·dor, *tp.*: king with hair; alt. to *Gil-galad* [find + taur[2]] *WJ*:56

Fin·'dui·las: meaning obscure; daughter of Arothir [probably contains *find* 'tress', and possibly *glas* 'joy'] called *Faelivrin Silm*

Fi·'nel·lach, *tp.*: flame of hair and eye; *Gil-galad* [fîn + hen + lach] *PME*:351

Fin·glas, *impr. tp. bv.*: having hair of leaves [find + las] *Names*:169

Fin·'gol·fin, *tp.*: Finu of knowledge; *fn.* of a son of Finu, king of the Noldor in Middle-earth [Finu + Golfin, based on Q *Nolofinwë*] also *Aran Hithlum*, *Taur Edledhryn PME*:344

Fin·gon, *tp.*: commander with hair; *fn.* of a son of Fingolfin, named for his long dark hair [find + caun[3], from Q *Findecáno*] *PME*:345

Fin·rod, *tp.*: champion with hair; *fn.* of a son of Finarfin, king of Nargothrond, named for his golden hair [find + raud[2]; from Q *Findaráto*] called *Felagund*, *Felagon*, *Edennil*, *PME*:346, *VT*41:9

Fi·nu: meaning unknown; the first king of the Noldor [expected CS form of Q *Finwë*] spelled Finw *LR*:381 *PHIN-*

'Fi·ri·el: mortal maiden; *epessë* of *Lúthien* [fair + -iel[2]] *LotR*, *ATB*
Flad·rif, *impr. tp. bv.*: having skin of bark; an Ent [flâd + rîf] *Names*:173

G

Gae·rys, *tp.*: fearful Ossë; the Maia Ossë (*Yssion*) [gaer[1] + Ys (name), OS *Gairossi, the last element from Valarin oššai 'foaming'] *WJ*:400
'Ga·la·dor, *tp.*: ?king of light; an early lord of Dol Amroth [galad + taur[2]] *UT*, *PME*:222
Ga·'lad·ri·el, *tp.*: maiden with crown of light; the Noldorin lady of Lórien [galad + riel; from Q *Altariel*] *LotR*, *Silm*, *MR*:182, *PME*:347, *Letters*:423
'Ga·la·dhon: tree-person; a Sinda of Doriath, akin to Thingol [galadh + -on[1]] *UT*:266
Ga·'ladh·ri·el, *tp.*: crowned maiden of the trees; a common misinterpretation of the name Galadriel [galadh + riel] *UT*:267
Ga·'ladh·ri·en, *tp.*: queen of trees; alt. to *Galadriel* [galadh + rien] *TI*:249
#Ga·'ladh·wen, *tp.*: maiden of the trees; a queen of Gondor of Northmannish origin [galadh + gwên; from the Northmannish name *Widumawi of the same meaning] spelled *Galadwen PME*:260
'Ga·la·thil, *tp.*: radiance of trees; a Sinda of Doriath, kin to Thingol [galadh + thîl] *UT*
'Ga·la·thir, *tp.*: lord of trees; alt. to *Celeborn* [galadh + hîr] *TI*:249
Gal·dor, *tp.*: king of light; an Elf of Gondolin and of the Grey Havens, also a lord of the house of Hador [gâl + taur[2]] called *Orchal* 'the tall' *Silm*, *WJ*:305
'Ga·li·on, *tp.*: son of light; the king's butler of Mirkwood [gâl + iôn] *Hobbit*
Ge·lir, *adj.*: merry; a son of Samwise (Perhael), in Westron called Merry [gelir] *SD*:128–31
Gel·mir, *tp.*: jewel of joy; a Noldo Elf of the people of Angrod, also an Elf of Nargothrond [gell + mîr] *Silm*
'Gil·ba·rad, *tp.*: tower of stars; a Dúnadan of Eriador, father of Ivorwen [gîl + barad[1]] *PME*:263
Gil·'bren·nil, *tp.*: lady of the stars; *Elbereth* [gîl + brennil] *LR*:358 *GIL-*
Gil·dis, *tp.*: woman of the stars; wife of Hador [gîl + dîs] *WJ*:234
Gil·dor, *tp.*: king of stars; a Noldo of Eriador [gîl + taur[2]] called *Inglorion LotR*
Gil-ga·lad, *gph.*: star of brilliance; *epessë* of *Rodnor* son of Arothir, High King of the Noldor in Middle-earth during the Second Age [gîl, galad] called *Ereinion*, *Finellach*, also *Findor LotR*, *RGEO*, *Letters*:425–26

Gil·mith, *impr. kd.*: grey star; a lady of Belfalas [gîl + mîth[1]] *UT*

Gil·raen, *tp.*: enlaced with sparks (referring to a hairnet with glinting jewels); a lady of the Dúnedain of Eriador, mother of Aragorn II [gîl + raen] *VT*42:12

Gil·'tho·ni·el, *tp.*: kindler (feminine) of stars; *Elbereth* [gîl + thoniel] *LotR*, *RGEO*, *MR*:388

Gil·wen, *tp.*: maiden of stars; a woman of the house of Bëor [gîl + gwên] *WJ*:231

'Gi·ri·on, *n.*: shuddering man; lord of Dale in Rhovanion [giri- + on[1]; possibly means 'man who causes others to shudder'] *Hobbit*

Gladh·wen, *tp.*: maiden who laughs; "true" CS form of *Lalwen* [gladha- + gwên] *PME*:359

Glau·rung: meaning uncertain; a dragon of the First Age [possibly contains *glaur* 'gold'] *Silm*

'Gló·re·dhel, *tp.*: Elf of gold; a woman of the house of Hador [glaur + edhel] *Silm*

Glor·'fin·del, *tp. bv.*: having tresses of gold; a noble Elf of Gondolin and Imladris [glaur + finnel; the form *-findel* is archaic] *LotR*, *Silm*

Glor·'fin·ni·el, *tp.*: maiden having hair of gold; a daughter of Samwise (Perhael) [glaur + find + -iel[1]] translation of Goldilocks *SD*:128–31

Gló·'rin·dol, *kd. bv.*: having a golden head; *epessë* of *Hador* [glóren + dôl] *WJ*:225

Goe·nor, *tp.*: fire of terror; "correct" CS equivalent of Q *Aicanáro* (*Aegnor*) [goe[1] + naur] *PME*:363

Go·'las·gil, *tp.*: star of leaves; lord of the Anfalas in Gondor [golas + gîl] *LotR*

Gon·'doth·rim, *tp.*: people of Gondost; the inhabitants of Gondolin [Gondost + rim[1]] *LR*:359 *GOND-*

Gor·thaur, *tp.*: detestable one of horror; Sauron [gôr[2] + thaur[1]] also *Thû*, *Gorthu*, *Morthu* *Silm*

Gor·thol, *tp.*: helm of dread; *cilmessë* of *Túrin* when he fought beside Beleg Cúthalion in the lands west of Doriath [gôr[2] + thôl; the name derived from the dragon-helm Túrin wore] *Silm*

Gor·thu, *tp.*: stench of horror; alt. to *Gorthaur* [gôr[2] + thû] *LR*:333

Gos·tir, *tp.*: countenance of dread; a dragon [gos + thîr] *LR*:359 *GOS-*

Goth·mog, *impr. kd.*: cruel enemy; Lord of the Balrogs [goth + baug] *LotR*, *Silm*, *LR*:359 *GOS-*, 372 *MBAW-*

Goth·rog, *tp.*: demon of dread; a monster [gos + raug] *LR*:359 *GOS-*

Gui·lin: meaning uncertain; an Elf, father of Gwindor and Gelmir [probably contains *lind* 'singer'] *Silm*

Gun·dor: meaning uncertain; a man of the house of Hador [probably contains *taur*[2] 'king'] *Silm*

Gw

Gwae·hir, *tp*.: lord of the wind; Lord of the Eagles [gwaew + hîr] also spelled *Gwaihir*; also *Gwaewar LotR*

Gwae·war, *tp*.: king of the wind; alt. to *Gwaehir* [gwaew + âr] *LR*:301

Gwe·nyn, i-We·nyn, *n*.: (the) twins; the youngest sons of Fëanor, twins, both named *Amros* [gwenyn] *PME*:353, 365

Gwin·dor, *kd*.: new king; an Elf of Nargothrond [gwain + taur[2]] *Silm*

H

Ha·dor, *n*.: warrior; chief of the tribe of Marach and Lord of Dor-Lómin [hador] called *Glórindol Silm*

Ha·'do·ri·on, *tp*.: descendant of Hador; *epessë* of *Húrin* [Hador + iôn] *WJ*:294

'Hal·ba·rad, *kd*.: tall tower; a Dúnadan of Eriador [hall[1] + barad[1]] *LotR*

Hal·dir, *kd*.: hidden man; an Elf of Lothlórien, also a son of Arothir [hall[2] + dîr] *LotR*

Hal·las, *n*.: ?tallness; a Steward of Gondor [hall[1] + -as] *LotR:AppA*

Hal·mir, *kd*.: hidden jewel; alt. to Haldir [hall[2] + mîr] *WJ*:137

Han·dir, *kd*.: intelligent man; a man of the house of Haleth [this name was probably in the tongue of the Haladin, but in CS it appeared to be a compound, *hand* + *dîr*] *Silm*

Har·thad U·'lui·thi·ad, *ajph*.: unquenchable hope; *epessë* given to Samwise Gamgee (*Perhael*) [harthad, uluithiad] *SD*:62

Ha·'thal·dir: perhaps a variant of Hatholdir; a man loyal to the house of Bëor *Silm*

Ha·thol, *n*.: axe; chief of the tribe of Marach [hathol] *Silm*

Ha·'thol·dir, *tp*.: man with an axe; a man of Númenor [hathol + dîr] *UT*

Hen·derch: meaning uncertain; a man of Númenor [may contain *hen(d)* 'eye'] *UT*

'He·ri·on, *tp*.: son of lords; a steward of Gondor [hîr + iôn] *LotR:AppA*

Hir·gon, *kd*.: commander who is a lord; a man of Gondor [hîr + caun[3]] *LotR*

Hi·ril, *n*.: lady; a woman of the house of Bëor, sister of Beren, also a lady of the Haladin [híril] *WJ*:270

Hir·luin, *impr. kd*.: blue lord; lord of the Pinnath Gelin in Gondor [hîr + luin] *LotR*

Hir·wen, *kd*.: maiden like a lord; a woman of the house of Bëor [hîr + gwên] *WJ*:231

Hu·an, *n.*: hound [from Q *huan* 'beast that barks' < CE *k^hugano √KHUG] *Silm*

Hu·or, *tp.*: vigor of heart, courage; a man of the house of Hador [hû- + gôr[1]; the name is also said to be from a Mannish language] *Silm*

Hú·rin, *tp.*: mind of vigor; a lord of the House of Hador [hûr + ind] called *Thalion, Hadorion Silm*

ˌHu·ri·'ni·o·nath, *tp. pl.*: descendants of Húrin; the house of stewards of Gondor, descended from Húrin, steward of King Minardil [Húrin + ionath, *pl.* of iôn] *PME*:202–3, 218

I

Id·ril, *kd.*: sparkling brilliance; daughter of Turgon [from Q *Itarillë*] called *Celebrindal Silm, PME*:346

Idh·ril: thoughtful woman; alt. to *Idril* [idhor + -il[1]] *LR*:361 *ID-*

In·glor, *impr. tp.*: Vanya of gold (color); Elf of the house of Finrod [from Q *Ingalaurë*, but also interpreted in CS as *ind* + *claur* 'mind of splendor' or *ind* + *glaur* 'mind of gold'] *UT*:255, *LR*:361 *ID- PME*:360

In·'glo·ri·on: son or descendant of Inglor; *anessë* of *Gildor* [Inglor + iôn] *LotR*

Í·reth: woman of desire; alt. to *Írith* [!ír- + -eth[2]] *PME*:345

Í·rith, *n.*: desire, beauty; *fn.* of a daughter of Fingolfin [although the meaning is not securely attested, the word has the shape of an abstract noun derived from the root √IR with the noun suffix *-th* following vocalic extension. From Q *Írissë*] called *Aredhel, Ar-Feiniel, Rodwen Los PME*:345, 362

I·'thil·bor, *tp.*: fist of the moon; a Nandorin Elf, father of Saeros [ithil + paur] *UT*

Ith·ryn Luin, *ajph.*: blue wizards; two of the five wizards (Ithryn) who went into the East of Middle-earth and never returned [ithron, luin] *UT*:390

I·von, *tp.*: giver of corn; the Valië Yavanna [MS *iƀaun < OS *jabǭna < CE *jabānā √JAB √AN] *PME*:404

I·'vor·wen, *tp.*: ?maiden of crystal; a woman of the Dúnedain of Eriador [ivor + gwên] *LotR:AppA*

Iv·'ri·ni·el, *kd.*: crystalline maiden; a daughter of Adrahil of Dol Amroth [ivrin + -iel[1]] *PME*:221

J

Iar·wain, *adj.*: eldest; the person known to the Periannath as Tom Bombadil [iarwain] called *Iarwain Ben-adar* (see *Pen-adar*) *LotR*

Iôn, *n.*: son; *Maeglin*, as he was called by his father [iôn] *WJ*:337

Io·reth: old woman; a woman of Gondor [iaur + -eth[2]] *LotR*

Ior·hael, *dv.*: old and wise; a son of Samwise (Perhael), in Westron called Frodo [iaur + sael] *SD*:128–31

Ior·las, *kd.*: old joy; a man of Gondor, uncle of Bergil [iaur + glas] *LotR*

L

'La·ba·dal, *tp. bv.*: one having a foot that hops; *epessë* of Sador, a servant of Húrin's [laba- + tâl] *UT*:60

'Lae·go·las, *kd.*: green foliage; an Elf of Mirkwood, son of the Elvenking Thranduil [laeg[1] + golas] dialectal form *Legolas LotR*, *Letters*:282, and *no.* 297 *p.*382

La·laith, *n.*: laughter; *epessë* of *Urwen* daughter of Húrin [lalaith] also *Lalaeth WJ*:235

Lal·wen, *kd.*: maiden who laughs; a daughter of Finu [from Q *Lalwendë*] cf. *Gladhwen PME*:343

Lam·thanc, *impr. kd. bv.*: having a forked tongue; a serpent or dragon [lam[1] + thanc] *LR*:388 *STAK-*

'Lân: lenited form of *Glân*; see *Curunír UT*:390

'Lan·dro·val, *kd. bv.*: having wide pinions; an eagle [land[1] + roval] *LotR*

Lan·hael, *dv.*: plain and wise; alt. to *Panthael* [land[1] + sael] spelled *Lanhail SD*:118

Lath·laeg, *impr. kd.*: one who listens acutely; application uncertain [lasta- + laeg[2], OS *lasthalaika] *LR*:368 *LAS-*

Legolas: see *Laegolas*

Le·vain tad-dail, *ajph.*: bipedal animals; opprobrious name given to the petty-Dwarves [lavan, tâd, tâl] *WJ*:388

Lin·dir, *tp.*: man of song; an Elf of Imladris [lind[1] + dîr] *LotR*

Lin·dis, *tp.*: woman of song; alt. to *Nimloth* [lind[1] + dîs] *WJ*

Lórindol: lenited form of *Glórindol* (q.v.) *Silm*

Lo·'thí·ri·el, *tp.*: lady of flowers; daughter of Imrahil of Dol Amroth [loth + hîr + -iel[1]] *PME*:221

'Lú·thi·en, *n.*: enchantress; daughter of Thingol [Doriath dialect form of *luithien*, OS *lukthiene] called *Firiel*, *Tinúviel LotR*, *Silm*

M

Mab·lung, *impr. kd. bv.*: having a heavy hand; a Sinda of Doriath, whose name (the only one by which he is known) is said to have derived from the falling of his hand beneath the weight of the Silmaril when he took it from the belly of Carcharoth [mâb + lung, DorS form of *long*] *LotR*, *Silm*

Maed·ros, *dv.*: shapely and red-haired; the eldest son of Fëanor, who had reddish-brown hair [maed[2] + ros[1]; from his Q *amilessë Maitimo* and *epessë Russandol*] also spelled *Maedhros, Maidros Silm, PME*:366, *VT*41:10

Maeg·lin, *kd. bv.*: having a penetrating glance [maeg + glind] also *Iôn WJ*:337

Ma·gor, *n.*: sword; chief of the tribe of Marach [magor] called *Dagorlind Silm*

'Mag·la·dhonn, 'Mag·la·dhûr, 'Mag·la·vorn, *impr. kd. bv.*: having a dark sword; *alt.* to *Mormegil* [magol + donn, dûr, morn] *LR*:371 *MAK-*

Mag·lor, *impr. tp.*: one who forges golden light (sc. music); *amilessë* of Fëanor's second son, a singer and harpist [*maga- + glaur, from Q *Macalaurë*] *Silm, VT*41:10

Mal·beth, *tp.*: word of gold; a seer of Arthedain in the days of king Arvedui [mall + peth] *LotR*

'Mal·ga·lad, *tp.*: light of gold; *alt.* to *Amdír* father of Amroth [mall + calad] *UT*

Mal·lor, *tp.*: ?(golden) light of gold; king of Arthedain [mall + glaur] *LotR:AppA*

'Mal·ve·gil, *tp. bv.*: having a sword of gold; king of Arthedain [mall + megil] *LotR:AppA*

Me·'gil·dur, *impr. kd. bv.*: having a dark sword; *alt.* to *Mormegil* [megil + dûr] *LR*:371 *MAK-*

'Meg·li·vorn, *impr. kd.*: black bear; application uncertain [medli + morn] *LR*:369 *LIS-*

Mel·dis, *kd.*: dear woman; wife of Malach Aradan [mell + dîs; her original name was the proto-Adûnaic *Zimrahin*]

Me·leth, *n.*: love; a woman of the house of Haleth [meleth] *WJ*:270

Me·li·an, *kd.*: dear gift; a Maia, wife of Thingol [mail + ann, OS *Melianna] *Silm:App mel-*

Me·'nel·dor, *tp.*: king of the sky; an eagle [menel + taur[2]] *LotR*

Me·ril, *n.*: rose; a *perian*, wife of Perhael [meril] *SD*:128–31

Mír n·'Ar·dhon, *prph.*: jewel of the world; Eärendil [CS translation of Eärendil's *amilessë Ardamírë*] *PME*:348

Mith·'ran·dir, *kd.*: grey pilgrim; name used by Elves and men of Gondor for the wizard Gandalf [mîth[1] + randir] *LotR*

Mith·'rel·las, *kd.*: grey-leaf; an Elf-woman, companion of Nimrodel and ancestress of the Lords of Dol Amroth [mithren + las] *UT*

Mor·goth, *kd.*: black enemy; name given to the evil Vala Melkor by Fëanor [môr[1] + goth; from Q *Moringoflo*] called *Bauglir, Belegurth Silm*; *MR*:108, 294

'Mor·me·gil, *kd. bv.*: having a black sword; *epessë* given to *Túrin* in Nargothrond [morn + megil] *Silm*; *WJ*:83, 256

Mor·thu, *kd.*: black stench; CS *alt.* to *Gorthaur* (*Sauron*) [môr + thû] *LR*:393 *THUS-*, *RS*:186

Mor·wen, *kd.*: dark maiden; a woman of the house of Bëor, married to Húrin: [môr + gwên] called *Edhelwen Silm*, *WJ*:409

N

Nei·than, *adj.*: deprived; *cilmessë* of *Túrin* among the outlaws [neithan] *Silm*

Nel·las, *dg. bv.*: ?having three leaves; Elf-woman of Doriath [nel- + las; possibly from a plant name] *UT*

Nim·loth, *kd.*: (like a) white blossom; Elf-woman of Doriath, akin to Thingol, wife of Dior [nimp + loth] *Silm*

'Ní·ni·el: maiden of tears; *epessë* given to his sister Nienor by Túrin in Brethil [nîn + -iel[1]] *WJ*:96

#Noe·naer, *impr. kd.*: woeful lamentation; S interpretation of the Q name *Nienor* 'mourning' [noe + naer] (N Nuinoer] *LR*:375 *NAY-*

Nú·neth: ?woman of the West; a woman of Númenor [!nûn (? < Q *nú*, *númen* 'west') + -eth[2]] *UT*

O

Or·'chal·dor, *kd.*: tall king; a nobleman of Númenor [orchall + taur[2]] *UT*

Or·nil: ?little tree; an Elf of Nargothrond [orn + -il[2]] *WJ*:86

O·'rod·reth: meaning uncertain; *alt.* to *Arothir* [orod + !reth, an element equated to the unidentifiable Q *resto*, presumably from a root √*RET, √*RED or √*RETH] *PME*:350

'O·ro·pher, *tp.*: ?beech of the mountain; a king of the Silvan Elves of Mirkwood [orod + fêr] *UT*

'O·ro·phin: meaning uncertain; an Elf of Lórien [probably contains *orod* 'mountain'] *LotR*

Oth·'ron·dir, *tp.*: man of the cave-fortress; a man of Gondor [othrond + dîr] *PME*:417

P

Pant·hael, *kd.*: completely wise; *epessë* given to Samwise (*Perhael*) Gamgee by Aragorn II [pant + sael] *SD*:128–31

Pen-a·dar, *pc. bv.*: without father; *epessë* of *Iarwain* [pen[1], adar] *LotR*

'Pen·go·lodh, *kd.*: Elf who is a Noldo; Elvish loremaster and linguist [pen[2] + golodh, in Q *Quendingoldo* or *Quengoldo*] also called

Thingódhel WJ:396, 417; *PME*:401, 404

'Pe·re·dhil, i-·'Phe·re·dhil, *n. pl.*: half-Elves; *Elrond* and *Elros*, who were descended from both the Edhil (Eldar) and Edain [peredhel] *Silm:Index, App edhel*; *PME*:256, 348

Per·hael, *kd.*: half wise; the *perian* (halfling) known in Westron as *Banazîr* (Samwise) [per- + sael] *LotR*, *SD*:128–31

R

Ras·mund, *tp.*: bull with horns; a bull [ras + mund] *Letters*:423

Rí·an, *n.*: queen; a woman of the house of Bëor, mother of Tuor [rían] *Silm*

Ro·'chal·lor: meaning uncertain; horse of Fingolfin [contains *roch* 'horse'] *Silm*

'Ro·he·ryn, *impr. tp.*: horse of the lady; Aragorn II's horse, given him by Arwen [roch + heryn] normal form *Rocheryn LotR*

Rod·nor, *kd.*: noble fire; *fn.* of *Gil-galad* [raud[1] + naur] *PME*:350

Rod·wen, *kd.*: noble virgin; *Írith* [raud[1] + gwên] called *Glos* (lenited '*Los*) 'the White' *WJ*:317–18

S

Sae·lind, *kd. bv.*: having a wise heart; *epessë* of *Andreth* [sael + ind] *MR*:305

Sae·lon: wiseman; a man of Gondor [sael + -on[1]] *PME*:409

Se·ron 'Ae·a·ron, *gph.*: friend of the sea; Eärendil [seron, aearon; CS translation of Q *Eärendil*] *PME*:348

T

Tar·gon, *kd.*: noble commander; a man of Gondor [taur[1] + caun[3]] *LotR*

Tar·mund, *kd.*: noble bull; a bull [taur[1] + mund] *Letters*:423

Taur, *adj.*: high, noble; CS name used for the *perian* Frodo [taur[1]; this may be incorrect, as the meaning of Frodo (Old English Fróda) is 'old, wise by experience'. The name actually appears in the lenited form *Daur* (cf. *Iorhael*) *LotR*

Taur Ed·'ledh·ryn, *gph.*: king of exiles; title of *Fingolfin* [taur[2], i, edledhron] (N Taur Egledhruin, misspelled *Egledhriur*) *LR*:389 *TA-*

Tau·ron, *n.*: forester; the Valië *Araw* [tauron; short for *Aran Tauron Forester King*] *PME*:358

Tin·fang, *tp. bv.*: having a beard of stars; an Elvish piper [tinu + fang] *LR*:387 *SPAN-*

Ti·'nú·vi·el, *tp.*: daughter of the twilight, nightingale; *epessë* given to Lúthien by Beren [tinnú + iell] *WJ*:62

Tor·hir, *kd.*: high master; a geographer of Beleriand, writer of the work *Dorgannas Iaur* [taur[1] + hîr] called *Iphant* 'the old' (also *Ifant*) *WJ*:192

Tu·or, *dv. bv.*: having strength and vigor; a man of the house of Hador [tû + gôr[1]; also said to be from a Mannish language] called *Eladar Silm*

'Tú·ram·arth, *impr. tp.*: master of doom; *cilmessë* of *Túrin* in Brethil [tûr[2] + amarth] *Silm*

'Tú·rum·arth, *impr. tp.*: master of evil fate; *alt.* to *Turamarth* [tûr[2] + úmarth] *WJ*:311

Tur·gon: ?master commander; *fn.* of a son of Fingolfin and King of Gondolin [tûr[2] + caun[3], from Q *Turucáno*] *Silm*, *PME*:345

Tú·rin, *tp. bv.*: having a mind (suitable) for victory; a great warrior of the house of Hador [tûr[1] + ind] called *Neithan*, *Gorthol*, *Agarwaen*, *Adanedhel*, *Thuringud*, *Thurin*, *Mormegil*, *Turamarth*, *Dagnir Glaurunga LotR:AppA*, *Silm*, *UT*

Th

'Tha·li·on, *adj.*: steadfast; *epessë* of *Húrin* [thalion] *Silm*

Thin·'gó·dhel, *kd.*: grey Noldo; *alt.* from *Pengolodh* [thind + gódhel; the name indicated that he came of both Sindarin and Noldorin ancestry] *WJ*:419

Thin·gol, *kd. bv.*: one with a grey cloak; *epessë* of King *Elu* of Doriath [thind + coll, OS *thindikollo] also *Aran Tinnu Silm*, *MR*:217, *WJ*:410, *PME*:337

Thin·rod, *tp.*: noble of the Sindar [thind + raud[2]] *VT*41:9

Tho·'ron·dir, *kd.*: man like an eagle; steward of Gondor [thoron + dîr] *LotR:AppA*

Tho·'ron·dor, *tp.*: king of eagles; chief of the Eagles of Beleriand in the First Age [thoron + taur[2]] *LotR*; *Letters*:427; *LR*:298

Tho·'ron·gil, *impr. tp.*: eagle of the star; *epessë* of Aragorn, when serving Rohan and Gondor [thoron + gîl, named for the 'star of the Dúnedain' (a star-shaped brooch) that he wore] *LotR*, *Letters*:427

Thû, *n.*: stench; *alt.* to *Gorthaur*

Thu·rin, *adj.*: secret; *epessë* given to *Túrin* in Nargothrond [thurin] *UT*

Thu·'rin·gud, *kd.*: hidden foe; a *cilmessë* of *Túrin* in Nargothrond [thurin + gûd] *WJ*:256

Thu·'rin·gwe·thil, *kd.*: secret shadowy woman; a vampire of Angband [thurin + gwâth + -il[1]] *Silm*

U

U·'dal·raph, *kd. bv.*: one without a stirrup; *epessë* of the rider *Borondir* of Gondor [ú + talraph] *UT*:313

Ul·bar: meaning uncertain; a man of Númenor [may not be Sindarin] *UT*
Ul·dor, *kd.*: hideous king; an Easterling of Beleriand [ul- + taur[2]] *UT*
Ul·fang, *kd. bv.*: having a hideous beard; chief of Easterlings in Beleriand [ul- + fang] *UT*
Ul·fast, *kd. bv.*: having hideous shaggy hair; an Easterling of Beleriand [ul- + fast] *UT*
Ul·warth, *kd.*: hideous betrayer; an Easterling of Beleriand [ul- + gwarth] *UT*
Úm·arth, *n.*: evil fate; a fictitious name given as patronymic by Túrin when in Nargothrond [úmarth] *UT*
Un·'go·li·ant: meaning uncertain; a primeval spirit of darkness in spider form [contains *ungol* 'spider'] also *Delduthling LotR*, *Silm*
Ur·wen, *tp.*: maiden of heat; sister of Túrin [ûr[1] + gwên] called *Lalaith UT*:57

Y

'Ys·si·on: the Valië Ossë [OS *Ossiondo < Valarin oššai 'foaming' + -on[1]] also *Balar*, *Gaerys WJ*:400

NAMES OF THINGS

A

Aeg·los, *impr. tp.*: thorn of snow (i.e., icicle); the spear of Gil-galad [aeg[2] + los] also spelled *Aiglos LotR:Index*, *Silm*
Aer·linn in-Edhil o Imladris, *gph.*: sea-song of the Elves of Imladris; a hymn to Elbereth *RGEO*:62 (written in tengwar only)
An·'ger·thas Dae·ron, *gph.*: rune alphabet of Daeron [angerthas, Daeron] *LotR*
An·'ger·thas 'Mo·ri·a, *gph.*: rune alphabet of Moria [angerthas, Moria] *LotR*
'An·gla·chel, *tp.*: iron of the star of flame; the sword *Gurthang* before it was reforged; [ang + lach + êl; the sword was made of iron from a meteor] *Silm*
An·grist, *tp.*: cleaver of iron; Beren's knife [ang + rist] *Silm*
An·'gui·rel, *tp.*: ?iron of the star of eternity; Eöl's sword, the mate of Anglachel [ang + ?uir + êl] *Silm*
Ann-then·nath, *n. dv*: longs and shorts; a mode of Elvish verse (iambic tetrameter, rhyme scheme ABACBABC) [and + thent; presumably so-called from its alternation of 'long' (stressed) and 'short' (unstressed) syllables] *LotR*

A·'ran·rúth, *tp*.: anger of the king; the sword of king Thingol [aran + rûth, dialectal form of CS *ruith* 'anger'; the CS form of this name would be Aradhruith] *Silm*

'Ath·ra·beth Fin·rod ah An·dreth, *gph*.: debate of Finrod and Andreth; title of a philosophical work on the fates of Elves and men [athrabeth, a[2], Finrod, Andreth] *MR*:329

B

Bal·choth, *kd*.: cruel horde; a nation from Rhûn that periodically attacked Rhovanion and Gondor [balch + hoth; the first element is also said to be Westron *balc* 'horrible'] *LotR*, *UT*:313

Bar 'Bë·o·ra, *gph*.: house of Bëor; the descendants of Bëor [bâr, Bëor] *WJ*:231

Bar Ha·dor, *gph*.: house of Hador; the descendants of Hador [bâr, Hador] *MR*:373

'Be·le·gast, *kd*.: great void; the emptiness beyond the world [beleg + gast] *LR*:366 *KUM-*

'Be·le·go, *kd*.: great void; the emptiness beyond the world [beleg + gaw] *LR*:357–58, *GAS-*

Bel·thil, *kd*.: divine radiance; a tree in Gondolin, made in the image of Telperion [bal + thîl] *MR*:155

Bor·gil, *kd*.: red-hot star; the star Betelgeuse (α Orionis) [born + gîl] *LotR*, *Letters*:427

C

'Ce·le·born, *tp*.: tree of silver; *Galathilion* [celeb + orn[2]] *MR*:155

Ce·'leb·rond, *tp*.: mace of silver; probably a weapon [celeb + grond] *LR*:384 *RUD-*

#Cerch i Me·lain, *gph*.: sickle of the Valar; the asterism of the 'Big Dipper' [cerch, i, balan] (N Cerch i mBelain) *LR*:365 *KIRIK-*

Cer·thas Dae·ron, *gph*.: rune-row of Daeron; *Angerthas Daeron* [certhas, Daeron] *LotR:AppE*

Cer·veth, *n*.: meaning unknown; the seventh month of the Númenorean year, corresponding approximately to July [based on a noun !*cerf* < OS *kerme] *LotR:AppD*

D

Dag·mor, *impr. tp*.: that which slays the dark; the sword of Beren [dag- + môr[2]] *LB*:344

Da·gor·'Ag·la·reb, *ajph*.: glorious battle; the third battle of Beleriand [dagor, aglareb] *WJ*:36

Da·gor Ar·'ne·di·ad, *ajph.*: countless battle; *Nírnaeth Arnediad* [dagor, arnediad] *WJ*:22

Da·gor Bra·'gol·lach, *gph.*, *kd.*: battle of sudden flame; the fourth battle of Beleriand [dagor, bragol + lach] also *Dagor Bregedúr* *WJ*:52

Da·gor Bre·ge·dúr, *gph.*: battle of wildfire; *alt.* to *Dagor Bragollach* [dagor, bregedúr] *WJ*:125

Da·gor 'Da·go·rath, *gph.*: battle of battles; the last battle between the Valar and Morgoth at the end of the world [dagor] *UT*:395

Da·gor nuin- 'Gi·li·ath, *prph.*: battle under the stars; the second battle of Beleriand [dagor, nu, i, gîl] *WJ*:17

Dan·gweth 'Pen·go·lodh, *gph.*: answer of Pengolodh; text in which Pengolodh answers a traveler's questions [dangweth, Pengolodh] *PME*:395

'Dan·ti·lais, *gph.*: fall of the leaves; *alt.* to *Firith* [dant + i + lais *pl.* of las] *PME*:135

Dor·'gan·nas Iaur, *ajph.*, *tp.*: former shaping of the lands; title of a geography of Beleriand made by Torhir Iphant [dôr + cannas, iaur] *WJ*:192, 206

E

'E·de·gil, *dg.*: seven stars; the asterism of the 'Big Dipper' or 'the Plough' [odog + gil, MS *ödögil < OS *otokoŋile] *LR*:379 *OT-*

'El·fa·ron, *tp.*: hunter among the stars; the moon [êl + faron] *LR*:387 *SPAR-*

G

ˌGa·lad·'ló·ri·el, *impr. kd.*: golden tree; Laurelin, one of the Two Trees [galadh + glóriel] also *Glewellin*, *Lasgalen*, *Mellinorn*, *Melthinorn* *MR*:155

ˌGa·la·'thi·li·on, *impr. kd.*: shining silver tree; Telperion, one of the Two Trees [galadh + thilion] also *Celeborn*, *Nimloth*, *Silivros* *MR*:155

Gil-Es·tel or **Gil-O·'res·tel,** *gph.*: star of hope or star of high hope; the star of Eärendil (cf. *Tengyl*) [gîl, or + estel] *WJ*:246

Gi·'rith·ron, *tp.*: month of shuddering; the twelfth month of the Númenorean year, corresponding approximately to December [girith + raun] *LotR:AppD*

Glam·dring, *tp.*: hammer of Orcs; a sword belonging to Turgon of Gondolin and later to Mithrandir [glam + dring] *Hobbit*, *LotR*, *WJ*:391

Gle·'wel·lin, *tp.*: song of golden light; *Galadlóriel* [glawar + lind] *MR*:155

Glin·gal, *kd.*: hanging flame; a tree in Gondolin, made in the image of Laurelin [gling + gâl] *MR*:155

Grond, *n.*: club; the mace used by Morgoth, and the battering ram used by the forces of Sauron in the battle of the Pelennor [grond] *LotR*, *Silm*

Gur·thang, *tp.*: iron of death; a sword borne by Túrin, formerly called Anglachel [gurth + ang] *WJ*:83

Gur·tholf or **'Gu·ru·tholf**, *tp.*: wand of death; *alt.* to *Gurthang* [gurth or guruth + olf] *WJ*:138

Gwae·ron, *tp.*: month of wind; the third month of the Númenorean year, approximately corresponding to March [gwaew + raun] *LotR:AppD*

Gwaith i-Mír·dain, *gph.*: people of the jewel-makers; a guild in Eregion led by Celebrimbor [gwaith, i, mírdan] *UT*

Gwin·gloth, *tp.*: flower of the foam; the ship of Eärendil [gwing + loth] *PME*:370

Gwi·rith, *n.*: meaning unknown; the fourth month of the Númenorean calendar, corresponding approximately to April [OS *wirittʰe √*WIR; Q *Víressë*] *LotR:AppD*

H

'Ha·dha·fang or **'Ha·va·thang**, *impr. tp.*: cleaver of the throng; a sword [hâdh + thang, MS*haðaɸaŋg] *LR*:388 *STAG-*, 389 *SYAD-*

Ha·'leth·rim, *tp.*: people of Haleth; the Haladin of Brethil [Haleth(name) + rim[1]] *UT*

'Hí·ri·lorn, *tp.*: tree of the lady; a great beech tree with three trunks in Doriath, probably named for Lúthien, who was kept captive in a house in the tree [híril + orn[2]] *Silm*

Hi·thui, *adj.*: misty; the eleventh month of the Númenorean calendar, corresponding approximately to November [hithui] *LotR:AppD*

I

'Í·ni·as Ba·'lan·nor, *gph.*: annals of Valinor; *alt.* to *Ínias Dor-Rodyn* [ínias, Balannor] *MR*:200

'Í·ni·as Be·'le·ri·and, *gph.*: annals of Beleriand; a chronology of events in Beleriand in the First Age, attributed to Pengolodh and others of the Sindar [ínias, Beleriand] *MR*:200

'Í·ni·as Dor-Ro·dyn, *gph.*: annals of the Land of the Valar; a chronology of events in Aman up to the rising of the Sun, attributed to Rúmil and revised by Pengolodh [ínias, Dor-Rodyn] *MR*:200

I·'van·neth, *n.*: giving of corn; the ninth month of the Númenorean calendar, corresponding approximately to September [iaw[1] + anneth, Q *Yavannië*] *LotR:AppD*

L

Laer Cú Be·leg, *gph., ajph.*: song of the great bow; a song made by Túrin in memory of Beleg Cúthalion [laer, cû, beleg] *Silm*

Lam·mas, *n.*: account of tongues; a linguistic work by the loremaster Pengolodh [lammas] *WJ*

'Las·ga·len, *adj.*: having green leaves; *Galadlóriel* [lasgalen] *MR*:155

'Lei·thi·an, *n.*: release (from bondage); a lay about Beren and Lúthien [leithian; the name probably refers to the release of Beren and Lúthien from Mandos to return to Middle-earth, though other applications are possible] *Silm*, *LR*:368 *LEK-*

Loth·ron, *tp.*: month of flowers; the fifth month of the Númenorean calendar, approximately corresponding to May [loth + raun] *LotR:AppD*

M

'Mel·li·norn, *kd.*: golden tree; *Melthinorn* [mallen + orn[2]] *LR*:386 *SMAL-*

'Mel·thi·norn, *kd.*: golden tree; *Galadlóriel* [malthen + orn[2]] *MR*:155

Me·'nel·va·gor, *tp.*: swordsman of the sky; the constellation Orion [menel + magor] *LotR*

Me·reth A·'der·thad, *gph.*: feast of reuniting; a meeting at which the Noldorin houses of Fëanor and Fingolfin were reconciled [mereth, aderthad] *Silm*

Min·'lam·ad thent/es·tent, *ajph.*: short initial sound; a Sindarin poetic form, probably alliterative, in which the Narn i-Chîn Húrin was written [mîn + lamad, thent] *UT*:146, *WJ*:311

Mîr in-Ge·lydh, *gph.*: jewel of the Noldor; Silmaril [mîr, i, golodh] (N Mîr in Geleidh) *LR*:377 *ÑGOLOD-*

N

'Nar·be·leth, *tp.*: fading of the sun; the tenth month of the Númenorean calendar, corresponding approximately to October [naur + peleth; Q *Narquelië*] *LotR:AppD*

Narn Be·ren ion·'Ba·ra·hir, *gph.*: tale of Beren son of Barahir; a Númenórean prose recension of *The Lay of Leithian* [narn, Beren, iôn, Barachir] *MR*:373

Narn e-Dant 'Gon·do·lin ar Or·thad en-Êl, *gph.*: tale of the fall of Gondolin and the raising of the star; the Númenorean story of Tuor linked to that of Eärendil [narn, en, dant, Gondolin, a[2], orthad, êl] *MR*:373

Narn e-Di·'nú·vi·el, *gph.*: tale of the nightingale; *Narn Beren ion Barahir* [narn, en, tinúviel] *MR*:373

Narn e-mbar Ha·dor, *gph.*: tale of the house of Hador; a collective name for legendary material dealing with the descendants of Húrin and Huor [narn, en, bâr, Hador] *MR*:373

Narn en-Êl, *gph.*: tale of the star; the Númenorean story of Eärendil [narn, en, êl] *MR*:373

Narn e-·'Rach Mor·goth, *gph.*: tale of the curse of Morgoth; *Narn i·Chîn Húrin* [narn, en, rhach, Morgoth] *MR*:373

Narn i-Chîn Hú·rin, *gph.*: tale of the children of Húrin; a long poem about Túrin and Nienor, attributed to Dírhaval [narn, i, hên, Húrin] *UT*, *MR*:373, *WJ*:313

Nar·wain, *impr. kd.*: (month of) new sun; the first month of the Númenorean year, corresponding approximately to January [naur + gwain; after the beginning of Narwain, the days began to lengthen again. Based on Q *Narvinyë*] *LotR:AppD*

Naug·la·mír, *tp.*: necklace of the Dwarves [naugol + mîr; given the form Nauglamír instead of expected Nauglavír, it is probable that this name is not CS but dialectal S or Ossiriandic] *Silm*

Nern in 'A·da·nath, *gph.*: tales of the Edain; the entire legendarium dealing with the heroic activities of Men in the First Age, as compiled in Númenor [narn, i, adan] *MR*:373

Nern in E·'de·ne·dair, *gph.*: tales of the fathers of the Edain; *Nern in Adanath* [narn, i, adanadar] *MR*:373

Nim·loth, *kd. bv.*: (tree) having white blossoms; *Galathilion* [nimp + loth] *MR*:155

Nim·phe·los, *impr. kd.*: white as snow; a pearl given by Thingol to the Dwarves [nimp + los[1], OS *nimphélosse, a very archaic name = CS !Nimlos] *Silm*

Ní·nui, *adj.*: watery (month); the second month of the Númenorean year, corresponding approximately to February [nínui[2]] *LotR:AppD*

Nír·naeth Ar·'ne·di·ad, *ajph.*: lamentation without count; the fifth battle of Beleriand [nírnaeth, arnediad] also *Ar·'noe·di·ad* (i.e., Arnödiad) *Silm*; *WJ*:71, 312

Nó·rui, *adj.*: sunny (month); the sixth month of the Númenorean calendar, corresponding approximately to June [nórui] *LotR:AppD*

Nos Fin·rod, *gph.*: family of Finrod; the descendants of Finrod [nos, Finrod] *LR*:378 *NO-*

Nost or **Noth·rim Fi·'nar·fin**, *gph.*: family of Finarfin; the descendants of Finarfin [nost, nothrim, Finarfin] *PME*:360

Noth·lir 'Ha·le·tha, *gph.*: family line of Haleth; a diagram of the descendants of Marach [nothlir, Haleth (name)] *WJ*:237

Noth·lir 'Ma·ra·cha, *gph.*: family line of Marach; a diagram of the descendants of Marach [nothlir, Marach (name)] *WJ*:234

O

Or·'ae·a·ron, *impr. tp.*: day of the Great Sea; the sixth day of the Númenorean week [aur + aearon] *LotR:AppD*

'O·ra·nor, *impr. tp.*: day of the Sun; the second day of the Eldarin and Númenorean week [aur + anor] *LotR:AppD*

'Or·be·lain, *impr. kd.*: day of the Valar, the sixth day of the Eldarin and seventh day of the Númenorean week [aur + !belain, !belain being an artificial CS equivalent of Q *valanya* 'of or having to do with the Valar' < CE *balanjā √BAL] *LotR:AppD*, *LotR*, *Letters*:427

Or·christ, *tp.*: cleaver of Orcs; an ancient sword borne by Thorin Oakenshield [orch + rist[2]] also spelled *Orcrist Hobbit*:51

'Or·ga·ladh, *impr. tp.*: day of the Tree; the fourth day of the Númenorean week [aur + galadh] *LotR:AppD*

Or·'ga·la·dhad, *impr. tp.*: day of the Two Trees; the fourth day of the Eldarin week [aur + galadh + -ad] *LotR:AppD*, *LotR*, *Letters*:427

Or·'gi·li·on, *impr. kd.*: day of stars, starry day; the first day of the Eldarin and Númenorean week [aur + gilion] *LotR:AppD*

'O·ri·thil, *impr. tp.*: day of the moon; the third day of the Eldarin and Númenorean week [aur + ithil] *LotR:AppD*

'Or·me·nel, *impr. tp.*: day of heaven; the fifth day of the Eldarin and Númenorean week [aur + menel] *LotR:AppD*

P

Pen·nas in-Ge·lydh, *gph.*: account of the Noldor; *Pennas Silevril* [pennas, i, golodh] (N Pennas in-Geleidh, Pennas na-Ngölöidh) *LR*:201

Pen·nas Si·'lev·ril, *gph.*: account of the Silmarils; CS name of the historical work called *Quenta Silmarillion* [pennas, silevril] *MR*:200

R

'Rem·mi·rath, *pl. n. kd.* or *tp.*: jewels like a net (or: jewels in a net); the asterism of the Pleiades [rem + mîr] *LotR*, *VT*42:29

Rin·gil, *kd.*: cold star; a sword used by Fingolfin [ring + gîl] *Silm*

Ro·chon Me·'thes·tel, *gph.*, *kd.*: rider of the last hope; a song about Borondir, rider of Gondor [rochon, meth + estel] *UT*:313

S

Si·gil 'E·lu·naeth, *gph.*, *tp.*: necklace of Thingol's woe; *Nauglamír* [sigil[2], Elu (name) + naeth] *WJ*:258

Si·'liv·ros, *tp.*: rain of silver light; *Galathilion* [silif + ros] *MR*:155

T

Ten·gyl, *tp.*: bearer of a sign; a star, possibly the Star of Eärendil [tann + cyll, OS *tannakolli] *MR*:385

U

Ú·rui, *adj.*: hot (month); the eighth month of the Númenorean calendar, corresponding approximately to August [úrui] *LotR:AppD*

NAMES OF PLACES

A

Ae·gais En·grin, *ajph. pl.*: iron peaks; *alt.* to *Ered Engrin* [aegas, angren] (N Oeges Engrin) *LR*:349 *AYAK-*

Ae·lin-ui·al, *gph.*: meres of twilight; region of pools and marshes at the confluence of Sirion and Aros [ael, uial] also *Hithliniath*, *Lîn Uial Silm*

Ae·luin, *impr. kd.*: blue pool, a mountain lake in Dorthonion [ael + luin] also *Tarn Aeluin* (*tarn* is English for a small mountain pool) *Silm*

'Ag·la·rond, *tp.*: vaulted cavern of radiance; caves behind Helm's Deep that contained remarkable mineral formations [aglar + rond] *LotR*

Ag·lon, *n.*: narrow pass; pass between Himring and Dorthonion [aglonn] *Silm*

'Al·pho·bas, *tp.*: haven of swans; the harbor of Alqualondë in Eldamar [alph + hobas] also called *Hobas in-Eilph LR*:364 *KHOP-*

Am·on Am·arth, *gph.*: hill of doom; *Orodruin*, so called because of its role as a portent of Sauron's return at the end of the Second Age [amon, amarth] *Silm*, *Names*:183

Am·on An·war, *gph.*: hill of awe; the Halifirien on the border of Gondor and Rohan, which was once the site of Elendil's tomb [amon, anwar] also *Fornarthan UT*:301

Am·on Ca·rab, *gph.*: hill of the hat; *alt.* to *Amon Rûdh WJ*:187

Am·on Dar·thir, *gph.*: ?hill of lofty view; a mountain in the east of Dor-lómin [amon, ?târ + tîr[2]] *UT*

Am·on Dîn, *gph.*: hill of silence; one of the beacon-hills of Anórien [amon, dîn[2]] *UT*:319

Am·on E·reb, *ajph.*: lonely hill; a hill standing alone in East Beleriand [amon, ereb] *Silm*

Am·on E·thir, *gph.*: hill of spies; an artificial prominence raised east of Nargothrond for the purpose of seeing to a distance [amon, ethir[2]] *Silm*, *WJ*:149

Am·on Gwa·reth or **Gwa·red**, *gph.*: meaning uncertain; hill in Tumladen on which Gondolin was built [amon, gwareth < OS *warett^{h}e, apparently an abstract nominal formation from a root √*WAR of unknown meaning; in early texts given the meaning 'hill of watch'] *Silm*, *WJ*:200

Am·on Hen, *gph.*: hill of the eye; a watch-hill to the west of Rauros [amon, hen(d)] *LotR*

Am·on Lanc, *ajph.*: naked hill; a hill with a bare summit in southern Mirkwood on which Dol Guldur was later built [amon, lanc[1]] *UT*

Am·on Lhaw, *gph.*: hill of the ears; a watch-hill to the east of Rauros [amon, lhaw] *LotR*

Am·on O·bel, *gph.*: hill of the *obel*; a hill in the forest of Brethil on which the *obel* (garth) of the Haladin stood [amon; the Haladic word *obel* may be derived from CS *gobel* 'enclosure'] *Silm*

Am·on Rûdh, *ajph.*: bald hill; a hill in West Beleriand where Mîm the Dwarf dwelt [amon, rûdh] *Silm*, *WJ*:187

Am·on Sûl, *gph.*: hill of the wind; a hill in Eriador, called Weathertop [amon + sûl[2]] *LotR*, *Silm*, *Names*:195

Am·on Ti·rith, *gph.*: hill of watching; hill on which Minas Tirith (2) was built [amon, tirith] *Names*:187

Am·on Ui·los, *ajph.*: eternally snow-white hill; the mountain of Taniquetil in Aman [amon, uilos[1]; from Q *Oiolossë*] also *Nimdildor*, *Ras Arphain* *Silm*; *RGEO*:62, 66; *Letters*:278; *MR*:154; *WJ*:403

A·nach: meaning unknown; a pass through the Ered Gorgoroth into Dorthonion *Silm*

An·dram, *kd.*: long wall; a line of hills crossing east Beleriand, falling steeply to the south [and[1] + ram] *Silm*

An·dras, *kd.*: long cape; a cape in the Falas west of Brithombar [and[1] + rast] *WJ*:184, 379

An·drast, *kd.*: long cape; cape in the far west of Gondor [and[1] + rast] also *Angast*, *Ras Morthil* *UT*

An·drath, *kd.*: long climbing way; low ground between the Tyrn Gorthad and the South Downs along which the Greenway passed [and[1] + rath] *UT*

An·droth, *kd.*: long cave; caves in Mithrim that served as refuge to some of the Sindar after the conquest of Hithlum [and[1] + groth] *Silm*

An·duin, *kd.*: long river; the great river of Wilderland [and[1] + duin] *LotR*

'An·fa·las, *kd.*: long shore; Langstrand, a province of Gondor, named after the long coast that bounds the Bay of Belfalas on the north [and[1] + falas] *LotR*, *Names*:188, *VT*42:15

An·'faug·lith, *kd.*: very choking dust; *Ard-Galen* after it was devastated in the Dagor Bragollach [an + faug + lith] also *Dor nu-Fauglith* *Silm*, *WJ*:52

An·gast, *kd.*: long cape; *Andrast* [and[1] + cast] *VT*42:14

Ang·band, *tp.*: prison of iron; fortress of Morgoth in the far north of Middle-earth [ang + band; possibly re-formed from *Angmand to recall the element *band*] *Silm*

'Ang·ha·bar, *tp.*: mine of iron; mine in the northern Echoriath [ang + habar] *Silm*

Ang·mar, *tp.*: land of iron; a kingdom at the north end of the Hithaeglir, long at war with Arnor [ang + bâr] *LotR*

'An·go·lonn: country of the Noldor; *Beleriand* [from Q *Ingolondë* < CE ŋgolondē] √ŋGOL + -(o)nd] also *Geleidhien LR*:377 *ÑGOL-*

An·gren, *adj.*: iron; *Sîr Angren* [angren] *UT*

'An·gre·nost, *kd.*: iron fortress; a fortress of extremely hard stone at the southern end of the Hithaeglir, originally belonging to Gondor [angren + ost] *Silm*, *Names*:187

An·'ner·chi·on, *impr. kd.*: orkish gate; door to the goblin tunnels underneath the Cirith Forn [and[2] + erchion] *TI*:114

An·non in-Ge·lydh, *gph.*: gate of the Noldor; secret entrance to a water-delved tunnel leading to Cirith Ninniach, made by the Noldor of Turgon [annon, i, golodh] also *An·non Ge·lydh UT*, *WJ*:181

An·non To·rath, *gph.*: gate of kings; *alt.* to *Argonath* [annon, taur[2]] *WR*:132

An·'núm·i·nas, *tp.*: tower of the West; ancient capital of Arnor [annûn + minas] *LotR*

A·'nó·ri·en: country of the sun; fief of Gondor north of the Ered Nimrais, called Sunlending by the Rohirrim [anor + -(ie)nd; named for the citadel of Minas Anor] *LotR*, *Names*:192

Ard-'Ga·len, *ajph.*: green region; a broad grassy plain north of Dorthonion [ardh, calen] also *'Ard·ga·len*, later called *Anfauglith Silm*

'Ar·dho·len, *impr. kd.*: hidden realm; *Doriath*, or perhaps *Gondolin* [ardh + dolen] *LR*:358 *GAT(H)-*

'Ar·go·nath, *kd. pl.*: royal stones; pillars carved with the likenesses of Kings Isildur and Anárion of Gondor, at the entrance to Nen Hithoel [arn + gôn + -ath] also *Annon Torath*, *Sern Ubed LotR*, *RGEO*:67, *Letters*:427

Ar·nen, *kd.*: by the water; a part of Ithilien across from Minas Tirith [Q *ar* 'beside' + nên] *LotR*, *VT*42:17

Ar·nor, *kd.*: (land of) royal people; northern kingdom of the Dúnedain in Middle-earth, founded by Elendil, the head of their royal dynasty [from Q *Arn(an)órë* or *Arn(an)or*] *LotR*, *Letters*:428

A·'ros·si·ach, *tp.*: ford of Aros; ford where a road crossed the river Aros and entered [Aros + iach] *Silm*

'Ar·the·dain, *kd.*: (land of) noble men; one of three kingdoms into which Arnor was divided during part of the Third Age [arth + edain, *pl.* of *adan*; a Sindarin translation of *Arnor*] *LotR*

Ar·'thó·ri·en, *impr. kd.*: country of the enclosed region; eastern portion of the forest of Region, between the rivers Limhir and Aros [ardh + thaur2 + -(ie)nd] *UT*, *WJ*:183, 189

Ar·'ver·ni·en: meaning uncertain; land west of the mouths of Sirion [contains -(ie)nd] *LotR*

Ath·rad An·gren, *ajph.*: iron crossing; ford across the river (Sîr) Angren (the Fords of Isen) [athrad, angren] *UT*

Ath·rad Daer or **Dhaer**, *ajph.*: great crossing; *Sarn Athrad* [athrad, daer1] *WJ*:335

Ath·rad i-Ne·gyth, *gph.*: crossing of the Dwarves; *Sarn Athrad* [athrad, i, nogoth] *WJ*:338

Ath·rad i-No·goth, *gph.*: crossing of the Dwarf, corrected to *Athrad i-Negyth*; *Sarn Athrad* [athrad, i, nogoth] *WJ*:338

B

Bair am Yrn, *prph. pl.*: dwellings upon the trees; *alt.* to *Caras Galadhon* [bâr, am, orn2] misread as Bair am Yru *TI*:243

Bair Nes·tad, *gph.*: houses of healing; hospital in Minas Tirith [bâr, nestad] also *Bair Nestedrin* *WR*:379–80

Bair Nes'ted·rin, *ajph. pl.*: healing houses; *Bair Nestad* [bâr, nestadren] misspelt Bair Nestedriu *WR*:379–80

Ba·'lan·nor, *tp.*: land of the Valar; Valinor [balan + dôr, OS *Balandore or Q *Valandor*] also *Dor Rodyn* *MR*:200

Ba·lar: meaning uncertain; bay into which Sirion flowed, and the island in that bay [named for the Maia Ossë, also called Balar] *WJ*:5

'Ba·rad-dûr, *ajph.*: dark tower; citadel of Sauron in Gorgoroth [barad1 + dûr] *LotR*

Ba·rad Ei·thel, *gph.*: tower of the well; principal fortress of Hithlum, at Eithel Sirion [barad1, eithel] *Silm*, *WJ*:168

Ba·rad Nim·ras, *gph.*, *kd.*: tower of the white cape; a tower in the Falas of Beleriand, on the shore west of Eglarest [barad, nimp + rast] *Silm*

Ba·'ran·duin, *kd.*: golden-brown river; the river Brandywine [baran + duin] *LotR:AppF*, *Names*:178

ˌBa·ran·'dui·ni·ant, *tp.*: bridge of Baranduin; the Bridge of Stonebows, where the East Road passed over the Brandywine [Baranduin + iant] *SD*:128–31

Bar en-Dan·wedh, *gph.*: house of the ransom; home of Mîm on Amon

Rûdh, so called because he revealed its location as ransom for his life [bâr, en, danwedh] *Silm*, *UT*

Bar in- 'Ni·bin-noeg, *gph*.: house of the petty-Dwarves; original name of *Bar en-Danwedh* [bâr, i, Nibin-noeg] misspelled *Bar-en-Nibin-noeg UT*

Bar E·rib, *gph*.: dwelling of the lonely people; outlaw stronghold south of Amon Rûdh [bâr, ereb] *UT*

Bar·goll, *impr. kd*.: hollow dwelling; *Nogrod* [bâr + coll[1]; from Kh *Tumunzahar*] *WJ*:414

Bar Ha·leth, *gph*.: house of Haleth; *alt.* to *Ephel Brandir WJ*:157

Bar i-Mŷl, *gph*.: home of the gulls; a cape in the Falas, south of Eglarest [bâr, i, mŷl] also *Bar in-Gwael, Ras Maewrim WJ*:379–80, 418

Bar in-Gwael, *gph*.: home of the gulls; *alt.* to *Bar i-Mŷl* [bâr, i, gwael] *WJ*:418

'Be·le·gaer, *kd*.: great sea; ocean between Middle-earth and Aman [beleg + aer or gaer] *PME*:363

'Be·le·gost, *kd*.: great fortress; a mansion of the Dwarves, east of the Ered Luin [beleg + ost; from Kh *Gabilgathol*] *WJ*:389

Be·'le·ri·and: country of Balar; lands on either side of the river Sirion in the far northwest of Middle-earth, later submerged [Balar + -(ia)nd, OS *Balariande] also *Be·'le·ri·an*; called *Angolonn, Geleidhien Silm*

'Bel·fa·las, *tp*.: coast of Bel; great bay southward in Middle-earth and a fief of Gondor on the bay [Bel(name) + falas] *LotR*

Be·raid Gon·drath, *gph*., *tp*.: towers of the causeway; the Causeway Forts on the Rammas Echor, where a causeway came in from Osgiliath [barad, gondrath] (N Bered Ondrath) *WR*:340

Bre·thil, *n*.: (wood of) beech trees; a wood of Doriath, between the Sirion and Taeglin Rivers [brethil] *Silm*

Bre·'thi·li·and: country of beeches; *Brethil* [brethil + -(ia)nd] *LR*:352 *BERÉTH-*

'Bri·thi·ach, *tp*.: ford of gravel; a stony ford across the Sirion just north of Brethil [brith + iach] *Silm*

Bri·'thom·bar, *tp*.: dwelling on the Brithon (river); a haven of the Falas, at the mouth of the Brithon [Brithon + bâr] *Silm*

Bri·thon, *adj*.: pebbly (river); river in the Falas [brithon] *Silm*

Brui·nen, *kd*.: loud water; a river flowing from the Hithaeglir into the Mitheithel, on one of whose branches Imladris was built [brui + nên] *LotR*

C

Ca·bed en-A·ras, *gph*.: leap of the deer; narrow and deep gorge in which the Taeglin ran, across which a deer could leap [cabed, en, aras] also *Cabed Naeramath, Mengas Dûr Silm*, *WJ*:98

Ca·bed Nae·'ram·arth, *gph.*: leap of dreadful doom; *Cabed en-Aras* after Nienor cast herself into the gorge [cabed, naer + amarth] *Silm*, *WJ*:100

Cair An·dros, *gph.*: ship of long foam; island in the Anduin shaped like a ship, against whose northern point the Anduin broke in foam [cair, and[1] + ros[1]] *LotR:AppA*, *AppE*

Ca·'lem·bel, *kd.*: green enclosure; township of Lamedon near the fords of Ciril [calen + pêl] *LotR*

ˌCa·le·'nar·dhon, *kd.*: green great province; grassland province of Gondor north of Ered Nimrais and west of Anduin [calen + ardh + -(o)nd] later *Rohan*; also spelt *Calenardon LotR:AppA*

Ca·'len·had, *kd.*: green spot; beacon-hill of Anórien [calen + sâd] *LotR*, *UT*, *VT*42:20

Ca·'len·hir, *kd.*: green river; river flowing from Pinnath Gelin into the lower Morthond [calen + sîr] *WR*:46

Ca·rach An·gren, *ajph.*: iron jaws; fortified gap between arms of the Ered Lithui and Ephel Dúath, leading from Gorgoroth to Udûn, closed by a fence of toothlike iron posts [carach, angren] *LotR*, *Names*:187, *Silm:App carak-*

Ca·'radh·ras, *kd.*: red horn; one of the Mountains of Moria [caran + ras; from Kh *Barazinbar*] also spelled *Caradras LotR*

#'Ca·rag-dûr, *ajph.*: dark spike (of rock); precipice on the north side of Amon Gwareth [carag, dûr] spelled *Caragdûr Silm*

Ca·ras 'Ga·la·dhon, *ajph.*: moated fortress of trees; principal city of the Galadhrim, on a tree-covered hill surrounded by a wall and ditch [SE karas < CE *karassē √KAR[1], galadhon] also spelled *Caras Galadon*; also *Bair am Yrn LotR*, *Letters*:426

Car·chost, *kd.*: fortress like a tooth; tower near the Morannon [carch + ost] *LotR*

Car·do·lan, *kd.*: land of red hills; one of the kingdoms arising from the breakup of Arnor [carn + dôl + -(a)nd] *LotR:AppA*

Carn Dûm, *ajph.*: red valley; capital of Angmar [carn, tûm] *LotR*

Car·nen, *kd.*: red water; river in Rhovanion, flowing from the Iron Hills to the Celduin [carn + nen] *LotR:AppA*, *UT*

Cel·duin, *kd.*: running river; river in Rhovanion, flowing from Erebor to Rhúnaer [cell + duin] called *River Running*; *LotR:AppA*

Ce·'leb·dil, *tp.*: sharp point of silver; one of the Mountains of Moria [celeb + till, from Kh *Zirak-zigil*] *LotR*, *Names*:191

Ce·'leb·rant, *tp.*: watercourse of silver; river flowing from Hithaeglir that may have carried silver from the mountains [celeb + rant] *LotR*, *Names*:191

Ce·'leb·ros, *tp.*: rain of silver; stream with a waterfall (Dimrost), flowing south through Brethil into the Taeglin [celeb + ros[2]] *Silm*, *WJ*:151

Ce·lon, *n.*: river; *alt.* to *Limhir* [celon] *Silm*

Ce·los, *n.*: river flowing out swiftly from a spring; river in Lebennin, flowing into the Sirith [celos] *LotR*

'Ce·lu·fain, *impr. kd.*: white spring; *alt.* to *Parth Galen*, perhaps because of the rill flowing through the lawn [celu + fain] *TI*:371

Ce·rin Am·roth, *gph.*: mound (or circle) of Amroth; a tree-planted mound in Lothlórien, where Amroth formerly dwelt [cerin, Amroth] *LotR*

'Cil·ga·lad, *impr. tp.*: pass of light; Calacirya, the pass from Eldamar into Valinor [cîl + calad] *LR*:365 *KIL-*

'Cil·tho·ron, *impr. tp.*: cleft of the eagle; *alt.* to *Cirith Thoronath* [cîl + thoron] *LR*:365 *KIL-*, 392 *THOR-*

Ci·ril: ?cleaving (river); river flowing through Lamedon into Ringló [OS ?*kirille √KIR] *LotR*

Ci·rith Dú·ath, *gph.*: cleft of dark shadow; former name of *Cirith Ungol* [cirith, dúath] *UT*

Ci·rith Forn en-An·drath, *kd.*, *gph.*: northern pass of the long climb; high pass across Hithaeglir above Imladris [cirith, forn, en, andrath] *UT*

Ci·rith Gor·gor, *gph.*: cleft of deadly fear; pass leading to the vale of Udûn in Mordor [cirith, gorgor] *LotR*

Ci·rith 'Nin·ni·ach, *gph.*: cleft of the rainbow; ravine containing a river flowing into Drengist, in whose spray the sun formed rainbows [cirith, ninniach] *Silm*

Ci·rith 'Tho·ro·nath, *gph.*: cleft of eagles; very high pass through the Echoriath north of Tumladen [cirith, thoron] also *Cristhorn*, *Cilthoron Silm*

Ci·rith Un·gol, *gph.*: cleft of the spider; a pass through the Ephel Dúath north of Minas Morgul, where a monstrous spider dwelt [cirith, ungol] *LotR*, *Names*:181

Côf gwae·ren Bêl *ajph.*, *gph.*: windy bay of Bêl; a poetic name for the Bay of *Belfalas* [côf, gwaeren] *VT*42:15

Cor·'mal·len, *impr. kd.*: golden circle; a field in which *culumalda* trees grew, on the east shore of Anduin above Cair Andros [corn + mallen] *LotR*

Cris·'saeg·rim, *tp. pl.*: peaks with clefts; high mountains south of Tumladen [cris + aeg + rim[1]] *Silm*

Cris·thorn, *impr. tp.*: cleft of the eagle; *alt.* to *Cirith Thoronath* [cris + thoron] also *'Cris·tho·ron PME*:379

D

Da·'gor·lad, *tp.*: plain of battle; flat barrens north of Mordor where the principal battle of the War of the Last Alliance was fought, defeating Sauron [dagor + lâd] *LotR*

Del·'dú·ath, *impr. tp.*: horror of nightshade; *Taur nu-Fuin* [del + dúath] also spelled *Delduwath Silm*

Dim·bar, *tp.*: land of sadness; region between Mindeb and Sirion north of Doriath [dim[2] + bâr] *Silm*

Dim·rost, *impr. kd.*: rainy stair; waterfall on the Celebros [dim[1] + rost] also *Nen Girith Silm*, *WJ*:151

Din-Ca·'radh·ras, *gph.*: pass of Caradhras; the Redhorn pass across Hithaeglir from Eregion into Nanduhirion [dîn[1], Caradhras] *LR*:354 *DEN-*

Din-'Dú·hir, *gph.*, *tp.*: pass of streams of darkness; *Din Caradhras* [dîn[1], dû + sîr] *LR*:354 *DEN-*

Dol Am·roth, *gph.*: hill of Amroth; chief city of Belfalas, anciently associated with the Silvan Elves of Amroth's kingdom who dwelt at Edhellond [dôl, Amroth] *LotR*

Dol Ba·ran, *ajph.*: brown hill; hill at the southern end of the Hithaeglir [dôl, baran] *LotR*

Dol Gul·dur, *gph.*: hill of dark sorcery; stronghold of Sauron on *Amon Lanc* [dôl, guldur] *LotR*

Dor Ca·'ran·thir, *gph.*: land of Caranthir; *Thargelion*, when it was ruled by Caranthir [dôr, Caranthir] *Silm*

Dor Cú·'ar·thol, *gph.*: land of bow and helm; land south of Taeglin and west of Sirion where Beleg (*<u>Cú</u>thalion*) and Túrin (*Gor<u>thol</u>*) fought the Orcs. It perhaps should be emended to *Dor Cúathol* [dôr, cû + ar + thôl; cf. a[2]] *Silm*

#Dor 'Dae·dhe·loth, *gph.*: land of great dread; *alt.* to *Dor na-Dhaerachas* [dôr, dae[1] + deloth] spelled *Daedeloth Silm*, *WJ*:183

Dor-'de·loth, *gph.*: land of dread; *Dor na-Dhaerachas* [dôr, deloth] *LR*:355 *DYEL-*

Dor Dí·nen or **Dhí·nen**, *ajph.*: silent land; region between Esgalduin and Aros north of Doriath [dôr, dínen] *Silm*; *WJ*:194, 333

Dor en-Er·nil, *gph.*: land of the prince; fief of Gondor ruled by the Prince of Dol Amroth [dôr, en, ernil] *LotR*

Dor Firn i-Gui·nar, *gph.*: land of the dead that live; *alt.* to *Dor Gyrth i-Chui·nar* [dôr, fern, i, cuina-] *Silm*

Dor Gyrth i-Chui·nar, *gph.*: land of the dead that live; region around Tol Galen in the south of Ossiriand, where Beren and Lúthien dwelt after their return from death [dôr, gorth[1], i, cuina-] *Letters*:417

Dor Hae·ron, *ajph.*: distant land; province of the ancient kingdom of Gondor, lying west beyond the Onodló River, later part of Rohan [dôr, haeron] *WJ*:273

'Do·ri·ath, *impr. tp.*: land of the fence; kingdom of Thingol and Melian in central Beleriand, consisting of the forests of Brethil, Neldoreth, and Region [dôr + iath] *Silm*, *WJ*:370

Dor·'lam·ren, *impr. kd.*: echoing land; *Dor-lómin* [dôr, glamren] *LR*:367 *LAM-*

Dor Lin·don, *kd.*: land known as Lindon; *Ossiriand* [dôr, Lindon] *WJ*:385

Dor-ló·min, *ajph.*: echoing land; CS rendition of NS name for the southernmost region of Hithlum, bounded on the west by Ered Lómin [dôr, NS lǭmin = CS ‡loven] translated into CS as *Dorlamren Silm*, *LR*:367 *LAM-*

#Dor na-·'Dhae·ra·chas, *prph.*: land of great dread; area north of Beleriand, controlled by Morgoth [dôr, na, daer[1] + achas] spelled *Dor na-Daerachas*; also *Dor Daedheloth WJ*:183, 187

Dor nu-Faug·lith, *prph.*: land under choking ash; *Anfauglith* [dôr, nu, faug + lith] *Silm*, *WJ*:239

Dor-Ro·dyn, *gph.*: land of the Valar; Valinor [dôr, rodon] also *Balannor MR*:200

Dor·'tho·ni·on, *impr. kd.*: land of pines; forested highland separating Ardgalen from Nan Dungortheb [dôr + thonion] also *Orod na-Thôn*; see also *Taur nu-Fuin LotR*, *Silm*

Dor·'wi·ni·on, *impr. kd.*: ?land of wine; region on the lower Celduin, known for its wines [dôr + *gwinion, *adj.* apparently formed from *gwîn (cf. Welsh *gwin* 'wine') + -on[3]] *Hobbit*, *UT*

Drann: see *Trann*

Dren·gist: meaning unknown; firth separating Lammoth from Nevrast *Silm*

'Dru·a·dan Forest: see *Tawar in-Drúedain LotR*

Drú·waith Iaur, *ajph.*: former wilderness of the Drúedain; region between Angren and Lefnui, once inhabited by the Drúedain [drû + gwaith, iaur] *UT*

Duin Daer or **Dhaer**, *ajph.*: great river; *Gelion* [duin, daer[1], translates Kh *Gabilân*] *WJ*:191, 336

Dur·thang, *kd.*: (fortress of) dark oppression; castle in Mordor [dûr + thang] *LotR*

E

E·chad i-Sed·ryn, *gph.*: camp of the faithful; refuge of Túrin's men on Amon Rûdh [echad, i, sedryn] *UT*

E·'cho·ri·ad, *kd.*: fence forming an outer circle; late alteration of *Echoriath* [echor + iâd] *WJ*:302

E·'cho·ri·ath, *kd.*: fence forming an outer circle; mountains surrounding the plain of Tumladen [echor + iath] also *Echoriad*, *Gochressiel Silm*, *UT*

#E·daib na Nes·tad, *prph.*: houses of healing; *alt.* to *Bair Nestedrin* [adab, na, nestad] (N Edeb na Nestad) *WR*:380

E·'dhel·lond, *tp.*: harbor of Elves; havens at the mouth of Morthond from which Elves sailed in the Second Age and part of the Third [edhel + lond] *UT*

'Eg·la·dil, *tp.*: point of Elves; narrow land at the tip of the Naith, where Celebrant flowed into Anduin [egol + till] *LotR*

'Eg·la·dor, *tp.*: land of the Eglain; that part of Beleriand bounded by Nevrast, the Narog, Sirion, and the sea [egol + dôr, OS *Eklandore; probably altered from *Eglanor to emphasize the element *dôr*] *WJ*:379

'Eg·la·hir, *tp.*: river of the Eglain; *Nenning* [egol + sîr, OS *Eklasīre] *WJ*:182, 187

'Eg·la·mar, *tp.*: home of the Eglain; central region of the Falas around Brithombar and Eglarest [egol + bâr, OS *Eklambar] *WJ*:365, 379

'Eg·la·rest, *tp.*: ravine of the Eglain; haven of the Falas at the mouth of Nenning [egol + rest, OS *Eklarista] *WJ*:365

Ei·thel Iv·rin or **Ei·thil Iv·rin**, *gph.*: well(s) of Ivrin; springs from which the Narog rose [eithel, Ivrin] *Silm*, *WJ*:85

Ei·thel Ní·nui, *ajph.*: well of tears; a fountain on the plain of Tumladen, said to have risen where Lúthien's tears fell as she passed over Gondolin borne by eagles [eithel, nínui[1]] *LR*:301

Ei·thel or **Ei·thil 'Si·ri·on**, *gph.*: well(s) of Sirion; sources of Sirion in the Ered Wethrin, and the nearby fortress of *Barad Eithel* [eithel, Sirion] *Silm*, *LR*:407

E·'len·nor, *tp.*: land of Elves; Eldamar [eledh + dôr] *LR*:356 *ELED-*

ˌEl·os·'ti·ri·on, *tp.*: fortress with watchtower of the stars; highest tower on the Emyn Beraid [êl + ostirion] *LotR*

Em·yn Ar·nen, *gph.*: hills beside the water; a small knot of hills in Ithilien, close to the Anduin [amon, Arnen] *LotR*

Em·yn Be·raid, *gph.*: hills of the towers; hills west of the Shire, on which stood three towers, including one containing a palantír [amon, barad[1]] also *Emyn Gwahaedir*, *Emyn Hen Dúnadan LotR*

Em·yn Duir, *ajph.*: dark hills; former name of *Emyn nu-Fuin* [amon, dûr] *UT*

Em·yn Eg·lain, *gph.*: hills of the Eglain; hills in the Falas, between Brithombar and Eglarest [amon, Eglan] *WJ*:189

Em·yn Gwa·'hae·dir, *gph.*: hills of the palantír; *alt.* to *Emyn Beraid* [amon, gwachaedir] *PME*:186

Em·yn Hen 'Dú·na·dan, *gph.*: hills of the eye of the Númenorean; *alt.* to *Emyn Beraid* [amon, hen(d), dúnadan] *PME*:186

Em·yn Muil, *gph.*: hills of dreariness; hills surrounding Nen Hithoel and part of the Anduin north of it [amon, muil] *LotR*

Em·yn nu-Fuin, *prph.*: mountains under night; mountains in the north of Mirkwood [amon, nu, fuin] formerly *Emyn Duir UT*

Em·yn Rain, *gph.*: hills of the border; *alt.* to *Emyn Muil* [amon, rain2] *TI*

Em·yn Ui·al, *gph.*: hills of twilight; hills north of Nenuial [amon, uial] *UT*:456, *Index Nenuial*

E·'nedh·waith, *tp.*: people (or wilderness) of the middle; region between Gwathló and Angren, midway between north and south [enedh + gwaith] spelled *Enedwaith LotR*; *UT*; *Letters*:223; *PME*:328, 330

En·nor, *n.*: middle land; the central lands of the world, east of Belegaer, called Middle-earth [ennor] *LotR:AppE*, *RGEO*, *Letters*:384

E·phel Bran·dir, *gph.*: outer fence of Brandir; stockade of the Haladin on Amon Obel, named for a lord of the people [ephel, Brandir] *Silm*

E·phel Dú·ath, *gph.*: outer fence of dark shadow; mountains bounding Mordor on the west and south [ephel + dúath] *LotR*

'E·re·bor, *kd.*: lonely mountain; mountain in northern Rhovanion, home of a kingdom of Dwarves [ereb + ôr] *LotR*

E·'reb·ras, *kd.*: 'lone horn', alt. to **Erebor** *VT*45:12

E·red or **E·ryd En·grin**, *ajph. pl.*: iron mountains; mountains of the far north under which Angband was delved [orod, angren] *Silm*, *WJ*:196

E·red 'Gor·go·rath, *gph.*: mountains of horrors; *Ered Gorgoroth* [orod, gorgor] *Silm*, *MR*:127, *WJ*:129

E·red or **E·ryd 'Gor·go·roth**, *gph. pl.*: mountains of terror; southern mountains of Dorthonion, north of Nan Dungortheb [orod, gorgoroth] *Silm*, *WJ*:15; also *Ered Gorgorath* (as if *pl.* of gorgor)

ˌE·red·'lem·rin, *impr. kd. pl.*: echoing mountains; *Ered Lómin* [orod, glamren] *LR*:367 *LAM-*

E·red or **E·ryd Lin·don**, *gph. pl.*: mountains of Lindon; *Ered Luin*, as mountains bordering on Lindon [orod, Lindon] *Silm*, *WJ*:385

E·red Li·thui, *ajph. pl.*: ashy mountains; mountains forming the northern boundary of Mordor [orod, lithui] *LotR*, *Names*:178

E·red or **E·ryd Ló·min**, *ajph. pl.*: echoing mountains; CS rendition of NS name for the mountains west of Hithlum [orod, NS lǭmin = CS ‡loven] translated into CS as *Eredlemrin*, *Eryd Lammad Silm*, *WJ*:196

E·red or **E·ryd Luin** or **E·'red·luin**, *ajph. pl.*: blue mountains; mountains forming the eastern boundary of Ossiriand [orod, luin] also *Ered Lindon LotR*

E·red Mith·rin, *ajph. pl.*: grey mountains; mountain range north of Mirkwood [orod, mithren] *LotR*

E·red or **E·ryd Nim·rais**, *gph.*, *kd. pl.*: mountains with white peaks; principal mountain range of Gondor [orod, nimp + ras] *LotR*

E·red or **E·ryd Weth·rin**, *ajph. pl.*: shadowy mountains; mountains east and south of Hithlum [orod, gwathren] *Silm*, *WJ*:196

E·'re·gi·on: country of hollies; realm of the Noldor west of the Hithaeglir, near Moria [ereg + -(io)nd] *LotR*

E·'ri·a·dor, *kd.*: wilderness; sparsely inhabited lands between Hithaeglir and Ered Luin [eriador] *LotR*, *VT*42:4

E·rui, *adj.*: first (river); easternmost of the rivers of Lebennin, and the "first" of the Seven Rivers of Gondor (Erui, Sirith, Serni, Morthond, Lefnui, Angren, Gwathló) [erui] *LotR*

Eryd: for names beginning with this word see also *Ered*

E·ryd Lam·mad, *gph.*: mountains of the echo; *Ered Lómin* [orod, lammad] *WJ*:192, 196

E·ryn Fuir, *ajph.*: north wood; the Firienwood on the border of Gondor and Rohan [eryn, fuir] *VT*42:20

E·ryn Ga·len, *ajph.*: green wood; original name of *Taur e-Ndaedhelos*, then called Greenwood the Great [eryn, calen] *UT*

E·ryn 'Las·ga·len, *ajph.*: wood with green leaves; *Taur e-Ndaedhelos* in the Fourth Age [eryn, lasgalen] *LotR:AppB*

E·ryn Vorn, *ajph.*: black wood; forest in northwest Minhiriath [eryn, morn] *UT*

Es·'cal·duin, *tp.*: river of the veil; a river running through Doriath, "veiled" or screened by the trees that overhung it [escal + duin, OS *Esk^{h}aladuine] *Silm* spelled Esgaldain

Es·'cal·i·ant, *tp.*: bridge of the veil; *Iant Iaur* [escal + iant; OS *Esk^{h}aliant^{h}a] *WJ*:333 spelled Esgaliant

'Es·to·lad: said to mean *encampment*; area in east Beleriand where the Edain first settled [exact meaning uncertain] *Silm*

E·thir An·duin, *gph.*: outflow of Anduin; delta at the mouth of the Anduin [ethir^{1}, Anduin] *LotR*

Eth·raid En·grin, *ajph. pl.*: iron crossings; *Athrad Angren* [athrad, angren] *UT*

Eth·raid E·rui, *gph.pl.*: crossings of Erui; crossing of the Erui river, site of a battle [athrad, Erui] *PME*:199

Eth·ring, *kd. bv.*: (town) across the cold (river; sc. Ringló); a town at a crossing of the Ringló river [ath- + ring] *LotR*

F

Fa·las, *n.*: coast, shore, strand, line of surf; esp. the western coast of Beleriand in the First Age [falas, OS *p^halasse] *Silm*

Fan·gorn, *impr. tp.*: beard of tree; the Entwood north of Rohan, named for its eldest Ent [fang + orn[2]] *LotR:AppF*, *Names*:175

Fa·'nui·dhol, *kd. bv.*: having a cloudy head; one of the Mountains of Moria [fanui + dôl, from Kh *Bundushathûr*] *LotR*

Fen Hol·len, *ajph.*: closed door; door in the rear wall of Minas Tirith leading to the royal tombs between Minas Tirith and Mindolluin, which was kept shut except during funerals [fen(d), hollen] also *Fen Uidafnen LotR*

Fen Ui·'daf·nen, *ajph.*: ever-closed door; *alt.* to *Fen Hollen* [fen(d), uidafnen] *WR*:341

Fo·'ran·nest, *kd.*: *impr. tp.*: north gate of the center; a northern gate in Rammas Echor, looking toward the road to Rohan [fôr + and[2] + nest] *WR*:354, 357

'For·fa·las, *kd.*: northern coast; northern part of the Falas [fôr + falas] *WJ*:186

For·'lin·don, *kd.*: northern Lindon; Lindon north of the gulf of Lhûn [fôr + Lindon] *LotR*

For·lond, *kd.*: northern haven; Elf havens in Forlindon [fôr + lond] *LotR*

For·lorn, *kd.*: northern haven; Elf havens in Forlindon, alt. to **Forlond** [fôr + lorn] *TI*:302

For·'nar·than, *kd.*: northern beacon; old name of *Amon Anwar* [fôr + narthan or forn + narthan] *VT*42:20

'For·no·bel, *kd.*: northern town; *alt.* to *Fornost Erain* [forn + gobel] *TI*:304

For·nost E·rain, *gph.*: northern fortress of the kings; capital of the kingdom of Arthedain [forn + ost, aran] *LotR*, *Names*:190

'Fo·ro·chel, *kd.*: northern mass of ice; cape and bay lying north of Lindon and Eriador [fôr + gochel] *LotR*, *Letters*:199

Fo·'rod·waith, *n. tp.*: northmen, north-folk, northerland [forod + gwaith] *LotR:AppA*, *UT*:14

Fuin 'Gor·go·roth, *gph.*: night of deadly fear; *Taur nu-Fuin* [fuin, gorgoroth] *LR*:377 *ÑGOROTH-*

G

'Gar·tho·ren, *impr. kd.*: fenced fortress; *Gondolin* [garth + thoren] *LR*:360 *GARAT-*

Gel·duin, *tp.*: river of joy; *Gelion* [gell + duin] *WJ*:336

Ge·'lei·dhi·en: country of the Noldor; *Beleriand* [golodh + -(ie)nd, MS*Gölöiðiend] also *Angolonn LR*:377 *ÑGOLOD-*

'Ge·li·on, *adj.*: joyful; river separating Beleriand and Ossiriand [as if from √GJEL + -ion[2], but said to be a modification of Kh *Gabilân* great (river)] also !'*Ge·li·an*, *Gevilon*, *Gelduin*, *Duin Daer Silm*

'Ge·vi·lon: great (river); *Gelion* [MS *Geƀilaun < OS *Gabilǭn < Kh *Gabilân*] also '*Ge·ve·lon*, '*Ge·wi·lan WJ*:336

Gil·rain, *impr. tp.*: wandering (river) with stars; river of Gondor, separating Lebennin from the Dor en-Ernil, which for part of its course meandered through a depression, finally forming a pool in which stars could be reflected [gîl + rain[1]] *UT*:242–43, *VT*42:12

Gin·glith: meaning unknown; tributary of Narog [may include *lith* 'sand'] *WJ*

Gla·'dui·al, *impr. tp.*: wood in twilight; *Nan Elmoth* [glâd + uial] *WJ*

Glan·duin *kd.*: river forming a boundary; river flowing from Hithaeglir into Nîn in-Eilph, formerly the northwestern boundary of Gondor [glân[2] + duin] *LotR:AppA*, *UT*:263–64

Glan·hír, *kd.*: stream forming a boundary; river flowing from Amon Anwar into Onodló, the boundary between Rohan and Gondor [glân[2] + sîr] *UT*:318

Gli·thui, *adj.*: meaning unknown; tributary of Taeglin [contains -ui] *UT*

Glor·nan, *tp.*: valley of golden light; *Lothlórien* [glaur + nan(d), from SE *Lórinand*] *UT*:253

Goch·'res·si·el, *adj.*: (mountains) with a group of peaks; *alt.* to *Echoriath* [go + rhass + iel[3], OS *wok^h^rassiela] *WJ*:239

'Gon·do·lin, *impr. tp.*: stone of song; hidden city on the hill of Amon Gwareth (from which sprang "singing" fountains), kingdom of Turgon [gond + lind[1], from Q *Ondolindë*, influenced by CS *gond* 'stone'; actual CS cognate would be *Gonglinn. Often interpreted as *gond dolen* 'hidden rock'] also *Garthoren*, *Gondobar*, *Gondost*, *Gondothrimbar Hobbit*, *LotR*, *Silm*, *WJ*:201, *PME*:374

Gon·dor, *tp.*: land of stone; southern kingdom of the Dúnedain in Middle-earth, founded by Isildur and Anárion, sons of Elendil, possibly so called from the abundance of usable stone in the region, much used by the Dúnedain in building [gond + dôr] *LotR*

Gon·dost, *tp.*: fortress of stone; *Gondolin* [gond + ost] *LR*:359 *GOND-*

ˌGon·doth·'rim·bar, *tp.*: dwelling of the Gondothrim; *Gondolin* [Gondothrim + bâr] *LR*:359 *GOND-*

'Gor·go·roth, *n.*: (land of) deadly fear; (1) *Taur nu-Fuin*; (2) waste plain in the north of Mordor [gorgoroth] *LotR*, *Silm*

Go·'roth·res, *tp.*: ravine of horror; probably, the pass by which Beren descended from Dorthonion into Nan Dungortheb [goroth + res] *WJ*:188

Grod·nof, *impr. kd.*: hollow excavation; *Nogrod* [grôd + naw[1]; from Kh *Tumunzahar*] *WJ*:414

Gwa·thir, *tp.*: river under shadows; former name of *Gwathló*, a river formerly deeply shaded by trees [gwâth + sîr] *UT*:263

Gwath·ló, *tp.*: (river from the) pool of shadow; river at the southeastern boundary of Eriador, named for the fenland of Nîn in-Eilph, above which the river was named Mitheithel [gwâth + lô] *UT*:263

H

Ha·'dhod·rond, *tp.*: vaulted cavern of Dwarves; *Moria* [hadhod + rond, from Kh *Khazad-dûm*] also *Hadhodrûd* *WJ*:389, 414

Ha·'dhod·rûd, *tp.*: cave of Dwarves; *alt.* to *Hadhodrond* [hadhod + rhûd] *WJ*:419

Hae·rast, *kd.*: far shore; the coast of Aman, west of Belegaer [hae + rhast] *Silm:Index*

Ha·rad, *n.*: the south; lands south of Gondor [harad] *LotR*

Ha·'rad·waith, *tp.*: folk of the south; *Harad* [harad + gwaith] *LotR*

Ha·'rath·rad, *kd.*: southern ford; *Sarn Athrad* [hâr + athrad] *WJ*:335

'Har·fa·las, *kd.*: southern coast; southern part of the Falas [hâr + falas] *WJ*:190

Har·'lin·don, *kd.*: southern Lindon; Lindon south of the gulf of Lhûn [hâr + Lindon] *LotR*

Har·lond, *kd.*: southern haven; (1) Elf havens in Harlindon; (2) port of Minas Tirith on the Anduin [hâr + lond] *LotR*

Har·lorn, *kd.*: southern haven; Elf havens in Harlindon, alt. to **Harlond** [hâr + lorn] *TI*:302

Har·nen, *kd.*: southern water; river separating Harondor from Harad [hâr or harn[1] + nên] *LotR*

Ha·'ron·dor, *kd.*: southern Gondor; former province of Gondor south of Ithilien [hâr + Gondor] *LotR*

Haudh en-Ar·wen, *gph.*: mound of the noble woman; barrow in Brethil where Haleth was buried [haudh, en, arwen; from Hal *Tûr Haretha*] *Silm*, *WJ*:223

Haudh en-El·leth, *gph.*: mound of the Elf-woman; barrow east of the crossings of Taeglin in which Finduilas was buried [haudh, en, elleth] *Silm*; *WJ*:92, 95, 148

Haudh i-nDen·gin, *gph.*: mound of the slain; great barrow in the middle of Anfauglith, containing those slain in Nírnaeth Arnediad [haudh, i, dangen] also *Haudh en-nDengin*, *Haudh en-Nírnaeth Silm*; *WJ*:73, 79

Haudh en·Nír·naeth, *gph.*: mound of lamentation; *Haudh i-nDengin* [haudh, en, nírnaeth] *Silm*

Haudh in-Gwa·nur, *gph.*: mound of the twins; barrow at the crossings of Poros, where Folcred and Fastred, twin sons of Folcwinë of Rohan, were buried [haudh, i, gwanur] *LotR:AppA*

'Hel·cha·rach, *tp.*: see **Helcharaes** [helch + carach, OS *k^{h}elk^{h}arakse] *VT*45:19

'Hel·cha·raes, *tp.*: hedge of spikes of ice; area of pack ice that connected Aman and Middle-earth in the north [helch + caraes, OS *k^{h}elk^{h}arakse < CE *k^{h}elkaraksē] *LR*:362 *KARAK-*

'He·le·vorn, *impr. kd.*: black glass; dark mountain lake in Thargelion [heledh + morn, partial translation of Kh *Narag-zâram* black lake] *Silm*

Hen·neth An·'nûn, *gph.*: window on the west; hidden refuge in Ithilien, in a cave whose opening looked westward through a waterfall [henneth, annûn] *LotR*

Him·lad, *kd.*: cool plain; plain in the north between Limhir and Aros [him^1 + lâd] *Silm*

Him·ring, *impr. kd.*: continually cold; exposed and windy hill in northeast Beleriand [him^2 + ring] *Silm*

Hi·'thaeg·lir, *tp.*: mountain range with mist; great mountain range separating Eriador from Rhovanion, called Misty Mountains [hîth + aeglir] also *Hithdilias LotR* (misspelled Hithaiglin) *Silm*, *UT*

Hith·'di·li·as, *tp.*: line of peaks with mist; *alt.* to *Hithaeglir* [hîth + tilias] *TI*:124

Hith·'li·ni·ath, *tp. pl.*: pools of mist; *Aelin-uial* [hîth + liniath, pl. of lîn] *LR*:364 *KHITH-*

Hith·lum, *tp.*: night of mist; lands north and west of the Ered Wethrin, so called by the Noldor who first came there [NS form < MNS *xiβlǭm < Q *Híβilómë*; the CS form of this name would (if borrowed from Quenya) have been *Hithlo < MS *xiβlau; the actual cognate compound would have been *Hidhu] *Silm*

Ho·bas in-Eilph, *gph.*: haven of the swans; *Alphobas* [hobas, i, alph] (N Hobas in Elph) *LR*:364 *KHOP-*

I

Im·lad Mor·gul, *gph.*: deep valley of sorcery; valley in which Minas Morgul was situated [imlad, morgul] *LotR*

Im·lad Rin·gló, *gph.*: deep valley of the Ringló; Ringló Vale in Gondor [imlad, Ringló] *WR*:287

Im·'lad·ris, *impr. tp.*: deep valley of the cleft; a secret fastness in a deep-cloven valley on an upper branch of the Bruinen [imlad + rist[1]] *Names*:156, 190

Im·loth Me·lui, *ajph.*: sweet flowering valley; a region of Lossarnach, known for its roses [imloth, melui] *VT*42:18

Im·rath Gon·draich, *gph.*: valley of stone wagons; valley in the Druadan forest through which an ancient wagon road to stone quarries had passed [imrath, gond + rach] *UT*:465

I·'thi·li·en: country of the moon; fief of Gondor between Anduin and Ephel Dúath, named for the fortress of Minas Ithil [ithil + -(ie)nd] *LotR*

I·'thil·duin, *tp.*: river of the moon; former name of *Morgulduin* [ithil + duin] *WR*:436

Iv·rin, *adj.*: ?crystalline; pool and fall at the head of the river Narog [ivrin] *Silm*

ˌIv·ri·'nei·thel, *tp.*: well of Ivrin; *Eithil Ivrin* [ivrin, eithel] *LR*:139

J

Iant Iaur, *ajph.*: old bridge; bridge over the Esgalduin north of Doriath [iant, iaur] also *Esgaliant* *WJ*:333

L

Lad·ros, *impr. tp.*: ?plain of rain; region of northeast Dorthonion [lâd + ros[2]] *Silm*

Lam·moth: great echo; a coastal region west of Hithlum, under the echoing hills of Ered Lómin [lam[2] + -oth] *Silm*

Lant·hir Lam·ath, *gph.*: waterfall of echoes; waterfall in Ossiriand by which Dior dwelt before he came to Doriath [lanthir, lam[2]] *PME*:349

Le·'ben·nin, *kd.*: five waters; a province of Gondor, containing the five rivers of Erui, Sirith, Celos, Serni, and Gilrain [leben + nîn, pl. of nên] *LotR*

Lef·nui, *adj.*: fifth (river); westernmost river flowing into the Bay of Belfalas, and the "fifth" of the Seven Rivers of Gondor (Erui, Sirith, Serni, Morthond, Lefnui, Angren, Gwathló) [lefnui] *LotR*

Lest 'Me·li·an, *gph.*: girdle of Melian; a zone of enchantment encircling the forests of Neldoreth and Region in Doriath, created by Melian [lest, melian], also called *List Melian* (where *list* may be the archaic English word meaning 'boundary') *WJ*:225, 228

Lim·hir, *kd.*: sparkling river; clear river flowing from Himring into the river Aros [lim[1] + sîr] also *Celon WJ*:337

Lim·lint, *dv.*: light and swift; a river flowing into Anduin from Hithaeglir, called Limlight [lim[1] + lint] also *Lim·laith* of uncertain meaning *UT*:318

Li·'nae·wen, *impr. kd.*: lake of birds; lake and wetland in Nevrast, much resorted to by birds [lîn + aewen] *Silm*

Lin·don: land of singers; *Ossiriand*, after it was inhabited by the Green-Elves (Glinnil, Laegil); also, that portion of Beleriand that remained unsubmerged [from Oss *Lindon* < *Lindānā < *Lindā, name of the Teleri for themselves] *LotR*, *Silm*, *WJ*:385

Lin·hir, *tp.*: ?stream of song; town at the fords below the inflow of Gilrain into Serni [lind[1] + sîr] *LotR*

Lîn Ui·al, *gph.*: pool of twilight; *Aelin-Uial* [lîn, uial] *LR*:374 *MUY-*

Lis·cardh, *tp.*: region of reeds; land at the mouths of Sirion [lisc + ardh or gardh] *UT*:34 spelled Lisgardh

Li·thir, *tp.*: stream of sand; tributary of the upper Sirion [lith + sîr] *WJ*

Lith·lad, *tp.*: plain of ash; plain in Mordor under Ered Lithui east of Barad-dûr [lith + lâd] *LotR*

Lô Dhaer, *ajph.*: great fen; *Nîn-in-Eilph VT*42:14

Loeg 'Nin·glo·ron, *kd.*: pool(s) of the gladden-flower; marshy land where Sîr Ninglor enters Anduin [loeg, ningloron] *UT*

Lond Daer E·nedh, *ajph.*, *gph.*: great haven of the middle; Númenorean harbor built at the mouth of Gwathló [lond, daer[1], enedh] also *Lond Daer ajph. UT*:264

Lon·nath Er·nin, *gph.*: havens beside the water; *alt.* to *Harlond* [lond, Arnen] *WR*:294

Los·gar: meaning unknown; place on the coast on the north side of the Firth of Drengist *Silm*

Los·'sar·nach, *tp.*: Arnach of flowers; fief of Gondor on the upper waters of Erui [los[2] + Arnach (pre-Númenorean name)] *LotR*, *VT*42:18

Loth·lann, *dv.*: wide and empty (land); (1) plains east of Ard-galen; (2) desert south of Mordor [lost + land] *LotR*

Loth·'ló·ri·en, *tp.*: dreamland with flowers; woodland realm of Elves centered on the confluence of Celbrant and Anduin, named to recall the gardens of Irmo in Valinor [loth + Q *lórien* 'land of dreams' √(O)L-OS] also *Glornan*, *Nan Laur LotR*, *UT*:253

Lh

Lhann: see *Trann PME*:45

Lhûn, *adj*.: (river) of sound; river flowing east of Ered Luin [lhûn] *LotR*

M

Mal·duin, *tp*.: river of gold; tributary of Taeglin [mall + duin] *Silm*

Me·'neg·roth, *dg*.: thousand caves; chief city of Doriath, built in underground halls [meneg + groth] *Silm*; *WJ*:11, 415

Me·'nel·rond, *tp*.: vault of heaven; domed throne-hall in Menegroth set with silver and gems in the shape of constellations [menel + rond] *PME*:371

Men·gas Dûr, *ajph*., *tp*.: dark gap in the way; *alt*. to *Cabed en-Aras* [mên + gas, dûr] *WJ*:157

Men i-Naug·rim, *gph*.: way of the Dwarves; road traversing Taur e-Ndaedhelos from Celduin to the Cirith Forn south of Emyn Duir [mên, i, naug] *UT*:280

Me·'reth·rond, *tp*.: vaulted hall of feasts; hall in Minas Tirith [mereth + rond] *LotR*

Me·thed en-Glad, *gph*.: end of the wood; outlaw stronghold at the edge of the forest of Brethil [methed, en, glâd] *UT*:153

Me·'thed·ras, *tp*.: peak at the end; mountain at the southern end of Hithaeglir [methed + ras] possibly should be *Me·'thedh·ras* [methen + ras] *LotR*

Me·'thi·ri·ad, *impr. tp*.: ?end of the two rivers; region between the lower waters of Narog and Sirion [meth + sîr + -ad^2] *WJ*:190

Mi·nas A·nor, *gph*.: tower of the sun; earlier name of *Minas Tirith* [minas, anor; named for King Anárion of Gondor] *LotR*

Mi·nas I·thil, *gph*.: tower of the moon; earlier name of *Minas Morgul* [minas, ithil; named for King Isildur of Gondor] *LotR*

Mi·nas Mor·gul, *gph*.: tower of sorcery; fortress built by Gondor in the Ephel Dúath east of Anduin, later controlled by the Ringwraiths [minas, morgul] *LotR*

Mi·nas Ti·rith, *gph*.: tower of vigilance; (1) fortress built on Tol Sirion; (2) fortress built by Gondor at the eastern end of the Ered Nimrais, maintained as a guard against Minas Morgul and Mordor [minas, tirith] *LotR*, *Silm*

Min·deb: meaning unknown; tributary of Sirion, flowing from the pass of Anach *Silm*

Min·'dol·luin, *kd*., *impr. kd*.: blue towering hill; mountain at the east end of Ered Nimrais, overlooking Minas Tirith [mîn + dôl + luin] *LotR*, *Silm:Index*

Min·'hi·ri·ath, *pc. bv.*: (land) between the rivers; region of Eriador between Baranduin and Gwathló [mi (or im) + in, prepositional form of i + siriath, *coll. pl.* of sîr] *LotR*, *Silm:App sîr*, *UT*

Min-·'Rim·mon, *gph.*: peak of Rimmon; beacon-hill of Anórien [mîn, Rimmon(pre-Númenorean name for a group of crags)] *LotR*, *UT:Index*

Mi·'thei·thel, *kd. bv.*: (river having a) grey spring; upper course of the Gwathló, from its source in the Hithaeglir to the fens of Nîn in-Eilph [mîth[1] + eithel] *LotR*

Mith·lond, *kd.*: grey harbor; havens at the head of the Gulf of Lhûn in Lindon, possibly so called because it belonged to the Sindar or Grey-Elves [mîth[1] + lond] *LotR*

Mith·rim, *kd.*: grey people; that portion of the Sindar that dwelt in Hithlum, also the region of Hithlum primarily inhabited by this people, named from the grey clouds and mist common in this northern region, or from the grey cloth that the Mithrim wore [mîth[1] + rim[1], OS *Mit^{h}irimbė] *WJ*:378, 410

Mo·'ran·non, *kd.*: black gate; rampart at the entrance to Cirith Gorgor [môr + annon] *LotR*, *Letters*:178

Mor·dor, *kd.*: black land; mountain-ringed land in the Southeast, realm of Sauron [morn + dôr; so called in the Second Age because of the devastating eruptions of Orodruin] *LotR*; *Letters*:178, *no.* 347 *p.* 427; *WJ*:370; *PME*:390

Mor·gai, *kd.*: black fence; secondary mountain range inside the northern Ephel Dúath [morn + cai] *LotR*, *UT*:282

Mor·'gul·duin, *tp.*: river of sorcery; river flowing from Imlad Morgul into Anduin [morgul + duin] *LotR*

'Mo·ri·a, *kd.*: black chasm; the great Dwarf-mansion in the Hithaeglir [môr + iâ] also *Hadhodrond*, *Hadhodrûd*, *Nornhabar*, *Letters*:178, 382

Mor·nan, *kd.*: black valley; valley of the Morthond [morn + nan] *UT*, *VT*42:14

Mor·thond, *kd.*: black root; river in western Gondor springing from a ghost-haunted region of the Ered Nimrais [môr or morn + thond] *LotR:AppE*, *Names*:179, *Letters*:178

N

Nag·lath Morn, *ajph.*: black teeth; the toothlike towers of *Narchost* and *Carchost* [nagol, morn] also *Nelig Myrn* *WR*:122

Naith, *n.*: spearhead; that part of Lórien in the angle between the Celebrant and Anduin rivers [naith] *LotR*, *UT*:282

Nan 'Cu·ru·nír, *gph.*: valley of the wizard; valley at the southern end of

Hithaeglir containing Angrenost, where the wizard Saruman dwelt [nan, curunír] *TT*:3.8, p. 159

Nan 'Don·go·roth, *gph., kd.*: valley of dark horror; *Nan Dungortheb* [nan(d), donn + goroth] *LR*:355 *DUN-*, 377 *ÑGOROTH-*

ˌNan·du·'hi·ri·on, *impr. kd.*: valley having streams of darkness; valley around the upper waters of the Celebrant, fed by streams in the mountain-shadow [nan(d) + dû + sîr + -on[3]] also *Nan Duhirion ajph.* of same meaning. *LotR*, *Names*:182

Nan Dun·'gor·theb, *ajph.*: black and horrible valley; low land between Ered Gorgoroth and the northern border of Doriath [nan(d), donn + gortheb] also *Nan Dongoroth*, *Nan Gorothvor Silm*

Nan El·moth, *gph., tp.*: valley of dusk with stars; wood east of Limhir [nan(d), êl + môth] also *Gladuial Silm:App moth*

Nan E·'reg·dos, *ajph.*: valley of the holly tree; *alt.* to *Eregion* [nan(d), eregdos] *TI*:166

Nan Go·'roth·vor, *gph., impr. kd.*: valley of black horror; *Nan Dungortheb* [nan(d), goroth + môr] (N Nann Orothvor) *LR*:355 *DUN-*, 377 *ÑGOROTH-*

Nan Laur, *gph.*: valley of golden light; *Lothlórien* [nan(d), glaur; from SE *Lórinand*] *UT*:253

Nan-tath·ren, *ajph.*: valley of willows; meadowlands at the juncture of Narog and Sirion [nan(d), tathren] *LotR*

Nar·chost, *tp.*: fortress that rends; tower near the Morannon [narcha- + ost] *LotR*

#Nar·dhol, *tp.*: hill with fire; hill of Anórien on which beacon fires were lit [naur + dôl] spelled *Nardol LotR*, *UT*:319, *WJ*:187

Nar·'goth·rond, *tp.*: fortified cave on the Narog; secret fortress of Finrod, and the extensive kingdom on both sides of the Narog whose capital it was [Narog + othrond] *Silm*, *WJ*:414

Na·rog, *adj.*: rushing (river); river of West Beleriand, flowing from Ivrin into Sirion [MS *Na·'raug < OS *Narǫka < CE *narākā] *Silm*, *LR*:374 *NÁRAK-*

'Na·ro·gardh, *tp.*: realm on the Narog; kingdom of *Nargothrond* [Narog + ardh] *LR*:374 *NÁRAK-*

'Nel·do·reth: ?forest of beeches; beech-wood of Doriath between Esgalduin and Mindeb [neldor + ?-eth[1]] also *Taur na-Neldor LotR*, *Silm*

Ne·lig Myrn, *ajph.*: black teeth; *Naglath Morn* [nêl or neleg, morn] *WR*:113

Nen Ce·'ned·ril, *gph.*: water like a mirror; a long lake in Nanduhirion [nên, cenedril; from Kh *Kheled-zâram*] *RS*:466

Nen E·chui, *gph.*: water of awakening; Cuiviénen, the lake in the East by which the Elves first awoke [nên, echui] *Silm:App cuivië*, *LR*:366 *KUY-*

Nen Gi·rith, *gph.*: water of shuddering; *Dimrost*, so called because Nienor shivered when coming there [nên, girith] *WJ*:96

Nen Hi·thoel, *ajph.*: water cool with mist; lake in the course of Anduin above Rauros [nên, (tp.) hîth + an obscure element ending in *-oel* (possibly oel, goel, hoel, soel, or thoel) meaning 'cool'] *LotR*

Nen La·laith, *gph.*: water of laughter; stream flowing into Dor-lómin from Amon Darthir [nên, lalaith] *UT*

Nen·ning: meaning uncertain; river flowing into the sea at Eglarest [?contains nên 'water'] also *Eglahir Silm*

Ne·'nui·al *impr. tp.* or **Nen Ui·al**, *gph.*: water of twilight; lake in Eriador, source of Baranduin [nên + uial] *LotR*, *Names*:188

Ner·wing, *kd.*: red foam, name of a river with reddish foaming water [naru + gwing √NAR √!WIŋ] *VT*45:36

Nev·rast, *kd.*: near shore; (1) the coast of Middle-earth, east of Belegaer; (2) region south of Drengist [nef + rhast] *WJ*:197

'Nim·bre·thil, *kd. pl.*: (land of) white birches; region of birch trees in Arvernien [nimp + brethil] *LotR*, *Silm*

Nim·'dil·dor, *impr. kd.*: high white peak; *Amon Uilos* [nimp + till + taur[1]] *LR*:389 *TA-*

Nin·dalf, *kd.*: wet flatland; marshy land east of Anduin, opposite the inflow of Onodló [nîn[1] + talf[1]] *LotR*, *Names*:195

Nîn in-Eilph, *gph.*: water(land)s of the swans; great fen at the confluence of Mitheithel and Glanduin [nên, i, alph] also *Lô Dhaer UT*

Nog·rod, *tp.*: excavation of Dwarves; Dwarf mansion east of Ered Luin [naug[2] + grôd; modification of earlier *Novrod*] also *Grodnof Silm*, *WJ*:389, 414

'Norn·ha·bar, *tp.*: mine of the Dwarves; *Moria* [norn + habar] *WJ*:206

Nov·rod, *kd.*: hollow excavation; *Nogrod* [naw[1] + grôd, MS*nauƀʒrod, from Kh *Tumunzahar*] *WJ*:389, 414

Nú·ath, *pc. bv.*: ?(wood) under shadow; woods in northwest Beleriand, between Narog and Nenning, perhaps so called from being underneath the Ered Wethrin [nu + gwâth] *UT*

Nurn: region of southern Mordor about the sea of Núrnen [from *Núrnen*] *LotR*

Núr·nen, *kd.*: sad water; inland sea in southern Mordor [nûr[2] + nên] *LotR*, *UT*:458

O

'O·do·thui, *adj.*: seventh (river); *alt.* to *Gwathló* [odothui] *WR*:437

O·'nod·ló, *tp.*: pool of the Ent; the river Entwash in Rohan, presumably named for a pool at or near its source at Wellinghall, home of the Ent Fangorn [onod + lô] *LotR*

Or·falch E·chor, *gph.*, *kd.*: high ravine of the outer circle; cleft through the Echoriath connecting Gondolin to the outer world [or + falch, echor] *UT*

O·rod na-Thôn, *gph.*: mountain of pine; *Dorthonion* [orod, na, thôn] *LotR*

O·'rod·ruin, *impr. kd.*: burning mountain; the great volcano of Gorgoroth [orod + ruin] also *Amon Amarth LotR:App F*, *Names*:182

Or·thanc, *impr. kd.*: split mountain; the tower of Angrenost, whose top divided into four horns [ôr + thanc] *TT*:3.8, p. 160; *Silm:Index*

'Os·fo·rod, *impr. tp.*: fortress of the north [ost + forod]; *alt.* to *Fornost Erain TI*:120

Os·'gi·li·ath, *impr. tp.*: fortress of stars; original capital of Gondor, on both sides of Anduin, having an astronomical name, as the city intermediate between Minas Anor and Minas Ithil [ost + giliath, pl. of gîl] *LotR*, *RGEO*, *Letters*:426

Os·sir, *kd.*: seven rivers; *Ossiriand* [Ossiriandic *oss *seven* + sîr] *LotR*, *Silm*

Os·'si·ri·and, *kd.*: land of seven rivers; land between the Gelion and Ered Luin, watered by seven rivers [Ossiriandic *oss *seven* + sîr + -(ia)nd] also *Lindon*, *Dor Lindon LotR*, *Silm*, *WJ*:385

Ost in-E·dhil, *gph.*: fortress of the Elves; chief city of *Eregion* [ost, i, edhel] *Silm*, *UT*

Oth·ram, *tp.*: wall of the fortress; outer wall of Minas Tirith [ost + ram] *WR*:288

P

Parth Ce·'leb·rant, *gph.*: field of Celebrant; grassland between Celebrant and Limlint [parth, Celebrant] *UT*

Parth Ga·len, *ajph.*: green lawn; grassy lawn on the banks of Nen Hithoel, near Amon Hen [parth, calen] *LotR*

Pe·'lar·gir, *impr. tp.*: enclosure for royal ships; great seaport of Gondor, at the confluence of Sirith and Anduin [pêl + arn + cîr, pl. of cair] *LotR*

Pe·'len·nor, *kd.*: land forming an enclosure; the land around Minas Tirith, surrounded by the Rammas Echor [pêl + dôr, as if < OS *pelehndore] *LotR*

Pen-Ar·duin, *gph.*: fall of the royal river; name of a dwelling in Emyn Arnen [pend, arn + duin; the Arduin was perhaps a river running from the Emyn Arnen into Anduin] *PME*:411

Pen·drath-dú·hir, *gph.*: stair of streams of darkness; the Dimrill Stair, the falls on the east side of the Redhorn pass at the head of Nanduhirion [pendrath, dû + sîr] (misread as Pendrethdulur) *RS*:433

Pin·nath Ge·lin, *ajph.*: green ridges; hills in western Gondor, and a fief containing them [pinnath, calen] *LotR*

Po·ros: meaning uncertain; river forming the southern boundary of Gondor [may contain *ros*[2] 'spray'] *LotR*

R

Ram·dal, *tp.*: foot (end) of the wall; eastern end of the Andram [ram + tâl] *Silm*, *WJ*:191

Ram·mas E·chor, *gph.*: wall of the outer circle; wall surrounding the Pelennor [rammas, echor] *LotR*

Ras Ar·phain, *ajph.*: high white peak; *Amon Uilos* [ras, ar-[1] + fain; from Q *Arfanyarasse*] *WJ*:403

Ras Maew·rim, *gph.*: cape of gulls; *Bar i-Mŷl* [ras, maew + rim[1]] spelled *Ras Mewrim* *WJ*:190, 418

Ras Mor·thil, *tp.*, *kd.*: cape of black peaks; *Andrast* [ras, môr[1] + till] *UT*

Rath a Che·'ler·dain, *prph.*: street for lampwrights; *alt.* to *Rath Celerdain* [rath, an, calardan] *WJ*:287, 388

Rath Ce·'ler·dain, *gph.*: street of lampwrights; a street in Minas Tirith [rath, calardan] *LotR*

Rath Dí·nen, *ajph.*: silent street; street in the area of the royal tombs behind Minas Tirith [rath, dínen] *LotR*

Rath·'ló·ri·el, *impr. kd.*: golden watercourse; northernmost of the seven rivers of Ossiriand (called Ascar by the Green-Elves), named for the dragon hoard that was drowned there by the Dwarves who had carried it from Doriath [rath + glóriel] also *Rathlórion*, *Rathmalad*, *Rathmallen* *Silm*, *WJ*:190, 353

'Rath·ma·lad, *impr. tp.*: watercourse of gold; *alt.* to *Rathlóriel* [rath + malad] *WJ*:191

Rath·'mal·len, *impr. kd.*: golden watercourse; *alt.* to *Rathlóriel* [rath + mallen] *WJ*:191, 353

Rau·ros, *tp.*: spray with a roaring sound; great cataract that poured the waters of Nen Hithoel into the lower reaches of Anduin [raw[3] + ros[2]] *LotR*

'Re·gi·on: country of hollies; forest of Doriath, between Esgalduin and Aros [rêg + -(io)nd] *Silm*

Rim·dad, *impr. kd.*: (river) rushing down; river flowing swiftly from Hithaeglir into Anduin [rimp + dad] (N Rhimdad) *TI*:296

Rin·gló, *kd.*: (river from the) cold pool; a river of Gondor, originating in an icy tarn in the Ered Nimrais [ring + lô] also *Ringnen LotR*, *UT*:461, *VT*42:14

Ringnen, *kd.*: cold water; former name of *Ringló* [ring + nen] *VT*42:14

Rin·gwil: meaning uncertain; stream entering the Narog at Nargothrond [may contain *ring* 'cold'] *Silm*

Ri·vil: meaning unknown; tributary of upper Sirion *Silm*

Ro·han: land of horses; kingdom of a horse-breeding nation settled in the province of *Calenardhon* [roch + -(a)nd] normal form *Ro·chann LotR*, *UT*, *Letters*:178, 382

Ros·fain, *impr. kd.*: white spray; *alt.* to *Rauros* [ros^2 + fain] (N Rhosfein) *TI*

Rh

'Rhos·co·bel, *kd.*: russet enclosure; home of Radagast in the western borders of Taur e-Ndaedhelos [rhosc + gobel] *LotR* (spelled Rhosgobel)

Rho·'va·ni·on: wild country; land east of the Misty Mountains and north of Gondor and Rohan [rhovan + -(io)nd] *LotR*

Rhu·daur, *kd.*: eastern wood; the eastern kingdom of the three into which Arnor was divided, possibly named for the woods there (the later Trollshaws) [rhû + taur^3] *LotR:AppA*

Rhûn, *n.*: (the) East; general name for lands to the east of Carnen and Celduin [rhûn] *LotR*

Rhú·naer, *tp.*: sea of the East; inland sea in the east of Middle-earth, fed by Celduin [rhûn + aer] *TI*:307

S

Sam·math Naur, *gph.*: chambers of fire; a delving in the side of Orodruin, in which Sauron forged the One Ring [sam, naur] *LotR*

Sarch ni·a Hîn Hú·rin, *prph.*: grave of the children of Húrin; a name given by Brandir to Brethil, when he believed both Túrin and Nienor dead [sarch, hîn, Húrin] *UT*. The word *nia* is almost certainly wrong, though also seen in *Glaer nia Chîn Húrin WJ*:160, 251. Perhaps for *nia* should be read *ina*, as in the early form *Haudh-ina-Nengin WJ*:79, in which case it should have become *Sarch i·Chîn Húrin*, as *Glaer nia Chîn Húrin* became *Narn i·Chîn Húrin*.

Sar·nas Fin·'gol·fin, *gph.*: cairn of Fingolfin; the burial place of Fingolfin in the mountains north of Gondolin [sarnas, Fingolfin] *LR*:406

Sarn Ath·rad or **Sarn-ath·rad,** *ajph.*: stony ford; (1) ford over Gelion near Rathlóriel; (2) Sarn Ford on Baranduin [sarn[1], athrad] also *Athrad Daer, Athrad i-Negyth, Harathrad Names*:190, *WJ*:335

Sarn Ge·bir, *ajph.*: stony spikes; rapids in Anduin north of Emyn Muil [sarn[1], ceber] *LotR, Silm:App sarn*

Se·rech: meaning unknown; fen at the confluence of Rivil and Sirion *Silm*

Sern 'A·ra·nath, *gph.*: stones of kings; *Argonath* [sarn[2], aran] *WR*:132, 137

Ser·ni, *n.*: shingle; river of Lebennin flowing into the bay of Belfalas, where its mouth was choked with pebbly deposits [serni] incorrectly spelled *Sernui ATB*:8

Sern U·bed, *gph.*: stones of denial; *Argonath*, statues raising their hands toward the north in a forbidding gesture [sarn[2], ubed] *WR*:132, 137

Si·'ran·non, *impr. tp.*: stream at the gate; a stream flowing from the west gate of Moria, probably a tributary of the Glanduin [sîr + annon] *LotR*

Sîr An·gren, *ajph.*: iron river; a river flowing west from the Hithaeglir, out of the valley in which was Angrenost [sîr, angren] *UT*

ˌSi·ri·'om·bar, *tp.*: dwelling on the Sirion; the havens at the mouths of Sirion at the end of the First Age [Sirion + bâr] *LR*:407

'Si·ri·on: great river; principal river of Beleriand [sîr + -on[2], OS *Siriondo] *Silm*

Si·rith, *n.*: flowing; river of Lebennin, flowing into Anduin at Pelargir [sirith] *LotR*

Sîr Nin·glor, *gph.*: river of gladden-flower(s); a tributary of the Anduin [sîr, ninglor] *UT*

T

Taeg·lin, *tp.*: singer on the boundary; a river forming the western boundary of the wood of Brethil [taeg + lind[2], OS *Taikalinde] also *Taiglin, Teiglin WJ*:309

Taen Nim·dil, *gph.*: summit of the white peak; hall of Manwë on Amon Uilos [taen[2], nimp + till] *LR*:389 *TA-*

Ta·lath Dir·nen, *ajph.*: guarded plain; plain northeast of Nargothrond, watched by its spies [talath, tirnen] *WJ*:85

Ta·lath Rhú·nen, *ajph.*: eastern vale; former name of *Thargelion* [talath, rhúnen] *Silm, WJ*:197

'Ta·ra·gaer, *impr. kd.*: ruddy horn; *alt.* to *Caradhras* [tarag, gaer[2]] *RS*:419

Ta·ras: meaning unknown; mountain in the west of Nevrast *Silm*

Tar·lang's Neck, *kd.*: tough neck; a rocky ridge connecting (as a neck) Ered Nimrais to an outlying group of hills; *Tarlanc* or *Tarlang* was the original name, later understood as a personal name after its meaning had been forgotten [tara + lanc[2]] *Names*:193.

#**Taur e-'nDae·dhe·los**, *gph*.: forest of the great fear; the great forest of Rhovanion called Mirkwood [taur[3], en, daedhelos] spelled *Taur e-Ndaedelos*; also *Eryn Galen*, *Eryn Lasgalen*, *Taur nu-Fuin LotR:AppF*

Taur en-Fa·roth, *gph*.: wood of the hunters; woodland west of Nargothrond [taur[3], en, faroth] earlier *Taur na-Fa·ras Silm*

Taur i- 'Me·le·gyrn, *gph*.: wood of the great trees; *Taur im-Duinath* [taur[3], i, beleg + orn[2]] *WJ*:193

Taur im-Dui·nath, *prph*.: wood between rivers; a great forest in the south of Beleriand [taur[3], im, duin] also *Taur i-Melegyrn*, *Taur na-Chardhîn Silm*, *WJ*:193

#**Taur na-Dhel·'dú·ath**, *prph*.: wood of the horror of nightshade; *Taur nu-Fuin* [taur[3], na, Deldúath] spelled *Taur na-Delduath*

Taur na-Nel·dor, *prph*.: wood of beech; *Neldoreth* [taur[3], na, neldor] *LotR*

Taur na-Char·dhîn, *prph*., *kd*.: wood of southern silence; *Taur im-Duinath* [taur[3], na, hâr + dîn[2]] *WJ*:193

Taur nan-E·rig, *prph*.: wood of the hollies; *Region* [taur[3], na, ereg] *LR*:356 *ERÉK-*

Taur nu-Fuin, *prph*.: wood under night-darkness; (1) the forest on Dorthonion, after it became the abode of evil creatures; (2) *Taur e-Ndaedhelos* [taur[3], nu, fuin], also *Deldúath*, *Taur na-Dheldúath*, *Fuin Gorgoroth WJ*:56

Tau·rost, *kd*.: lofty fortress; the *akrópolis* or citadel of Minas Tirith [taur[1] + ost] *WR*:260

'Tav·ro·bel, *tp*.: enclosure of woodpeckers; *alt*. to *Ephel Brandir* [tavor + gobel] *LR*:390 *TAM-*

Ta·war in- 'Drú·e·dain, *gph*.: forest of the Drû-folk; the Druadan forest at the eastern end of Ered Nimrais [tawar, i, drúadan] *UT*:319

Teig·lin, *kd*.: boundary-marking singer: *Taeglin* [taig + lind[2]] *Silm*

Ti·rith Ae·ar, *gph*.: guard of the sea; the 'Sea-ward Tower' in Dol Amroth that watched the coasts *ATB*:8

Tol Bran·dir, *gph*.: island of Brandir; island at the southern end of Nen Hithoel, above Rauros falls; the origin of the name is obscure [toll, Brandir(name); when first devised this name referred to Amon Hen, and *brandir* probably meant 'high sight' (brand + tîr[2]); this translation seems inapplicable to the later Tol Brandir, which was completely inaccessible and could not be used for keeping watch] *LotR*

'Tol·fa·las, *impr. tp.*: island of the coast; large island in the bay of Belfalas [toll + falas] also *Tol Fa·las LotR*

Tol Fuin, *gph.*: island of night; that part of *Dorthonion* (Taur nu-Fuin) that rose above the water after the drowning of Beleriand [toll, fuin] *TI*:301–2

Tol Ga·len, *ajph.*: green island; island in south Ossiriand, in the midst of the river Adurant [toll, calen] also *'Tol·ga·len. WJ*:195

Tol in-Gaur·hoth, *gph.*: island of the wolves; *Tol Sirion*, after it was taken by Sauron and became the abode of werewolves [toll, i, gaur] *WJ*:54, 239

Toll E·reb, *ajph.*: lonely island; Tol Eressëa in the bay of Eldamar [toll, ereb]

Tol·'lon·dren, *impr. kd.*: stony island; *alt.* to *Tol Brandir* [toll, gondren] *TI*:270

Tol Mor·wen, *gph.*: island of Morwen; island supposedly existing on the site of Morwen's grave after the downfall of Beleriand [toll, Morwen] *Silm*

Tol 'Si·ri·on, *gph.*: island of Sirion; island in the midst of the upper waters of Sirion, on which was built Minas Tirith [toll, Sirion] later *Tol in-Gaurhoth Silm*

To·rech Un·gol, *gph.*: lair of the spider; den of the monster-spider Shelob in Cirith Ungol [torech, ungol] *LotR*

Trann, i **Drann**, *n.*: (the) Province; the Shire of the Periannath in Eriador, whose name seems to have been used in general of the provinces of the Númenorean kingdoms [*trann*] also *Lhann SD*:128–31

'Tum·ha·lad: meaning uncertain; field in West Beleriand on which the army of Nargothrond was destroyed [contains *tûm deep valley*]

'Tum·la·den, *impr. kd.*: wide valley; (1) the valley in which Gondolin was situated; (2) a valley of the Ered Nimrais [tûm + laden] *Silm*

Tûn: high hill; hill in Eldamar on which the city of the Noldor was built [Q *Túna*, √TUN] *LR*:395 *TUN-*

Tyrn Gor·thad or **Tyrn Ger·thaid**, *gph.*: downs of barrow(s); downs in northern Cardolan, on which grave mounds were anciently built [torn, gorthad] *LotR:AppA*, *PME*:194

Th

ˌThan·go·'rod·rim, *tp. pl.*: mountains of oppression; immense hills of earth and refuse in front of Ered Engrin, raised by Morgoth during the excavation of Angband [thang + orod + rim[1]] *Silm*, *MR*:298

Thar·bad, *n.*: crossway; port city where the North-South Road crossed Gwathló [tharbad] *LotR*, *Silm:App thar-*, *UT*

Thar·'ge·li·on, *pc. bv.*: (land) across Gelion; region between Gelion and the Ered Luin north of Rathlóriel [thar- + Gelion] also *Talath Rhúnen, Dor Caranthir, Thargelian, Thorewilan Silm*

'Then·fa·las, *kd.*: short beach; shoreland between Ethir Anduin and Dol Amroth [thent + falas] also *Belfalas VT*42:15

Tho·'re·wi·lan, *pc. bv.*: (land) across Gewilan; *Thargelion* [thor-, variant of thar- probably < OS *t^{h}ǭr- √THAR + Gewilan, variant of Gelion] *WJ*:336

U

U·'dûn, *n.*: hell; deep valley in northwestern Mordor [udûn] *LotR*, *Silm*, *MR*:382

Ui·los: see *Amon Uilos*

U·'van·waith, *tp.*: wilderness of monsters; the No-man's-lands on the borders of Mordor [úan + gwaith] *TI*:281

Appendix 6

Miscellanea

SINDARIN NAMES FOR THE VALAR, VALIER, AND MAIAR

Many names for the most prominent Valar, Valier, and Maiar exist in Sindarin and Noldorin. The actual usage of these names is, however, somewhat limited; only Manwë, Varda, Orome, and perhaps Yavanna had names that were regularly used. Since the remaining names are for the most part recorded in the Noldorin dialect of Sindarin, and in many cases must be derived from Quenya (and show the influence of the language of the Valar), their source might be sought in Gondolin, where Noldor and Sindar mixed freely and the use of Quenya was not prohibited. For differences between the Noldorin and Sindarin names, see §§ 4.221–36.

The Valar

Manwë

Manwë's most frequent Sindarin name was *Aran Einior* 'Elder King'. But he was also simply called *Manwë*, a direct borrowing from Q *Manwë*, originating from *Mānawēnuz* in the language of the Valar. It fit Sindarin in style and structure well enough, however; it might be interpreted in Sindarin as 'holy person'.

Ulmo

The Quenya name *Ulmo* was derived from the Valarin *Ulubōz* but was often interpreted as **Ulumō*, 'the pourer', from a root √ULU 'pour'. A Sindarin equivalent was created on this basis, *Ulu*, which could be derived from a Middle Sindarin **Uluv̄*.

In Noldorin Ulmo was also called *Guiar* or *Uiar* (CS *Goear*), corresponding to Quenya *Vaiaro*. Both came from Common Eldarin **wājārō* 'lord of the ocean that enfolds the world', from the root √WAJ 'enfold, envelop'. The Sindarin forms evolve as they would have if they were derived from an Old Sindarin name **wǭjarō*.

Aulë

The Quenya name *Aulë* was derived from the Valarin *Aȝulēz*; but the equivalent *Gaul* was assigned to it in Noldorin, as if it were related to the root √GAW 'devise, contrive', corresponding to Quenya *aulë* 'invention' [CE **ȝaulē*]. This was often seen in shortened and lenited form *-ol*, as in the name *Belegol* [S *beleg* + *Gaul*] *Aulë the Great*—a name that certainly seems to show the sympathies of the Noldor.

Another name given to him was *Barthan*, 'the world-maker', equivalent to Quenya *Martano*; this phonologically sophisticated equivalent is a correct Sindarin derivation from a deduced Common Eldarin form *mbartanō (see Appendix 2, *bâr*, *tân*).

Aulë and *Yavanna*, together called in Quenya *veru*, the two spouses [CE **bedū*]. From this was derived the Noldorin adjective *Bedhwen* 'of or relating to Aulë and Yavanna together'.

Oromë

Oromë was most often known by his Sindarin name *Araw*, a direct derivative from his Valarin name *Arǭmēz* (through OS **Arǭme* and MS *Arauṽ*] and cognate to the Quenya name *Oromë*. It was often, however, associated with the root √ROM 'horn'.

Oromë was also called *Tauron* 'the Forester', or *Aran Tauron* 'the Forester King', since he often rode in the forests (S *taur* 'forest') of Middle-earth. In Noldorin he was also called *Galadhon*, 'the Tree-Vala' (S *galadh* 'tree') and *Tauros* 'the forest terror' (S *taur* + *gos* 'terror') *MR*:124.

The Fëanturi

The brothers Valar, Námo, and Irmo, were in Quenya collectively called *Fëanturi*, 'masters of spirits', since the souls (*fëar*) of dead Elves dwelt in both the prisons of Mandos and the gardens of Lórien. In Noldorin this was altered to *Fannor*, pl. *Fennyr* or *Fennuir*, a word of obscure meaning but possibly to be interpreted as 'lord of cloud' or 'lord of fana' (the chosen appearance of a Vala or Maia).

Mandos

The formal equivalent to the Quenya *Mandos*, the common name of the Vala Námo, was *Bannos*, as if from **m̃bandogosse* 'dread imprisoner'. *Bannost* (from **m̃bandosto* 'fortress of duress') would have been more correct but is not actually recorded. Námo was also called *Gurfannor*, 'Fëantur of Death'; the first element, *gur-*, may be either S *gurth* or a borrowing from Quenya *nuru* [CE *ŋ̃gurū].

Lórien

The formal equivalent of Quenya *Lórien* (from **lōsiende* 'land or dwelling of sleep and dreams') was *Luien* (Noldorin *Lhuien*). This is the form **lōsiende* would have taken if it had developed through Old Sindarin **lūhiende*. It was commonly used as a proper name for the Vala Irmo. He was also called *Olfannor*, 'Fëantur of Dream'.

Tulkas

Tulkas was known in Noldorin as *Enner* 'the masculine', corresponding to Quenya *Ender*, as if from an Old Sindarin **endero*; both would be from Common Eldarin **endero*, from the root √E-NDER, itself a derivative of the root √NDER 'male, man'.

The Three Kings

In Noldorin Tulkas, Oromë, and the Maia Ossë (see below) were called *Neleduir* (S *Neledoer*) 'the three kings' [*neledh* + *taur*, pl. *toer*] or *Nethwelain* 'the young Valar' [*neth* + *balan*, pl. *belain*]; they presumably appeared in forms that seemed younger than those of the other Valar.

The Valier

Varda

Varda was most often called *Elbereth* 'queen of the stars' [*êl* + *bereth*], since the creation of the stars was attributed to her; for this reason she was also called *Gilthoniel* 'kindler of the stars' [*gîl* + *thoniel*]. She was also called *Fanuilos* 'having an eternally white fana'; this referred to a vision of Varda appearing clothed in white, standing on the mountain of Oiolossë (*Amon Uilos*) in Valinor.

Other, less-common names for Varda were *Berethil* 'spouse', from Old Sindarin **barat*^{h}*ille* and *Gilbrennil* [*gîl* + *brennil*] 'lady of the stars'.

Yavanna

Yavanna was known in Sindarin by the name, possibly of ancient form, *Ivon* [OS **jabāna*], or by a form closer to that of Quenya, *Ivann* [OS **jabanna*]. Both names mean 'giver of fruit' (i.e., the edible produce of any crop, especially wheat-corn) and come from the roots √JAB 'fruit' and √AN 'give'.

Estë

Estë, whose name was originally the common noun for 'rest' in the Eldarin languages [CE **Esdē*, **Ezdë* √SED] was known by the cognate noun in

Sindarin, *Îdh*; the word *estë* was, however, no longer used as a common noun in Quenya.

Vairë

Vairë's name originally meant 'weaver'; from Common Eldarin **weirē* (root √WEJ 'weave') or **waigrē* (root √WIG 'weave']. The Noldorin equivalent, *Gwîr*, was the expected development of Old Sindarin **weire*, but it could also come from Old Sindarin **wigre*, both formed with the feminine agent suffix *-re* (CE **-rē*).

Vána

Vána was known in Noldorin as *Banwen*, which was a compound containing the equivalent *Ban* to Common Eldarin **Bana* (from the root √BAN 'fair'), and the Sindarin suffix *-wen* 'maiden' or 'virgin'.

Nessa

Although Nessa's name was thought to come from Common Eldarin **neresā* 'manly, courageous', in Noldorin her name was rendered *Neth* 'the young', probably by association with the Quenya words *nessë* 'youth', *nessa* 'young', from the root √NETH. She was also called *Dineth* 'the young bride' [*dî* + *neth*].

Nienna

No Noldorin or Sindarin equivalent name is known for Nienna.

The Maiar

Ossë

Best known of the Maiar was Ossë, whose name came from the Valarin *Oššai* 'foaming' (OS **ossī*) but which was often confused with Sindarin *gos* 'terror'. Ossë was sometimes called *Yssion* (OS **ossiondo*), a lengthening of his proper name, or by the compound names *Gaerys* (OS **gairossi*) 'fearful Ossë' and *Aeros* [aer + gos] 'terror of the sea', the latter in Noldorin form being *Oeros*. Ossë was also known as *Balar*, a name of uncertain meaning but possibly related to the root √BAL 'ability, power'.

Uinen

Uinen, whose name was originally Quenya (*Uinen*, *Uinend-*) was also known in Noldorin as *Uinen*. This name was of uncertain origin even in Quenya, but in Noldorin it might have been associated with the root √UJ, also seen in Sindarin *uil* 'seaweed' and possibly also with *nen* 'water' or *nend* 'wet'.

Tilion

The Maia of the Moon was known as *Tilion* in both Noldorin and Quenya, which could be interpreted in both languages as 'the horned one', probably in reference to the "horns" or points (S *till*, Q *tildë*) of the crescent moon. Tilion was also known in Noldorin as *Elfaron*, 'the hunter of stars' [*êl* + *faron*], perhaps thinking of the crescent moon being shaped like a bow.

SINDARIN NUMBERS

Numbers in the Eldarin languages were originally based on a duodecimal system, with unique names for every number up to twelve. This appears to have been altered by the Dúnedain to a decimal system. The known cardinal and ordinal numbers were these:

Cardinals: 1 *mîn* or *êr*, 2 *tâd*, 3 *neledh* or *neled*, 4 *canad*, 5 *leben* (Noldorin *lheben*), 6 *eneg*, 7 *odog* (DorS *odo*), 8 *toloth* or *tolodh*, 9 *neder*, 10 *caer* or *pae*.

These reflect the following Old Sindarin forms: 1 *minė*, 2 *tata*, 3 *nelede*, 4 *kanata*, 5 *lepene*, 6 *eneke*, 7 *otoko* or *otoho*, 8 *toloto* or *tolodo*, 9 *netere*, and 10 *kaire* or *paia* (< *k^{w}ajā).

Ordinals: 1st *main*, *minui*, *erui*; 2nd *taid*, *tadui*, or *edwen*; 3rd *nail*, *nelui*; 4th *cannui*; 5th *lefnui*; 6th *engui* or *enecthui*; 7th *othui* or *odothui*; 8th *tolthui*, *tollui*, *tolothen*; 9th *nedrui*; 10th *caenen* or *paenui*.

These forms reflect Old Sindarin 1 *minia*, 2 *tatia*, *atwina*, 3 *nelia*, 4 *kant^{h}uia*, 5 *lepnuia*, 6 *eŋk^{h}uia*, 7 *ott^{h}ūia*, 8 *toltuia* or *tolduia*, 9 *netruia*, 10 *kainina* or *painuia*. The ordinal forms *cannui* and *engui* are actually cited as *canthui* and *enchui*, reflecting a Sindarin dialect in which -*nt^{h}*- and -*ŋk^{h}*- were not changed to -*nn*-, -*ŋŋ*- (> -*ŋg*-) but to -*nβ*-, -*ŋx*-.

Although the cardinal numbers for 11 and 12 are not recorded in Sindarin, possible forms can be deduced from their Common Eldarin forms *minik^{w}ē (or *minikē?) and *rasatā: *minib* or *minig* for 11, *rast* (N *rhast*) or *rahad* (N *rhachad*) for 12.

Very few higher numbers are known, one being the ordinal *nelchaenen*. *Nelchaenen* is a special problem in that it is intended to represent *thirty-first* but actually combines the prefix for 'three' (*nel*-) with an ordinal derived from an alternative root for 'ten' (√KAJAN, CE *kaininā > S !*caenen* 'tenth') without any indication of the -*first*. *Nelchaenen* would actually seem to mean 'thirtieth', and 'thirty' would be *nelchaen* in the decimal system of the Dúnedain.

The structure of *nelchaen* suggests that forms of the cardinal numbers were prefixed to -*caen* (and perhaps in the duodecimal system to -*rast*) to show multiples of ten or twelve, as follows: 10 *caer*, 20 *tadgaen* or *adgaen* [OS **tatakaina* or **atakaina*], 30 *nelchaen* [OS **nelk^{h}aina*], 40 *cangaen* [OS **kaŋk^{h}aina*], 50 *lebengaen* [OS **lepeŋk^{h}aina*], 60 *engaen* [OS **enekaina* or **eŋk^{h}aina*], 70 *odgaen* [OS **otokaina*], 80 *tolgaen* or *tolchaen* [OS **tolokaina* or **tolk^{h}aina*], 90 *nederchaen* [OS **neterk^{h}aina*]. Substituting *-pae* for *-caen* yields 10 *pae*, 20 *tadbae* or *adbae*, 30 *nelphae*, 40 *cammae*, 50 *lebemmae*, 60 *embae* or *emmae*, 70 *odbae*, 80 *tolbae* or *tolphae*, 90 *nederphae*.

Based on the word *canath* 'fourth, quarter', we can reconstruct the following Sindarin words for fractions: 3 **nelest* 'third' [OS **nelest^{h}a* < CE **neledtā*]; 4 *canath* 'fourth, quarter' [OS **kanatt^{h}a*]; 5 **lebent* 'fifth' [OS **lepent^{h}a*]; 6 **enaith* 'sixth' [MS **eneiꞵ* < OS **enekt^{h}a*];[1] 7 **odost* 'seventh' [OS **otost^{h}a*] or *odauth* [OS **otokt^{h}a*]; 8 **tolost* 'eighth' [OS **tolost^{h}a* < CE **tolodtā*, **tolot^{h}tā*]; 9 **nederth* 'ninth' [OS **netert^{h}a*]; 10 **caerth* 'tenth' [OS **kairt^{h}a*] or **paed* [OS **paita*]; 11 **minith* 'eleventh' [OS **minikt^{h}a*]; 12 **rahath* 'twelfth' [OS **rahatt^{h}a* < CE **rasattā*]. 'Half' is *perin*, *per-*.

The only larger numbers known are *host* 'one hundred forty-four' (i.e., twelve twelves) and *meneg*, conventionally translated 'thousand' but perhaps referring to twelve cubed, i.e., 1,728.

SINDARIN MONTH AND DAY NAMES

Both Elves and Edain used calendars with Sindarin names for days and months. The Elvish calendar used six long "months" of variable length, *Laer* and *Rhîw* being seventy-two days long and the other months fifty-four days long. At the end of the Third Age the year began about six days after the spring equinox. The months were these:

Ethuil 'spring'. OS **ett^{h}uile*, from an old nominal **tuile* 'springing, sprouting' (from √TUJ) and the prefix *et-* 'up, out'.

Laer 'summer'. OS **laire*, from the root √LAJ 'grow green'.

Iavas 'autumn'. OS **jabasse*, indicating the season in which fruits (**jabi*) grew. Also called *Dannas* 'fall' or *Dantilais* 'fall of the leaves'.

Firith 'fading'. OS **p^{h}iritt^{h}e* 'fading, withering', from the root √PHIR.

Rhîw 'winter'. OS **srīwe* 'winter'.

---

1. A form *eneith*, apparently meaning 'a sixth part', is found in the Marquette University Memorial Library, Department of Special Collections and University Archives, Mss. 4, Box 11, Folder 18.

Echuir 'stirring'. OS **ekk^{h}uire*, from an old nominal **koire* 'coming to life' and the prefix *et-* 'up, out'.

The Dúnedain used a calendar composed of twelve months, beginning around the winter solstice, each of the months having thirty-one days (Nórui and Cerveth) or thirty days (all the others).

Narwain (January): *Narwain* is composed of the element *nar-*, usually 'fire' but here standing for the related *anor* 'sun' and *gwain* 'new'. *Narwain* is thus the 'month of the new sun', i.e., the time when the days begin to lengthen again or (in very northerly climates) when the sun returns after having been obscured by the horizon during the period surrounding the winter solstice. *Narwain* was also called *Cathriw* (OS **katar̭r̭īwe*), apparently meaning 'the second or later month of winter', from a prefix *cad-* (OS **kata-*) and *rhîw* 'winter'.

Nínui (February): *Nínui* simply means 'watery (month)', an adjectival form derived from *nen* 'water', indicating the month when snow begins to melt.

Gwaeron (March): *Gwaeron* is a compound of *gwaew* 'wind' and *raun* 'moon' and so means 'month of wind'.

Gwirith (April): The meaning of *Gwirith* is obscure. Comparison with the Quenya *Víressë* indicates that it is an abstract noun from a root √WIR (OS **wiritt^{h}e*), but the meaning of the root is unknown. It may refer to the budding of trees in the early spring, but this is only a guess.

Lothron (May): *Lothron* is a compound of *loth* 'flower' and *raun* 'moon', and so means 'month of flowers', the time when flowers start to open.

Nórui (June): As in *Narwain*, the element *nór-* (from *naur*) here means not 'fire' but 'sun', and *Nórui* is just the 'sunny (month)', the time of year when the days are long. *Nórui* was also called *Eblaer* (OS **epelaire*), apparently meaning 'the first or earlier month of summer', from a prefix *eb-* (OS **epe-*) and *laer* 'summer'.

Cerveth (July): Comparison with Quenya *Cermië* indicates that *Cerveth* (OS **kermett^{h}e*) is a derivative from a noun **kerme*, probably from a root √KER or possibly √KEREM. However, the meaning of the root is unknown and cannot be guessed. *Cerveth* was also called *Cadlaer* (OS **katalaire*), apparently meaning 'the second or later month of summer', from a prefix *cad-* (OS **kata-*) and *laer* 'summer'.

Úrui (August): From the adjective *úrui*, simply meaning 'the hot (month)'.

Ivanneth (September): This month-name is related to a Sindarin form of the name of the *Valië* Yavanna but can also be taken as an old compound meaning '(month of) giving of fruits', i.e., the month of the fruit harvest.

Narbeleth (October): As with *Narwain* and *Nórui*, *nar-* here signifies the sun, compounded with *peleth* 'fading, waning'; *Narbeleth* thereby means 'the (month of the) waning of the sun', the time when the days shorten.

Hithui (November): From the adjective *hithui*, simply meaning 'the misty (month)', a time of year when the cooling of the air creates fogs.

Girithron (December): *Girithron* is a compound of the noun *girith* 'shivering, shuddering' and *raun* 'moon, month', meaning 'the month of shivering', the time of year when it is cold enough to induce shivers. *Girithron* was also called *Ephriw* (OS **epeṛ̭ṛ̭īwe*), apparently meaning 'the first or earlier month of winter', from an otherwise unattested prefix *eb-* (OS **epe-*) and *rhîw* 'winter'.

The Sindarin weekday names are loose compounds of which the second element is a genitive or adjective, in either case unlenited. The first element is always *aur* 'day', which shows compound reduction to *or-* (see §§ 4.168, 15.31). The Elves used a "week" or repeated cycle of six days, the Edain a week of seven days similar to our own:

Orgilion 'Day of Stars': The first day of the week, named after the stars in the sky, compounding *aur* with an adjective *gilion* 'stellar, starry, of stars'.

Oranor 'Day of the Sun': Named after the sun, compounding *aur* with the noun *anor* 'sun'.

Orithil 'Day of the Moon': Named after the moon, compounding *aur* with the noun *ithil* 'moon'.

Orgaladhad 'Day of the Two Trees': Named after the Two Trees in Valinor, compounding *aur* with the archaic dual *galadhad* 'two trees', from *galadh* 'tree'. The Edain used, instead of *Orgaladhad*, the name *Orgaladh* 'Day of the Tree', referring to the White Tree from which came the White Trees that grew in Númenor or Gondor.

Ormenel 'Day of Heaven': Named for the sky, compounding *aur* with the noun *menel* 'the heavens'.

Oraearon 'Day of the Great Ocean': Named for the ocean, this day was not used by the Elves but only by the Dúnedain, who were mariners; it compounds *aur* with the noun *aearon* 'great sea, ocean', augmentative of *aear* 'sea'.

Orbelain 'Day of the Valar': Named for the Valar, compounding *aur* with an adjective (only used here) *belain* 'of the Valar', modeled on the Quenya adjective *Valanya*. *Orbelain* was also called *(Or) Rodyn* 'day of the Valar', using the Sindarin word *Rodon* (earlier **Raudon*), *Vala*, related to the Quenya *Arata*. *Orbelain* was the chief day of the week, a kind of holiday.

GLOSSARY OF LINGUISTIC TERMS

This glossary is intended to help those readers who may be unfamiliar with some linguistic terminology and other terms found in this book. Explanatory examples are given primarily in English.

ablaut: the relationship between forms of a single root that differ as a result of changes in the root vowel. The relationship between English *sing*, *sung*, and *song* is one of ablaut.

absolute initial: the position of the first sound of a word standing alone, or at the beginning of a sentence, with no preceding words or prefixes.

abstract nouns: nouns that do not denote definite people or objects but qualities or states imagined to collectively inhere in a variety of things or that are seen in separate actions. E.g., *height*, *freedom*, *life*, or *sight*, which do not exist as visible entities but can be seen in things that are *high* or *free* or that *live* or *see*.

accusative: the case of a noun or pronoun that is the direct object of a sentence. In English pronouns, which are marked for case, *me*, *us*, and *him* are accusative.

adverbials: adverbs and phrases (such as prepositional phrases) that function to qualify an action represented by a verb.

adverbs: words that qualify an action represented by a verb, such as *now*, *here*, *quickly*, *soon*.

affection: a mutation of vowels in which the vowel changes quality because of the presence of another sound (at least originally) which "affects" it. In Sindarin there are two main types: *i*-affection, which raises and fronts vowels because of the original presence of an *i*, and *a*-affection, which lowers vowels because of the original presence of a final *a*. See also **umlaut**.

affix: any morpheme that is attached to a stem; includes prefixes, suffixes, and infixes.

action noun: an abstract noun signifying an action, usually derived from a verb; *building* (from *build*) and *construction* (from *construct*) are action nouns.

agent noun: a noun signifying the person or thing that performs an action; *actor* and *jogger* are agent nouns.

allative: a relationship indicating the direction of motion toward a point distant from the speaker; usually translatable by *to* + noun or *toward* + noun.

analogy: the formation of forms that may not be the result of regular historical developments, based on the resemblance of those forms to other words that (at some point) were similar. In English, for instance, the regular past tense of *help* would have been *halp*; and the past passive participle would have been *holpen*. However, both *halp* and *holpen* became *helped* by analogy with more common verb forms such as *yelp*, past tense *yelped*.

antepenultimate syllable: the third syllable from the end of a word.

antihiatic: a sound inserted to avoid *hiatus*, a sequence of two or more vowels with no intervening consonant, particularly where the vowels are identical.

aorist tense: a tense that does not indicate whether the action of the verb is in the past, present, or future, or whether it is continuing, repeated, or punctual, but merely records the fact of the action.

aphaeresis: the loss of an initial sound; e.g., in the pronunciation *gainst* for *against*.

apocope: the loss of a sound or sounds at the end of a word; e.g., in pronunciations such as *lis* for *list*.

apposition: the juxtaposition of one noun or noun phrase to another, when both nouns or noun phrases refer to the same thing, and the two nouns or noun phrases come together to form a single appositive noun phrase. In the English phrase *my son John*, *my son* is in apposition to *John*.

article: a word used to indicate the definiteness or indefiniteness of an accompanying noun, like English *a* (indefinite) or *the* (definite). In general, use of the definite article indicates a reference to something already introduced into the discourse.

aspiration: the accompanying of a stop with a strong out-breath or *h* sound, due to not beginning to make the vowel sound voiced for some time after releasing the stop. Aspiration is symbolized in IPA by a raised lower-case h. In English, initial voiceless stops are slightly aspirated (e.g., *teal* is [t^{h}il]), whereas following an *s* they are unaspirated (e.g. *steal* is [stil]).

assimilation: the change of one sound to make it more like (or, often, identical) to a neighboring sound.

augment: the reduplicated prefix of Sindarin reduplicated past verbs.

augmentative suffix: a suffix indicating that the word derived via suffixation is of greater size or higher status or otherwise superior to the word from which it is derived.

auxiliary verb: one of a small class of verbs, such as English *have*, *will*, *can*, *may*, *must*, and *shall*, that occur together with other verbs and that modify their semantics. New verb forms have been formed in many languages by the merging of a verb and their associated auxiliary.

back vowel: a vowel in which the highest part of the tongue is toward the back of the mouth. The vowels in *loon*, *loan*, and *lawn* are back vowels.

bahuvrihi: a compound in which neither of the elements of the compound directly refers to the person or thing described; e.g., a *redcoat* is neither a 'red' nor a 'coat' but 'a soldier wearing a red coat'.

bipartite: having two parts.

calque: a word coined for one language based on the existence of a word in another language; typically the coined word will resemble the source word in sound or structure.

case: a characteristic of nouns, pronouns, and (in Sindarin) articles that reflects the word's function in a sentence. Cases found in English are nominative, accusative, and genitive, which are clearly distinguished in the pronouns. *I*, *we*, and *he* are nominative; *me*, *us*, and *him* are accusative; *my*, *our* and *his* are genitive.

causative verb: a verb indicating that something else is made to perform or undergo an action. A causative verb can often be translated by *cause to* + verb. English *lay* (cause to lie down) and *fell* (cause to fall) originated as causative verbs.

characteristic adjective: an adjective indicating that the noun it modifies is characterized by possession or association with some person or thing. Characteristic adjectives in English are often indicated by the suffix *-y*; as in *starry*, meaning 'characterized by stars', or *stony*, meaning 'characterized by stones'.

closed syllable: a syllable containing a vowel followed by two or more consonants.

coalescence: the merging of two sounds into a single sound.

cognate: one of a set of words in different languages that share a common ancestor; e.g., English *father* is cognate to Latin *pater*.

collective plural: also called general plural. A plural formation that indicates a number of items considered together as a single group rather than as separate individuals. The English word *person* has *persons* as a particular plural but *people* as a collective plural; likewise, *cow* has *cows* as a particular plural but *cattle* as a collective plural. Like some Sindarin collectives, *people* can be construed as either grammatically singular or plural.

comitative: a relationship indicating that one person or thing accompanies or goes along with another person or thing. Usually expressed by *(together) with* + noun.

complement: a word or phrase that forms a new phrase when joined with a head.

complementizer: a word that introduces a sentence and functions to allow that sentence to be "embedded" into another sentence. The complementizer and the following sentence together form a *complementizer phrase*. In Sindarin, complementizer phrases are only attested as parts of a noun phrase.

composition: the putting together of two elements to form a compound. Adjective form: **compositive.**

compound: a word formed by putting together two or more other words; *blueberry* is an English compound.

conjunct sentence: a sentence formed by the joining of two other sentences using a conjunction.

conjunction: a word that connects two other words, phrases, or sentences, like English *and*, *or*, or *but*.

consonant cluster: a group of two or more consonants placed next to each other with no intervening vowels.

dative: a case indicating the recipient or beneficiary of some action, the person or thing *to* or *for* which something is done. See *indirect object*.

defective singular: a singular form of a noun that has lost a syllable (through apocope) that appears in the plural.

demonstrative: a word (pronoun, adjective, or adverb) that points out the relationship, in space or time, of some person or thing to the speaker. English *this* and *that* are demonstrative pronouns and adjectives; pronouns when they stand alone as subjects or objects (*this is good*), adjectives when they modify nouns (*this ring*).

dependent determinative: see *tatpurusha*.

derivative root: a root that is derived (through addition of prefixed and suffixed elements) from another root.

derivation: the process of forming a word by adding prefixes and suffixes, by reduplication or any other process that produces (derives) an entirely new word; contrasted with inflection.

derivational affix: an affix that creates an entirely new word *derived* from another by the addition of the affix. *Kindness* is derived from *kind* by the addition of the derivational affix *-ness*.

determinative: a type of compound in which one of the elements of the compound indicates, in a less qualified way, the kind of person or thing to which the compound refers. Determinative compounds include *tatpurushas* and *karmadharayas*.

determiner phrase: a syntactic unit consisting of a determiner (article) and a noun phrase.

dialect: any one of a number of mutually intelligible varieties of a language that nonetheless have regular differences from each other

diminutive suffix: a suffix indicating that the word derived via suffixation is of smaller size or lower status or otherwise inferior to the word from which it is derived, such as English *-ling* in *duckling* or *princeling*.

diphthong: a group of two adjoining vowel sounds in the same syllable. The vowel sounds in *line*, *loin*, and *loud* are diphthongs.

direct object: the person or thing directly affected by an action. In the sentence *June touched me*, *me* is the direct object. See also *accusative*.

disjoin: the separation of two words or phrases into either alternative or exclusive categories (e.g., *hot or cold*, *eat or sleep*). The *disjunctive* conjunction in English is *or*.

distant demonstrative: a demonstrative that indicates a relation in space or time distant from the speaker but possibly close to the person addressed. English *that* is a distant demonstrative pronoun and adjective; *there* and *then* are distant demonstrative adverbs.

disyllable: a word with two syllables.

double affection: the change in vowel of a word due to both *i*-affection and *a*-affection operating simultaneously.

double comparative: a kind of compound in which a person or thing is compared to two different things. Sindarin *ithildin* 'starmoon' and *elanor* 'sunstar' are examples.

doublet: one of a pair of words in a single language that have different forms but a single common ancestor. In English, pairs such as *yard* and *garth* or *road* and *raid* are doublets.

dual: a number indicating two (or a pair) of anything.

dvandva: a compound word that is the collective name for the different elements contained in the compound, like *bittersweet* meaning 'bitter' and 'sweet'. They can normally be translated by joining the two elements with *and*.

dvigu: a compound word consisting of a number and the word for the thing enumerated: *sixpack* is a dvigu compound.

exocentric: referring to something external; of compounds, ones in which neither element directly refers to the person or thing described. See *bahuvrihi*.

extrasentential: outside the (normal) sentence structure.

far distant demonstrative: a distant demonstrative that indicates a relation in space or time distant from all persons involved in a conversation. English *yonder* and the phrase *over there* may be considered far distant demonstrative adverbials.

feature (phonemic): one of several distinctive characteristics of a range of sounds, such as back, high, low, rounded (of vowels), sonorant, continuant, nasal, labial, coronal, velar, anterior, voice (of consonants). Features are usually given two values (+ and –) and are represented in square brackets, e.g. [+ voice]. Adjective form: **featural.**

final: the position of a sound at the end of a word. *n* is the final sound in *spoon* [spun].

fricative: a consonant produced by creating a narrow space in the mouth that the air makes noise in passing through. All the consonants in the words *this, sea, fish, shaves* are fricatives.

front vowel: a vowel pronounced with the highest part of the tongue toward the front of the mouth. The vowels in *lean*, *lane*, and *land* are front vowels.

fronting: changing a back vowel into a front vowel.

future tense: the tense of a verb indicating action that will happen in the future.

genitive: the case of a noun or pronoun used to indicate a close relationship with another noun; frequently possession, but also material, agency, objects of action, subject matter, habitual inhabitants or users, creators, spheres of rule or control, associated emotions, associated persons and places, characteristic qualities, constituent elements, intensifiers, and so on. Usually translated by *of* + noun, though in some instances noun + *'s* is also an appropriate translation.

genitive phrase: a noun or noun phrase followed by another noun or noun phrase in the genitive case, which together form a new noun phrase.

gerund: a noun referring to an action or event and derived directly from a verb. The noun *rising* in the phrase *the rising of the sun* is a gerund. The word *rising* in *the rising sun* isn't a noun but an adjective, and so is not a gerund (it is a participle).

glide: a consonant produced with only a slight obstruction of the air flowing through the mouth; the *w* in *wield* and the *y* in *yield* are both glides.

grade of ablaut: the quality (in terms of backness, length, height, etc.) possessed by vowels in a root that undergoes ablaut. See *long grade*, *normal grade*, *strong grade.*

haplology: a form of syncope in which one of two identical or similar sequences of sounds is omitted, shortening the word by a syllable. For instance, in Old English *Englaland* the first *la* is omitted to avoid the repetition of two consecutive *la*'s; the result is Middle and Modern English *England*.

head: In syntax, the main word of a phrase, after which the phrase is named; a noun is the head of a noun phrase, a determiner of a determiner phrase, a preposition of a prepositional phrase, etc. In morphology, the part of a compound word that indicates, in a less qualified way, the kind of person or thing to which the compound refers. For instance, the head of the compound *blueberry* is the element on the right, *berry*, because "berry" is the category to which *blueberry* belongs.

hiatus: a transition between two vowels in different syllables that do not have a consonant between them. Adjective form: **hiatic**.

high vowel: a vowel in which the tongue is raised toward the roof of the mouth. The vowels in *lean* and *loon* are high vowels.

heavy syllable: a syllable that is either *closed* or contains a long vowel or a diphthong, usually of longer duration.

immediate suffixes: suffixes attached directly to a root, usually with some phonological change to either the form of the root or of the suffix.

improper compound: a compound whose head is on the left rather than, as is generally the case, on the right.

indefinite pronoun: a pronoun that does not refer to any specific person or thing, like *one* in *one can see it's raining*.

indirect object: a noun or pronoun indicating a person or thing indirectly affected by an action. In the sentence *we gave them books*, *books*, the item actually given, is the direct object, but *them*, the recipient of the gift, is the indirect object.

infinitive: a derived verb form that is not marked for tense or person or other inflections. Usually translated by *to* + verb, but the meaning can overlap with that of the gerund.

infix: an affix inserted into the middle of a root.

inflection: the morphological alteration of a word such as a noun, pronoun, verb, or adjective to express categories such as number, tense, person, or case, which do not alter the basic category of the word. Contrasted with derivation. *blinked*, *blinking*, and *blinks* are all inflected forms of the verb *blink*; *cats* and *cat's* are inflected forms of the noun *cat*.

initial: the position of a sound at the beginning of a word. *t* is the initial sound of *too* [tu].

instrumental: a relationship indicating that an action is performed by means of a person or thing who acts as the tool or instrument of the subject. It is usually rendered by *by* + noun or *by means of* + noun.

karmadharaya: a compound in which the first element is used adjectivally or in apposition to qualifying the second element. English examples of karmadharayas include *blackbird* and *girlfriend.*

lenited initial: the first sound of a word that has undergone lenition.

lenition: a change in the initial consonant of a word due to syntactic position or morphology, e.g., by virtue of being a direct object or by following a particular preposition. Adjective form: **lenited.**

light syllable: a syllable of usually short duration and consisting of a syllabic onset (the initial consonant or consonants of the syllable) and a single short vowel.

liquid: a group of sounds including *l* and *r* and their voiceless counterparts *lh* and *rh*. These are the only liquids in the Elvish languages.

liquid mutation: a change in the initial consonant of a word resulting from its being preceded by either of the liquids *l* or *r*.

locative: a relationship indicating the place where something is located; usually translated by *in* + noun or *at* + noun.

long grade: a grade of ablaut that, in Elvish languages, originally involved a lengthening of the root vowel.

low vowel: a vowel pronounced with the tongue lowered. The *a's* in *hat* and *fall* are low vowels.

medial: in the middle; not initial (at the beginning) or final (at the end).

mediate suffixes: suffixes separated from the root by a vowel, usually preserving the form of both the root and the suffix.

metathesis: the reversal of the positions of two consonants, e.g., the pronunciation *aks* for *ask*.

mid vowel: a vowel in which the tongue is raised about halfway between the positions for low and high vowels. The *e* in *bet* is a mid vowel, as is the *o* in *more*.

mixed mutation: a change in the first consonant of a word that, in Sindarin, originally resulted from any consonant being preceded by a vowel that was itself preceded by a nasal.

morpheme: the smallest unit of meaning into which a word can be separated. For instance, the word *unkindness* consists of three morphemes; the stem *kind*, the suffix *-ness*, and the prefix *un-*. Adjective form: **morphemic.**

morpheme boundary: the boundary between two morphemes. In *un* + *kind* + *ness*, the + marks the morpheme boundaries.

morphological: having to do with morphemes.

mutation: generally, any change in the value of a sound; particularly lenition (of consonants) and affection (of vowels).

nasal: any sound characterized by the flow of air out through the nose. *n*, *m*, and the *ng* sound in the word *sing* are all nasal consonants.

nasal infix: in Elvish languages, the insertion of a nasal sound before a stop.

nasal mutation: a change in the first consonant of a word that was originally preceded by a nasal consonant with no intervening vowel.

nasalization: pronunciation of a sound with some air flowing out through the nose. Adjective form: **nasalized.**

near demonstrative: a demonstrative that indicates a relation in space or time close to the speaker. English *this* is a near demonstrative pronoun and adjective; *here* and *now* are near demonstrative adverbs.

nominal: of or relating to nouns.

nominalizing suffix: a suffix that turns a word of another part of speech into a noun.

nominative: the case of the noun or pronoun that is the subject of a sentence. In English pronouns, which are marked for case, *I*, *we*, and *he*, *she*, and *it* are nominative.

normal grade: one of a number of contrasting ablaut grades, taken to be the one from which others are derived. In Sindarin, the normal grade is the one most commonly found for most roots and consists of a short vowel.

object: the person or thing affected by the action indicated by the verb. See *direct object*, *indirect object*. Also used for the noun complementing a preposition in a prepositional phrase.

open syllable: a syllable containing a vowel (or diphthong) followed by only one or no consonant at all.

ordinal number: a number that indicates order rather than amount. *First*, *second*, *third*, and so on are ordinal numbers.

palatalized: pronounced with the front of the tongue touching the front part of the roof of the mouth, often caused by a following *y* sound or front vowel. Represented in IPA by a raised lower-case *j*. The sound of *k* in *key* [kʲi] is palatalized compared to the sound of *k* in *kite* [kajt].

past passive participle: an adjective derived from a verb that indicates a state arising from the completion of an action. *Eaten*, *hidden*, *seen* are all past passive participles.

penultimate: immediately preceding the last; *s* is the penultimate sound in *lost*.

perfect tense: a verbal form indicating the completion of an action; i.e., that it either is no longer going on or that, at least, it had entirely ceased before beginning again. English verb forms with the auxiliary *have* can have a perfect meaning; e.g., *I have spoken* in the sense *I have finished speaking and I am done.*

phoneme: a basic or underlying sound intuitively known by native speakers of a language but that may be produced in several different but predictable ways when spoken, depending on neighboring sounds. Adjective form: **phonemic.**

phonetic: relating to the description or transcription of the sounds actually produced in speech, without regard to which phonemes they represent.

phrase: a syntactic unit composed of a head and its complement.

polysyllabic: having many syllables.

prefix: an affix that precedes the stem to which it is attached. The *un-* in *unkind* is a prefix.

prenasalized stop: a stop preceded by a nasal, when the two sounds function as a single phoneme in a language.

preposition: a word indicating position in space or time, direction, possession, and other forms of relationship. Together with a noun phrase or determiner phrase complement, it forms a *prepositional phrase.*

present participle: an adjective directly derived from a verb indicating ongoing action at the present time. *rising* in the phrase *the rising sun* is a present participle.

present tense: the tense of a verb indicating action presently taking place.

preterite tense: the tense of a verb indicating action taking place in the past. Also called past tense. In English, *saw* is the preterite of *see.*

pronominal: related to pronouns.

raising: the change of a low or mid vowel to a mid or high vowel, or the change of a mid vowel to a high vowel.

reduplication: the repetition of some part of a word or stem to derive a new word. The relationship of the words *mention* and *memento* involves reduplication; *memento* has the reduplicated prefix *me-*, which repeats the first two sounds of the stem *ment.* Adjective form: **reduplicated.** See also *augment, vocalic extension.*

relative pronoun: traditional name for a word linking a subordinate (relative) clause to the main clause of a sentence and referring back to some word in that phrase. English *who, which, that* can function as relative pronouns; in the phrase *the bread that we ate*, the relative pronoun *that* refers back to *the bread.* In syntactic terms the relative pronoun is a *complementizer.* In Sindarin, as in English, the relative pronoun tends to immediately follow the noun or pronoun to which it refers.

root: an abstract sequence of sounds from which all members of a group of related words can be derived; e.g., in English the words *lose, loose, lost,* *less* all come from a single root, which can be reconstructed as √LEUS. In Elvish languages the root normally consists of two or three consonants and one vowel. These roots may, but need not, have existed as independent words at one time.

root vowel: in Elvish languages the single vowel that is an intrinsic part of the root.

secondary affection: a change in the quality of a vowel induced by the affection of another vowel; in Sindarin this involves fronting and raising of back vowels.

shortening: the change of a long vowel or consonant to a short one.

soft mutation: a change in the initial consonant of a word, originally (and in many cases still) due to its having been placed between two vowels.

stem: in the derivation of a word, that part of a word to which an affix is attached. The word *unkind* is formed by attaching the prefix *un* to the stem *kind*; the word *unkindness* is formed by attaching the suffix *ness* to the stem *unkind*.

stop: a consonant whose production involves complete blocking of air flowing through the mouth followed by its sudden release. The consonants in *Dad, Bob got a backpack* are all stops.

stop mutation: a change in the initial consonant of a word due to its being preceded by a word ending in a stop with no following vowel.

strong grade of ablaut: a grade of ablaut that, in the Elvish languages, is originally characterized by the change of the root vowel into a diphthong.

subject: the person or thing that performs an action or exists in a state indicated by the verb. See also *nominative*.

suffix: an affix that follows the stem to which it is attached. The *-ness* in *kindness* is a suffix.

syllabic: related to the sounds that form the nucleus of a syllable.

syllable: a unit of prosodic organization. A syllable is divided into three parts: (1) onset, the consonant or consonants at the beginning of the syllable; (2) nucleus, the part of the syllable, usually a vowel, that is pronounced with the greatest energy; (3) coda, the end of the syllable (at the end of a word or preceding another syllable).

syncope: the omission of medial sounds, usually a vowel between two consonants, resulting in contact between the consonants, as in the common pronunciation *evry* for *every*.

tatpurusha: a determinative compound in which the first element has a genitive or other relation (indicating place, time, motion, beneficiary, instrumentality) relation to the noun. Also called dependent determinative.

topicalization: the placing of a word in a *topic position* of particular emphasis. There are no close analogies in English.

trill: a sound produced with the rapid vibration of the tongue against the roof of the mouth. Elvish trilled *r*'s are produced by vibrating the tip of the tongue on the ridge just behind the top front teeth (alveolar ridge). Adjective form: **trilled.**

trisyllable: a word containing three syllables.

ultimate: last or final, especially used of syllables. *las* is the ultimate syllable of *Legolas*.

umlaut: a systematic change in a subset of vowels, usually resulting from fronting or raising of the vowels. The relationship between the vowels in *man* and *men*, *food* and *feed*, *tooth* and *teeth*, *full* and *fill*, *mouse* and *mice*, *proud* and *pride*, is the result of umlaut.

vocalic: of or relating to vowels.

vocalic extension: the reduplication of the root vowel immediately following the root.

vocative: the case of a noun used for direct address, e.g., in calling someone or something by its proper name.

voiced: the characteristic feature of sounds produced by vibrating the vocal folds (a pair of muscular flaps in the throat).

voiceless: the characteristic of sounds produced without vibrating the vocal folds.

ANNOTATED BIBLIOGRAPHY

Works frequently cited here and elsewhere in the text have been identified by the following abbreviations:

AI	*J. R. R. Tolkien: Artist and Illustrator*
ATB	*The Adventures of Tom Bombadil*
FR	*The Fellowship of the Ring* (vol. 1 of *LotR*)
HME	*The History of Middle-Earth* (12 vols.)
Hobbit	*The Hobbit, or There and Back Again*
ItE	*An Introduction to Elvish*
LB	*The Lays of Beleriand*
Letters	*The Letters of J. R. R. Tolkien*
LotR	*The Lord of the Rings*
LR	*The Lost Road and Other Writings*
LTME	*The Languages of Tolkien's Middle-earth*
MR	*Morgoth's Ring*
Names	*A Tolkien Compass*
PME	*The Peoples of Middle-earth*
RGEO	*The Road Goes Ever On*
RK	*The Return of the King* (vol. 3 of *LotR*)
RS	*The Return of the Shadow*
SD	*Sauron Defeated*
Silm	*The Silmarillion*
TI	*The Treason of Isengard*
TT	*The Two Towers* (vol. 2 of *LotR*)
UT	*Unfinished Tales*
VT	*Vinyar Tengwar*
WJ	*The War of the Jewels*
WR	*The War of the Ring*

CONTEMPORARY PUBLICATIONS OF J. R. R. TOLKIEN

The Adventures of Tom Bombadil. 1963. Boston: Houghton Mifflin. A collection of poetry related to *The Lord of the Rings*; comments of interest occur mostly in the preface, pp. 7–9, including the otherwise unmentioned place-name *Tirith Aear*.

The Hobbit, or There and Back Again, first published 1937. Available in many editions; text cited is 1978 (Boston: Houghton Mifflin). *The Hobbit* contains Tolkien's first published use of Sindarin in the names *Elrond*, *Gondolin*, *Orcrist*, *Glamdring*, *cram*, and perhaps *Galion*, *Girion*, *Bladorthin*, including translations of the names *Orcrist* and *Glamdring* in chapter 3.

The Lord of the Rings. Published in three volumes: 1. (*FR*) *The Fellowship of the Ring* (first pub. 1954); 2. (*TT*) *The Two Towers* (first pub. 1955); 3. (*RK*) *The Return of the King* (first pub. 1955). Available in many editions; text cited is 1983 (Boston: Houghton Mifflin). *The Lord of the Rings* contains a large number of Sindarin personal and place-names in both the main text and Appendices A and F in *RK*. It also includes information on the writing system and pronunciation, including several cited words (Appendix E), and discusses the calendar used by Elves and by Sindarin-speaking Númenóreans (Appendix D).

There are also several small Sindarin quotations in the text: Glorfindel's call to Aragorn (*FR*:1.12, p. 222), Glorfindel's call to Asfaloth (*FR*:1.12, p. 225), the Hymn to Elbereth (*FR*:2.1, p. 250), Gandalf's fire spells (*FR*:2.3, pp. 304, 312), the inscription on the doors of Moria (*FR*:2.4, p. 319) given in both Roman letters and *tengwar*, Gandalf's door-opening spell (*FR*:2.4, p. 320), some short exclamations (*FR*:2.4, p. 321; 2.6, pp. 356, 359; 2.9, p. 402), Samwise's invocation of Elbereth (*TT*:4.10, p. 339), Peregrin's "title" (*RK*:5.1, p. 41; 5.4, p. 80), praises of Frodo and Samwise (*RK*:6.4, p. 231), Gilraen's Linnod (*RK*:AppA, p. 342).

The Road Goes Ever On. 1967. New York: Ballantine. A collection of poetry, with music by Donald Swann. Includes tengwar transcriptions of and extensive linguistic notes on the hymn *A Elbereth Gilthoniel*, pp. 62–67, and a translation of Samwise's invocation of Elbereth, p. 64. Only here is the title of the hymn found written in tengwar: *Aerlinn in Edhil o Imladris*. The section on the Quenya poem *Namárië* also includes comments on the words *gloss*, *loss*, *lossen*, *Lossoth*, *Uilos*. At the end is found the translation of part of Gandalf's door-opening spell (*FR*:2.4, p. 320), *fennas nogothrim*.

POSTHUMOUS PUBLICATIONS

"Guide to the Names in *The Lord of the Rings*." In *A Tolkien Compass*, ed. Jared Lobdell, pp. 155–201. La Salle: Open Court, 1975. This text was prepared for translators in which Tolkien comments on the names in *The Lord of the Rings* that he regards as "translatable." A few Sindarin names are given translations in this text, often with citations of the Sindarin words of which they are composed: *Amon Amarth* (183), *Amon Sûl* (195), *Amon Tirith* (187), *Anfalas* (188), *Angrenost* (187), *Anórien* (192), *Baranduin* (178–79), *Bregalad* (172), *Carach Angren* (187), *Celebdil* (191), *Celebrant* (191), *Cirith Ungol* (181), *Ered Lithui* (178), *Eregion* (187), *Fangorn* (175), *Finglas* (169), *Fladrif* (173), *Fornost* (190), *Imladris* (156, 190), *Mitheithel* (187), *Nan Duhirion* (182), *Nen Uial* (188), *Nindalf* (195), *Onodrim* (165), *orch* (171), *Orodruin* (182), *Sarn-athrad* (190), *Tarlang* (193).

The History of Middle-Earth. Consists of texts by J. R. R. Tolkien, edited and with commentary (sometimes very extensive) by Christopher Tolkien. 12 vols. Volumes 1, 2, and 4 contain little or no material relevant to the study of Sindarin (though much that is relevant to the various languages that preceded it) and therefore are not reviewed here.

The Lays of Beleriand (vol. 3 of *HME*). 1985. Boston: Houghton Mifflin. Most of the texts contained in this book are very early, and the names are often of archaic and obsolete form. However, *LB* also contains a late Sindarin text as part of the rewritten *Lay of Leithian*, p. 354, ll. 99–104; the rewritten parts of the *Lay*, pp. 331–63, also contain a few Sindarin names not found elsewhere (e.g., *Dagmor*, the sword of Beren).

The Letters of J. R. R. Tolkien, selected and edited by Humphrey Carpenter, with the assistance of Christopher Tolkien. 1981. Boston: Houghton Mifflin. A collection of letters written by J. R. R. Tolkien to various recipients, including many items of linguistic interest. These items are, however, found in a fairly small number of letters, and most of the information relevant to Sindarin is found in only five of them. The relevant letters are listed below, with a general characterization of their contents:

Major Letters

Letter no. 144, pp. 177–78 (1954): This letter briefly discusses the relationship between Quenya and Sindarin, comments on the words *orch*, *onod*, *rochir*, *rim*, and the names *Morannon*, *Mordor*, *Moria*, *Morthond*, *Rohirrim*, *Haradrim*, and *Rohan*, and adds some remarks on the contrast between collective and partitive plurals.

Letter no. 211, p. 278, 281–83 (1958): This letter, an answer to several miscellaneous questions, includes a translation of Samwise's invocation of Elbereth (*TT*:4.10, p. 339), which differs from that in *RGEO* only by translating *sí* as 'now' instead of 'here'. It also provides explanations of the names *Amon Uilos*, *Elladan*, *Elrohir*, *Elrond*, *Elros*, and *Legolas* and for the words *êl*, *eledh*, *golas*, *hîr*, *laeg*, *las*, *roch*, *rochir*, *rond*, *ros*, and *uilos*.

Letter no. 230, p. 308 (1961): This answer to a number of questions about language in *LotR* translates Glorfindel's greeting to Aragorn *mae govannen* (*FR*:1.12, p. 222) and also translates the Sindarin praises of Frodo and Samwise (*RK*:6.4, p. 231).

Letter no. 297, pp. 383–84, 386 (1967): This letter discusses various guesses made about Tolkien's nomenclature and offers corrections. Included are remarks about the names *Ennor*, *Legolas*, *Rohan*, and *Moria* and the words *aear*, *golas*, *hîr*, *iâ*, *laeg*, *môr*, *morn*, *rim*, and *roch*.

Letter no. 347, p. 424–28 (1972): This long and important letter contains remarks on the social use of Quenya and Sindarin, the names of the kings of Arthedain and chieftains of the Dúnedain, the Sindarin soft and nasal mutations, the (mis)spelling of *dh* as *d*, the collective plural *-ath* and the dual *-ad*, and the history and meanings of the words and names *celeb*, *galadh*, *orn*, *perian*, *Arathorn*, *Gil-galad*, *Thorondor*, *Thorongil*, *Borgil*, *Orbelain*, *Orgaladhad*, *Argonath*, *Arnor*, *Mordor*, and *Osgiliath*.

The original text of this letter contained a footnote, heavily struck through, which was not published in *Letters*. It followed a reference to the name *Gil-galad* in section 3 and read "In which medial *g* is not removed, since the hyphen is meant to show it is a genitival compound which in S does not affect the 2nd element. Cf. ennyn Durin" (unpublished correspondence of J. R. R. Tolkien, Dec. 17, 1972 [photocopy]).

Minor Letters

Letter no. 154, p. 199 (1954): Glosses the name *Forochel*.

Letter no. 168, p. 223 (1955): Discusses the words and names *onod*, *ennorath*, *Enedwaith*, and *Forodwaith*.

Letter no. 312, p. 402 (1969): Describes some flowers with Elvish names and glosses the name *alfirin*.

Letter no. 324, pp. 409–10 (1971): Explains the meaning and origin of the name *Gondor*.

Letter no. 332, p. 417 (1971): Uses the name *Dor Gyrth i Chuinar*.

Letter nos. 342, 345, pp. 422–23 (1972): Provides the Elvish root for the word *bull*, glosses the names *Galadriel* and *Celebrían*, and proposes several names for bulls.

Letter no. 348, p. 428 (1973): Briefly explains the meaning of the name *Galadriel.*

The Lost Road and Other Writings (vol. 5 of *HME*). 1987. Boston: Houghton Mifflin. Virtually none of part 1 of this book, and little of part 2, is relevant to the study of Sindarin. Although there are many names in part 2, they are mostly either met with in *Silm* and elsewhere or represent obsolete forms. Of some interest are the Sindarin titles of the *Quenta Silmarillion*, pp. 201–2; a brief description of the soft consonant mutation, p. 298; and the name *Eithel Nínui,* not seen elsewhere, p. 301.

Part 3, on the other hand, "The Etymologies" (pp. 347–400), is the single most important text yet published for the study of the Elvish languages, including Sindarin. This text is a glossary organized by root words. Readers should also recognize before using it that words are cited in a variety of forms; e.g., verbs are sometimes cited as infinitives (ending in *-o* or *-i*), sometimes as stems, sometimes as first-person or third-person singular presents. It should also be noted that the romanized orthography is slightly different in places from that used for Sindarin; e.g., *f* between vowels may represent the sound of *v* (where *v* is used in Sindarin), e.g., *Afor* for *Avor* and *rhofal* for *rhoval*, and final *f* represents *f* (where *ph* is used in Sindarin), e.g., *alf* for *alph*. *oe* is sometimes used to represent a diphthong (when derived from **ai*) and sometimes to represent *ö*, (when derived from **o*). Other differences in spelling from Sindarin usually reflect the fact that a dialect of Sindarin ("Noldorin") is being quoted that is different from the form of Sindarin used in *The Lord of the Rings* (in real-world terms, this reflects a shift in Tolkien's ideas of how to realize the surface structure of the language).

"The Etymologies" is unfortunately marred by many miscopyings that took place before printing. These can be recognized as unsystematically divergent from other data or as anomalies from the structures that "The Etymologies" itself sets out. The data are also very inconsistently set out. There is no need to list all the errors or difficulties here, but the following are directly relevant to Sindarin:

p. 358, root GIL-: *geil* is identified as the plural of *gîl* but is actually the direct descendant of the Eldarin word **gilya* quoted before it. *gîl* could be the plural of *geil* but not the other way around. This concept of the history of the word *gîl* was later abandoned.

p. 359, root GLIN-: Noldorin *glin* should read *gliri.*

p. 363, root KHAL-: Noldorin *orchel* should read *orchal.*

p. 363, root KHAP-: Noldorin *hamnia-* should read *hamma-.*

p. 363, root KHAT-: Noldorin *hennin* and *hant* should be identified as first- and third-person singular forms, respectively.

p. 364, root KHOR-: Noldorin *hoeno, heno* should read *hoerio, herio.*

p. 365, root KHYEL(ES)-: Old Noldorin *khelelia* should read *kheleha.*

p. 366, root KWAT-: Noldorin *pannod* should probably read *panno.*

p. 368, root LED-: Noldorin *eglehio* should read *egleðio* (i.e., *egledhio*).

p. 373, root MERÉK-: Noldorin *brerg* should read *breig.*

p. 373, root MIS-: Noldorin *mistrad* should probably read *mistad*; *-str-* is not a possible sequence of sounds in Noldorin.

p. 373, root MOR-: Noldorin *moru* should read *morn.*

p. 374, root NAR2-: The Noldorin forms *nennar* and *trener* are very doubtful, but it is uncertain what should replace them.

p. 375, root NDAM-: Noldorin *damna-* should read *damma-.*

p. 376, root NEL-: *neltildi* should be identified as a pre-Noldorin form.

p. 379, root ORO-: *oronte* should be identified as a pre-Noldorin form.

p. 380, root PEL(ES)-: Old Noldorin *peleki* should read *pelehi.*

p. 383, root RAS-: Noldorin *rhaes* should read *rhass.*

p. 385, root SED-: Old Noldorin *Ezda* should probably read *Ezde.*

p. 386, root SKAL-: Noldorin *hall* derives from Old Noldorin *skhalla*, but Noldorin *haltha-* should be from Old Noldorin *skhaltha-*, not *skhalia-*; the latter should produce Noldorin *helia-.*

p. 386, root SKEL-: Noldorin *helta* should read *heltha-.*

p. 387, root SNAS, SNAT-: The form *natsai* should be identified as an Old Noldorin plural, from which the Noldorin form *naith* is derived. This etymology of *naith* was later abandoned.

p. 388, root SUK-: Noldorin *asogant* should read *sogant*, and *sogennen* should read *sogannen.*

p. 389, root TA-: Noldorin *egledhriur* should read *egledhruin.*

p. 390, root TAM-: Noldorin *tamno* should read *tammo.*

p. 391, root TARÁK-: 'mountain path' should read 'mountain peak'.

p. 392, root THE-: *Gorsthir* should read *Gosthir.*

p. 392, root THIN-: Noldorin *thinna* should read *thinna-* and therefore should be grouped with the following Quenya word *sinta-* 'fade'.

p. 397, root WAR-: Noldorin *gwerio* appears to derive from Old Noldorin *warie*, although the form that should have developed is *gweri*. This is not an error but reflects a change in the conjugation class of the Noldorin verb from the *-i* stems to the *-ia* stems.

p. 397, root WED-: Noldorin *gwedi* should read *gweði* (i.e., *gwedhi*).

p.398, root WEG-: the word *gweth* should probably read *gweith*.

p. 399, root YA-: Noldorin *gem* should read *gern*.

p. 400, root YUL-: *iolf* is misidentified as Old Noldorin; it is actually Noldorin.

Section 2 of the appendix to *LR*, "The List of Names" (pp. 404–7), contains a few words and names in Sindarin that are not met with elsewhere. These include *Sarnas Fingolfin* and *Siriombar*.

Morgoth's Ring: The Later Silmarillion, Part One (vol. 10 of *HME*). 1993. Boston: Houghton Mifflin. Contains a large number of words and names in Sindarin. Notable are the list of the names of the Two Trees (p. 155); a glossary of words in the *Athrabeth Finrod ah Andreth* (pp. 349–50); and the names of the "Great Tales" (p. 373).

The Peoples of Middle-earth (vol. 12 of *HME*). 1996. Boston: Houghton Mifflin. Contains yet more names of persons and places. Notable sections include the early forms of the Sindarin month and day names (pp. 130, 135–36); the Sindarin names of the princes of Dol Amroth (p. 221); the essay "The Shibboleth of Fëanor" (pp. 331–66), which includes glosses and history of many Sindarin personal names; and the essay "The Problem of Ros" (pp. 367–76), which discusses the names *Elwing*, *Elrond*, and *Elros*.

The Return of the Shadow: The History of The Lord of the Rings, Part One (vol. 6 of *HME*). 1988. Boston: Houghton Mifflin. This volume contains extracts from early drafts of *LotR*, some of which include several older or alternative versions of names found there. The most important information in this volume is the translation of Gandalf's door-opening spell from *FR* on p. 463. Very little else in this text is relevant to Sindarin, as most of the names are of very archaic or obsolete form, and the text, in any case, covers a part of the story where Sindarin names are rare. Two exceptions are *Pendrathduhir* (misread Pendrethdulur), the Sindarin name of the Dimrill Stair (p. 433), and *Nen Cenedril* (from a later text), the name of Mirrormere (p. 466). There is also an earlier version of the hymn to

Elbereth (p. 394) and of the words on the doors of Moria (p. 451). One short text of pre-Sindarin form is *Gurth i Morthu* (Death to Sauron) on p. 186.

Sauron Defeated: The End of the Third Age, including The History of The Lord of the Rings, Part Four (vol. 9 of *HME*). 1992. Boston: Houghton Mifflin. Part 1 of this volume, the last discussion of the *LotR* drafts, contains previously unknown Sindarin nicknames for Frodo and Samwise, *Bronwe athan* [*sic*] (for *athar*) *Harthad* and *Harthad Uluithiad* (p. 62). There is also a shorter and slightly different version of the praises of Frodo and Samwise from *RK* (pp. 46–47). The most significant Sindarin text in this book, however, is the "King's Letter" (pp. 128–31), the longest known text written in Sindarin, given in two of three versions written in tengwar, which is invaluable for the study of Sindarin syntax and also provides two otherwise unknown modes of writing Sindarin. There is very little Sindarin in part 2 of this book ("The Notion Club Papers"): the only point at which Sindarin is discussed is on pp. 302 and 306, where forms of the words *dû*, *dúlinn*, *galadh*, *orn*, *anor*, and *ithil* are mentioned.

The Silmarillion. 1977. Boston: Houghton Mifflin. Tolkien's legendary history of the First Age, as revised and condensed by Christopher Tolkien. A great many words and names are encountered here for the first time. Of especial interest are the "Index of Names" and the appendix, "Elements in Quenya and Sindarin Names," which, though unsystematically organized, contains much useful information. The only Sindarin text found here is the brief inscription on Túrin's grave given at the end of chapter 21, but the appendix (under *quen-*) includes a translation of part of Gandalf's door-opening spell, *lasto beth lammen*.

The Treason of Isengard: The History of The Lord of the Rings, Part Two (vol. 7 of *HME*). 1989. Boston: Houghton Mifflin. Many Elvish names appear in this book, most of them variants on names found in *LotR*, but many of them are still archaic or obsolete, and others add nothing to our knowledge of Sindarin. However, some show previously unknown or poorly attested words or inflections: *Annerchion* 'Goblin gate' (p. 115), *Hithdilias* 'Misty Mountains' (p. 124), *Nan-eregdos Hollin* (p. 166), *Bair am Yrn* (p. 243, misspelled *Bair am Yru*), *Emyn Rain* 'Border Hills', later *Emyn Muil* (p. 268), *Toll-ondren* (p. 268), *Uvanwaith* 'No-man's-lands' (p. 281), *Rhimdad* 'Rushdown River' (p. 296), *Fornobel* 'Northbury', later *Fornost* (p. 304), and *Rhúnaer* 'Sea of Rhûn' (p. 307). Other notable inclusions are a translation of Gandalf's fire spells (pp. 169, 175, 187), an early drawing of the words on the Doors of Moria (p. 182), an explanation of the word *cerin* (p. 242), the first maps for *LotR* and a listing of Gondor's rivers (pp. 295–323).

Unfinished Tales. 1980. Boston: Houghton Mifflin. A collection of late unpublished material relating to Middle-earth. *UT* contains a large number of new names and text in Sindarin and an excellent index, which adds some etymological material not found in the main text. Important sections of the main text include portions of a long essay on the river-names of Gondor, which are found out of sequence in two places: pp. 240–45 and 261–65. There are also a few short phrases in Sindarin: an exclamation by Tuor (39), one by Voronwë (40, with translations on p. 54), and a battle cry (65).

The War of the Jewels: The Later Silmarillion, Part Two (vol. 11 of *HME*). 1994. Boston: Houghton Mifflin. Contains many more words and names in Sindarin. Notable are the map of Beleriand (pp. 180–91), family trees of Bëor and Marach (pp. 231, 234), and the phrase *tôl acharn* (p. 254). Especially notable is the very important essay "Quendi and Eldar" (pp. 360–420), which discusses the names used by Elves for themselves and other peoples and includes a large number of new words in Sindarin.

The War of the Ring: The History of The Lord of the Rings, Part Three (vol. 8 of *HME*). 1990. Boston: Houghton Mifflin. As in *TI*, most of the names in this volume are either obsolete in form or found in *LotR*, but there are a few significant new ones: the names of the Towers of the Teeth (*Nelig Myrn, Naglath Morn*, pp. 113, 122), the Argonath (*Sern Aranath, Sern Ubed, Annon Torath*, pp. 132, 137), the City Wall (*Othram*, p. 288), the Causeway Forts (*Bered Ondrath*, p. 340), the Houses of Healing (*Bair Nestedrin*, p. 380, misspelled *Bair Nestedriu*), and the Lampwrights' Street (*Rath a Chalardain/Chelerdain* pp. 287, 388). Also of note are an earlier text of Samwise's invocation of Elbereth (p. 218), the names of the "Seven Rivers of Gondor" (pp. 434–37), and the Sindarin "passwords of Minas Tirith" (p. 293), although a slightly different reading of the last, based on the original manuscript text, is adopted at appendix 1, § A1.20 of the present volume.

OTHER SOURCES

Hammond, Wayne G., and Christina Scull. 1995. *J. R. R. Tolkien: Artist and Illustrator*. Boston : Houghton Mifflin. Contains the text of the "Thror's Map Inscription" in Noldorin (illustration no. 85, p. 92); five versions of the inscription on the Doors of Durin (illustration nos. 150–54, pp. 158–59); the name *Lúthien Tinúviel* written in tengwar (illustration nos. 194–95, p. 197); and the second version of the "King's Letter" (illustration no. 199, p. 202).

Vinyar Tengwar. A number of essays, or extracts from essays, by J. R. R. Tolkien have been posthumously published in the irregular publication *Vinyar Tengwar*. Some of these are relevant to the study of Sindarin.

Vinyar Tengwar, no. 39 (July 1998). "From Quendi and Eldar," appendix D: Sections omitted from *Quendi and Eldar* in *WJ*. Page 10 contains the single Sindarin word *caul*; p. 15 briefly mentions *lam*.

Vinyar Tengwar, no. 41 (July 2000): This issue includes extracts omitted from *WJ* and *PME*. The following are relevant to Sindarin:

Etymological Notes on the *Ósanwe-kenta*: page 6 provides the root √KHEP for the verb *hebi-*.

From "The Shibboleth of Fëanor": page 9 of this extract cites the names *Finrod*, *Arothir*, *Thinrod*, and *Thindrim* and provides more details of Sindarin phonology; page 10 discusses the Sindarin names of Fëanor's sons with some new words related to the root √RUS.

"Notes on *Órë*": page 11 of this essay includes the short Sindarin sentence *guren bêd enni*; page 14 cites the name-form *Eignor* (otherwise *Aegnor*) and its etymology.

Vinyar Tengwar, no. 42 (July 2001): "The Rivers and Beacon-Hills of Gondor." This article (pp. 6–20) includes the omitted portions of an essay frequently cited in *UT*; it contains several new Sindarin roots, words, and names related to the geography of Gondor and elaborates on some of the etymologies cited in *UT*. This issue also contains a brief note on the meaning of the name *Eriado*r (p. 4).

Vinyar Tengwar, no. 44 (June 2002): "Ae Adar Nín: The Lord's Prayer in Sindarin." This article (pp. 21–30) contains Tolkien's translation of the Lord's Prayer into Sindarin, which contains several new words and syntactic constructions.

Vinyar Tengwar, no. 45 (November 2003): "Addenda and Corrigenda to the Etymologies, Part One." This article (pp. 5–38) is a much needed set of corrections and additions to the text of "The Etymologies" as found in *LR*. It covers the root entries from AB- to NEI- (the rest is to be published in a future issue of *VT*) and includes a considerable number of new entries not provided in the text in *LR* (but found in the same handwritten text). Among these new roots that are relevant to Sindarin are DUS-, GRAWA-, IMBE-, KEN-, KHAR-, KHES-, KWÆ-, LOP-, LUB-, LUR-, MIW-, MBATH-, NE-, NEG-, and NDI-. These shed new light on the meanings of the element *im-* in the words *imlad*, *imloth*, and *imrath*; the preposition *di*; and the place-name element *-lorn*. There is an even larger number of new Noldorin words related to roots already found in "The Etymologies." There are also several entries that were apparently deleted at an early stage in the composition of "The Etymologies"; since most of them were evidently replaced by new entries of the same meaning, those have been disregarded in this book. Several misreadings have been corrected, many of which had already been detected by close scrutiny of the published text (including those mentioned in the entry for *LR*). It is now apparent that the "irregular" forms *bronio-* and *dammint* (in which *i*-affection does not appear) were simply misreadings of the expected forms *brenio* and *dammant*, and the impossible form *brerg* was an error for *breig*. It is also amply demonstrated that there existed a Noldorin past tense formed with the ending *-as*, previously only attested in the one past tense verb *mudas*.

This text is necessary reading for anyone who wants to study the text of "The Etymologies." However, it is likely that a few errors may have been retained in the new text. On p. 11, the word *dost* is given, with the tentative gloss 'brown' or 'burn'. As the facsimile of the page on which this word is found is given on p. 10, it seems possible to verify the reading 'burn' (which is also the meaning of the root DUS-), in which case the word ought to be the verbal form dosta-. One of the derivatives of the root KHAYA- is given as *haen*; it probably ought to be read *haer*, cognate to the Quenya *haira-*. The form *degant*, given as a past tense of the stem *dag-*, is implausible, even as an analogical form, and ought to be read *dagant*; likewise, the past tense *eglant* of *egledhi* should be read *eglent*.

SECONDARY RESOURCES ON SINDARIN

The number of secondary works published about Sindarin is very small. Leaving aside a number of self-published and usually severely flawed "dictionaries," only two books have attempted to deal with Sindarin structures: Jim Allan's *Introduction to Elvish* (ItE) and Ruth Noel's *Languages of Tolkien's Middle-earth* (*LTME*). Since *ItE* is still cited by some commentators on Sindarin, and since *LTME* is the only work on the Elvish languages that remains in print and widely available, I provide a full review of each.

Allan, Jim, et al. 1978. *An Introduction to Elvish*. Somerset: Bran's Head Books. *ItE* includes a twenty-three-page essay (pp. 47–70) on Sindarin, its brevity probably justified at the date of publication, when *The Silmarillion* had just been published and its data had not yet been taken into account. *ItE* deserves notice as one of the earliest efforts to analyze Tolkien's languages on their own terms, rather than as distortions or adaptations of real-world languages (a common mistake among early critics of Tolkien's work). Unfortunately, the old tendency to look to real-world languages for parallels still surfaces in a number of not particularly helpful asides about Welsh, such as a long list of Welsh words that sound vaguely similar to Sindarin words (p. 50) or a discussion of Welsh spelling conventions (p. 54). There is also a genuine attempt to apply some linguistic knowledge to Tolkien's work; unfortunately, some of it goes astray.

ItE remains a highly misleading source of information about Sindarin. Since many people who study Sindarin may have read *ItE*, or may have heard mistaken claims made about Sindarin ultimately derived from *ItE*, it is necessary to point out these errors.

Phonology: Consonant Mutations. *ItE*'s understanding of consonant mutations is frequently faulty, although it identifies two of the main types of mutation (soft mutation and nasal mutation). Many details of the mutations were not well understood at the time of *ItE*, including the existence of a separate class of nouns with (underlying) nasalized voiced stops as initials.

ItE looks on the quasi-compounds *Orbelain* and *Orgilion* (and presumably *Orgaladhad*, though it isn't mentioned) as exceptions to lenition (p. 58), not perceiving that they are to be understood as adjectival and genitive phrases in construction rather than pure compounds, equivalent to *Aur Belain*, *Aur Gilion*, and *Aur Galadhad*.

The word *Argonath* is also cited as an exception (p. 58), although in this case the development is the loss of *n* between a liquid and a voiced stop (*Arn* + *gonath* > *Argonath*).

The word *lembas* is also cited as an exception to nasal mutation (p. 60). It is taken as derived from *len* and *bas* (it is actually from OS **lende* 'way' and **mbasse* 'bread'). In any case, the combination *len* + *bas* could not possibly result in *!lebas*, as *ItE* maintains; if contact of **len* and **bas* produced **lembas*, this would surface in Sindarin as *!lemmas* (cf. **rambasse* > *rammas*); if, however, it were, as it in fact is, from **lende* and **mbasse* (or even *!basse*), it would produce *lembas*. *!lebas* is an impossible shape except from OS **lepasse*.

The explanation of the shape of *Ancalagon* (rather than *Angalagon*) as deriving from *anc* + **calagon* (p. 58) is incorrect, since the second element contains *alag* 'rushing wind', and, in any case, **calagon* would have lenited to **galagon*, producing *Angalagon*. *Anc* is preserved unchanged before the morpheme boundary of a compound word.

The explanation of the transformation of *w* to *gw* (p. 59), a development familiar from Welsh and many other languages, is both mistaken and barely intelligible. It is certainly not the case that *w* can be characterized as [γβ]; it is true, however, that it is a *labialized velar* and can become *gw* by alteration of the features [+ sonorant] and [+ continuant] to [–sonorant] and [–continuant].

ItE wrongly states that *n* followed by a voiced stop will double that stop (p. 60) and that *Aragorn* comes from **Arangorn* > **Araggorn*. Allan expends too much effort trying to extract valid data from the *Ar-* and *Ara-* names in Appendix A, although the proper forms and meanings of the meaningful elements are still largely unknown, and the treatment is clearly idiosyncratic, as Tolkien admitted (see *Letters*, p. 426). In the name *Aragorn*, *Ara-* is merely a prefix that does not affect the element *gorn*. It is likewise not the case, as is stated with regard to names like *Aravir* (p. 60), that an *mm* arising from *n* + *m* will reduce to *m* and be lenited to *v*; in fact, the reverse is true, *mm* being resistant to lenition, as in *lam* 'echo' from **lamma*, *Annúminas* from *annûn* + *minas*. If *Aravir* contains the element *mîr*, then it is lenited following the element *ara-* and is not composed of *aran* and *mîr*.

Allan asserts that the *d* in words such as *pedo* and *Udûn* arises from a combination of *n* and *d* resulting in a geminate **dd* (p. 61). This is incorrect; in both cases the *d*'s arise from an original **t*, *pedo* arising from **k^{w}et-ā* and *udûn* from **utupnu*.

Likewise, the underlying form of the preposition *na* is incorrectly stated to be *!nan* (p. 61). This is said to produce, together with the word *!caered*, the form *na-chaered* 'to a distance'. Although this is phonetically possible, the actual elements are *na* and *haered*, with the latter showing a simple soft mutation to *chaered*.

The explanation of *na vedui* as resulting from *!nan* + *medui* is mistaken. *!nan* + *medui* would have to result in *na(m) medui*, just as *an* + *Meril* results in *am Meril* 'to Rose'.

The preposition *di* 'beneath' is also characterized as being from *!din* (p. 61) in order to explain the form *di-nguruthos* (unlenited form *guruthos*). In fact, this is simply the soft mutation appropriate after a preposition ending in a vowel. *guruthos* lenites as *nguruthos* [ŋuruβos] and not *!uruthos*, not because of any *n* in the preposition but because the underlying form of the noun is /ŋguruβoss/. Had the preposition been *!din*, we should have had *!din guruthos*. The same error is made with regard to the lenition *gaurhoth* > *ngaurhoth* (p. 61).

Because of confusion over the nasal mutation, *ItE* was forced to distinguish two phonemes, an *n* that did not induce nasal mutation and an *(n)* that did (pp. 60–61). The cases of *n* without nasal mutation arise sometimes from instances such as *palan-díriel*, in which the nasal mutation was not used to avoid confusion between verbal roots (e.g., √TIR and !√THIR, or √KAT and √KHAT), where there was no distinctive nasal mutation for verbs beginning with fricatives; see *Letters*, p. 427. More often it arises from the faulty assumption that *n* + a voiced stop results in a geminate voiced stop. There is therefore no basis for distinguishing between *n* and *(n)*.

Phonology: Vowel mutations. The treatment of vowel mutations is defective in several ways; in general, it appears that Allan had not worked out the historical developments in any depth nor considered the phonetic reasons for mutations like *i*-affection.

For instance, *eryd*, the plural of *orod* 'mountain', is given an impossible "historical" form **oröd* (p. 52), and it is said that this *ö* sometimes became *e* and sometimes *y* = *ü* (p. 63). In fact, no such form as **oröd* ever existed. The *i*-affection of nonhigh vowels involved an initial stage of raising, and **oroti* had become **oruti* before fronting of the back vowels took place. The subsequent stages of development were **öryti* > **öryit* > **öryid* > *öryd* > *oeryd* > *eryd*. The form *ered*, appearing in names of mountain chains such as *Ered Wethrin*, may actually be in composition (= *Eredwethrin*) and so may show a secondary *i*-affection (see § 5.9), as the plural of *!Orodwathren*.

ItE claims (pp. 53, 64, 66) that the Sindarin sound *ae* undergoes *i*-affection to *ai*. This conclusion is based on the comparison of *Gwaihir* to *Gwaeron*, both containing *gwaew* 'wind', and perhaps on *Hithaiglir*. In fact, the forms *Gwaehir* and *Hithaeglir* are also found; also *Aiglos* (in which there is no opportunity for *i*-affection) beside *Aeglos*. In a passage commenting on the names *Gilraen* and *Gilrain* (*Vinyar Tengwar*, no. 42, p. 11), Tolkien explained that he had not always carefully distinguished between *ae* and *ai* and that the latter was sometimes used in the text of *The*

Lord of the Rings when the former was strictly correct, and he cites *Hithaiglir* and *Aiglos* as examples. In general, *ai* in nonfinal syllables can be taken as a mere variant of *ae*.

The treatment of plural *i*-affection, despite several pages being given to it, is very incomplete, and some mutation patterns are absent. In addition, *ItE* provides various reconstructed extensions of the basic pattern, most of which are wrong.

ItE correctly predicts the *i*-affection change of *u* to *y* in final syllables but provides no examples of this change (p. 63), nor is it able to predict how *u* mutates in nonfinal syllables (p. 65). One example now known showing both mutations is *tylys*, the plural of *tulus* 'poplar'. However, some of the *i*-affection changes of *o* to *y* are actually changes of *u* to *y*, the *o* in the singular having changed from **u*, e.g., *yrch* < **urk*^{h}*i*, plural of *orch* 'orc' < **urk*^{h}*o*.

ItE takes the relationship of Sindarin **ei to í* (seen, for example, in the relationship of *cair* 'ship' to *cîr* 'ships') to be an example of *i*-affection of the *e* in **keir* (p. 64). This is an intrinsically improbable change; the completion of the diphthong *ei* or *ai* already anticipates the high and front features of any following *i*, and there is no need for any other anticipatory realization of those features. It is also incorrect in Sindarin. The original vowel is actually **i* in OS **kiria* (cf. Q *cirya*), and this remains in the plural, with *i* > *í* as a result of metathesis of the *i* with the preceding consonant: **kiri* > **kiiri* > *kīr* (*cîr*). The vowel **ei* > *ai* is derived by *a*-affection: **kiria* > **keria* > **keira* > **keir* > *kair* (*cair*). *I*-affection does not induce a change in quality in the *e* because in the plural it was never there in the first place.

ItE also assumes that the long *í* in the name *Círdan* indicates that the name includes a plural. This is incorrect. The name is regularly derived from OS **kiriatano* > **kiiratano* > **kīradano* > *kīrdan* 'Círdan'; the first element is a stem form, which is not inflected for number.

A similar erroneous assumption is made about the word *celerdain*, plural of *calardan* 'lampwright'. *ItE* suggests that it comes from a plural *celair* + *dan* (p. 65). *ItE* is unaware of the principle of vowel harmony that would change all *a*'s and *o*'s in a word to *e* under the influence of *i*-affection (for more detail see § 5.9 of the present volume); cf. *edegil*, in which the first element is *odog* 'seven', and there is no question of a plural form being compounded.

ItE wrongly suggests that the vowel of adjectives ending in *-ui* would undergo *i*-affection, e.g., *fanui* 'cloudy' would have a plural form *fenui* (p. 67). In fact, the unmutated *u* of the suffix insulates the remainder of the word from *i*-affection; thus we have *Bair Annui* 'Western Dwellings' instead of *!Bair Ennui.*

ItE hypothesizes a plural of the word *aear* 'sea' of the form *!eir* or *!air* (pp. 65–66). There is no evidence for such a plural form; the *ae* could not be expected to change, and there is no reason to suppose any form other than the regular *aeair.*

ItE states that the diphthong *au* is not susceptible to *i*-affection (p. 65), but, in fact, it is; the *i*-affected plural of *naug* 'Dwarf' is *noeg. ItE* further hypothesizes, without evidence, an *i*-affection of *oe* to *ui* (p. 65), but *oe*, like *ae*, does not, in fact, undergo affection, even when it is not itself the result of *i*-affection; e.g., *loeg* 'pools', plural of *loeg* < OS **logika* 'pool'.

Vocabulary. There are a number of errors in *ItE*'s providing of the meanings of words and in relating them to other words in Elvish languages. For instance, Allan does not realize that the word *gwanûr* means '(a pair of) twins'. Instead, it is compared to Quenya *vanwa* (p. 59) and given the hypothetical Quenya form **vanóri*, as if from the root *van* + *óri*, under the impression that the word meant 'departed spirits'. In fact, the Sindarin word is based on the roots √WA 'together' and √NO 'born', and there is no relationship to *vanwa*, which comes from the root √(A)WA-N 'go away' or to *órë*, which comes from the root √GOR.

The word *arth* (seen in *Arthedain*) is identified as meaning 'realm' (p. 60). This is an unlikely interpretation. Though *arth* could conceivably be a form of *ardh* 'region, realm', showing final devoicing, in *The Lord of the Rings dh* was not devoiced between vowels; cf. *Calenardhon.* The word *arth* has a greater likelihood of meaning 'royal', cognate to Quenya *arta*, the meaning 'royal men (of Númenórean ancestry)' being close to that of Quenya *Arnanórë*, 'royal people'.

The name *Roheryn* is explained as meaning 'horse of the wood' (p. 60); in fact it means 'horse of the lady', the second element being *heryn* 'lady', not *eryn* 'wood'.

The element *ened* in *Enedwaith* is mistakenly taken to be a variant of *enyd*, the plural of *onod* 'ent' (p. 63). In fact it is a spelling variant of *enedh* 'middle'; the name of the area has nothing to do with Ents.

The word *galen* (p. 63) is taken as a basic form in names such as *Parth Galen*, *Pinnath Gelin.* In fact it is the lenited form of the adjective *calen* (plural *celin*) 'green'.

The name *Hithaiglin* is repeatedly cited (pp. 65, 66) for 'Misty Mountains', but *Hithaiglin* is actually a spelling error on the map to *The Lord of the Rings* for *Hithaiglir* or *Hithaeglir.* The last element is not a plural ending in *-in*, as suggested on p. 66 of *ItE*; it is a compound of *aeg* 'peak' and *lîr* 'line'.

The name of a scribe *Findegil* is analyzed as containing an element *-degil* related to Quenya *-ndacil*, 'slayer, conqueror' (p. 66), usually used with first elements indicating the object that is slain or conquered. Although this is phonologically possible, the interpretation of the name as either *hair-slayer* or *skill-slayer* (the latter being an older meaning of the root √PHIN) is very unsatisfactory. The name of a scribe is more likely to contain the word *tegil* 'pen'.

The place-name *Doriath* is said to contain a plural suffix *-iath* (p. 67). In fact it is singular, a compound of *dôr* 'land' and *iath* 'fence'.

Morphology. ItE wrongly identifies a plural ending *-in* in the words *elin* 'stars', plural of *êl* 'star' and *cerin* (p. 66). The ending on *elin* is not an inflectional suffix but an *i*-affected form of the stem *elen-*; *cerin* is not plural but is a singular noun 'mound, circular enclosure' with a derivational suffix *-in*.

The endings *-on* and *-ion* (seen in words like *galadhon* 'of trees', *gilion* 'starry, of stars') are not genitive plural suffixes, as *ItE* suggests on pp. 66–67, but adjectival suffixes found in words that cannot be interpreted as genitive plurals, e.g., *erchamion* 'one-handed' (not 'of single hands') or *brithon* 'pebbly'.

ItE considers the plural suffixes *-ath* and *-iath* to have the following distribution: *-iath* following metrically light monosyllables and *-ath* in all other cases (p. 67). This is not the case; there are examples like *lamath* 'echoing voices' and *torath* 'kings', whereas the vowel in *siriath* 'rivers' was originally long (**sīr-*), and the singular form of *firiath* is *fair*.

The actual distribution is *-iath* after monosyllables whose stems contain *i* and end in a coronal resonant (*l*, *r*, *n*). Thus we have *giliath*, *firiath*, *liniath*, *siriath*, *siniath*. The insertion of an *i* after these consonants is found before several other suffixes and is perhaps due to palatalization of the resonants. The plural form suggested in *ItE* for *gôn*, *!goniath* (p. 67), is therefore impossible.

ItE confusingly refers to a "Pre-Sindarin" dual suffix *-at* (p. 62) but never says anything more about it. Allan should have noted that in Sindarin this suffix is found as *-ad*, and it is only known from the name *Orgaladhad* 'Day of the Two Trees'.

A serious error occurs on pp. 61 and 68, in which *ItE* asserts that *en* is the singular article for all nouns. In fact *en* is only used in the genitive case. *ItE* also states (p. 68) that the article *i* marks direct objects. In fact, it marks both determined subjects and objects. *ItE* also does not explain that *en* takes a distinct form of consonant mutation, the *mixed mutation*, and wrongly predicts the form *e-mbarad* for 'of the tower' rather than *e barad* (cf. *e dant* 'of the fall').

The treatment of pronouns and verbs (p. 69) is extremely sketchy (both covered in a single page), as it had to be, given the small amount of material available. However, it is now possible to say somewhat more about the pronouns and a great deal more about the Sindarin verb system; see chapters 8 and 9 of this volume.

Syntax. *ItE* has little to say about syntax, but what it says is erroneous. On p. 70 we are told that Sindarin has SVO word order. In fact, the predominant order is VSO, with VS order appearing in most of the sentences of the Sindarin corpus. SVO and OVS structures can be easily derived from the basic VSO, but OVS cannot be simply derived from an SVO structure (see chapter 17). SVO is rather the result of topicalization of the subject.

Noel, Ruth S. 1980. *The Languages of Tolkien's Middle-earth*. Boston: Houghton Mifflin. Although *LTME* was published in 1980, it clearly did not make use of the earlier *Introduction to Elvish*. Some use was made, however, of the materials in *The Silmarillion*. At only 207 paperback pages it is a much more limited effort than *ItE* and consequently finds fewer opportunities for error. Only pp. 35–41 "Quotations Translated" and pp. 62–74 "Using Elvish" contain materials relevant to Sindarin.

"Quotations Translated" contains several inaccurate translations. The word *na* in the sentence *Ai na vedui Dúnadan* is translated as 'is' (p. 36); in fact it is a preposition 'to', 'of', or 'at'. This error is repeated on p. 71.

The words *noro lim* are translated as 'ride on' (p. 37). Since the imperative is addressed to the horse Asfaloth, this is an unlikely interpretation; the meaning may be 'run swiftly' or 'run lightly', though this is not certain.

The word *dan* in *naur dan i ngaurhoth* is translated as 'take' (p. 38). This error is repeated on p. 71. The word is actually a preposition meaning 'against'.

The word *lammen* in *lasto beth lammen* is translated as 'my voice' (p. 38); it actually means 'my tongue'.

The words *hi ammen* in *edro hi ammen* are untranslated (p. 38); they mean 'now for us'.

LTME takes *aglar'ni* as a verbal form meaning 'glorify'; it actually means 'glory to the' (plural).

The word *diriel* in Samwise's invocation of Elbereth is miswritten *díriel* on p. 40. As a result *LTME* appears not to distinguish between the present participle (e.g., *tiriel* 'gazing') and the past active participle (e.g., *tíriel* 'having gazed').

The Quenya lines among the cries at the field of Cormallen (p. 40) are not clearly distinguished from the Sindarin ones.

In the "Using Elvish" section the word *ambartanen* is misidentified as Sindarin; it is Quenya, 'by doom' (p. 65). The opposite mistake is made in identifying the Sindarin word *amrûn* as Quenya (pp. 72–73).

On p. 66 *LTME* attempts to describe the Sindarin verb. The analogies made in this section are poorly extended. *LTME* takes the future third-person singular ending to be *-ath*, e.g., *!edrath* 'he will open'. In fact it is *-atha*, e.g., *anglennatha* 'he will approach'. The participial forms are not distinguished, and nothing is said about the formation of the past passive participle. *LTME* has found an "auxiliary" ("perfect" is probably intended) ending *-i*, which does not exist. It is apparently deduced from *ú-chebin*, translated as 'I have kept no' (sc. 'I have not kept'), but this is simply a normal present form of the verb *heb-* 'keep'. *LTME*, like *ItE*, makes no distinction between *a*-stem and *i*-stem verbs.

On pp. 67–68 some very misleading statements are made about compound words. *LTME* does not explain the role that consonant mutations play in forming compounds. It is said that compounds can be freely made of Quenya and Sindarin elements; an example given is *Noldothrond*, translated as 'Halls of Knowledge'. In fact, such compounds are improperly formed. Although there are a few names, such as *Fëanor*, that blend Quenya and Sindarin elements, these are properly regarded as incomplete adaptations of Quenya words to Sindarin. They are rare and cannot be freely formed.

LTME has no characterization of consonant mutations at all. Words are frequently quoted in mutated form, e.g., *pheriannath* quoted as the word for 'halfling' and *dan* quoted as 'wright'. The correct (unlenited) forms are *periannath* and *tân*.

Pages 72–73 contain a list of sound relationships between Quenya and Sindarin, but there is no actual analysis of the phonology of the languages, whether historical or synchronic. The relationship between Sindarin *echuir* and Quenya *coirë* is presented as a simple instance of sound correspondences; in fact, *echuir* contains the prefix *ed-* 'out'. The relationship between Sindarin *gw* and Quenya *v* and *b* is taken to be dependent on the environment (based on a sample of two words); in fact, there are different underlying sounds (CE **w* and **b*) for the pairs *gw:v* and *gw:b* respectively. Other generalizations, like "d becomes dh when it is the first letter"

(*LTME* 73), are neither useful nor accurate. A fuller account of Sindarin phonology is found in chapter 4 of the present volume.

Both *ItE* and *LTME* suffer from similar flaws resulting in large part from a lack of data. In the time since they were published a great deal of new material has become available, which allows statements to be made about the development of the Elvish languages with much greater precision.

ADDENDUM

NOTE: *Vinyar Tengwar*, no. 46 (July 2004) published new additions and corrections to *The Etymologies*, which form the basis for the following list of additions and corrections to the text of *A Gateway to Sindarin*:

CORRECTIONS TO APPENDIX 2

#Ad·lann/ change "**#Ad·lann**" to "**#Ad·lod**"; change "OS *atlanda" to "OS *atlǭta"; change "(‡adland)" to "(‡adlaud)"; at end add "*VT*46:17"

Ar'ne·di·ad/ after "**Ar'ne·di·ad**" add ", **ar'nei·di·ad**"; at end add "*VT*46:6"

Dad·benn/ change "prone" to "prone (to do)"; at end add "*VT*46:8"

'E·ri·a-/ change "'**e·ri·ant**" to "'**e·ri·as**"; at end add "*VT*46:7"

Hwind/ change "*adj.* whirling" to "*n.*: eddy"; at end add "*VT*46:16"

Hwiniol/ after "fantastic" add "mad"; at end add "*VT*46:16"

Iâr/ change entire entry to "**Iûr**, *n.*: blood [OS jūr < CE *jōr √JOR] *VT*46:22"

Iaw[1]/ after "**Iaw[1]**" add ", *pl.* **ioe**"; at end add "(N *pl.* iui) *VT*46:22"

Orch/ after "**yrch**" add ", ‡**yr·chy**"; at end add "*VT*46:7"

Oth·ronn/ after "stronghold" add "or city"; at end add "*VT*46:12"

Pa·thu/ change "space" to "place"; at end add "*VT*46:8"

Rain[1]/ after "wandering" add ", free"; at end add "*VT*46:10"

Rind[1]/ change **Rind[1]** to **Rend**; at end add "*VT*46:11"

Rind[2]/ change **Rind[2]** to **Rind**

Rhaw[1]/change "*n.*: wilderness" to "*adj.*: wild, untamed"; at end add "*VT*46:10"

Rho·van/ change "*adj.*: wild" to "*n.*: wilderness"; at end add "*VT*46:10"

To·bas/ before "roofing" add "roof,"; at end add "*VT*46:19"

The·nid/ change entire entry to "**Thand**, *adj.*: firm, true, abiding [OS *st^{h}anda √STAN] *VT*46:16"

The·nin/ delete entire entry
Thond/ change "√THUD" to "√STUD"

ADDITIONS TO APPENDIX 2

Bre·thorn, *n.*: beech-tree [OS bret^{h}orne √BERÉTH √ÓR-ON] *VT*46:3
Duir·ro, *n.*: riverbank [duin+raw^{1}] *VT*46:10
Faur, *n.*: beach, shore [OS sp^{h}ǭra √SPAR^{2}] *VT*46:15
#Fei·ri·a-, *v.*: suffice [OS *p^{h}aria- √PHAR] spelled feira- *VT*46:9
Fer·vain, *adj.*: northern [OS *p^{h}ormenia √PHOR √MEN] *VT*46:10
Gwae·da-, *v.*: enfold [OS *waita- √WAJ] *VT*46:21
Ial·la-, *v.*: cry [OS *jalla- √JAL] *VT*46:22
Îr, *n.*: sexual desire [OS *jīre < CE *jērē √JER] *VT*46:23
Noen, *n.*: sense, wisdom [OS nuhina < CE nusinā √NUS] *VT*46:7
No·roth, *n.*: giant [OS norot^{h}a √NOROTH] *VT*46:6
Pes·sa-, *v.*: affect, concern [OS *persa- √PÉRES] *VT*46:8
Rîdh, *n.*: sown field, acre [OS *rīda < CE *rēdā √RED] *VT*46:11
Roth, *n.*: cave, delving, large excavation [OS *rott^{h}o √ROT] *VT*46:12
Rhîf, *n.*: brink, brim [OS *r̭īma √SRI] *VT*46:11
Rho·'van·nor, *n.*: wilderness [rhovan+dôr] *VT*46:10
!Têwdi, *n.*: 'letter-row,' alphabet [têw+tî] *VT*46:18
Tes, *n.*: fine pierced hole [OS *tersa √TER-ES] *VT*46:18
Thon·nas, *n.*: root [OS *st^{h}undasse √STUD] *VT*46:16
Thost, *n.*: smell [OS *t^{h}ust- √THUS] *VT*46:19
Thos·ta-, *v.*: stink [OS *t^{h}usta- √THUS] *VT*46:19
Thund, *n.*: root [OS *st^{h}undó < CE *stundu √STUD] *VT*46:16

CORRECTIONS TO APPENDIX 3

change √**THUD** to √**STUD**
change "√**JAR blood:** iâr" to √**JOR blood:** iûr"

ADDITIONS TO APPENDIX 3

√**JAL (cf. √!NAL) cry out:** ialla-
√**JER feel sexual desire:** îr
√**NOROTH giant:** noroth
√**NUS sense, wisdom:** noen
√**SPAR^{2} strew, spread:** faur
√**SRI edge:** rhîf

√TER-ES: tes
√WIR new, fresh, young: Gwirith

CORRECTION TO APPENDIX 6

change "*the hunter of stars* [êl+faron]" to "*the hunter of the sky* [ell-^{2}+faron]"